A History of Legislation in the Past 70 Years in China

Chunyao Shen · Anbiao Xu · Tiewei Zang ·
Yunlong Liu
Editors

A History of Legislation in the Past 70 Years in China

The Wise Who Makes Law

经典中国国际出版工程
China Classics International

法律出版社
LAW PRESS·CHINA

Springer

Editors
Chunyao Shen
Legislative Affairs Commission
Standing Committee of the National
People's Congress
Beijing, China

Anbiao Xu
Legislative Affairs Commission
Standing Committee of the National
People's Congress
Beijing, China

Tiewei Zang
Legislative Affairs Commission
Standing Committee of the National
People's Congress
Beijing, China

Yunlong Liu
Legislative Affairs Commission
Standing Committee of the National
People's Congress
Beijing, China

Translated by
Jixu Zhan
East China University of Political Science
and Law
Shanghai, China

Wensheng Qu
Zhejiang University
Hangzhou, China

ISBN 978-981-95-3798-3 ISBN 978-981-95-3799-0 (eBook)
https://doi.org/10.1007/978-981-95-3799-0

Jointly published with Law Press China
The print edition is not for sale in China (Mainland). Customers from China (Mainland) please order the print book from: Law Press China. ISBN: 978-751-97-3862-4

Translation from the Chinese language edition: "大智立法:新中国成立70年立法历程" by Chunyao Shen et al., © Law Press China 2019. Published by Law Press China. All Rights Reserved.

Originally published by Law press, China, 2019

This Springer imprint is published by the registered company Springer Nature Singapore Pte Ltd.
The registered company address is: 152 Beach Road, #21-01/04 Gateway East, Singapore 189721, Singapore

Notes

The year of 2019 marks the 70th anniversary of the founding of People's Republic of China. Over the past 70 years, under the leadership of the Communist Party of China ("CPC"), China has made historic achievements in socialist modernization, successfully advancing socialism with Chinese characteristics, and the development of the socialist system with Chinese characteristics has been continuously strengthened. The socialist rule of law system with Chinese characteristics has been under steady progress, and great achievements have been made in legislation. The Chinese socialist legal system, with the Constitution as the core, which conforms with the modernization of state governance system and capacity has been established as scheduled and under continuous amelioration.

Never forget why you started, and your mission can be accomplished. As pointed by General Secretary Xi Jinping, "we can grasp the essence of many problems only by looking back over the path we have taken, comparing it with other paths, looking to the road ahead, and by understanding where we came from and where we are going." Over the past 70 years, especially over the past 40 years since the reform and opening-up, under the strong leadership of the Party, the National People's Congress ("NPC") and its Standing Committee have closely focused on the undertakings of the Party and state and carried out the work on legislation by innovating their working methods. In this extraordinarily historical period, they not only make tremendous achievements, but also accumulated valuable experience. Since the Eighteenth CPC National Congress, the Central Committee with Xi Jinping as the core has attached great importance to fully advancing rule of law, insisted on the integration of the Party's leadership, people's position as masters of the country and rule of law, steadfastly followed the socialist path of rule of law, kept a close eye on holding onto and developing socialism with Chinese characteristics, promoted institutional innovation by practice-based theoretical innovation, and advanced a complete, scientific, regulated and effective institutional system so as to make the systems in all respects more mature and well-defined and promote the continuous improvement and development of Chinese socialist legal system in line with the modernization of state governance system and capacity. On the occasion of the 70th anniversary, it is of special importance to theoretically elaborate and promote China's achievements in rule of law, especially in legislation over the past 70 years and the Eighteenth Congress in particular for, in addition to voluntary service for rule of law construction in China, maintaining political integrity, big picture thinking, following the leadership core, and keeping in alignment with the Central Committee's leadership, for holding full confidence onto the path, theory, system, and culture of socialism with Chinese characteristics, upholding General Secretary Xi Jinping's core position in the Central Committee and in the Party as a whole and the Central Committee's authority and its centralized and unified leadership.

As the adviser to the national legislature, the Legislative Affairs Committee guarantees the service for the National People's Congress and its Standing Committee. Over the past 70 years, especially over the past 40 years since the reform and opening-up, generations of legislators have directly joined and witnessed the inception, formation and improvement of the Chinese socialist legal system in a great sense of responsibility for the Party, the people and the history. They have upheld the majestic ideal of developing socialist democracy and improving the socialist legal system and dedicated themselves to this cause with perseverance. Consequently, they are also liable to tell the stories about the National People's Congress and the legislation to demonstrate the advantages, features and effectiveness of China's fundamental political system, and about the history, achievements and experience of the work on legislation. To this end, the Research Office of the Legislative Affairs Committee organized the editing of this book, which mainly focuses on the National People's Congress' dedication to upholding, improving and developing the Chinese socialist system, and promoting the modernization of state governance system and capacity. It has 14 chapters on the history, achievements and experience in legislation during the 70 years with a special relevance to theoretical development, change of times and wide use of historical archives as a celebration of the 70th anniversary of the founding of People's Republic of China.

The editors of this book are Shen Chunyao and Xu Anbiao, the Director and Deputy Director of the Legislative Affairs Committee of the National People's Congress, the associate editors are Zang Tiewei and Liu Yunlong from the Research Office thereof. The chapters and their contributors are as follows:

Liu Yunlong	Preface, Chap. 1, Epilogue and general editing
Wang Hongyu	Chaps. 2 and 13
Luo Huanxing	Chap. 3
Da Ji	Chap. 4
Hu Jian	Chaps. 5 and 8
Ren Caifeng	Chaps. 6 and 12
Luo Huanxing and Qu Di	Chap. 7
Hou Xiaoguang and Wang Yuanyuan	Chap. 9
Mao Yu	Chap. 10
Luo Xiaoman and Zhao Zhenhong	Chap. 11
Hou Xiaoguang	Chap. 14

All the comments are welcome. And all the errors that are found in this book remain with the editors and contributors.

Preface

On October 1, 1949, in China, in the East of the world, a peal of spring thunder sounded over the world: Mao Zedong, the great leader of the CPC and the Chinese people, and Chairman of the Central People's Government, solemnly declared on Tian'anmen Square that the People's Republic was founded. As the bright five-star red flag was raised on the Tiananmen Square, a brand new China stood firm in the East, marking the beginning of the Chinese people's historic drive toward national rejuvenation and building a prosperous and strong socialist country. Under the strong leadership of the CPC, the Chinese people have, with great determination, embarked on a great journey of national rejuvenation. China's history has turned a new page, which has made great change to the world.

Over these 70 years, China has achieved historic transformations under the CPC's leadership.

The founding of a nation entails a fundamental choice of system. The past 70 years is not only a decisive breakthrough with the backward and autocratic system that had prevailed in China for several thousand years, but also the exploration of a new type of state system, the state governance methods based on it and the path for realizing the rejuvenation of Chinese nation. After its founding, a transition from a new democratic society to a socialist society was achieved, which contributed to the establishment of socialist system in China; after the reform and opening-up was initiated, the productive forces have been actively released and developed, which helped to eliminate poverty and construct the Chinese socialism. As the socialism with Chinese characteristics enters a new era, by focusing closely on common prosperity, great efforts have been made to deepen reform and expand opening-up in all respects and to coordinate the implementation of the Five-Sphere Integrated Plan and the Four-Pronged Comprehensive Strategy and lay down the two centenary goals. Along this new journey, the progress will be more steady and the measures and programs will be more mature.

Great changes have taken place in China over the past 70 years.

Over the past 70 years, the generations of the Party's leadership represented by Mao Zedong, Deng Xiaoping, Jiang Zemin, Hu Jintao and Xi Jinping have, under arduous explorations through difficulties, trials and hardships, successfully pioneered, persisted in and developed socialism with Chinese characteristics. In the new era, the socialism with Chinese characteristics has been walking steadfastly towards the two centenary goals and delivered on the most magnificent chapter in the history of human development.

Over the past 70 years, in order to realize the Chinese dream of rejuvenation cherished since the advent of modern China, the generations of the Central Party leadership have united and led the Chinese people to integrate the Marxist basic principles with China's experience in revolution, development and reform, draw on the historical experience of socialism in the world, make explorations to answer what is socialism, how to develop socialism in China, and what kind of socialism China desires both from the perspectives of theory and practice. In this process, the Party has made achievements in the theory, practice and system of socialism with Chinese characteristics, adhered to the aspirations and mission of the Chinese Communists, ensured the socialist direction of China's development, created the socialist path in China, and successively ushered socialism with Chinese characteristics in the 21st century.

Over the past 70 years, the generations of the Central Party leadership have united and led the Chinese people to found the new China, open a new chapter in China's history of development, and continue to develop China in the new century. In this process, new systems have been established, new initiatives have been carried out on the new starting point and the socialism with Chinese characteristics have entered a new era. Under the Party's leadership, China has achieved tremendous transformation from standing up and growing prosperous to becoming strong. These glorious achievements have been made amid difficulties, trials and hardships.

Over the past 70 years, the legislation in China has taken the integration of the Party's leadership, people's position as masters of the country and rule of law as the goal, evolved with the changes of the history, times, reform and practice, dedicated itself to the formation, consolidation, improvement and development of socialist system with Chinese characteristics, and drawn on the great practice of Chinese socialist modernization to promote the modernization of state governance system and capacity. In this process, through unremitting efforts, achievements that attract world attention have been attained.

Over the past 70 years, the legislation has insisted on the Party's leadership. China's revolution has demonstrated that the core that leads China's undertakings is the CPC. Its leadership is the choice of history and people, and the most essential feature of socialism with Chinese characteristics. Since the founding of People's Republic of China, the work on legislation has been carried out under the Party's leadership to establish the socialist system, develop socialist economy, improve people's well-being and strive for s great modern socialist country, which not only serves as the Party's proposals but also conforms with the fundamental interests and the will of Chinese people. The Common Program, 1954 Constitution and 1982 Constitution along with its Amendments have reflected the objectives and missions of China's socialist construction in different historical stages, and collectively represented the fundamental interests of the Party and the people. Regardless of changing circumstances, the essential feature of the Party's leadership remains unchanged.

The legislation has always been subject to the guidance of the Party's innovative Marxist theories that adapt to Chinese context, that is, to take Mao Zedong Thought, Deng Xiaoping Theory, the Theory of the Three Represents, the Scientific Outlook on Development and Xi Jinping Thought on Socialism with Chinese Characteristics for a New Era as the scientific action guidelines, resolutely implemented the Central Committee's major decisions and arrangements in different historical stages, adhered to the integration of legislative decision-making with the decisions on national reform and development, and made proactive responses to the various problems faced by the Party under the conditions of long-term governance and reform and opening-up. Since the reform and opening-up in particular, by paying special attention to the constitutional principle that the Party should act within the scope of the Constitution and law, the work on legislation has strived to connect law-making with the Party's laws and regulations and connect the rule of law with the governance of the Party in accordance with the law, steadfastly adhered to the socialist rule of law with Chinese characteristics while not being swayed by the so-called Western constitutionalism, and unswervingly promoted the construction of the socialist rule of law system with Chinese characteristics.

Over the past 70 years, the legislation has unwaveringly adhered to the socialist path. The history of China's revolution has demonstrated that only socialism can save China, and only the socialism with Chinese characteristics can develop China. Since the founding of the People's Republic of China, no matter how Chinese economy and society has developed and what twists and turns it has gone through, the principle of socialism is an important one that the state's fundamental law never wavers. The fundamental system of the People's Republic of China is the socialist system; China is a socialist state governed under the people's democratic dictatorship that is led by the working class and based on an alliance of workers and peasants, and its government system is the system of people's congresses. These constitutional foundations have not only remained intact but have been continuously enriched and refined alongside the evolving theory and practice of socialist modernization, and their socialist features have become more pronounced. No matter how things change, in whatever stage of socialist construction, and whatever the twists and turns the socialist construction has gone through, China's legislation has consistently adhered to and represented the principles and essential requirements of socialism. The work on legislation has always stood firm on the great practice of socialist construction and reform and opening-up. Neither should it follow the old path of a rigid and closed-door policy nor an erroneous path of abandoning socialism. It has insisted on and developed socialist democratic politics with Chinese characteristics, and consolidated and improved the system of people's congresses to make it play an even more important role in national political and social life; it has adhered to the fundamental economic system under which public ownership is the mainstay and diverse forms of ownership develop together to stimulate to the greatest extent the initiative for economic and social production, promoted the release and development of productive forces, resolutely eradicated the system of exploitation of man by man, practiced the principle of "from each according to his ability, to each according to his work", and strived to eliminate the exploitation and polarization to promote the ultimate common prosperity. It has also followed the socialist direction of cultural development, placed emphasis on presvering and carrying forward China's fine traditional culture and the contemporary revolutionary culture, persisted in learning from other countries and looking into the future without forgoing its own history and heritage, spread core socialist values and boosted the confidence in national culture according to law.

Over the past 70 years, the legislation has always adhered to the system of people's congresses. It is the fundamental political system for integrating the Party's leadership, people's master position with rule of law and the most central component and the most decisive element for the socialist system with Chinese characteristics. Since the founding of People's Republic of China, the principle that all the state powers belong to people has been unwaveringly upheld so that all the people can exercise the state power through the National People's Congress and the local people's congresses, and participate in the management of state, economic, cultural and social affairs through various channels and methods according to the provisions of law. After the First National People's Congress, the composition of both the national and local people's congresses has fully reflected and safegarded the broadest people's participation, thereby contributing to the democratic system with people as the true masters, no parallel in other countries, and laying solid foundation for the development of the Party and state's undertakings. Since the reform and opening-up, alongside the continued progress of Chinese society, the people's congresses at all levels have been further improved: the election of deputies to people's congresses based on the same population in urban and rural areas is gradually realized; the equality of nationalities are fully guaranteed; the standing committee are established at the county or above people's congress; the legislative power are granted to the people's congresses and their standing committees of the provinces, autonomous regions, cities directly under the Central Government and the cities with subordinate districts; the state agencies are made sound; the powers and functions of the people's congress and its standing committee are better exercised. In a whole, the socialist system with Chinese characteristics have been continuously consolidated, improved and developed. It has been the focus of the legislature to uphold the system of people's congresses and the democratic centralism, oppose bicameralism and separation of powers, take the firm hold of the direction of reform, keep confidence in system and take full political advantage of the system of people's congress so as to ensure the complete exercise of the powers and functions of people's congresses and their standing committees at all levels, and realize true integration of the Party's leadership, people's master position and rule of law. With these in hands, there will be strong institutional guarantee for adhering to the essence of socialism, ensuring national security, enhancing national unity, and realizing national prosperity, rejuvenation, people's better life, and the modernization of state governance system and capacity.

Over the past 70 years, the legislation has always adopted the people-centered thought. To regard people as the center is of the Party's very existence. The original aspiration and the mission of Chinese Communists is to seek happiness for the Chinese people and rejuvenation of the Chinese nation. Since the founding of People's Republic of China, the legislation has unswervingly upheld the position of people as the masters of the country, adopted the people-centered approach, believed and relied on the people, insisted on the fundamental principle of serving the people wholeheartedly and voluntarily put into practice the Party's mass line in all the undertakings for state governance. Considering the proper protection and handling of people's long-term, overall and real interests, the legislature has drawn aspirations from the people and made laws for the people, respected and safeguarded human rights, listened to the call and expectations of the people, adapted to the people's demands for better life, for material and cultural progress, and for democracy, rule of law, fairness, justice, security and environment, and protected citizens' economic, political, cultural and social basic rights in all respects. The legislature has also strengthened efforts in improving people's well-being and advanced the legislation to ensure people's access to childcare and social assistance, and the right to education, employment, medical and old-age care, and housing, never faltered in the legislation on ecological civilization and environment protection for enhanced governance of ecology and environment, the harmonious co-existence between man and nature and a beautiful world, attached importance to stimulating to the greatest extent the people's enthusiasm for participating in the decisive reforms to improve the life and increase well-being for people, and spared unremitting efforts to build a moderately prosperous society in which the fruits of reform and opening-up and social development are shared with people and to realize well-rounded development of man.

Over the past 70 years, the legislature has never faltered in its pursuit for rule of law and the modernization of state governance system and capacity. The founding of People's Republic of China marked the establishment of a new type of state system, infused new vitality and vigor into state governance and created a new type of rule of law country in China. Begining with the adoption of Common Program as the provisional constitution, which made provisions on the legal status of new China, its system of government and organization, China has embarked on a unique path of building a socialist civilization, which is different from China's traditional legal system and the capitalist rule of law in the modern times with respect to the social system and state governance. It is a new state governance model which stands on contemporary China's realities and embodies the modern rule of law concepts and the fine traditional Chinese civilization of law. China has been exploring and then practicing the best rule of law methods, from the role of law in the state governance as prescribed in the 1954 Constitution to the provisions that "the state shall safeguard the unity and dignity of the socialist legal system" and "the People's Republic of China shall practice law-based governance and build a socialist state under the rule of law" in the 1982 Constitution. Under these principles, the legislature has aligned its work with the major decisions and arrangements of the Central Committee on building China into a rule of law country, adhered to the guidance of the Chinese socialist rule of law theory, actively promoted the construction and continuous development of socialist legal system with Chinese characteristics and dedicated itself to achieving the objective of rule of law and the modernization of state governance system and capacity. In this period, the legislation has undergone several transitions:

from the Organic Law of the Central People's Government, Marriage Law, Agrarian Land Reform Law, and Trade Union Law enacted in the early stage of the People's Republic of China to the seriously damaged legal system during the Cultural Revolution;

from the Law on the Organization of the Local People's Congresses and Local People's Governments at All Levels ("Local Organization Law"), Criminal Law, Law on Chinese-Foreign Equity Joint Ventures and other four laws enacted in the early reform and opening-up period marking the new stage of legal system construction to the proposal that "legislation should be started on China's actual circumstances, and an independent legal system with Chinese characteristics can only be gradually established according to the principles for socialist legal system" put forward in 1982;

from the proposal that "to establish socialist legal system with Chinese characteristics by 2010" put forward in the Fifteenth CPC National Congress, the objective of promoting law-based governance, establishing socialist rule of law system with Chinese characteristics and building socialist rule of law country as advocated in the Fourth Plenary Session of the Eighteenth CPC Central Committee to the proposal of the two centenary goals, ultimate realization of modern state governance system and capacity, a more mature theory on socialist rule of law with Chinese characteristics and well-defined objectives for establishing a law-based China.

Over the past 70 years, the legislation has proceeded from the national conditions and realities. Social practice is the basis for law, while law is a summary of the practical experience. Law is determined by economic foundation and serves it. In different countries, the different ethnicity, history, territory, economy and culture determines that its legal system is completely different from other countries. To proceed from the realities is an important principle for law-making in China. A populous country with a weak economic foundation and uneven development has been an acute problem for China. Since the founding of the People's Republic of China, the legislation has always freed the minds, sought truth from facts, kept pace with the times and adopted a pragmatic attitude, while never submitted to authority, the western and external pressure. It has adapted itself to the realities and the characteristics in different phases of social economic development, properly and actively dealt with the various contradictions and problems during development and made significant progress in rule of law for restoring national economic and political order, consolidating national defense and promoting socialist economic and cultural undertakings. Since the reform and opening-up, the legislation has taken a firmer hold of the great practice of reform and opening-up and socialist modernization, closely focused on economic development as the central task, kept a close eye to the goal of completely building a moderately prosperous country, and strengthened the efforts for realizing the Chinese dream. The legislature has properly handled the relationship between law-making and reform, persisted in the connection of legislative decision-making with reform decisions, made legislation proactively serve the needs of social economic development and ensured law-based major reforms, improved rule of law in reform and reform through rule of law, advanced the Chinese socialist legal system with the Constitution as the core and worked towards the socialist rule of law system and country with Chinese characteristics. The legislature has also adapted itself to the actual needs of national reunification and unswervingly adhered to the advancement of the great cause of peaceful reunification. The state may establish special administrative regions when necessary. To this end, the legislature made it clear in the Constitution that "the state may establish special administrative regions when necessary. The systems instituted in special administrative regions, in light of specific circumstances, shall be prescribed by laws enacted by the National People's Congress"; and to implement the "One Country Two Systems", the Basic Law of the Hong Kong Special Administrative Region and the Basic Law of the Macao Special Administrative Region were formulated to ensure the smooth return of Hong Kong and Macao to the motherland in accordance with the law and to realize the peaceful reunification. Moreover, the legislature has attached importance to learning from and drawing upon the valuable achievements in the development of rule of law worldwide, applied the modern rule of law concepts to support the work on legislation, proactively made legislation connected with WTO rules and observed the international conventions that China is a signatory and other international rules. In a word, China's legislation has drawn on the benefits from others, but never blindly copied them. In China's legislation, the legal systems of some western countries are never applied to the Chinese socialist legal system. For some of their laws that do not conform with China's conditions and realities, the legislature will never enact them. For the laws that are not found in their legal systems but are needed for China, the legislature will make a haste to enact them. In addition, the traditional Chinese legal system is also the sources for legislation, from which the legislature may draw aspirations and promote the ancient rule of law concepts and institutions that are still in line with contemporary China for innovating state governance models.

Over the past 70 years, the legislation has consistently adhered to the practice of scientific and democratic law-making. Since the New Culture Movement in the 20th century, democracy and science has taken deep root in the hearts of Chinese people, and they were also the two banners upheld by the revolutionary movements in modern China. In the meantime, they have been practiced in the undertakings of the Party and state during China's socialist revolution, development and reform and opening-up, contributing to China's transition from a semi-colonial and semi-feudal state to a people's republic. The new republic has adhered to the principle of people's master position, insisted on scientific and democratic law-making, attracted people to participate in legislation as much as possible through favorable institutional designs, and dedicated the legislation to be more scientific and democratic. The scientific and democratic legislation has also experienced several changes as follows: from the Common Program adopted under the negotiation among the democratic parties and people with no party affiliations to the draft 1954 Constitution which was discussed among over 8000 people and over 1.18 million suggestions solicited from more than 150 million people nationwide; from the legislative forums, seminars and hearings under a regular basis, to the disclosure of some draft laws for public opinions, and then to the provision of the Law on Legislation prescribing that "for a bill which has been put on the agenda for the session of the Standing Committee, after the deliberations by the Standing Committee, the draft law and an explanation of the drafting or amendments shall be released to the public for opinions...A report shall be made to the public on the solicited opinions", which realized the disclosure of all law bills to the public except for the ones related with state secrets and expanded the channels for citizen's orderly participation in the legislation; and from the provision that "preparation of legislative plans and the annual legislative program should be made by studying the delegate's proposals and suggestions, broadly soliciting opinions, scientifically debating and evaluating", to the rule that "a bill which has been put on the agenda of the Standing Committee session shall in general be deliberated three times in the current session of the Standing Committee before being voted on" and then to the provision that "legislation shall, in a scientific and reasonable manner, prescribe the rights and obligations of citizens, legal persons and other organizations, and the powers and duties of state agencies".

Over the past 70 years, the legislation has consistently upheld the unity of socialist legal system. China is a centralized, unified, unitary and multi-ethnic country. As soon as it was founded, the new republic chose the state governance structure and methods based on China's conditions, historical traditions and realities, i.e. the centralized and unified state governance model in which the local initiative is fully stimulated and mobilized under the centralized and unified leadership of the central authorities. To safeguard ethnic equality and unity, the regional autonomy is practiced in the places where the ethnic minorities live together, which was made into a basic political institution of China. Additionally, to protect the unity of socialist legal system, the National People's Congress was designated as the highest national authority and the only authority of state legislative power as stipulated in the 1954 Constitution, while the self-governance authorities of the autonomous regions, prefectures and counties may draw up statutes governing the exercise of autonomy or separate regulations suited to the political, economic and cultural characteristics of the nationality or nationalities, which are reported to the Standing Committee of the National People's Congress for approval. Since the reform and opening-up, to meet the needs of socialist modernization and legal institutions and mechanisms for local social and economic development and to resolve the contradiction that legislation cannot meet the rapid economic and social development, the 1982 Constitution granted the power of enacting laws to the Standing Committee of the National People's Congress and, at the same time, the power to formulate administrative regulations to the State Council and the power to draw up local regulations to the provincial people's congresses and their standing committees. Later, the enacted and revised Local Organization Law and the Law on Legislation, step by step, gave the legislative power to the people's congresses and their standing committees of all the cities with subordinate districts, that is, the people's congresses of cities with subordinate districts and their standing committees may make regulations on the urban and rural development and administration, environment protection, and historic and cultural protection, so long as the local provisions do not contravene the Constitution, laws, administrative regulations, or the local provisions and regulations of that province or autonomous region, which are to be reported to the provincial people's congress for approval. Over the past 40 years since the reform and opening-up, the State Council and local people's congresses and their standing committees at all levels with legislative power have upheld the unity of national legal system, carried out legislation according to the Constitution and law, made innovations within the statutory limits, enacted new laws timely and revised, repealed and reviewed the outdated regulations according to national laws. Guided by the principle of conformity, characteristics and practicability, they have contributed to the formation and improvement of the socialist legal system with Chinese characteristics and maintained the inherent logic, harmony and unity within the socialist legal system.

Over the past 70 years, the socialist system has profoundly changed China, Chinese nation, Chinese people and the Party. The legislation in the past 70 years have taken a firmer hold of the great practice of Chinese socialist modernization. The difficulties, trials and hardships that China's legislation has undergone demonstrated the Party's deepening understanding of the laws of governance by the Party, laws of building socialism, and laws of the development of human society, which have advanced the improvement and development of the socialist system with Chinese characteristics, and given impetus to the fundamental transformation of state governance methods. Also in this process, the socialist legal system with Chinese characteristics, the socialist rule of law system with Chinese characteristics, rule of law practice, the construction of China into a law-based country and the modernization of state governance system and capacity have been under continuous improvement and development. The goal of fully deepening reform is gradually attained. The legislation of the past 70 years is creating a new modern socialist rule of law country that is full of Chinese wisdom, displays Chinese civilization and exemplifies Chinese characteristics, and helps to offer Chinese solution to the world based on its success in governance.

The legislation of the past 70 years has also fully demonstrated that rule of law provides the ballast for national and social stability and progress, signifies the awakening, profound revolution and mission of the Party's governance, which is integral to improving and developing the socialist system with Chinese characteristics, and is an important approach for realizing the two centenary goals and the great rejuvenation of Chinese nation.

The valuable experience in the legislation of the past 70 years has left the Party and people with a precious asset, and is of great significance for sustaining and developing the socialist system with Chinese characteristics and promoting the modernization of state governance system and capacity. This experience should be cherished and unwaveringly applied so as to write a new chapter in the development of socialist rule of law system with Chinese characteristics and in the building of socialist rule of law country.

Beijing, China

Chunyao Shen
Anbiao Xu
Tiewei Zang
Yunlong Liu

Contents

About the Translators

Jixu Zhan, Ph.D in Law, is a Lecturer and Master Supervisor at East China University of Political Science and Law (ECUPL). His research focuses on comparative legal history, the translation of Chinese legal classics, and legal translation studies. He has authored multiple scholarly articles in academic journals, including the Journal of East China University of Political Science and Law and Foreign Languages and Their Teaching. Currently, he is the Principal Investigator for a National Social Science Fund (NSSF) project involving the translation of Shen Jiaben's A History of Crimes and Punishments in China. With over a decade of expertise in legal translation for legislative and judicial authorities, he also served on secondment to the Standing Committee of the Shanghai Municipal People's Congress in 2025.

Wensheng Qu Qiushi Distinguished Professor at Zhejiang University, Doctoral Supervisor, Dean of the School of International Studies. He is also a Doctoral Supervisor at the Guanghua Law School. He previously taught for many years at East China University of Political Science and Law. He has published more than 80 original and interdisciplinary articles in leading academic journals, including Social Sciences in China, Historical Research, and Chinese Journal of Law. His monograph Unequal Treaties and Non-equivalent Translations: A Translation History of Sino-foreign Treaties (1842–1902)was selected for the National Achievements Library of Philosophy and Social Sciences and received the Second Prize of the Ninth Ministry of Education Outstanding Achievements in Humanities and Social Sciences Award. His article From Extraterritoriality to Extraterritorial Regulation: A Jurisdiction Theory Perspective won the First Prize of the 16th Shanghai Philosophy and Social Sciences Outstanding Achievement Award. His representative translations, including Chinese translations of A General Survey of Events, Sources, Persons and Movements in Continental Legal History and China's Entrance into the Family of Nations, have had a broad impact in the academic field. He has chaired numerous projects,including a National Social Science Fund Major Project, which was rated "excellent" upon completion. He has been selected for the inaugural National Youth Scholar Program for High-level Talents and the Leading Talent Program of the Oriental Scholar Project (Shanghai Leading Talent Program). His honors include a nomination for the Tenth National Outstanding Young Jurist Award, among others.

Chapter 1
A Glorious Past: Legislation of the People's Republic of China in Seventy Years

Liu Yunlong

Abstract This chapter reviews the 70-year legislative history of the People's Republic of China, emphasizing the role of legislation in advancing socialism with Chinese characteristics and modernizing state governance. China's legislation has evolved through two key phases: the first 30 years after 1949, marked by socialist revolution, institution-building, and setbacks during the Cultural Revolution; and the reform and opening-up era since 1978, characterized by economic transformation, legal reconstruction, and constitutional development. It highlights the integration of Party leadership, people's sovereignty, and the rule of law as the core principle of China's legal system. The legislative achievements have enabled the transition from a planned economy to a market economy, from policy-led governance to rule-based governance, and from social instability to stable, law-based order. The socialist legal system with Chinese characteristics has been a strong institutional guarantee for China's development, national unity, and the great rejuvenation of the Chinese nation.

Keywords Socialist legal system with Chinese characteristics · Reform and opening-up · 1982 constitution · People's congress system · State governance modernization · Rule of law in China

As General Secretary Xi Jinping pointed out, "the state governance system and capacity of a state epitomize not only its many systems but also how well it can enforce them".[1] To promote the modernization of state governance system and capacity is essential for improving and developing the socialist system with Chinese characteristics and necessary for realizing socialist modernization.[2] The purpose of

[1] Xi Jinping, *The Governance of China*, Foreign Languages Press, 2018, p. 101.

L. Yunlong (✉)
Beijing, China
e-mail: liujixuan@lawpress.com.cn

[2] Translator's Notes: For the sake of readability, the translator chooses to simplify the expression of 中国特色 into "Chinese" in most parts of this book except for the emphasis needed. The controversy

C. Shen et al. (eds.), *A History of Legislation in the Past 70 Years in China*,
https://doi.org/10.1007/978-981-95-3799-0_1

reform is to better the Chinese socialist system, to make it mature and enduring, to provide stronger institutional support for realizing the dream of the rejuvenation of the Chinese nation, and deliver on a happier and better life for Chinese people. As advocated in the Third Plenary Session of the Eighteenth CPC Central Committee, "(we must take) improving and developing the Chinese socialist system and modernizing our state governance system and capacity as the general goal of continuing the reform comprehensively". It is a scientific summary made by the Party on the experience of the road to national development, institutional development and the way of governance since the founding of the People's Republic of China ("PRC") especially since the reform and opening up, and also a development of the Party's strategy for building a prosperous country in the new era.

Over the past 70 years since the founding of the PRC, the Party has led the Chinese people to focus on the dream of national strengthen, national rejuvenation and people's well-being. Guided by the theory of scientific socialism, it has chosen the socialist path, blazed the trail for the socialism with Chinese characteristics, established the socialist system with Chinese characteristics, created and developed the socialist theory system with Chinese characteristics. In the past 70 years, the socialist revolution, development and reform undertaken by the people under the Party's leadership have served as the foundation of making all innovations in theory and practice by the Party. Improving and developing the Chinese socialist system and advance the modernization of state governance system and capacity are the choice of strategic significant to advance the realization of the historical tasks and goals at the current stage and to improve the quality of the achievements from realizing the goals. It is necessary to realize the historical tasks and goals and to meet the essential requirements of socialism. In the past 70 years, China's legislation has also walked on a winding road: it stood behind glorious past of the socialist revolution, development and reform and opening-up led by the Party and withstood the ups and downs along with the Party and the Chinese nation. On this road, the new China saw the birth of legal system, the Cultural Revolution caused severe setbacks to legal development among social chaos and disorder, the early period of reform and opening-up witnessed the construction of socialist legal system, and then a law-based socialist country was advocated. Also on this path, the understandings about the law of the Party's rule, the socialist construction and the development of human society have continuously moved forward.

Over the past 70 years, legislation in China has adhered to the integration of the Party's leadership, people's master position of the country, and the rule of law, taken the socialist modernization as the foundation, and aligned steadfastly with the Party's basic line in which the economic development is the center, the Four Cardinal Principles are the bedrock and the reform and opening up is the long-standing path. With the awareness of historical mission, China's legislation has progressed in pace with the time, kept the same pace with the reform and opening-up, and developed

---

in its translation has long been debated, but the choice in this book did not affect the understanding of foreign audience in this regard. Some laws mentioned here, the Civil Code in particular, have been promulgated since this book was published in 2019.

as the social practice evolved. From crossing the river by touching the stones to independently emphasizing the top-level institutional design, it has persisted in integrating decisions related to reform with legislative decision-making, actively adapted to the needs of reform and economic and social development, advanced reform under the rule of law, and improved the rule of law through reform. Through unremitting efforts, the Chinese socialist legal system with the Constitution as the core has been formed and continuously improved, which has effectively promoted the transition of China's economic development from a planned economic system to a market economy, the social order from chaotic and lawless to sound and law-based, and the state governance from policy-led to rule of law. It has also provided strong legal guarantee for improving and developing the socialist system with Chinese characteristics, promoted the modernization of the state governance system and capacity, and advanced the construction of China into a law-based country along a more glorious path.

1 Twists and Turns in the First Thirty Years After PRC'S Founding

A socialist society, so far established under the guidance of Marxist theory of scientific socialism, is the most advanced form of society in human history. What social system a country may choose is based on whether it can resolve the historical problems to which it has to respond. Both history and reality have told us that only socialism can save China and only socialism with Chinese characteristics can bring development to China. As remarked by Xi Jinping in his speech at the First Session of the Twelfth National People's Congress on March 2013, "we are able to embark on this path thanks to the great endeavors of reform and opening-up made in the past 30 years and more, the continuous quest made in the 60-plus years of the PRC, a thorough review of the evolution of the Chinese nation in its 170-plus years of modern history, and carrying forward the 5,000-plus years of Chinese civilization. This path is deeply rooted in history and broadly based on China's present realities."[3] His remarks fully summarized Chinese people's explorations for the socialist path with Chinese characteristics, revealing the historical necessity, foundation, and cultural origins that lead the Chinese people to choose it.

As Xi Jinping pointed out, "the process by which the people build socialism under the leadership of the Party can be divided into two historical phases – one that preceded the launch of reform and opening-up in 1978, and a second that followed on from that event. The two phases – at once related to and distinct from each other – are both pragmatic explorations in building socialism conducted by the people under the leadership of the Party." He continued that "Chinese socialism was initiated after the launch of reform and opening-up and based on more than 20 years of development since the socialist system was established in the 1950s", "we should not deny the

[3] Xi Jinping, *The Governance of China*, Foreign Languages Press, 2018, p.41–42.

pre-reform-and-opening-up phase vis-à-vis the post-reform-and-opening-up phase, or *vice versa*. The socialist explorations in the former phase opening-up contributed to the latter, while the socialist explorations in the latter period exemplified the legacy, reform and development of the former".[4] To make a defining judgment on the legislative practices in the past 70 years requires unremitting adherence to the epistemology and methodology of dialectical and historical materialism, and a comprehensive and correct understanding of the history of socialist revolution, development and reform under the leadership of the Party. In retrospect of the history before the reform and opening-up, the Party, when leading the socialist revolution and development, has made theoretical and practical thinking and explorations on its own on what is socialism, how to develop socialism in China, and what kind of socialism China desires.

1.1 Theoretical Reflections and Explorations for Socialism in China

The goal of the Party that led the whole Chinese people in the New Democratic Revolution (1919–1949) was to achieve national independence, liberation, democracy and freedom, build a new China with socialism, make China prosperous and strong, rejuvenate the nation, and bring happiness to the Chinese people through socialism, realize the rejuvenation of the Chinese nation and finally achieve communism. This goal has determined the eventual success of Chinese revolution, which would inevitably bring about the fundamental changes towards Chinese social system and the state governance model.

The nation-building equals to a choice-making of (socio-political) system. In the past several thousand years, China's socio-political system and governance were compatible with the economic foundation for an agricultural society characterized by the small-scale peasant economy. However, when the West entered the era of industrial civilization in the modern period, China withered and was reduced to the colony of Western powers, so the former economic foundations could not meet the demands of China's social change and development. Since then, Chinese socio-political system has undergone two transformations: the first was 1911 Revolution led by Dr. Sun Yat-sen, which ended the feudal imperial dynasty, completed the bourgeois revolution and established the Republic of China; but it did not change the status quo of China as a poor and backward country, nor accomplish the historical task of saving China from subjugation and fighting against colonialism and feudalism. The second was in 1949 when the Party with President Mao Zedong as the great leader led the Chinese people to win the great victory of New Democratic Revolution and founded the PRC after the long-drawn-out military struggles and other fights, ending the imperialist, feudal and crony capitalist rule. Chinese people have taken hold of state power and become the masters of the country ever since. Following the

[4] Xi Jinping, *The Governance of China*, Foreign Languages Press, 2018, p.24–25..

founding of the PRC, it chose the principle of people's democracy and followed the direction of building socialism, which was a fundamental transformation of China's socio-political system and state governance. China has started explorations for a modern path characterized by democracy and rule of law as it was transformed from the feudal rule.

As a populous country with a weak economic foundation characterized by backward and uneven development, the Party has proactively explored both the theory and practice for building socialism. In the early stage of the PRC, Mao Zedong pointed out that the socialist revolution and development in China could not copy the Soviet Union. In 1957, he proposed to "make China a socialist country with modern industry, modern agriculture, and modern science and culture." In 1959, he added "modern military defense", which finally set out the "four modernizations". He emphasized that the road that China had walked for economic development needed to be "somewhat different from that of Soviet Union", which means "the light industry and agriculture developed in the first, and the heavy industry if permitted"; "to study Chinese issues should be based on the features and realities of China", "to make explorations down to earth to help find the path for China building its own socialism". Mao also particularly emphasized that the Marxism and China's reality "be integrated for the second time to find the path to build socialism in China", "now we should strive to find the path".[5]

From the Great Leap Movement, Mao Zedong realized that to explore and find the law for building socialism was not easy, gradually recognizing the complexity and long-term nature of socialism. Between December 1959 and February 1960, he organized several reading groups to read and discuss the parts on socialism in the Political Economy, a textbook from the Soviet Union. From these readings and discussions, he concluded that the socialism "is divided into two stages. The first is the underdeveloped socialism, and the latter is the relatively developed socialism. This latter stage may take even longer than the first." He then wrote the *Summing Up Ten Years*, in which he confessed that China's socialist construction "still has a big blind spot".[6] These are the theoretical summaries about building China's socialism and exploring China's own path and the vivid description of the socialism with Chinese characteristics. In a word, the exploration for socialism with Chinese characteristics was initiated by the Party as soon as the PRC was founded. As Deng Xiaoping believed, since the Third Plenary Session of the Eleventh CPC Central Committee, "in many respects, we are doing things Comrade Mao suggested but failed to do himself, setting right his erroneous opposition to certain things and accomplishing some things that he did not. All this we shall continue to do for a fairly long time. Of course, we have developed Mao Zedong Thought and will go on developing it."[7]

---

[5] Mao Zedong Thought Study Group and First Section of Party Literature Research Office of CPC Central Committee ed., *To Understand Chinese Path from the Annals of Mao Zedong (1949–1976)*, Central Party Literature Press, 2017, p. 197, 38–39, 78, 213, 215.

[6] *Ibid.*, p. 188–189.

[7] DENG Xiaoping, *Selected Works of Deng Xiaoping (Vol. 2)*, Foreign Languages Press, 1995, p. 299.

Deng's comments have been proved correct by the socialist practices since the reform and opening-up.

1.2 To Establish the Socialist Democratic System for China

Since the PRC's founding, the exploration for socialist China's political system that is different from other socialist countries had been started, and "the three basic political systems, i.e. the system of people's congresses, the system of multiparty cooperation and political consultation under the leadership of the CPC, and the system of regional ethnic autonomy, all of which have laid solid and long-lasting political foundation for China's enduring peace and order".[8]

When looking back at China's history, that what type of political system should be established in China had been a historical question for the Chinese people since the modern period. To resolve it, Chinese people had made painstaking efforts. After the Opium War (1840–1842), China was reduced to a semi-colonial and semi-feudal society. To save China from subjugation and realize the rejuvenation of the Chinese nation, the Chinese people and the people with lofty ideals rose up and spared unswerving efforts to search for the political system that suited China's reality, but they all failed.

In 1921 when the Party was founded, it has taken the realization of Chinese people being the masters of this country and the rejuvenation of Chinese nation as its mission, and led the Chinese people, after arduous revolutionary battles and struggles, to establish a new China in which the master position of the people can be assured. After the victory of Chinese revolution, how should the new regime be organized? How should the country be governed? They were fundamental questions whose answers were directly concerned with China's future and Chinese people's fate. They were also important questions that confronted the Chinese communists. However, the Chinese communists represented by Mao Zedong had made profound thinking both from the theory and practice since the Revolutionary War Period. In July 1945, in discussing with Huang Yanpei, a prominent educator, in Yan'an, Shaanxi Province, on how to find a way out of the cycle of dynastic rise and collapse, Mao stated clearly that "we have found a new path; we can break free of the cycle. The path is called democracy. As long as the people have oversight of the government then government will not slacken in its efforts. When everyone takes responsibility there will be no danger that things will return to how they were even if the leader has gone."[9] In fact, as early as in 1940, Mao ever wrote in plain words, "there is no state which does not have an appropriate apparatus of political power to represent it.

---

[8] Mao Zedong Thought Study Group and First Section of Party Literature Research Office of CPC Central Committee ed., *To Understand Chinese Path from the Annals of Mao Zedong (1949–1976)*, Central Party Literature Press, 2017, p. 137.

[9] *Ibid.*, p. 221. Translation adapted from http://www.chinaheritagequarterly.org/features.php?searchterm=026_yanan.inc&issue=026

China may now adopt a system of people's congresses, from the national people's congress down to the provincial, county, district and township people's congresses, with all levels electing their respective governmental bodies."[10]

On September 29, 1949, on the eve of the founding of the PRC, the members of other political parties and those without party affiliation who ever fought with the Party, jointly convened the First Plenary Session of the Chinese People's Political Consultative Conference ("CPPCC"). This session adopted the Common Program of the Chinese People's Political Consultative Conference ("Common Program") which put Mao Zedong's thought on the system of people's congresses into practice It made provisions on China's state system, the system of government and other basic systems in all respects, and it also solemnly proclaimed that China should adopt the system of people's congresses. This conference also marked the establishment of the system of multiparty cooperation and political consultation under the leadership of the Party, following the principle of long-term coexistence, mutual supervision, mutual understanding, and shared honor and disgrace It has played an important and irreplaceable role in developing China's democratic politics. The 1982 Constitution[11] provides that the system of multiparty cooperation and political consultation under the Party's leadership will exist and develop for a long time to come, which makes it an inseparable part of the socialist system with Chinese characteristics. The Common Program also established the system of regional ethnic autonomy, the basic policy for the Party to deal with the ethnic issues after the founding of the PRC and another important basic political system established under the Party's leadership This system is in line with China's national conditions with a vision for the future, laying the political foundation for forming socialist ethnic relations characterized by equality, solidarity, mutual assistance and harmony, strengthening ethnic unity, and maintaining national unity.

In the First Session of the First National People's Congress held on September 20, 1954, the Constitution of the People's Republic of China was adopted. It prescribed that "the People's Republic of China is a people's democratic state led by the working class and based on the alliance of workers and peasants", and "all power in the people's republic of China belongs to the people. The agencies through which the people exercise power are the National People's Congress and the local people's congresses". These provisions confirmed the system of government and the system of people's congresses as first prescribed by the Common Program. They also established the principle of people's democracy and socialism. Under the guidance of the Common Program and the 1954 Constitution, China has gradually transitioned from a new democratic society to a socialist society. The socialist transformation of the private ownership of the means of production was accomplished, the exploitation of man by man was abolished and the socialist system was gradually established. China

[10] Translation is from MAO Zedong, *Selected Works of Mao Zedong (Vol.2)*, Foreign Languages Press, 1965, p 352.

[11] It is abbreviated for the Constitution of the People's Republic of China adopted at the Fifth Session of the Fifth National People's Congress on December 4, 1982.

has walked on the path of socialism since then. Socialism, thereafter, has become the unshakeable bedrock of Chinese nation.

1.3 To Establish Socialist Economic System for China

In the early stage of PRC, the whole country was impoverished. And the poverty also drove people for change, in desperate need to get rid of their situation and live a happy life. The Chinese communists represented by Mao Zedong united and led the Chinese people to strive for establishing the socialist economic system different from those of other socialist countries.

From the founding of the PRC to the completion of socialist transformation, China realized two historical changes: one was the change from an old semi-colonial and semi-feudal society to a new society in which the people are their own masters, and the second was the change from new democratic society to the socialist society. Based on the Common Program and other laws, between 1949 and 1952, the Party led the people of all ethnic groups to consolidate the people's democratic government, finished the agrarian land reform and other democratic reform missions, won the battle against the American aggressors and provided aid to Korea which motivated the people to engage in revolution and development. The national economy was quickly rehabilitated and the conditions were created for the transition to socialism and then to socialist industrialization of China. In 1953, the fundamental task in the transition period set up by the Party was written down in the 1954 Constitution. According to the 1954 Constitution and other laws, the economic construction led by the Party would complete the socialist transformation of the means of production in the utmost and establish the basic socialist systems in the initial stage, which laid the political and institutional foundation for all the development and progress made in contemporary China.[12] As Xi Jinping pointed out in his speech at the symposium to commemorate the 120th anniversary of Mao Zedong's birth, "the first generation of the central collective leadership with Mao Zedong at the core led the people, when healing the wounds of war and rehabilitating the national economy, to seize the opportunity to propose the idea of transition period, completed the creative transformation from the new democratic revolution to socialist revolution, and turned the big country in the East with a quarter of world's population into the socialist country, which realized the greatest and the most profound social change in Chinese history".[13]

From 1956 to 1966, marked by the eventful Eighth CPC National Congress, the Party led the Chinese people to carry out massive and full-scale socialist construction and made arduous efforts to search for the socialist path that suited China's

---

[12] Party History Research Center ed., *Ninety Years of the Communist Party of China (Socialist Revolution and Development Period)*, History of Chinese Communist Party Publishing House and Party Building Readings Press, 2016, p. 356.

[13] Party Literature Research Office ed., *Selection of Important Documents since the Eighteenth CPC National Congress*, Central Party Literature Press, 2014, p. 690.

reality. In this period, the Party made a correct judgment on the principal contradiction in Chinese society and set out the goals of "four modernizations" and building China into a modern socialist country, which offered guidance for Chinese people marching toward socialism. However, due to the lack of the grasp of the law about and the experience in socialist construction, the Party made left-line mistakes in the guiding principles of economic development, and the Great Leap Forward and the people's commune movement were started. China's politics and culture were impacted by these mistakes, and the legal system construction was also put aside, which planted the seeds for Cultural Revolution. However, through the efforts of the Party and Chinese people, a relatively complete and independent industrial system and national economic framework were also established, providing important material and technology foundation for socialist modernization.

The Cultural Revolution between 1966 and 1976 caused the Party, the country, and the people to suffer the most serious losses. This long-lasting left-line mistake across the nation inflicted serious setbacks for China's economic development and major destruction of social order and legal system. From October 1976 when the Gang of Four was smashed to the end of 1978, the Party and the state revived for progress, some corrections had been made in some areas, the work on economic development, social affairs and diplomatic relations was resumed and made progress to a certain degree. However, the left-line guiding principles remained uncorrected from the deepest, the Party and the country were hovering.[14] It was not until the reform and opening-up was initiated that China opened a new chapter itself for the socialist modernization with Chinese characteristics. After a decade's serious setback, "the nature of the Party, people's government, people's army and the entire society did not change. History has demonstrated the strong vitality of the Party and the socialist system".[15]

It should be emphasized that the law of value was respected considering that the planned economy system was still practiced in this period. The Party paid attention to agriculture's fundamental status and its role in advancing China's transition from an agricultural country to an industrial country. For example, from the lessons of absolute egalitarianism ("gong chan feng"), Mao Zedong further elaborated on two theories: one was that the socialist country should respect the law of value and encourage commodities exchange; the other was that the scope of socialist collective ownership could not be excessively expanded. During the CPC Central Committee's Meeting on Correcting Left-line Mistakes held between May 21 and June 12, 1961, he said, "Comrade Chen Yun ever said that the market should be put in the first place. A lot of people opposed at that time, but I did not say a word. Now, are we not marching to that direction?" When correcting the mistakes in Great Leap Forward, he also said that if the commodity exchange and the law of value were not understood,

[14] Party History Research Center ed., *Ninety Years of the Communist Party of China (Socialist Revolution and Development Period)*, History of Chinese Communist Party Publishing House and Party Building Readings Press, 2016, p. 650.

[15] *Ibid.*, p. 560.

there would be no correct understanding about socialism.[16]It is fair to say that the socialist construction led by the Party experienced twists and turns in this period, but some positive thinking and theoretical summaries were also made, which laid the foundation for launching and implementing the reform and opening-up and provided material guarantee and safeguarded the smooth progress of reform and opening-up.

1.4 To Start Exploring the Socialist Legal System in China along a Winding Road

The founding of the PRC provided the political premise and foundation for pursuing the rule of law in China. The application of law-based governance is an unprecedented move in Chinese history for it fundamentally guarantees the people as the masters of the country, and puts an end to the feudal rule for over two millennia and the rule of the Kuomingtang ("KMT") reactionaries.

After its founding, to ensure that political missions and economic development were carried out in an orderly manner under sound regulation, the Party led the Chinese people to create the legal system with Chinese characteristics at the same time. The outdated legal practices were abolished, declaring that the old laws and legal systems during the feudal and KMT rule be non-existent. The Party then led the representatives of other political parties to formulate the Common Program in lieu of the constitution, which reiterated the revolutionary fruits made by the Chinese people under the Party's leadership and stated the nature of new China and the system of government. In 1950, based on the provisions of Common Program, the Central People's Government formulated the provisional laws on customs, marriage, trade union, land reform and the regulations on punishing counterrevolutionaries. In 1954, the First Session of the First National People's Congress also adopted the laws on the organization of National People's Congress, State Council, people's courts, people's procuratorates, local people's congresses and local people's committees, and set out the principles of democratic centralism, democratic supervision and equality before the law and others. These new laws and legal principles had played an important and positive role in consolidating the powers of new government, accelerating the transition from new democratic society to socialist society, and promoting the transformation and development of state governance from feudal rule by man to democracy and rule by law. According to statistics, from 1949 to the eve of Cultural Revolution, the Chinese People's Political Consultative Conference (according to Article 13 of Common Program, "pending the National People's Congress", "exercises the functions and powers of the NPC"), the Central People's Government, the NPC and its Standing Committee formulated 127 documents in total in the forms of laws, decrees, resolutions and answers to certain legal issues, which gradually established,

[16] Mao Zedong Thought Study Group and First Section of Party Literature Research Office of CPC Central Committee ed., *To Understand Chinese Path from the Annals of Mao Zedong (1949–1976)*, Central Party Literature Press, 2017, p. 185, 42, 78.

consolidated, improved and developed socialism in China. During this period, the political affairs were handled with integrity, harmony was felt across the country, peace and order were maintained, and desire for progress and prosperity was well pronounced; the socialism in China had demonstrated its strength and vigor. All the promulgation of laws and principles shows that PRC paid due attention to legislation and the law-based governance even though in its puberty.

However, since the NPC was the only national legislative body as prescribed in the Common Program, the construction of legal system could not meet the demands of national economic and social development. In 1956, in his *On the Major Ten Relationships*, Mao Zedong stated, to "enlarge the powers of the local authorities to some extent, give them greater independence and let them do more, all on the premise that the unified leadership of the central authorities is to be strengthened. This will be advantageous to our task of building a powerful socialist country". "According to our Constitution, the legislative powers are all vested in the central authorities. But, provided that the policies of the central authorities are not violated, the local authorities may work out rules, regulations and measures in the light of their specific conditions and the needs of their work, and this is in no way prohibited by the Constitution."[17] His remarks reflected the Party leader's theoretical thinking on the governance of China from the perspective of the national system.

But the complex domestic and international situations influenced and changed the Party leader's focus. The left-line thinking gradually took hold of China's politics, causing serious setbacks to the socialist exploration and eventually the decade-long Cultural Revolution. The Party and the State had suffered greatly. From 1966 to 1978, the NPC and its Standing Committee adopted 9 pieces of legal documents including the Constitution, laws, rules, resolutions and decisions (the 1975 Constitution and 1978 Constitution are deemed as one document). Though the laws adopted before the Cultural Revolution were still in force, they could not meet the rising demands. During the Cultural Revolution, the massive democratic movements such as "kicking out the party committee to make revolution" and "smashing the public organs of security, procuratorates and courts" have paralyzed the state agencies at all levels, and caused premature death to the construction of socialist legal system that had just started in PRC. Between 1964 and 1974, the NPC rarely convened meetings, let alone made laws; the work on legislation was in stalemate.

The First Session of the Fourth National People's Congress convened in 1975 adopted a new constitution, i.e. the 1975 Constitution. It amended its predecessor in a full scale and made reflections on the mistaken theories and practices of the Cultural Revolution. Though it upheld the principles of people's democracy and socialism and advocated building "socialism with greater, faster, better, and more economical results", it took class struggle as the key link and the theory of continued revolution under the dictatorship of the proletariat as its guiding principles, established a system that confused the Party with government organizations, which weakened the functions of state agencies and judicial departments and abrogated the provisions

[17] MAO Zedong, *Selected Works of Mao Zedong (Vol.5)*, Foreign Languages Press, 1977, p.292, 294.p.

about the equality before the law and the state's guarantee for citizen's basic rights. Whether in form, style or contents, it was seriously defective, neither could it guarantee the socialist democratic politics, the socialist construction in which economic development takes the central priority, nor could it protect people's legitimate rights and interests. The eventual fate awaiting was to be abandoned by history. The wrong theories and practices developed in the Cultural Revolution had cost the Party and the country a big and disastrous price, and made the socialist construction suffer grave setbacks. The Party learned the lesson that institutional development was of utmost importance. In his speech titled *On the Reform of the System of Party and State Leadership*, Deng Xiaoping pointed out that "it is true that the errors we made in the past were partly attributable to the way of thinking and style of work of some leaders. But they were even more attributable to the problems in our organizational and working systems. If these systems are sound, they can place restraints on the actions of bad people; if they are unsound, they may hamper the efforts of good people or indeed, in certain cases, may push them in the wrong direction". He further emphasized that the problems in the national systems were more fundamental, widespread and long-lasting which should therefore command the attention of the entire Party.[18]

In October 1976, the Central Committee smashed the Gang of Four and ended these theories and practices, ending the disruption in legal system and helping redress the wrongs in guiding principles, steering China's socialist course into the right direction and constituting the solid foundation for developing socialist democracy, improving socialist legal system, carrying out socialist economic development and the law-based governance. The Eleventh National Congress of the CPC convened in August 1977 declared the end of the decade-long Cultural Revolution and reiterated the central task of building China into a socialist modern powerful country in the twentieth century.

To correct the mistakes made in the Cultural Revolution and eradicate the impact of the Gang of Four on China's political life, the Central Committee decided in 1977 to amend the 1975 Constitution. In March 1978, the First Session of the Fifth National People's Congress adopted the new constitution (1978 Constitution). Given the fact the Gang of Four was smashed not long ago and China was on the way to a new historical period, the time was not sufficient to summarize the experience and lessons from the socialist revolution and development since the founding of the PRC and to eliminate the malignant influence of Cultural Revolution. The 1978 Constitution was unavoidably characterized by such insufficiency. Since it embodied the initial achievements for correcting wrongs and inherited the 1975 Constitution, it was sitll a transitional one. Specifically, it restored the provisions of the system of people's congress, the apparatus of state agencies, and the principle of socialist democracy and legal system. It prescribed the setup of people's procuratorates again to realize its constitutional supervisory function, proposed the principal task and general objective of the Chinese people in the new stage, i.e. to "make a great, powerful, socialist country with modern agriculture, modern industry, modern national defense and

[18] DENG Xiaoping, *Selected Works of Deng Xiaoping (Vol.2)*, 1995, Foreign Languages Press, p.331–332..

modern science and technology by the end of the century". It added a provision that "(the state undertakes) high-speed development of the national economy, and it continuously develops the productive forces." It also promoted the development of science, education and the protection of environment and natural resources, prevention of pollution and other hazards to the public. These new amendments were well received by the people. Nevertheless, it failed to fundamentally get rid of the influence of the left-line guiding principles and to correct the wrong theories, policies and slogans of the Cultural Revolution, and still followed the continued revolution under the dictatorship of the proletariat. Therefore, comprehensive amendment was still awaiting.[19] The 1982 Constitution superseded the 1978 Constitution, laying the foundation for future rule of law development.

However tortuous as the road China had trodden in exploring the socialist development in the first 30 years since the founding of the PRC, the Party engaged in proactive theoretical thinking and put these theories into practice to identify the correct socialist direction, and made foundational achievements, which accumulated the experience for exploring the path with Chinese characteristics and laid a solid theoretical foundation, especially through the establishment of the socialist political system, the fundamental political and institutional premise for all the subsequent development in contemporary China.

2 Reform and Opening-up: A New Path Created for Chinese Socialist Cause

As directed by Xi Jinping, "reform and opening-up is a new great revolution of the Chinese people led by our Party in the new era. It is the most outstanding characteristic of contemporary China, and the distinctive feature of our Party." "Reform and opening-up plays the decisive role in determining the destiny of contemporary China. It is also the key to realizing the two centenary goals and the great rejuvenation of the Chinese nation." "Since the introduction of the reform and opening-up policy some three decades ago, our Party has begun to ponder the issue of state governance system from a new perspective, and come to the conclusion that the issues of leadership and organizational systems are fundamental, comprehensive, stable and permanent ones. Today, we are tasked with an important historic mission, that is to make our socialist system with Chinese characteristics more mature and better established, and provide a set of more complete, more stable and more effective systems for the development of the Party and the nation, the well-being of the people, social harmony and stability, and the enduring prosperity and stability of the country."[20] Reform and opening-up is the epoch-making event and historical turn after the founding of the PRC. It abandoned the Party's long-held left-line thinking and the guiding principles of taking

---

[19] ZHANG Jintan, *The History of Chinese Constitution (revised edition)*, China Legal Publishing House, 2016, p. 376.

[20] XI Jinping, *The Governance of China*, Foreign Languages Press, 2018, p.77, 97, 116–117.

class struggle as the key link and the theory of the continued revolution under the dictatorship of the proletariat and rejected the old massive and stormy struggles, while it transformed the governance of the country and put the economic and social development in a regulated and orderly manner.

2.1 Chinese Socialist Economic System as the Basis for Theory and Practice of Chinese Socialist System

According to classical Marxist writers, the base determines the superstructure. The unswerving adherence to implement reform and opening-up and the Party's basic line reflect this axiom, which can be specifically summarized as taking economic development as the central task, upholding the Four Cardinal Principles and continuing reform and opening-up. If we look back to the path we have trodden, we may find that reform and opening-up was initially launched as the breakthrough and principal task for establish and improve the Chinese socialist economic system with Chinese characteristics. It stands for the improvement and development of the Chinese socialist system and is the driving force for promoting comprehensive and deepened reform and opening-up. If there is no such an economic system, there will be no democratic, political and legal systems with Chinese characteristics that can follow its development, neither will the Chinese socialist system be improved and developed.

However, the course that has been pursued to improve and develop the economic system with Chinese characteristics is not without twists and turns; rather, the economic system was the result of long-term explorations and practices and later confirmed in the Constitution. During this course of history, China has transformed from the planned economy to market economy, from agricultural society to modern industrial and information society, from policy-led guarantee to law based guarantee for economic development. The Chinese socialist economic system has been targeted at releasing and developing the productive forces, and improving the people's livelihood and wellbeing. Deng reiterated that "pauperism is not socialism".[21] To take advantage of the superiority of socialism, eradicate poverty and make the country and its people prosper, Deng emphasized the importance of developing the socialist economic system with Chinese characteristics from several different angles.

With regard to the essence of socialism, Deng said, "the essence of socialism is liberation and development of the productive forces, elimination of exploitation and polarization, and the ultimate achievement of prosperity for all", "in building socialism we must do all we can to develop the productive forces and gradually eliminate poverty, constantly raising the people's living standards", "the fundamental task for the socialist stage is to develop the productive forces. The superiority of the socialist system is demonstrated, in the final analysis, by faster and greater development of those forces than under the capitalist system. As they develop, the people's material and cultural life will constantly improve", "socialism means eliminating

[21] DENG Xiaoping, *Selected Works of Deng Xiaoping (Vol.3)*, Foreign Languages Press, 1994, p.73.

poverty. Pauperism is not socialism, still less communism" and "(t)he primary task in the socialist period is to develop the productive forces and gradually improve people's material and cultural life. Our experience in the 20 years (1958–1978) teaches us that poverty is not socialism, that socialism means eliminating poverty. Unless you are developing the productive forces and raising people's living standards, you cannot say that you are building socialism".[22]

When talking about the direction of reform, he said, "this reform is part of the self-perfecting process of the socialist system, and in certain areas and to a certain extent it is also a revolutionary change...In the reform we have consistently followed two fundamental principles. One is the predominance of the socialist public sector of the economy; the other is common prosperity", "China's determination to adhere to socialism will not change", "since the very beginning of the reform we have been emphasizing the need for seeking common prosperity; that will surely be the central issue someday. Socialism does not mean allowing a few people to grow rich while the overwhelming majority live in poverty. No, that's not socialism. The greatest superiority of socialism is that it enables all the people to prosper, and common prosperity is the essence of socialism", "we are working hard to build socialism not only because socialism provides conditions for faster development of the productive forces than capitalism, but also because only socialism can eliminate the greed, corruption and injustice that are inherent in capitalism and other systems of exploitation".[23]

In contemplating the means for developing socialist economy, Deng pointed that "one way in which socialism is superior to capitalism is that under socialism the people of the whole country can work as one and concentrate their strength on key projects. A shortcoming of socialism is that the market is not put to best use and the economy is too rigid. How should we handle the relation between planning and the market? If we handle it properly, it will help greatly to promote economic development; if we don't, things will go badly", "there is no fundamental contradiction between socialism and a market economy. The problem is how to develop the productive forces more effectively", "Actually they are both means of developing the productive forces. So long as they serve that purpose, we should make use of them. If they serve socialism they are socialist; if they serve capitalism they are capitalist", and "the proportion of planning to market forces is not the essential difference between socialism and capitalism. A planned economy is not equivalent to socialism, because there is planning under capitalism too; a market economy is not capitalism, because there are markets under socialism too. Planning and market forces are both means of controlling economic activity".[24]

The Deng Xiaoping Theory has liberated China from ideological shackles and established the socialist economic system with Chinese characteristics which has been improved and developed along with the deepened reform and opening-up.

---

[22] *Ibid.*, p.21, 73, 122, 361.

[23] *Ibid.*, p. 145, 146, 334, 351.

[24] *Ibid.*, p.26–27, 151, 203, 361.p.

Xi Jinping's elaborations when reviewing the glorious past of the four-decade reform and opening demonstrate the leading role of the Chinese socialist economic system in improving and developing the Chinese socialist system. This socialist economic system contributes to the theory and practice of its socialist system and lays the foundation for rule of law in China.[25]

2.2 *To Start Socialist Legal System Construction to Promote Complete Transformation of State Governance*

In 1978, the Third Plenary Session of the Eleventh Central Committee decided to steer the course of the Party and state's focus on socialist modernization, opening a chapter for the reform and opening-up history. In this conference, Deng Xiaoping said, "to ensure people's democracy, we must strengthen our legal system. Democracy has to be institutionalized and written into law, so as to make sure that institutions and laws do not change whenever the leadership changes, or whenever the leaders change their views or shift the focus of their attention", and "from now on, legislation should be an important agenda on the work of the NPC and its standing committee", as emphasized in this conference.[26]

Confronted with this historical mission, how should the socialist legal system be promoted? And how should the work on legislation be carried out?

Deng's speech crystallized the direction for the Party and China's future development and laid out the path for China's legal system construction. He said, "the trouble now is that our legal system is incomplete, with many laws yet to be enacted.... So we must concentrate on enacting criminal and civil codes, procedural laws and other necessary laws concerning factories, people's communes, forests, grasslands and environmental protection, as well as labor laws and a law on investment by foreigners. These laws should be discussed and adopted through democratic procedures. Meanwhile, the procuratorial and judicial organs should be strengthened. All this will ensure that there are laws to go by, that they are observed and strictly enforced, and that violators are brought to book. The relations between one enterprise and another, between enterprises and the state, between enterprises and individuals, and so on should also be defined by law, and many of the contradictions between them should be resolved by law. There is a lot of legislative work to do, and we don't have enough trained people. Therefore, legal provisions will have to be less than perfect to start with, then be gradually improved upon". To ensure effective implementation of laws, he further emphasized, that "just as the country must have laws, the Party must have rules and regulations. The fundamental ones are embodied in the Party Constitution. Without rules and regulations in the Party it would be hard to ensure that the laws

[25] Xi Jinping, *Speech at the Grand Gathering to Celebrate the 40th Anniversary of Reform and Opening-up*, Qiushi Journal, Vol. 24, 2018.

[26] Deng Xiaoping, *Selected Works of Deng Xiaoping (Vol.2)*, Foreign Languages Press, 1995, p.156.

of the state are enforced".[27] He illustrated the important role of strengthening the socialist legal system construction, the relationship between the Party's rules and regulations and national laws in developing socialist rule of law, and the essence of Chinese socialist rule of law. In a word, China's socialist rule of law inherently reflects the essential requirements of adhering to the Party's leadership, observe the Party's rules and regulations and strictly disciplining itself. In the Twelfth CPC National Congress held in 1982, the Constitution of the Communist Party of China (the "Party's Constitution") was amended, adding that "the Party must be bound by the Constitution and other laws", which made the Party's leadership and socialist rule of law construction into an organic whole. "Adhering to the Party's leadership, respecting and following the people's will and strictly observing law when carrying out our work are consistent and integrated with each other", all of which are still under great undertakings and are inherent to the socialist legal system construction in the early stage of reform and opening-up. Therefore, to develop socialist democracy and a sound socialist legal system has been the unwavering basic line of the Party and the state at the start of reform and opening-up, and the fundamental principle that the Party never gives up.

The integration of the Party's leadership, the position of the people as masters of the country, and the rule of law is a self-portrait that tells the story of the great practices in developing socialist democracy, and is marked as the new transformation of China towards a modern state governance under the Party's leadership. On February 23, 1979, in the Sixth Session of the Fifth National People's Congress, the Standing Committee adopted the provisional Forest Law and the Regulation on Arrest and Detention, marking the entry of China into a new stage where laws were enacted for promoting reform. On July 1, 1979, the decision to amend several provisions of the 1978 Constitution was made in the Second Session of the Fifth National People's Congress. The amendments included the establishment of the standing committees at or above the county level people's congresses and the provisions that the people's congresses at all levels convene regular conferences and exercise some functions and powers. This session also adopted the Law on the Organization of Local People's Congresses and Governments, Electoral Law, Law on the Organization of People's Court, Law on the Organization of People's Procuratorate, Criminal Law, Criminal Procedure Law, and Law on Chinese-Foreign Equity Joint Ventures. These legislations ushered the reform and opening-up in a new stage characterized by rapid legal system development, and restored the social order. For a country whose rule of law had failed due to the decade-long Cultural Revolution, legislation took the initiative to boost national development, and the change of laws started to promote reform. By taking it as an opportunity, the socialist cause in China explored a new path that enabled China to walk with its own characteristics and gradually towards a sound and orderly rule of law. China was met with unprecedented change.

[27] Ibid., pp.156–157.

2.3 1982 Constitution: A Compass for Reform and Opening-up and Socialist Modernization Practice

As Xi Jinping put it, the Constitution is enacted and improved based on a thoughtful summary of the successes of China's socialist revolution, development and reform, and the logical outcome of history, theory, and practice based on the strenuous efforts of the Chinese people in modern times.

Socialism has been the bedrock of Chinese nation on which the Party has unswervingly rested itself since the founding of the PRC. The Common Program as the provisional constitution in 1949 stipulated China's state system, the system of government and other basic policies in all respects; the 1954 Constitution, based on the Common Program, added the principles of people's democracy and socialism. The 1975 Constitution, though still plagued by the left-line thinking, the 1978 Constitution, and the 1982 Constitution adopted during the reform and opening-up never gave up socialism.

Based on the spirits and main provisions of Common Program and 1954 Constitution, the enactment of the 1982 Constitution inherited, improved and developed the old constitutions under new historical conditions. It fully exemplified the guidelines, principles and policies formulated since the Third Plenary Session of the Eleventh Central Committee, stipulated "one central task, two basic points" (taking economic development as the central task, upholding the Four Cardinal Principles and continuing reform and opening) as the basic line, clarified the fundamental task, basic programs, direction for development, and goal, made additions to citizen's basic rights and obligations, and restored and improved the state authorities and systems. These provisions calibrated the compass for directing the reform and opening-up and the socialist modernization, complied with the constitutional provisions, and formed constitutional basis for them. They are also the basic political principles that China's legislation has persistently upheld in the past 4040 years' reform and opening-up.

Since its promulgation, the NPC have made 52 pieces of amendments in 1988, 1993, 1999, 2004 and 2018 under the Party's leadership. These amendments reflect the success and experience in reform and opening-up and socialist modernization carried out by the Chinese people under the Party's leadership. They are the achievements made when exploring the socialist path with Chinese characteristics, and developing the socialist theory, system and culture with Chinese characteristics. They are also the increasingly deepened understanding and knowledge of the laws of governance by the Party, the laws of building socialism, the laws of socialist market economy and the laws of socialist rule of law.

The 1982 Constitution and its five amendments laid the foundation for the steady progress of reform and opening-up and the socialist modernization, and played an important role in consolidating, sticking to, improving and developing socialist system with Chinese characteristics, and promoting the modernization of state governance system and capacity. This conclusion is made by considering the following aspects: first, the 1982 Constitution and its five amendments set out and improve the tasks and goals of national development, guiding principles, basic line, and basic program, and establish the Deng Xiaoping Theory, the important thought of the Three Represents, the Scientific Outlook on Development, and Xi Jinping Thought on Socialism with Chinese characteristics for a New Era as the guidelines for political and social development in China; they adjust the overall plan for building Chinese socialism and the second two-centenary goal and make additions to them; they nourish and improve the content of the development of revolution and progress in China, put "reform and opening-up" with "revolution and development" in equal terms, faithfully describing the glorious course of the Party and Chinese people's concerted efforts to promote reform and opening-up. Second, the 1982 Constitution and its five amendments state the nature of the country that the People's Republic of China "is a socialist state under the people's democratic dictatorship led by the working class and based on the alliance of workers and peasants. The socialist system is the basic system of the PRC. Disruption of the socialist system by any organization or individual is prohibited". Third, they provide for the attribution of state powers and the organization of government, "all power in the PRC belongs to the people", "The National People's Congress and the local people's congresses at various levels are the organs through which the people exercise state power", "all administrative, judicial and procuratorial organs of the state are created by the people's congresses to which they are responsible and by which they are supervised" (Article 2 and Article 3). The regional autonomy system is pursued in these provisions, and the establishment of the self-government organs and their powers and functions are also provided for. The provision that "the state may establish special administrative regions when necessary", which provides constitutional basis for accomplishing peaceful reunification of the motherland and resolving the remaining historical issues concerning Hong Kong, Macau and Taiwan in a flexible and proactive way. It effectively safeguards national sovereignty and territorial integrity. Fourth, they clearly state and improve basic national economic system, i.e. "the basis of the socialist economic system of PRC is socialist public ownership of the means of production", "in the primary stage of socialism, the state upholds the basic economic system in which the public ownership is dominant and diverse forms of ownership develop side by side", "the non-public sectors of the economy such as the individual and private sectors of the economy, operating within the limits prescribed by law, constitute an important component of the socialist market economy", and "the state protects the lawful rights and interests of the non-public sectors of the economy such as the individual and private sectors of the economy. The state encourages, supports and guides the development of the non-public sectors of the economy and, in accordance with law, exercises supervision and control over the non-public sectors of the economy". It is further stipulated that the state "practiced market economy" to replace "planned economy", and "strengthens economic legislation, improves macro-regulation and control". Fifth, the 1982 Constitution and its five amendments clarify and improve the protection of property rights as "socialist public property is inviolable", "citizens' lawful private property is inviolable", "the state, in accordance with law, protects the rights of citizens to private property and to its inheritance" and "the state may, in the public interest and in accordance with law, expropriate or requisition private property for its use and make compensation for the private property expropriated or requisitioned". Sixth, they clearly state and improve the state governance as "the people administer state affairs and manage economic, cultural and social affairs through various channels and in various ways in accordance with the law", the state "governs the country according to law and makes it a socialist country under rule of law", and "uphold the uniformity and dignity of the socialist legal system". Seventh, they set out and improve the citizen's fundamental rights and obligations, as "the state respects and protects human rights", "no citizen may be arrested except with the approval or by decision of a people's procuratorate or by decision of a people's court, and arrests must be made by a public security organ. Unlawful detention or deprivation or restriction of citizen freedom of the person by other means is prohibited, and unlawful search of the person of citizens is prohibited". The residence of citizens and the personal dignity are inviolable, and the citizens enjoy the freedom of speech, of the press, of assembly, of association, of procession, of demonstration, of religious belief and of correspondence. Last, the 1982 Constitution and its five amendments clarify and improve the organization of government and its responsibilities, i.e. the NPC Standing Committee was empowered to exercise the legislative power, the presidency of the PRC was resumed, the standing committees could be established at or above the county level people's congresses, the provincial people's congresses and their standing committees and the people's congresses of cities with subordinate districts and their standing committees were granted with certain legislative power on local affairs, the term of state leadership was prescribed, the national and local supervisory commissions were established, and the like. These provisions have been followed by China's legislation since the reform and opening-up.

In the past 40 years, the guidelines and policies formulated by the Party and the State have been grounded in the basic line of the Party as affirmed by the Constitution and have reflected the spirit of the Constitution. All the achievements made since reform and opening-up are the inevitable results of upholding and implementing the Constitution. During this period, the Constitution has been amended several times, thereby continuously providing a strong constitutional guarantee for advancing reform and opening-up and socialist modernization in the new era. These amendments themselves are also the most important achievements of reform and opening-up and socialist modernization. The history of the past 40 years has demonstrated that the Constitution upholds the Party's leadership, convincingly ensures that the Chinese people are the masters of the country, vigorously promotes reform and opening-up and socialist modernization, advances the building of a law-based socialist country, and safeguards national reunification, national unity and social stability. It is a good Constitution that accords with China's national conditions and realities, and keeps abreast of the times.

2.4 System of People's Congresses: A Fundamental Political Guarantee for Building Chinese Socialist System and Modernizing State Governance System and Capacity

Xi Jinping pointed out that "the system of people's congresses is an important component of the system of socialism with Chinese characteristics, and the fundamental political system underpinning China's governance system and governance capacity."[28] This argument demonstrates the status and important role of the system of people's congresses as the state's fundamental political system in improving and developing socialist system with Chinese characteristics, and modernizing state governance system and capacity.

The revolution, development and reform led by the Party have always carried forward the belief and pursuit of socialism and adhered to the fundamental principle of people's master position. Since the founding of the PRC, the socialist democratic system with Chinese characteristics has remained unchanged in its fundamental nature, but has undergone improvement and development after initiating the reform and opening-up, although the socialist path was tortuous during certain periods. The decision to amend several provisions of the 1978 Constitution was made in the Second Session of the Fifth National People's Congress held in 1979. The amendments included the establishment of the standing committees at or above the county level people's congress, and the provisions that the people's congresses at all levels should convene regular sessions and exercise some functions and powers. This session also adopted the Local Organization Law, Electoral Law, Law on the Organization of People's Court, Law on the Organization of People's Procuratorate and other laws concerning the state system construction. The Local Organization Law made it clear that the provincial people's congresses and their standing committees had certain legislative power, on the basis of which they could formulate local regulations on local affairs. These provisions were helpful in restoring, improving and developing the system of people's congresses.

The 1982 Constitution and its five amendments expand the scope of functions and powers of the NPC and its Standing Committee, better the construction of local state powers, and provided reliable constitutional guarantee for advancing, developing and improving the system of people's congresses. With regard to the national legislation, the NPC and its Standing Committee co-exercise the legislative powers; as the permanent body of NPC, its Standing Committee may exercise such legislative power frequently. Based on the division of functions and powers, the NPC amends the Constitution, supervises the enforcement of the Constitution, and enacts and amends basic laws governing criminal offences, civil affairs, the state agencies and other matters, while its Standing Committee interprets the Constitution and supervises its enforcement, enacts and amends laws except those which should be enacted by the NPC, partially supplements and amends, when the NPC is not in session, laws enacted

[28] Xi Jinping, *Speech at the Ceremony Marking the 60th Anniversary of the National People's Congress*, People's Publishing House, 2014, p. 9. The English text can be found at http://en.qstheory.cn/2020-03/20/c_489248.htm

by the NPC provided that the basic principles of these laws are not contravened, and interprets laws. In the local legislation, the 1982 Constitution and its five amendments clearly provided for that the provincial people's congresses and their standing committees may adopt local regulations, which must not contravene the Constitution, the law and administrative rules and regulations; the people's congresses of the cities with subordinate districts and their standing committees may also adopt local regulations, which must not contravene the Constitution, the law, administrative rules and regulations, and the local regulations of the province and the autonomous region, and report such local regulations to the standing committee of the province or the autonomous region. These arrangements of the legislative system reflect the spirits of reform and opening-up, and provide constitutional guarantee for mobilizing the initiative of both the central and local authorities. They are major acts to advance and improve the system of people's congresses that also improve and develop the socialist system with Chinese characteristics. In the past four decades, whether the NPC and its Standing Committee or the local people's congresses and their standing committees, they have earnestly exercised the functions and powers conferred by the Constitution, deepened legislation in a scientific, democratic, and law-based manner by taking the legislative quality as the key, better the legislation's institutions and procedures, and strived to make each and every legislation conform with the spirits of the Constitution, reflect the people's will and win people's support. Their exercise of functions and powers has provided strong legal guarantee for promoting socialist modernization and solid foundation to modernize the state governance system and capacity.

The system of people's congresses in China is the product of integrating the Marxist theory on the state with the realities of China, as developed and refined by the Party. It also reflects the achievements in adapting the theory of scientific socialism to China's conditions. As pointed out by Xi Jinping, "China's implementation of the system of people's congresses represented a monumental innovation in human political history made by the Chinese people, and reflected all the painful lessons drawn from China's political process since modern times began. It was the result of Chinese society's dramatic transformation and development over more than a century, and the inevitable choice made by the Chinese people who had finally become masters of their country and taken control of their own density."[29] Over the past 70 years Since the founding of the PRC, especially over the past 40 years since the reform and opening-up, the system of people's congresses has been consolidated and developed along the socialist modernization practices, representing tremendous vitality. The NPC and its Standing Committee, and the local people's congress and their standing committees that have legislative power, have made full use of their functions and powers in this regard, which, as a legal system, provides strong support for promoting the high-speed social and economic development and securing the prosperity of all the undertakings carried out by the Party and the State. The system itself is also developed and improved during the course of realizing rule of law. It has been proven by history that this system is a sound one that accords with

[29] *Ibid.*.

China's national conditions and realities, embodies China socialist character, safeguards people's master position, and guarantees the rejuvenation of Chinese nation. It also integrates the Party's leadership, people's master position and the rule of law into an organic whole, advances and improves the socialist system with Chinese characteristics, and guarantees the modernization of state governance system and capacity. As we embark on new endeavors, we must continue to uphold and improve the system of people's congresses, fully make use of its role as our fundamental political system, and continue to use it as a means of keeping the future of the country and nation safely in the hands of Chinese people.

3 Socialist Legal System with Chinese Characteristics: Basis for Promoting Modernization of State Governance System and Capacity

The Third Plenary Session of the Eleventh CPC Central Committee made a thoughtful summary of the experience and lessons of socialist construction after the founding of the PRC, cleared the haze clouding the China's politics and society, put the state governance into the track of rule of law again, and set out the tasks and objectives of socialist legal system. The spring has come for China to build rule of law. Since then, China's rule of law construction has progressed in a sound and orderly manner. In the past 40 years, the NPC and the Party have spared no effort to advancing and improving the Chinese socialist legal system. In November 1982, the NPC's work report made its first mention: "legislation should be based on the realities of China, and an independent legal system with Chinese characteristics should be gradually established by adhering the principle of socialist legal system", and in the Seventh Five-year plan period, "a rather complete system of laws and regulations on economic affairs should be build"; in the Third Plenary Session of the Fourteenth CPC Central Committee convened in 1993, "the legal system of socialist market economy should be set in the preliminary stage", and then in the Fifteenth CPC National Congress, "the Chinese socialist legal system should be established". In the Seventeenth and Eighteenth CPC National Congress, "the Chinese socialist legal system should be improved", and in the Nineteenth CPC National Congress, "the Chinese socialist legal system at the heart of which is the Constitution should be improved and a Chinese system of socialist rule of law should be established, and the socialist country based on the rule of law should be established". The NPC and its Standing Committee adheres to the correct political direction, persist in connecting legislative decision-making with reform decisions, set out the focus and objectives of legislation at the time when the CPC Central Committee laid its major work and made decisions and arrangements on the work. They have made great achievements in strengthening and improving the work on legislation. Through concerted efforts, by the end of August 2019, the NPC and its Standing Committee had adopted the Constitution and its five amendments, formulated or amended 643 pieces of laws, 25 pieces of interpretations and 258 pieces of decisions concerning some legal and other major issues. By that time, China had 274 pieces of laws and 119 pieces of decisions in force that were incorporated in the Collection of the Laws of the People's Republic of China (2018 Edition). In addition, the State Council had formulated over 600 pieces of administrative regulations, the people's congresses and their standing committees that have legislative power had adopted over 12,000 pieces of regulations on local affairs. With the formation, improvement and development of the Chinese socialist legal system with the Constitution as the core, the socialist system with Chinese characteristics has also been consolidated, improved and developed according to law, which effectively promotes the modernization of state governance system and capacity.

First, between 1979 and 1989, the focus of the work on legislation was to quickly formulate laws to restore the national system and initiate the reform and opening-up.

At the start of reform and opening-up period, everything was left undone. To adapt to the needs for quickly restoring the national political and economic order, maintaining a peaceful and cohesive political environment and starting socialist modernization, on July 1, 1979, the Second Session of the National People's Congress adopted seven laws at one time, which marked the full restart of the work on legislation. The whole legal system in this period was underscored by the fact that China still practiced a system dominated by planned economy and supported by market adjustment, so a combination of planning and market was still adhered to at that time. The NPC and its Standing Committee adopted the new Constitution, formulated and amended 98 laws and issued 64 decisions on legal issues. Apart from the 1982 Constitution and the constitutional amendment in 1988, to restore the national political, economic and social order, the NPC adopted the Law on the Organization of National People's Congress, Law on the Organization of State Council, Regional Ethnic Autonomy Law, Law on the Organization of the Villagers' Committees, Law on the Organization of the Urban Residents' Committees, Marriage Law, Individual Income Tax Law, Regulation on Administrative Penalties for Public Security, Law on Assemblies, Processions and Demonstrations, Urban Planning Law, Economic Contract Law, General Principles of Civil Law, Trademark Law, Patent Law, Civil Procedure Law (Provisional), Enterprise Bankruptcy Law (Provisional), Administrative Procedure Law, Law on the Prevention and Control of Water Pollution, Law on the Prevention and Control of Air Pollution, and Environment Protection Law; to enhance opening-up, after the Law on Chinese-Foreign Equity Joint Ventures was formulated in 1979, it adopted successively the Income Tax Law for Enterprises with Foreign Investment and Foreign Enterprises, Law on Economic Contracts Involving Foreign Interest, Law on Wholly Foreign-Owned Enterprises, Law on Chinese-Foreign Contractual Joint Ventures, Law on Control of the Entry and Exit of Aliens, Law on Frontier Health and Quarantine, Customs Law, and Law on Import and Export Commodity Inspection. These laws made fundamental changes to many important areas where no law could be resorted to previously, provided a legal guarantee for rapidly restoring the state and the social order, enhancing sound and orderly economic and social development, and carrying out the open strategy. They also marked the gradual transition from policy-oriented to law-based governance, laying the foundation for economic transformation. Given these achievements, the report of the Thirteenth CPC National Congress stated that "the socialist legal system in which the Constitution is the core has come into form".

Second, between the early 1990 to the end of 2002, the focus was to strengthen the legislation in economic sectors to satisfy the needs of socialist market economy, improve the national macro-regulation and control, proactively establish the legal system for socialist market economy and lay the foundation for the Chinese socialist legal system.

In 1989, China was struck by a grave political turmoil. The Party led the Chinese people in withstanding the domestic and international pressure from a trend of opposing the Party's leadership and socialism, as well as from the disintegration of socialist countries in East Europe led by the Soviet Union, and the serious setbacks to socialism consequently. However, China successfully rectified deviations and corrected the course and, continued to deepen reform and opening-up. In 1992, Deng Xiaoping made the famous south tour speeches, which marked the entry of China into a new phase of reform and opening-up. The planned economy was transformed to socialist market economy, and the rule of law as a fundamental principle was put forward. The Fourteenth CPC National Congress set out the objective of practicing the socialist market economy, and the Third Plenary Session of the Fourteenth CPC Central Committee advanced that "the legal system that adapts to the socialist market economy should be established by the end of this century". In the Fifteenth CPC National Congress, the basic principles of "rule of law and establishing a socialist law-based country" was put forward, and the task then was to "strengthen the work on legislation, improve its quality and form a legal system with Chinese characteristics by 2010". In this period, after a long-march of arduous negotiations, China was acceded to the World Trade Organization ("WTO"), and the entry into the international social and economic system laid out the requirements on China's law-based modernization. Therefore, the NPC and its Standing Committee lost no time to promulgate and amend the laws concerning market economy. For example, they adopted the constitutional amendment, formulated and amended 186 pieces of laws, made 94 pieces of decisions on legal issues, and issued 9 pieces of interpretations. In the 1993 constitutional amendment, it was clearly stated that "the state practices socialist market economy", and "the state strengthens economic legislation, improves macro-regulation and control". The 1999 constitutional amendment furthered the improvement of the national economic system, clarified that the non-public sectors of the economy such as the individual and private sectors of the economy are the important components of the socialist market economy, and provided for the basic principles of "rule of law and establishing a law-based socialist country". The two amendments had provided constitutional guarantee for establishing socialist market economy and socialist rule of law.

The NPC also enacted laws with regard to the constitutional concerns, such as the National Flag Law, National Emblem Law, Martial Law, Law on Legislation, State Compensation Law, Basic Law of Hong Kong Special Administrative Region and Basic Law of Macao Special Administrative Region; in market economy, it adopted Company Law, Contract Law, Partnership Enterprise Law, Anti-Unfair Competition

Lawn, Law on the Protection of Consumer Rights and Interests, Law on Urban Real Estate Management, Auction Law, Guaranty Law, Budget Law, Price Law, Foreign Trade Law; it formulated the Administrative Penalty Law and the Administrative Reconsideration Law; on people's livelihood and wellbeing, the Labor Law, Law on the Protection of Minors, Law on the Protection of Women's Rights and Interests, Trade Union Law, Law on the Promotion of Privately-run Schools, Work Safety Law were also formulated. Meanwhile, the Criminal Law, the Criminal Procedure Law and the Civil Procedure Law were amended. Considering the improved legal system in all respects, the NPC Standing Committee declared in 1998 that the law in China "presented a preliminary legal framework for socialist market economy". After five year's efforts, in 2003, the NPC Standing Committee announced that "the Chinese socialist legal system with the Constitution as the core has come into form". The construction of Chinese socialist legal system has made milestone progress.

Third, from early 2003 to the end of 2012, the focus was to actively promote a harmonious society to accomplish the goal of building a moderately prosperous society in all respects and to ensure that the Chinese socialist legal system will be established and improved as scheduled.

The Sixteenth and the Seventeenth National CPC National Congresses convened in 2002 and 2007 set the goal of building a moderately prosperous society in all respects. To ensure it would be attained, the Sixteenth CPC National Congress emphasized the goal of the work on legislation that was already advocated in the previous congress, which was to "form a Chinese socialist legal system". The Seventeenth CPC National Congress updated the goal, "to deepen legislation in a scientific and democratic manner and improve the Chinese socialist legal system" as it was phrased. Guided by this goal and the indispensable importance of quality, the NPC in this period mainly focused on the laws that were the pillars of the Chinese socialist legal system and urgently needed and mature for legislation. The NPC and its Standing Committee adopted the constitutional amendment, formulated and amended 138 laws, made 41 decisions on legal issues and issued 7 interpretations.

In this decade, the 2004 constitutional amendment was the most important, for it clearly stipulated that the state respects and preserves human rights, the citizens' property right and the right to succession are protected by law, and other important issues. It was another milestone for socialist democracy. In the meantime, some theoretical research on the Chinese socialist legal system was made, the results of which made a division of the departments of law for the first time. For example, in the laws concerning constitutional concerns, the NPC formulated or amended Anti-Secession Law, Law on the Supervision of Standing Committees of People's Congresses at Various Levels, Regional Ethnic Autonomy Law, and Law on the Organization of the Villagers' Committees; in civil and commercial laws, it formulated or amended the Property Rights Law, Tort Law, Company Law, Securities Law, Law on Chinese-Foreign Equity Joint Ventures, Law on Wholly Foreign-Owned Enterprises, Law on Chinese-Foreign Contractual Joint Ventures; in the economic laws, it formulated or amended the Anti-Monopoly Law, Vehicle and Vessel Tax Law, Product Quality Law, Law on Anti-Money Laundering, Law on Tax Collection and Administration. The Regulation on Agricultural Tax was abolished. In administrative laws, it formulated or amended the Administrative Reconsideration Law, Administrative Licensing Law, Law on Administrative Penalties for Public Security, Administrative Supervision Law, Civil Servants Law, Food Safety Law, Drug Administration Law, and Law on the Protection of Cultural Relics; in social legislation, it formulated or amended the Work Safety Law, Social Insurance Law and Labor Contract Law. In criminal legislation, it adopted the Fifth to Eighth Amendments to and three interpretations on criminal law. In procedure and non-litigation procedure law, it formulated the Special Maritime Procedure Law, Law on the Mediation and Arbitration of Rural Land Contract Disputes and Law on Labor Dispute Mediation and Arbitration. The NPC also carried out several special operations to sort out the obsolete laws that did not conform to the social and economic development and inconsistency among the laws to ensure the scientific nature, harmony and unity in the legal system.

By the end of 2020, the number of the effective laws, including the Constitution, were 237 in total, administrative regulations 690 and local rules and regulations over 8600. In the Fourth Session of the Eleventh National People's Congress held on March 10, 2011, Wu Bangguo, Chairman of the NPC Standing Committee stated that "we have established the Chinese socialist legal system that adapts to the conditions of this country, the needs of reform and opening-up and socialist modernization and reflects the will of the Party and Chinese people. In this system, the Constitution plays the central role, the relevant constitutional, civil, commercial, and other departmental laws are the pillars, and the legislation can be divided into law, administrative regulations and local rules and regulations. The economic, political, cultural, social, and ecological development and others in China are able to be well-founded on law. The goal of the work on legislation put forward in the Fifteenth CPC National Congress is attained as scheduled."[30] It is an important milestone for China's socialist democracy, a critical indicator for the advancement and improvement of the socialist system with Chinese characteristics, and a lively example of China's gradually modernizing governance system and capacity.

Fourth, in the period from the early 2013 to this day, the work on legislation has focused on adapting the new situations created by China's entry into a new era and on the key areas. In this period, the Chinese socialist legal system with the Constitution as the core has been improved, the Chinese socialist system been further developed, and the modernization of state governance system and capacity made steady progress.

The Eighteenth CPC National Congress put forward the objective and task of building China into a moderately prosperous society in an all-round way. At the same time, the Party proposed to comprehensively promote the rule of law, legislation in a scientific manner, strict law enforcement, impartial justice, and law-abiding by all people, improve the Chinese socialist legal system, and strengthen key areas legislation. Since the conference, the undertakings of the party and the state have undergone historic changes. At the beginning of 2013, when the Twelfth NPC Standing Committee was established, it formulated a legislative plan based on the goals and tasks proposed by the conference, and make corresponding adjustments to the legislative plan based on the reform proposals in the Third and Fourth Sessions of Eighteenth

[30] For the full text of Wu's report, see http://www.gov.cn/2011lh/content_1827143.htm

CPC National Congress. The Twelfth NPC and its Standing Committee adhered to the centralized and unified leadership of the Central Committee over legislative work, focused on implementing the decisions and arrangements made by the CPC Central Committee, ensured the prioritized function of legislation, and gave full play to the leading and motivational role of legislation and the role of the NPC and its Standing Committee in the work on legislation. Legislation in key areas has been continuously strengthened. Great new achievements have been made in all these areas. For example, In the field of national security, the National Security Law, Anti-Espionage Law, Anti-Terrorism Law, and Cyber Security Law were formulated; on market economy, the compilation of civil laws was under steady progress, the General Principles of Civil Law, Tourism law, Environment Protection Tax Law were promulgated, and the Anti-Unfair Competition Law, Law on the Promotion of Small and Medium-Sized Enterprises were amended. For people's livelihood and wellbeing, the Charity Law, Traditional Chinese Medicine Law, Anti-Domestic Violence Law were formulated, and the Food Safety Law was revised. For cultural development, the Law on the Guarantee of Public Cultural Services, Public Libraries Law and Film Industry Promotion Law were promulgated. In the field of ecological civilization, the Environment Protection Law, the Law on the Prevention and Control of Air Pollution, and the Law on the Prevention and Control of Water Pollution were revised. At the same time, the authorization decision and legal decisions are used to ensure that major reform measures are well grounded on law. In the past five years, a total of 25 pieces of laws have been formulated, 127 revised, 46 pieces of decisions on legal issues and major issues passed, and 9 legal pieces of interpretations made. It has made a significant contribution to the construction of the socialist rule of law system.

In 2017, the Nineteenth CPC National Congress clearly put forward the Two centenary goals and made a "two-step" strategic arrangement for China's development after 2020. The Thirteenth NPC Standing Committee, established in March 2018, is in the historical conjuncture of the two centenary goals. The NPC Standing Committee firmly grasped the new opportunity of socialism with Chinese characteristics entering a new era, earnestly implemented the strategic goals and tasks proposed by the Central Committee, accelerated the pace of legislation, proactively formulated the legislative plan, and reported it to the Central Committee for approval and implementation. Apart from the amendments to the Constitution adopted at the First Session of the Thirteenth National People's Congress, as of the end of August 2019, the NPC and its Standing Committee had formulated the Supervision Law, Law on the Protection of Heroes and Martyrs, People's Assessors Law, E-commerce Law, and Law on the Prevention and Control of Soil Pollution, Law on International Criminal Judicial Assistance, Regulation on Fire and Rescue Ranks, Law on Farmland Occupation Tax, Law on Vehicle Purchase Tax, Foreign Investment Law, Vaccine Management Law, and Resource Tax Law. The Standing Committee revised the Individual Income Tax Law, Criminal Procedure Law, Law on the Organization of People's Court, Law on the Organization of People's Procuratorate, Company Law, Social Insurance Law, Rural Land Contract Law, Civil Servants Law, Judge Law, Prosecutor Law, Drug Administration Law, Land Administration Law, Law on

Urban Real Estate Administration and other 47 laws. At the same time, it also made 13 decisions on issues such as the adjustment of the administrative responsibilities as stipulated by law when advancing the institutional reform of the State Council, the establishment of Shanghai Financial Court, the responsibilities of the Constitution and the Law Committee, the functions and responsibilities of the China Coast Guard in maritime rights protection and law enforcement, and the authorization to the State Council to implement the drug marketing authorization holder system in some places and litigation procedures for intellectual property rights cases, and the Resolution of the Standing Committee of the National People's Congress on Comprehensively Tightening Ecological and Environmental Protection and Lawfully Promoting Triumph in the Uphill Battle for Prevention and Control of Pollution. These decisions and resolutions marked a good start for the work on legislation.

Improving and developing the socialist system with Chinese characteristics is the inevitable requirement and fundamental task of building China into a socialist rule of law country, on which all the laws and regulations and related systems and mechanisms are based. The legislative history over the past 40 years is a course of progress that the NPC and its Standing Committee, and the local people's congresses and its standing committees with legislative power, by strictly adhering to the Chinese socialist path, following the centralized and unified leadership of the Party and respecting the dominant position of the people, promote the legal development consistent with the national economic, political, cultural, social and ecological progress in all respects and make the socialism prosper and enduring. In the past 40 years, the Chinese socialist legal system with the Constitution as the core has gradually taken its shape and achieved uninterrupted progress; a deeper integration of decisions related to development and reform with legislative decision-making has been achieved for motivating the unfatigued reform and opening-up. The legislative system and institutions have progressed with increasing improvement underpinned by a more scientific and democratic manner. Over the past four decades, the capacity of the legislature has achieved significant progress and the team of legislators continued to grow stronger. In the meantime, the Chinese socialist system has also been consolidated, improved, and developed through the increasingly intact normative structure for legal system, and such normative structure also in turn pushes forward the state agencies in all levels and the officials and cadres to improve their expertise in legal thinking and application of law to improve the modernization of the state governance system and capacity.

4 Overall Goal of Comprehensively Deepening Reform: Guidance of Legislation

The Constitution declares that the socialist system is the basic system of China. In the Third Plenary Session of the Eighteenth CPC National Congress, "the general purpose of deepening its all-round reform is to develop socialism with Chinese characteristics, to advance modernization in the state governance system and governance capability". This statement has illuminated the direction of comprehensively deepening reform and opening-up, and played a leading role in the work on legislation.

Law is crucially important for state governance, and the rule of law is the important pillar of building state governance system and capacity. Legislation is an important political activity of the state and the premise and foundation for rule of law; therefore, it should adhere to correct political direction and take the Party's line, principles and policies as its base to reflect the needs of the Party's undertakings and national development as well as the fundamental interests of the majority of Chinese people. This is the basic starting point and the mission for the work on legislation.

4.1 Chinese Socialist System and Modernization of the State Governance System and Capacity: For a Better Relationship

As emphasized by Xi Jinping, "reform and opening-up is an in-depth revolution, and we must follow the correct direction and stay on the correct path." The direction we follow determines the path we take, and that path we take determines our fate. He further emphasized, "which path should we follow? This is the paramount question for the future of the Party and the success of its cause. Socialism with Chinese characteristics is the integration of the theory of scientific socialism and social development theories of Chinese history. Socialism has taken root in China. It reflects the wishes of the people and meets the development needs of the country and the times. It is a sure route to success in building a moderately prosperous society in all respects, in the acceleration of socialist modernization, and in the great renewal of the Chinese nation."[31] The reason why the reform and opening-up has made such tremendous success is the steadfast adherence to the socialist path with Chinese characteristics, the firm standing on the Party's leadership, and the Party's basic line as the lifeline of the Party and the state. Meanwhile, economic development as the central task, the adherence to the Four Cardinal Principles and the continuing reform and opening-up have been integrated with the development of socialism with Chinese characteristics. Rule of law should be pursued as the best way to ensure this integration, and the old path of a rigid closed-door policy or an erroneous path by abandoning socialism has never been an option.

In the beginning, it would not be true reform and opening-up if it was not a conversion to western universal values and political system. This is a major misinterpretation. To address it, in 1986 when meeting with Radovan Vlajkovic, President of the Presidium of the Socialist Federal Republic of Yugoslavia, Deng Xiaoping made a clear statement, "when the policies of reform and opening to the outside world were adopted at the Third Plenary Session of the Eleventh Central Committee

[31] Xi Jinping, *The Governance of China*, Foreign Languages Press, 2018, p. 23,73.

of our Party, people all over the world, particularly in the Western countries, thought that we were going to adopt capitalism, or that our policies would ultimately lead to capitalism. But witnessing the realities of reform over the past few years, they have come to realize that we are keeping to socialism. Keeping to socialism is of vital importance for China. If China, with its one billion people, took the capitalist road, it would be a disaster for the world. It would be a retrogression of history..." In that year, he also made it further clear in "Take A Clear-Cut Stand Against Bourgeois Liberalization" that "without the Communist Party's leadership and without socialism, there is no future for China. This truth has been demonstrated in the past, and it will be demonstrated again in future", and then emphasized, "we must with confidence keep to the socialist road and uphold the Four Cardinal Principles."[32]

We should correctly grasp the two goals in comprehensively deepening the reform, because they are integrated whole that cannot be separated. The socialism with Chinese characteristics is the institutional foundation for modernizing state governance system and capacity. To improve and develop Chinese socialist system is the premise and purpose of promoting the modern state governance system and capacity. Without this premise and purpose, any discussion about modernizing state governance system and capacity would be reduced to mere arguments on legal instrumentalism, which is distanced from the essence of comprehensively deepening the reform and the path we have followed. Without the modernization of state governance system and capacity, any talk on improving and developing socialism with Chinese characteristics would fall into putchism, eventually abandon rule of law or even resort to another Cultural Revolution. If so, there is no legal foundation for socialist system and the socialist cause would go backwards and even fail. These are the lessons we have learned from the socialist revolution and development since 1949.

As an important state activity, legislation has its own political aspirations. There is no country in the world whose legislation is independent of political purposes. Over the past four decades, the reason why the work on legislation has made such tremendous success is that the Party's line, principles and policies have been taken as the basis to continuously promote the self-improvement and development of socialist system, rather than to change it. Legislation cannot ignore that China is a socialist country and socialism is the path that is followed. Legislation should, from the start, benefit the promotion and development of the socialist system with Chinese characteristics, the release and development of socialist productive forces and the improvement of overall national strength and people's livelihood and well-being. As Deng Xiaoping said, "in the reform of the political structure, our general objectives are as follows: (1) to consolidate the socialist system, (2) to develop the socialist productive forces and (3) to expand socialist democracy in order to bring the initiative of the people into full play. The chief purpose of mobilizing the people's initiative is to develop the productive forces and raise living standards. This in turn will help increase the strength of our socialist country and consolidate the socialist

---

[32] DENG Xiaoping, *Selected Works of Deng Xiaoping (Vol.3)*, Foreign Languages Press, 1994, p.160–161, 195.

system."[33] All the reform measures adopted are to consolidate, improve and develop the socialist system with Chinese characteristics. The work on legislation has been adherent to the principles of the Constitution and to the service of socialism. It should not presume that legislation is only purported to "modern state governance system and capacity". Without socialism, state governance system and capacity would be ill-founded and may cause a disaster.

4.2 *Aspirations and Goal of Legislation: For Better Chinese Socialist System*

To improve and develop socialism is a long historical process. Socialism is an unprecedented undertaking, and there is no ready-made experience for reference. The Party has led the Chinese people to make painstaking efforts to explore the way toward socialism, and from the lessons learned since the founding of the PRC, have explored the socialist path with Chinese characteristics. Since the reform and opening-up, the great achievements of China's society and economy have demonstrated again that only socialism can save China, and only reform and opening-up can develop China, socialism and Marxism. The socialism with Chinese characteristics is the only way for China to develop and prosper.

In his talks during the southern tour in 1992, Deng Xiaoping clearly stated that "If we did not adhere to socialism, implement the policies of reform and opening to the outside world, develop the economy and raise living standards, we would find ourselves in a blind alley".[34] From the beginning of reform and opening-up to the inception of comprehensively deepening reform, in every important moment of reform and development, the Party has to make a choice on which direction should be followed. In a word, the Party has to answer the question, what kind of flag we choose to raise and what path we should pursue in new conditions. As early as in 1985 Deng gave his answer, "our general principles are that we should keep to the socialist road, uphold the people's democratic dictatorship, uphold leadership by the Communist Party and uphold Marxism-Leninism and Mao Zedong Thought. These principles have been written into China's Constitution".[35] The Constitution's provisions on the Four Cardinal Principles are the basic spirit and principle that have been the fundamental guidelines for the Party and the state's undertakings.

Over the past 40 years, we have kept abreast with the times, and applied the Deng Xiaoping Thought, the Three Represents, Scientific Outlook and the Xi Jinping Thought on Socialism with Chinese characteristics for a New Era, and have consolidated a shared understanding to guide and promote the work on legislation. We carry out the work on legislation based on the reality that China is still in the primary stage of socialism and will remain in this stage, and that it remains the largest developing

---

[33] *Ibid.*, p.180.

[34] *Ibid.*, p. 358.

[35] *Ibid.*, p. 138.

country in the world, and we take the reform and opening-up and socialist modernization as the fundamental consideration for legislation and adapt law-making to the new problems in different phases of social and economic development. By strictly adhering to the central task of economic development and the aspiration for rejuvenation of the Chinese nation, the work on legislation has been carried out with much enthusiasm for ensuring coordinated implementation of the Five-Sphere Integrated Plan and the Four-Pronged Comprehensive Strategy. We have insisted on the integration of the Four Cardinal Principles with the reform and opening-up, the improvement and development of Chinese socialism with market economy, the advancement of change in economic base with the reform of superstructure, the economic and social development with the people's aspiration for a better life, the promotion of reform with the deepened law-based governance, and the persistence of independence with the active participation in global governance reform and development. Such insistence is to ensure the laws and regulations are beneficial to improving and developing the socialist system with Chinese characteristics, to unleashing and developing socialist productive forces, to giving full play to the advantages of the socialist system and to building China into a great modern socialist country that is properous, democratic, culturally advanced and harmonious.

4.3 Standards for Evaluating Legislation Quality: State Governance System and Capacity

As Xi Jinping pointed out, "to modernize our state governance system and capacity we should adapt properly to the changing times, and reform outdated systems, mechanisms, laws and regulations, while building new ones to make our institutions in all respects more appropriate and complete and the governance of Party, state and social affairs more institutionalized, standardized and procedure-based."[36]He further emphasized that "shrewd people of petty mind attend to trivial matters, of medium wisdom attend to the rule of people, while people with vision attend to legislation. The key to the governance of a country and a society is to make, respect and observe rules. Law is the most important rule for governance of a country. To modernize the state governance system and capacity should strictly follow the rule of law, which is the fundamental, comprehensive, and long-lasting institutional guarantee for the Party and the state's undertakings."[37]

To put it simply, the state governance system is the institutional arrangements for managing a country. In China, it refers to the institutional arrangements as required by state governance under the Party's leadership, including the institutions, mechanisms, laws and regulations and other arrangements for economic, political, cultural, social, and ecological progress and Party building. These institutions also constitute a set of

---

[36] Xi Jinping, *The Governance of China,* Foreign Languages, Press, 2018, p.103.

[37] The Central Literature Research Office ed., *The Law-based Governance of China,* Central Compilation and Translation Press, 2017, p.14.

interconnected and coordinated national systems. The national governance capacity refers to the capability to apply national systems to administer the affairs in all social respects. For China, this capacity refers to the Party and government's ability to effectively administer the social affairs, including reform, development and stability, national defense and domestic and foreign affairs, and running the Party, the country and the military. The state governance system and capacity are integrated. A good governance system is the basis for improving state governance capacity, while the capable state governance will take full advantage of the governance system in return.

Legislation is sacred because it sets the rules for the country and the society, and it is foundational for establishing various institutional mechanisms, laws and regulations for the country. The quality of legislation directly concerns the state governance system, and the modernization of national governance capacity. The modernization of state governance system and capacity should adapt to the changes with the times, and the new developments of social practices. The mechanisms, institutions, laws and regulations that are not suitable for practical requirements will be reformed, and new ones will be established for more scientific and comprehensive systems, which will make the Party, state and social affairs more institutionalized, standardized and procedure-based with a sound legal system and a well-functioning governance system.

In 1992, when visiting the southern provinces and cities, Deng Xiaoping stated, "it will probably take another thirty years for us to develop a more mature and well-defined system in every field. The principles and policies to be applied under each sub-system will also be more firmly established."[38] Based on Deng's vision, in the Third Plenary Session of the Eighteenth CPC National Congress, it was proposed that to modernize the state governance system and capacity is the objective of development for the new era based on the achievements of China's legal development since the founding of the PRC, especially the reform and opening-up, a summary of the experience of the winding road that China's socialist legal system have walked, positive confirmation, generalization and refinement of the work on legislation over the past 40 years, and a new higher standard for this work in the new era. The modernization of state governance system and capacity is a realistic standard for evaluating the quality of legislation in the new era. The key to the work on legislation is whether the laws and regulations can guarantee the correct and effective implementation of the Party's line, guidelines and policies; whether they can improve and develop the socialist system with Chinese characteristics and ensure that people can administer the national, social, economic and cultural affairs to guarantee the position of masters of the country; whether they can assure the steady, healthy, sound and orderly operations of the state machine; whether they can effectively promote the liberation of socialist productive forces and improve the overall strength of a socialist country; and whether they can effectively improve people's material and cultural lives, continuously satisfy people's aspiration for a better life, and promote social fairness and justice.

---

[38] DENG Xiaoping, *Selected Works of Deng Xiaoping (Vol.3)*, Foreign Languages Press, 1994, p.360.

Over the past 40 years, under the Party's leadership, the work on legislation has been put in the correct political orientation: it starts from the essential requirements of Chinese socialism and its actual conditions, aims to help unleash and develop the social productive forces, implements the Party's basic line with respect to rule of law, takes the socialist modernization with Chinese characteristics as the basis, and adheres to the law of development, the law of social and economic development and the law of legislative affairs to continue improving the quality of legislation. A lot of laws are formulated and revised to improve the systems of the state, which has provided a strong legal guarantee for the various undertakings of the State and has played an active and irreplaceable role in promoting the modernization of state governance system and capacity.

5 The Overall Goal of Rule of Law Consolidates and Promotes China into a Great Modern Socialist Country

The goal of comprehensively advancing the law-based governance was proposed in the Third Session of the Eighteenth CPC National Congress, then in the Fourth Session the Resolution of the Central Committee of the CPC on Major Issues Concerning the Enhancement of All-round Law-based Governance ("Resolution") proposed that the overall goal of comprehensively deepening rule of law is to establish the Chinese rule of law system and transform China into a socialist law-based country. To be specific, this goal cannot be achieved without the Party's firm leadership, upholding the socialist system with Chinese characteristics, putting the theory on Chinese socialist rule of law system into practice, and establishing a complete system of laws, a highly effective enforcement system, a stringent scrutiny system and effective supporting measures, and a sound system of Party regulations. It also cannot be achieved without the consolidated efforts to develop the law-based governance of the country, the law-based exercise of state power, and the law-based administration of government, the integrated development of the country, the government and the society where the rule of law is firmly established, the holistic approach through which the laws are made scientifically, enforced strictly, applied impartially and observed by everyone and the modernization of state governance system and capacity.

5.1 To Unswervingly Uphold Chinese Socialist Rule of Law for Consolidating Legislation

As Xi Jinping put it in his explanations on the Resolution, "to comprehensively advance rule of law is a major strategic issue concerning the Party in the governance and rejuvenation of China, people's wellbeing, and the endurable peace and stability of the Party and the State; it is also an important aspect for improving and developing Chinese socialist system and modernize the state governance system and capacity".[39] A society of moderate prosperity in all respects, comprehensively deepened reform, great rejuvenation of the Chinese nation and a modern socialist powerful country that is prosperous, strong, democratic and culturally advanced and harmonious cannot be realized without advancing overall law-based governance in China.

This overall goal identifies the nature and direction for comprehensively advancing the rule of law, and pinpoints its working focus: the nature and direction for China's rule of law is to uphold Chinese socialist rule of law, not any other kind of rule of law, and the working focus is to establish a socialist law-based system with Chinese features, not the so-called Western rule of law characterized by "universal values". It highlights the socialist nature of Chinese law-based system, and further clarifies that the Chinese socialist system is fundamental to Chinese socialist law-based system and advance overall rule of law, which mandates its institutional nature and direction for Chinese rule of law. To build the Chinese rule of law system and build China into a socialist law-based country is essential for and conducive to the modernization of state governance system and capacity and the comprehensively deepened reform, and carrying out the work on law-based governance within the general framework of comprehensively deepening reform and advancing reform by observing the law.

To promote the rule of law requires the observance of the Constitution in the first place. The Constitution has stipulated the socialist road that China follows and the theoretical system on Chinese socialism, which is a summary of the common will and fundamental interests of Chinese people from all ethnic groups and the most authoritative expression of the Party and the country's central undertakings, basic principles, major guidelines and important polices in law. More importantly, in the First Session of NPC's Thirteenth National Congress, an amendment to the Constitution was adopted to confirm the major innovation of the theory, practice and institution made, under the firm leadership of the CPC with Xi Jinping as the core, by the Party and the Chinese people in the new era for the socialist cause. Such confirmation has become the guiding principles that the people across China should observe in all their undertakings for the country. The amendment establishes the highest standard for all the causes of the Party and the country and provides guiding principles for the work on legislation in the new era; and it also consolidates the work on legislation. The work on legislation should uphold the Xi Jinping Thought

[39] *A Reader's Guide to Resolution of the Central Committee of the Communist Party of China on Major Issues Concerning the Enhancement of All-round Law-based Governance*, People's Publishing House, 2014, p. 44.

on Socialism with Chinese characteristics for a New Era, follow the socialist rule of law with Chinese characteristics, put the theory on socialist rule of law into practice, play the role of the people's congress system, integrate the Party's leadership, people's master position and the law-based governance, and provide effective and scientific institutional guarantee for improving and developing Chinese socialist system and modernizing state governance system and capacity.

5.2 *To Establish Chinese Socialist Law-Based Governance for Defining the Tasks of Legislation*

As pointed out by Xi Jinping, "to comprehensively advance law-based governance of China has many concerns, so in our work there should be a leverage that covers all aspects and guides all practical objectives. It is the establishment of the socialist law-based governance of China. All our work should take it as the central task."[40] The work on legislation, as the foundation for comprehensively advancing law-based governance, is also the principal concern.

In the Fourth Session of the Eighteenth CPC National Congress, it was stated that "to establish the socialist law-based governance of China requires that legislation precede reform, playing the leading role of legislation and focusing on the key task of improving the legislation's quality". Insisting on the preceding role of legislation is necessary for improving the Chinese socialist legal system with the Constitution as the core and establishing a complete system of laws. The relation between reform and rule of law should be correctly dealt with: the systems and the rules should be established in the first place to ensure that every major reform decision should have legal basis and reform should be carried out according to law; and the decisions and arrangements of the Central Committee should be implemented earnestly to ensure that legislation and reform decision be interconnected and the legislation adapt to the needs of reform and social economic development. When considering the reform program and reform measures, the issues on legislation concerning it should also be taken into account, and the needs and possible proposals for legislation should then be stated to ensure the Party's reform decision can be turned into a legal institution through statutory procedures and then promoted into a norm that binds all the people. The experience from and measures of reform that have been proven by practice should be quickly turned into law, while they are underdeveloped or need pilot programs, authorization should be made according to law. Reform cannot be carried out by breaking the law or delayed on the excuse of lack of legal basis. The laws and regulations that cannot adapt to or even put obstacles to reform should be amended or repealed. In a conclusion, to ensure that legislation precedes reform is also necessary for comprehensively deepening reform and inherent to improving and

---

[40] *A Reader's Guide to the Resolution of the Central Committee of the Communist Party of China on Major Issues Concerning the Enhancement of All-round Law-based Governance*, People's Publishing House, 2014, p. 52.

developing Chinese socialist system and modernizing state governance system and capacity.

As Wang Anshi, a statesman in the Song Dynasty, wrote, "when the law of the land under heaven is good, there will be order in the land under heaven; when the laws of the state are good, there will be order in the state". Not all the laws are intended for governance, and not all the laws are capable of delivering sound governance. To modernize state governance system and capacity needs good law to promote sound governance. In this sense, to ensure that legislation precedes reform needs to establish correct ideas for legislation and put legislation's quality as a priority. Legislation should be carried out for the people and the core socialist values be upheld, and then every legislation will conform with the principles of Constitution, reflect people's will and win people's support. Now the people's expectations for legislation are not the call for new law but for good, effective and practical law. The central task of legislation is to improve quality, therefore, the work on legislation should be carried out in a scientific and democratic manner, the working mechanisms and procedures for legislation need calibrating, people's participation should be expanded for a fuller consideration of opinions, the principle of justice, equality and transparency should be thoroughly adhered to, and the formulation, revision, repealing and interpreting of laws should be put in equal footing. Moreover, for taking advantage of the leading role and motivating effect of legislation, it should put more emphasis on solving problems to ensure that laws and regulations are manifest with the social and economic development needs, better coordinate the relationships of varied interests, and make the laws and regulations more responsive, systematic, targeted and effective.

5.3 New Tasks and Demands for Legislation Raised by the Objective of Establishing Rule of Law China in New Era

At the Party's Nineteenth National Congress, a new critical statement was made upon the assessment of the past circumstances: that with decades of hard work, socialism with Chinese characteristics has crossed the threshold into a new era. This is a new historic juncture in China's development. This new era presents many new characteristics, new circumstances and new issues. In this congress, a two-stage plan was formulated for completing the strategic goal of China's social and economic development between 2020 and the middle of twenty-first century. Specifically, for law-based governance, in stage one between 2020 and 2035, the rights of the people to participate and to develop as equals are adequately protected. The rule of law for the country, the government, and society is basically in place. Institutions in all fields are further improved; the modernization of China's system and capacity for governance is basically achieved. In stage two between 2035 and the middle of the twenty-first century, China will be built into a great modern socialist country which is prosperous, democratic, culturally advanced, harmonious and beautiful. At that time, new heights are reached in every dimension of material, political, cultural and ethical, social, and ecological advancement, and modernization of China's system and capacity for governance is achieved. This new statement has proposed new tasks for the work on legislation.

Between the 19th and the 20th Party National Congress, the timeframes of the two centenary goals converge. In this period, not only must we finish building a moderately prosperous society in all respects and achieve the first centenary goal; we must also build on this achievement to embark on a new journey toward the second centenary goal of fully building a modern socialist country. In the congress, based on the judgment that China is still and will long remain in the primary stage of socialism has not changed, it was proposed that the principal contradiction facing Chinese society has evolved into one between unbalanced and inadequate development and the people's ever-growing needs for a better life, and China's economy had been transitioning from a phase of rapid growth to a stage of high-quality development. Therefore, on a demanding and higher standing from which to plan and promote the comprehensive and deepened reform, a lot of new reform initiatives and major reform tasks were laid down, most of which were closely related with law, such as new demands for the work on legislation and the formulation of laws based on the urgency and circumstances that the matters require. In this critical period, the work on legislation needs to adapt to new trends to solve new problems and make new breakthroughs to ensure the quality of legislation and continuous contribution to sound social and economic development.

The Thirteenth NPC Standing Committee has thoroughly studied and implemented the Xi Jinping Thought on Socialism with Chinese Characteristics for a New Era, put Xi Jinping's new ideas, thoughts and strategies on comprehensively advancing law-based governance into practice, closely followed the gist of the Nineteenth CPC National Congress and its second and third plenary sessions and adhered to the new circumstances in the Party's and the country's causes on development, the new expectations of the people for better life, and the new demands for quality development. The NPC Standing Committee then made the legislative plan and reported it to the CPC Central Committee for approval. The plan, by centering on the Five-Sphere Integrated Plan and the Four-Pronged Comprehensive Strategy, reflects the legislation work's adherence to new development ideas. It specifically arranged the work of the NPC Standing Committee and proposed 116 items subject to legislation by putting them into two categories according to emergency. In category one, there are 69 items mature for legislation and pending for deliberation within the period of the Thirteenth NPC. There are 47 items in category two which still needs hard work to enable the circumstances for deliberation. In category one, there are 33 new legislation and 34 amendments apart from the formulation of the Constitution's amendment and the Civil Code, including Supervision Law, People's Assessors Law, Law on the Protection of Heroes and Martyrs, Energy Law, Rural Revitalization Promotion Law, E-commerce Law, Value Added Tax Law, Real Estate Tax Law, Cultural Industry Promotion Law, Preschool Education Law, Personal Information Protection Law, Social Assistance Law, Community Correction Law, Law on the Prevention and Control of Soil Pollution. The laws subject to amending include Local Organization

Law, State Council Organization Law, People's Court Organization Law, People's Procuratorate Organization Law, Patent Law, Rural Land Contract Law, Securities Law, Administrative Penalty Law, Administrative Reconsideration Law, Criminal Procedure Law, Law on Administrative Penalties for Public Security, Drug Administration Law, Land Administration Law, Safe Production Law. The areas of these legislation and amendments are delicately important which present unusual pressure. To complete these legislation and amendments, the Standing Committee needs to continue to apply the legislative methods of enactment, revision, repeal, interpretation, authorization, decision and re-examination to help make good laws for sound governance and lay the legal foundation for reform and opening-up.

6 Practice-Oriented Legislation for Socialist Cause with Chinese Characteristics

Over the past 70 years, especially over the past 40 years, under the Party's leadership, legislation in China has walked in its own path. Along this path, the integration of Party's leadership, people's master position, and rule of law has been pursued, and the legislation has strived to serve the Party and the state's initiatives for development and the goal of establishing China into a great modern socialist country. Meanwhile, the work on legislation draws inspirations from the great practices of the socialist cause with Chinese characteristics and, by being referred to the characteristics of China's different social and economic development phases, has been undertaken step by step, a plan after a plan and a program after a program. In only several decades, a legal system with Chinese characteristics has taken shape and developed with continuous improvements. It has provided effective legal guarantee for improving and developing China's socialist system and the modernization of state governance system and capacity, which closely follows the practices of the socialist cause with Chinese characteristics. These achievements are not made with ease.

6.1 Reflecting the Nature and Demand for Improving and Developing Chinese Socialist System

The social system determines the legal system and the nature of law-based governance. Legislation is an important political activity for a state, hence the process of law-making is political. China is a socialist state under the people's democratic dictatorship led by the working class and based on the alliance of workers and peasants. The nature of China's state system determines that legislation in China should be subject to the Party's leadership, follow a correct political direction laid by it, and its fundamental mission is to improve and develop the Chinese socialist system. Over the past 70 years, especially over the past 40 years, the work on legislation has always upheld the Party's leadership illustrated and characterized by Marxism-Leninism, Mao Zedong Thought, Deng Xiaoping Theory, the Three Represents, and the Scientific Outlook on Development, and steadfastly followed the socialist path. The systems of people's congresses, of multiparty cooperation and political consultation under the leadership of the CPC, of regional ethnic autonomy and the system of community level self-governance, the Chinese socialist legal system, the basic economic system in which public ownership is dominant and diverse forms of ownership develop side by side, and other mechanisms and institutions of economy, politics, culture, society and ecology based on the preceding systems have drawn strength from the work on legislation for their own establishment, improvement and development. Meanwhile, these systems are inseparable parts of the Chinese socialist system, and in return they consolidate the construction, improvement and development of it. They reflect the common will of the people, safeguard the fundamental interests of the people, and ensure the integration of the Party's leadership, people's master position, and the law-based governance of the state.

6.2 *Reflecting the Aspiration of the Socialist Modernization and Reform and Opening-up*

Reform and opening-up is the greatest social practice for China's socialist modernization, providing a fertile ground for the development of the Chinese socialist legal system. In the past 70 years, the work on legislation has undertaken numerous explorations to serve the overarching goal of establishing China into a great socialist modern country. In the past 40 years, the development of legislation in China has progressed in tandem with the practice of socialist modernization with each reinforcing each other, reflecting the distinctive contemporary features of the reform and opening-up. On one hand, the socialist modernization has created demands and provided momentum for developing and improving legal system, while also supplying valuable experience for the work on legislation. As the reform and opening-up has made more progress, the economy and society will face more changes, cerating an urgent need for a complete state governance system and raising higher requirements for improving state governance according to law. These developments have laid a solid foundation for finally establishing a Chinese socialist legal system. On the other hand, the progress of legislation has mirrored the evolving features of different phases of reform and opening-up, properly balancing the stability of law and the instability of reform and opening-up. In the work on legislation, great efforts have been made to integrate the decisions related to development and reform with legislative decision-making and to adapt to the needs of reform and social economic development to ensure that every reform decision is made according to law. In the past several decades, legislation has provided effective legal guarantee and helped build a good legal environment for assuring the smooth economic and social development and the advancement of reform and opening-up.

6.3 Reflecting the People-Centered Approach to Law-Making

A people-centered approach lies at the very heart of the Party's very existence. The original aspiration and the mission of Chinese Communists are to seek happiness for the Chinese people and rejuvenation of the Chinese nation. In the past seven decades, the Party has always put into practice its mass line in all aspects of governance and regard as our goal the people's aspirations to live a better life, and rely on the people to move history forward. This practice reflects the Party's adherence to its fundamental purpose of wholeheartedly serving the people. Over the past 40 years, the Party has always taken the protection of the fundamental interests of the majority of Chinese people as the starting for the work on legislation. It has adhered to the people-centered approach in legislation, respected the people's master position and their pioneering spirit, and expanded the channels for participating in legislation. Furthermore, the Party has practiced democracy in legislation and gathered people's wisdom to ensure that people can actively participate in the state and social governance through all kinds of legal channels. Guided by the principles of aligning with people's aspirations, showing respect to their views and ideas, caring about their worries and concerns, and improving their livelihood, laws and regulations have been enacted to respect and secure their human rights, protect their lawful rights and interests, and ensure their rights on economic development, politics, culture, social development, and ecology. In the final analysis, great efforts have been made to ensure that the citizens have broad, sufficient and real freedoms and rights whether in substantive law or in procedures. The work on legislation have also persisted in promoting common prosperity and social fairness and justice to advance people's wellbeing. To be specific, a lot of laws and regulations have been made to ensure people's access to childcare, education, remunerable employment, health care, old-age care, housing and social assistance, and to boost new forms of social governance for the purpose of giving people a greater sense of fulfillment, happiness and security as they contribute to and gain from development and promoting well-rounded human development. The work on legislation also paid attention to ensuring social stability and harmony and people living in peace and happiness to effectively realize, safeguard and develop the fundamental interests of all the people and promote common prosperity for everyone.

6.4 Reflecting the Requirements for Comprehensive Rule of Law and Modernization of State Governance System and Capacity

To comprehensively advance law-based governance is a major strategic issue directly concerned with the Party's governance of China, people's happiness and wellbeing, the enduring stability of the Party and the lasting peace of the country. It is also important for improving and developing Chinese socialist system and the modernization of state governance system and capacity. Since the founding of the PRC, a lot of explorations have been undertaken to build China into a socialist country, and the socialist legal system also evolved from the basic establishment of legal system, the rule of man to the rule of law. In the past 70 years, the Party, by putting emphasis on reform and opening-up on one hand and the establishment of legal system on the other hand, has defined rule of law as the fundamental principle by which the Party leads the people in governing the country, the exercise of political power in the framework of law as the basic method by which the Party governs the country, and the law-based governance as the concern for the cause of Party and the country. Coordinated efforts have been made to exercise law-based governance, political power and administration, while a holistic approach has been adopted to establish a law-based country, government and society. With regard to legislation, laws and regulations have been enacted in a scientific manner, and the Chinese socialist legal system has been under progress and development through unremitting efforts from all respects. The Chinese socialist legal system with the Constitution as the core has provided effective constitutional and legal basis for the Party to exercise political power and helped improve the Party's expertise in exercising the political power in a scientific, democratic and law-based manner. It also provides constitutional and legal guarantee for the people to participate in the management of state and social affairs and the work on economy and culture to ensure the position of the people as the masters of the country. It serves as a strong effective constitutional and legal weapon for the Party and the state to weather against any urgent problems and risks, improves the capacity of applying law to and transforming institutional advantage into the capabilities for state governance. Comprehensive rule of law ensures the vitality and stability in responding to profound social changes, the vigor of socialism, the continuous improvement of the national overall strength and people's wellbeing, and the presentation of socialism's superior advantages.

6.5 Reflecting the Initiative to Inherit Traditional Legal Culture and Learn from Outstanding Human Civilization of Law

Culture is the soul of a country and a nation. When the culture thrives, the country will prosper; when the culture becomes strong, the nation will be strong as well. Over the past 70 years, especially over the past 40 years, the work on legislation has stayed true to the Chinese socialist culture, and taken a firm standing in Chinese culture by inheriting historical traditions, promoting socialist culture and combining the achievements of human civilization of law with institutional innovation. And the past has been harnessed to serve the present and the foreign to serve China. All these efforts have been made to ensure the legislation advanced, inclusive and widest scope of legislative concerns. Chinese legal system draws its strength from socialist practice. On one hand, it is subject to the guidance of Marxism and the results of adapting Marxism to Chinese context, including the Mao Zedong Thought, Deng Xiaoping Theory, the Three Represents, the Scientific Outlook on Development, and Xi Jinping Thought on Socialism with Chinese characteristics for a New Era, takes the evolving social realities and the new era's demand as its basis, and integrates the core socialist values into the Constitution and law as people's norms, which transforms them into people's emotional affiliation and habits. On the other hand, the excellent Chinese traditional culture should be studied for more inspirational ideas, spirits and moral norms to help build people's cultural identity and confidence through proper institutional innovation as required by the new era. Moreover, the human civilization of law, the foreign legal systems and experience of law-based governance are good lessons we can learn but not copy directly. The legal systems that are established by the people of other nations based on their own realities are respected but not blindly adopted, i.e. the foreign legal systems cannot be simply put in equal with the Chinese socialist legal system, and their laws are not used to evaluate Chinese legal system. The international rules are respected, but Chinese laws are made based on China's own needs and realities.

6.6 Reflecting the Coordinated Efforts to Promote the Five-Sphere Integrated Plan

China's socialist modernization has gradually evolved into a complete system both in theory and practice. At the time of the PRC founding, it was proposed to build China into a socialist country with modern industry, agriculture, science, culture and national defense. From the reform and opening-up to current period, it has transitioned from "crossing the river by touching the stones" to the formulation of top institutional design. To achieve the four modernizations, China has transformed from the pursuit of socialist material and cultural progress to the development of material, cultural and political progress, from the Chinese socialist economic, political, cultural and social development to the integrated development of five aspects including Chinese socialist economic, political, cultural, social and ecological progress. These transformations are the results of the Party's increasingly deepened understanding of and continuous contribution to socialist modernization. Over the past 70 years, especially over the past 40 years, as the Party and the nation's undertakings for development progressed, the work on legislation has also made progress and experienced ups and downs: from the initiation of legislation in the early stage of PRC, the stagnation, rejuvenation, rapid development to continuous upgrading. These progress and experience have helped to establish and enhance the awareness and consciousness of top institutional design. And also in this process, initiatives have been carried out to coordinate the implementation of Five-sphere Integrated Plan based on different phases of development, which contributes to the establishment of a compatible legal system that improves and develops Chinese socialism and the modernization of state governance system and capacity. The legislation of political institution's reform started to restore and improve the state governments and their powers and authorities, which sailed the boat of Chinese socialist modernization; as an engine to this boat, the economic legislation has established and improved the mechanisms and institutions for socialist market economy, which laid the foundation for forming a socialist legal system. The legislation on social affairs and people's livelihood is aimed to improve people's life, ensure that the achievements of reform and development can be shared among all the people with greater benefits and fairness, and satisfy people's demands for material and cultural progress and their aspirations for better life. The legislation on cultural affairs is a direction for social values; it inherits Chinese traditional culture and traditions and advance the socialist culture to facilitate cultural confidence and lead the direction for socialist cultural development. The legislation on ecological affairs is a weapon to fight against pollution and for the blue sky; it incorporates the idea of green development into law and contributes to building an ecological environment that is conducive to living and harmony between people and the nature. The legislation during the reform has fully reflected the requirements of coordinating and promoting the Five-Sphere Integrated Plan.

6.7 Reflecting the Coordinated Promotion of Four-Pronged Comprehensive Strategy

At the founding of the PRC, the Party proposed the strategy of building China into a great modern socialist country. After 30 years' explorations, reform and opening was enshrined as a principle in the Third Plenary Session of the Eleventh CPC Central Committee with the goal of a moderately prosperous country by the end of the twentieth century. In the end of twentieth century, the Party laid down the mission of building a high-level moderately prosperous country when the initial goal was achieved ahead of schedule. After the Eighteenth Party Congress, based on the strategic goal of making China prosper and the outline of Chinese socialism, the Party proposed the Four-Pronged Comprehensive Strategy which is the integration of completing a moderately prosperous society in all respects, furthering reform, advancing rule of law and strengthening the CPC discipline. In the past four decades, the work on legislation has been carried out based on the Party's decisions and arrangements and closely adherent to the Four-Pronged Comprehensive Strategy for the implementation of specific strategies and initiatives to promote and improve the Chinese socialist legal system. The work on legislation has taken a moderately prosperous society in all respects as the strategic goal and established relevant legal systems to liberate people from many taboos and motivate people to participate in the fulfilment of this goal. It takes comprehensively advancing deepened reform as the strategic focus by accentuating the legislation in economy, politics, culture, society and ecology to maintain a combination of focus and balanced development for mutually strengthening reform of various areas and stimulating the vigor and vitality across the country. It collaborates with the practice of promoting all-rounded law-based governance, and strengthens people's capability in applying legal thinking and approaches to deepen reform and development, resolve disputes and maintain social stability to ensure the smooth operations of state affairs and social activities and facilitate the transformation of state governance. It also takes the improvement of Party discipline as the strategic leverage; the earlier expression of Party discipline's importance emphasized that "the Party's Constitution is the fundamental law for the party's activities. If there are no party regulations, the laws of the state cannot be guaranteed", later it is stressed that the Party's regulations should be incorporated into the Chinese socialist legal system to ensure the effective connection between the two. The new proposal can promote the modernization of state governance system and capacity, and resolve the disconnection problem between Party's leadership and the enforcement of Party discipline in state governance, which will consolidate the Party's governance of the state and improve the Chinese socialist system.

6.8 *Reflecting the Requirements of Seeking Truth from Facts and Moving Forward with the Times*

Practice is the lifeline of law. Law is the summary of experience accumulated through practice, and develops as the practice evolves. Practice never ceases, and law can not remain unchanged forever. Law must advance with the times and innovate to keep its vital heat. No matter in the early stage of the PRC's founding or after the reform and opening-up was initiated, the work on legislation has undergone a tortuous path, but it has never deviated from the Party's leadership. By focusing on the implementation of Central Committee's decisions and arrangements, Chinese legislation has secured the party's proposals to be state's will through statutory procedures. Especially since the reform and opening-up, the work on legislation has been carried out by upholding the principle of seeking truth from facts and moving forward with the times. It adapts itself to the features and requirements of different social and economic development phases, formulates and establishes the legal institutions that best suit the need at that time, and provides necessary legal guarantee for social progress. The socialist cause is a process of never ceasing practice, improvement and development, hence the socialist system needs improvement and development, and the socialist market economy system also needs uninterrupted development. In return, the norms that reflect these systems and institutions are also subject to continuous improvement and development. The idealist legislation will never succeed because it oversteps the social reality, and cannot be enforced, and the approach of stationary legislation should not be adopted either, because it sticks to the old which will let the current legal systems hinder reform and opening-up. Therefore, the work on legislation should be carried out in a scientific manner by observing the law of development, the law of social and economic development and the law of legislative activities. The relationships between reform and rule of law, between stability and instability of law and between phased development and long-term planning for law should also be properly addressed. Various legislative methods including new enactment, amendment, repeal, judicial interpretation, authorization, decision and reform decision should be adopted. The work on legislation should also adapt itself to the new demands raised by changing social and economic development. And the reform should be improved under the rule of law, while the rule of law is improved through reform. Law should boost and blaze the trail for reform and opening-up and actively promote the modernization of state governance system and capacity.

Over the past 70 years, especially over the past 40 years, remarkable achievements have been accomplished in the cause of Chinese socialism, a miracle in human history and a magnificent chapter in the history of human civlization. The socialist system with Chinese characteristics has provided the fundamental institutional foundation for socialist practice and has itself benefited from that practice. In this sense, the greatest progress and achievement of Chinese socialist cause lies in the socialist system itself. It is firmly believed that China, with modern a state governance system and capacity, will stand firmly in the East of the world and make even greater contributions to human progress and civilization as the socialist system with Chinese characteristics continues to be improved and developed.

Chapter 2
Development and Innovation of Theory and Practice of Party's Leadership in Legislation

Wang Hongyu

Abstract This chapter explores the history of how the CPC has steered legislative development since 1949. It argues that CPC leadership is the defining feature of socialist rule of law and the key to building a modern Chinese legal system. Reviewing historical milestones, it shows that Party-led legislation has translated policy into binding national law while balancing central direction and local initiative. Since the 18th CPC Congress, the Party has improved institutional mechanisms to ensure law-making serves the people's interests and the rejuvenation of the Chinese nation. It concludes that embedding the Party's leadership throughout the legislative process safeguards socialist rule of law, advances state governance modernization, and offers an alternative path to legal development distinct from the Western models.

Keywords CPC leadership · Socialist rule of law · Legislative system · Modernization of state governance · Theoretical development · Innovation

As Xi Jinping pointed out, "the relationship between Party leadership and the rule of law is an issue of fundamental importance; if dealt with properly, the rule of law will develop smoothly, and our Party and country will flourish; if dealt with poorly, the rule of law will become weaker and our Party and country will fall into decline". He further emphasized, "as we fully advance the country's law-based governance, our direction must be correct, and our political guarantees must be strong. Our ancestors said, 'when Dao is used to govern, even with few laws, it shall serve to moderate behavior; when Dao is not introduced, even with a profusion of laws, there shall be public disorder'".[1] The Party's leadership is the most essential feature of socialism with Chinese characteristics, and is the Dao of socialist rule of law in China. It is also the basic experience for the practice of Chinese socialism to incorporate the

[1] The Party Literature Research Office ed., *The Law-Based Governance of China*, Central Compilation and Translation Press, 2017, pp. 38–39.

W. Hongyu (✉)
Beijing, China
e-mail: liujixuan@lawpress.com.cn

C. Shen et al. (eds.), *A History of Legislation in the Past 70 Years in China*,
https://doi.org/10.1007/978-981-95-3799-0_2

Party's leadership into the whole process and all the aspects in rule of law. To insist on the Party's leadership in the work on legislation means that, under the Party's leadership, the Party's polices will be translated into the State's will through statutory procedures, and then make it into the common goal and the norms of behavior of the people, all of which are intended to achieve the Party's mission. To insist on the Party's leadership is also a political advantage of Chinese socialist system and the fundamental political requirement for the Party to govern the country and create the law-based governance according to law. In the past several decades, it is the Party's leadership that helps the work on legislation make historical progress, establish and continuously improve the Chinese socialist legal system. The Party has insisted on uniting and leading the Chinese people to stay on and develop Chinese socialism, spare efforts to engage in Chinese socialist modernization, pave the road for creating law-based governance with Chinese characteristics, develop the theoretical system on Chinese socialist rule of law and form such a culture compatible with rule of law. Such insistence has helped and improved the Chinese socialist legal system with the Constitution as the core, which provided an effective legal guarantee for establishing, consolidating, improving and developing Chinese socialist system and promoted the modernization of state governance system and capacity.

1 The Political Mission for Improving and Developing Chinese Socialist System

1.1 Political Necessity for Establishing, Consolidating, Improving and Developing Chinese Socialist System

The fundamental issue of revolution is about state power. What the state power should be after the PRC was founded was a serious political problem that confronted the Party, and the answer to this question also reflected the nature of the Party. Since the founding of CPC, the Party has taken communism as its highest and eventual goal and also defined socialism as its ideal and objective. From the First Civil War, Agrarian Revolutionary War and the War of Liberation, the Party had taken a firm leadership in the state power, from which it established legal systems and made explorations for people's democracy. In the eve of the PRC's founding, based on the experience of the legal systems of the revolutionary base areas, the Party issued the Instructions concerning Abolishing the Six Codes of the KMT and Determining Judicial Principles for the Liberated Areas, and the Common Program was adopted in First Plenary Session of the Chinese People's Political Consultative Conference, declaring the abolition of KMT's constitution and legal systems and enactment of law and decrees to protect the people. In the Common program, the new China was defined as "a New Democratic or a People's Democratic State. It carries out the people's democratic dictatorship lead by the working class and uniting all democratic classes and all nationalities in China", "the state power of the People's Republic of China belongs to the people. The people's congresses and the people's governments of all levels are the organs for the exercise of state power by the people". These provisions provided guarantee for the establishment of state power for the newly founded PRC. The 1954 Constitution, as the fundamental law of the state, confirmed the Party's role in governing the state, the leadership in state's politics and social life, and the legitimate status in the Constitution. It also established the principle of people's democracy and socialism and confirmed the people's congress system as the fundamental political system. The history has proven that the road of socialism is the only correct one for a prosperous and strong China and national rejuvenation. The socialist system with the people's congress system as the core is the most effective one to ensure the people's position as masters of the country. In the Eighth CPC National Congress, it was further stated that "we should further strengthen the people's democratic legal system and consolidate the order for constructing socialism", "the state must, as it necessitates, gradually establish a complete set of laws"[2] to ensure that "there are laws to abide by, and laws are observed and strictly enforced".[3] The formulation of constitutions and laws were crucial for establishing and consolidating China's socialist system and people's democratic dictatorship. As Xi Jinping pointed out, "in the early stage of PRC, when abolishing the old legal system, the Party took advantage of the success and experience in the base areas' legal establishment in helping create the socialist law-based governance, which laid foundation for future development. however, when the left-line thinking took over the Party's guiding principles, law was no longer a focus of its main job, especially during the Cultural Revolution, when the legal system was badly damaged. We have paid a heavy price for it, and it is a lesson we should learn."[4]

In the early stage of reform and opening-up, under the Party's leadership, the work on legislation took the establishment of socialist rule of law as its objective and aimed to promote a mature and well-developed socialism, which has laid the foundation for modernizing the state governance system and capacity. The Third Plenary Session of the Eleventh CPC Central Committee, by summarizing and learning the lessons from the Cultural Revolution, the Party decided to shift the focus from "class struggle as the key link" to "economic development as the central task" and to transform from the rule of man to rule of law. In the past four decades, the work on legislation has always adhered to the Four Cardinal Principles, and by centering on the objectives and tasks on legal development raised by the Central Committee in different phases,

---

[2] For the full text of The Political Report of the Central Committee of the Communist Party of China to the Eighth National Congress of the Communist Party of China, see http://cpc.people.com.cn/GB/64162/64168/64560/65452/4526551.html. For its English translation, see LIU Shaoqi, *The Political Report of the Central Committee of the Communist Party of China to the Eighth National Congress of the Party*, Foreign Languages Press, 1956.

[3] DONG Biwu, *On Further Strengthening People's Democratic Legal System and Ensuring the Socialist Undertakings*, in Collection of Dong Biwu's Writings on Politics and Law, Law Press, 1986, pp. 479–480.

[4] Central Party Literature Research Office ed., *Selected Speeches of Xi Jinping On Socialist Political Construction*, Central Party Literature Press, 2017, pp. 82–83.

adopted a scientific and democratic manner to promote a well-planned and step-by-step approach for establishing and improving the Chinese socialist legal system. The legislation in this period has consolidated the state power, secured the direction for Chinese socialism and ensured the continuous improvement of Chinese socialist system.

Since the Eighteenth CPC National Congress, the Central Committee with Xi Jinping as the core has made coordinated efforts for promoting Five-Sphere Integrated Plan and the Four-Pronged Comprehensive Strategy, and to expand and deepen reform and opening-up. The third and fourth sessions of the Eighteenth CPC Central Committee set forth the overall goal of comprehensively advancing reform and law-based governance. With regard to how to promote comprehensive reform, Xi pointed out that "Today, we are tasked with an important historic mission, that is to make our socialist system with Chinese characteristics more mature and better established, and provide a set of more complete, more stable and more effective systems for the development of the Party and the nation, the well-being of the people, social harmony and stability, and the enduring prosperity and stability of the country."[5] This set of systems is mainly manifested in the continuous improvement of Chinese socialist legal system with Constitution as the core, the advancement of comprehensive law-based governance, the establishment of Chinese socialist rule of law and China into a socialist country under the rule of law, the improvement of Chinese socialist system, and the eventual attainment of the grand goal of modern state governance system and capacity by the middle of twenty-first century as advocated in the Nineteenth CPC National Congress.

1.2 Solemn Mission of Seeking Happiness for People and Rejuvenation of Chinese Nation

As pointed out by Xi Jinping, "the original aspiration and mission of the Chinese Communists is to seek happiness for the Chinese people and rejuvenation of the Chinese nation".[6] China's modern history tells that the PRC would not exist without CPC. The CPC has been the political force that truly burdened the mission of seeking happiness for people, making China prosperous and strong and achieving national rejuvenation. It comes from the people; hence it is part of the people, which makes it represent the fundamental interests of the overwhelming majority of the people. Only the work on legislation is under the Party's leadership can the laws and regulations always serve the people and cause of national rejuvenation, take their aspirations

---

[5] Xi Jinping, *To Improve and Develop Chinese Socialist System and Promote the Modernization of State Governance System and Capacity*, People's Daily, February 18, p. 1.

[6] *Secure a Decisive Victory in Building a Moderately Prosperous Society in All Respects and Strive for the Great Success of Socialism with Chinese Characteristics for a New Era*, Report Delivered by Xi Jinping at the Nineteenth CPC National Congress. The Chinese-English text can be found at http://www.chinadaily.com.cn/interface/flipboard/1142846/2017-11-06/cd_34188086.html. For the reports of previous national congresses, see http://www.bjreview.com/90th/node_53448.htm

for better life as its objective, and take the realization, safeguard and advancement of their interests as the highest standard. A complete set of legal systems can make reform and development benefit more to all the people in a much fairer manner, which is the very principle and the political pursuit and mission of the Party.

To insist on the Party's leadership in the work on legislation requires adherence to the people-centered approach, which is the fundamental principle of the Party. The Party's policies and the state laws are both the reflections of the people's will, consistent in nature. The origin of the Party's policies comes from people, serve the people and seeks happies for the people. Only the Party's leadership in legislation is upheld can the legislation fulfil the integration of Party's will and the people's will, reflect the fundamental interests of the majority of the people, and serve the people's interests and happiness. Only under the Party's leadership can the laws and regulations be supported, observed and enforced, and can rule of law be the inviolable force that is defended by all the people. The history of the past several decades has demonstrated that it is the persistence in the Party's leadership in the work on legislation that helps maintain the socialist direction in creating law-based governance, uphold the principle of serving the people whole-heartedly and preserve the original aspiration and mission of the Party. Though the Party deviated from the path of socialist rule of law for some time, it relied on the people to correct its mistakes, which finally steered a correct direction for rule of law construction. Along this path, that there were no laws to abide by is changed; the laws were made to govern people, and observed and strictly enforced; the mere existence of a legal system is transformed to law-based governance; the way in which the Party governs the state is promoted to be scientific, democratic and law-based; and the Chinese socialist legal system is upgraded to the Chinese socialist rule-of-law system. All these changes have been the strong legal guarantees for the Party to lead Chinese people to make three historic leaps from liberation, prosperity and growing strong along this path.

To insist on the Party's leadership in the work on legislation requires unswerving efforts to serve the rejuvenation of Chinese nation, which is the current goal of the Party's mission. To build China into a great modern socialist country of prosperity, democracy, civility, harmony and beauty is the common ideal of the Chinese people, which requires cohesion and the people-centered approach. The Party is the core leadership of the Chinese socialist cause and is the backbone for uniting the people to realize Chinese dream. The Party unites and leads the people by its original aspiration and the spirit to fight for such aspiration, by its historical mission to formulate the correct principles and policies that conform to people's fundamental interests and the spirit to put them into practice, and by the spirit to seek truth from facts and seek benefits, interests and happiness for people based on the actual circumstances. The insistence on the Party's leadership in the work on legislation requires a firm standing on China's realities and actual circumstances, a full grasp of changing demands raised by the primary social contradiction in China, and a comprehensive understanding of the risks and challenges during China's reform, development and stability. The work on legislation under the Party's leadership is to address the issues that may hinder development, overcome departmental and regional protectionism, address people's major problems and concerns in education, employment, distribution of income, social security, health, housing, safety and ecology, and promote social justice and fairness. In a word, it is to integrate the Party's tasks with the Party's principles and policies and the people's aspirations, and combine the Party's proposals with people's will through statutory procedures, which is then turned into state's legal system and the people's belief and institutional guarantee for universal compliance, coordinated efforts, spread of positive energy and Chinese dream.

1.3 Essential Requirement for Constructing Socialist Law-Based Country

Xi Jinping pointed out that "the Party's leadership is the most essential feature of socialism with Chinese characteristics and the most fundamental guarantee for socialist rule of law in China."[7] Legislation should play a leading role in comprehensively promoting rule of law, establishing Chinese socialist rule of law system and building China into a law-based socialist country. Its leading role cannot be manifested without the Party's leadership in the work on legislation, which is the fundamental requirement for building socialist rule of law and the lifeline of the Party and the State. It also concerns the fundamental interests of all the Chinese people and the cause of comprehensively promoting rule of law.

To persist in the Party's leadership in legislation requires a clear understanding of the core principle for the overall goal of comprehensively promoting rule of law: under the Party's leadership to insist on the Chinese socialist system, put the theory of Chinese socialist law-based governance, establish a complete system of laws, a highly effective enforcement system, a stringent scrutiny system and effective supporting measures, and a sound system of Party regulations; coordinated efforts are made to exercise law-based governance, political power and administration, a holistic approach adopted to establish a law-based country, government and society and efforts made to ensure that law is strictly enforced, justice impartially administered, and law is observed by everyone; and the state governance system and capacity are modernized. The important statements on comprehensive rule of law made in the Fourth Plenary Session of the Eighteenth CPC Central Committee illustrated the essential feature of Chinese socialist rule of law: on one hand, the Party's leadership is exercised over the whole process and in every aspect of China's law-based governance, which demonstrates the Party's leadership in legislation, its guarantee of law enforcement, its support for judicial justice, its rigorous observation of the law and the requirement for enforcing Party discipline. On the other hand, the Party's leadership and the socialist rule of law are consistent: the socialist rule of law should persist in the Party's leadership, while the Party's leadership is exercised by relying on the socialist rule of law. The work on legislation should make sure that the normative

[7] The Party Literature Research Office ed., *The Law-based Governance of China*, Central Compilation and Translation Press, 2017, p. 38.

system of law is connected with the complete system of Party regulations. Third, the Party's leadership is the basic guarantee for socialist rule of law, the Chinese socialist system is the basic institutional foundation for Chinese socialist rule of law system and the basic institutional guarantee for comprehensively advancing rule of law. Therefore, legislation should be intended to improve and develop Chinese socialist system. Fourth, the theory on Chinese socialist rule of law is the theoretical guide and support for the Chinese socialist rule of law system, and is the guidance for comprehensively promoting rule of law. In this sense, legislation should be carried out under its guidance, especially the new concepts, new thinking and new strategies of Xi Jinping on comprehensively promoting rule of law. Fifth, the eventual outcome of comprehensive rule of law is the making of China into a law-based nation and the modernization of state governance system and capacity. Hence the work on legislation should reflect the requirements of the "coordinated efforts made to exercise law-based governance, political power and administration, a holistic approach adopted to establish a law-based country, government and society and efforts made to ensure that law is strictly enforced, justice impartially administered, and law is observed by everyone" and promote the development of Chinese socialist legal system with the Constitution as the core which is suitable for the modern state governance system and capacity.

To insist on the Party's leadership in legislation requires clarifying the core principles of comprehensive rule of law, fulfiling the essential requirements of socialist rule of law, closely following the path of Chinese socialist rule of law and firmly grasping the nature and direction for developing Chinese socialist system. It should also be clear with regard to the Party's leadership that the CPC Central Committee's important strategies and decisions on reform and opening-up should be earnestly implemented, and that the decisions related to reform should be integrated with the legislative decisions. It becomes further clear that legislation should proactively adapt to the needs of reform, economic and social development, translate the Party's proposals into the will of state through statutory procedures, and put into practice the requirements of "legislation in a scientific manner, law being strictly enforced and observed by everyone, justice being impartially administered".

2 Fundamental Guarantee for Modernizing State Governance System and Capacity

The Party's understanding of how to govern China after the PRC was founded has developed over time, especially as it was not clear about the distinction between rule of man and rule of law in the beginning. Due to the limitations of history, China's socialist modernization followed a tortuous road in the beginning which came at a big price. History is the greatest teacher. Experience and lessons have made the Party keenly aware that rule of law is indispensable as a means of governance and an important basis for establishing modern state governance system and capacity.

3 Political Awakening for Party's Law-Based Administration and Governance

As Xi Jinping stated, "the rule of law or rule of man question has been a fundamental one throughout the history of human political civilizations. It is a major issue that all countries must face and solve as they modernize. Modern world history tells us that of those countries that have successfully modernized, every one of them has dealt with this issue well. In contrast, some countries have failed to reach full modernization despite experiencing periods of rapid development. instead, they fell into various traps which resulted in economic and social stagnation or even regression. The experiences of these countries are largely due to a lack of rule of law".[8] As emphasized in the Nineteenth CPC National Congress, "comprehensively advancing law-based governance is a profound revolution in China's governance, and rule of law should be strictly carried out". To put rule of law into the four-pronged comprehensive strategy and state that rule of law is basic to governance are another wave of profound revolution, which has also been a preliminary conclusion for the Party's practice of rule of law and governance of China since the reform and opening-up.

To persist in the Party's leadership in legislation is a manifestation of political consciousness in strengthening the Party's governance capacity, which will develop as the practice changes. Between 1949 and the reform and opening-up, China's law-based governance experienced twists and turns, which made the Party realize the important role of rule of law in state governance. In the Third Plenary Session of the Eleventh CPC Central Committee, the tasks of strengthening socialist democracy and improving the socialist legal system were proposed. After 20 years' explorations, in the Fifteenth CPC National Congress, the Party's understanding of rule of law was upgraded to a new level, based on which the work on legislation also turned its focus from legislation primarily in economic affairs to comprehensively advancing socialist rule of law. In this congress, rule of law and building China into a socialist rule of law country were advocated; it was emphasized that to carry out rule of law is the basic principle for the Party to lead people to govern China; the work on legislation should be strengthened and a Chinese socialist legal system would be established by 2010. In the Sixteenth CPC National Congress, it was put forward that to integrate the Party's leadership, the people's position as masters of the country with the rule of law was fundamental to developing socialist democratic politics; the objectives and tasks stated in the preceding congress were reiterated; the guarantee that legislation and decision-making should better reflect the people's will was also emphasized. In the Party's Seventeenth National Congress, the basic principle of comprehensive rule of law should be carried out in every aspect; the construction of socialist rule of law country should be faster; the Party's proposals should be turned into the will of the state; the legislation in a scientific and democratic manner should be continuously carried out, and the Chinese socialist legal system should be improved. Since the Eighteenth CPC National Congress, the Central Committee

[8] *Ibid.*, p. 14.

with Xi Jinping as the core has made uninterrupted efforts in fulfilling the basic principle of comprehensive rule of law, paid more attention to the important rule of law-based governance in state governance and social management, and clearly stated that rule of law is a basic means of governance, promoted a well-designed approach in which legislation is well-conceived, laws are enforced strictly, justice is impartially administered, and everyone abides by the law. It also further stated that Chinese socialist legal system should be improved, the legislation should focus on key areas, and more channels are created for expanding people's orderly participation. Therefore, "law-based governance of the country is something that was introduced by our Party; making this the fundamental policy by which, with Party leadership, the people govern the country was also an idea introduced by our Party, and the Party has, all along, been leading the people in advancing the country's law-based governance in practice".[9] As pointed out by Xi Jinping in this regard, "since the Third Plenary Session of the Eleventh Central Committee, our Party has adopted law-based governance as its fundamental policy for leading the people in governing the country, has treated the law-based exercise of state power as the basic means by which it governs, and has always considered, planned, and advanced the rule of law in light of the work of the Party and country", "advancing law-based governance of the country comes from the desire of the Party itself to improve its capacity for governance, and not from outside pressure", and "our moves to comprehensively advance the law-based governance of the country must help strengthen and improve the Party's leadership and be conducive to bolstering the party's position as governing party and to helping the Party fulfill its mission of governing the country. In absolutely no way does it mean weakening Party leadership."[10]

As the Party deepens its understanding of how to govern a country, its leadership in the work on legislation has also been strengthened. As stated in the Fourth Plenary Session of the Eighteenth CPC Central Committee, to establish the rule of law system in China, legislation should precede reform, and its role in leading and motivating reform should be played. Such statement is the first ever made in the Party's Central Committee's document to establish the role of legislation and also enhance the strategic foundation of comprehensive rule of law for building China into a moderately prosperous country, comprehensive advancing China's reform, and strengthening the Party's discipline, which is essential for the Party's overall leadership in state and social affairs. To implement the basic line of comprehensive rule of law, it was further stated in the Nineteenth CPC Central Committee that legislation should be made in a scientific, democratic manner according to law to make sure that good laws are enacted to promote development and rule of law. In this conference, it was decided by the Central Committee to establish a Central Leading Group for Advancing Rule of Law for strengthening Party's leadership in building China into a law-based country. Moreover, to strengthen the Party's leadership in the work on legislation requires improved awareness of governance according to law, reliance on the ideas, institutions and procedures for law, and innovative methods of

[9] *Ibid.*, p. 31.

[10] *Ibid.*, p. 9, 30, 31.

Party's exercise of its leading role and governing the country. To better play its core role, the Party should always exercise overall leadership and coordinate all efforts of relevant parties, and firmly stand on the basic line of comprehensive rule of law and law-based governance of the country. The Party should also be adroit at turning the Party's proposals into the state's will, training candidates recommended by Party organizations to become leaders of agencies of state power, and exercising the Party's leadership over the country and society through state agencies, and maintaining both the Party and the state's authority and the unification of the Party and the country by the democratic centralism.

In return, the work on legislation requires the profound consciousness of the Party's leadership in legislation and the full-scale implementation of the Party's leadership throughout every aspect and procedure of legislation. The work on legislation should also make sure that a complete system of laws is set to implement the Constitution and the polices of the CPC Central Committee so that the activities for advancing governance are institutionalized in the framework of law. Moreover, as time changes, the legislation should also change. The laws and regulations that fail to conform with the development and practice should be amended or abolished and the plan of the work on legislation should be made at the same time to ensure the legal systems scientific and comprehensive and make the mechanisms and institutions for the Party, state and social affairs institutionalized, regulated and procedure-based. The people's congress system is China's fundamental political system through which the Party leads the people to govern the country; it is also a fundamental political arrangement to ensure the integration of the Party's leadership, achieving people's position as masters of the country and law-based governance. Therefore, the legislation should firmly adhere to the Party's leadership which is manifested in turning the Party's proposals into the will of state and national law and putting the principle of the people running the country in China's political and social activities. In addition, legislation is also the foundation for carrying out and advancing the undertakings of the state and the specific work, the guarantee for the full and effective implementation of Party's guidelines, policies and decisions and the pillar for improving and developing the Chinese socialist system.

3.1 Party's Leadership Contributes to the Creation of Chinese Socialist Legislative System

In the early years of the PRC, the Party established the legislative system based on the nature and realities of China. However, as the economy and society were gradually transformed as they developed further, the inadequacy of this system was exposed. Since the Third Plenary Session of the Eleventh Central Committee, to play the role of both the central and local initiatives, the Party has set up a new legislative system based on China's realities, and developed and improved it through practices.

The 1954 Constitution prescribed that the National People's Congress is the only legislative authority in this state, and has the power to amend the Constitution and enact laws. The NPC Standing Committee had the power to interpret the laws and adopt decrees. The State Council is authorized to formulate administrative measures, issue decisions and orders according to the Constitution, laws and decrees. Locally, only the people's congresses of the autonomous regions are authorized to draw up statutes and separate regulations, and those of other regions could only adopt and issue decisions according to statutory authority but had no legislative power.

On July 1, 1979, in the Second Session of the Fifth National People's Congress the Law on the Organization of Local People's Congresses and Governments (Local Organization Law) was adopted, which prescribed that the standing committees should be established for the county or above people's congresses and that the people's congresses and their standing committees at the provincial, autonomous region and cities directly under the Central Government may, according to the realities and demands of their respective administrative areas and not contrary to the Constitution, laws, policies, decrees and administrative decrees, formulate and issue local regulations and report them to the NPC Standing Committee and State Council for approval. Such provisions were the first time to grant the local people's congresses and governments to make regulations on local affairs as explicitly stated in law, a major progress for the people's congress system. The 1982 Constitution confirmed this arrangement, and also reserved the power of the autonomous region, autonomous prefecture and autonomous county to make self-government and separate regulations but changed the approval authority to the NPC Standing Committee and the standing committees of the provincial or autonomous region's people's congresses.

As the reform and opening-up deepened, the legislative system was also changed to respond to development and changes for improvement. In 1982, the NPC Standing Committee amended the Local Organization Law which allowed that the people's congresses and their standing committees of the cities where the provincial or autonomous region's people's government reside and of the large cities subject to State Council's approval may formulate draft local regulations and report them to the provincial or autonomous region's people's congresses. In 1986, it amended the Local Organization Law again, which then allowed that the said people's congresses and their committees may formulate local regulations and implement them subject to approval of provincial or autonomous region's people's congresses after reporting. The local legislative authority was then extended to the cities with subordinate districts. From 1988 to 1996, the NPC made decisions to set up Hainan Province and Chongqing Municipality and granted them with provincial legislative authority. It also granted the people's congresses and their standing committees of Hainan Province, Shenzhen, Xiamen, Shantou and Zhuhai, the five special economic zones, to make regulations according to their own realities and demands. With the promulgation of the Law on Legislation in 2000, 31 provinces, autonomous regions, and municipalities, and 49 large cities were granted with local legislative authority.

In addition, the Constitution and the Law on Legislation authorized the State Council to make administrative regulations, the provincial people's governments and the large cities' people governments to make rules, and also the State Council's departments and committees, the People's Bank of China, National Audit Office, and the directly affiliated agencies that can exercise administrative functions to make rules based on provisions of the laws and the State Council's administrative regulations, decisions and decrees within their own administrative power. These provisions help establish a unified and hierarchical legislation system in China.

Since the Eighteenth CPC National Congress, the Central Committee with Xi Jinping as the core has made new contributions to the legislative system's theory and practice to adapt to a modern state governance system and capacity, people's expectations for a better life, and both the central and local initiatives. In its third plenary session, the number of the large cities with legislative power was increased, and in the following session, the scope and limits of this power were further clarified and the cities with subordinate districts were granted with the legislative power. To better implement the Central Committee's major decisions and arrangements, in the Third Session of the Twelfth NPC National Congress held in 2015, the Law on Legislation was revised to grant all the cities with subordinate districts the legislative power. According to this new law, the people's congresses and their standing committees may make regulations on the urban and rural development and administration, environment protection, and historic and cultural protection, so long as the local provisions do not contravene the Constitution, laws, administrative regulations, or the local provisions and regulations of that province or autonomous region. These local regulations are subject to the approval of the provincial or autonomous regions' people's congress standing committees for effective implementation. In 2018, in the First Session of the Thirteenth National Congress, an amendment to the Constitution was adopted, which added the provision that grants the local legislative power, a Constitutional basis for this change. Up to now, there are 353 local legislators, including 31 provinces, autonomous regions, and municipalities, 288 cities with subordinate districts, 30 autonomous prefectures, and 4 cities with no subordinate districts. In this period, China's legislative system has made important progress.

The history of such progress has demonstrated the current one is suitable for the circumstances and meet the demands of China, and both of the central and local initiative are mobilized. In the coordinated efforts of the central and local governments with other related aspects, China's socialist rule of law has opened a new chapter and made tremendous progress, which contributes to that modernization of state governance system and capacity and effectively promotes the sound and orderly development of national economy and society.

3.2 Party's Leadership Contributes to the Historical Achievements in Creating Chinese Socialist Legal System

Since the founding of the PRC, especially since the launch of reform and opening-up, the most salient feature has been the role of legislation in serving and motivating reform and the development of socialism with Chinese characteristics under the

Party's leadership. It has dismantled the mechanisms and institutions that constitute obstacles to reform and opening and, in the meantime, adjusted and improved the institutions for developing the Chinese socialist system by promoting step-by-step work on legislation in focus areas according to plan. In this process, the Chinese socialist legal system with Constitution as the core, which is conducive to modernizing state governance system and capacity, has been gradually established and improved, providing effective institutional guarantee for building China with a socialist rule of law system and then into a law-based country.

The Party's theories and its initiative to advance with the times have made strong leadership in legislation possible. Without scientific theories on rule of law, there can be no well-coordinated practices of rule of law. In the early 30 years after PRC's founding, the Party did not develop a complete and mature theory on law-based governance, so there were twists and turns. Since the Third Plenary Session of the Eleventh CPC Central Committee, the Party has turned a new page in its dedication to Chinese socialist cause by standing firm on China's realities, which has become a central thesis of the Party's theory and practice since the initiation of reform and opening-up. From this unprecedented move, the Party has, by relying on collective wisdom, developed Deng Xiaoping Theory, the important thought of Three Represents, the Scientific Outlook on Development, and the Xi Jinping Thought on Socialism with Chinese Characteristics for a New Era. It has thereby established and developed a theoretical system on Chinese socialism and the theory on Chinese socialist rule of law as the time changes.

The Party is full of innovation. As the Chinese socialist cause moves a step further, the goal of rule of law will be nearer. From the PRC's founding to the initiation of reform and opening-up, the Party's lack of understanding of law-based governance and its failure to set a goal for rule of law and the disruptive force of Cultural Revolution created the stalemate in rule of law. In the Third Plenary Session of the Eleventh CPC Central Committee, the Party declared that "from now on, we should put in the agenda of the NPC and its Standing Committee the work on legislation". However, the goal set was not ambitious, as it primarily focused on the issue of having laws rather than having good laws. Put forward by Deng Xiaoping, the work on legislation was to make sure that there were laws to abide by, "legal provisions will have to be less than perfect to start with, then be gradually improved upon. Some laws and statutes can be tried out in particular localities and later enacted nationally after the experience has been evaluated and improvements have been made. Individual legal provisions can be revised or supplemented one at a time, as necessary; there is no need to wait for a comprehensive revision of an entire body of law. In short, it is better to have some laws than none, and better to have them sooner than later,"[11] "the legal system will be improved only gradually in the course of practice, and we can't wait for that".[12]

---

[11] DENG Xiaoping, *Emancipate the Mind, Seek Truth From Facts and Unite As One In Looking to the Future*, in Selected Works of Deng Xiaoping (Vol. 2), Foreign Languages Press, 1995, p. 156.

[12] *Ibid.*, p. 255.

At the Twelfth National Congress, the Party proposed that "from now on, the Party should lead the people to formulate laws and make them complete". In the Fifth Session of the Fifth National People's Congress, it was further proposed to "gradually establish an independent legal system with Chinese features". In the Thirteenth CPC National Congress, it should be quickened to establish and improve the socialist market system and to ready a complete set of economic regulations. It was then emphasized in the following national congress that "the work on legislation should be hastened, especially the enactment of laws and regulations on improving and securing reform and opening-up, strengthening macro-economic administration and regulating micro-economic activities, for they are urgent for establishing socialist market economic institution". Later, in its third plenary session, the Decision of the Central Committee of the CPC on Some Issues Concerning the Improvement of the Socialist Market Economy proposed that "by the end of 20th century the legal system for socialist market economy at preliminary stage be established". In the Fifteenth CPC National Congress, the goal of rule of law and to build China into a socialist rule of law country were advocated, and "by 2010, the socialist legal system with Chinese characteristics should be formed"; it was further demanded that the rule of law be established "under the Party's leadership step by step in an orderly manner", and "the key is to insist on, strengthen and improve Party's leadership". This goal was then reiterated in the sixteenth and seventeenth CPC national congresses, adding an emphasis that "the rule of law as a principal strategy should be implemented in all respects and to build China into a socialist rule of law country should be accelerated". Based on the decisions and arrangements made by the Party in different periods of time, the NPC and its Standing Committee adjusted the tasks for legislation accordingly. Through the joint efforts of relevant parties, in the Fourth Session of the Eleventh National People's Congress held in March 2011, it was declared that the socialist legal system with Chinese characteristics was established as scheduled, a new milestone of China's rule of law after 1949.

Since the Eighteenth CPC National Congress, to build a more mature and well-defined system, the CPC Central Committee with Xi Jinping as the core has upgraded and improved the existing Chinese socialist legal system, blazed the trail for Chinese socialist rule of law, and laid out the mission and measures for establishing the rule of law system and country, and issued a bigger strategic goal of modernizing state governance system and capacity. The new mission, measures and goal have made new contributions and developments to the theory on Chinese socialist rule of law, acting as the beacons for rule of law construction in the new era. Since the Nineteenth CPC National Congress, the principle strategy of comprehensive rule of law has, guided by the Xi Jinping Thought on the Socialism with Chinese Characteristics for the New Era, met with a systemic set of implementing arrangements, and it was emphasized that "the Party's leadership be exercised at every point in the process and over every dimension of law-based governance". In the first meeting of the Commission for Law-based Governance under the CPC Central Committee held in 2018, Xi Jinping made a complete narration on his new concepts, thinking and strategies for comprehensive rule of law, which can be summarized as Ten Persistence: to persist in the Party's leadership in law-based governance; the people's principal position and the path of Chinese socialist rule of law; the unwavering efforts to build Chinese socialist rule of law system; the coordinated efforts to exercise law-based governance, political power and administration and a holistic approach to establishing a law-based country, government, and society; the governance of country and state affairs based on the Constitution; an overall practice of scientific law-making, strict law enforcement, impartial justice and all-around observation of law; a well-considered grasp of the relationship between comprehensive rule of law and the advancement of reform; the training of talents with strong moral integrity and high professional competence for rule of law; and the key role of the small-number officials for implementing rule of law.

He also made many new requirements for the work on legislation. First, to amend the Constitution. The amending of the Constitution is a major political and legislative act that concerns the overall situation, so it must be done under the collective leadership of the Central Committee. Meanwhile, the Constitution is for the people, so its amendment should take the people's situation, opinions and wisdom seriously to reflect the people's will. It should also adapt to the needs of the Party and people's cause for development, and follow the logic of the constitutional and legal development. Second, the leading role of the people's congress and its standing committee in the work on legislation; the mechanism for drafting, argument, coordination and deliberation should also be improved; the legislation plan needs to be improved to focus on important areas; law-making in key areas should be strengthened to better reflect the Party and national undertakings and people's concern and expectations. Third, more statements were made on legislation: legislation should precede reform; new formulation, revision and repeal and interpretation should be put on equal footing; the system of laws, administration regulations and local regulations should be improved quickly; to improve quality is key to legislation, which should be made in a scientific, democratic and law-based manner with wider people's participation in an orderly manner; a mindset of problem solving should be adopted for the work on legislation to make it more responsive, systematic, targeted and effective and guarantee its role in leading and motivating reform; the legislation and reform decision should be interconnected to ensure that every reform decision is made according to law and the law meets the demand of reform and development; if development is characterized by quality, the legislation's quality should also be high-quality for the latter can promote and secure quality social and economic development; every enactment should be pursued to conform to Constitutional principles and people's will, and win people's support; and development and governance of country should be guaranteed by good law.

Since the Eighteenth CPC National Congress, the NPC and its Standing Committee have earnestly implemented the Central Committee's decisions and arrangements on legislation, spared efforts to ensure the interconnection of legislation with reform decision and legislation serve the making of reform decision and meet the demands of reform and social and economic development. They also amended the Constitution in a proper time, actively promoted the compilation of Civil Code, and made more efforts on the law-making in key areas including market economy, social welfare, culture and ecology, which marked important progress for the work on legislation. The Twelfth NPC and its Standing Committee made 25 pieces of laws, 127 pieces of revisions, 46 pieces of decisions and 9 pieces of interpretations. From March 2018 when the Thirteenth NPC was elected to August 2019, it adopted 1 constitutional amendment, made 12 laws and 60 revisions, and issued 14 decisions. At present, China 274 pieces of laws, over 600 pieces of administrative regulations, and more than 12,000 pieces of local regulations in force. The Chinese socialist legal system with the Constitution as the core has made further progress, which provides effective legal guarantee for modernizing state governance system and capacity.

4 New Developments in Adhering to Party's Leadership in Legislation

4.1 Meaning of Adhering to Party's Leadership in Legislation

To adhere to the Party's leadership has been a basic principle in China's legislation since the PRC's founding. From Common Program, the early legislations in marriage, labor union, land reform and election, to the 1954 Constitution and a series of laws and decrees made based on it, all of them were formulated under the Party's leadership, whose collective action reflected the people's will and their fundamental interests. Since the reform and opening-up, how to uphold and improve Party's leadership has been a theme that the Party high values and never stops explorations through practice. During the Chinese socialist modernization, as the Party improves its understanding of how to govern a country and build socialism in China as well as the law of human development, its conception about the socialist rule of law also deepens.

The Party has reflected on the experience and lessons of socialist development since the reform and opening-up, and improved its understanding of its leadership in fulfilling the socialist modernization, thereby expanding the meaning of such leadership in the work on legislation. As proposed in the Twelfth National Congress, the Party mainly exercised leadership in ideology and formulation of guiding principles and policies, so it should "concentrate on studying and making important policies, inspect the implementation of these policies and strengthen the work on the ideology of the Party and government officials and the people". Then in the thirteenth congress, it was stated as "the Party's leadership is political one, especially on the political principles, direction, major decision-making and recommendation of important officials to state authorities". The Party's exercise of leadership in state affairs is mainly: by turning the Party's proposals into the will of state through statutory procedures, and through the Party's activities and the role models of Party members to motivate people to put into practice the Party's line, principles and policies. In the sixteenth congress, "the Party exercises its leadership in politics, ideology and organization, formulating overall principles and guidelines, proposing legislative opinions, recommending important officials, conducting ideological publicity, playing the role of Party organizations and its members, and governing the country according to law to specifically achieve its leadership over the state and society". In 2004, the Decision of the CPC Central Committee on Improving Party's Governance Capabilities made it clear "to put forward and apply correct theories, principles, policies and tactics to lead the enactment and implementation of Constitution and law" is essential to the enhancing the Party's governance capabilities. All these evolving statements about its own role of leadership have shown that the Party's leadership in the work on legislation has been improved in line with the changing times.

The Party has placed greater emphasis on the important role of rule of law for state and social governance since its Eighteenth National Congress. At its fourth session, the Resolution of the Central Committee of the CPC on Major Issues Concerning the Enhancement of All-round Law-based Governance, a first overall statement on the Party's role in advancing rule of law in a party's central committee's document. It clearly stated that the Party's leadership in advancing rule of law should be strengthened and improved to carry out it in the whole process and all aspects of promoting rule of law, and asked for making sound institutions and working mechanism for exercising such leadership and improving the working mechanism and procedures for the implementation of Party's principles, policies, decisions and arrangements for rule of law. The mechanism and institutions for exercising Party's leadership in the work on legislation changed as the proposal, which the Party's leadership in comprehensively advancing rule of law should be improved, was made. The meaning of the Party's leadership in legislation is broadened, and its leadership becomes more specific on working mechanism, especially about the methods and procedures.

At the Nineteenth National Congress, a general requirement for the Party's development in the new era was set forth, emphasizing "the Party's supreme political leadership", "upholding and strengthening the Party's overall leadership" and "integration of Party's leadership, the position of people as masters of the country, and rule of law". It further stated that "the Party's leadership is the fundamental guarantee for ensuring that the people run the country and governance in China is law-based; that the people run the country is an essential feature of socialist democracy; and law-based governance is the basic way for the Party to lead the people in governing the country", "We will improve the way the Party exercises leadership and governance to ensure that it leads the people in effectively governing the country", "we should see to it that people's congresses and their standing committees play the leading role in lawmaking, and improve the organizational and working systems of people's congresses to support and ensure the exercise of their statutory powers of enacting laws, conducting oversight, making decisions, and appointing and removing officials". A central leading group for advancing law-based governance in all areas was set up to exercise unified leadership over the initiative to build rule of law in China. The Resolution and measures have secured the Party's leadership in the work on legislation, deepened and broadened the meaning of this leadership and improved the systems and mechanisms for the exercise of leadership.

4.2 *Adhering to the Party's Overall Leadership in the Work on Legislation*

To adhere to the Party's overall leadership means that every line, principle and policy should be implemented throughout the work on legislation, and every major decision and arrangement should be carried out to ensure the correct political direction of legislation.

First, to uphold the Party's basic line, which means that the Party leads and unites the people of all ethnic groups, upholds the Four Cardinal Principles, continues to reform and open up, remains self-reliant, hardworking, and enterprising, and strive to build China into a great modern socialist country that is prosperous, strong, democratic, culturally advanced, harmonious, and beautiful. It was reiterated in the nineteenth congress that "the Party must be completely clear about this fundamental dimension of our national context, and must base our work on this most important reality – the primary stage of socialism. We must remain fully committed to the Party's basic line as the source that keeps the Party and the country going and that brings happiness to the people." To uphold the Party's basic line for legislation is to keep committed to the Party and the state, and seeking happiness for the people. To uphold development as the primary task requires to improving the legal systems for supporting and promoting sound social and economic development; to keep confident in the socialist path and its system to continue to establish sound legal systems for socialist democracy, promote Chinese socialist system and the modernization of state governance system and capacity by a complete normative system of law. To take the Party's basic theories as the guidelines and stay true to the theory of Chinese socialism, especially the Xi Jinping Thought on Socialism with Chinese Characteristics for a New Era, the latest achievement of adapting Marxism to China's realities. To uphold people's democratic dictatorship, the people's congress system and ensure the people's position as masters of the country. The work on legislation should be carried out by centering on the implementation of the Five-sphere Integrated Plan and the Four-pronged Comprehensive Strategy, strictly adhering to new development concepts and promoting scientific and democratic law-making according to law in order to improve the Chinese socialist legal system, and rule of law system and the position of China as a law-based one.

Second, to adhere to the Party's principle of relying on and serving the people (or the "mass line" principle). This Party principle means everything the Party does is to serve the people wholeheartedly, rely on the people and act for the people. To adopt the people's approach is the Party's fundamental political standing. Therefore, law should be made by implementing this principle, for serving the people wholeheartedly. To adhere to this principle also requires democratic legislation, in which the cities have more access to participating in the legislation activities, and listening to people's opinions and collecting their wisdom to turn the Party's proposal into the will of the state so as to realize integration of Party's proposals with people's will and make it common behavioral norms abided by all the people. A complete set of legal systems can make it possible for the people, under the Party's leadership, to administer the affairs of the state, its economy, cultural and society as true masters of the country.

Third, to adhere to the Party's guiding principles. This means to start everything from reality, associate theory with practice, seek truth from facts, and test and then develop the truth through practice. To adhere to it in legislation means to uphold the theory of Chinese socialist rule of law as the guide, insist on the circumstances and realities of the state, make full use of investigation and research, study and take an accurate grasp of the contradiction in China's reality and development, formulate specific measure to solve problems, make institutional arrangements through legislation's procedures and make law more practicable and effective. Meanwhile, it also means to learn and borrow any good experience from other civilizations of law, promote the traditional Chinese legal heritage, try to achieve the interconnection of Chinese rule of law discourse with the ideas and concepts of other civilizations of law to continuously strengthen China's discourse power in rule of law so as to demonstrate Chinese wisdom to international community governance and offer Chinese solution.

Last, to adhere to the Party's line on organization. This refers to the general principles and guidelines that the Party establishes regarding the organizational work as required by the political line in certain period. In the new era, that the legislation adheres to this line means to fully implement the Xi Jinping Thought on Socialism with Chinese Characteristics for a New Era, to strengthen the establishment of legal systems for the work on organization, to make the training and management of officials more scientific and regulated, to an honest, clean and responsible team of officials with competence, and to improve the officials' to apply legal thinking and approaches to deepen reform and development, resolve disputes and maintain social stability to provide strong and reliable guarantee for the organization of developing the Party's cause.

4.3 To Adhere to the Central Committee's Centralized and Unified Leadership in Legislation

That the Party's overall leadership in the work on legislation means to adhere to the Central Committee's centralized and unified leadership in legislation, firmly uphold its authority and ensure its decision is thoroughly implemented. The Central Committee's unified leadership is key to the destiny of the Party and the state and fundamental to the interests of all the people.

To adhere to the centralized and unified leadership has been a political discipline of the Party. Since the founding of the Party, a set of strict organizational disciplines has been established. The Party's discipline is the basic guarantee to fight against all the difficulties and make achievements. To overcome the negative influence of extreme democracy brought by Cultural Revolution and restore the Party's traditions and good practices, the Party issued the Several Principles on Political Life in the

Party in the Fifth Plenary Session of the Eleventh CPC Central Committee held in 1980, which emphasized "maintaining the centralized and unified leadership of the Party" and set out a principle that "individual Party members defer to Party organizations, the minority defers to the majority, lower-level Party organizations defer to higher-level Party organizations, and all organizations and members of the Party defer to the Central Committee of the Party." In the Sixth Plenary Session of the Eighteenth CPC Central Committee held in 2016, the Several Principles on Political Life in the Party under New Situation reiterated these disciplines and principle. In the new era, to abide by the Party's discipline is to follow the Party's political discipline and political leadership of the Party. In 2018, Xi Jinping stated in the sixth group study session of the Political Bureau that to adhere to the Central Committee's authority and its centralized and unified leadership was most important for standing firm on the Party's political leadership. The work on legislation requires enhanced political integrity, a better understanding of the general picture, adherence to the core leadership of the Central Committee, and be consistent with the CPC Central Committee's policy; it also calls for comprehensive and accurate implementation of the Party's line, guidelines and polices and unwavering implementation of the decisions and arrangements made by the Central Committee to make sure that the Party's proposals can be turned into the will of the state and closely follow the Central Committee in terms of our thinking, political orientation, and actions. To adhere to the Party's leadership in local legislation also requires the Central Committee's centralized and unified leadership in the first place, and the implementation of local Party's committee's decision is also intended for ensuring the Central Committee's decision implementation, other than for the local and partial interests. The local interests are by no means local characteristic, and the authority of the Central Committee and its centralized and unified leadership should always be upheld.

5 Institutions and Mechanisms for Upholding the Party's Leadership in Legislation

The Party's leadership in legislation has never been clearly identified in documents since the reform and opening-up. As an alternative, its leadership has been exercised through formulation of policies. The NPC Standing Committee and its party group, with infinite loyalty to the Party, practice the Party's leadership to ensure that the Party's line, guidelines, and policies in different periods of time can be implemented through law. In the early stage of reform and opening-up, the CPC Central Committee summarized the experience and lessons from its exercise of leadership for socialist revolution and development, and started to pay attention to the institutional construction in all respects. In 1979, Peng Zhen drafted a report, requiring that the issues and opinions for drafting and revision of laws and regulations should be reported to the Central Committee, which established the instruction-seeking and reporting system. In 1991, the Central Committee issued a document on the Party's leadership in legislation based on past experience and proposed the following aspects to exercise leadership: in defining the principles of the work on legislation and the guiding principles of important laws, deliberating on and adopting the NPC Standing Committee's legislative plan, proposing the legislator to turn the Party's long-term proven guidelines and policies into law (the suggestion to amend Constitution and make laws); and deciding on the issues concerning important guidelines and policies that rely on the Central Committee for the work on legislation. The two documents have made the Party's leadership in legislation more specific and institutionalized.

In the Fourth Plenary Session of the Eighteenth CPC Central Committee, it was for the first time to clarify the system and working mechanism for improving the Party's leadership in advancing comprehensive rule of law through a central committee's resolution which stated that "any adjustment of major institution or policy by the legislation should be reported to the CPC Central Committee for discussion and final decision. The CPC Central Committee proposed suggestion on amending the Constitution to the NPC which amended the Constitution according to the procedures as stipulated in the Constitution. The major issues of law-making and revision should be reported to the CPC Central Committee by the NPC Standing Committee". In a document on strengthening the Party's leadership in legislation issued by the Central Committee in 2016, it further stated the guiding philosophy, principles, mechanism, contents and methods for exercising its leadership in the work on legislation.

5.1 Basic Principles

The Party's leadership in the work on legislation includes the Party's Central Committee's leadership in overall work on legislation nationwide, study and decide on the major issues in legislation, and the party committees of the regions whose people's congresses and their standing committees have local legislative power exercise leadership in local legislation according to the Central Committee's decisions and guidelines. The documents on strengthening the Party's leadership in the work on legislation has clarified the basic principles: to uphold the political leadership, to adhere to democratic decision-making and collective leadership, to fully play the role of legislative authorities, and to carry out work according to laws and regulations. To uphold the political leadership refers to the exercise of Party's leadership mainly in political sphere, especially the guidelines and policies. Specifically, the Party formulates the guidelines for the work on legislation, makes suggestions on legislation, clarifies major legislative issues and strengthens the training and teambuilding of professional legislative talents to ensure that the work on legislation fully reflects the Party's proposals, demonstrate people's will, win people's support and take a firm standing on the correct political direction. To adhere to democratic decision-making and collective leadership means to implement democratic centralism and to adopt a people's-oriented approach in exercising Party's leadership in legislation. It also means to focus on legislation quality, promote scientific and democratic legislation, follow the Party's decision-making rules on major issues, and study and decide on the major issues in legislation through the leadership group. To fully play the role of legislative authorities means that Party's leadership in legislation should conform with the requirements of law-based exercise of state power and properly deal with the relationship between the strengthening of Party's leadership and its support and guarantee for the legislative authorities to make law. Except for the legislation on political matters and major social and economic issues, the legislative authorities draft the laws and deliberate on them according to statutory provisions. To carry out work according to laws and regulations means that the Party's leadership in legislation should be exercised within the scope of Constitution and law, and not voluntarily intervene with or even replace legislation itself.

5.2 To Improve Leadership Institutions and Mechanisms

First, to make suggestions on Constitutional amendment and interpretations. Every Constitution was drafted under the organization of Party's Central Committee and delivered to the NPC as legislative opinions since the PRC's founding. It is an important practice for the Party to exercise its leadership. The 1982 Constitution and its amendments were drafted under the organization of the Party's Central Committee and then reported to the NPC for revision. Some legislative programs including the enactment of Anti-Secession Law were advocated and decided by the Party's Central Committee which then organized their drafting. In 2018, the Party's Central Committee with Xi Jinping as the core made the great decision to amend the Constitution based on the general situation and strategic importance of upholding and improving Chinese socialism for the new era. The Second Plenary Session of the Nineteenth Central Committee deliberated on and approved the suggestive constitutional amendment. The Twelfth NPC Standing Committee pushed forward the constitutional amendment by strictly following the statutory procedures, convened meetings of the NPC Standing Committee to discuss the suggestion, formulate a draft amendment and reported to the First Session of the Thirteenth NPC for deliberation.

Second, to formulate the guidelines and strategies for legislation. In each national congress of the Party, it made new arrangements for realizing the strategic development goals in different periods of time as the time changed, and the objectives and missions of legislation in these periods were also set out. For example, in the Fifteenth CPC National Congress held in 1997, it was stated that rule of law is the basic principle for the Party to lead people in governing the country, and the objective of legislation that Chinese socialist legal system was to be established by 2020 was also set out. The Fourth Plenary Session of the Eighteenth CPC Central Committee was the first one to take rule of law as its conference theme in the Party's history and adopted the Resolution, which provided for the general goal of establishing a Chinese socialist rule of law system and building China into a law-based country. In the Nineteenth CPC National Congress it was then emphasized that legislation should be carried out in a scientific, democratic manner according to law, and good law be applied to promote development and guarantee good governance. This conference also proposed a two fifteen-year goals in state governance after China is built into a moderately prosperous country: one is, between 2020 and 2035, to basically realize law-based governance of the country, the law-based exercise of state power, and the law-based administration of government, establish well-designed institutions in all respects, and achieve the basic modernization of state governance system and capacity. The other is, between 2035 and the middle of the twenty-first century, to build China into a great modern socialist country in all respects and realize modernization of state governance system and capacity. The Central Committee's arrangements for the key links of rule of law construction have served as the guidelines and strategies for the work on legislation in later periods.

Second, to deliberate on and then approve the legislative plan and make suggestions about important legislation programs. The NPC Standing Committee formulates its legislative plan at its early term of office to define its focus, objectives and tasks of legislation and make arrangements for the future five years' legislation based on the social and economic development objectives, missions, principles and guidelines in different phases set out by the Central Committee, which also adheres to the central task of the whole Party. From the Seventh NPC Standing Committee in 1988, every NPC Standing Committee would formulate a legislative plan and issue it upon the Central Committee's approval after reporting, which has helped form an important way of Party's leadership in legislation. To formulate and implement the legislative plan by referring to the Party and the state's central is an important leverage for the NPC Standing Committee to play the leading role of legislation, which are conducive to strengthening the integration, coordination and reasonableness.

Fourth, to study and discuss important draft and decide on the major issues related with the draft. The important draft laws and their major issues are often concerned with the core of political decision-making, which should be subject to the Central Committee's decision. Not all the draft laws submitted to the NPC and its Standing Committee are reported to Central Committee for discussion. Only the important ones that concern an important topic, a highly political issue, complicated matters or wide public attention are subject to this procedure. Since the Eighteenth CPC National Congress, the Central Committee with Xi Jinping as the core has strengthened its leadership in the work on legislation and innovated its way of exercising leadership: to incorporate the important legislative programs and matters into the annual work guidelines of Political Bureau's Standing Committee of the Central Committee. Such a procedure can be understood from two aspects: on one hand, if the Central Committee thinks important, it will incorporate them into its annual work guidelines and require the relevant departments or parties to submit to the Central Committee for discussion according to the scheduled timetable. On the other hand, if the NPC Standing Committee, State Council and other state authorities that organize the law drafting and deliberation think the drafts are in need of the Central Committee's study and discussion, they can also suggest an ad hoc submission to Political Bureau's Standing Committee though the concerned drafts are not listed in its annual working guidelines.

Fifth, to deliberate on the instructions-seeking reports on important legislative matters. It includes the deliberation on the working reports of the Party Group of NPC Standing Committee, the instructions-seeking reports on important draft laws and the instructions-seeking reports on important legislation. To uphold the Central Committee's centralized and unified leadership means to strictly follow the instructions-seeking and reporting system, for it is not only the requirement laid out by the Party Constitution and regulations, but also a Party discipline. To strictly implement this system by reporting fully and timely the circumstances and issues in the legislation to the Central Committee and asking for the Central Committee's support is conducive to resolving the major controversies for smoothly promoting legislation, to reflecting the wishes and demands of the people's congress representatives and people for legislation for better responding to people's will, and to guaranteeing the Party's leadership exercised throughout the whole process and all aspects for promoting the integration of Party's leadership, people's position as masters of the country and rule of law. Since the reform and opening-up, the work on legislation has always been adherent to the instructions-seeking and reporting system. After the Eighteenth CPC National Congress, the party groups of NPC Standing Committee, State Council, National Committee of the CPPCC, Supreme People's Court and Supreme People's Procuratorate have made reports to the Central Committee. Xi Jinping has chaired the meetings of the Political Bureau's Standing Committee to deliberate on the reports of the NPC Standing Committee's Party Group for consecutive years. He also convened several meetings of this kind to study and discuss the major legislative issues and matters, and deliberate on the instructions-seeking reports on some important draft laws and revisions submitted the NPC Standing Committee's Party Group. On these meetings, he has made a lot of important decisions and arrangements for the concerned issues and matters. This procedure has been evolved into a system. The NPC and its Standing Committee have always upheld the instructions-seeking and reporting system to ensure that the enactment and revision of important laws and other major issues in legislation are subject to this system, and put in practice the Party's directives on legislation. Since the Eighteenth CPC National Congress, the NPC has reported every important legislative matter to the Central Committee for seeking instructions in the name of its Party Group, an institutionalized and routine practice.

Last, to strengthen the construction and leadership of the Party groups of people's congresses. Party group is a leadership authority set up in the leadership departments of the central and local state authorities and the people's, economic organizations, cultural, social and other organizations, which played a core leading role in its own organization. The Party's Constitution was adopted in the Eighth CPC National Congress held in 1956. It stipulated that party groups should be established in state authorities and people's organizations. Since the Eighteenth CPC National Congress, the Central Committee has continued to strengthen the capacity of party group. On May 29, 2015, in the Political Bureau's meeting convened by Xi Jinping, the Working Regulations for the Party Group of the CPC (for trial implementation) was adopted after deliberation. In 2017, the Party's Constitution was revised in the Nineteenth CPC National Congress, which further improved the provisions on the role of party group.

According to relevant provisions, the Party Group of NPC Standing Committee decided to establish sub-party groups in its special committees upon the consent of the CPC Central Committee's Organization Department. On October 17, 2016, the Party Group of NPC Standing Committee convened a meeting on the party development of the special committees. In this meeting, it was declared that sub-party groups be established in nine special committees and many arrangements were also made to strengthen the party development in these committees. It is a historical move for NPC. The party group and sub-party group are responsible to "control the direction, overall plan, and strict implementation" in the work on legislation; they are key organizational links between Party's leadership and people's position as masters of the country and also exemplify the Party's unique political, organizational and institutional advantage.

6 Experience and Reflections

To strengthen and improve the Party's leadership in the work on legislation is essential to advancing Constitution-and-law based governance and modernizing the state governance system and capacity, and important for implementing Xi Jinping Thought on Socialism with Chinese Characteristics for a New Era and enhancing and improving the work on legislation in all respects. Over the past 70 years, especially over the past 40 years, valuable experience has been gained in upholding the Party's leadership in legislation, which should be cherished, inherited and carried forward.

6.1 To Exercise Party's Leadership Throughout Legislation

As explicitly expressed by Xi Jinping, "the Party's leadership is the soul of the socialist rule of law with Chinese characteristics".[13] Legislation is the premise and foundation for rule of law. To adhere to the Party's leadership in legislation is a major political principle that the work on legislation should uphold, and is also a piece of basic experience in making achievements and progress in legislation. The advantage of Chinese socialist system is mostly represented by the core and leading role of the Party in exercising overall leadership and coordinating efforts from all parties. To fully play this role is to adhere to the Party's exercise of state power according to law in the first place. The Constitution and law are the most powerful and important ruler of state governance. The key to upholding the Party's exercise of state power according to laws is the Party's firmer leadership in legislation and better

[13] Xi Jinping, *Speech at a seminar for principal provincial and ministerial level leaders on the guiding principles from the Fourth Plenary Session of the 18th CPC Central Committee and on comprehensively advancing the law-based governance of China, February 2, 2015*, in The Party Literature Research Office ed., *The Law-based Governance of China*, Central Party Literature Compilation and Translation Press, 2017, p. 40.

at governing the country according to the Constitution and law. Therefore, to adhere to the Party's leadership in legislation needs to integrate the Party's role of leading people to legislate and implement the provisions of Constitution and law with the Party's exercise of its leadership within the limit of Constitution and law. Moreover, in order to continuously strengthen and improve the Party's leadership, improve the expertise of the Party's law-based exercise of state power, and ensure a law-based approach to the Party's leadership in state and social affairs, it also needs to improve capacity in turning the Party's proposals into the will of the state through statutory procedures, in exercising leadership over the state and society through agencies of state power, and maintaining the authority of both the Party and the state and the unification of the Party and the country under the principle of democratic centralism.

6.2 To Adopt a People-Centered Approach

To seek happiness for the Chinese people and rejuvenation of the Chinese nation is the original aspiration and mission for the Chinese Communists. The reason why the people's congress system has shown great vitality and advantage is its being deeply rooted in the people. Since the Eighteenth CPC National Congress, the NPC and its Standing Committee has adopted a people-centered approach in which the people's interests are the pursuit of the work of people's congresses, insisted on legislation for the people and responded to social concern and people's will through legislation. For example, in 2018 Changchun Changsheng Bio-Technology was found to produce illegal vaccines, Xi Jinping made several directives and asked for putting people's health and safety in the first place. The NPC Standing Committee then took an active role in coordinating and promoting the legislation on vaccine administration based on these directives, organized deliberations and then adopted it, which created a long-term institution of comprehensive supervision on vaccine in an unprecedented pace in legislation. To better perform in legislation, the NPC has always made the people's aspiration for better life as its objective, people's support, approval, satisfaction, and consent as the fundamental criteria for appraising all of its work and the improvement of people's wellbeing as the focus. It also respects the people's position as masters of the country in every possible and practical aspect of state, political and social life to ensure that every legislation reflects and safeguards people's interests and wishes and promotes their wellbeing.

6.3 To Give Full Play to the Advantages of the People's Congress System

The people's congress system is the fundamental political system that guarantees the integration of the Party's leadership, the people's position as masters of the country and rule of law, which demonstrates the features and advantages of socialist democracy. In the past sixty years, it has been continuously consolidated and developed, kept with time neck and neck and made innovation in the practice of building Chinese socialism, and played an important role in promoting state governance. Since the Eighteenth National Congress, the Central Committee with Xi Jinping as the core has made contributions to the practice and theory on it as time changes. Xi Jinping pointed out that the people's congress system is an important component of the Chinese socialist system and is also the fundamental political system that supports the state governance system and capacity. He also emphasized that people's congress exercises the state power in a unified way to ensure that the state authorities exercise powers and perform duties according to statutory provisions and procedures, and that the Party exercises unified leadership to give full play to the initiative and enthusiasm of the local authorities and ensure the all the causes of the state can be promoted in an efficient way. He further emphasized that this system should never been abandoned and require continuous improvement, and its role as the fundamental political system should be fully played to ensure that the people take a strong hold of the country and nation's destiny. Xi's remarks re-positioned the people's congress system for the new era, added new in-depth ideas to the basic principle of democratic centralism and served as the beacon of light for promoting and improving it. Practice never stops, and system never ceases to upgrade. The people's congress system should adapt to the changes of time, meet the challenges and make new achievements for building the Chinese socialism. Under the Central Committee's leadership with Xi Jinping as the core, the NPC should, with the tireless aspirations and relentless spirits, embrace its mission, strive for innovation, continue to innovate the theory and practice of the people's congress system to make it more mature and perfect and give a full play to the political and institutional advantages in Chinese socialism.

6.4 To Comprehensively Advance Rule of Law

To build a comprehensive rule of law is the essential requirement and important guarantee for Chinese socialism, the foundation for maintaining long-lasting peace of the Party and the state, and a profound and all-around revolution for state governance. As a complete set of institutions and mechanism for Party's leadership in legislation is in place, a uniform but multi-tiered legislative system is continuously improved, and the legislative procedures and authorization is under steady progress, the NPC and its Standing Committee take a comprehensive rule of law as the basic principle and an important task for their work on legislation, strive to promote legislation in a scientific and democratic manner according to law, accelerate law-making in key areas. They have adopted a large number of important laws quickly which caused positive social effect. The NPC and its Standing Committee are burdened with great responsibilities in building a socialist law-based country for China, so they should be under the strong leadership of the Central Committee, assume the powers granted by the Constitution and law, and improve the Chinese socialist legal system with Constitution as the core, so as to ensure the effective implementation of the Constitution and law and make greater contributions to comprehensive rule of law and law-based socialist country.

Chapter 3
History of the Constitution of the People's Republic of China

Luo Huanxing

Abstract This chapter examines the legislative history of China's constitution from the enactment of the Common Program, the 1954 Constitution, the 1975 Constitution, and the 1978 Constitution to the 1982 Constitution, discusses the contents, features and significance of these constitutional documents. It highlights the importance of the CPC leadership for China's Constitutional change for safeguarding people's role as the masters of the country, advancing reform and modernization, strengthening socialist rule of law, and maintaining national unity and stability. It concludes that the Xi Jinping Thought on Socialism with Chinese Characteristics should act as the guide to implement the new ideas, thoughts and strategies and the requirements of strengthening the constitutional enforcement and supervision, promoting constitutional review and safeguarding the Constitution's authority.

Keywords Constitutional history · Common Program · 1954 Constitution · 1982 Constitution · CPC leadership · Constitution-based governance

Constitution is the fundamental law of the state and the general charter for governing the country and the state. It has the highest legal status, legal authority and legal effect. In 1954, when the Committee of Central People's Government discussed about drafting the first constitution, Mao Zedong clearly stated that "an organization must have rules, and so must a state. A constitution is a set of general rules; it is the fundamental law".[1] It is the fundamental law, because it provides for the fundamental systems and missions of the state, and provides people's basic rights and obligations and provides rule of behavior for people of all ethnic groups, state authorities, armed forces, political parties, social organizations and corporations and non-profit institutions. In China, this fundamental law has evolved from the Common Program in 1949, 1954 Constitution, 1975 Constitution, 1978 Constitution to 1982

[1] MAO Zedong, *Selected Works of Mao Zedong (Vol. 5)*, Foreign Languages Press, 1977, p. 145.

L. Huanxing (✉)
Beijing, China
e-mail: liujixuan@lawpress.com.cn

C. Shen et al. (eds.), *A History of Legislation in the Past 70 Years in China*,
https://doi.org/10.1007/978-981-95-3799-0_3

Constitution and its several amendments. Since 1949, though it was amended for several times, the nature, path of development, system and mission have never been changed: socialism is the wish for which the Chinese people is united and fight.

1 Common Program

1.1 Formulation

As the War of Liberation came to an end with victory, on April 30, 1948, the Central Committee issued the "May Day" slogans, the fourth of which called for "all the Chinese workers united, collaborating with the intellectuals, liberal bourgeoisie, all democratic parties, community leaders and other compatriots, consolidating and the expanding the united front to fight against the imperialism, feudalism, and crony capitalism, beating down Chiang Kai-shek and fighting for establishing a new China". Its fifth one further called for "all democratic parties, people's organizations, and community leaders to convene a political consultative conference as soon as possible to discuss and convene the people's congress and establish a coalition government!" In his letter addressed to the leaders of democratic parties, Mao Zedong pointed out that "in current circumstances, it is opportune and necessary to convene a congress of people's representatives, establish a coalition government, strengthen the cooperation with other democratic parties and people's organizations, and formulate a program for the new government to exercise state power. However, to realize it, it is essential to convening a meeting with the representatives of the democratic parties and people's organizations." These calls received with welcome from Chinese people, democratic parties, people's organizations, nonpartisan democrats, people of minority ethnic groups, and overseas Chinese. Many democrats issued declarations and took an active part in preparing the upcoming political consultative conference.

In 1949, as the decisive Three Campaigns of the War of Liberation and the Yangtze River Crossing Campaign were to close with victories, the liberation army marched towards south, southwest and northwest China. The China mainland was to be liberated, and the circumstances for establish a new China and central people's government were mature. In September 1949, after thorough preparations the First Chinese People's Political Consultative Conference (CPPCC) was held in newly liberated Peking (later named Beijing), which consisted of 622 representatives from democratic parties, regions, people's groups, ethnic groups, army, overseas Chinese and other compatriots. The CPC members took 44%, and the rest were the democratic parties' members, workers, peasants and nonpartisan people. It was a convention of unity among the whole Chinese people. In the opening speech, Mao Zedong said, the CPPCC was held under completely new basis; it represented the whole Chinese people, and won their trust and support. On September 27, the Organic Law of the Chinese People's Political Consultative Conference, the Organic Law of the Central People's Government of the People's Republic of China and four resolutions on designating capital, national calendar, national anthem and flag were adopted at the first plenary session of CPPCC.[2] Two days later, the Common Program was also adopted. The two organic laws and Common Program were the legal basis for new China. On September 30, the president, vice president, and councilors of the People's Republic of China were elected at the CPPCC's first plenary session. On October 1, the People's Republic of China was declared, and the councilors of the Central People's Government were announced to assume office in Peking (then changed to Beijing), the capital; the Common Program was unanimously accepted as the guidelines for the Central People's Government to exercise state power.

1.2 Nature

However, the military operations and land reform were not completed yet, and the people were not fully motivated, the circumstances for convening a national people's congress based on universal suffrage were not ripe yet. The CPPCC was not a state authority, but it could perform the powers and functions of the national people's congress, and its first plenary session was functioned in part as a constitutional convention. Article 7 of the CPPCC's Organic Law stipulated that the CPPCC shall be "performing the functions and exercising the powers of the All-China (National) People's Congress prior to its convocation by means of universal franchise", for example, to enact or amend the Organic Law of the CPPCC, elect the Central People's Government Council of the People's Republic of China and vest it with the power of exercising state power. Hence, the first CPPCC's plenary session was concerned with political consultation and exercise of state power in respect of its nature. It was a form of organization for maintaining people's democratic united front and a state authority that exercised certain supreme power of a state. The Common Program adopted in this session made many provisions that should be stipulated in a constitution, which made it the fundamental law that performed the functions of a constitution in the early stage of PRC. Mao Zedong also stated clearly that the fundamental law at that time was Common Program.

1.3 Contents

Apart from its preamble, the Common Program was divided by seven chapters with 60 articles in total. These chapters included general principles, organs of state power, military system, economic policy, cultural and educational policy, policy towards nationalities, and foreign policy. Its formulation, form, contents and structure were

[2] The official English translation of these documents can be found in *The Important Documents of the First Plenary Session of the Chinese People's Political Consultative Conference*, Foreign Languages Press, 1949. The translations of the citations are adapted accordingly.

similar with those of a constitution, and many of its provisions were constitutional. For example, Article 1 stated the nature of the country, as "the People's Republic of China is a New Democratic or a People's Democratic state. It carries out the people's democratic dictatorship led by the working class, based on the alliance of workers and peasants, and uniting all democratic classes and all nationalities in China". It also stipulated an extensive array of people's rights and freedoms, as stated in Article that "the people of the People's Republic of China shall have the right to elect and to be elected according to law", in Article 5 that "the people of the People's Republic of China shall have freedom of thought, speech, publication, assembly, association, correspondence, person, domicile, change of domicile, religious belief and the freedom of holding processions and demonstrations", in Article 6 that women shall enjoy equal rights with men in political, economic, cultural, educational and social life, and in Article 8 that "it is the duty of every national of the People's Republic of China to defend the motherland, to abide by the law, to observe labor discipline, to protect public property to perform public and military service, and to pay taxes". Article 12 made provisions on the organs of state power: "the state power of the People's Republic of China belongs to the people. The people's congresses and the people's governments of all levels are the organs for the exercise of state power by the people. The people's congresses of all levels shall be popularly elected by universal franchise. The people's congresses of all levels shall elect the people's governments of their respective levels. The people's governments shall be the organs for exercising state power at their respective levels when the people's congresses of their respective levels are not in session. The All-China (National) People's Congress shall be the supreme organ of state power. The Central People's Government shall be the supreme organ for exercising state power when the All-China (National) People's Congress is not in session". Article 15 stipulated that the organs of state power at all levels shall practice democratic centralism. Article 16 clarified the central-local relation: "the jurisdiction of the Central People's Government and the local people's governments shall be defined according to the nature of the various matters involved, and shall be prescribed by decrees of the Central People's Government Council so as to satisfy the requirements of both national unity and local expediency". Additionally, the Common Program made provisions on state and government systems and provides specific rules on important matters of military affairs, economy, culture, education, nationalities and diplomacy.

These matters prescribed in the Common Program were important for the state and often subject to the provisions of Constitution, which made it an important document for its historical significance and profound practical relevance and was the reason why it was called the interim Constitution.

2 1954 Constitution

2.1 Background

Article 6 of the CPPCC's Organic Law prescribed that "a plenary session of the Chinese People's Political Consultative Conference shall be summoned once every three years", and according to it, the second plenary session should be convened around September 1952, however, the situation in China changed rapidly in this period. When the PRC was founded in October, China mainland still awaited a complete liberation. Between the end of 1949 and the beginning of 1950, the south, southwest and northwest of China were liberated, in May 1950, Hainan island was finally liberated, and in 1951, a peace accord was made between the central government and the Tibetan government after several negotiations, which delivered the People's Liberation Army to Lhasa. The military operations in China mainland were basically to an end. The land reform was simultaneously carried in the newly liberated areas. From the winter of 1950 to the spring of 1953, the reform was completed in the villages of the newly liberated areas which took a bigger half of China's population except from some ethnic minority areas. The social order was also restored by the Campaign to Suppress Counterrevolutionaries initiated in 1950 and basically ended in October 1951. Until 1952, the war-devastated national economy gained vitality in all respects after several campaigns including increased production and economy, three-antis and five-antis. The first five-year plan was started from 1953, which strived for a systemic socialist industrialization and pushed forward the socialist transformation in agriculture, handicraft, and capitalism industry and commerce. The new China was met with a thriving future.

Article 14 of the Common Program stated that "in all places where military operations have completed ended, agrarian land reform has been thoroughly carried out and people of all circles have been fully organized, elections based on universal franchise shall be held immediately for the purpose of convening local people's congresses." Upon the proposal of the Central Committee and the suggestion of CPPCC made to the Council of Central People's Government, based on the duties and powers stipulated in the Organic Law of the Central People's Government, the NPC and the local people's congresses were to be held in 1953. On January 1953, Zhou Enlai made a report on convening the NPC and the local people's congresses in the twelfth session of the Council, stating that the Constitution was to be made on the basis of the Common Program for the latter had incorporated provisions on the national system, social structure and people's rights and other matters. A Resolution on Convening the NPC and Local People's Congresses was adopted. It was estimated that the NPC was to be held in 1953, however, it was eventually convened in September 1954 to formulate the Constitution due to the community-level elections and the convocation of local people's congresses.

2.2 Formulation

In the twelfth session, the drafting commission for the Constitution of the People's Republic of China was established, which consisted of 33 members with Mao Zedong as the president. According to a plan, the draft constitution was made by the Party as the basis for the committee's discussion. In early 1954, the Party's Central Committee set up a constitutional drafting committee, and Mao Zedong joined as the responsible person. The committee members also include Chen Boda, Hu Qiaomu and Tian Jiaying. They gathered in Hangzhou, and worked from January 7 to March 9 of 1954 to complete the constitution's draft. After consulting the commission members who were not CPC members for opinions, they wrote down the first draft which was later submitted for discussion in the commission's first plenary meeting. Between March 23 and June 11, the Commission held seven plenary meetings to discuss it. Some departments also organized over 8000 people to give opinions on it, which solicited over 5900 revision opinions, a great help to its improvement. On June 14, the Council decided to issue the draft Constitution of the People's Republic of China for all Chinese people's opinions. It was widely studied, discussed and popularized among over 150 million people, and the people's congresses at the provincial, city and county level were held to discuss it. From June 15 to September 10, there were over 1.18 million pieces of opinions collected from the Chinese people on revising and making additions to the Constitution, which, after the commission's office made classifications and compilations, were published as Collection of Public Opinions in 16 volumes. The drafting committee then made some revisions and improvements based on these opinions. The commission convened the eighth plenary meeting on September 7 and made a thorough discussion on the draft Constitution. Two days later, it was adopted by the Council's meeting and would be submitted to the NPC for adoption.

After the meetings of local people's congresses, the First NPC, consisting of 1226 members, was convened between September 15 and 28. One of its most important issues in the conference's agenda was to discuss and deliberate on the draft Constitution and the report on it. On the afternoon of September 20, 1197 members present at the meeting unanimously adopted the Constitution by casting anonymous votes. At the same day, an announcement in the name of the National People's Congress of the People's Republic of China was issued, which marked the birth of the general charter as well as the fundamental law of new China.

2.3 Contents

The structure of 1954 Constitution[3] consisted of a preamble, general principles, state structure, people's basic rights and duties, and the national flag, emblem and

[3] Its official English translation can be found in the *Constitution of the People's Republic of China*, Foreign Languages Press, 1954.

capital in five parts and 106 articles. It inherited the Common Program in some part and made some changes: it followed the structure of setting up a preamble and general principles, and the state structure were also similar with those of the Common Program. The change was the absence of separate provisions on military affairs, economy, culture and education, nationalities, foreign policy and other systems and policies. The Constitution also made detailed provisions on citizen's basic rights and duties. As clearly stated in the Preamble, "this Constitution is based on the Common Program of the Chinese People's Political Consultative Conference of 1949, and is an advance on it".

The contents of the Preamble include: that the people's revolution under the Party's leadership was completed with a victory and, People's Republic of China, a people's democratic dictatorship was established; that from the founding of the PRC to the attainment of a socialist society was a period of transition, and the fundamental task of the state during the transition was, step by step, to bring about the socialist industrialization of the country, and, step by step, to accomplish the socialist transformation of agriculture, handicrafts and capitalist industry and commerce; that the people of China had forged a broad people's democratic united front, composed of all democratic classes, democratic parties and groups, and popular organizations, and led by the Party; and that China had made guidelines and policies on national unity and foreign affairs.

Article 1 makes a provision on the nature of the country that the People's Republic of China is a people's democratic state led by the working class and based on the alliance of workers and peasants. Article 2 provides that the system of government is the national people's congress which practices democratic centralism. Article 3 states that China is a single multi-ethnic state and all the nationalities are equal. Articles 4–16 make provisions on economic system and policies. Article 17 provides for the relationship between state agencies and people. Article 18 provides that the servants of the state must be loyal to the people's democratic system, observe the Constitution and the law and strive to serve the people. Article 19 emphasized dictatorship, stating that all treasonable and counter-revolutionary activities are to be suppressed and all traitors and counter-revolutionaries are to be punished. Article 20 makes a provision on the nature and task of armed forces.

Its third part is on the state structure, which is based on the Common Program. This part is divided in six sections with 64 articles, taking up 60% of the articles.

Section 1 is on the NPC: that the NPC is the highest authority of state authority and is the only legislative authority in the country; that the Standing Committee is a permanently acting body of the NPC; that specific provisions are made on the election, composition, session, powers and duties. It is clearly stated in this section that amendments to the Constitution require a two-thirds majority vote of all the deputies to the NPC.

Section 2 is on the chairman of the People's Republic of China: that the election, term of office, powers and duties were clarified; that the chairman commands the armed forces, is the chairman of the Council of National Defense and convenes a Supreme State Conference when necessary and acts as its chairman.

Section 3 makes provisions on the State Council: that the State Council is the Central People's Government, the administrative organ of the highest state authority and the highest administrative organ of state.

Section 4 is on the local people's congresses and the local people's councils: that China practices a three-tiered system, namely the provinces, autonomous regions, to municipalities directly under the central authority in the provincial level, from autonomous prefectures, counties, autonomous counties and municipality in the city level, and township, autonomous townships and towns. The autonomous prefecture is divided into counties, autonomous counties and municipalities; that provisions were also made on the nature, election, powers and duties of the local people's congresses and councils.

Section 5 provides for the self-government of national autonomous areas: that the organs of self-government of all autonomous regions, autonomous prefecture and autonomous counties may draw up statutes governing the exercise of autonomy or separate regulations suited to the political, economic and cultural characteristics of the nationality or nationalities in a given area, which statues and regulations are subject to endorsement by the Standing Committee of the NPC.

Section 6 is about the people's courts and the people's procuratorate: that in administering justice the people's courts are independent, subject only to the law, and local organs of the people's procuratorate are independent in the exercise of their authority and are not subject to interference by local organs of state.

Part 4 is on the citizens' fundamental rights and duties. Compared with the five articles of the Common Program, it has increased the number which reaches 19. It states that the citizens are equal before the law, provides the citizens' right to vote and stand for election, the freedoms of speech, the press, assembly, association, procession and demonstration, religious belief, and the person, and the right to work, rest and leisure, material assistance, education, bring complaints and compensation. It also provides protection for women, children, marriage and family. When enjoying the rights, the citizens should also abide by the Constitution, law, and public order, respect and protection public property, pay taxes and perform military service according to law. The proper rights and interest of Chinese resident abroad are also protected by the state which also grants the right of asylum to foreign nationals.

Part 5 provides the national flag, emblem and capital: that the national flag of the People's Republic of China is a red flag with five stars, the national emblem is Tian An Men in the center under the light of five stars framed with ears of grain and with a cogwheel at the base, and the capital is Beijing.

2.4 Function

The 1954 Constitution was the first of its kind since the founding of PRC, the first people's constitution since the Preparative Constitutionalism Movement in Late Qing, all of which made it historically important. It established all the basic systems practiced by the Party after it won the state power to ensure the exercise of state power was well organized and under smooth operations. It provided a large array of citizens' fundamental rights and duties, and the fundamental task in the transition period was also written down in it. As pointed by Mao Zedong, "there will be a clear course before the people of the whole country and they will feel sure they have a clear, definite and correct path to follow". The 1954 Constitution, characterized by its socialist nature, guarantees the transition of China from new democratic society to socialist country.

However, only after a few years of implementation, its authority and implementation were severely impacted due to the rising leftist thinking since the late 1950s, especially when the Cultural Revolution started in 1966. It was finally replaced by the 1975 Constitution despite its scientific and democratic features.

3 1975 Constitution

3.1 Background and Process

After the Cultural Revolution was started in 1966, the political situation was enormously changed, and the democratic legal system and social order were disrupted. Many provisions of the 1954 Constitution were shelved. On March 8, 1970, Mao Zedong suggested a convocation on the fourth NPC, amending the Constitution, and change of government system in which a chairman was not needed. The Political Bureau established a team on the work on the Constitution (Constitution team). Between March 17 and 20, the Central Committee held a meeting to discuss the issues about convening the NPC and amending the Constitution. In an announcement made after the meeting by the responsible person of the team, it was explained that the Constitution should adapt to the continuous revolution theory advocated Mao Zedong, which asked for a change of current Constitution into a socialist one. In July 1970, the Central Committee established a constitutional drafting commission consisting of 55 members with Mao Zedong as the director. In its first plenary meeting, Zhou Enlai pointed out that, based on Mao Zedong's requirements, the Constitution should be concise, and easy to read and understand. Two prepared drafts, one with 60 articles in 6000 Chinese characters and the other one with 30 articles in 4000 Chinese characters, were discussed in the meeting. After several meetings, the latter one was taken as the basis for amending the Constitution.

On August 23, 1970, the Second Plenary Session of the Ninth CPC Central Committee was convened in Lushan, an important agenda was to discuss the amendment of the Constitution. However, Lin Biao, Chen Boda and others colluded to insist the setup of chairman in the forthcoming Constitution even though they knew Mao's proposal. It sparked fierce discussions on this issue in the meetings. Mao Zedong made an opportune speech, criticizing Chen as "fear that the world is not in chaos, and potentially blow up Lushan and stop the earth". The draft Amendment to the Constitution of the People's Republic of China was then adopted at this plenum, which consisted of a preamble and four chapters with 30 articles. However, the Rectification of Chen Boda Movement, September 13 Incident, Criticize Lin and Criticize Confucius Campaign and other political changes, the Fourth NPC that was planned in September 1970 was postponed, and the draft was also put in abeyance. As late as in 1974, it was designated as the basis for discussing the amendment in the forthcoming Fourth NPC.

From January 8 to 10, 1975, the Second Plenary Session of the Tenth CPC Central Committee was convened, which adopted the draft Amendment to the Constitution of the People's Republic of China, the Report on Amending the Constitution and the Report on the Work of the Government. The First Session of the Fourth National People's Congress was held between January 13 to 17, and the Report on Amending the Constitution was delivered. It stated that the 1954 Constitution was correct, and some of its basic principles were still applicable. However, tremendous changes had taken place in national politics, economy, culture and international relations, and some of its provisions were outdated. It also explained that the main task of amending the Constitution was to summarize experience, consolidate victories, and reflect people's common wish of upholding the continuous revolution based on the proletariat dictatorship. In the last day of the conference, the Constitution of the People's Republic of China was adopted unanimously by all the delegates. It had been 5 years since the start of this constitution amendment.

3.2 Contents and Appraisal

The 1975 Constitution[4] shared the structure with the 1954 Constitution. However, for the sake of being concise, its article number was reduced from 106 to 30. According to the Report and its text, the changes include: (1) to strengthen the Party's leadership; in Article 2, it was prescribed that "the CPC is the core of leadership of the whole Chinese people"; (2) the people's democratic dictatorship was changed to the proletariat dictatorship; it stated that "the People's Republic of China is a socialist state of the dictatorship of the proletariat" in Article 1, and emphasized that the proletariat must exercise all-around dictatorship over the bourgeoisie in the superstructure, including all spheres of culture, which strengthened the dictatorship; (3) changes on citizens' rights; the people had the right to speak out freely, air views fully, hold great debates and write big-character posters and the freedom to strike as stipulated in Article 13; (4) Article 5 prescribed two kinds of ownership of the means of production: socialist ownership by the whole people and socialist collective ownership by working people; (5) the Preamble stated that "China will never be a superpower" considering the US-Soviet Cold War. In addition, it abolished the provision that citizens are equal before the law, and the setup of Chairman and people's procuratorate.

---

[4] Its official English translation can be found in the *Constitution of the People's Republic of China*, Foreign Languages Press, 1975.

The 1975 Constitution was made during the Cultural Revolution, aimed for adapting to changing circumstances and implementing the theory of continuous revolution under the dictatorship of the proletariat, which were plainly manifested in its contents. It was impacted by leftist thinking, an apparent retrogression compared with 1954 Constitution. A year later, China's political situation changed greatly. In September 1976, Mao Zedong passed away. In October, the Central Committee with Hua Guofeng, Ye Jianying and Li Xiannian as the leaders smashed the Gang of Four. Later, the guidelines and policies adopted in that period were adjusted, rectifications were made for the wronged cases and injustice and the purged cadres and officials went back to work. As the situation changed, it was eventually replaced by a new Constitution.

4 1978 Constitution

After the fall of the Gang of Four and a lot of preparations, the Eleventh CPC National Congress, the first party conference after the Cultural Revolution ceased, was convened in August 1977, which solemnly declared the end of Cultural Revolution, mobilized and call for the Party and Chinese people to build China into a modern socialist country. In October, the Central Committee issued a notice, which decided to convene the Fifth NPC in early spring of 1978, ahead of the designated date, considering the great victories made in all social respects in a year and the changes and developments of circumstances. The notice also asked the local governments and relevant departments to take proper means to collect opinions on amending the Constitution inside and outside the Party and then report them to the Central Committee. In November, the Central Committee issued another notice on opinions collection. In the Second Plenary Session of the Eleventh CPC Central Committee held in February 1978, the draft Constitution of the People's Republic of China and the Report on Amending the Constitution were approved and would be submitted for deliberation in the First Session of the Fifth National People's Congress. According to the report made by Ye Jianying in the congress, the draft Constitution was formulated by the commission for amending constitution which consisted of all the members of the Political Bureau.

In February 1978, the First Session of the Fifth National People's Congress was convened. On March 5, the amended Constitution of the People's Republic of China was adopted and its full text was released. It was the third constitution since the founding of PRC, often referred as 1978 Constitution.

The 1978 Constitution also shared the structure with the preceding constitutions. It had 60 articles, a double of the 1975 Constitution but less than the 1954 Constitution. It generally inherited some basic principles of 1954 Constitution and added a provision on the task of realizing four modernizations and building China into a great socialist country with modern agriculture, industry, national defense and science and technology by the end of the twentieth century. In the General Principles of the Constitution, a provision was made to adhere to the principle of socialist democracy and ensure the people's right to participate in the management of state affairs and of all economic and cultural undertakings based on the lessons of Cultural Revolution. The provisions on state structure were more complete and detailed compared with those of the last preceding one, and it restored the system of the people's procuratorate, the system of public trial and the right to defense. It also added new provisions, 16 in total, to the people's fundamental rights and duties, such as the right to lodge complaints and to appeal.

However, due to the limit of the situation at that time, the left-line, guidelines and polices practiced in the Cultural Revolution were not totally discarded, and some Central Committee's leaders still insisted on Two Whatevers ("we will resolutely uphold whatever policy decisions Chairman Mao made, and unswervingly follow whatever instructions Chairman Mao gave"), the 1978 Constitution was still seared by the Cultural Revolution. For example, in the Preamble, the wrong statement of "the continuous revolution under the dictatorship under the proletariat" was kept, and the statement that "the triumphant conclusion of the first great proletariat cultural revolution has ushered in a new period of development in China's socialist revolution and socialist construction", an affirmative attitude towards Cultural Revolution, was proposed. The position of chairman was still absent in the part of state structure, while the local revolutionary commissions were still kept. Moreover, the part of citizens' rights and duties preserved the provisions on the rights to speak out freely, air views fully, hold great debates and write big-character posters. Therefore, the time when the Constitution was adopted, it was not able to meet the needs of economic and social development in China. In the following 2 years, it was amended twice.

On July 1 1979, the Resolution on Amending Several Provisions of the Constitution of the People's Republic of China was adopted in the Second Session of the Fifth NPC. The Resolution set out that the standing committees should be established in the people's congresses at or above the county level, the local revolutionary committees were changed to local people's governments, the county people's congresses were elected directly by the voters, and the relationship between the upper and lower people's procuratorates was changed from supervision to leading. All these provisions improved the Constitution's provisions on state structure. On September 10, 1980, the Third Session of the Fifth NPC amended Article 45, which deleted the provision on people's right to speak out freely, air views fully, hold great debates and write big-character posters, helped to maintain the social peace and unity. As the socialist modernization and the Reform and Opening-up were carried out in full swing, it became obsolete and was then superseded by the 1982 Constitution.

5 1982 Constitution

5.1 Formulation

In early 1979 when the Third Plenary Session of the Eleventh CPC Central Committee was closed, the Central Committee envisaged a complete revision of the Constitution. In October 1079, Deng Xiaoping directed that the Constitution should be amended after the Political Bureau's discussions. In the Political Bureau's expanded meeting held in August 1980, Deng Xiaoping further directed the first item subject to significant reform that was considered by the Central Committee was to suggest amending the Constitution to the NPC to make it more complete, detailed and accurate in his speech, On the Reform of the System of Party and State Leadership. On August 30, 1980, the Central Committee submitted the Suggestion on Amending the Constitution and Establishing a Constitution Amendment Committee to the Presidium of the Third Session of the Fifth National People's Congress. It was pointed out in the Suggestion that the 1978 Constitution was not suitable for the political and economic life for some of its provisions and for the need of modernization due to the limits of the situation at that time and the great changes after its adoption, so it called for a comparatively systemic amendment. On September 10, the Third Session of the Fifth NPC adopted a resolution to approve Central Committee's Suggestion and the list of members for the Constitution Amendment Committee and decide that the Committee be in charge of amending the 1978 Constitution and submitting a draft. In the Committee, Ye Jianying was the director, while Song Qingling and Peng Zhen deputy directors, who were responsible for reporting to the NPC. A separate secretariat was established under the Committee as its working body, and Hu Qiaomu was the secretary. After the Resolution on Certain Questions in the History of Our Party since the Founding of the People's Republic of China was adopted, Peng Zhen was appointed by Deng Xiaoping to take charge of the constitution amendment due to Hu's illness.

After assuming this position, Peng made it clear that the amendment should be based on the 1954 Constitution, summarize experience and resolve the problems to make the new Constitution adaptable to the new situation. Peng's considerations had three reasons: first, the basic principles of the 1954 Constitution were still suitable. After a study on the preceding three constitutions, it was concluded that the 1954 Constitution was better, while the other two were seared by the Cultural Revolution; second, the reference to the 1954 Constitution may avoid many unnecessary arguments. Many discussions were made around the main issues in this constitution amendment, however many such issues were given due consideration when formulating the 1954 Constitution. A consensus would be easier to reach if the 1954 Constitution was taken as the basis. Third, the 1954 Constitution was generally mature. After widely discussed among over 8000 people that represented all social walks and then the among the whole Chinese people, it had revealed a strong consensus was well recognized by the people, which made it possible to complete the amendment quickly. Peng also stated that the amendment should be based on the newly adopted Resolution on Certain Questions, because it had made definitive statements on some long-lasting arguments after the Central Committee's consideration, discussion and revision, while amending the Constitution was not to make arguments but to settle down the issues free from arguments. Though the 1982 Constitution was amended on the 1978 Constitution in terms of its form, its basis was the 1954 Constitution.

From September 1980 to April 1982, under the Party's strong leadership and through the diligent efforts made by the Constitution Amendment Committee and its Secretariat, after soliciting opinions as organized by local governments, departments and other relevant organizations, the draft Constitution was submitted to the 23rd plenary meeting of the Fifth National People's Congress Standing Committee, and then released by the NPC Standing Committee for discussions of the whole Chinese people. Later, the Committee made improvements based on these opinions. In September 1982, the draft Constitution was adopted after deliberation in the Fifth Plenary Session of Fifth National People's Congress, which declared the birth of the new Constitution.

It should be noted that the 1982 Constitution was not a new one but a newly amended one based on the explanations on the draft Constitution and the report on the draft Constitution made by Peng respectively in April and August 1982, all of which followed the Suggestion.

5.2 Contents

The 1982 Constitution,[5] which is still in force, makes a summary of the socialist revolution, construction and reform since the founding of PRC, and reflects the demands in a full scale for development in the new phase and people's will. It, in the form of fundamental law, represents the achievements made for adhering to Chinese socialist path, the theoretical system on Chinese socialism, and the Chinese socialist system, reflects the common will and fundamental interests of Chinese people, and constitutes the mission statement for the central task, basic principles, important guidelines and policies of the Party and the state in new historical phase. Its main contents can be summarized as follows:

1. To uphold the Four Cardinal Principles

To uphold the four Cardinal Principles means to uphold the Marxism-Leninism and Mao Zedong Thought, adhere to the people's democratic dictatorship and follow the socialist road, which are also the guiding principles for formulating, amending and implementing the Constitution.

As stated in the Preamble, "both the victory in China's New-Democratic Revolution and the successes in its socialist cause have been achieved by the Chinese people

[5] Its official English translation can be found at http://www.npc.gov.cn/englishnpc/constitution2019/201911/1f65146fb6104dd3a2793875d19b5b29.shtml

of all nationalities, under the leadership of the CPC...by...surmounting numerous difficulties and hardships", "under the leadership of the CPC and the guidance of Marxism-Leninism and Mao Zedong Thought, the Chinese people of all nationalities will continue to adhere to the people's democratic dictatorship and the socialist road, ..., to turn China into a socialist country with a high level of culture and democracy". Preamble, as an expression of the Constitutional spirits, is an important part of the Constitution and has legal force. The CPC's leading role in China is confirmed by the Constitution. It has been proven through practice that the incorporation of the four Cardinal Principles is very necessary, for it is the common political foundation for promoting unity of all the Chinese people and fundamental political guarantee for realizing long-lasting peace, withstanding risks and challenges and promoting smooth reform and opening and socialist modernization.

2. To prescribe the people's democratic dictatorship as state system and the people's congress system as the government system

The state system and government system are closely related. The system of state refers to the status of social classes, i.e. the state power is controlled by what kind of social class, while the government system refers to the organization of state power, i.e. in what way does the controlling social class exercise state power. The state system determines the government system, and the latter serves the former. And it is a relation between contents and form, while the state system is the contents and the government system is the form.

Mao Zedong ever said, "the question under discussion here is that of the 'state system'. After several decades of wrangling since the last years of the Qing Dynasty, it has still not been cleared up. Actually it is simply a question of the status of the various social classes within the state". Paragraph 1 of Article 1 stipulated that "the People's Republic of China is a socialist state under the people's democratic dictatorship led by the working class and based on the alliance of workers and farmers", which clarified the nature of PRC and the status of all social classes. The nature of people's democratic dictatorship determines that only people are the masters of the country and society. Paragraph 2 of Article 2 stated that "all power in the People's Republic of China belongs to the people", which is the core and fundamental principles for the state system.

The government system, as mentioned before, refers to the type of organization to exercise the state power for administering the state, which concerns what kind of state department should exercise the legislative, executive, judicial and other powers, how to elect and organize these departments and what are their relations. According to the Constitution, all power in the People's Republic of China belongs to the people, and the organs through which the people exercise their power are the NPC and the local people's congresses, which means that the people's congress system is PRC's government system. To be brief, the people's congress system refers to an organization of state power, in which the democratic centralism is the principle, the NPC and the local people's congresses are formed through democratic elections, and the entire state agencies are established based on the people's congress to ensure people's position as masters of the country.

3. To provide the basic line for the primary stage of socialism

The CPC's basic line for the primary state of socialism is confirmed by the Constitution, making it a guide for Chinese people to fight together as prescribed that "the basic task of the nation in the years to come is to concentrate its effort on socialist modernization. Under the leadership of the CPC and the guidance of Marxism-Leninism and Mao Zedong Thought, the Chinese people of all nationalities will continue to adhere to the people's democratic dictatorship and the socialist road, steadily improve socialist institutions, develop socialist democracy, improve the socialist legal system, and work hard and self-reliantly to modernize the country's industry, agriculture, national defense and science and technology step by step to turn China into a socialist country with a high level of culture and democracy".

4. To make provisions on the socialist economic system

The Constitution reflects the fact that the socialist economy system has already been established and is developing in strong momentum. As stipulated in Article 6, "the basis of the socialist economic system of the People's Republic of China is socialist public ownership of the means of production, namely, ownership by the whole people and collective ownership by the working people. The system of socialist public ownership supersedes the system of exploitation of man by man; it applies the principle of 'from each according to his ability, to each according to his work'".

5. To enrich the provisions on socialist culture

In a working conference held on December 1980, Deng Xiaoping stressed that "the socialist China we are building should have a civilization with a high cultural and ideological level as well as a high material level. When I speak of a civilization with a high cultural and ideological level, I refer not only to education, science and culture (which are of course indispensable) but also to communist thinking, ideals, beliefs, morality and discipline". An important feature of the 1982 Constitution is the emphasis on socialist culture in two aspects: one is to develop education, science and culture, the other is to stress the education on ideology and morality.

The draft Constitution only made two articles on education, science and culture. After the discussions, it was changed into four articles from 19–22, one article for each respect with more specific provisions. Article 24 makes an important provision on ideology and morality education, stating that "the state strengthens the building of socialist cultural progress through spreading education in high ideals and morality, general education and education in discipline and the legal system, and through promoting the formulation and observance of rules of conduct and common pledges by different sections of the people in urban and rural areas. The state advocates the civic virtues of love for the motherland, for the people, for labor, for science and for socialism; it educates the people in patriotism, collectivism, internationalism and communism and in dialectical and historical materialism; it combats the decadent ideas of capitalism and feudalism and other decadent ideas".

6. To improve the provisions on citizens' fundamental rights

The people's fundamental rights and duties are the core of the Constitution for it is the fundamental guarantee for every citizen to enjoy rights and perform duties. The PRC is a socialist country under the people's democratic dictatorship, and as the masters of the country, the people have an extensive array of rights and freedoms. However, the democracy and legal order were seriously damaged during the Cultural Revolution, which also jeopardized the ordinary and even the officials' rights. After making a genuine summary of experience from 1949 and especially the lessons of the 10 years, the 1982 Constitution prescribed in details the citizens' rights and freedoms by moving this chapter between the General Principles and State Structure as the second one and increasing its number from 19 in 1954 Constitution, 16 in 1978 Constitution to 24 articles in it.

The provisions on citizens' rights and freedoms are extensive and detailed, which include the following: first, it recovers the provision of 1954 Constitution that all citizens are equal before the law; second, the right to elect and to stand for election; third, the freedom of speech, of the press, of assembly, of association, of procession and of demonstration; fourth, the freedom of religious belief, including the freedom of believing in or not believing in any religion; fifth, the freedom of person is inviolable. Considering the unlawful and arbitrary arrest of people, the Constitution provides that "unlawful deprivation or restriction of citizens' freedom of person by detention or other means is prohibited; and unlawful search of the person of citizens is prohibited"; sixth, the personal dignity is inviolable, and any insult, libel, false charge or frame-up directed against citizens by any means is prohibited; seventh, the home of citizens is inviolable. Any unlawful search of or intrusion into a citizen's home is prohibited; Eighth, the freedom and privacy of correspondence of citizens are protected by law; ninth, the citizens have the right to criticize and make suggestions to any state organ or functionary, and it also prescribed that "in case of complaints, charges or exposures made by citizens, the state organ concerned must deal with them in a responsible manner after ascertaining the facts. No one may suppress such complaints, charges and exposures, or retaliate against the citizens making them. Citizens who have suffered losses through infringement of their civil rights by any state organ or functionary have the right to compensation in accordance with the law".

The basic social rights enjoyed by the citizens include: first, the right as well as the duty to work and the state creates conditions for employment; second, the right to rest; third, the livelihood of the retired is ensured by the state and society; fourth, the right to material assistance from the state and society when they are old, ill or disabled, and the state and society ensure the livelihood of disabled members of the armed forces, provide pensions to the families of martyrs and give preferential treatment to the families of military personnel, and help make arrangements for the work, livelihood and education of the blind, the deaf and other handicapped citizens; fifth, the duty as well as the right to receive education. The preceding constitutions all prescribed the right to receive education, but the new Constitution further makes a duty of the citizens; sixth, women enjoy equal rights with men, and the state protects marriage, family, mother and child and protects the legitimate rights and interests of Chinese nationals residing abroad and the lawful rights and interests of returned overseas Chinese and of the family members of Chinese nationals residing abroad; seventh, the freedom to engage in scientific research, literary and artistic creation and other cultural pursuits.

The Constitution also makes provisions on the duties of the citizens. It clearly prescribes that the exercise by citizens of their freedoms and rights may not infringe upon the interests of the state, of society and of the collective, or upon the lawful freedoms and rights of other citizens, and must perform the duties as prescribed by the Constitution. These duties include: first, to safeguard the unity of the country and the unity of all its nationalities; second, the citizens must abide by the constitution and the law, keep state secrets, protect public property and observe labor discipline and public order and respect social ethics; third, to safeguard the security, honor and interests of the motherland; they must not commit acts detrimental to the security, honor and interests of the motherland. This article was added to the Constitution in 1982. Fourth, to perform military service and join the militia according to law to defend the motherland and resist aggression.

7. To improve the provisions on state structure

The Constitution reforms and develops the state structure, which can be summarized as follows:

First, to strengthen the people's congress system. Some of the NPC was changed to the hands of its Standing Committee to expand its authorities and powers and improve its organization. The NPC and its Standing Committee exercised the legislative power of the state; except for the basic laws that should be made by the NPC, other laws are to be made by its Standing Committee. The members of the Standing Committee cannot hold any post in any of the administrative, judicial or procuratorial organs of the state. The chairmanship meeting consists of the chairman of the Standing Committee, the vice-chairman and the secretary-general to handle the daily matters of importance. To better do the job, some special committees are established under to the leadership of the NPC and its Standing Committee in charge of studying, deliberating on and drafting some bills. According to the Constitution, the NPC established the Nationalities Committee, Law Committee, Finance and Economic Committee, Education, Science, Culture and Public Health Committee, Foreign Affairs Committee, Overseas Chinese Committee and such other special committees as are necessary.

Second, to recover the positions of president and vice-president of the state. The practice since PRC's founding has proved that the establishment of a state president is necessary for a sound state system, and it is also more in line with the habits and aspirations of the people of all ethnic groups. The Constitution makes provisions on the establishment and powers and duties of president and vice-president, and explicitly states that the President and Vice-President of the People's Republic of China are elected by the NPC.

Third, to improve the system of the leadership of the State Council. The premier has overall responsibility for the State Council, and the plenum of the State Council consists of the premier, vice premiers, State Councilors and secretary general. The premier convenes and presides over the executive meetings and plenary meetings of the State Council.

Fourth, to establish the central military commission to direct the armed forces of China. Its Chairman has overall responsibility for the commission, while it is elected by the NPC and is responsible to the NPC and its Standing Committee. To strengthen supervision over revenue and expenditure, the State Council establishes an auditing body, which independently exercises its supervisory powers according to law without any interference. The local governments also establish local auditing bodies.

Fifth, to impose limits on term of office. The Constitution prescribes that the President and Vice President of the state, Chairman and Vice Chairman of the NPC Standing Committee, and Premier and Vice Premiers of the State Council shall not serve for no more than two consecutive terms of office.

Sixth, to strengthen local government authority and self-government at the community level, and establish special administrative regions. The people's congresses at or above the county level establish standing committees. The people's congresses of provinces and cities directly under the Central Government and their standing committees may adopt local regulations. Local people's governments at different levels practice the system of overall responsibility by governors, mayors, county heads, district heads, township heads and town heads. The system of regional autonomy is practiced in the areas of minority ethnic groups. The provisions on local government authority and self-governance at the community level also apply to the autonomous regions. The people's commune in rural areas is changed to township. The status and functions of the self-management organizations at the community level including the residents' committees and villagers' committees that have been long established and proved effective are incorporated in the Constitution.

To address the issues on Taiwan, Hong Kong and Macao, Deng Xiaoping proposed the "one country with two systems". Article 31 provides that "The state may establish special administrative regions when necessary. The systems to be instituted in special administrative regions shall be prescribed by law enacted by the National People's Congress in the light of the specific conditions". This provision gives another legislative power to the NPC.

8. To make provisions on the symbol of the state

It prescribes that the national flag is a red flag with five stars, the national emblem is Tian An Men in the center illuminated by five stars and encircled by ears of grain and a cogwheel, and the capital is Beijing.

9. To strengthen the socialist legal system

According to the requirement of developing socialist democracy and socialist legal system made in the Third Plenary Session of the Eleventh CPC Central Committee, the 1982 Constitution took the improvement of socialist legal system as an important part of its fundamental task, and made detailed provisions on legislation, law enforcement, judiciary, observance of law and constitutional and legal supervision.

First, the 1982 Constitution reforms the legislation system to strengthen the work on legislation, which can be summarized as following: (1) the NPC Standing

Committee has the power to make laws. The legislative power was only exercised by the NPC, and its Standing Committee may only make decrees. However, it cannot meet the demand for fast legislation and improving legal system. The provisions of the Constitution expanded the Standing Committee's powers by prescribing that the NPC and its Standing Committee are legislators, and the basic laws are formulated by the NPC while other laws can be formulated by its Standing Committee. (2) The State Council may formulate administrative regulations while in the past could only make administrative measures. (3) The people's congresses of provinces, their capital cities and the large cities approved by the State Council and their standing committees may formulate local regulations, which must not contravene the Constitution, the statutes and the administrative regulations. (4) The people's congresses of national autonomous areas have the power to formulate autonomous regulations and specific regulations according to their political, economic and cultural characteristics. To maintain the unity of the legal system is a basic principle for constructing socialist legal system though it is a multi-tiered one in China, as Article 5 prescribes that "the state upholds the unity and dignity of the socialist legal system. No law or administrative or local regulations shall contravene the Constitution."

Second, strict law enforcement requires the administrative departments to exercise their powers and functions according to law. As stipulated in the Constitution, the State Council, that is, the Central People's Government, is the executive body of the highest authority of state power, while the local people's governments are the executive bodies of local agencies of state power. Most of Chinese laws are related with administrative management, directly concerning the people's life; these laws are enforced by the administrative departments and their working staff. The Constitution prescribes that all state agencies, the armed forces, all political parties and public organizations and all enterprises and undertakings must abide by the Constitution and the law. All acts in violation of the Constitution and the law must be investigated.

Third, with regard to judiciary, as prescribed in Article 126, "the people's courts shall, in accordance with the law, exercise judicial power independently and are not subject to interference by administrative departments, public organizations or individuals", and "the People's procuratorates shall, in accordance with the law, exercise procuratorial power independently and are not subject to interference by administrative organs, public organizations or individuals".

Fourth, in observation of law, paragraph 3 of Article 33 prescribes that "every citizen enjoys the rights and at the same time must perform the duties prescribed by the Constitution and the law", and "citizens of the People's Republic of China must abide by the constitution and the law" as in Article 53. To make people know law and enhance their awareness of law, the expression of "the education in discipline and the legal system" was added in Article 24 as an important component for promoting socialist cultural and ethical progress.

Last, specific measures were also made to ensure the supervision by the Constitution and the law. People cared a lot about how to guarantee the enforcement of the Constitution given the high price for the Cultural Revolution. The preceding constitutions prescribed that the NPC supervise the constitution's enforcement. However, only one session in a year was not suitable for supervision. Therefore, the 1982 Constitution prescribes that the NPC and its Standing Committee supervise its enforcement. This arrangement of supervisory power is more suitable for the Standing Committee is the permanent body of the NPC. Article 99 also further provides that local people's congresses ensure the observance and implementation of the Constitution, the statutes and the administrative regulations in their respective administrative areas.

5.3 Five Amendments

The 1982 Constitution conforms with the situations and realities of China and responded to the call of the times. It also presents strong vitality because it reflects the historical progress in the causes of the Party and the people, adapts itself to changing circumstances, draws on new experience, confirm the new achievements and makes new norms. In retrospect of PRC's constitutional history, it can be felt that the constitution is closely linked with the arduous endeavors and glorious achievements made by the Party and the people, and with the road for development and valuable experience explored by the Party and the people. China's constitution should never stop developing as the Chinese socialist practice of Chinese people led by the Party never stops. It is an essential requirement for the Constitution to confirm the Party's and the people's great achievements and valuable experience to better play the role of Constitution in regulating, leading, promoting and guaranteeing the socialist practice. This is a feature and a basic law for PRC's constitutional history.

1. Four Amendments before 2014

As the reform and opening-up and socialist modernization develops, the NPC made four important and necessary revisions on the Constitution in 1988, 1993, 1999 and 2004 with 31 amendments in total: two amendments for the first revision as in Article 1 and 2, nine amendments for the second revision as in Articles 3 to 11, six amendments for the third revision as in Articles 12 to 17, and 14 amendments as in Articles 18 to 31.

The four amendments can be summarized as follows: (1) Paragraph 7 of the Preamble was revised for three times by incorporating the expressions of Deng Xiaoping Thought, the Important Thought of Three Represents, the primary stage of socialism, Chinese socialist path, development of socialist market economy, coordinated development of the material, political and spiritual civilizations and turning China into a socialist country that is prosperous, powerful, democratic and culturally advanced; (2) Paragraph 2 of the Preamble was revised twice by writing in the Constitution the system of the multi-party cooperation and political consultation led by the CPC and a broad patriotic united front composed of all socialist working people, people involved in building socialism and all patriots; (3) Article 5 was revised, which incorporated the statement of rule of law and building China into a socialist country under rule of law; (4) Article 6 was revised, which incorporated the fundamental economic system and income distribution system in the primary stage of socialism; (5) Article 8 was revised twice, which provided a two-tiered system of both unified and separate operations with household contract management as its basis; (6), Article 11 was revised for three times, which prescribed the status and guidelines and policies for non-public economic sectors; (7) Article 14 was revised, which prescribed the establishment of a sound social security system compatible with the level of economic development; (8) Article 15 was revised, which prescribed that the state practiced socialist market economy; (9) Article 33 was revised, prescribing that the state respect and protect human rights; (10) Article 81 was revised, providing that the president of PRC could engage in activities for foreign affairs. These amendments also made new additions to or improved the provisions on the transfer of land use right according to law, the inviolability of citizens' lawful private property, the expropriation or requisition of citizens' land and accruing compensation, a three-year to five-year term of office for county and township people's congresses, a state of emergency, and national anthem. Such amendments reflected the successes in promoting reform and opening-up and the socialist modernization by the people under the Party's leadership and manifest the achievements in developing the Chinese socialist road, theory, system and culture.

2. 2018 Amendment

Many great changes have taken place in the cause of the Party and the state since the last constitution's amendment in 2004. Since the Eighteenth CPC National Congress, the Central Committee with Xi Jinping as the core has united and led the Chinese people of all ethnic groups to unswervingly stay on and develop the socialism with Chinese characteristics, implement the Five-Sphere Integrated Plan and the Four-Pronged Comprehensive Strategy in a coordinated manner and improve the Party's leadership with new initiatives, which have generated a lot of new ideas, thoughts and strategies for state governance and promoted new historical achievements and transformations. The socialism with Chinese characteristics is ushered into a new era. Standing on the start of a new era, the nineteenth congress made new strategic arrangements on upholding and developing the Chinese socialism and defined the new objective for national development to guide and lead the undertakings of the Party and the state. Therefore, it was very necessary to make new amendments to the Constitution by referring to the spirits of the nineteenth congress, confirmed in the fundamental law the achievements of the Party and the people made in theory, practice and institutions to make them the common rules observed by the Chinese people of all ethnic groups and the code of conduct for the cause and work of the state. It would better reflect the will of people, show the advantages of Chinese socialist system and meet the demands for modernizing state governance system and capacity. These amendments are crucially important for fully implementing the gist of the nineteenth congress and mobilizing and organizing Chinese people to fight for new victories on Chinese socialism in the new era.

On March 2018, in the First Session of the Thirteenth NPC the amendment was adopted after deliberation, which produced new 21 revisions.

First, to establish the leading role of the Scientific Outlook on Development and the Xi Jinping Thought on Socialism with Chinese Characteristics for a New Era in national political and social life. In the seventh paragraph of the Preamble, "the guidance of Marxism-Leninism, Mao Zedong Thought, Deng Xiaoping Theory and the Three Represents" is amended to read "the guidance of Marxism-Leninism, Mao Zedong Thought, Deng Xiaoping Theory, the Theory of Three Represents, the Scientific Outlook on Development and Xi Jinping Thought on Socialism with Chinese Characteristics for a New Era"; before "work hard in a spirit of self-reliance", the words "apply the new development philosophy" are inserted.

Second, to make adjustments and enrichments to the statements on the overall plan for building Chinese socialism. In the seventh paragraph of the Preamble, "promote coordinated material, political and cultural-ethical advancement, in order to build China into a socialist country that is prosperous, strong, democratic and culturally advanced" is amended to read "promote coordinated material, political, cultural-ethical, social and ecological advancement, in order to build China into a great modern socialist country that is prosperous, strong, democratic, culturally advanced, harmonious and beautiful, and realize the great rejuvenation of the Chinese nation."

Third, to improve the measures for rule of law and the enforcement of the Constitution. In the seventh paragraph of the Preamble, "improve the socialist legal system" is amended to read "improve socialist rule of law". And in Article 27 of the General Principles, a new paragraph is added as paragraph 3 to read: "state employees, when assuming office, should make a public pledge of allegiance to the Constitution in accordance with the provisions of law."

Fourth, to consolidate and improve the narration on the historical process of China's revolution and development. In the tenth paragraph of the Preamble to the Constitution, "Through the long process of revolution and development" is amended to read "Through the long process of revolution, development and reform"; and in the twelfth paragraph of the Preamble to the Constitution, "The achievements of China's revolution and development would have been impossible without the support of the world's people" is amended to read "The achievements of China's revolution, development and reform would have been impossible without the support of the world's people".

Fifth, to consolidate and improve the narration on patriotic united front and ethnic relations. In the tenth paragraph of the Preamble to the Constitution, "a broad patriotic united front, including all socialist working people, people involved in building socialism, patriots who support socialism, and patriots who support China's reunification" is amended to read "a broad patriotic united front, including all socialist working people, people involved in building socialism, patriots who support socialism, and patriots who support China's reunification and are dedicated to the rejuvenation of the Chinese nation." In the eleventh paragraph of the Preamble to the Constitution, "Socialist ethnic relations of equality, unity and mutual assistance are established and will continue to be strengthened" is amended to read "Socialist ethnic relations of equality, unity, mutual assistance and harmony are established and will continue to be strengthened". Accordingly, in paragraph 1 of Article 4 of the Constitution, "uphold and promote relations of equality, unity and mutual assistance among all ethnic groups." is amended to read: "uphold and promote relations of equality, unity, mutual assistance and harmony among all ethnic groups".

Sixth, to consolidate the narration on peaceful foreign policies. In the twelfth paragraph of the Preamble to the Constitution, after "China pursues an independent foreign policy, and observes the five principles of mutual respect for sovereignty and territorial integrity, mutual nonaggression, mutual noninterference in internal affairs, equality and mutual benefit, and peaceful coexistence" the words "keeps to a path of peaceful development, follows a mutually beneficial strategy of opening-up," are inserted; and "works to develop diplomatic relations and economic and cultural exchanges with other countries" is amended to read "works to develop diplomatic relations and economic and cultural exchanges with other countries, and promotes the building of a human community with a shared future".

Seventh, to consolidate the narration on upholding and strengthening of the Party's overall leadership. In paragraph 2 of Article 1 of the Constitution, after "the socialist system is the fundamental system of the People's Republic of China." a new sentence is inserted to read: "Leadership by the CPC is the defining feature of socialism with Chinese characteristics."

Eighth, to add provisions on promoting core socialist values. In paragraph 2 of Article 24 of the Constitution, "The state shall advocate the civic virtues of love for the motherland, for the people, for work, for science and for socialism" is amended to read: "The state shall champion core socialist values; advocate the civic virtues of love for the motherland, for the people, for work, for science and for socialism."

Ninth, to revise the provision on the president's term of office. Paragraph 3 of article 79 of the Constitution, which reads "The president and the vice president of the People's Republic of China shall have the same term of office as that of the NPC and shall serve no more than two consecutive terms." is amended to read: "The president and the vice president of the People's Republic of China shall have the same term of office as that of the NPC."

Tenth, to add a provision on the power of cities divided into districts to formulate local regulations. In article 100 of the Constitution, a new paragraph is added as paragraph 2 to read: "The people's congresses of cities divided into districts and their standing committees may, provided there is no conflict with the Constitution, laws or administrative regulations, or with the local regulations of their province or autonomous region, formulate local regulations in accordance with the provisions of law, which shall go into force after submission to the standing committee of the people's congress of their province or autonomous region and the receipt of approval."

Eleventh, to add provisions on the Commissions of Supervision. To reflect the deepened implementation of national supervisory system and provide constitutional basis for establishing Commissions of Supervision, a new section is added as section 7 titled "Commissions of Supervision", prescribing the nature, status, name, composition, term of office, leadership system and working institution. Other revisions are also made to conform with this section.

Twelfth, to improve the provisions on the NPC's special committees. In paragraph 1 of Article 70 of the Constitution, "The NPC shall establish an Ethnic Affairs Committee, a Law Committee, a Financial and Economic Committee, an Education, Science, Culture and Public Health Committee, a Foreign Affairs Committee, an

Overseas Chinese Affairs Committee and such other special committees as are necessary." is amended to read "The NPC shall establish an Ethnic Affairs Committee, a Constitution and Law Committee, a Financial and Economic Committee, an Education, Science, Culture and Public Health Committee, a Foreign Affairs Committee, an Overseas Chinese Affairs Committee and such other special committees as are necessary."

6 The Role of Constitution in Strengthening Rule of Law in All Respects

On June 14, 1954, in his speech on the draft constitution delivered in the Thirtieth Session of the Central People's Government Council, Mao Zedong said, "to codify the principles of people's democracy and socialism in the form of a fundamental law, in the form of the constitution, so that there will be a clear course before the people of the whole country and they will feel sure they have a clear, definite and correct path to follow – this will heighten their enthusiasm."[6] The great battles and achievements in revolution, development and reform made by the people under the Party's leadership are confirmed in the form of the constitution. The Constitution also confirms the state system as a socialist state under the people's democratic dictatorship led by the working class and based on the alliance of workers and peasants and the government system as the people's congress system, and the fundamental mission, core of leadership, guiding principles, road for development and objectives, and prescribed the system of the multi-party cooperation and political consultation led by the CPC, the system of regional ethnic autonomy and the system of community-level self-governance. It also specifically makes provisions on the principle of socialist rule of law, the democratic centralism and the principle of respecting and guaranteeing human rights. All these confirmations, provisions and principles reflect the will and fundamental interests of Chinese people of all ethnic groups.

The history of the past 40 years has demonstrated in all respects that China's constitutions are good ones: they have effectively upheld the Party's leadership, secured the position of people as masters of the country, vigorously promoted reform and opening-up and socialist modernization, advanced the process of building China into a socialist law-based country, and effectually safeguarded China's unification, ethnic unity and social stability. They have conformed with the circumstances and realities of China and respond to the call of time. They have comprehensively reflected the common will of the people, guaranteed the people rights to democracy, safeguarded people's fundamental interests. They have promoted national development and progress, secured a happy life for the people, and assured the rejuvenation of Chinese nation. They have also provided a fundamental legal guarantee for the country and its people to withstand all kinds of difficulties, risks and challenges and to unswervingly follow the socialist road with Chinese characteristics. The systems,

[6] MAO Zedong, *Selected Works of Mao Zedong (Vol. 5)*, Foreign Languages Press, 1977, p. 145.

principles and norms established and the guidelines and policies formulated by the constitutions manifest their advantages, foundational character and strong vitality, which call for unfaltering implementation in all respects.

The life of the Constitution is in its implementation, and so is its authority. The force of the Constitution comes not only from its supreme status but also from its effective implementation. As the development of Chinese socialism enters a new era, new requirements for comprehensive rule of law, governance of the country according to the Constitution and enhanced enforcement of the Constitution are made. On August 24, 2018, in his important speech made in the meeting of the Party's Central Commission for Comprehensive Law-based Governance, Xi Jinping summarized the new ideas, new thoughts and new strategies for comprehensive rule of law after the Eighteenth CPC National Congress into ten points, one of which was to the emphasis on adhering to governance and administration according to the Constitution. The Xi Jinping Thought on Socialism with Chinese Characteristics for a New Era should act as the guide to help earnestly put in practice these new ideas, thoughts and strategies and the requirements of strengthening the constitutional enforcement and supervision, promoting constitutional review and safeguarding the Constitution's authority as proposed in the Nineteenth CPC National Congress, advancing the enforcement of the Constitution in a high level.

First, to quickly improve the Chinese socialist legal system with the Constitution as the core and push forward the enforcement of the Constitution through a complete system of laws. It is a basic approach to promote and guarantee the Constitution's enforcement by establishing a sound system of laws and regulations. The Constitution is the center of the Chinese socialist legal system, and all the laws are formulated based on it and are specific expression of the Constitutional spirits, principles and systems. Through legislation and legal enforcement, the major systems and important subjects prescribed by the Constitution can be turned into specific legal systems as later stated in the legal provisions that are practically effective, interconnected and complementary. The Constitutional spirits, principles and norms can be implemented by these legal systems in the cause of the state and all respects of social life. The overall plan and the objective of the socialist cause should be the focus for improving the quality of legislation and the Chinese socialist legal system with the Constitution as the core and advancing the enforcement of the Constitution with a complete system of laws.

Second, to further put in practice relevant legal systems for the enforcement of the Constitution. Since the Eighteenth CPC National Congress, the NPC Standing Committee has earnestly implemented the decisions and arrangements made the Party's Central Committee and improved the legal systems to ensure its enforcement. For example, it successively adopted the decisions to set up the National Constitution Day, to practice the public pledge of allegiance to the Constitution, and to grant special pardons to some prisoners. To focus on the implementation of the important systems and measures are crucial to demonstrating the Constitution's authority, spreading its spirits and improving the people's awareness of the Constitution across the country. Therefore, it is still an imperative to better organize the practice for enforcing the Constitution to enliven the text of the Constitution.

Third, to actively and steadily advance the work on constitutional review to safeguard the dignity and authority of the Constitution. Since the Eighteenth National Congress, the Party's Central Committee with Xi Jinping as the core has paid extraordinary attention to the important status and role of Constitution in state governance and taken a lot of effective measures to strengthen the enforcement of the Constitution enforcement and its supervision. To put the requirements of the Party's Central Committee in practice, the NPC Standing Committee has made efforts to strengthen the system and capacity of recording and review, to accelerate the establishment of an integrated national information platform for recording and review and to increase the supervision and correction, which have produced fruitful results. In December 2017, in the Thirty-First Session of the Twelfth National People's Congress, the Report on the Work Since the Twelfth NPC and the Work on Recording and Review in 2017 was for the first time delivered and deliberated, which advanced the work on recording and review into a higher level.

To safeguard the authority of the Constitution, the work on constitutional review was explicitly laid out in the Nineteenth CPC National Congress. The amendment adopted in the First Session of the Thirteenth NPC changed "a Law Committee" to "a Constitution and Law Committee". The purpose of this revision is to, based on the work on deliberating on the draft laws, impose more responsibilities on the Committee to promote the enforcement of the Constitution, carry out constitutional interpretations, push forward the work on constitutional review, strengthen the constitution's supervision and support the dissemination of the Constitution. The third session adopted a decision on the responsibilities of the Constitution and Law Committee, which further clarified its responsibilities through the law. To establish a sound system for constitutional review and actively and steadily promote the work on it cannot be achieved without upholding the Party's leadership and following the correct political direction, and is also inseparable from a keen sense of political responsibility, arduous work, prudent research and cautious opinions, all of which are intended to strive for the unification of political effect and legal outcome and exert the role of the Constitution as the fundamental law for governing the country and the state.

Chapter 4
A Legislative System for China's Conditions and Realities

Da Ji

Abstract This chapter traces the evolution of China's legislative system from 1949 to the present, showing how it has been shaped by China's unitary structure, socialist character and the leading role of the CPC. After abolishing the Kuomintang legal order, the new China first experimented with a dispersed pattern of law-making to consolidate power and revive the economy. The highly centralized model established by the 1954 Constitution matched the planned economy but stifled local initiative. Reform and opening-up brought a decisive turn, changing the centralized model into a unitary yet multi-tiered system, which allocates exclusive national powers to the NPC, grants the State Council power to enact administrative regulations, and allows provinces, larger cities and cities with subordinate districts to adopt local regulations. It also highlights the 2018 constitutional amendment which further improved this structure. It concludes that the current system balances national unity with local diversity, supplies rules for rapid socio-economic change, and underpins the modernization of China's governance capacity while preventing fragmentation and local protectionism.

Keywords Unitary legislative system · Local legislative power · Socialist rule of law · Governance modernization · Tiered law-making · Realities

Legislative system collectively refers to the authorities which make laws, division of legislative powers and exercise of legislative powers. The legislative system of a country is determined by its state system and government system, and also influenced by its traditional politics, history and culture, geography, and customs of all ethnic groups. Traditional China is a unified, multi-ethnic and unitary centralized state, and in ancient Chinese society, the supremacy of emperor and the feudal rule characterized by heaven under one family were practiced. The founding of the People's Republic of China set up a completely new state power, i.e. the socialist country under the people's democratic dictatorship. This characterization of PRC's nature

D. Ji (✉)
Beijing, China
e-mail: liujixuan@lawpress.com.cn

C. Shen et al. (eds.), *A History of Legislation in the Past 70 Years in China*,
https://doi.org/10.1007/978-981-95-3799-0_4

promises a new path for its social system and state governance. The people's democracy and the principle of socialism are fundamental to this path. The system of people's congresses is the fundamental political system of PRC, while the Party's leadership is the most essential feature of Chinese socialism, which manifest the nature of people's democracy and the principle of socialism. The system of people's congresses and the Party's leadership asks China's legislative system to be conducive to strengthening Party's leadership and people's position as masters of the country based on reasonable and sound division of legislative powers between the central and local people's congresses and the legislative authorities and executive organs according to China's circumstances and realities. In the past seven decades, the establishment, development and improvement of China's legislative system has reflected the continuous development of China's democratic political system, especially the system of people's congresses, and the modernization of China's state governance system and capacity.

In February 1949, the Party's Central Committee issued the Instructions concerning Abolishing the Six Codes of the KMT and Determining Judicial Principles for the Liberated Areas, which declared the end of KMT's law. It prescribed that, under the people's democratic dictatorship led by the proletariat and with on the alliance of workers and peasants, the Six Codes of the KMT be abolished since the people's judicial work could no longer be based on KMT's Six Codes but should be on the new laws of the people. Before such new laws were promulgated systemically, the policies of the CPC and the various programs, laws, decrees, regulations and resolutions made by the people's governments and people's liberation army should be basis for administering justice. These Instructions not only declared the end of KMT's traditions of law and legal system in the liberated areas and the impending people's democratic government, but also removed the obstacles for new China to establish a new legal system for socialism.

1 Evolution of PRC's Legal System

Since the founding of PRC, the Party has led the Chinese people of all ethnic groups to fight for establishing a great modern socialist country, and through arduous and unswerving efforts, created a socialist road for Chinese rule of law. The legislative system has also evolved along this road, which can be summarized into the following four phases.

Phase 1: From the Founding to pre-1954 Constitution period

In this period, the exercise of legislative powers was diverse and scattered. In the central authority, the CPPCC's plenum, the Central People's Government Council and the Government Administration Council (later State Council) could exercise the legislative powers, while in the local authority, the local people's governments, from the county level to the greater administrative areas enjoyed a certain degree of legislative powers.

In September 1949, the Common Program was adopted, which formally declared in a legitimate way the full abolition of the Six Codes and set out the objective of making new laws and decrees, as stated in Article 17 that "all laws, decrees and judicial systems of the KMT's reactionary government which oppress the people shall be abolished. Laws and decrees protecting the people shall be enacted and the people's judicial system shall be established". Its Article 13 also prescribed that "pending the convocation of the All-China People's Congress elected by universal franchise, the Plenary Session of the Chinese People's Political Consultative Conference shall exercise the functions and powers of the All-China (National) People's Congress, enact the Organic Law of the Central People's Government of the People's Republic of China, elect the Central People's Government Council of the People's Republic of China and vest it with the authority to exercise state power". The Organic Law of the Central People's Government of the People's Republic of China was also adopted at the same time, and it made provisions on the legislative power of the Central People's Government. According to these provisions, the Central People's Government Council had the authority to enact and interpret the laws of the state, promulgate decrees and supervise their execution; to determine the administrative policies of the state; to annul or revise any decisions and orders of the Government Administration Council, which do not conform to the laws and decrees of the state; to formulate the organization regulations on the Central People's Government Council; to enact or ratify the organization regulations on the Government Administration Council and its Committees, Ministries, Commissions, Academy, Administrations, Bank and Secretariat; to issue decisions and orders and verify their execution; and to annul or revise the decisions and orders of the Committees, Ministries, Commissions, Academy, Administrations, and Bank and governments of all levels, which do not conform to the laws and decrees of the state and of the decisions and orders of the Government Administration Council.

On December 16, 1949, the Government Administration Council adopted the General Rules on the People's Government Council of the Greater Administrative Area, which granted the councils the power to enact interim regulations on local administrative affairs and report to the Government Administration Council for approval or record. Their legislative powers were not abolished until June 19, 1954 when the Decision of the 32rd Meeting of the Central People's Council declared the revocation of the greater administrative area. On January 6, 1950, the general rules on the organization of the provincial, municipal and county people's governments were adopted by the Government Administration Council. According to these rules, the provincial people's government had the authority to enact interim decrees or regulations related with its administration and then report to the greater administrative area's people's government to submit to the Government Administrative Council for approval or recording. The people's governments of the municipalities directly under the council, the cities under the greater administrative area and the cities under the province were authorized to enact interim decrees and regulations concerning the municipal administration, and report to the upper level people's government for approval or recording. The county people's governments had the authority to enact separate regulations related with the county's administration, and report to the provincial people's government for approval or recording. These interim decrees, regulations, or separate regulations could not be categorized as local legislation in today's discourse of legislation; they were more of the extension of executive authority in certain period, but they represented the inception of local legislation.

The autonomous regions also enjoyed the legislative power in enacting separate regulations in this period. In August 1952, the Program for the Implementation of Ethnic Regional Autonomy of the People's Republic of China was approved in the Eighteenth Meeting of the Central People's Government Council. Its Article 23 prescribed that "within the scope determined by laws and decrees of the Central People's Government and upper people's governments the self-government organs of autonomous regions may formulate separate regulations based on their own jurisdictions, and make a level-by-level report to the Central People's Government for record". It should be emphasized that the "autonomous regions" in this provision are different from the current use of this expression in the Constitution for they are more of the equivalents of township (village), district, county, special area or above as defined by the population and administrative area.

This scattering of legislative powers in the early period was out of the need for consolidating the state power. When the PRC was founded in 1949, the country was in total ruins and everything was waiting to be done. The state power needed to be established and consolidated, the national economy was about to be recovered and developed, and the people's position as masters of the country should be secured. The legal vacuum emerged as the old KMT's legal system was completely abolished, however, it was an impossible mission for the central authority to quickly formulate laws and decrees on its own to restore social order of new China. Moreover, since the time of liberation was different in different areas, considering their regional differences, the Central People's Government was unable to directly administer the provincial areas or the areas below. It was an essential requirement to grant the six greater administrative areas with the legislative power. The newly liberated areas, provincial or county level, were also granted with such power to consolidate the state power as expediency requires, quickly restore production and carry out reforms.

Phase 2: From 1954 Constitution to the Second Session of Fifth National People's Congress in 1979

In this period, the legislative power was highly centralized. In the central authority, the NPC was the only legislative authority. After July 1955, some legislative authorities were exercised by the NPC Standing Committee. In the local level, the local authorities, except in autonomous regions, did not have any legislative power. The state administrative organs also did not have the legislative power.

The 1954 Constitution prescribed that the National People's Congress was the only legislature of the country. According to its provisions, the NPC had the authority to amend the Constitution and enact laws, and its Standing Committee had the authority to interpret the laws, adopt decrees and annul decisions and orders of the State Council which contravene the Constitution, laws or decrees. Similar provisions could also be found in the 1975 Constitution and the 1978 Constitution. Though the decrees may be adopted by the NPC Standing Committee, distinguished from laws, they were normative documents that may have legal force issued by the state authorities within their own duties and functions. "Decrees" was deleted from the 1982 Constitution.

The NPC could not be convened frequently, and neither did the meeting last long, which could not meet the demands of "formulating various laws for national development and the work on the state", especially "when the NPC is not in session, some laws are inevitably in need of its Standing Committee to adopt". Therefore, in July 1955, the Second Session of the First National People's Congress adopted a resolution to authorize the Standing Committee, based on the spirits of the Constitution and actual needs, formulate some regulations in a timely manner, i.e. separate regulations. In April 1959, the First Session of the Second National People's Congress adopted another resolution to authorize the Standing Committee to make revisions to the outdated articles of the laws and adopt new provisions based on the development of circumstances and actual needs when the NPC was not in session to better meet the socialist transformation and the socialist cause. In fact, between September 1954 and the first half of 1957, the NPC and its Standing Committee went full steam ahead with over 80 laws, decrees and decisions on the issues of law as every cause of the state was carried out vigorously. However, since the Anti-Rightist Campaign initiated in the second half of 1957, as the top leader's ideas changed and his attention diverted, the rule of man emerged, which damaged the authority of the Constitution and law. China's cause of promoting democracy and establishing legal system was halted. From 1966 to the autumn of 1968, revolutionary committees were established in 29 provinces, autonomous regions and municipalities directly under the State Council, and the system of people's congresses was seriously damaged. In the eight and half years between July 1966 and January 1975, the NPC and its Standing Committee never convened a session. Apart from some resolutions and decisions, the NPC Standing Committee never adopted any law after April 1959; therefore, the resolution adopted in 1959 was never implemented. However, the grant of legislative authority by the NPC to its Standing Committee in two resolutions made an addition to the 1954 Constitution, which changed its provision on the NPC's sole and only legislative authority.

According to the 1954 Constitution, the State Council had the authority to formulate administrative measures, issue decisions and orders and verify their execution, in accordance with the Constitution, laws and decrees; to revise or annul inappropriate orders and directives issued by the Ministers or by Heads of Commissions; and to revise or annul inappropriate decisions and orders issued by local administrative organs of state, but these organs had no legislative power. In local authority, only the autonomous regions were authorized to legislate, "the organs of self-government of all autonomous regions, autonomous prefecture and autonomous counties may draw up statutes governing the exercise of autonomy or separate regulations suited to the political, economic, and cultural characteristics of the nationality or nationalities in a given area, which statutes and regulations are subject to endorsement by the Standing Committee". The former legislative authority in administrative affairs were also abolished.

This centrality of legislative power reflected the highly planned economy system that China practiced at that time. It provided strong support for the central authority to exercise collective and unified leadership over the cause of the state, but it impacted the local initiative and hindered the development of China's legal system. This issue was also found shortly after the implementation of the 1954 Constitution. Therefore, in his On Ten Major Relationships, Mao Zedong wrote, "it was subsequently decided to abolish the greater administrative areas and put the various provinces directly under the central authorities; that was a correct decision. But neither was the outcome so satisfactory when matters went to the length of depriving the localities of their necessary independence. According to our Constitution, the legislative powers are all vested in the central authorities. But, provided that the policies of the central authorities are not violated, the local authorities may work out rules, regulations and measures in the light of their specific conditions and the needs of their work, and this is in no way prohibited by the Constitution."[1] His view provided theoretical guidance for local legislative power.

Phase 3: Between the Second Session of Fifth National People's Congress in 1979 and the Third Session of the Twelfth NPC in 2015

In this period, a unified but multi-tiered legislative system was established by the Constitution and the laws. The Constitution, Law on Legislation and other laws granted the NPC and its Standing Committee to exercise legislative power of the state. The State Council may enact administrative rules and regulations in accordance with the Constitution and the statutes. The people's congresses of the provinces, municipalities and large cities and their standing committees may adopt local regulations. The people's congresses of the autonomous regions, prefectures and counties have the power to enact self-governance regulations and separate regulations in the light of the political, economic and cultural characteristics of the nationality or nationalities in the areas concerned. The people's congresses of the provinces and cities that established special economic zones and their standing committees may have power to enact regulations on the affairs of special economic zone based on the authorization of the NPC and implement them within the scope of these zones. The ministries, committees, People's Bank of China, the National Audit Office and the departments directly charged with certain administrative functions may formulate rules within their own limit according to the laws, and administrative regulations, decisions and orders of the State Council.

The Third Plenary Session of the Eleventh CPC Central Committee marked a new stage of the reform and opening-up and the development of socialist legal system. As early in December 1978, Deng Xiaoping put forward in Emancipate the Mind, Seek Truth From Facts and Unite As One In Looking to the Future, "there is a lot of legislative work to do...some laws and statutes can be tried out in particular localities and later enacted nationally after the experience has been evaluated and improvements have been made."[2] Based on his proposition, the Local Organization Law was adopted in the Second Session of the Fifth NPC convened in July 1979. It proposed an important reform of China's legislative system. According to its

[1] Mao Zedong, *Selected Works of Mao Zedong (Vol. 5)*, Foreign Languages Press, 1977, p. 294.

[2] Deng Xiaoping, *Selected Works of Deng Xiaoping (Vol. 2)*, Foreign Languages Press, 1995, p. 156.

provisions, the people's congresses of the provinces, autonomous regions and municipalities directly under the State Council and their standing committees were granted with the legislative power, allowing them "to enact and issue local regulations which do not contravene the Constitution, laws, policies, decrees and orders, and report to the Standing Committee and State Council for the record". The 1982 Constitution also reformed the legislative system, as in Article 89 the State Council was authorized to enact administrative rules and regulations, in Article 90 the ministries and commissions of the State Council to issue orders, directives and regulations, in Article 100 the people's congresses of provinces and municipalities directly under the State Council and their standing committees to adopt local regulations, and in Article 116 the people's congresses of national autonomous areas to enact regulations on the exercise of autonomy and other separate regulations. In the Fifth Session of the Fifth National People's Congress held in December 1982, the resolution on amending the Local Organization Law was adopted, which allowed "the people's governments of provinces, national autonomous areas, municipalities directly under the State Council, cities where the people's governments of provinces and national autonomous areas reside and the large cities approved by the State Council may also enact rules and regulations based on the laws and administrative regulations of the State Council". When the Local Organization Law was revised in 1986, in paragraph 2 of Article 7 and paragraph 2 of Article 38 the people's congresses of the cities where the people's governments of provinces and national autonomous areas reside and the large cities approved by the State Council and their standing committees were granted with the power to make local regulations which "shall be reported to the standing committees of the people's congresses of the provinces and national autonomous areas, and then reported to the Standing Committee and the State Council by these standing committees for the record". It was revised again in February 1995, and its Article 60 further regulated the local governments' power in formulating regulations, i.e. "the people's governments of provinces, national autonomous areas and municipalities directly under the State Council may formulate rules according to the laws, administrative regulations and the local regulations made by provinces, national autonomous areas and municipalities directly under the State Council, and report to the State Council and their corresponding people's congresses. The people's governments of the cities where the provincial people's governments reside and the large cities approved by the State Council may formulate rules according to laws, administrative regulations and the local regulations of provinces and autonomous regions, and report to the State Council, the standing committees of the people's congresses and people's governments of provinces and national autonomous areas and the corresponding standing committees of the people's congresses for the record". When the Law on Legislation was adopted in 2000, China's legislative system was already well refined, making the laws, regulations and rules more regulated and institutionalized. New provisions were made on the division and grant of legislative power, and further clarification were laid down on the matters subject to the exclusive legislative power of the state. The law also granted the cities where the special economic zones were located and large cities with the legislative authority. China's legislative system was basically established.

The legislative system founded on the 1982 Constitution served "to resolutely put the focus of the work of the state on socialist economic development". The work on legislation had made remarkable progress in this phase, but it also showed its shortcoming as the society and economy developed for it could not effectively meet the local demands for legislative power, which, to a certain degree, undermined the initiative of the localities. Though some cities were granted with this authority, the problem still existed because the legislative power was not divided or clearly divided. The authorization of legislative power was made very often, for example the NPC and its Standing Committee had authorized the people's congresses of Guangdong, Fujian, Hainan, Shenzhen, Xiamen, Shantou and Zhuhai and their standing committees to formulate regulations on special economic zones. The 2000 Law on Legislation provided further that "the people's congresses of provinces and cities where special economic zones are located and their standing committees have the power to make regulations based on the authorization of the NPC, which are implemented in the special economic zones".

In addition, Hong Kong and Macau were returned to PRC in 1997 and 1999 respectively. According to "One Country, Two Systems", based on the provisions of the two basic laws, the legislators of Hong Kong and Macau have the power to enact laws and report to the Standing Committee for the record.

Phase 4: After the Third Session of the Twelfth National People's Congress in 2015

In the twenty-first century, especially since the Eighteenth CPC National Congress, China has entered a decisive stage of building China into a moderately prosperous country, and its reform is sailing in uncharted waters faced with tough challenges. Rule of law has played an even more obvious and important role in the overall work of the Party and the state. To better mobilize the initiative of both the central and local governments, modernize the state governance system and capacity, and promote comprehensive law-based governance, many new objectives and missions are set out with regard to legislative power. For example, in the third and fourth plenary sessions of the Eighteenth Central Committee, the Party proposed "to gradually increase the number of the large cities which have local legislative power" and "to define the scope of local legislative power and give it to the cities with subordinate districts according to law". In the fourth session, it was also proposed to "define the boundary of legislative power and prevent the departmental interests and local protectionism according to our mechanism, institutions and procedures". Following these requirements made by the Party's Central Committee, the NPC and its Standing Committee revised the Law on Legislation in the Third Session of the Twelfth National People's Congress convened in 2015. Through this revision, the scope and limits of local legislative power were further elaborated, and the people's congresses of the cities with subordinate districts and their standing committees were authorized to make local regulations, which helps to improve the current legislative system.

First, to grant the cities with subordinate districts, autonomous prefectures and four cities with no subordinate districts with the legislative power. The amended Law on Legislation prescribed that the people's congresses of the cities with subordinate districts, autonomous prefectures, and Jiayuguan, Dongguan, Zhongshan and Sansha which do not have districts and their standing committees may enjoy legislative power over urban and rural development and administration, environmental protection, and historic and cultural protection, "to formulate local regulations and implement them after reporting to the standing committees of the people's congresses of provinces and national autonomous areas for approval; the people's governments of the cities with subordinate districts (including four cities with no subordinate districts) and autonomous prefectures may make rules according to the laws, administrative regulations and the local regulations of the provinces, national autonomous areas and municipalities directly under the State Council".

Second, to implement the principle of statutory taxation and improve the system on specific legislative matters. Article 8 of the old law only prescribed the matters subject to laws, and taxation was one of the matters included in a general provision of "the basic economic system and the basic institutions of treasury, taxation, customs, finance and foreign trade". The revised Article 8 gave a separate item for taxation, declaring that "the establishment of a tax, determination of tax rates, tax collection administration and other basic taxation rules" are only subject to the jurisdiction of laws.

Third, to improve the system of authorized legislation. To achieve the interconnection between legislation and reform decision, and ensure that every reform decision is made according to law and law meets the demand of reform and development, the revised Article 13 prescribed that "the NPC and its Standing Committee may, as reform and development requires, decide to adjust or temporarily suspend the application of some provisions of law in specific authorization matters in areas such as administrative management, for a set period of time in some areas". Considering the comparative principle in legislative authorization, vagueness in authorized scope of legislation and lack of time limit, the revised law also made provisions. For example, the authorization should specify the purpose, subject matter, scope and term of authorization and the principles to be observed by the authorized that implements the authorization decision; the authorization shall not exceed 5 years, except as otherwise specified in the authorization decision; the authorized should, 6 months before expiry of the authorization, report the implementation of the authorization decision to the authorizing, and submit an opinion on whether or not it is necessary to formulate law; where it is necessary to continue the authorization, an opinion may be submitted to that effect, and the NPC and its Standing Committee will make a decision.

Last, to regulate the rules made by departments and governments. The revision was read, concerning the departmental rules, as "the matters decided by departmental rules shall be within the scope of the laws, administrative regulations, decisions, or orders of the State Council being enforced. Departmental rules not based on the laws, administrative regulations, decisions, or orders of the State Council must not impair the rights of citizens, legal persons or other organizations, or increase the scope of their duties, nor increase the power of that department or reduce that department's legally provided duties". The revision also considered the local needs: "where local regulations should be formulated but the conditions are not yet ripe, to satisfy the urgent administration's needs, local governmental rules may be enacted first. Where it is still necessary to implement administrative measures provided for by local rules that have been in effect for two years, the local people's congress or its standing committee shall be requested to enact local regulations".

The 2018 Constitution's amendment also provided the fundamental basis for confirming the authority of the cities with subordinate districts to make local regulations. It added a paragraph to Article 100 which was read as "the people's congresses of cities divided into districts and their standing committees may, provided that there is no conflict with the Constitution, laws or administrative regulations, or with the local regulations of their province or autonomous regions, formulate local regulations in accordance with the provisions of law, which shall go into force after submission to the standing committee of the people's congress of their province or autonomous region and the receipt of approval."

The development and improvement made for legislative system in this period highlighted the expansion of local legislative power by granting legislative power to the cities with subordinate districts, including 30 autonomous prefectures and 4 cities with no subordinate districts. The specific legislative matters subject to law and the local legislative matters were also improved, which gave a clear-cut division of legislative authority. These highlights and improvements are important steps to advance comprehensive rule of law and law-based governance, and are also important institutional arrangements for improving China's legislative system and promoting local legislation. They are significant for mobilizing the aspirations and initiative of the cities with subordinate districts, accelerating the efforts on local legislation and promoting the locality in modernizing state governance system and capacity.

2 Effects and Reflections

2.1 Superiority of China's Legislative System

In general, China's legislative system is in conformity with its national circumstances and practical needs. Its establishment and improvement are grounded on the experience accumulated in developing Chinese socialist modernization. It has given full play to the initiative of both the local and central governments, inspired the localities to make joint efforts for promoting socialist modernization, which has helped to improve and develop Chinese socialism and modernize the state governance system and capacity. If the legislative power is exclusively exercised by the central authority, the subjectivist attitude and bureaucracy will rise, and the local circumstances will be overlooked, and the laws could be detached from social realities and thus ill-suited to diverse circumstances. However, if the local legislative power is unscrupulous, wide disparities among local regulations would emerge, which does not conform with the traditions of China as a long-lasting unitary country and may undermine the unification of socialist legal system. Only a unified but multi-tiered legislative system can both prevent over-centralized power and fully harness the initiative of both the local and central authorities. The principles of this unified and multi-tiered legislative can be elaborated as follows:

First, to define the principle of legal reservation. Under this system, the state and local legislative authorities are clearly delineated, while the matters exclusively subject to state legislation are expressly prescribed. The exclusive legislative power by the NPC and its Standing Committee is committed to resolving the fundamental, general and long-term issues concerning stability during national development, setting out the fundamental legal systems for national economic, political, cultural, social and ecological development, laying the foundation for national legal system and providing basis for administrative and local regulations.

Second, to define the State Council's power to make administrative regulations. To grant the State Council with a certain degree of legislative power outside the NPC and its Standing Committee may remedy the inadequacy of national legislation in responding promptly to social practice. It will help the implementation of pilot initiatives for comprehensively deepening reform, ensure the unity of national decrees, specify the legal systems, make supplements to law, secure the effective implementation of Constitution and law, and urge the people's governments at all levels to administer according to law.

Third, to clarify the scope of local legislative power. The local matters outside the reach of national legislation are subject to local legislation, which may, out of the need for social governance, formulate local regulations that are compliant with upper level legislation, practicable and reflect local characteristics. With the local legislative power, the local governance can be improved and innovated by referring to legal thinking and available laws, which may address the issues of no law to resort, and the differences, imbalances and inadequacies in local social and economic development. It can also guarantee the effective implementation of Constitution, law and administrative regulation in local governance on one hand, and provide legal guarantee for refined and delicate local governance and administration.

Last, to provide the opportunity to explore possible local legislative matters. The law prescribes that the local legislation may be carried out in areas that the state does not makes laws or administrative regulations. These legislative explorations not only fill the legislative vacuum but also will gain experience to better the local governance capabilities and capacity and implement the programs for comprehensively advancing rule of law. In addition, the ministries and commissions of the state council and the local people's governments granted with legislative power may formulate rules to promote the effective implementation of laws and administrative regulations, decisions and orders of the state council, improve the law-based governance, push forward the integrated development of law-based country, government and society and promote the modernization of state governance system and capacity.

2.2 *Reflections*

Although China's legislative system has already taken initial shape and achieved significant accomplishments, it still faces certain problems and leaves room for futher improvement.

First, to establish a concept of overall consideration. Constrained by their own circumstances, local legislators may seek to protect local interests and departmental interests through legislation. On one hand, the local legislators often give priority to local interests, which may lead to local protectionism and market fragmentation, thereby disrupting the establishment and improvement of unified national market to a certain extent. On the other hand, the formulation of administrative regulations and rules is largely undertaken by relevant government departments, making departmental control and struggles over powers and responsibilities during legislation particularly prominent. Those who do not have a concept of overall consideration will not take control of any part of overall situation. In the future legislation, the legislative authorities should adhere to a overall perspective fully recognize the importance of legislation in promoting the socialist law-based country, plan the legislation within their own scope of authority and make coordinated efforts to safeguard the unity and coherence of the national legislative system.

Second, to uphold legislation based on law. To introduce legislation according to law is the requirement of the Constitution and law, the essential characterization of rule of law, and the political mission proposed in the Nineteenth CPC National Congress. However, unauthorized legislation often happens in various forms: first, legislation may exceed the scope of statutory authority. Sometimes in local legislation, due to an inaccurate understanding of the relevant provisions, the matters not subject to legislation are nonetheless regulated, resulting in provisions that go beyond national law and infringe upon citizens' legitimate rights and interests. Second, in the absence of clear legislative authority, the legislative vacuum is exploited and the legislators solely rely on the local needs to introduce legislation out of nothing to circumvent existing provisions of laws and regulations, such as in the case of legislation on local renowned trademarks. Third, breakthroughs are made in disregard of the limits on local legislative power by the laws and regulations. If the laws or regulations do not regulate or make provisions but not impose administrative punishments on certain acts, the local people's congresses and their standing committees may regard such acts as harmful to the society or consider existing national laws or regulations outdated and incapable of meeting practical needs As a resulti, they also go beyond the provisions of the Administrative Penalty Law by adding new acts subject to administrative punishment or introducing new punishments, or by prescribing punishments exceeding the statutory limits. For example, by May 2014, among the 14 local regulations on radio administration across China, eight of them exceeded the provisions of the Regulations on Radio Administration adopted by the State Council in 1993. Last, abuse of legislative power and infringements of citizens' legitimate rights and interests often occur.

The feudal rule, which tended to emphasize the obligations over rights of the people and the state power over citizens' rights, has a long history in China. The local regulations, especially governmental rules, have long been focusing on administration rather than service. If the old means are still pursued for administration, the citizens', legal persons' and other organizations' rights will be damaged or their obligations will be increased. Therefore, the principles for local legislation should be changed, and the local legislators should adhere to a people-centered approach, guarantee the people's position as masters of the country, cautiously exercise the local legislative power, make the laws more target-oriented, and proactively safeguard the unity of national legal system. Moreover, coordinated efforts should be made for state legislation, and the imbalance and inadequacy of local development should also be fully considered. Some matters that are not suitable to be regulated in a unified way should be left to local legislation for specific and detailed norms. The state should also establish sound mechanism for record-filing and review, strengthen the review of legislation and spare more efforts to correct the legislation that goes beyond authority to safeguard people's rights and interests and the unity of socialist legal system.

Third, to improve capacity for legislation. An important feature of China's horizontal allocation of legislative authority is the overlap of legislative scope and ompetence. If the local legislation seeks to incorporate everything into the regulations or rules, or pursue political performance or excessive completeness of provisions, the indiscriminate copying among laws and regulations, whether within the same level of legislation or across different local rules and regulations, would happen. The more detailed the provisions are, the more likely redundancy will happen. For example, by comparing the tourism regulations of some provinces with the Law on Tourism, the duplication rate reached a stunning 62%! To address such indiscriminate copying, it is imperative to improve the professionalism of legislative personnel by strengthening training in legislative work, and improve the legislator's understanding of policy, legal judgment and drafting language. Legislation is a sacred task that aims to lay down the rule of the state and society. To better legislate, the legislators should maintain correct political standing, possess solid professional expertise, and most importantly, be capable of translating the major decision and arrangements of the Party into law and transforming the Party language into language of law. The legislators should also take the initiative to follow the law of legislative activities and try to make every legislation conform with practical needs and the rules on legislative techniques.

At the second meeting of the Party's Central Commission for Comprehensive Law-based Governance, Xi Jinping emphasized that development should be high-quality, while legislation should also be high-quality; quality legislation is aimed for securing and promoting continuously sound economic development. However, to realize quality legislation, the legislators at all levels should deepen the scientific and democratic legislation according to law, continuously perfect the mechanisms and institutions for the work on legislation, improve legislation through institutional innovation and provide quality and effective provision of institutions for social and economic development through quality legislation. The legislators should also take the lead in and promote the reform and opening in the new era to make new contributions to the improvement of Chinese socialist legal system with the Constitution as the core and the modernization of state governance system and capacity.

Chapter 5
A History of Chinese Socialist Legal System: Its Inception, Formation and Improvement

Hu Jian

Abstract This chapter focuses on the evolution of China's socialist legal system, reviewing the NPC's evolving mandate, from early post-1949 emergency decrees, through the 1954 Constitution's concentration of legislative power, to the reform-era expansion of delegated and local legislation. It details the procedures by which the NPC and its Standing Committee initiate, deliberate, revise and enact laws. It also pays attention to the constitutional supervision and filing-review system, and the characteristics of the socialist legal system during this evolution. It concludes that the NPC's institutional design, combining broad representation, centralized decision-making and increasingly transparent processes, has enabled rapid, large-scale legislation that underpins China's modernization.

Keywords Evolution · Socialist rule of law · Characteristics · Reform and opening-up · 1982 Constitution · Legislative authority allocation

As emphasized by Xi Jinping at the Fourth Plenary Session of the CPC Central Committee, "since the founding of PRC, especially since the reform and opening-up, the Chinese socialist legal system has been established through arduous efforts, through which all the respects of national and social life are generally guaranteed by law. It is a remarkable achievement".[1] Only by reviewing the legislative development of the past 70 years, particularly since the reform and opening-up, of legislation can we have a deeper understanding of the role of Chinese socialist legal system in

[1] Xi Jinping, *Explanations on the Draft Resolution of the Central Committee of the Communist Party of China on Certain Major Issues Concerning Comprehensively Advancing the Law-Based Governance of China*, in The Party Literature Research Office ed., Selection of Important Documents Since the Eighteenth CPC National Congress (Vol. 2), Central Compilation and Translation Press, p. 148–149.

H. Jian (✉)
Beijing, China
e-mail: liujixuan@lawpress.com.cn

C. Shen et al. (eds.), *A History of Legislation in the Past 70 Years in China*,
https://doi.org/10.1007/978-981-95-3799-0_5

advancing and improving the Chinese socialist system and the modernization of state governance system and capacity.

Since the founding of PRC, especially the reform and opening-up, under the Party's firm leadership, the work on legislation has waded through an extraordinary historical process and made tremendous achievements. By the end of August 2019, there were 274 pieces of laws in force and 119 pieces of decisions on legal issues and other major issues, later incorporated in the Collection of Laws of the People's Republic of China (2018); in addition, there are over 600 pieces of administrative regulations and over 12,000 pieces of local regulations. The Chinese socialist legal system with the Constitution as the core has thus been established and continuously improved, providing strong legal guarantee for reform and opening-up and socialist modernization. Therefore, it is of crtitical importance and great significance for further strengthening and improving the work on legislation and continuously improving the Chinese socialist system with the Constitution as the core to make a omprehensive review of and carry out an in-depth research on the background, process, features and experience from its inception and formation to its ongoing improvement.

1 Background

The Chinese socialist legal system has developed in tandem with the continuous rooting of socialism with Chinese characteristics. However, the pursuit of the socialist path began as early as in the early period following the founding of PRC, when some legal institutions were also established. From the perspective of the history of Chinese socialist practice, the political system suited to China's circumstances was established upon the PRC founding, the national economy was soon recovered, the planned economic development was pursued, the private ownership of the means of production was basically transformed into socialist ones, the new democracy was transformed into socialism step by step, and the socialist production forces were unleashed, bringing refreshed vitality to the socialist cause. However, due to the lack of experience in socialist development and the later left-line mistakes in guiding principles for national development, a lot of correct lines and policies that conformed with China's circumstances proposed by the Party were not consistently implemented. What made the matter worse is the Cultural Revolution that caused serious setbacks and losses to the cause of the Party, the state and the people and led to a nearly broken economy. When the Cultural Revolution came to an end, as Deng Xiaoping ever said, "the overall political situation was chaotic, and the economy either grew slowly or stagnated".[2] Therefore, to strengthen the vigor of Chinese socialism, unleash and develop socialist productive forces and improve people's livelihood must be achieved by reform and opening-up.

---

[2] DENG Xiaoping, *Selected Works of Deng Xiaoping (Vol.3)*, Foreign Languages Press, 1994, p.259.

From the perspective of outside world, the new technology revolution that emerged worldwide in the 1970s drove the economic development much faster, which widened the gap of China's economic and technological strength with the international leading powers and confronted China with great pressure of international competition. At that time, what lay ahead of us was to the mission to break through the Western blockades, emancipate our minds, reach the outside world and look to the future, carry out reform and opening-up in an all-round way, and actively participate in economic globalization so as to make us stronger. The intentional political landscape also changed as the East-West confrontation was eased, and the peace and development became two major themes of global development. With a keen sense of these changes and vision for future, Deng Xiaoping thought that the peace and development were the mainstream of the world, and decisively shifted the focus of state to economic development, which presented China with a perfect strategic opportunity for long-term development.

Such a historical shift and transformation were made possible at the Third Plenary Session of the CPC Central Committee held in 1978. In this conference, the basic line of One Central Task with Two Points was proposed along with a series of new lines and policies, ushering in a new historical period for reform and opening-up. The institutional reform of the agricultural economy was designated as the first breakthrough; a two-tiered system of both unified and separate operations with household contract management was then established, which promoted the professional, commercial and modern agricultural production, released socialist productive forces and laid the foundation for China's transitioning from traditional agricultural society to a modern industrial society. Building on this success, various reforms, in both the rural and urban areas, were carried out, extending from the pilot programs of state-owned enterprises to the promotion of modern enterprises, from the establishment of special economic zones to the opening in all respects These reforms helped advance China's socialist cause.

The reform and opening-up has provided China with a historical opportunity and testing ground for establishing its own legal system. The socialist practice demonstrated that the Party had made due consideration and planning for how to build a socialist legal system with Chinese characteristics when the Party was committed to promoting socialist democracy and enhancing socialist legal system. As the reform and opening-up deepens and the socialist democratic rule of law is gaining momentum, the Party and the state's understanding of legal system also evolves. In the Fifteenth CPC National Congress held in 1997, it was proposed that the general objective of the work on legislation should be the establishment of Chinese socialist legal system by 2010. This objective was reiterated in the Sixteenth CPC National Congress in 2002. Five years later, a new mission for improving the Chinese socialist legal system was laid out. In 2010 when the general objective was successfully achieved as scheduled, another new objective that the Cheese socialist legal system needed refining was stated unambiguously in the Eighteenth CPC National Congress in 2012, while the focus on legislation in key areas and expansion of people's participation in legislation in an orderly manner were highlighted. To better the Chinese socialist legal system, in the Third Plenary Session of the Eighteenth Central Committee, the Party emphasized that the mechanism for legislative drafting, argument, coordination and deliberation should be consolidated to improve the quality of legislation and prevent institutionalized local protectionism and departmental interests. In its fourth plenary session convened in 2014, according to the objective of establishing a Chinese socialist rule of law system, it called for improving the Chinese socialism with Constitution as the core, establishing Chinese socialist rule of law system and promoting the modernization of state governance system and capacity. The two centenary goals were set out in the Nineteenth CPC National Congress, which reiterated the objective laid out in 2014 and called for "achieving the modernization of state governance system and capacity". In a conclusion, the inception, improvement and development of Chinese socialist legal system is gradually made along with the explorations for Chinese socialist system, reform and opening-up and the strengthening of socialist democratic legal system. It is the fruit of the Party's gradual recognition and summary of its governance, the essential and inevitable achievement of social and economic development, and an important part of the cause of Chinese socialism.

2 Preparations

The Chinese socialist legal system was proposed, established and improved following the launch of reform and opening-up representing a major achievement of the work on legislation in the past 40 years. It was not out of nothing, but drew strength from history. This achievement cannot be made without reflecting on the valuable experience and lessons from the arduous tasks of establishing socialist legal system after the PRC founding These experience and lessons can be summarized as follows:

First, the 1982 Constitution inherited, improved and developed the 1954 Constitution, which provided fundamental legal guarantee for China and Chinese people to withstand all kinds of difficulties and risks.

The convocation of the Third Plenary Session of the Eleventh CPC Central Committee ushered in the period of reform and opening-up and China's socialist democratic legal system. In the Fifth Session of the Fifth National People's Congress, the Constitution was opportunely promulgated which is still in force. The 1982 Constitution, based on the reflection on successes and failures in China's socialist development, inherited the basic principles and major provisions of the Common Program and the 1954 Constitution, adapted itself to the new requirements for reform and opening-up, socialist modernization and the socialist democratic legal system, established the line, principles, and policies after the third session. According to the provisions of 1982 Constitution, the fundamental mission of the state was to concentrate on socialist modernization, and correspondingly a lot of provisions were made for socialist democratic legal system to consolidate the legal foundation for reform and opening-up and socialist modernization.

As pointed out by Xi Jinping, the current Constitution was promulgated on the basic principles and major provisions of the Common Program and the 1954 Constitution, from which many of its systems and principles were originated. It inherited, improved and developed the two documents by referring to the new circumstances. The reason why the 1982 Constitution is regarded as a sound Constitution lies precisely in the fact that the 1954 Constitution itself was a good one. As the first socialist constitution formulated by the Chinese people under the Party's leadership, it not only played an important role in securing the consolidation of socialist state power and stimulating the socialist cause, but also laid the foundation for promulgating and improving the later constitution for reform and opening-up. For its weight and significance in history, the 1954 Constitution is often called the founding constitution by many scholars.

The 1954 Constitution was promulgated under Mao Zedong's direct guidance. During its drafting, opinions and suggestions were solicited from all relevant respects, and its draft was also published on June 14, 1954 for the discussion of Chinese people. Two months later, a total of 15 million people joined in the discussion, while the number of people over 18 years old was only 33.8 million. People warmly welcomed the draft Constitution, which demonstrated the unity of Party's correct proposal with people's will. It was a people's constitution. Guided by Marxism-Leninism and Mao Zedong Thought, this Constitution summarizes in a practical and realistic manner the revolutionary experience of the Chinese Communist Party in uniting and leading the Chinese people against imperialism, feudalism and bureaucratic capitalism and of the experience from social reforms, economic development, cultural progress and work of government in the early years of PRC. Its promulgation consolidated the achievements of people's revolution and the new victories made in politics and economy since the PRC founding, made provisions on the mission and road for Chinese people's socialist construction and transformation, and presented the collective vision of Chinese people and their fundamental interests.

The 1954 Constitution established two fundamental principles in the form of the basic law: one is the principle of people's democracy as the people are the masters of the country, not bourgeois democracy; the other is the principle of socialism as the road of socialism not the road of capitalism was chosen. Based on two principles, it established people's democratic dictatorship as the state system and the system of people's congresses as the system of government. It prescribed that the People's Republic of China practice the democratic centralism, make provisions on the status, powers and functions of the president of PRC, allowed the National People's Congress to make a reasonable distribution of legislative, executive and judicial powers based on its unified exercise of state power and stipulated the basic principles of the relationship between the central and local governments. The 1954 Constitution also determined that all ethnic groups are equal and the regional autonomy is practiced, and further stipulated that all the Chinese people are equal before the law as the basic principle for people's democratic legal system. Lastly, this Constitution also empowered the citizens with extensive and true rights and basic obligations to the state and society. These provisions and principles are the founding principles of the new PRC, which shall not be waived at any time.

The first problem confronted in the drafting of 1982 Constitution was whether it was based on the 1978 Constitution or the 1954 Constitution. According to general practice, a Constitutional amendment was often made based on the immediately preceding one, i.e. the 1978 Constitution. However, this constitution was promulgated under special circumstances and failed to make a summary of the lessons from the decade-long Cultural Revolution and the complete rectifications of the left-line mistakes. Though it recovered some provisions of the 1954 Constitution, its basis was the 1975 Constitution, a rough text with only over 60 articles absent from many necessary provisions. Therefore, while the 1982 Constitution took the form of revision of the 1978 Constitution, it was substantively based on the 1954 Constitution. Under the Party's leadership and after the discussion of all the Chinese people, the 1982 Constitution was adopted through strict legal procedures to integrate the Party's correct proposals with the people's will. It is precisely because the 1982 Constitution inherited, improved and developed the principles and spirits of the 1954 Constitution, which provided the fundamental legal guarantee for China and Chinese people to withstand all kinds of difficulties and risks and the basis from the fundamental law for the state governance system in the new era.

Second, the important ideas and working methods adopted by the older generation of proletarian revolutionaries on legislation have provided valuable assets for the work on legislation in the 40 years of reform and opening-up.

After the PRC was founded, the first generation of CPC leadership with Mao Zedong as the core led the Chinese people to quickly heal the wounds of war, rehabilitate the national economy and develop the new democratic economy, carry out various social reforms, seize the opportunity to propose the idea of transition period, establish the basic socialist systems and then start the arduous explorations for socialist road in all respects. The old generation of proletarian revolutionaries, especially Mao Zedong, Liu Shaoqi, Zhou Enlai, Zhu De, Chen Yun, Deng Xiaoping and Peng Zhen took charge of the work on drafting the Constitution and other important legal texts, led the establishment of legal systems across the country, and contributed to a lot of important ideas and working methods for legislation, which are valuable assets for the work on legislation in the 40 years of reform and opening-up.

Mao Zedong took charge of drafting the PRC's first Constitution and acted as the president of the drafting commission. He ever told his staff before departing for Hangzhou where the drafting commission was located, "Constitution is the fundamental law of the state. Whether the Party's president or ordinary people, they should abide by it. Even if I will no longer be the president, whoever takes it should abide by it. It is a rule that must be observed."[3] He devoted a lot of efforts to the drafting of the constitution: he not only proposed many guiding principles and specific provisions of drafting a constitution, but also revised all the drafts, wrote comments and made speeches and directives at the meetings of the constitutional drafting commission and the Central People's Government Council.

[3] Mu Zhaoyong, *Mao Zedong chaired the drafting of the first republic's constitution*, General Review of the Communist Party of China, No.10, p.46–50 (2003).

Liu Shaoqi is one of the founders of Chinese socialist legal system. Upon the founding of PRC, he proposed to carry out the work on legislation step by step based on China's realities. He said, "now we can formulate all kinds of separate regulations, and then promulgate formal codes based on the implementation of these regulations".[4] As the first Chairman of the Standing Committee, he chaired five plenary sessions of the NPC and 109 meetings of the Standing Committee, took charge of formulating over 80 laws and decrees and joined the promulgation of the 1952 Constitution for which he chaired its drafting and made the Report on the Draft Constitution of the People's Republic of China in the First Session of the First National People's Congress; he also took charge of the formulation of the Land Reform Law, revised and finalized the marriage law, labor law and other draft laws. Liu Shaoqi played a foundational role in establishing and improving the legal systems of the newly founded PRC.

Peng Zhen is also one of the founders. In the early stage of PRC, especially after a lot of initiatives were carried out for economic development, the fundamental mission of the Party and the state was changed. As Peng Zhen thought, as the historical mission changed, the establishment of legal system should be among the Party and the state's agenda, and the work should be carried out not only by relying on policy but also on law. In 1953, as these economic development initiatives were being implemented, Peng Zhen said that "as the social revolution and movements for completely eliminating the remaining forces of the three major enemies went to an end, the legal system should be strengthened. Only a complete legal system can guarantee the socialist construction, so the important work that the state is confronted is to formulate laws".[5] Until 1956, the socialist system was basically established. He then pointed out to strengthen the people's democratic legal system needed laws to abide, to rely on and work with, as he said that "the problem is that we still lack a set of complete and urgent-needed basic laws, such as criminal law, civil law, procedural law, labor law and land use law. So it is necessary to quickly formulate the important laws that the country needs".[6] These important reflections and practices pushed forward the work on legislation.

Third, the drafting of important laws, including civil law and criminal law, laid the foundation for the lawmaking in the period of reform and opening-up.

In 1954, the first socialist Constitution was adopted, together with the Organic Law of the National People's Congress, Organic Law of the State Council, Organic Law of the People's Court, Organic Law of the People's Procuratorates, and Organic Law of the Local People's Congresses and Local People's Councils were also passed. However, some basic laws were still absent. Peng Zhen, the deputy chairman of the NPC Standing Committee and its General Secretary, suggested the criminal law, civil

[4] WANG Hanbin, *The Great Significance of Liu Shaoqi's Thought on Guiding the Development of Socialist Democracy and Legal System*, in Central Party Literature Office ed., Essays in Commemorating the 100th Birthday of Liu Shaoqi, Central Party Literature Press, 1999, p. 31.

[5] WANG Hanbin, *Peng Zhen's Outstanding Contribution to the Construction of China's Socialist Democracy and Legal System*, China Legal Science, No.6, p.3–17 (1997).

[6] *Ibid.*

law and other basic laws upon the formulation of these five laws. He immediately started the work on drafting these laws and invited experts in Soviet law and old laws.

As an important component of the Chinese socialist legal system, civil law is the foundational and comprehensive one in civil life, which is often referred as the encyclopedia of social life. It regulates the relationships of person and property, involving every aspect of people's social and economic life and concerning all the people. To promulgate a civil code for Chinese people has been the common aspiration of Chinese people since 1949. The codification of civil laws was initiated in 1954, 1962, 1979 and 2001. After the 1954 Constitution was issued, the NPC Standing Committee started the work on civil code. On February 1946, the draft Civil Law, consisting of the general principles, ownership, obligations and inheritance, were completed. Since it was based on the 1922 Civil Code of the Russian Soviet Federated Socialist Republic (RSFSR), it excluded the family part. Marriage was also considered not a part of civil law, and only ownership not property right was included in this draft. However, the political movements stopped the work on the promulgation of civil law. The second try was in 1962. In the Anti-Rightist Campaign started in 1957, the supremacy of law was criticized, and the legal nihilism rose. In 1960, the Party and the state began to rectify the left-line mistakes and decided to implement the principle of adjustment, reform, reorganization, improvement in national economy. In 1962, Mao Zedong criticized the legal nihilism and pointed out that "not only criminal law was needed, but also civil law. It is lawless now. It is impossible to have no laws, so the criminal and civil law should be made". Then the civil law made new progress. On September, the second civil was drafting was started and completed in July 1964. The draft civil law was divided into three parts: general principles, ownership of property and transfer of property with 24 chapters and 262 articles. It excluded the inheritance and torts but incorporated the budget, taxation and other financial relations and labor relations such as wages and remuneration. It was characterized by the planned economic system. However, the drafting work was also stopped by the Four Cleanups Movement (also known as Socialist Education Movement). It was not until 1979 when the work on drafting civil law was started for the third time. After the Third Plenary Session of the Eleventh CPC Central Committee, the civil code was put into the legislative agenda. In November 1979, the Law Committee of the NPC Standing Committee established an expert team on civil law drafting, which started the third trial. By May 1982, five drafts had been issued consecutively: the 1980 draft (for opinions) with 6 parts and 501 articles, the April 1981 draft (second draft for opinions) with 6 parts and 426 articles, the July 1981 draft (third draft for opinions) with 8 parts and 501 articles, and the 1982 draft (fourth draft for opinions) with 8 parts, 43 chapters and 465 articles. However, the conditions for drafting a civil code were still not ripe as the reform and opening-up were still under explorations. Therefore, under the working principle of adopting one when conditions are satisfied, the separate civil laws were designated to be first made. The later Law on Marriage, General Principles of Civil Law, Guaranty Law and Contract Law were consecutively formulated under this principle. In 2001, the codification of civil laws was started again. The draft Civil Law of the People's

Republic of China was prepared by the Standing Committee of the Ninth National People's Congress and was submitted for discussion in 2002. After discussion, it was decided to continue the promulgation of separate civil laws. In the term of the Tenth National People's Congress and its Standing Committee, the Property Law, Tort Law and Law on the Laws Applicable to Foreign-related Civil Relations were formulated. In the Fourth Plenary Session of the Eighteenth CPC Central Committee, to enact the Civil Code was proposed as the major legislative task. According to the decisions and arrangements made by the CPC Central Committee, the Civil Code should consist of a part of general principles and separate parts, such as personality, property right, contract, tort, marriage and inheritance as considered to be incorporated. Acceding to a two-step strategy, the first step was to enact the general principles part, which was the General Provisions of the Civil Law adopted in the Fifth Session of the Twelfth National People's Congress on March 2017; the second step was to enact the other parts, all of which were submitted to the NPC Standing Committee for deliberation in 2018, and in 2019 were deliberated on by the NPC Standing Committee and then submitted for adoption in 2020. After the two steps, a complete Civil Code would be made ready. In review of history of civil legislation, though the two drafting of civil code produced no practical results due to various reasons, they had made preparations for the initiation of codification of civil laws after the reform and opening-up was started. In a conclusion, since 1949, especially the reform and opening-up period, Chinese civil legislation has made fruitful achievements, helping to establishing a rather complete set of civil law system and lay the foundation for the final enactment of Civil Code.

Criminal law concerns national security, social stability, people's peaceful and happy life, and citizens' freedom, life and property, and is also the cornerstone of the rule of law. Peng Zhen attached great importance to its drafting. After the First Session of the First National People's Congress, he proposed to start the drafting of criminal law. During the drafting, he listened to the reports many times and put forward suggestions. In May and June 1957, he summoned many leaders and officials who participated in the drafting of criminal law to report at his residence for over six times. In the discussions, he made many insightful opinions, which were critical for the smooth drafting. Under Peng Zhen, the drafting made rapid progress. In June 1957, the 22nd draft was submitted to the NPC Bill Committee and issued for opinions at the Fourth Session of the First National People's Congress. The draft was revised for many times which made preparations for the enactment of criminal law. However, when the Anti-Rightist Campaign was started, the drafting was stopped. It was not restarted until 1961. Two years later, the 33rd draft were prepared. But the Socialist Education Movement and the Cultural Revolution stopped the work on criminal legislation. In July 1979, the criminal law, the criminal law was one of the seven laws adopted in the Second Session of the Fifth NPC. As remarked by Deng Xiaoping, "For the 29 years since the founding of New China we have had no criminal law. Though we tried repeatedly to draw up such a code and it went through more than 30 drafts, nothing ever came of the project. Now a code of criminal law and a code of criminal procedure have been adopted and promulgated and are being implemented. The whole nation sees in them the hope for a strictly enforced socialist legal system. This is no small achievement."[7] That sSeven laws, including the criminal law, were adopted within only several months vividly reflects the Chinese people's urgent desire for legal order in the aftermath of the Cultural Revolution. It marked a breakthrough in the establishment of Chinese legal system, and also showed that the drafting of criminal law before had laid solid foundation for quickly formulating the criminal law upon the initiation of reform and opening-up.

Fourth, the important laws and principles before had exerted profound influence on the legislation in the reform and opening-up period.

On November 24, 1987, the NPC Standing Committee made a decision to approve the report of the Legislative Affairs Committee on the situation and opinions on re-examining the laws promulgated before 1978. According to this report, the 134 laws adopted or approved by the first CPPCC, the Central People's Government Council, the National People's Congress and its Standing Committee, 111 of them were invalid, and 23 of them were still effective or under study for revision. Most of the laws and decrees before the reform and opening-up had expired because they were taken place by new laws, appealed, not applicable or not implemented for new circumstances and situations or obsolete governing legal issues. However, it is undeniable that some important laws and principles still exert significant influence on legislation in the reform and opening-up period. The Law on Election and its basic principles were typical of such significant influence. After the founding of PRC, the Electoral Law was promulgated twice, from which the principles of universality, equality and a combination of direct and indirect election were established. These principles have been the red line running through the legislative history, the essence of the election system and the vivid description of people's democracy.

To guarantee the equal right of people to election and to stand for election has been the political aspiration. In 1953 when the first Electoral Law was formulated, it was clearly required that a true democracy election should be established based on the circumstances of China. Acceding to this requirement, the principle of universality and equality was adopted in the election. Considering the low urbanization with 13.26% of the population in China urban areas and the concentration of working class in urban areas, the Electoral Law prescribed different ratios of deputies based on the rural and urban population to reflect the leading role of working class and the national industrialization initiative and to maintain the number of deputies among all the social classes and ethnic groups equal with their status. For example, the number of deputies to be elected from a province to the National People's Congress shall be on the basis of one deputy for every 800,000 people, while the number of deputies to be elected to the National People's Congress from a municipality directly under the Central People's Government and from a municipality with a population of more than 500,000 directly under a provincial government shall be on the basis of one deputy for every 100,000 people. The number of deputies elected to the provincial, city and county people's congresses was also based on the ratio of urban and rural population. These provisions were necessary because they were in line with PRC's government system and its realities at that time. In his Explanations on Draft Electoral

[7] DENG Xiaoping, *Selected Works of Deng Xiaoping (Vol.2)*, Foreign Languages Press, 1994, p.244.

Law, Deng Xiaoping also pointed out, "these provisions on different ratios are not completely equal to a certain extent, but only with such provisions can truly reflect China's reality and make every social class and ethnic have their own deputies equal with their status", "with China's politics, economy and culture makes progress, we must adopt…a more complete election system in the future", and "evolves into a more equal and even completely equal election".

Before the reform and opening-up, China's urbanization barely made any progress due to various reasons. The urban population reached only to 18.96% when the new Electoral Law was enacted in 1979. Therefore, it continued the provisions of the 1953 Electoral Law and clarified the ratio of urban and rural deputies elected to the people's congresses of each level: 8:1 to National People's Congress, 5:1 to people's congresses of provinces and national autonomous areas, and 4:1 to the people's congresses of the autonomous prefectures, counties and autonomous counties. After the reform and opening-up was initiated, the society and economy has developed rapidly, the urbanization also gains momentum, which led to the change of urban-rural population. In the revision of Electoral Law in 1995, the National People's Congress changed it to 4:1 regardless of the level of people's congress.

In the Seventeenth National Congress, the Party suggested that the goal of electing deputies to people's congresses based on the same population in urban and rural areas be gradually realized. To implement the gist of this congress, the NPC started its work on revising Electoral Law in a timely manner. During the research and investigations, the Party's Central Committee's proposal were welcomed throughout the country and by all social respects. However, opinions differed as to how to implement it, to formulate it once for all or step by step. After in-depth research, based on most of the local opinions, the revision of Electoral Law in 2010 would be the once for all approach, which granted the equal representation without regard to the population for the following reasons: first, the conditions were ripe. Since 1995 great changes had taken place in China's social structure as the industrialization and urbanization was accelerating, and the rural economic and cultural development made great progress. The ratio of urban population had increased from 29.04% in 1995 to 46.6% in 2009 (according to the Sixth National Census, this number was 49.68% in November 2010). At the same time, a lot of experience was gained from the various elections by the people's congresses at all levels, the socialist democratic politics and legal system had made tremendous achievements, and the foundation for the social classes and people's support under the Party's leadership in people's democratic dictatorship were consolidated. The conditions for granting equal representation without regard to urban and rural population were ripe. Second, it was practicable to make it in full swing. Jiangsu and Shanghai had carried out pilot programs in granting equal or nearly equal representation in county, district or city's elections of people's congresses based on their actual circumstances. These pilot programs brought about good results. Third, it would make the work on legislation more proactive by adopting the once for all approach.

In a conclusion, it changed the history when the election of deputies to the people's congresses were carried out based on the ratio of urban and rural population. It is the requirement of China's economic, political, cultural and social progress, an important measure to integrate the urban and rural development and eliminate the dual structure of urban and rural areas, and a historical step to implement the principle of equality in election as established and emphasized when drafting the 1953 Electoral Law.

Last, the achievements and mistakes made in socialist construction, especially in building the democratic legal system before the reform and opening-up provided historical reference for the work on legislation.

As pointed out by Xi Jinping, the Constitution in force was promulgated during the reform and opening-up, which reflected on the achievements and mistakes of socialist construction. From the later 1950s, the left-line mistakes and other mistakes, the process of building a socialist democratic legal system was halted and stagnant. Especially the Cultural Revolution, which led to serious disruptions and catastrophic losses to the cause of the Party and the state, left the Constitution on the shelf. This is a grave lesson we should learn. In December 1979, the Third Plenary Session of the Eleventh CPC Central Committee made a historical shift by correcting the mistakes and putting things right, starting the reform and opening-up and establishing the basic principles for developing socialist democracy and a sound socialist legal system. In the Sixth Plenary Session, the achievements and lessons after the PRC's founding were reflected, especially with regard to why the Cultural Revolution happened and why it lasted so long. One of its conclusions was to gradually establish and improve the highly democratic socialist political system and make it one of the fundamental missions for socialist revolutions. The report made in the Twelfth CPC National Congress affirmed this conclusion by emphasizing that "only a highly democratic socialist democracy is established can the various causes conform with people's will, interests and needs, enhance people's responsibility of masters and give full play to their initiative and enthusiasm". The report also stated that "we should adhere to the principle of democratic centralism and continue the reform and improvement of China's political system and leadership system to make people better exercise the state power and the governmental departments to better lead and organize the socialist construction". Therefore, to develop socialist democracy and improve the socialist legal system concerns people's position as masters of the country, long-lasting peace and order of the country, prevention of the second Cultural Revolution, and smooth reform and opening-up and socialist modernization. These emphasis and statements posed a great task for promulgating the Constitution and improving legal systems related with socialist democratic politics.

According to the Central Committee's decisions and arrangements and the directives of Deng Xiaoping, based on these achievements and lessons, the 1982 Constitution reformed and developed the political system and leadership system. In his Report on the Draft Constitution of the People's Republic of China, Peng Zhen made several key illustrations. For example, to enlarge the functions and duties of the NPC Standing Committee, and strengthen the organization of NPC and its Standing Committee; second, to recover the position of president and vice-president of the state; third, the premier has overall responsibility for the State Council; fourth, to establish the central military commission; fifth, to establish people's congresses at or above the county level; sixth, to separate the administration from social functions and strengthen the exercise of state power among the communities; last, to abolish the life tenure of leaders that had been actually practiced. These important institutional designs closely related with political system reform were correct conclusions made by learning from the historical lessons, which had significant and far-reaching influence on a sound state system, ensuring people's position as masters of the country and guaranteeing the efficient and sound operations of state authorities.

3 Conceptual Evolution

3.1 Systematization of Law: An Initial Idea

At the Third Plenary Session of the Eleventh CPC Central Committee, the lessons from Cultural Revolution were reviewed and summarized, and it was decided to turn the focus of the Party and the state's work to economic development and reform and opening-up. To strengthen the establishment of a socialist democratic legal system was designated as a unswerving principle which emphasized the development of legal system and made the socialist democracy institutionalized by law, so that these institutions and laws would not be changed as the leaders' opinions or attention changed and there were laws to abide by, observed and strictly enforced and any violation of laws were punished. This conference ushered China into a new stage of developing socialist democratic legal system. In response to the urgent need to maintain political stability and unity and to carry out socialist modernization, Deng Xiaoping and other leaders paid special emphasis on the need of accelerating the work on legislation. On December 13, 1978, as Deng Xiaoping pointed out, "the trouble now is that our legal system is incomplete, with many laws yet to be enacted…So we must concentrate on enacting criminal and civil codes, procedural laws and other necessary laws concerning factories, people's communes, forests, grasslands and environmental protection, as well as labor laws and a law on investment by foreigners. These laws should be discussed and adopted through democratic procedures. Meanwhile, the procuratorial and judicial organs should be strengthened. All this will ensure that there are laws to abide by, that they are observed and strictly enforced, and that violators are to be punished. The relations between one enterprise and another, between enterprises and the state, between enterprises and individuals, and so on should also be defined by law, and many of the contradictions between them should be resolved by law."[8]

At the closing meeting of the Second Plenary Session of the Fifth National People's Congress, Ye Jianying, chairman of the NPC at that time, said, "after this meeting, the NPC Standing Committee will, based on the opinions of many deputies, organize experts of all fields to speed up the work on formulating civil law and the laws of civil procedure, marriage, family planning, factory, labor, contract, energy and environmental protection. The State Council along with the people's congresses

[8] *Ibid.*, p.156.

and local governments of all levels should also formulate necessary rules and regulations within their own jurisdictions".[9] In his talk with the eighth delegation for visiting China of the Komeito Party of Japan headed by Yoshikatsu Takeiri in June 1979, Deng further required, "we shall formulate a series of laws. We lack many necessary civil laws. We also need to enact many laws governing economic development, such as those pertaining to factories. The laws that we have made are too few. We need about one hundred of laws which we do not presently have. Therefore, we have much work to do and this is just the beginning. We must promote our democracy and our legal system. They are like a person's two hands; if either one is weak, the person will not be able to accomplish anything."[10]

According to Deng's remarks, the work on legislation was fully recovered and made rapid progress. In July 1979, the Local Organization Law, Electoral Law, Organization Law of the People's Courts, Organization Law of the People's Procuratorates, Criminal Law, Criminal Procedure Law, and Law on Chinese-Foreign Equity Joint Ventures were adopted in the Second Plenary Session of the Fifth National People's Congress, marking a major breakthrough in China's legislation after suspension of over 20 years and a decisive step to be taken to develop the socialist legal system. The promulgation of the 1982 Constitution and other important laws made the socialist democratic legal system fully regain recovery. On September 6, 1982, in his speech made in the National Experience Exchange on the Work of Legislative Affairs, Peng Zhen proposed the concept of the systematization of law for the first time, as he said, "whether people admit it or not, the productive forces and relations have developed in China. And as the society develops, the circumstances also change, so does the law and the system of law".[11] Peng explicitly raised the issue of legal systematization, which fully demonstrated that China had already adopted a long-term perspective in considering this issue as soon as the work on legislation was restored and recovered.

When the reform and opening-up wasfirst launched, the practical experience in this regard was insufficient, so the work on legislation was to formulate the primary laws urgently needed for guaranteeing the restoration of social order and implementing the initiatives for reform and opening-up. Therefore, given the small number and scale of laws, regulations and administrative regulations, the concept of "the system of law" was still a very forward-looking goal of legislation. As analyzed by Peng, "the change of the circumstance that the focus of the Party and the state's work was turned to socialist modernization called for economic legislation as the priority in the legislative agenda, which should be actualized faster and better. However, could it be done once for all? No. it was not because this goal was not desirable but impracticable. The guiding principles and polices were under transformation and correction, adjustments were made for economy, and reforms were carried out for institutions. Legislation

---

[9] YE Jianying, *Selected Works of Ye Jianying*, People's Publishing House, 1996, p. 510.

[10] DENG Xiaoping, *Selected Works of Deng Xiaoping (Vol.2)*, Foreign Languages Press, 1994, p.196.

[11] PENG Zhen, *On the Work of Politics and Law in New China*, Central Party Literature Press, 1992, p. 297.

could not be made only by wishes and assumptions or by one's own like."[12] Therefore, "legislation is only the summary of social practice, and the institutionalized polices expressed in article by article that have proven by practice. The practice determines the resolution of problems, and the contradictions, whether subjective or objective, can also be resolved in practice".[13] In December 1982, the NPC's annual report proposed that "legislation should be started on China's actual circumstances, and an independent legal system with Chinese characteristics can only be gradually established according to the principles for socialist legal system. "[14]

3.2 Start: "to establish a relatively complete system for economic legislation"

In the Twelfth CPC National Congress held in September 1982, it was proposed that the Party should lead the people to continue enacting and improving all the laws to fixate more norms on economic relationships and activities into laws and make laws the important method to regulate these relationships and activities. In the Third Plenary Session of the Twelfth CPC Central Committee held in October 1984, it was stated that more and more economic relationships and activities needed to be fixated into law as the reform of economic institutions and national economy deepened, and the state legislators should accelerate legislation's pace. In the second CPC National Representative Conference held between September 18 and 23, 1985, the Party's Central Committee proposed in its suggestions for making the Seventh Five-year Plan that "due emphasis be paid to economic legislation and the justice of economic disputes…a relatively complete system for economic regulations will be established by making unremitting efforts to make sure that every economic activity is carried out with law to abide by, and that the law should be strictly enforced and any violation of law will be punished". In the Thirteenth CPC National Congress convened in November 1987, it was further emphasized that the construction of legal system be carried out throughout the reform, guarantee the order for development and reform and consolidate the achievements of reform; it was necessary to incorporate the matters subject to development and reform into the framework of law or institutions.

According to these principles, the work on legislation was carried out in full swing. The first amendment to the 1982 Constitution made in 1988 clarified the status of non-public economic sectors and that the land use right may be transferred according to law; a lot of economic legislation, including the Law on Chinese-Foreign Equity Joint Ventures, Foreign-funded Enterprise Law, Law on Chinese-Foreign Contractual Joint Ventures, Law of Industrial Enterprises Owned by the Whole People, Patent

---

[12] *Ibid.*, p. 298–299.

[13] *Ibid.*

[14] YANG Shangkun, "Report on the Work of the Standing Committee of the National People's Congress of People's Republic of China", in *Gazette of the Standing Committee of the National People's Congress of People's Republic of China*, China Legal Publishing House, 2004, p. 577.

Law, Copyright Law, Law on Economic Contracts Involving Foreign Interest, Technology Contract Law, Maritime Law and Land Administration Law, were revised or enacted. The State Council was authorized to reform the taxation system in industry and commerce, issue relevant draft taxation regulations and formulate interim rules or regulations concerning the reform of economic institutions and opening-up. Some laws on civil affairs were also adopted, including the General Principles of Civil Law, Civil Procedure Law, and Inheritance Law. Laws for protecting the environment and resources were also promulgated, such as the Environment Protection Law, Law on the Prevention and Control of Water Pollution, Law on the Prevention and Control of Air Pollution, Mineral Resources Law, Water Law, Grassland Law, Fisheries Law, and Forest Law. Additionally, some laws for improving state authorities, protecting citizens' rights, punishing violations of laws, developing the education, strengthening military development and enhancing social administration were formulated or revised. However, Wan Li, Chairman of the Standing Committee of the Seventh National People's Congress, pointed out in the first meeting of the Standing Committee held in April 1988, these legislation "still have a long way to go to meet the demands of current social life and a complete legal system", because "our legal system was just in inception, not complete, and a lot of important laws need to be enacted…in the following five years, our work on legislation will be tough…the work of legislation of this National People's Congress requires a comprehensive consideration…this Standing Committee will…make a five legislative plan, and then implement it step by step. Once the conditions for a law is ripe, we will formulate the law opportunely. If not, the government may continue to make administrative regulations".[15]

In a meeting of party members from the Third Plenary Session of the Seventh National People's Congress and the Third Plenary Session of the Seventh CPPCC held in March 18, 1990, Jiang Zemin emphasized the need to further strengthen the work on legislation. He said, "since the founding of the People's Republic, and especially during the last ten years, our country has made outstanding legislative achievement, and we basically already have laws to observe in the main areas of political, economic, and social life. However, our body of laws is still not complete, and there remains much legislative work to do. At present, we need to promptly enact new and improve existing laws guaranteeing civil rights and safeguarding social stability and people's normal lives; enact laws guaranteeing reform and opening up and establishing macro-control; enact las concerning the development of agriculture, transport, energy, education, science and technology; and enact new and improve existing laws governing criminal punishment and promoting clean government.".[16] At the end of 1990, in the Recommendations for Formulating the Plan for Economic and Social Development and the Eighth Five-year Plan, the Party's Central Committee stated that "the construction of economic legal system should be accelerated to promote the regulation and institutionalization of economic adjustment and control. In the Eighth Five-year Plan, a relatively complete system for economic regulations shall

[15] WAN Li, *Selected Works of Wan Li*, People's Publishing House, 1995, p. 583–584.

[16] JIANG Zemin, *Selected Works of Jiang Zenmin (Vol. 1)*, Foreign Languages Press, 2010, p. 109.

be gradually established to make sure that every economic activity carried out and every economic relationship established have laws to abide by".

The conception of "establishing a relatively complete system of economic regulations" represents both an elevation and extension of Peng Zhen's "systematization of law" and the essential requirement as the reform of economic institutions deepened and the reform and opening-up sped up. It also demonstrated that the need for systematization of law became urgent as the practice for legislation developed rapidly and made more achievements.

3.3 Development: "to establish a legal system for socialist market economy"

In the Fourteenth CPC National Congress convened in October 1992, the report stated that "to strengthen the work on legislation, especially to accelerate the formulation and improvement of the laws and regulations for ensuring reform and opening-up, enhancing micro economic administration and regulating macroeconomic behaviors is the urgent need of establishing socialist market economic system". On March 29, 1993, the Constitutional Amendment adopted at the First Plenary Session of the Eighth National People's Congress prescribed that "the state practices the socialist market economy" and "the state strengthens economic legislation and improve micro control". Two days later, Qiao Shi, the successor to Wan Li as the Chairman, declared in the closing session that "the pace of legislation should be accelerated by following the aspiration for reform, especially the economic legislation should be placed in the most important position…by sparing unremitting efforts, the legal system for socialist market economy should be established within this term of NPC to promote and safeguard the development of socialist market economy". Qiao further directed that "the National People's Congress within this term should take economic legislation as the first mission and formulate laws for socialist market economy as soon as possible…in this decade, we will establish an initial system for market economy, and we should gradually the legal system for socialist market economy".[17] In the second meeting of NPC Standing Committee held on July 2, 1993, Qiao Shi said that "the framework of legal system for socialist market economy will be established with an initial form within the term of this NPC Standing Committee. This is an arduous task".[18] Qiao's remarks had decomposed the task of establishing the legal system for socialist market economy into several steps, one of which was to formulate its framework within the term of his office.

In the Decision of the CPC on Several Issues Concerning the Establishment of the Socialist Market Economic System issued on November 14, 1993, it was stated that "to observe the principles stipulated by the Constitution, to step up the economic

[17] The Party Literature Research Office ed., *Selection of Important Documents since the Fourteenth CPC National Congress (Vol. 1)*, Central Party Literature Press, 1996, p. 230.

[18] *Gazette of the Standing Committee of the National People's Congress*, Vol. 4, 1993.

legislation, to further improve the civil, commercial and criminal laws and other laws on state authorities and administration, and to establish an initial legal system that adapts to the socialist market economic system by the end of the 20th century". On March 15, 1994 the NPC Standing Committee proposed that "to continue taking the economic legislation as the first priority and gradually establish the legal system that adapts to the socialist market economy. The Standing Committee has made a five-year legislative plan...if this plan was realized, the framework of legal system for socialist market economy will be generally established, and the legal systems in other respects will also be improved".[19]

The NPC Standing Committee in these years had formulated a lot of laws on socialist market economy based on the requirements, its first priority and the conformity of legislation with reform and development. The NPC and its Standing Committee deliberated on 129 pieces of drafts of law and the decisions on related legal issues and adopted 118 pieces of decisions on laws and related legal issues.

The Constitutional Amendment adopted in this NPC made provisions on China's adherence to the primary socialist stage, the theory on establishing Chinese socialism and upholding reform and opening-up. It also established the leading position of the theory on Chinese socialism, prescribed that "the state practices socialist market economy", "strengthens economic legislation and improve micro control", providing constitutional basis for establishing and improving socialist market economy. By focusing on the key links of the market economic system, the NPC and its Standing Committee had spared efforts to step up economic legislation. In respect of regulating market entities, the Company Law, Partnership Enterprise Law, Town/Township Enterprise Law, and Commercial Banking Law were enacted. For establishing market rules and maintaining market order, the Anti-Unfair Competition Law, Law on the Protection of Consumer Rights and Interests, Law on the Administration of Urban Real Estate, Advertising Law, Auction Law, Guaranty Law, Negotiable Instruments Law, and Insurance Law were set ready for implementation, and the Economic Contract Law was revised accordingly. To better macro control, the NPC and its Standing Committee had put the Budget Law, Audit Law, Law on the People's Bank of China and Price Law on the table while made revisions to Statistics Law and Individual Income Tax Law. The Labor Law and the like were enacted to establish the social security system, while the Foreign Trade Law and others made for further opening-up. In revitalizing basic and pillar industries, laws such as the Agricultural Law, Civil Aviation Law, Electricity Law, Highway Law, Coal Law, Energy Conservation Law and Construction Law were formulated, and Mineral Resources Law and the like were revised. In addition, a number of important laws were enacted or revised with respect to socialist democratic political construction and education, science and technology, health, sports, environmental protection, national defense and litigations.

[19] TIAN Jiyun, *Report on the Work of the Standing Committee of the National People's Congress*, in Collection of the Documents on the Second Session of the Eighth National People's Congress, People's Publishing House, 1994, p. 135.

From these legislation, it can be seen that the Party and the state's conception of legal system has deepened as the reforms, especially of the economic institutions and socialist democratic legal system were gaining momentum. As the Party and the state set up the goal of establishing socialist market economic system, they would propose new requirements of legal system. From "establishing an initial legal system that adapts to socialist market economy", "generally establishing the framework for the legal system for socialist market economy", to "establishing an initial legal system that adapts to the socialist market economic system", and then to "gradually establishing the legal system that adapts to socialist market economy", these statements manifested such evolving understandings. Through concerted efforts of all parties, between the end of 1996 and the beginning of 1997, it was declared that "important strides have been made in establishing the legal system for socialist market economy", and "an initial framework for the legal system for socialist market economy", laying the foundation for the Party's Central Committee to plan on the "socialist legal system with Chinese characteristics".

3.4 Orientation: "to establish socialist legal system with Chinese Characteristics by 2010"

In the Fifteenth CPC National Congress held in 1997, the basic line of "governing the country according to the law and making it a socialist country ruled by the law" was set out, and it also proposed a general legislative mission of "strengthening the work on legislation, improving its quality, establishing the socialist legal system with Chinese characteristics by 2010". The Chinese legal system was put forward for the first time by the Central Committee. By the end of Eighth National People's Congress, "the framework of the legal system for socialist market economy has been initially established, providing an important legal environment for nurturing and developing socialist market economy", and "laying the foundation for socialist legal system with Chinese characteristics".

To better understand the background of "establishing the socialist legal system with Chinese characteristics by 2010" put forward in the fifteenth congress report, the staff of the Research Office of Legislative Affairs Committee visited Wang Chuanfu who participated in preparing the draft report. Wang recalled that they had emancipated their minds and engaged in heated discussions when preparing the part on democracy and law, and finally decided to incorporate two statements, i.e. "respect and protect human rights" and "governing the country according to the law and making it a socialist country ruled by the law". They have ushered China into a new starting line for rule of law. It was also a great achievement of China's legal development and a major progress of scientific socialism that no other socialist countries had made. There were some considerations concerning this general legislative mission:

First, a relatively sound legal system was the precondition for governing the country according to law. To this end, a scientific and integrated legal system was necessary that was able to regulate all kinds of social relations by applicable norms to ensure that every aspect of social life had laws to abide by.

Second, the general legislative mission was proposed as a political objective for governing the country according to law, for the wish at that time was to realize the rule of law and prevent the lawlessness. It was not purported as an ultimate or a doctrine-delicate one but was left for future development and improvement. The research then made was no that in-depth but to make it complete without any blanks and to ensure every aspect have laws to abide by.

Third, with regard to the proposal of "legal system", it first came out as "the legal system for socialist market economy", then changed to "the legal system with Chinese characteristics" in the report. The primary concern for making this change was the fact that different social relations should be subject to different laws, not just one category of laws since social life were diverse for its various sectors. Therefore, a legal system that was complete and integrated to regulate social relations from various sectors, not only "for socialist market economy".

Wang thought that the timing to declare the formation of the legal system was opportune after 30 years' efforts, especially in the latest decade when primary laws including the Property Law and Tort Law were enacted and the Social Insurance Law was around the corner. But it did not mean that legislation was complete and the work on legislation was finished. In the context of globalization, as reform and opening-up deepens, the legal system will also evolve with the development of society and change of social relations. There is a lot of work to do for legislation to promote Chinese civilization and progress, advance people's happiness, strengthen its soft power and ameliorate its international standing and image.

4 Formation

4.1 Foundation

As the general legislative mission was put forward in the Fifteenth CPC National Congress, the work on legislation had entered a new phase. On April 29, 1998, Li Peng, successor to Qiao, continued to emphasize that "this NPC and its Standing Committee has been dedicated to establishing the initial form of legal system with Chinese characteristics. To fulfil this task, we have to strengthen the work on legislation and improve its quality". On March 15, 1999, the Constitutional Amendment adopted at the Second Plenary Session of the Nineteen National People's Congress made a provision that "the People's Republic of China governs the country according to law and makes it a socialist country under rule of law". On October 31, 2000, Li further proposed that "we should strengthen the construction of legal system, and the focus is to establish and improve the legal system that adapts to socialist market economic system".[20] In November, Li said in a meeting on legislative work that "we should summarize the experience of the past twenty years' work on legislation to further strengthen and improve our work on legislation, improve its quality and efficiency and strive for the Chinese socialist legal system to ensure the smooth development of reform and opening-up and socialist modernization by sound laws and institutions and achieve the ambitious goal set out in the fifteenth party congress and its fifth session."[21] In November 2002, the report of the Sixteenth CPC National Congress put forward that "to adapt to the new situation characterized by the development of a socialist market economy, all-round social progress and China's accession to the WTO, we will strengthen legislation and improve its quality and will have formulated a socialist system of laws with Chinese characteristics by the year 2010.", which reiterated the requirement in the previous report.

The term of Standing Committee of the Ninth National People's Congress was key to completing this mission. In its term, the NPC and its Standing Committee deliberated on 124 pieces of law drafts, legal interpretations and decisions related with legal issues and adopt 113 pieces, a move that further enriched and improved the departmental laws of the Chinese socialist legal system.

The Law on Legislation was enacted, which made provisions on China's legislative system and procedures to better regulate the work on legislation and perfect Chinese system of legislation. The Regional Ethnic Autonomy Law was revised to reiterate the system of regional autonomy and promote the social and economic development in national autonomous areas. The Law on the Organization of the Villagers' Committees was also revised to improve the community-level self-government. All these enactments and revisions had consolidated and improve the socialist democratic political system in China.

To better improve the civil and commercial laws for market economic development, the Contract Law was promulgated to standardize the rules on market transactions. The Marriage Law was also revised propitiously for new circumstances and situations in family life. The Rural Land Contract Law guaranteed farmers with the right to use land for a long term to boost agricultural and rural development and maintain rural stability. In response to the joining of WTO, the Patent Law, Trademark Law and Copyright Law were revised for further improving the intellectual property protection system. To better the legal institutions for market economy, the Securities Law, Bidding Law, Trust Law and Individual Proprietorship Enterprises Law were enacted.

With regard to economic laws, Seed Law, Law on the Administration of the Right to Use Sea Areas, Law on the Promotion of Small and Medium-Sized Enterprises, and Government Procurement Law, among others, were promulgated, while the Product Quality Law, Accounting Law, Law on Tax Collection and Administration, Agricultural Law, Land Administration Law, Law on Chinese-Foreign Equity Joint Ventures, Law on Chinese-Foreign Contractual Joint Ventures, Foreign-funded

---

[20] *Gazette of the Standing Committee of the National People's Congress*, Vol. 6, 2000.

[21] The Party Literature Research Office ed., *Selection of Important Documents since the Fifteenth CPC National Congress (Vol. 2)*, People's Publishing House, 2001, p. 630.

Enterprise Law and Customs Law were revised to improve the legal institutions for economic development and opening-up.

In respect of regulation on administration, Administrative Consideration Law was formulated, making sound supervisory systems for administrative acts to promote law-based administration. The Population and Family Planning Law was formulated to control population and improve its quality. The promulgation and revision of the Higher Education Law, National Defense Education Law, Law on the Promotion of Privately-run Schools, National Common Language and Writing Law, Law on the Promotion of Science and Technology, Medical Practitioners Law, Drug Administration Law and Law on the Protection of Cultural Relics and others carried out the strategy of promoting science and education for national development, and promote the sound development of education, science, culture and health. The enactment of Law on the Prevention of Control of Sand, Law on Environmental Impact Assessment and Law on the Promotion of Clean Production and the revision of Law on the Prevention and Control of Air Pollution and Marine Environment Protection Law were intended to protect natural resources, improve ecological environment and boost sustainable social and economic development.

In terms of social laws, the NPC and its Standing Committee adopted the Safe Production Law and Occupational Disease Prevention Law to ward off and reduce safety accidents, prevent, control and eliminate occupational hazards and protect the workers' safety and health. To better regulate the labor relations under market economy and safeguard employees' legitimate rights and interests, the NPC and its Standing Committee also revised the Labor Union Law.

The NPC Standing Committee also issued the Decision Concerning Punishment of Criminal Offenses Involving Fraudulent Purchase, Evasion and Illegal Trading of Foreign Exchange and adopted the First, Second, Third and Fourth Amendments to the Criminal Law and legal interpretations on criminal law to improve the criminal legislation.

A lot of litigation and non-litigation procedural laws were enacted, such as Special Maritime Procedure Law. The Extradition Law was also set ready to providing basis for international cooperation in punishing crimes.

From this term the legal interpretation had risen to the legislative agenda. Apart from the legal interpretations made to address several issues concerning the implementation of Nationality Law in Macau and articles of the Hong Kong Basic Law, the NPC Standing Committee also adopted six interpretations on the provision of Criminal law to clarify the application of law and maintain the unity of the authority of law and socialist legal system.

It should also be noted this Standing Committee also organized research on the socialist legal system with Chinese characteristics and made important achievements. After efforts from all relevant parties, the seven departments of law that consisted of this legal system was formally put forward, i.e. Constitution and its related laws, civil and commercial laws, administrative laws, economic laws, social laws, criminal laws and litigation and non-litigation procedural laws. The three milestones for establishing such a legal system were also set out, i.e. the departments of law should be complete; the basic and major laws from each department of law should be enacted;

and within the legal hierarchy with the law as the pillar, the administrative regulations, local regulations, autonomous regulations and separate regulations should be formulated to strengthen the laws. These conclusions have enriched the conception and understanding of the Chinese socialist legal system with Chinese characteristics.

On March 10, 2003, Li declared that "based on the work of our predecessors and through unremitting efforts, the departments of law consisting the Chinese socialist legal system have been made complete, and the major laws of each department have been basically enacted. The administrative regulations of the State Council and local regulations of the people's congresses have all be set ready. The Chinese socialist legal system with the Constitution as the core has been initially established".[22]

4.2 *Rapid Development: "to basically establish the socialist legal system with Chinese Characteristics"*

As the report of the Sixteenth CPC National Congress reiterated the general legislative mission, the tenth Standing Committee of the National People's Congress had made clear its legislative task of "basically establishing the socialist legal system with Chinese characteristics as the goal and improving legislative quality as the focus".[23] It put emphasis on many legislation programs that were pillars to the system, urgently needed for social realities and satisfied with conditions. Through arduous efforts, this Standing Committee had fixated the successes and experience of reform and opening-up and socialist modernization in the form of law, paid attention to both the economic legislation and social legislation, and emphasized the revision of existing laws while formulating new laws. A lot of important legislation programs were completed one after another, paving the road for a more sound socialist legal system. During its terms, it had deliberated on 106 pieces of drafts of Constitutional amendment, laws, legal interpretations and decisions on related legal issues, 100 of which were adopted.

First, through the amendment to the Constitution, some major theories, thoughts, lines, principles and polices determined by the Sixteenth CPC National Congress were confirmed by the Constitution. This amendment also made clear that the state respect and protect human rights, and protect citizens' property rights and right of succession, which reflected the unity of the Party's proposals and people's will, another important milestone made for China's democracy and rule of law.

Second, the laws intended for national unification and democratic politics were enacted. This Standing Committee enacted the Anti-Secession Law, a move to incorporate the Party and the state's principles and policies on Taiwan into a law and

---

[22] Li Peng, *Report on the Work of the Standing Committee of the National People's Congress*, in the Party Literature Research Office ed., Selection of Important Documents since the Sixteenth CPC National Congress (Vol. 1), Central Party Literature Press, 2005, p. 195.

[23] Wu Bangguo, *Under the Guidance of the Important Thought of Three Represents to Strive for a New Chapter of the People's Congress Work*, in the Party Literature Research Office ed., Selection of Important Documents since the Sixteenth CPC National Congress (Vol. 1), Central Party Literature Press, 2005, p. 233–234.

provide legal guarantee for opposing and deterring Taiwan independence separatist activities and promote China's peaceful reunification. The Law on the Supervision of Standing Committees of People's Congresses was formulated to improve the supervision and supervision procedures and promote an institutionalized, standardized and procedure-based supervision. The Civil Servants Law were also promulgated to better implement the principles and policies on cadres and promote the reform of cadre system.

Third, the construction of economic legal system was advanced in all respects. The Standing Committee enacted the Property Law to define the attribution of property and utilize property to protect the right holder's legitimate rights and improve the legal system on property protection. The Enterprise Bankruptcy Law was enacted to regulate the procedures on bankruptcy and provide a legal system for the enterprise to exit in an orderly manner. The Anti-Monopoly Law established a legal system that conformed with China's economic development, prevented and stopped the monopoly acts, and protected and promoted fair competition. The financial legal system was also enhanced with the promulgation of the Banking Supervision Law and the Law on Anti-Money Laundering and the revision of Law on the People's Bank of China, Commercial Banking Law, and Securities Law. The Corporate Income Tax Law was formulated, Individual Income Tax Law revised, Regulation on Agricultural Tax abolished, all of which contributed to the improvement of taxation law system. The Specialized Farmers' Cooperatives Law promoted the agricultural industrialization. The Renewable Energy Law was formulated and the Energy Conservation Law revised to promote coordinated development of economy and environment.

Fourth, social legislation was also enhanced. The Labor Contract Law and Law on Labor Dispute Mediation and Arbitration were made to regulate labor relations, resolve labor disputes in a timely manner and protect the employees' legitimate rights and interests. The Employment Promotion Law was intended for coordinating economic development with expansion of employment and maintaining social harmony and stability. The Compulsory Education Law, Law on the Protection of Women's Rights and Interests and Law on the Protection of Minors were also revised.

Last, laws that regulated the exercise of administrative power to promote law-based administration were enacted. For example, Administrative Licensing Law was enacted to help establish an administrative management system characterized by regulated behaviors, coordination, fairness, transparency, integrity and efficiency for establishing and developing a unified socialist market. Law on Penalties for Administration of Public Security was made to regulate and secure the law-based performance of public security administration by the public security departments and people's police, protect the legitimate rights and interests of citizens, legal persons and other organizations, and maintain social public order and security.

On March 2008, Wu Bangguo, successor to Li Peng, pointed out in his report of the NPC Standing Committee that the socialist legal system with Chinese characteristics had already been basically established. The Constitution is the core, while the laws are pillars; by incorporating the administrative regulations, local regulations and other normative documents, it consists of seven departments of law and three levels of legal norms.

4.3 Formal Establishment of Socialist Legal System with Chinese Characteristics

The general legislation mission was set out in the Fifteenth CPC National Congress and reiterated in its following congress. In the Seventeenth CPC National Congress, it was proposed to adopt a scientific and democratic manner in the work on legislation for improving the Chinese socialist legal system. On March 19, 2008, Wu stressed in the closing session that "by following the spirit of the 17th Party congress, we should improve the quality of legislation and then ensure that the socialist legal system with Chinese characteristics will be established by 2010 and keep it under continuous improvement".[24] By focusing on this goal, the Standing Committee of the Eleventh NPC had lost no time to enact the laws important and necessary for social and economic development, revise the laws that were no longer compatible with the situations, and carry out initiatives to clean up the laws, urge the relevant legislative authorities to formulate and revise regulations corresponding with the laws, and conduct publicity activities and in-depth research on the theory of socialist legal system with Chinese characteristics.

First, to enact important laws. For example, the Tort Law was enacted to protect the legitimate rights and interests of the persons of the civil law, prevent and sanction tort acts and reduce social frictions. The new Social Insurance Law regulated the relations concerning social insurance, protected the legitimate rights and interests in participating social insurance and the insurance benefits incurred, and hastened the establishment of social security system covering both the residents of rural and urban areas. The People's Mediation Law was promulgated to effectively prevent and resolve social disputes and frictions and enhance social harmony and stability. The NPC Standing Committee also enacted the Circular Economy Promotion Law, State-Owned Assets in Enterprises Law, Food Safety Law, Law on the Mediation and Arbitration of Rural Land Contract Disputes, People's Armed Police Law, Island Protection Law, Vehicle and Vessel Tax Law, Intangible Cultural Heritage Law and Law on the Laws Applicable to Foreign-related Civil Relations.

Second, to continue the revision of existing laws. For example, the Electoral Law was revised to promote the self-improvement and development of socialist election system with Chinese characteristics; and the law on deputies was also enacted to further regulate and secure the law-based performance of the people's congress deputies, give full play to the features and merits of the system of people's congresses. The NPC standing committee also revised the Law on the Organization of the Villagers' Committees, State Compensation Law, Administrative Supervision Law, Soil and Water Conservation Law, State Secrets Protection Law and Military Service Law.

Third, to re-examine the existing laws and regulations in concerted efforts. From the latter half of 2008, the special committees of the NPC and the working agencies of

[24] Wu Bangguo, *Report on the Work of the Standing Committee of the National People's Congress*, Party Literature Research Office ed., *Selection of Important Documents since the Seventeenth CPC National Congress (Vol. 1)*, Central Party Literature Press, 2009, p. 350–351.

its Standing Committee worked in concerted efforts with the State Council, Central Military Commission, Supreme People's Court and Supreme People's Procuratorate to sort out and clean up the existing laws and regulations. According to the data, the Standing Committee made decisions to abolish or revise some laws, which basically addressed the issue in incompatibility, inconsistency and disconnection of law. It also urged the State Council and other state authorities to quickly formulate regulations for the implementation of laws. Based on the arrangements of the NPC Standing Committee, some state authorities also carried out initiatives to clean up regulations and legal interpretations to ensure the compatibility, consistency and connection within the legal system.

Last, to conduct theoretical research and publicity activities. To make preparations in theory, thoughts and public opinions, the Legislative Affairs Committee had been engaged in theoretical research and publicity activities since 2009, including the collection and study of the opinions on establishing and improving legal system by the NPC deputies and staff of the Standing Committee, the collection of opinions of the local people's congresses, the government departments on legal affairs and experts and scholars for guiding and promoting theoretical research and discussions, the preparation of research reports to gradually deepen the understanding of legal system and make theoretical summaries. The Law Committee also convened two meetings on legal system.

To strengthen the work on theoretical research and publicity activities dedicated to legal system, the Legislation Affairs Committee issued the Working Plan on the Theoretical Research and Publicity on the Establishment of Socialist Legal System with Chinese Characteristics, later approved by the NPC Standing Committee. According to the directives of the Standing Committee made following this working plan, the Law Committee and Legislative Affairs Committee convened a forum on socialist legal system in August 2010, and Li Jianguo, deputy Chairman and General Secretary of the Eleventh National People's Congress, laid out the requirements for establishing the socialist legal system as scheduled. Then in November 2010, the Legislative Affairs Committee convened the sixteenth national forum on local legislation, in which Wang Zhaoguo, the deputy Chairman elaborated on the issues concerning the formation of socialist legal system. In November 2011, the NPC Standing Committee held a forum to establishing the system, and Wu Bangguo made a speech on its history, significance, experience and tasks to call for a wave of public opinions and publicity activities. One after another, these forums and leaders' speeches had made a progressive narration and contributed to a rigorous atmosphere for declaring the establishing of the socialist legal system with Chinese characteristics.

By the end of 2010, there were 237 pieces of laws in force including the Constitution, over 690 pieces of administrative regulations and more than 8600 pieces of local regulations, and the work on re-examining the outdated laws, administrative regulations and local regulations were finished with a success. The departments of law that regulated all social relations were complete, the basic and major laws for each department were enacted, the regulations that corresponded with laws were also relatively complete, making a generally harmonious and unified system within itself. On March 3, 2011, Hu Jintao, President of PRC, pointed out at a meeting of party responsible persons that the establishment of the socialist legal system with Chinese characteristics was an important milestone in China's history of socialist legal system construction and a significant symbol of the mature Chinese socialism; it was of great practical significance and far-reaching historical significance.[25] Seven days later, in the Fourth Session of the Eleventh National People's Congress, Wu declared that "a socialist system of laws with Chinese characteristics has been formed which is based on the situation and realities in China; complies with the requirements for reform, opening-up and socialist modernization; represents the will of the Party and the people; is rooted in the Constitution; has several types of laws including laws related to the Constitution, civil laws and commercial laws, as its backbone; and has different levels of legal force, reflected in laws, administrative regulations, and local statutes. There are laws to cover every area of economic, political, cultural, social and ecological development in the country. The legislative goal set forth at the Fifteenth National Congress of the CPC of forming a socialist system of laws with Chinese characteristics by 2010 was attained on schedule."[26]

5 Improvement

5.1 An Analysis of New Trends

Practice is the foundation of law, and practice never stops to evolve. The Chinese socialist legal system is dynamic and open-ended, so it will develop as the socialist practice develops. The legislative task is still arduous, and the work on legislation can only be strengthened,[27] of which the Central Committee has kept a keen awareness. On March 17, 2011, Hu Jintao chaired the meeting of the Standing Committee of the Political Bureau, listened to the report made by the Party Group of the NPC Standing Committee on establishing the socialist legal system. The Central Committee then forwarded this report. According to it, the Central Committee asked for "further improving the socialist legal system with Chinese characteristics, and proving stronger legal guarantee for advancing a moderately prosperous country in all respects and Chinese socialism" on the new starting line.[28]

---

[25] Cited in Li Jianguo, *To Strengthen and Improve Local Legislation for Improving the Socialist Legal System with Chinese Characteristics: A Speech Made in the Sixteenth National Forum On Local Legislation*, National People's Congress of China, No. 22, p.8–12 (2011).

[26] *Report of Wu Bangguo on the Work of the Standing Committee in the Fourth Session of the Eleventh National People's Congress*, People's Daily, March 11, 2011, p. 2.

[27] Wu Bangguo, *The Great Significance and Basic Experience in Forming the Socialist Legal System with Chinese Characteristics*, Qiushi Journal, Vol. 3, 2011.

[28] Cited in Li Jianguo, *To Strengthen and Improve Local Legislation for Improving the Socialist Legal System with Chinese Characteristics: A Speech Made in the Sixteenth National Forum on Local Legislation*, National People's Congress of China, No.22, p.8–12 (2011).

To effectively implement the gist of the Party's guidelines and the arrangements of the NPC Standing Committee, the Law Committee convened a meeting on theoretical work to enhance the initiative of the work on legislation and strive for an in-depth discussion on the regular, long-term and prevalent issues in the work on legislation and the construction of rule of law. The meeting was dedicated to improving the socialist legal system with Chinese characteristics. The Legislative Affairs Committee the made arrangements on resolving the major issues on the theory of socialist legal system with Chinese characteristics. Though it was universally acknowledged that the fruits and achievements were abundant, the mission ahead for a comprehensive socialist legal system was still laborious. China is still at the early stage of socialism and the start of a moderately prosperous country in all respects with incomplete market economic system, continuous reform and transformation and imbalance of economy, culture and society, therefore, it is necessary to grasp the long-term nature and difficulty of this mission from the perspective of strategic importance, and with a strategic vision, clear-headed thinking and innovative minds, pay special attention to, study and actively respond to the new situations and challenges in the work on legislation after the socialist legal system was established.

First, the mission of the work on legislation is changed. After the socialist legal system was established, the mission is to improve it. To be specific, the work on legislation needs to pay more attention on the soundness of institutional design and strive for a more refined and detailed perspective, to focus on the effective implementation of laws and regulations and make it more target-oriented, timely and practicable, and to also pay more attention to the guiding function of legal system to make it a booster to sustainable economic and social development.

Second, the focus of the work on legislation is transformed. After its establishment, the focus of the work on legislation was transformed from the legislation on economy and social affairs to all areas and more to coordinated and sustainable development of economy and society. Of special importance is the legislation on social areas, the innovation in institutions and mechanisms for social administration, and the deepened construction of the cause of society, and the sharing of development fruits with strenuous efforts. In addition, the legislation on ecological civilization should also be strengthened to meet the demands for a resource-conservation and environment-friendly society, and the legal systems on energy and resources conservation and ecological environment protection should also be improved to resolve the conflict between social and economic development and energy and resource protection. Finally, based on the demands raised in the Sixth Plenary Session of the Eleventh CPC National Congress, the legislation on culture should also be enhanced to develop and enrich socialist culture with better legal institutions.

Third, more requirements of the work on legislation are raised. The requirements of the work on legislation has changed from the establishment of a framework to refined development. More and more sticky issues arise as the legislation tends to concern the reform, development and stability, so a once-for-all approach is increasingly impracticable. Moreover, the desire to utter the interest demands through legislation becomes urgent, the consensus is more difficulty to reach, and the requirements for adjusting social relations through legislation are increasingly higher. Therefore, legislation should be more scientific, democratic, target-oriented and practicable with actual quality improvement; legislation should also be refined, detailed and quality to more accurately reflect the objective law of things and balance different interests in a more sound and reasonable way; and furthermore, legislation should quickly respond to and solve the new problems arising from all respects.

Last, new areas are explored in legislation. As the reform and opening-up deepens and economy and society develops quickly, more and more problems are subject to the jurisdiction of legal systems, and increasingly diverse interest relationships are also within the authority of legal systems. The areas subject to legislation are thus expanded. Since legislation has played an important role implementing the Party's decisions and arrangements and advancing all the work of the state under law-based framework, the emerging new situations and new areas call a higher standing, wider vision, in-depth thought and sound planning for the work on legislation, pay close attention to the development and changes of domestic and international situations, keep a keen grasp of these new situations and their problems, and take initiative to study them and propose countermeasures.

5.2 Planning: To Define the Mission and Tasks for Improving Legal System

Fully aware of the new trends after the legal system was established, the Standing Committee of the Eleventh National People's Congress made a comprehensive analysis of the new tasks and challenges in China's construction of rule of law, emphasized the work on legislation should be strengthened and improved, spare more efforts to revising the laws and regulations, enact new laws to meet the demands of social and economic development, and continuously improve the socialist legal system with Chinese characteristics. Its analysis also stressed that the lifeline of law is implementation. The establishment of this legal system resolved the problem of which laws to abide by, the next step is to give more attention to the effective implementation of the Constitution and law to ensure the laws are strictly observed and enforced and any violations will be punishment by law and to safeguard the dignity and authority of the Constitution and law.[29] According to this analysis, the work on legislation should take China's needs of social and economic development as the starting point, focus on the improvement of legislative quality, promote an increasingly complete legal system and provide solid guarantee for effective implementation. The NPC Standing Committee put legislation into the general planning of social and economic development, review the work on legislation by referring to the evolution of reform and opening-up, put forward sound institutional designs to ensure the major decisions and arrangements made by the Party's Central Committee are fully adhered to and

[29] *Report of Wu Bangguo on the Work of the Standing Committee of the National People's Congress*, People's Daily, March 21, 2013, p. 1.

implemented, and spare no efforts to actively respond to and effectively resolve all kinds of problems during economic and social development.

First, to revise and improve existing laws and enact new laws. The establishing of legal system means the provision of primary and basic laws for the state and all the respects of social life, so the focus is changed to revise and improve the existing laws according to the changing practice and new demands. As laid out by the NPC Standing Committee, the new goal and mission for the work on legislation is to timely revise the laws not compatible with reform and opening-up to make them better serve the needs of reform and opening and socialist modernization. Meanwhile, facing the new situations and tasks, new laws should be enacted, especially the laws for securing and improving livelihood. Thus the legislation on social affairs should be strengthened with greater efforts, aiming for the social security law system that gradually incorporates labor, employment, social insurance, social assistance, welfare, education and health. The legislation on finance and taxation is another pivot for adjusting income distribution and takes advantage of fiscal and taxation system's regulation in promoting the transformation of means of economic development.

Second, to take various measures to secure the unification and integration of socialist legal system. As advocated by the NPC Standing Committee, when considering the formulation of new laws, the potential inconsistency between the new laws and existing laws or provisions of these existing laws and the possible revision or abolition of these provisions should be taken into consideration. Consistency should be maintained when the enactment, revision and abolition are carried out at the same time. If not, the laws or provisions of laws should be revised or abolished after the laws, especially the important ones, are enacted. The work on recording and review of normative documents should also be enhanced to address the inconsistency or contradiction between the Constitution and law and the regulations, judicial interpretation and other normative documents and maintain the unification of socialist legal system. The work on evaluating after laws or regulations are formulated should be continued to provide basis for enacting, revising or abolishing laws and regulations and to improve legislative quality. Before the laws or regulations are formulated, sound argumentation should be made to reasonably arrange the legislative programs, accentuate the pivotal legislation, make use of legislative resources and improve legislation quality.

Third, to provide guarantee for implementation of law through the work on legislation. As pointed out by the NPC Standing Committee, the regulations intended to implement the newly enacted or revised laws may be formulated when the draft laws are prepared through coordinated efforts, and published when these laws are issued. Some regulations that fail to be promulgated simultaneously should be subject to following supervision to assure early issuance. The work on legislative interpretation should be strengthened; if the provisions of new laws need more detailed explanations and clarify their applicable basis for new circumstances, the legislative interpretation should be issued to make the articles of law more accurate and detailed and assure the effective implementation of law. If the circumstances are ripe, the work on codification should also be timely carried out to systematize the laws to embrace new situations and changes.

Fourth, to promote scientific and democratic legislation. The NPC Standing Committee has made it clear that more efforts should be made on scientific and democratic legislation. To be specific, the leading role of the people's congress deputies should be respected, and their role in legislation be enhanced. The methods of participation, including symposium, demonstration meeting, hearing, issuance of draft laws and regulations and citizens' sitting in standing committee's meetings and others for scientific and democratic legislation should be explored to improve a sound mechanism for voicing opinions and feedback during legislation. Survey is inseparable from legislation; in this regard, the work on legislative survey should dive deep into the communities to listen to the people and follow the practice in order to improve the efficacy of public participation and to reflect people's wisdom, opinions and realities in legislation.

Last, to carry out in-depth research on legal theory. More and higher requirements are raised to carry out in-depth research on legal theory for improving the Chinese socialist legal system from a new starting line. As clearly stated by the NPC Standing Committee, theoretical research on it should be made to better grasp the overall, long-term and regular problems that affect or restrict the further advancement of the work on legislation. The new ideas and measures should also be made to improve and strengthen the work on legislation through a profound contemplation of new circumstances. The ability to put the theoretical achievements into resolving practical issues should be improved to better serve the legislative decision and provide reliable support for improving legal system.

5.3 Upgrade: To Incorporate Legal System into the Socialism with Chinese Characteristics

On July 1, 2011, in his speech at the meeting commemorating the 90th anniversary of CPC,[30] Hu Jintao made a systemic elaboration of the Chinese socialism, and for the first time, incorporated legal system into it. This move has demonstrated that CPC had been paying attention to rule of law and building China into a socialist law-based country and made the development and improvement of legal system as its pivot in state governance system. His remarks made clear the path and direction for improving the legal system.

Since the founding of PRC, especially since the reform and opening-up, the Party has led the Chinese people to promote the self-reform and development of socialist system, which contributed to a complete set of interconnecting and closely related systems and institutions in economy, politics, culture and social affairs, i.e. the system of people's congresses as China's fundamental political system, the multiparty cooperation and political consultation under the leadership of the CPC, regional ethnic

[30] Hu Jintao, *Speech at A Meeting Commemorating the 90th Anniversary of the Founding of the Communist Party of China*, in Selection of Important Documents of the Party and State since the Fourteenth CPC National Congress (Vol. 1), Central Party School Press, 2015, p. 529–543.

autonomy and community level self-governance as the basic political systems, the socialist legal system with Chinese characteristics, the dominant public ownership with diverse forms of ownership as the basic economic system, and the economic, political, cultural and social institutions established based on these systems. Most of these systems and institutions are established by the Constitution, law and regulations, and their formation, improvement and development are closely related with the construction of legal system. Their relationship can be illustrated in the following two aspects: first, legal system in an important component of Chinese socialist system, which is the relationship between the whole and the part; second, the Chinese socialist legal system is manifested in legal system, which is a relationship between form and contents. Under new historical circumstances, the adherence and improvement of Chinese socialist system and the advantages of socialist system can be realized to a great extent through the construction of rule of law and improvement of legal system, the legal system also needs to advance as the time changes. The key to achieving institutionalization is to legalization, and the key to institutional development is to build a legal system. The legal system, if understood within the framework of Chinese socialism will endow us a wider vision and a more in-depth understanding of the work on legislation, which burdens us with great responsibility, arduous tasks and honor. The work on legislation will never be loosened.

The Chinese socialist system takes its shape as the practice develops, so it should be enriched and improved as new practice are carried out. Under strict adherence to the fundamental political system and basic political and economic systems, our minds should continue to be liberated to promote the reform and innovation of economic, political, cultural and social institutions. And people's enthusiasm, initiative and creativity will be fully mobilized to promote the self-improvement and development of socialist system and to provide a more comprehensive institutional guarantee for the prosperity and long-lasting peace of the Party and the state. The practice develops, so does the legal system, so that it can catch up with the time and reflect the demands of social development. Therefore, we should proceed from China's circumstances and realities, correctly understand and grasp the relationships between adherence and improvement, inheritance and development, stability and change, and spare efforts to improve the socialist legal system with Chinese characteristics to maintain this legal system as the foundation of Chinese socialism, the fruit of innovation for and the guarantee for the prosperity of Chinese socialism.

5.4 *Innovation: New Concepts and Initiatives for Improving Legal System*

The deep-seated problems of the legislative system and institutions will be touched when the work on legislation is strengthened and the socialist legal system with Chinese characteristics is continuously improved from the new starting line after it was established. From early 2011 when its formation was announced to the end of the Eleventh NPC Standing Committee, great efforts have been made to innovate the theoretical research and explorations with a special focus on the sustainability of the work on legislation. New ideas and initiatives were put forward illustrated as follows:

First, to play the role of legislation in promoting development. In the meeting dedicated to the socialist legal system with Chinese characteristics held in March 24, 2011, Wu Bangguo pointed out that "we lose no time to upgrade the experience in reform and opening-up and socialist modernization into law, and formulate and improve the legal system to respond to the new circumstances and new issues arising from reform and opening-up...to give full play to the role of law in regulating, leading, securing and promoting development". On November 3, Li Jianguo also pointed out in the seventeenth national forum on local legislation that "the role of legislation in leading and promoting reform and opening-up and stability should be stimulated...the legislation should be coordinated with the making of reform decision; and legislation should lead and promote the reforms of various areas, give strong impetus for deepening reform, and provide strong guarantee for scientific development". In the following national forum on local legislation convened September 3, 2012, Wang Zhaoguo stressed that "we should deepen our understanding of law's functions, and give more attention to taking advantage of law to lead and advance reform and development", "strive for aligning the legislation with the making of reform decision, strengthen the role of legislation in serving reform and development, comprehensively take advantage of various functions of law, continuously improve the system and institutions, and spare efforts to make law lead development and promote reform."

The emphasis on the role of legislation in promoting reform and opening-up is the natural result of an evolving understanding of law's functions and the relation between law and practice, and is also the new demand raised as China's modernization is gaining momentum, state systems become more complete, new situations arise, and new tasks and challenges confront the reform and opening-up. Over 30 years' reform and opening-up, the socialist modernization has made tremendous success and achievements and accumulated massive experience from practice, especially on the formation of legal system, which has resolved the fundamental, overall and long-term problem in national development and subject all the causes of the state progress to the socialist legal system. In this case, the conditions are ripe and the law of development can also be correctly grasped, which makes it impossible to set a scientific development goal and carry out top design and master planning of the work on legislation; it is also necessary and practical to play the role of legislation in leading and promoting reform and development when reflecting on the experience from practice.

Second, to play the leading role of NPC and its Standing Committee. In the same meeting, Wu Bangguo said "the NPC and its Standing Committee should give full play to its role as the top legislator in China, exercise the legislative power according to law, strengthen the organization and coordination of the work on legislation, urge relevant authorities to study the major difficulties in legislation, innovate the working methods, improve the working mechanism for the work on legislation, improve the legislator's organization and capabilities, and continuously improve the quality and expertise in legislation." Li Jianguo also remarked, "facing new circumstances and problems, we should stick to the requirements of the Party's Central Committee and reflect on how to better play the leading role of the people's congress and its standing committee in the work on legislation. Under the leadership of the Party committee at the same level, the people's congress and its standing committee should fully play its role as a legislative authority, take sound steps to strengthen the coordination of legislation, and strive for the implementation of legislative programs and plan." Wang Zhaoguo made it further by stressing that "to enact laws is an important function and power of the people's congress and its standing committee granted by the Constitution. It is especially meaningful to adhere to and improve the system of people's congresses and strengthen the work on legislation in new circumstances by enhancing the party's leadership and giving full play to the leading role of people's congress and its standing committee.", "the leading role of the people's congress deputies should be respected", "its leading role should be continuously strengthened", and "the special committees and the standing committee's agencies should actively participate in, guide and supervise the drafting of laws and regulations."

The emphasis on the leading role of people's congress and its standing committee is made to respond to the increasing difficulty, demands and burden of legislation and the practical requirement for improving legislative system and institutions. Since the primary and basic laws are readily made after the establishment of legal system, the laws and regulations subject to urgent revision or formulation concerned the interests of different parties and the working mechanism or institutions od various departments, so their legislation is difficulty. The pursuit of interests and power but evasion of responsibility often make it difficult to resolve the practical issues, which lead to lower practicability and efficiency in legislation. As a result, the laws that are urgently needed or revised cannot be enacted or revised, the regulations that correspond with the laws are delayed, and some laws and regulations are put on the shelf. The emphasis on the leading role of the people's congress and its standing committee is the result of a problem-based approach which aims to resolve the problems in legislative mechanism and institutions.

In general, the NPC Standing Committee makes an in-depth study on the new circumstances arising after the establishment of legal system, adapts to the changes of legislative goal, focus and areas, consolidate the consensus, carries out legislative planning and lays the foundation for the work on legislation in the new period. Against this backdrop, the NPC and its Standing Committee have paid attention to the role of legislation in leading and promoting practice and their leading role in legislation, and make great strides in pushing forward the implementation of the legal system. First, the revision and improvement of existing laws are accentuated, and the Criminal Procedure Law, Criminal Law, Civil Procedure Law, Individual Income Tax Law, Military Service Law, Occupational Disease Prevention Law, Law on Resident Identity Cards, Law on the Promotion of Clean Production and other important laws. Second, the NPC and its Standing Committee took every opportunity to enact new laws to respond to the needs of social and economic development, including the Administrative Compulsion Law, Intangible Cultural Heritage Law,

Vehicle and Vessel Tax Law, Exit and Entry Administration Law, Military Insurance Law and others. Third, the NPC and its Standing Committee made new achievements in promoting scientific and democratic legislation and proactively carried out argumentation before legislation and review after legislation, which provided solid basis for determining legislative programs and improving legal system. Fourth, the NPC and its Standing Committee paid special attention to the effective implementation of law, coordinated to simultaneous revision of various laws, strengthened the work on legal interpretation and recording and review of normative documents, guided and supervised the State Council, local people's congresses and their standing committees to formulate corresponding regulations in a timely manner, guided and supervised the activities in re-examining the obsolete administrative regulations and local regulations for better implementation of Administrative Compulsion Law, urged the Supreme People's Court and Supreme People's Procuratorate to clean up the judicial interpretations, and made active explorations for connecting legislation with supervision.

Meanwhile, the local people's congresses and their standing committees also played their leading role in the work on legislation, spared efforts to promote scientific and democratic legislation and dedicated themselves to improving the legal system. For example, they have strengthened economic legislation to better serve the transformation of economic development and industrial structuring, put emphasis on social legislation to secure and improve people's livelihood and innovate social administration with more efforts, and paid special attention to ecological legislation to ensure the sustainable social and economic development. To ensure the effective implementation of law, they have also promulgated regulations, carried out inspections, reviewed special working reports, and cleaned up local regulations that contravened the Administration Compulsion Law. Their work and efforts are inseparable from the dedication to improving the socialist legal system.

5.5 *Great Strides and New Progress in Legislation*

As the Chinese socialism entered a new era, the socialist legal system is also confronted with new circumstances and assigned with new goals and missions. Since the Eighteenth CPC National Congress, the Party's Central Committee with Xi Jinping as the core highly valued the socialist rule of law, paid keen attention to adhering to and developing Chinese socialist system, promoted the modernization of state governance system and capabilities, put forward the overall law-based governance and made detailed arrangements for it. According to the congress's decision and arrangements, Zhang Dejiang, the Chairman of the NPC Standing Committee, stressed that "we should continuously improve the socialist legal system, and provide a stronger legal guarantee for the moderately prosperous country in all respects and the deepening of reform and opening-up. The role of legislation in leading and promoting reform and development and the legislation in key areas should be strengthened to better enhance the economic, political, cultural, social and ecological progress. The organization and coordination in the work on legislation should also be improved to expand channels for people's participation in legislation, improve legislation quality, and secure that the laws adopted better reflect the Party's proposals and people's will." Guided by the Xi Jinping Thought on Socialism with Chinese Characteristics for a New Era, the NPC and its Standing Committee has been dedicated to implementing the major decisions and arrangements made by the Party's Central Committee and unswervingly adhered to the Five-sphere Integrated Plan and coordinated the plan of Four-pronged Comprehensive Strategy to continue innovative initiatives and make great strides and new progress in the work on legislation, which are abundant, important and quickly made, opening a new chapter of the work on legislation for the new era.

First, to amend the Constitution in a timely manner to make available a sound legal system for the implementation of the Constitution. The Constitutional amendment adopted in the First Session of the Thirteenth National People's Congress included the important ideas, lines, principles and policies proposed in the Party's congress, especially the Xi Jinping Thought on Socialism with Chinese Characteristics for a New Era into the state's fundamental law, made adjustments to the overall plan for building Chinese socialism and the second centenary goal, improved the measures for rule of law and Constitution's implementation and enriched the adherence to and advancement of the Party's overall leadership. The change of provisions on the president's term of office and addition of provisions on the commission of supervision have demonstrated the new achievements, experience and requirements made from the causes of the Party and the state, which have provided strong legal guarantee for advancing and developing Chinese socialism in the new era. The legal systems that are intended to enforce the Constitution are also continuously improved. For example, the setup of the National Constitution Day was aimed to enhance the awareness of Constitution and spread the spirits of Constitution among the public. The practice of public pledge of allegiance to the Constitution calls for steadfast loyalty to the Constitution, country and people. The special pardons as prescribed in the Constitution made it possible to issue two consecutive decisions to release some prisoners. The Law on National Medals and Titles of Honor was enacted to implement the provision of the Constitution on national medals and titles of honor. To commemorate the 70th anniversary of PRC, the decision of granting national medals and titles of honor were made in the Thirteenth Meeting of the Standing Committee of the Thirteenth National People's Congress, and Xi Jinping then signed the presidential order to grant 42 people with national medals and titles of honor, the first time since the 1982 Constitution came into force, and also an important step for fully advancing the Constitution. It was of both historical and practical significance. The National Anthem Law, along with the already adopted National Flag Law and National Emblem Law, are intended to secure the national symbols and dignity as required by the Constitution. The NPC and its Standing Committee also made decisions to assign the responsibilities of the Law Committee to the Constitution and Law Committee and burden it with the responsibilities of advancing the implementation of the Constitution, making Constitutional interpretations, carrying out constitutional review, enhancing supervision of the enforcement of the Constitution and supporting the publicity of the Constitution.

Second, to focus on the legislation in key areas and accelerate the readiness of a complete normative system. The NPC and its Standing Committee have made important progress in legislation of national security. The National Security Law, Anti-Espionage Law, Anti-Terrorism Law, National Defense Traffic Law, Cyber Security Law, Law on Exploration for and Development of Resources in the Deep Seabed Area and Nuclear Safety Law were consecutively adopted and the Criminal Law revised to safeguard the national core interests and other important interests. The compilation of Civil Code was also actively promoted. To compile the Civil Code was a major legislative task laid out in the Fourth Plenary Session of the CPC Central Committee. The adoption of the General Principles of Civil Law in the Fifth Session of the Twelfth National People's Congress marked the first step to accomplish this task. The Thirteenth National People's Congress continued this task and hastened the compilation of the parts of Civil Code, and then submitted a draft Civil Code divided into 6 parts with 1034 articles to the Standing Committee for deliberation. Now all the parties concerned in this task are working arduously to ensure that a socialist Civil Code with a scientific system, a rigorous structure, reasonable standards and consistency would be enacted by 2020. The NPC and its Standing Committee have also been dedicated to enhancing the legislation in ecology and environment protection. The Environment Protection Law, Law on the Prevention and Control of Air Pollution, Marine Environment Protection Law, Law on the Prevention and Control of Water Pollution were successively revised, and the public interest litigation system for ecology, environment and resource protection was also established, both of which are initiatives to try to set up the strictest ecological and environmental protection system of law. In the special meeting purported to put into practice the Xi Jinping thought on ecological civilization and the arrangements of the Party's Central Committee on pollution prevention and control convened by the NPC Standing Committee, the inspection report on the implementation of the Law on the Prevention and Control of Air Pollution was deliberated, questions were asked, and the Resolution on Comprehensively Strengthening Ecological Environment Protection and Promoting the Fight of Pollution Prevention and Control was issued. There efforts to devoted to using the strictest institutions and laws to protect the ecology and environment, establishing a more closely knit legal system, supervising all the parties concerned to assume their legal responsibilities in this regard, and making the legal institutions rigid and untouchable. The Law on the Prevention and Control of Soil Pollution was enacted to resolutely contain the worsening of soil and carry out the work on preventing and controlling pollution in soil, water, air, sound, slag and light with joint efforts. The legislation in culture has made breakthroughs. The Law on the Guarantee of Public Cultural Services, Film Industry Promotion Law and Public Libraries Law were enacted to accelerate a sound cultural law system that inspire cultural vitality and safeguard people's rights and interests in culture. The NPC and its Standing Committee also strengthened the legislation in social affairs and people's livelihood. The Charity Law, Anti-Domestic Violence Law, Special Equipment Safety Law, Traditional Chinese Medicine Law, Vaccine Administration

Law were enacted, and the Food Safety Law, Population and Family Planning Law, Red Cross Law, Law on the Promotion of Privately-run Schools and Drug Administration Law were amended, helping to protect the legitimate rights and interests of the people. The legislation in taxation has been actively advanced. The Environmental Protection Tax Law, Vessel Tonnage Tax Law, Cultivated Land Occupation Tax Law, Vehicle Purchase Tax Law and Natural Resources Tax Law were enacted to adhere to the principle of statutory taxation.

Since the First Session of the Thirteenth National People's Congress in particular, the NPC and its Standing Committee have enacted the Foreign Investment Law and E-Commerce Law, and revised Rural Land Contract Law and Land Administration Law to promote quality development. They have revised the Criminal Procedure Law, Organization Law of the People's Courts Organization Law of the People's Procuratorates, formulated the Law on International Criminal Judicial Assistance and made several decisions to build a better litigation system and advance reform of judicial system. They have also revised the Public Servants Law, Judges Law and Public Prosecutors Law and promulgated the Regulation on Fire and Rescue Ranks to improve the law on national public servants.

Third, to adapt legislation to reform and social and economic development to ensure the law serves reform in all respects. First, if the implementation of reform measures needs new legislation, the NPC and its Standing Committee will promote the work on such new laws and make relevant decisions in a timely manner. For example, to carry out the major decisions and arrangements of the Party's Central Committee on deepening the supervisory institution reform, the NPC and its Standing Committee made decisions on the pilot programs in Beijing, Shanxi and Zhejiang and then the nation-wide programs, providing support for the implementation of pilot programs for reform. The NPC and its Standing Committee also amended the Constitution, added provisions on the supervision committees, enacted the Supervision Law, and innovated and improved the state's supervisory institutions to establish a full coverage of supervision, strengthen the supervision over the exercise of public power by the public servants and push forward the work on anti-corruption. The Individual Income Tax Law was also revised to transform China's taxation on personal income from a classification-based one to a combination of classification and integration to better play its role in adjusting income and promoting social and economic development. Second, the NPC and its Standing Committee timely revised or abolished the laws not in line with reform. For example, to cater for reform, the NPC and its Standing Committee adopted an overall approach to revise certain provisions of laws, deliberated on 22 decisions of revision, revised 142 pieces of laws and continued the reforms in administrative approval, professional qualification and the agencies of the State Council to stimulate market and social vitality. The relevant parties are not studying the modification of existing legal provisions and the transfer of administrative responsibilities before relevant laws were revised to ensure the agency reform is carried out according to law. The NPC and its Standing Committee also proactively revised the law if the circumstances for revision are mature. Third, the NPC and its Standing Committee timely made decisions to grant pilot programs if the circumstances do not permit. The NPC Standing Committee has issued 27 authorization decisions since the Eighteenth CPC National Congress, including the free trade pilot zone, administrative approval institution reform, agricultural collective land use right reform, financial institution, judicial institution and marine police. It authorized relevant parties to adjust the implementation of laws temporarily or carry out pilot programs according to law. In addition, the NPC Standing Committee has strictly observed both the rule of law and rule of virtue, and highly valued the transformation of core socialist values into legal spirits and principles. General Principles of Civil Law, Ninth Amendment to Criminal Law, Ant-domestic Violence Law, Law on the Guarantee of Public Cultural Services, Film Industry Promotion Law, National Anthem Law and others manifested the Chinese traditional culture, ethics, and moral principles and absorbed the core socialist values. In particular, the Law on the Protection of Heroes and Martyrs focused on the punishment on distorting, vilifying, insulting or slandering heroes and martyrs, and by resolutely resisting historical nihilism, inheriting and carrying forward the spirit of heroes and martyrs and patriotism across the nation to gather strong spiritual strength for achieving the Two Centenary Goal and the realization of Chinese dream.

Fourth, to deepen legislation in a scientific, democratic and law-based manner for better legislation quality. The Standing Committee has strengthened organization and coordination and played the leading role of people's congress and its standing committee in the work on legislation. Since 2015, the Standing Committee had submitted important law drafts to the National People's Congress for deliberation five consecutive years. The special committees and working agencies for Standing Committee were set up to organize the law drafting, and they have carried out or submitted for deliberation for over 70 pieces. The NPC and its Standing Committee have been dedicated to expressing, balancing and adjusting social interests and tried their best to reach the legislative consensus. They have held meetings to argue about the potential legislative projects and coordinate the major interests involved in legislation, and also introduced third-party agency to review the important legislative matters. Experts have been introduced as advisors during legislation, the liaison office for legislation in the communities established one by one, nearly a hundred draft laws for deliberation by the Standing Committee disclosed to the public. From Tourism Law, the first one adopted by the Twelfth National People's Congress, the NPC and its Standing Committee has carried out a review system of the law drafts in order to make legislation more scientific and ensure the validity, feasibility and effectiveness of legal provisions.

Fifth, to actively advance the recording and review of normative documents to maintain the unification of socialist legal system. The NPC Standing Committee has been actively engaged in connecting the recording of normative documents with review system, issued the working rules on the work in recording and review and established a national recording and review platform to make sure that each normative document is recorded, each recorded one is reviewed and each reviewed one is subject to corrections if any mistakes are found. The work on recording and review of normative documents is unceasingly enhanced. During the term of the Twelfth National People's Congress, the NPC and its Standing Committee deliberated on, for the first time, the report on the work of recording and review of normative documents, accepted 4778 normative documents for recording and review, proactively reviewed 188 administrative regulations and judicial interpretations, inspected the local regulations with special focus on certain areas, studied 1527 review suggestions submitted by citizens and other organizations and urged for corrections by legislative authorities if any inconsistency or inappropriateness are found. All of these efforts have guaranteed the effective implementation of the Party's Central Committee's orders and decisions, and the Constitution and Law to safeguard the unification of China's legal system. In the first year of the Thirteenth National People Congress, its Standing Committee accepted 1238 pieces of normative documents, including administrative regulations, local regulations and judicial interpretations for recording and review; all the normative documents were subject to recording and review system. It also accepted 1229 letters on review suggestions from citizens and organizations, 112 of which are subject to the Standing Committee's recording and review. The Legislative Affairs Committee studied the problems in the normative documents as suggested, communicated with the legislative authorities and issued written suggestions to enhance the work on supervision and correction of normative documents. Based on the decision of the Party's Central Committee, the Standing Committee has been making efforts to strengthen the implementation and supervision of the Constitution, actively promoted constitutional review, and enhanced the recording and review system and its expertise.

The year of 2018, the first year of the new people's congresses at all levels, the 40th anniversary of reform and opening-up, initiated the implementation of the Party's Nineteenth National Congress in all respects. As the causes of the Party and state flourish, new higher demands are raised for the work of the people's congress and legislation. To promote local legislation as time changes, the NPC Standing Committee has convened two important meetings on legislation on September 7 in Beijing and September 15 in Zhejiang. Li Zhanshu, successor to Zhang Dejiang, made speeches on implementing Xi Jinping's new ideas, concepts and strategies on advancing comprehensive rule of law, and put forward his arrangements and requirements on strengthening and improving the work on legislation for the new era and promoting the development of legislation. His remarks can be summarized into five points: first, to adhere to the Party's leadership in the work on legislation; second, to continue playing the role of the people's congress and its standing committee in the work on legislation; third, to hasten the work on legislation with a sense of responsibility and great initiative; fourth, to support reform and guarantee reform with the rule of law; fifth, to promote legislation in a scientific, democratic and law-based manner to continuously improve legislation quality. Survey and research are also inseparable; sixth, to enhance the implementation and supervision of the Constitution and maintain the unification of socialist legal system.

The year of 2019 marks the 70th anniversary of PRC, the 40th anniversary of the establishment of standing committees in the people's congresses at or above the county level and the grant of local legislative power to the provincial people's congresses and the standing committees. The NPC Standing Committee also convened two meetings on July 18 and September 4 to commemorate the latter two anniversaries. In his speeches, Li emphasized the importance of the guidance of Xi Jinping Thought on Socialism with Chinese Characteristics for a New Era, the upholding of the Party's leadership in the work on legislation, the advancement of the people's congress work on legislation for the new era, and improvement of legislation quality. He also directed that the people's congress and its standing committee should make each legislation with a solid foundation to better serve the social and economic development and respond to challenges in reform. Li's remarks have given directives to the following specific initiatives for the work in legislation and improving legal system.

China's legislature is now working, according to the decisions and arrangements of the Party's Central Committee, for implementing the new ideas, concepts and strategies of Xi Jinping on advancing comprehensive rule of law, especially his important elaborations on legislation, carrying forward the work on legislation as time changes, and writing a new chapter with a sense of responsibility and new initiatives to celebrate the 70 anniversary of PRC with brilliant achievements.

6 Conditions for Its Inception, Establishment and Improvement

In the socialist legal system with Chinese characteristics, the Constitution is the center, law is the pillar, and the administrative and local regulations are important components. The laws about the Constitution, civil and commercial laws, administrative laws, economic laws, social laws, criminal laws, litigation and non-litigation procedure laws are integrated into one system. The conditions for its inception, establishment and improvement can be summarized as follows.

First, the strong Party's leadership provides the political guarantee, especially the correct decisions on socialist democratic legal system made by several generations of the leadership group based on China's actual circumstances. Jiang Zemin ever made an illuminating idea when concluding the Party's history that two changes had been made after the Party's revolution, development and reform: it has changed from a party that led Chinese power to take state power to one that has been leading Chinese people to exercise such state power permanently; second, its has been transformed from a party that led the state construction with external blockade and planned economy to one that engages opening-up and developing socialist market economy. By following the changes of the time, the party's tasks and circumstances of governance, it has adapted itself to the need for building the socialist democratic legal system, made every opportune major decision, and proposed the ideas of law-based work, governance and administration, through which the understanding of the socialist legal system has been deepened. As proven by practice, only the Party's leadership and unwavering adherence to the fundamental principle of rule of law can the socialist legal system form and develop by following the correct political direction, stick to China's circumstances and realities and reflect the fundamental rights and interests of the majority of people.

Second, the theoretical system has provided guidance for the inception, formation and improvement of the Chinese socialist legal system. After the Third Plenary Session of the Eleventh CPC Central Committee, the second generation of leadership group with Deng Xiaoping as the core explicitly put forward the mission of "enhancing socialist democracy and improving the socialist rule by law", determined the principles for socialist legal system, i.e. there were laws to abide by, observed and enforced, and any violations would be punished, which later was developed as an important part of Deng Xiaoping Thought on legal system. The third general of leadership group with Jiang Zemin as the core established the fundamental principle of rule of law and building China into a socialist law-based country during the reform and opening-up in all areas and socialist modernization, which was then incorporated into the Theory of Three Represents. During his term, the general legislative mission of establishing the Chinese socialist legal system by 2010 was laid out. The Party's Central Committee with Hu Jintao as the core adhered to the Deng Xiaoping Thought and the Theory of Three Represents, proposed the Scientific Outlook on Development, put emphasis on the integration of Party's leadership, people's position as masters of the country and rule of law, continued to r improve the methods for leadership and governance, persisted in law-based administration, took lead in legislation and guaranteed the enforcement of law to promote the institutionalization and standardization in national economy, politics, culture and social life. During his term, the ideas, systems and procedures of rule of law have secured the successful state governance under the Party's leadership, and the fundamental principle of rule of law has been carried out with solid theoretical and practical basis. Since the Eighteenth CPC National Congress, the Party' Central Committee with Xi Jinping as the core has led the whole party and people of all ethnic groups to forge ahead and make historical achievements and transformations of the causes of the Party and state, which ushered Chinese socialism into a new era. The Chinese Communist members led by Xi Jinping has contributed to the formation of Xi Jinping Thought on Socialism with Chinese Characteristics for a New Era with unprecedented theoretical innovation, superb political wisdom and insightful vision, which was later defined as the guiding principle of the Party that should be always adhered to in the Nineteenth CPC National Congress and incorporated in the Constitution as the major guidance in national political and social life. Xi Jinping addressed the question of positioning, planning and practicing rule of law with a view to the long-lasting peace and stability of the Party and state, advanced the comprehensive rule of law into the Four-pronged Comprehensive Strategy, and made the historical, decisive and overall transformation of rule of law construction in China and contributed to the achievements in major theoretical, practical and institutional innovation. The new ideas, thoughts and strategies put forward by him have laid out the guiding principles, path, reliable force, working planning, major tasks and important measures for advancing law-based governance in all respects, and answered the questions of what banner should raise, which path should follow, what kind of law-based country should aim for, how to build law-based country, and turned a new chapter for comprehensive rule of law. The socialist legal system with Chinese characteristics has been firmly and steadfastly advanced under the guidance of Chinese socialist theoretical system.

Third, the Chinese socialist construction has provided inexhaustible supply of strength from practice. Law comes from practice. As Peng Zhen ever said, "does law serve the practice or *vice versa*? Who is the mother and who is the son? Practice makes law, so practice is the mother, and law is the son. Law has its own system and logic, but it should proceed from practice and be subject to the test of practice." Under the Party's guidance, Chinese people of all ethnic groups, through various methods and channels, manage state affairs and social, economic and cultural affairs according to law, and devote themselves to the causes on reform and development and socialist modernization, which provides practical foundation for its formation. It comes from and lives with reform and opening and socialist modernization. The further the reform and opening and socialist modernization advances, the more profound changes the social and economic development make, the more urgent the requirements to improve the legal system, and the more solid the foundation on which the legal system is built. Meanwhile, the relationship between the stability of law and instability of reform will be properly handled in improving the legal system, which will affirm the success and consolidate the fruits of reform and opening-up and promote the role of legislation in leading and stimulating reform and development to ensure that every reform decision is made according to law.

Fourth, the unremitting efforts made by generations of the legislators provided intellectual support. In the past 70 years, especially in the past 40 years when the reform and opening-up was started, generations of legislators have dedicated themselves to advancing socialist democracy and strengthening socialist legal system with a great sense of responsibility to the Party, Chinese people and history. Their persistence in these aspirations, dedication without complaints and concerted efforts have made enduring contributions to the establishment and improvement of the socialist legal system. In the legislative activities over the past 40 years, China has nurtured a lot of capable legislators, who directly participated in and witnessed the establishment and improvement of the socialist legal system with Chinese characteristics and also were trained and developed in this process.

7 Main Features

The features in the inception, establishment and improvement of socialist legal system with Chinese characteristics are salient illustrated as follows:

First, it is proposed, established and improved along with the reform and opening-up. In the beginning of reform and opening-up when the country was left with ruins, it was in urgent need of restoring state order, maintaining a peaceful and united political environment, developing socialist democracy and advancing reform and opening-up. In the Second Plenary Session of the Fifth National People's Congress, the adoption of Electoral Law, Local Organization Law, Organization Law of the People's Courts, Organization Law of the People's Procuratorates, Criminal Law, Criminal Procedure

Law, and Sino-Foreign Equity Joint Venture Enterprise Law, all of which concerned the state political system, criminal justice and opening-up, initiated the large-scale legislation. It should also be noticed that the contradictions and problems that have risen during the development of western countries in the past several hundred years also emerged in the reform and opening-up, which presented the work on legislation with unprecedented complexity and difficulty. For example, the enactment of Property Law was confronted with tremendous difficulty for it was highly political and professional and involved with policies. From its inception to adoption, the NPC and its Standing Committee had held, except for the ones dedicated to the property part of draft civil codes, over a hundred meetings and forums to listen to the opinions from all fields and make endless revisions, which cost 13 years and 7 deliberations for adoption. On that account, the work on legislation should properly handle the relationship of reform, development and stability when dealing with the contradictions and problems that occur during the reform and opening-up, and take initiative to address the important issues and difficulties arising from legislation. To adhere to the principle of coordinating legislation with reform means that a law can be enacted if the experience accumulated from practice can be collectively expressed in the form of law; if not, the principles should be ascertained in case any provisions will be turned to, and the space for reform should also be reserved when defining these principles for future legislation. To take the example of establishing an orderly exit system of law for enterprises, the Enterprise Bankruptcy Law (for Trial Implementation) was adopted for the bankruptcy of the wholly-owned enterprises in 1986. As the state-owned enterprise reform went further and the rise of other ownerships, the NPC Standing Committee made a summary of experience, and enacted a new practicable Enterprise Bankruptcy Law applicable to all kinds of organizations and enterprises of all ownerships, which regulated the bankruptcy procedures, addressed the significant issues in satisfying the employee's wages and social insurance premiums first and maintained the legitimate rights and interests of employees. In addition, the formulation of certain pushed forward the reform measures, for example, the Social Insurance Law contributed to the reform on transferring the old-age insurance.

Second, it was proposed, established and improved according to the plans, schedules and focuses. The work on legislation is always carried out based on the legislative planning and annual legislative tasks in line with the priorities of the Party and state. To coordinate the formulation of urgently needed laws, the Law Committee suggested a five-year legislation plan in June 1988. Three years later, the Standing Committee of the Seventh National People's Congress made a legislative plan for the first time and planned for the legislation more than 1 year before its term expired. The Standing Committee of the Eighth National People's Congress made a lot of legislative programs in its plan to fulfil the goal of establishing and improving the socialist market economic system as advocated by the Party's Central Committee. From the beginning of 1993 to the end of 1997, in 82 laws enacted by the NPC and its Standing Committee, 36 were about market economy. The Standing Committee of the Ninth National People's Congress made legislative plans and annual legislative schedule to complete the general goal of establishing the socialist legal system with Chinese characteristics put forward in the Fifteenth CPC National Congress, which stepped up the work on legislation. The standing committees of the tenth and eleventh National People's Congress also made legislative plans and annual legislative schedules, and focused on enacting the laws to promote scientific development and building a socialist harmonious society. For example, the Renewable Energy Law, Law on the Promotion of Circular Economy and other laws were intended for scientific development, while the adoption of Labor Contract Law, Employment Promotion Law and Law on Labor Dispute Mediation and Arbitration Law in 2007 were for social development.

Standing in the new starting line, the legislative plan of the Standing Committee of the Twelfth National People's Congress was intended to improve legislative quality, continued to improve the socialist legal system, and focused on the Five-sphere Integrated Plan. It laid down the legislative programs dedicated to promoting the transformation of means of economic development, following the Chinese socialist path, securing and ameliorating people's livelihood, advancing the prosperity of socialist culture and deepening ecological progress. In these 68 legislative programs, there were 47 level-1 programs, 21 level-2 programs. It also put forward some legislative programs for discussion. In the third and fourth plenary sessions of the Eighteenth CPC Central Committee the decision to fully deepen reform and opening-up and advance the rule of law was made and a lot of reform measures were also put forward. To implement these reform measures, the Standing Committee of the Twelfth National People's Congress adjusted its legislative plan by increasing the legislative programs from 68 to 102. After reporting it to the Party's Central Committee, the changed legislative plan was issued and published by the CPC General Office, the first move of its kind in NPC's history.

As Chinese socialism has entered a new era, the vision for deepening and expanding reform and opening-up was renewed in the Nineteenth CPC National Congress by standing on a higher starting point. A lot of important reform measures and tasks were laid out in this conference. Then the legislative plan made by the Standing Committee of the Thirteenth National People's Congress incorporated the concerned reform measures into key programs, accounting for 85% of its total legislative programs. It also laid out some principles for future legislation. For example, the laws to be enacted, revised or abolished, or the decisions awaiting the NPC Standing Committee to make for the purpose of deepening reform in all respects would be deliberated in a proper timing, which retained flexibility for the changes of circumstances and tasks in the following 5 years. This was the first time that the principles of prospective arrangements in a legislative plan were laid down when reform was concerned, making a tighter connection between legislative plan and the reform measure of the Party's Central Committee.

Third, as a multi-tiered legal system, its inception, formation and improvement has been advanced by different legislators. To meet the needs of reform and opening-up, the laws, administrative regulations and local regulations have been promulgated in a coordinated manner. The expansion of national legislative power from the National People's Congress in 1954 Constitution to the NPC Standing Committee in 1982, and the grant of State Council with legislative power in administrative regulations have also confirmed the legislative power in local regulations of the people's congress and its standing committee of the province, national autonomous area and municipality as prescribed in 1979 Local Organization Law. Such power was then granted to the people's congress and its standing committee of larger cities in the following revised Local Organization Law. The 2000 Law on Legislation made provisions to specify the unified but multi-tiered legislative system. Its revised version in 2015 granted legislative power to the cities with subordinate districts. Different legislators at their corresponding levels work towards a better socialist legal system with Chinese characteristics according to the division of authorities and responsibilities. The socialist practice has proven the practicability of such unified but multi-tiered system because it not only maintains the unity of national legal system for better carrying out the tasks of the Party and state, but also takes care of the regional differences to better cater for the comprehensive social and economic development. It also guarantees the smooth progress of reform and opening-up and accelerates the construction of legal system.

8 Achievements

Since the founding of PRC, especially over the past 40 years since the reform and opening-up was initiated, the NPC and its Stand Committee have been adhering to the strong Party's leadership, dedicated to the central tasks of the Party and state and the work with focus in different phases, and carried out pioneering work on legislation. It is a very extraordinary history of development, which is also in line with the inception, establishment and improvement of the socialist legal system with Chinese characteristics. The achievements made during this period can be summarized as follows:

First, the legislative goals are more specific.

As advocated in the Third Plenary Session of the Eleventh CPC Central Committee, "in order to safeguard people's democracy, it is imperative to strengthen the socialist legal system so that democracy is systematized and written into law in such a way as to ensure the stability, continuity and full authority of this democratic system and these laws; there must be laws for people to follow, these laws must be observed, their enforcement must be strict and law breakers must be dealt with. From now on, legislative work should have an important place on the agenda of the National People's Congress and its Standing Committee." It was a declaration on the democratic legal system especially the work on legislation. The Chinese Communist members have been dedicated to exploring and strengthening the construction of socialist democratic rule by law, and made unwavering efforts to realize the general goal of gradually establishing and improving the socialist legal system with Chinese characteristics.

When elaborating the concept of systemization of law, Peng said, "in human history, once the law comes out, it will evolve into a system and aspire for more independence. When enacting laws, we have to consider the system and logic of law, and prevent the contradiction in law, such as some provisions in A law contravenes the those of B law", "when the production force and relationship develops, the society and reality will change accordingly, and law should change, the system of law should also change".

From the party congress in 1982 to the one held in 1995, as the reform of economic institutions and socialist democratic rule of law continued to develop in particular, the Central Committee deepened its understanding of legal system. As the goal of establishing socialist market economic institution was proposed, the legal system was met with new demands. From "establishing a legal system for socialist market economy", "generally establishing a framework of legal system for socialist market economy", to "establishing an initial legal system for socialist market economy", and then to "gradually establishing a legal system for socialist market economy", the evolution of socialist legal system demonstrated its adaptation to socialist market economic development. Through concerted efforts, by the end of 1996 and the beginning of 1997, "we have made important progress in establishing a legal system for socialist market economy", and "a framework of legal system for socialist market economy was set ready", which laid the foundation for the Party's Central Committee to plan the socialist legal system with Chinese characteristics.

From the proposal of the overall legislative mission in 1997, it has been reiterated in the successive Party's national congresses and was declared a success in 2011, which marked the tremendous achievement in the history of China's rule of law.

To take the success as the starting point, in the Eighteenth CPC National Congress, another new objective that the Chinese socialist legal system needed refining was laid out, while the focus on legislation in key areas and expansion of people's participation in legislation in an orderly manner were highlighted. In the Third Plenary Session of the Eighteenth CPC Central Committee, the goal of compressively deepening reform was to improve and develop the Chinese socialist system, and modernize the state governance system and capacity. New requirements of the work on legislation were also proposed as new goal came out. It was emphasized that the mechanism for legislative drafting, argument, coordination and deliberation should be consolidated to improve the quality of legislation and prevent institutionalized local protectionism and departmental interests. In its following session, the objective in comprehensively advancing the law-based governance was the establishment of a socialist rule of law system with Chinese characteristics and the building of China into a socialist rule of law country. This means that under the Party's leadership, it needed to uphold socialism with Chinese characteristics; put into practice the theory of socialist rule of law with Chinese characteristics; form a complete system of laws and regulations, a highly effective system to ensure the rule of law is put into effect, a stringent system to oversee the implementation of the rule of law, and a robust system to guarantee the rule of law; put in place a well-defined system of Party rules and regulations; make coordinated efforts to promote law-based governance, law-based exercise of state power, and law-based administration of government; adopt a holistic approach to the development of a rule of law country, government, and society; ensure that a scientific approach is taken to legislation, that law is enforced strictly, that justice is administered impartially, and that the law is observed by everyone; and modernize our country's governance system and capacity for governance. As stated in the Nineteenth CPC National Congress, it should improve the Chinese socialist system of laws, at the heart of which is the Constitution, establish a Chinese system of socialist rule of law, carry out lawmaking in a well-conceived and democratic way and in accordance with law, so that good laws are made to promote development and ensure good governance, and the eventual goal of national rejuvenation is to modernize state governance system and capacity. All these statements have the goal of the work on legislation more specific. The NPC and its Standing Committee has been dedicated to implementing the major decisions and arrangements made by the Party's Central Committee and unswervingly adhered to the Five-sphere Integrated Plan and coordinated plan of Four-pronged Comprehensive Strategy to continue innovative initiatives and make great strides and new progress in the work on legislation, made sound measures to continuous improve the Chinese socialist legal system and help achieve the goal of modernizing state governance system and capacity.

Second, the concepts driving the work on legislation are more explicit.

Before the reform and opening-up, especially during a long period after the founding of PRC, the mission for the work on legislation was to establish legal institutions and administrative institutions for the state in all fields. After the Cultural Revolution broke out, the socialist democratic legal system was seriously disrupted, and these institutions in particular were also destructed. When the reform and opening-up was initiated, the whole country was in ruins, and the mission of legislation was also to re-establish the systems and institutions already in destruction. As reform and opening-up deepens, the primary task of legislation also took change, not only to establish the new systems and institutions to adapt new needs, but also to reform the old ones not compatible with reform and opening-up. To properly handle the relationship between reform and legislation is the central task for the work on legislation in the 40 years of reform and opening-up.

In the early reform and opening-up period, the socialist market economic system was yet to come, a lot of principles, policies and arrangements were "touching the stones to cross the river". Therefore, stability of law was crucially important. Generally, any major reform measure always came out first as a policy, and by weighing the typical cases and interests after relatively successful local explorations and experiments, it would be upgraded into a legislation proposal. Reform came first and legislation followed, which was very common in this period. The deepening of reform and opening-up pushed forward the socialist practice and presented much abundant experience. As a result, people's awareness of law was raised, and the emphasis of the work on legislation was turned to the coordination of legislation with reform, which contributed to the rise of new patter: legislation and reform were carried out simultaneously. If the experience were abundant and a consensus could be reached over the matter of legislation, specific provisions would make it more practicable to carry out reform; if the circumstances were not ripe, but it needed law, to lay out some principles would not only regulate and guarantee the practice but also allow future enactment to deepen reform. This pattern coordinates the stability of law and instability of practice, ensuring legislation is compatible with reform and opening-up and socialist modernization and helping to lay the foundation for the establishment of socialist legal system with Chinese characteristics as scheduled.

Since the Eighteenth CPC National Congress, the Party's Central Committee with Xi Jinping as the core has pursued coordinated progress in law-based governance, law-based exercise of state power, and law-based government administration, particularly focused on the legal thinking and legitimate and application of law to promote development, deepen reform and strengthen Party discipline, and paid special attention to "the role of legislation in leading and promoting development" to ensure that "every major reform measure is made according to law". As advocated in the Fourth Plenary Session of the Eighteenth CPC Central Committee, legislation and reform decision should be interconnected to ensure legislation proactively adapts itself to the needs of reform and social economic development. If the latter is proved effective by practice, it should be enacted into legal provisions; if not, pilot programs should be carried out with proper authorization according to legal procedures; the laws and regulations not compatible with reform should be revised or abolished in a timely manner. This has become a common practice for the NPC and its Standing Committee since the conference. The adaptation for reform, role in leading and stimulating, initiative, revision in package, authorization for pilot programs and other means have helped to integrate decisions related to reform with legislative decision-making, promote law-based reform, and strive for enhanced systemization, integration and coordination of reform. Wherever the tasks and measures of the Party's Central Committee for deepening the reform are aimed for, the work on legislation will keep closely. The depth and breadth of its participation in reform is unprecedented in the history of China's legislation.

Third, the distribution of legislative power is more reasonable.

After 70 years of uninterrupted explorations, reform and refining, China's legislative system is now basically finalized. According to the Common Program, the legislative system then was a combination of central legislative power and partial power exercised by the greater administrative areas: the Central People's Government Council had the power to formulate and interpret the national laws or issue decrees, and the Council of the Greater Administrative Area had the power to enact interim decrees and regulations on their own local administration, and then reported for the State Council's approval or recording. The 1954 Constitution changed this model. According to its provisions, China exercised a highly centralized legislative system in which only the NPC had the legislative power; neither the NPC Standing Committee nor the State Council and local authorities were granted with this power. The 1975 and 1978 constitutions followed suit. However, there were also two exceptions: in 1955 and 1959 the NPC authorized its Standing Committee to enact and revise certain laws considering the inconvenience of convening a meeting due to its large number of deputies and the heavy burden of law-making incurred.

This distribution of legislative power was reformed after 1978, and these reform measures were laid down in the 1982 Constitution. The 2000 Law on Legislation and its revision in 2015 improved it again. These changes can be illustrated as follows:

First, to reasonably arrange the legislative powers for the NPC and the Standing Committee. The NPC has the power to make amendments to the Constitution, enact and revise the basics laws in criminal justice, civil affairs, state agencies and others, while the Standing Committee has the power to interpret the Constitution, enact and revise the laws outside of the NPC's jurisdiction, and may make additions and revisions to the laws made by the NPC, which shall not contravene the basic principles of the law concerned.

Second, to grant with State Council and regulate its exercise of legislative power in administrative regulations. The State Council is empowered to, according to the Constitution and law, formulate administrative regulations over the matters of the exercise of law and its administrative authorities. It may also first make administrative regulations over some matters that should be regulated by law under the NPC and its Standing Committee's authorization. The programs listed in the annual legislative schedule of the State Council should be in line with the NPC Standing Committee's legislative plan and annual legislative schedule.

Third, to grant local authorities with legislative power and continue to increase the scope of legislature. The 1979 Local Organization Law made provisions on establishing standing committees in the people's congresses at or above county level and granting the people's congresses and their standing committees of the province, national autonomous areas and municipalities directly under the State Council with the power to promulgate local regulations. This was the first time that the local authorities had the legislative power. The 1982 Constitution confirmed these new reform measures. The 1982 Local Organization Law added provisions, which allowed the drafting of local regulations by the people's congresses of the capital cities of provinces and the large cities approved by the State Council. Its 1986 revision made a further step by allowing the people's congresses of the cities where the people's governments of provinces and national autonomous areas reside and the large cities approved by the State Council and their standing committees to make local regulations and then reported to the standing committees of the people's congresses of the provinces and national autonomous areas for approval.

The 2000 Law on Legislation added a new provision that the people's congresses and their standing committees of the cities where the special economic zones were located may also make administrative regulations. According to the decision of the Party's Central Committee, the people's congresses of the cities with subordinate districts and their standing committees were empowered by make local regulations in its revision in 2015, a big step made for China's legislative system. The 2018 Amendment to the Constitution added again a provision on the cities with subordinate districts to exercise the legislative by making local regulations. The expansion of legislature is to implement Paragraph 4 of Article 3 of the Constitution, as it prescribed that "the division of functions and powers between the central and local state institutions shall honor the principle of giving full play to the initiative and motivation of local authorities under the unified leadership of the central authorities." This expansion inspired the local initiative for deepening reform and opening-up and overall development. It not only made explorations and accumulated experience in national legislation and contributed to the establishment and improvement of socialist legal system with Chinese characteristics, but also strengthened and improve the work of local people's congresses and gave impetus to the upholding of the system of people's congresses.

Fourth, to empower the State Council agencies and local governments to make rules and regulate the scope of their exercise. The State Council agencies and the local people's governments of the cities with subordinate districts may formulate rules and regulations according to law, which shall not impair the rights of citizens, legal persons or other organizations or increase the scope of their duties without the basis of laws or regulations.

In the past 40 years, the number of legislative bodies has rapidly increased, from the NPC and its Standing Committee to 31 provinces, then from 49 large cities (including cities where the special economic zones were located) to 239 cities with subordinate districts, 30 autonomous prefectures and 4 cities with no subordinate districts. The most profound and far-reaching reforms of legislative system were carried out in these years after the PRC was founded. Every reform and improvement were the result of the major decision made by the Party based on the in-depth analysis of its governance and of the important measure for developing and improving the Chinese socialist system and modernizing state governance system and capacity. These decisions and measures have consolidated the state power, mobilized the initiative of all parties to join the national governance and demonstrated the evolving governance system and capacity as times change.

Fourth, the working mechanism for legislation is more complete.

The Cultural Revolution and other political movements caused serious disruption and damage to the application of experience and workable mechanisms for legislation obtained through arduous explorations. After the reform and opening-up was launched, the stable environment and the emphasis on the construction of democratic legal system provided good atmosphere for carrying out the work on legislation. Led by Peng Zhen, Xi Zhongxun, Wang Hanbin and other proletariat revolutionaries, the staff of legislature had been actively engaged in exploring for more complete and sound legislative procedures and mechanisms.

Based on the legislative practices and the experience on them after the founding of PRC especially after the reform and opening was initiated, a clearer set of provisions on legislative procedures were laid down by the Law on Legislation. First, it prescribes the bodies that can propose a bill. According to its provisions, the presidium of the National People's Congress and other 7 bodies may introduce a bill to the National People's Congress, and the Chairman's Committee and other 6 bodies may introduce a bill to the Standing Committee. Second, it improved the mechanisms on deliberation. It established three-times deliberation and the uniform deliberation by the Legislative Committee and make explicit provisions on the circumstances of postponed voting and termination of deliberation. Third, it improved the voting for adoption. The law bills and other bills deliberated by the NPC and its Standing Committee shall be enacted if more than half of the votes cast by all the deputies. The separate voting on important individual clauses is practiced when the differences are great; when the revision of individual clauses involving the same matter in several laws and the bills are submitted together, they may be voted together or separately. Fourth, it clarified the promulgation of law. The laws shall be promulgated by way of a presidential order signed by the state president. The State Council issued the procedures on the formulation of administrative regulations and rules, the local people's congresses with legislative power also made measures on making local administrative regulations and rules. According to the Law on Legislation, these procedures and measures continued to make explicit provisions on the proposal, deliberation and voting procedures of regulations and rules to improve legislation quality and maintain the unification of state legal system.

The legislation in a well-conceived and democratic way has been continuously advanced. The mass line in legislation has been put into practice since the founding of PRC. For example, the draft 1954 Constitution was published for soliciting public opinions for 3 months with 150 million people joining the discussion, and over 1.38 million pieces of opinions were collected. The NPC Standing Committee also published the draft 1982 Constitution, draft Contract Law and other important law drafts for public opinions. However, most of the law drafts were only open for the local people's congresses, experts and relevant parties for opinions. With the deepening of reform and opening-up, the development of society and economy, and the advancement of democracy and rule of law, the public awareness of political participation, the enthusiasm for participation in legislation and the aspirations for expressing their interest demands and resolving interest conflicts through legislation have been continuously ramped up. To follow this trend, the NPC Standing Committee has been committed to expanding the orderly participation of the public in legislation, guaranteeing people's rights to be informed, to participate, to express and to supervise, promoting transparent, scientific and democratic decision-making related with legislation and gradually realizing the full-scale participation of the public in legislation. On April 2008, the Second Chairman Committee of the Eleventh NPC Standing Committee decided to disclose the law drafts after the first deliberation to the public for their opinions, a welcome move that significantly improves legislative transparency and public participation. After several years' efforts, the NPC and its Standing Committee have developed a lot of sound practices, such as legislation forums, meetings, hearings, review after law-making, and disclosure of law drafts for public opinions, all of which have been the basic characteristic and necessary procedures for legislation. Progress has been made in the legislation in a scientific, democratic and law-based manner since the 18th CPC National Congress. The importance of people's congress and its standing Committee in organizing, coordinating and leading the work on legislation has been heightened.

As of 2015, the Standing Committee has submitted the important law drafts to the NPC for deliberation for five consecutive years, established special committees under the NPC and working agencies to organize the drafting of important legislation, and organized drafting and submitted drafts for deliberation for over 70 times. The NPC and its Standing Committee have been dedicated to expressing, balancing and coordinating social interests and tried their best to reach legislative consensus. They have held meetings to argue about the potential legislative projects and coordinate the major interests involved in legislation, and also introduced third-party agency to review the important legislative matters. Experts have been introduced as advisors during legislation, the liaison office for legislation in the communities established one by one, n draft laws for deliberation by the Standing Committee disclosed to the public for opinions. The NPC and its Standing Committee has also carried out a review system of law drafts in order to make legislation more scientific and ensure the validity, feasibility and effectiveness of legal provisions. They have disclosed law drafts for over a hundred times to attract over 200 thousand people to make over 500 thousand suggestions, and the goods ones were adopted in the legislation.

As pointed out by Xi Jinping, the successful practice of China's construction of law-based governance has unambiguously demonstrated that China has found a path of socialist rule of law with Chinese characteristics grounded in China's conditions and trend of times. In the past 70 years when the PRC was founded, especially in the past 40 years when the reform and opening-up was started, the socialist legal system with Chinese characteristics with the Constitution as the core has been developed and finally established as scheduled. In this process, the decision-making concerned with legislation is more interconnected with the decision-making for reform, the legislative institutions and mechanism continue refining, a well-conceived, democratic and law-based legislation is advanced further, the capabilities of the state authorities in legislation are steadily enhanced, and the team of legislative professionals becomes bigger and stronger. Its inception, establishment, development and improvement have provided robust guarantee for adhering to and improving Chinese socialist system and modernizing state governance system and capacity.

Chapter 6
Administrative Regulations: History, Status and Function

Ren Caifeng

Abstract This chapter traces the evolution of administrative regulations of the State Council. From 1949, emergency ordinances filled the legislative vacuum left by the abolition of Republican-era laws. During the planned-economy decades, the State Council still issued rules, but without formal statutory power. The 1982 Constitution and 2000 Legislation Law finally granted express authority to issue "administrative regulations", creating a distinct tier below NPC legislation. It details the historical phases from the birth to the development of administrative regulations, with a special emphasis on translating Party policy into administrative regulation promulgations. It concludes that administrative regulations are indispensable to building a rule-of-law government and modernizing state governance under the CPC leadership.

Keywords Administrative regulations · State council · Delegated legislation · Rule-of-law government · Modernization of governance · CPC leadership

After the People's Republic of China was founded, the system of people's congresses, the state system that was adapted to the socialist people's democratic dictatorship, was established accordingly. The National People's Congress and the local people's congresses are the authorities to exercise state power. The legislative power, the most important component of state power, was wholly vested in the National People's Congress. Over the past 70 years, as profound changes have taken place in China's society and economy, a unified and multi-tiered legislative system has been gradually established to adapt to the needs of socialist modernization. In this system, while the National People's Congress remains the supreme authority of state power, the Standing Committee is granted with the power to enact laws, the State Council may make administrative regulations, the people's congresses and their standing committees of the province, national autonomous areas, cities directly under the Central Government and the cities with subordinate districts may formulate local regulations, and the departments of and the agencies directly controlled by State Council

R. Caifeng (✉)
Beijing, China
e-mail: liujixuan@lawpress.com.cn

C. Shen et al. (eds.), *A History of Legislation in the Past 70 Years in China*,
https://doi.org/10.1007/978-981-95-3799-0_6

and people's governments of the province, national autonomous areas, cities directly under Central Government and the cities with subordinate districts are empowered to make rules.

The power of the State Council to make administrative regulations is an important part of national legislation. According to statistics, there are over 600 pieces of administrative regulations currently in force, covering the matters on politics, economy, culture, society and ecology.[1] Over the past seven decades, the State Council has been adhering to the Constitution as the fundamental law, responded to social and economic development and actual needs of administration, carried out the work on administrative legislation based on statutory power and procedures, guaranteed the coordination of administrative regulations with laws and other regulations and made sure that administrative regulations do not contravene the Constitution or laws to maintain the unification of socialist legal system. The achievements made in this aspect can be summarized as follows:

[1] The Regulation on the Administration of Foreign-Funded Banks, Regulation on the Administration of Foreign Exchange, Regulation on the Administration of Futures Trading, Regulation on the Administration of Foreign-Funded Insurance Companies, and the Regulation on Implementing Individual Income Tax Law were promulgated to strengthen macro adjustment and control. The Regulation on Implementing Food Safety Law, Regulation on the Administration and Supervision of Dairy Products Quality Safety, Regulation on the Recall of Defective Auto Products were formulated to strengthen market regulations. The Regulation on Implementing Law on Environment Protection Tax, Regulation on the Energy Conservation of Public Institutions, Regulation on Environmental Impact Assessment of Planning, Regulation on the Safety Administration of Radioactive Waste and Regulation on the Prevention and Control of Pollution from Large-scale Breeding of Livestock and Poultry were intended for energy and environment conservation and environmental protection. The Regulation on the Prevention and Treatment of Medical Disputes, Regulation on Disability Prevention and Rehabilitation of Persons with Disabilities, Regulation on the National Social Security Funds, Regulation on the Work on Five Guarantees, Regulation on Work-related Injury Insurance, Provisional Measures on Social Assistance, Regulation on Implementing the Labor Contract Law, Special Provisions on Labor Protection of Female Employees to improve people's livelihood and social security. The Regulation on Implementing the Law on the Promotion of Privately-run Schools, Regulation on the Protection of Traditional Arts and Crafts, Regulation on the Protection of the Great Wall, and Regulation on National Science and Technology Awards to develop the education, technology and culture. The Regulation on Volunteering Service, and Regulation on the Administration of Credit Investigation Services were intended to promote social progress. In response to emergencies, the State Council made the Regulation on Handling Urgent Public Health Emergencies, Regulation on the Assistance of Natural Disasters, Regulation on Emergency Responses to Production Safety Accidents. They were either detailed provisions for carrying out the systems as stipulated by the Constitution and laws, or the guidelines for law-based administration of the governments at all levels, or the pilot rules to accumulate experience for law making. They created a sound legal environment for sustainable social and economic development, and provided institutional guarantee for modernizing state governance system and capacity.

1 State Council's Exercise of Legislative Power: Evolution and Achievements

The mission and evolution of the State Council's exercise of legislative power can be generally illustrated as in following five phases.

1.1 Early Stage (1949–1978)

The history of State Council's regulation-making could be traced back the founding of the People's Republic of China in 1949. On the eve of its founding, the Party declared the abolition of KMT's old legal system and organized the CPPCC's first plenum where the Common Program was adopted, which started the construction of PRC's legal system. As stipulated by the Common Program, pending the convocation of the National People's Congress elected by universal franchise, the Plenary Session of CPPCC exercised the functions and powers of the National People's Congress and enacted the Organic Law of the Central People's Government, based on which the Government Administration Council (later known as State Council), as the supreme organ for exercising state administrative power, had the power to "issue decisions and orders". To meet the needs of stabilizing state power and restoring economic development in the early days of the founding of PRC, the State Council issued or approved the Directive on Production and Disaster Relief, National Guidelines on Implementing Taxation, Interim Measures on Collecting Industrial and Commercial Tax from Public-owned Enterprises, Decision on Integrating the Work on National Finance and Economy, Provisional Regulation on Deed Tax, Industrial and Commercial Tax, Goods Tax, Stamp Tax, Interest Income Tax, Slaughter Tax and Agricultural Tax in Newly Liberated Areas, General Order on Prohibiting Opium, Provisional Regulation on Protecting Invention and Patent Rights, Measures On Prohibiting Exit and Entry of National Currency, and Decision on Customs Policies and Customs Work. Relying on relevant national laws and decrees, these documents were important for consolidating the state power, realizing the fast recovery and development of national economy and facilitating the transition from new democratic revolution to socialist construction.

The 1954 Constitution established a highly centralized legislative system in China. According to its provisions, the National People's Congress was the only legislative authority in China, and the State Council could formulate administrative measures, issue decisions and orders according to the Constitution, laws and decrees. After the socialist transformation of ownership of the means of production was completed in 1956, China entered the primary stage of socialism. In the Eighth CPC National Congress held in 1956, it was proposed that the main mission of the Party and the Chinese people was to concentrate all their efforts on developing socialist productive force and realize national industrialization, and decided that the state should gradually ready complete laws as the realities required.

The full-scale socialist construction and the development of various undertakings were subject to legislation. However, due to domestic and international interference, the Party made left-line mistakes in guiding principles, which erred in making guidelines for carrying out these undertakings from 1957 when the Anti-Rightist Campaign was initiated to 1976 when the Cultural Revolution came to an end. The class struggle was seriously escalated and a lot of left-line rural and urban economic policies and policies on class struggle were made, which undermined and even damaged the principle of collective leadership and democratic centralism in the Party and the state's political life. The democratic practices in the Party and the state's political and social life failed to be institutionalized or legalized. Even some of them were enacted as laws, but did not have authority.[2] During this period, apart from the Outline on National Agricultural Development (1956–1967) and 1975 Constitution, the National People's Congress, as the only legislative authority, did not enact any other laws. China's legislation thus hit rock bottom. It was not until March of 1978, when the amendment to the Constitution was adopted, that the NPC's legislation was resumed.

Though the State Council was explicitly authorized by the 1954, 1975 and 1978 Constitutions to make administrative regulations, it had made a lot of Regulation on organization and administration of the undertakings on economy, culture and education and on anti-corruption according to the powers and functions granted by the Constitutions and laws in order to help establish a new order.[3] Even in times of Cultural Revolution, the State Council also made some Regulation on economy, environment and resources, culture, health, sports and foreign affairs to maintain the basic normal operations of the economy and society.[4] These regulations filled the vacancy left out by the National People's Congress as the national legislature during this period, and they actually functioned as administrative laws.[5]

1.2 Recovery (From the End of 1978 to 1987)

At the end of 1978, it was decided in the Third Plenary Session of the Eleventh CPC Central Committee to turn the focus to socialist modernization and carry out reform

[2] The Party Literature Research Center ed., *Selection of Important Documents Since the Third Plenary Session of the Eleventh CPC Central Committee*, People's Publishing House, 1982, p. 1123.

[3] Though the State Council did not have the power to formulate administrative regulations, its provisions, measures, decisions and other normative documents functioned as administrative regulations. Since 1978, the State Council have titled the collection of these normative documents made after the founding of PRC as regulations.

[4] YUAN Shuhong, *To Enhance the Work on Administrative Legislation and Continuously Improve Socialist Legal System with Chinese Characteristics*, in A Reader's Guide to Socialist Legal System with Chinese Characteristics, Xinhua Publishing House, 2011, p. 151.

[5] The administrative regulations formulated during this period include: Provisional Regulation on the Organization of the Public Security Committee in 1952, Provisional Regulation on the Management and Use of Welfare Fees for the State Employees in 1957, Procedures on the Coal Delivery in 1965, and the Regulation on the Protection of Submarine Cables in 1973.

and opening. At this conference, "to advance socialist democracy and deliver on a sound socialist legal system" was designated as a basic principle. After the seven laws were adopted in the Second Plenary Session of the Fifth National People's Congress, Ye Jianying pointed out in the closing meeting that this meeting had made important achievements in strengthening socialist democracy and perfecting socialist legal system and the State Council and people's congresses and people's governments at all levels should make necessary rules and regulations at their own scope of authority, which marked an important step that the construction of China's socialist democratic legal system had made. During this period, to meet the demands for reform and opening and social and economic development, the state had made propitious changes to the legislative system, and empowered the State Council to make administrative regulations and the provincial people's congresses and their standing committees to formulate local regulations.

These changes and major achievements can be outlined as follows:

First, the adjustment of legislative power. The 1984 Constitution made new provisions on the national legislative system: the NPC and its Standing Committee exercise the legislative power of the state, the State Council may adopt administrative regulations according to the Constitution and law, and the ministries and committees of the State Council may formulate departmental rules. The Organization Law of the State Council adopted later also made it explicit that it was the State Council and its departments' statutory obligations to make administrative rules and regulations.[6] The new Constitution and the Organization Law confirmed the State Council as a legislative body, which moved the State Council from behind the scenes to the forefront of administrative legislation under steady progress.

Second, a focus on economic and administrative legislation. In the beginning of reform of opening-up, the economic management system was also gradually reformed, and the State Council also made the regulations necessary for socialist economic and planning management by adhering to the Party's principles and guidelines based on the experience and lessons of domestic and international economic development. It strengthened economic and administrative legislation, used economic, administrative and economic laws to administer the economic activities to promote the undertakings related with foreign trade.

As economic institutional reform deepened and national economy made new progress, it became increasingly important to consolidate the economic relationships and rules on economic activities in the form of law and make law the important means to coordinate these relationships and activities.[7] The application of economic

[6] According to Article 3 of the Organic Law of the State Council, the State Council shall exercise the functions and powers prescribed in Article 89 of the Constitution. Its Article 5 prescribed that the Premier shall sign the decisions, orders, and administrative rules and regulations issued by the State Council, and the competent ministries or commissions may, within the limits of their authority and in accordance with the law and decisions of the State Council, issue orders, instructions and regulations as prescribed by Article 10.

[7] For example, the 1986 working report called for gradually improving the economic and legal means with necessary administrative means to control and adjust the operations of economy in the seventh five-year plan. A few years ago, the NPC and its Standing Committee enacted a lot

and legal means and other necessary administrative means to control and adjust the economic operations was important for establishing new socialist economic institutions.

Third, authorized legislation and pilot programs to accumulate legislative experience. The making of guidelines and policies were still touching the stones to cross the river in the early start of reform and opening-up. To align legislation with reform and progress, Deng Xiaoping proposed that the legal provisions be less than perfect to start with, then be gradually improved upon. Following this suggestion, the legislation in the early period did not adopt a holistic approach, but the NPC and its Standing Committee authorized the State Council and local legislative authorities to carry out pilot programs in line with national law-making. For example, the State Council was granted with the power to formulate relevant taxation regulations and issue the draft regulations for trial implementation when it implemented the tax for profits scheme in the state-owned enterprise and reformed the industrial and commercial tax as stated in a decisions made in the Seventh Meeting of the Sixth National People's Congress held in September 18, 1984.[8] In the Third Session of the Sixth National People's Congress convened in 1985, the State Council was again authorized to formulate provisional measures or regulations which did not contravene the Constitution and the basic principles of relevant laws and the NPC and its Standing Committee's decisions to address the issues on economic institutional reform and opening-up.[9]

Fourth, to cater for administrative and economic management, the legislation was still within the framework of planned economy. The complexity and speed of economic reform required more government's control to ensure economic administration in the early reform and opening-up period. Therefore, the administrative legislation was emphasized more on granting powers to the administrative departments to manage economic, culture and social affairs, for example, the formulation of the Measures on the Management of Urban and Rural Market Trade and the Measures on the Management of Imported Films. These regulations were characterized by management and planned economy, and the conception of regulating administrative behaviors through administrative legislation was not yet recognized.

---

of important laws, and the State Council also made some necessary administration regulations. The work on legislation, especially on economic legislation should be accelerated to strive for a rather complete system of economic laws during the seventh five-year period, and to ensure every economic activity is carried out according to law.

[8] The State Council then issued the drafts of Regulation on Product Tax, Regulation on Valued-added Tax, Regulation on Salt Tax, Regulation on Sales Tax, Regulation on Resources Tax, and Regulation on State-owned Enterprise Income Tax and the Measures for Collecting the State-Owned Enterprise Regulation Tax, which came into force on October 1, 1984.

[9] The State Council formulated a number of Regulation on taxation and foreign investment. For example, in 1985 the State Council issued the Regulation on Import and Export Tariffs, Custom Import and Export Tariff, and Provisional Regulation on Collective-owned Enterprise Income Tax. A year later, the State Council issued the Provisional Regulation on the Administration of Banks, Provisional Regulation on the Administration of Tax Collection, Provisional Regulation on Individual Income Regulation Tax, and Provisions on Encouraging Foreign Investment.

Last, the legislation on administrative procedure was started. The State Council issued the Provisional Regulation on the Formulation of Administrative Regulations, laying out the procedural rules on the principles, planning, drafting, deliberation and issuance. It marked the beginning of pursuing balanced development of both substantive and procedural legislation.

The practice has proved that the unified and multi-tiered legislative system as defined in the Constitution, Organic Law of the State Council, Local Organization Law and others reflect China's conditions and real needs, and the promulgation of laws, administrative regulations and local regulations in all respects met the needs of reform and opening-up for a better socialist legal system and hastened law-making. As the State Council advanced administrative legislation, a lot of important regulations were promulgated in a timely manner.[10]

1.3 Rapid Development (1988–1998)

The 1988 Constitutional Amendment make clarification on the legal status of private sector. The 1993 Constitutional Amendment introduced the provisions that "the State practices socialist market economy" and "the state strengthens economic legislation and improves macro-regulations and control". In the Fourteenth CPC National Congress, to establish to socialist market economic system was taken as a reform objective. Then in the Third Plenary Session of the Fourteenth CPC Standing Committee, it was stressed that "the establishment and improvement of the socialist market economic system should be regulated and guaranteed by a complete legal system. Therefore, it is of great importance to focus on the legal system, to ensure the unification of reform and opening with the establishment of legal system, and learn how to use legal means to regulate economy", "to follow the principles laid down by the Constitution, accelerate economic legislation... by the end of the 20th century the legal system for socialist market economy should be basically established", "the governments at all levels should administer and act according to law." In the Fifteenth CPC National Congress, "rule of law and establish a socialist rule of law country" was set out as a fundamental principle. According to the decisions, arrangements, mission and tasks of the Party's Central Committee on strengthening

[10] According to the 1987 Report on Government Work, based on the legislative work in the past few years, the NPC Standing Committee deliberated on and adopt 11 laws, and the State Council formulated and issued 59 administrative regulations in 1986. The situation had gradually improved. The 1988 Report on Government Work made a summary of the main achievements in the past 5 years, and pointed out the governments at all levels and relevant departments had made great efforts to achieve the goal of the construction of legal system. In these 5 years, 30 laws were adopted by the NPC Standing Committee after deliberation under the Staten Council's proposals, and the State Council formulated and issued 225 pieces of administrative regulations. The legal system was also gradually improved.

the socialist legal system, the administrative legislation of the State Council gained momentum.[11]

The major achievements of the State Council's administrative legislation can be elaborated as follows:

First, to put into practice the two Constitutional amendments and carry out legislation to help achieve the goal of establishing the legal system for socialist market economy. The 1988 Constitution Amendment confirmed the legal status of private sector in the fundamental law.[12] In April, the State Council made the Provisional Rules on Prohibiting Apportionment of Charges in Enterprises, forbidding any kind of requests to the enterprises to provide financial, material and human resources outside the scope of provisions of the laws and regulations to protect the legitimate rights and interests of enterprises. Two months later, the State Council issued the Provisional Rules on Private Sector Enterprises to regulate the types, opening and closing, rights and obligations, labor management, finance and taxation, and supervision and punishment of the enterprises.

In the 1993 Government Work Report of the State Council, it was stated that "the construction of legal system should be strengthened, especially with regard to economic legislation, through which the successful policies and experience for the reform can be institutionalized into law…the law drafts aimed for regulation market operations should be quickly submitted, and the relevant administrative regulations should also be formulated quickly to better coordinate economic relationships through law." In the second national legislative affairs meeting held in 1993, some responsible persons of the State Council pointed out that there was a large number of law drafts, drafts of local regulations that should be submitted by the governments and the administrative regulations and rules already made, so the task was burdensome. It was necessary to set out the focus according to the legislative urgency, for example to plan the legislative programs on regulating market entities, on coordinating relationships among market entities for fair market competition, on improving and enhancing macro regulation and control for coordinated economic development, on establishing and perfecting social security system, and on the legal system compatible with socialist market economy.[13] The State Council formulated the Regulation on the Administration of National Budget and Regulation on the Administration of

[11] According to the 1988 Report on the Work of Government, during the sessions of the Eighth National People's Congress, the State Council made 66 pieces of draft laws and 197 pieces of administrative regulations. The law-based administration was ameliorated.

[12] According to this Amendment, Article 11 of the Constitution was added a new paragraph, which reads, "The State permits the private sector of the economy to exist and develop within the limits prescribed by law. The private sector of the economy is a complement to the socialist public economy. The State protects the lawful rights and interests of the private sector of the economy, and exercises guidance, supervision and control over the private sector of the economy."

[13] LUO Gan, *To Further Enhance Government's Work on Legal System and Promote and Guarantee the Establishment and Continuous Improvement of Socialist Market Economic System*, in Office of Legislative Affairs Bureau of the State Council ed., Review of Government's Work on Legal System and its Future: Second National Legislative Affairs Meeting, China Legal Publishing House, 1993, pp. 6–8.

Foreign Exchange to enhance macro regulation and control, the Provisional Regulation on the Issuance and Trade of Stocks, Regulation on the Administration of Enterprise Registration and Rules on Domestic Listed Stocks for Foreign Investors to regulate the development of the securities market, the Provisional Regulation on Value-added Tax, Provisional Regulation on Consumption Tax, Provisional Regulation on Resource Tax and Provisional Regulation on Deed Tax to enhance the legislation on taxation.

Second, to strengthen legislation regulating and supervising administrative behaviors to provide norms and guidelines for law-based administration. In the Thirteenth CPC National Congress, "to consolidate the achievements in institutional reform and ensure that the administrative management follows a law-based path, the administrative legislation should be strengthened to provide norms and procedures for administrative activities". To put it into practice, the 1989 Administrative Procedure Law, 1994 State Compensation Law and 1996 Administrative Penalty Law were enacted, and a lot of regulations compatible with laws were also formulated by the State Council to regulate and supervise the administration's performance of duties, protect and remedy the rights of citizens and organizations, for example, Regulation on Administrative Supervision, Regulation on Administrative Reconsideration, Procedures on the Recording of Regulations and Rules and the Measures for Separating Penalty Decisions From Penalty Payments Collection.

Last, the administrative legislation in other areas was accelerated. For example, the Provisional Regulation on Assignment and Transfer of Urban State-owned Land Use Rights, Regulation on the Administration of Urban House Demolition and Relocation and Regulation on the Administration of Urban Real Estate Development and Operation to regulate the order of housing market, and the Regulation on the Protection of Wild Animals to protect, develop and reasonably use the wild plant resources and to maintain ecological balance.

1.4 Full-Scale Development (from 1999 to 2011)

In the 1990s, China accelerated its accession to the WTO. In the 1999 Constitution Amendment, it was plainly stated that "the People's Republic of China governs the country according to law and makes it a socialist country under rule of law." At the same time, the State Council resolved to promote law-based administration, proposing to strengthen and improve the government's work on legislation and improve its quality. In 2004, the State Council issued the Outline for Promoting Law-based Administration in an All-round Way, stated the objective of law-based government and clarified the guidelines, goals, basic principles, requirements, major mission and measures. Three years later, in the Seventeenth CPC National Congress, it was stated to "comprehensively implement the rule of law as a fundamental principle and speed up the building of a socialist country under the rule of law", and "persist in scientific and democratic legislation to improve the socialist law system with Chinese characteristics". In 2010, the State Council issued the Opinions On

Strengthening the Law-Based Government, proposing to "enhance and improve institutional construction", accentuate the focus of government's legislation, improve the efforts in institutional construction, strengthen the re-examination of administrative regulations, rules and normative documents, make sound procedures for formulating normative documents, and impose strict recording and review of the rules and other normative documents. In this year, the socialist legal system with Chinese characteristics was successfully established as scheduled. The State Council responded to the social and economic development and the implementation of laws by formulating administrative regulations in a timely manner, which had made important contribution to the formation of socialist legal system with Chinese characteristics.

The changes of the scope of administrative legislation and the main achievements made by the State Council can be summarized as follows:

First, the scope of the State Council's legislative authority was changed. The 2000 Law on Legislation made detailed provisions regarding the basis, scope and procedures for making administrative rules and regulations, and delineated the legislative powers of the NPC, its Standing Committee and the State Council, which were helpful for the State Council to better exercise administrative authority through the making of administrative regulations. Matters that can be subject to administrative regulations are extremely varied. Except for those matters reserved to law under Article 8 of the Law on Legislation, the State Council may formulate administrative Regulation on the matters concerned with national politics, economy, culture, society and ecology. Article 9 made a clarification that the NPC and its Standing Committee has the power to make a decision to authorize the State Council to formulate, according to actual needs, administrative regulations first on part of those matters, except for the affairs concerning criminal offences and their punishment, mandatory measures and penalties involving deprivation of citizens' political rights or restriction of personal freedom, and the judicial system. As a result, the scope of the matters subject to administrative regulations was substantially expanded. Some standards on dividing the line between the law and administrative regulations had been established with certain successful experience from the legislative practice. For example, the matters related with criminal offences and civil disputes and state departments are subject to the scope of law, while the nationally unified working mechanisms and procedures that are essential for the administrative departments may be set out by administrative regulations. The matters on fundamental administrative institutions and systems are mandated by the law, while the specific matters and operations of these institutions and systems may be subject to administrative regulations. The law exercises its jurisdiction on the matters on fundamental economic system and management systems, while the operations of these systems and their economic and technical standards may fall into the jurisdiction of administrative regulations.[14]

Second, the State Council formulated, re-examined, revised and repealed the regulations, rules, policies and measures inconsistent with the WTO rules. For example,

[14] Office of State Law of the Legislative Affairs Committee of the National People's Congress ed., *Interpretations on the Law on Legislation of the People's Republic of China*, Law Press, 2015, p. 40.

to better import and export administration, the State Council formulated the Regulation on the Administration of Goods Import and Export and Regulation on the Administration of Technology Import and Export. The State Council also made the Anti-Dumping Regulations, Anti-Subsidy Regulations and Safeguard Measures Regulations to ensure trade remedial measures. The Rules on Implementing the Foreign-Funded Enterprises Law and the Regulation on Implementing the Law on Chinese-Foreign Contractual Joint Ventures were revised to ensure consistency with their corresponding revised laws. The Regulation on the Administration of the China-based Representative Offices of Foreign Law Firms was revised; the Regulation on the Administration of Foreign-Invested Telecommunications Enterprises, Regulation on the Administration of Films, and Regulation on the Administration of Audio-Visual Products were formulated, and the Regulation on the Administration of Foreign-Funded Financial Institutions were revised; the Regulation on the Administration of Foreign-Funded Insurance Companies was formulated, Regulation on the Administration of Travel Agencies were revised, Regulation on International Shipping was formulated, the Rules on Implementing the Patent Law, Rules on Implementing Trademark Law, Rules on Implementing Copyright Law were revised, the Regulation on the Protection of Computer Software and Regulation on the Protection of Integrated Circuit Layout Design were formulated, the Regulation on the Administration of Pesticides, Regulation on the Administration of Veterinary Drugs and Regulation on Implementing the Law on the Administration of Drugs, Regulation on the Administration of Feed and Feed Additives were revised, the Regulation on the Collective Administration of Copyright were formulated to better implement the Copyright Law, Regulation on Sino-Foreign Cooperation in Running Schools and Regulation on Certification and Accreditation were formulated.[15]

Third, the State Council made regulations to regulate the administrative legislation and behaviors. For example, it formulated the Regulation on the Procedures on the Formulation of Administrative Regulations, Regulation on the Procedures on the Formulation of Administrative Rules and Regulation on the Recording of Regulations and Rules in 2001 to standardize the procedures and maintain the unification of socialist legal system. Compared with the 1987 provisional regulations, the Regulation on the Procedures on the Formulation of Administrative Regulations made detailed provisions on the principles, forms of legislation, initiation of legislative programs, drafting, reviewing, decision, issuance and interpretation. The implementation of these three administrative procedural regulations promoted the law-based administrative legislation. The Regulation on Implementing the Administrative Reconsideration Law laid down the details on the basic administrative reconsideration systems to ensure more practicability and secure smooth channels for it.

---

[15] Li Shishi, *What Are the Adjustments China's Legal System and Institutions Make After Joining WTO?*, World Market, No. 1, pp. 10–11 (2004); Li Fuying, *China Actively Observed its WTO Commitments to Accelerate Adjustments of Domestic Legal System*, Chinese Law, Vol. 2, pp. 22–24 (2003).

Fourth, while continuing legislation for better economic adjustment and market regulations, the State Council also paid attention to the legislation in social management and public services, highly valued the law-making directly concerned people's own interests, and focused on the legislation in emergency response, securing peasants' rights and interests, labor and employment, social security and public affairs. For example, to address the problem in custody and repatriation, the State Council issued the Measures for the Administration of Relief for Vagrants and Beggars without Assured Living Sources in Cities and other corresponding measures. To improve legal institution in emergency administration, the State Council formulated the Regulation on Handling Major Animal Epidemic Emergencies and Regulation on Handling Urgent Public Health Emergencies, and submitted the Law on Prevention and Control of Infectious Diseases (Draft revision), Law on Animal Epidemic Prevention (Draft revision) and Law on Responding to Emergent Events (Draft) to the NPC Standing Committee. The State Council also made the Special Provisions on the Prevention of Coal Mine Production Safety Accidents to provide legal guarantee for identifying safety risk and protecting mine worker's life safety and production safety. The Regulation on Unemployment Insurance, Regulation on Guaranteeing Minimum Living Standards for Urban Residents and Regulation on Work-related Injury were made to strengthen the labor protection and improve people's livelihood. The Regulation on Letters and Visits were revised to smooth the channels and regulate the order of letters and visits. To ensure the implementation of Population and Family Planning Law and help achieve coordinated development of population with the economy, society, resources and environment, the State Council issued the Measures on the Administration of Collection of Social Maintenance Fees. The Regulation on the Marriage Registration were re-issued based on the revised Law on Marriage. The State Council formulated the Regulation on Legal Aid to ensure the citizens', especially the poor people's right to judicial relief. To put the Labor Contract Law into practice, the Regulation on Implementing the Labor Contract Law were formulated to make it more practicable. The Regulation on Nurse was also made to protect the legitimate rights and interests of nurses, regulate nursing behaviors and promoting the nursing sector.

The State Council also formulated the Regulation on Prohibiting Pyramid Selling, Regulation on the Administration of Direct Selling, Regulation on the Protection of Cultural Relics, Regulation on the Protection of Great Wall, and Regulation on the Protection of Renowned Cultural Cities, Towns and Villages. The State Council formulated the Regulation on National Science Funds, to regulate the use and administration of national science funds and improve its use efficiency. The Regulation on the Administration of Geological Data to strengthen the regulation on national land resources.

Fifth, the State Council adhered to scientific and democratic legislation to improve its quality. The State Council established sound institutions and mechanism to ensure scientific and democratic legislation, proposed that the law drafts and administrative regulations and rules should conform with the provisions of the Constitution and law, followed the law of social and economic development and made administrative legislation more target-oriented and practicable to effectively resolve the problems. The

State Council also made efforts to improve the transparency and public participation in the work of administrative legislation. Except for those that cannot be disclosed according to law, all the draft administrative regulations and rules were issued for public opinions.

To increase transparency of legislation, the Legislative Affairs Office of the State Council may convene hearings to solicit opinions if the administrative regulations were directly concerned with the interests of natural persons, legal persons or other organizations according to the provisions of the Regulation on the Procedures on the Formulation of Administrative Regulations; and it may issue the administrative rules for public opinions or convene hearings if the administrative authorities, organizations and citizens had major difference in the administrative rules that were directly concerned with the interest of natural persons, legal persons or other organizations according to the Regulation on the Procedures on the Formulation of Administrative Rules. All draft administrative regulations, except those involving state secrets or national security, have been issued for public opinions through the Chinese Legal Information Portal (also the Portal for Ministry of Justice in Chinese version) since 2008. During the sessions of the Tenth National People's Congress, a total of 15 draft laws and administrative regulations were open for public opinions, a major step to establish the institution and mechanism for public participation in administrative legislation.[16]The more the draft laws or administrative regulations concern public issues or special interest relationships, the more the public shows enthusiasm for participation.[17]

[16] On October 22, 2002, the Legal Affairs Office of the State Council issued the draft Regulation on the Administration of Property in the Legal Daily for public opinions. The revision of this draft incorporated nearly half of the suggestions, which was a trial to improve transparency of administrative legislation. On October 12, 2006, the Legal Affairs Office of the State Council, for the first time, published the Regulation on the National Science Funds on the Chinese Legal Information Portal for public opinions. By following this practice, 11 draft administrative regulations were published in this portal for public opinions in 2007, and 25 in 2008. From 2009, the rules formulated by the State Council were also published in it for the first time, and 73 in this year, 67 in 2010, and 117 in 2011. See QING Feng, *Analysis of the Status of Public Participation in Administrative Legislation for Decision-making*, Journal of Shanghai University of Political Science and Law, No. 6, pp. 1–13 (2012).

[17] The Regulation on the Expropriation of Houses on State-owned Land and Compensation (for public opinions) attracted 13,437 people to participate in the online discussion, which generated 130,356 opinions for the public were very concerned with the expropriation of houses. The second draft for public opinions still attracted 10.429 people and generated 74,266 opinions. The Regulation on School Bus Safety (for public opinions), though the issue of school bus was not a public concern, attracted 2737 people with 23,411 opinions. The public have shown great enthusiasm for participating in the decision-making of administrative legislation closely related with their own interests. For example, the Regulation on Labor Protection of Female Employees (for public opinions) attracted 6.503 people, who gave 35,234 suggestions, the Regulation on Implementing Labor Contract Law (for public opinions) attracted 7473 people with 76,136 suggestions, Regulation on Paid Annual Leave for Employees, 8387 people with 14,234 suggestions; Regulation on Work-related Injury Insurance, 5030 people with 29,876 suggestions. If not, such enthusiasm would be subdued. For example, the Regulation on Reporting of Balance of Payments Statistics only gathered 8 people who made 44 suggestions. *Ibid.*

In 2008, the State Council suggested that the administrative legislation should extensively listen to the public opinions and disclose in principle the draft administrative regulations and rules that were closely related with people's interests for public opinions in order to improve the mechanism, procedures and methods of public participation and deliver on more transparency. Two years later, the State Council issued opinions on strengthening law-based administration, which called for strict observance of statutory authority and procedures, a more scientific and practical legal system and improved system and institutions for public participation in administrative legislation. In addition, the State Council also proposed a legislation's cost-benefit analysis scheme to realize the greatest benefits in legislation. The system of reviewing administrative regulations and rules after formulation was also advocated by the State Council.[18]

Last, the initiative to re-examine regulations was carried out to adapt to the socialist legal system with Chinese characteristics. With a view to establish the socialist legal system with Chinese characteristics, the revision and improvement of laws and regulations were put in the equal foot with legislation. When new laws and regulations were enacted, the old ones that did suit the new development circumstances were also revised. In this period, the State Council carried out several initiatives to re-examine regulations to address the conflicts between rules and their upper level laws, local regulations between departmental rules, and among the departmental rules themselves. It also resolved the issue in disconnection between legislation and the making of reform decision and the untimeliness in revision and abolition.

Such efforts may be better summarized as follows:

1. the State Council made a re-examination on 756 pieces of administrative regulations formulated before the end of 2000 by referring to the requirements of socialist market economy and WTO accession, which lead to 71 abolished and 80 invalid. The State Council departments re-examined 2300 pieces of rules, policies and measures related with foreign affairs; 803 of them were abolished and 325 were revised.
2. to promote the effective implementation of the Administrative Licensing Law, 9 pieces of laws were revised and 11 licensing matters were abolished in the Eleventh Meeting of the Standing Committee of the Tenth National People's Congress. The State Council make reforms in administrative approval system by issuing decisions to abolish 1749 licensing matters, 121 matters on methods of administration and delegated 46 matters to lower level governments. (3) The State Council made another initiative to re-examine 691 administrative regulations formulated by the end of 2009 based on the achievements of past four-times re-examination initiatives and the new circumstances and requirements for social economic development and deepening reform to advance rule of law, maintain the unification of socialist legal system and promote law-based administration in all respects. In this initiative, the State Council made decisions to abolish 7

[18] Cao Kangtai, *Promoting Law-based Administration is the Basic Theme of Government's Legislation: Reflection on the Experience of Law-based Administration in the Past 30 years and Its Prospect*, People's Tribune, No. 19, pp. 8–10 (2008).

pieces of administrative regulations and revise some provisions of 107 pieces of administrative regulations. These re-examination initiatives basically addressed the inconsistency in administrative regulations and ensured a more scientific and harmonious system of law.

The administrative legislation in this period could be generally characterized in the following: law-based administration was the pursuit of administrative legal system with special emphasis on the regulation and constraint on the exercise of administrative power to make the administrative behaviors have laws to abide by; the status and function of legislative procedures were more stressed during law-making, and the scope of democratic legislation was increased by opening door for public opinions; the standards and accuracy of legislative technique were more emphasized to make regulations and rules more practicable; the comparative study on the foreign administrative legislation was more emphasized to actively introduce advanced foreign legislative concepts; the social legislation was stressed to provide institutional support for improving people's livelihood and building a harmonious society. However, problems still existed in administrative legislation in this period, which can be summarized into several aspects: the determination of legislative programs was not reasonable enough; it did not fully reflect the law of economy and social development and paid too much more attention to administrative than service; the cost-efficiency analysis was made rarely during law-making, which caused high cost for law-enforcement and law observing; it needed to strengthen the transparency and improve the public participation in law-making. Considering these achievements and problems in this period, it was then proposed to do the following work: to define the standards for evaluating the quality of administrative legislation; to grasp the regular pattern and opportunity for law making; to improve the transparency and public participation in administrative legislation; to explore a scheme on conducting cost-efficiency analysis on legislative programs, especially on economic legislation; to establish sound mechanisms on revision and abolition of administrative regulations and rules and the system on regular re-examination of rules and other normative documents.[19]Some supporting regulations clearly stipulated in the laws and essential for the implementation of the laws were either delayed in promulgation, or were only announced and implemented after many years, which seriously affected the implementation and authority of the law.

---

[19] CAO Kangtai, *To Promote Law-based Administration in All Respects and Establish a Law-based Government: Several Reflections on Learning Deng Xiaoping Thought on Democracy and Law*, in Committee for the Forum of Deng Xiaoping's Life and Thoughts ed., Commemoration of the 100th Birthday of Deng Xiaoping: Collection of Papers in the Forum of Deng Xiaoping's Life and Thoughts (Vol. 2), Central Party Literature Press, 2005, pp. 865–866.

1.5 Administrative Legislation in the New Era (After 2012)

The guiding principles for the socialist law-based governance in the new era were laid out in the Eighteenth CPC National Congress, namely to "make laws in a scientific law, enforce them strictly, administer justice impartially and ensure that everyone abides by the law" and to "improve the socialist system of laws with Chinese characteristics, strengthen legislation in key areas and expand channels for people's orderly participation in the legislative process", and regard "a law-based government be basically in function" as an important goal of achieving moderately prosperous country in 2020. In 2015, the Party's Central Committee and the State Council jointly issued the Outline on the Implementation of a Law-Based Government (2015–2020) which proposed to improve government legislation institution and mechanism in general. In particular, it proposed to: strictly implement the provisions in the Law on Legislation; carry out establishment, amendment, abolishment and interpretation concurrently, improve procedures for formulating administrative regulations and rules; refine the initiation, drafting, demonstration, coordination and review mechanisms of government legislation; promote government legislation refinement and make government legislation more timely, more systematic, better targeted, and more effective. It further clarified the need to improve the system by which public opinions are openly sought for legislation programs, use methods such as pre-legislation assessment to establish systems for hearings on legislative programs. In addition, as advocated by the Outline, important administrative laws and regulations shall be drafted by government's legislative affairs agency to effectively prevent legalization of departmental benefits and regional protectionism. For important legislative affairs involving significant interdepartmental disputes, the decision-making department shall introduce third party assessment and give full consideration to opinions of all parties concerned for a coordinated solution, and such issues shall not remain unsolved for a long time. It was also proposed to explore appointing third parties to formulate drafts of laws, regulations and rules, and regularly conduct post-legislation assessment of regulations and rules periodically to improve rationality of government legislation. Laws, regulations and rules that were not suitable for reform and economic and social development requirements should be promptly amended and abolished and efforts to interpret administrative regulations and rules should be strengthened as required by the Outline.

Higher requirements of the work on administrative legislation had been proposed to improve the socialist legal system after it was established. Since the Eighteenth CPC National Congress, the State Council has paid more attention to legislation quality, strengthened legislation in key areas, promoted reform according to the demands of rule of law, advanced law-based governance through reforms and steadily pushed forward legislation in a more scientific, democratic and law-based manner, which helped to deliver more outstanding achievements in law-based government. From 2013 to 2018, the State Council submitted 186 law bills to the NPC Standing Committee for deliberation, promulgated and revised 333 administrative regulations, proposed the bills to terminate re-education through labor and other matters, and revised and abolished a lot of departmental rules.[20]

The changes of the scope of administrative legislation and the main achievements made by the State Council can be summarized as follows:[21]

First, to improve the institution on the scope of legislative power. The 2015 Law on Legislation adhered to the principle of statutory taxation put forward in the Third Plenary Session of the Eighteenth CPC National Congress, improved the system of exclusive legislative power in taxation, and made the provision that "the establishment of a tax, determination of tax rates, tax collection administration and other basic taxation rules" are only subject to the jurisdiction of laws. To implement the decisions made in the fourth plenary session, it established a system of authorization based on specific matters and clarified the content and time limits of such authorizations, improved the power of formulating rules, and clearly prescribed that departmental rules not based on the laws, administrative regulations, decisions, or orders of the State Council must not impair the rights of citizens, legal persons or other organizations, or increase the scope of their duties, nor increase the power of that department or reduce that department's legally provided duties.

Second, to focus on legislation quality. The State Council and its departments put quality at the forefront of legislation. It required that the drafting of laws, administrative regulations and rules should start from national situations, conduct in-depth research to be informed of the most important issues and take into account of the interest demands of various parties and the pros and cons of different institution proposals in order to design the institutions that could practically solve problems and coordinate these interest demands and could deliver on laws, regulations and rules urgently needed for reform, development and stability in a timely manner.

Third, to strengthen legislation in key areas. By centering on the Five-sphere Integrated Plan and the Four-pronged Comprehensive Strategy, the State Council enhanced its work on legislation in key areas, such as the comprehensive reform, national security, economic development, people's livelihood, social governance and regulation of administrative behavior and others.[22]

In terms of national security, the State Council proposed to the NPC Standing Committee to enact or revise the National Security Law, National Intelligence Law, Anti-espionage Law, National Defense Traffic Law and the like. The State Council also submitted proposals to the NPC Standing Committee to formulate or make revisions to the Law on Transformation of Scientific and Technological Achievements, Film Industry Promotion Law and Commercial Banking Law to promote economic

---

[20] According to statistics of the State Council's working reports, the 2013 one did not indicate the data on legislation in 2012, so the data calculation starts from 2013.

[21] This part is written by referring to Li Mingzheng ed., *New Achievements in Law-based Government: A Transcript of Law-based Administration since the Eighteenth CPC National Congress*, China Legal Publishing House, 2007, pp. 87–90.

[22] From November 8, 2012 to August 31, 2017, a total of 45 pieces of law bills were submitted by the State Council to the NPC Standing Committee, and it also made or revised 48 pieces of administrative regulations and made revisions to 130 pieces of administrative regulations by adopting the package legislation method.

development. In terms of administrative regulations, the State Council made the Regulation on the Administration of Credit Investigation Services, Regulation on the Deposit Insurance, Regulation on the Administration of Approval and Recording of Enterprise Investment Projects, Provisional Regulation on Enterprise Information Publicity, Provisional Regulation on Express Delivery, and Measures for the Administration of Scrapped Vehicles Recycling to ensure regulated economic development. The State Council proposed to the NPC Standing Committee to enact or revise the Food Safety Law, Law on Environment Protection Tax, Production Safety Law, Advertising Law, Law on the Prevention and Control of Air Pollution, and Law on the Prevention and Control of Water Pollution to ensure and improve people's living environment for better development. Accordingly, the State Council itself formulated or revised the Regulation on the Administration of Water Supply of the South-to-North Water Diversion Project, Provisional Regulation on the Immovable Property Registration, Provisional Regulation on Social Assistance, Regulation on National Social Security Funds, Regulation on Urban Drainage and Sewage Treatment, Regulation on the Administration of Vaccine Distribution and Vaccination, Regulation on the Education of the Disabled, and Regulation on Implementing the Individual Income Tax Law. To better social governance, the State Council made proposals to NPC Standing Committee on the enactment or revision of the Law on Anti-Domestic Law, Traditional Chinese Medicine Law, and Drug Administration Law. In this case, the State Council made or revised the Regulation on Farmland Water Conservancy, Regulation on the Administration of Pesticides and Regulation on the Prevention and Treatment of Medical Disputes. To regulate administrative behaviors, the State Council formulated the Regulation on Implementing the Government Procurement Law, Regulation on the Administration of Construction of State Institution's Buildings, and Provisional Regulation on the Major Administrative Decision-making, and made revisions to the Regulation on the Disclosure of Government Information, Regulation on the Procedures for the Formulation of Administrative Regulations, and Regulation on the Procedures for the Formulation of Rules.[23]

In addition, the State Council also took the making of administrative regulations and rules as required by law as a focus of administrative legislation. When planning the legislative programs and drafting laws, the State Council coordinated the efforts to achieve synchronous drafting, promulgation and implementation of laws and their supporting administrative regulations and rules. For example, on August 31, 2018, the Individual Income Tax Law was adopted at the Fifth Session of the

[23] The main contents of the revised Regulation on the Procedures for the Formulation of Administrative Regulations and Regulation on the Procedures for the Formulation of Rules include: to implement the Party's leadership in the whole process and all the aspects of the work on government legislation, and turn the successful experience of streamlined administration and optimized service into institutions, practice the institution of collecting public opinions and review after promulgation, improve the institution on collecting legislative programs and argumentation, improve the procedures on interpretation and abolition of regulations and rules. See *Li Keqiang Signed the Decree of State Council to Issue the Decision on Revising the Regulation on the Procedures for the Formulation of Administrative Regulations and Regulation on the Procedures for the Formulation of Rules*, People's Daily, January 17, 2018, p. 1.

Thirteenth National People's Congress, and the State Council made timely revisions to its supporting regulations, which came into force on January 1, 2019, the date on which the Law was also effective. It also applied to the Law on the Environment Protection Law and its supporting Regulations and others.

Fourth, to promote reform according to the demands of rule of law and advance law-based governance through reforms. As pointed out by Xi Jinping, every reform decision should be law-based. If the provisions were needed or the laws and regulations needed to be revised to support the reform decisions or arrangements made by the Party's Central Committee and the State Council, the State Council often submitted them for being included in the legislative programs. Since 2015, the State Council has set aside a part for the urgently needed legislation for comprehensively deepening reform in its legislative annual plan. For example, in order the carry out the separation of certification from licensing in some regions and other reform measures, the State Council issued the Decision on Temporarily Adjusting in Shanghai Pudong New Area the Implementation of Provisions of Relevant Administrative Regulations and Decision of the State Council on Temporarily Adjusting Relevant Special Administrative Measures for Administrative Examination and Approval and Market Access in Beijing, and submitted to the NPC Standing Committee to issue the Decision on Authorizing the State Council to Temporarily Adjust the Implementation of the Provisions of Relevant Laws in the Administrative Regions of 33 Counties (Cities and Districts) under the Pilot Program Including Daxing District of Beijing Municipality. In addition, to implement the Party's Central Committee's decision on two-child policy, which required the timely revision of the Population and Family Planning Law, the National Health and Family Planning Commission and the Legislative Affairs Office of the State Council made a detailed legislative schedule to accurately calculate the timing for each legislative procedure, and kept close communication with the General Office of the NPC Standing Committee and the General Office of the State Council. They completed all the work necessary for the revision in less than 1 month to ensure that the draft revision to the Population and Family Planning Law was adopted as scheduled and to provide legal guarantee of the implementation of this policy.

Fifth, to promote legislation in a scientific, democratic and law-based manner. As advocated by the Fourth Plenary Session of the Eighteenth CPC Central Committee, the institution for administrative legislation should be strengthened and perfected, the procedures for making administrative regulations and rules and the public participation in government law-making should also be improved. The making of important laws and regulations should be organized by the legislative affairs body of the government. When formulating the administrative regulations and rules, the State Council should expand the channels for public participation, and extensively collect opinions from all the parties to gather their wisdom and strengthen and increase the level of scientific and democratic legislative decision-making. The public participation in government legislation should be expanded by providing more means and ways of participation. The practice of collecting the opinions from the people's congress deputies in making regulations should be made better, and CPPCC members, other political parties, federations of industry and commerce, people with no party affiliation, people's organizations and social organizations should also be taken into accounting during legislative consultations. An argumentation and consultation mechanism for coordinating major interests during administrative legislation should be established by incorporating relevant state departments, social organizations and experts. If the proposed institution or mechanism concerned people's interests or were confronted with divergent opinions, the State Council should extensively collect opinions by convening forums, meetings, hearings and surveys. The draft regulations and rules should be disclosed for public opinions through the Internet or newspapers except for those subject to confidentiality. The State Council should strengthen the communication with the public, make sound feedback mechanisms and help achieve social consensus during legislation. In 2012, the Legislative Affairs Office selected 4–6 administrative regulations or specific legal institutions to organize implementation assessment by entrusting relevant departments or local government legislative affairs bodies to gradually promote a regulated, standardized and scientific set of post-assessment criteria.

Last, to proactively defend the unity of national legal system, and improve the institution and mechanism for supervising the recording of regulations and rules. According to the provisions of the Constitution and the Local Organization Law, the local regulations should be reported to the NPC Standing Committee and the State Council for recording. If such local regulations contravene its upper-line laws, the NPC Standing Committee has the power to rescind them; if such contravention is found by the State Council, it may propose its solution to the NPC Standing Committee. Based on some statistics from November 2012 to August 2017, the Legislative Affairs Office registered 6619 pieces of administrative regulations (3248 pieces of local regulations, 2519 pieces of local government rules and 852 pieces of departmental rules), and urged the local governments and its departments to revised, abolish and re-exam over 500 pieces of regulations and rules according to the results of its supervision.

The working mechanism for re-examining administrative regulations, rules and normative documents was established. Referring to the needs of reform in all respects and social and economic development and the status of their upper-line laws, the State Council carried out initiatives to re-examine relevant administrative regulations, rules and normative documents in a timely manner. In early 2015, the State Council made arrangements to re-examine the documents issued by the State Council or its General Office since the founding of PRC. Through this initiative, the State Council decided to declare the invalidity of 995 pieces of documents made by the end of 2016.[24]The State Council also carried out special initiatives to re-examine regulations, rules and

[24] The purpose of re-examining documents is to make the State Council's policies and regulations better serve the socialist market economy, distribute the benefits of policies, accelerate the transformation of government functions, deepen the reform of streamlined administration and optimized services, better promote stable growth, reform, economic structuring, people's livelihood and risk prevention and maintain the fundamental interests of the majority of people.

normative documents.[25] For example, in 2017, to put into practice the Announcement on the Supervision and Treatment of Ecological Environment Problems in Qilian Mountain National Nature Reserve in Gansu Province and the Lessons Learned, the State Council made decisions to revise or abolish the local regulations, local government rules and normative documents issued by the people's governments and their departments at or above the county level which did not conform with the laws and administrative Regulation on ecological environment protection. In July 2018, the Resolution on Comprehensively Strengthening Ecological Environment Protection and Promoting the Fight of Pollution Prevention and Control was promulgated at the Fourth Session of the Thirteenth NPC Standing Committee. It stressed the urgency in re-examining the ecological environment protection regulations, rules, judicial interpretations and normative documents and called for timely abolition or revision if they were found to contravene legal provisions or fail to conform with the principles of Party's Central Committee and the needs of times. To put it into practice, the State Council issued a notice to carry out this re-examination initiative.[26]

2 Administrative Legislation of the State Council: Status and Function

The administrative authorities are the main executors of national legal system and the important force for institutional development. As the highest administrative authority in China, the State Council makes administrative regulations to perform one of its duties as stipulated in the Constitution and law. The formulation of administrative regulations is essential to establishing and improving the socialist legal system with Chinese characteristics, assuring the correct and effective implementation of the

[25] According to disclosed information, after the socialist legal system with Chinese characteristics was establishing, the State Council carried out 13 initiatives to re-examine the documents: in 2012, it revised 5 and abolished 5 administrative regulations to maintain unification of socialist legal system and promote law-based administration; from 2013 to 2014, it conducted 3 initiatives, which revised 62 administrative regulations and abolished 1 administrative regulation to advance the reform of administrative approval and transform government functions; in 2014, it revised 8 and abolished 2 administrative regulations to promote the transformation of government functions according to law, further alleviate the restrictions on market entry and stimulate social investment vitality. From 2016 to August 2019, it carried out 6 initiatives to revise 143 and abolish 8 administrative regulations to promote streamlined administration and optimized services according to law; from 2018 to August 2019, it conducted two initiatives to put into practice the reforms of the Party and state agencies.

[26] The scope of re-examination is the administrative regulations on ecological environment protection, rules made by the people's governments of the province, national autonomous regions, municipalities directly under the State Council, cities with subordinate districts and autonomous prefecture, and the departments of State Council, and the normative documents by the people's governments at or above the county level and their departments and the departments of State Council. It focused on addressing their incongruence and inconsistency with the Xi Jinping thought on ecological civilization, the spirits of relevant documents on ecological environment protection issued by the Party's Central Committee and the State Council after the 18th Party Congress, and the laws on ecological environment protection.

Constitution and laws, regulating the operations of administrative power, promoting law-based government, and ensuring and advancing the reform and opening-up and the orderly and healthy development of socialist modernization.

2.1 Overview

1. Administrative regulations are an important component of the socialist legal system with Chinese characteristics

Since the founding of the PRC, the State Council has assumed an important and indispensable responsibility in China's rule of law. In the early days of PRC, it issued administrative decrees and orders to help promote national economy and restore social order. After the reform and opening-up was started, as the socialist rule of law was under steady progress, the State Council was empowered by the Constitution and laws to make administrative regulations. Apart from making these Regulation on its own, it also proposed law bills to the NPC and its Standing Committee, and most of the laws came from the bills proposed by it for final enactment by the NPC Standing Committee. Therefore, the State Council's timely formulation of administrative regulations and proposal of law bills according to law to cater for China's social and economic development and the implementation of laws have made great contribution to the establishment and improvement of socialist legal system with Chinese characteristics.

2. It bears the responsibility to guarantee the implementation of the Constitution and laws

Since the founding of PRC, especially since the reform and opening-up, the State Council made exercise of its legislative powers via ex officio legislation, legislation for enforcement and authorized legislation to effectively guarantee the effective implementation of the Constitution and law. Since the Eighteenth CPC National Congress, the State Council has been keen on transforming government functions, promoting simplified administration, streamlined procedures and optimized services, making solid progress in scientific and democratic legislation, proposing law bills, revising and abolishing administrative regulations, strengthening the regular regulations re-examination and paying attention to formulating supporting regulations responsively. The State Council has also insisted on promoting reform based on the demands of rule of law, advanced law-based governance through reforms, made every exercise of government power, from decision-making, implementation and supervision, law-based, standardized and institutionalized, and established a complete set of institutions for law-based administration to strive for a new level of the implementation of the Constitution and law.

3. It bears the responsibility to maintain the unification of state legal system

To maintain a unified system of laws is an important responsibility for governments at all levels. Therefore, it is indispensable for the State Council to deal with the inconsistency among laws, regulations and rules. It has carried out the following work: first, to carry out the recording and review of regulations and normative documents; second, to carry out initiatives to re-examine the administrative regulations, rules and normative documents in a timely manner according to law. Although the State Council and its departments and local governments also formulated a lot of normative documents, it has been difficult to ensure their legality. Under the State Council's guidance, the local governments have gradually established an institution in which each government is subject to its immediate upper level government in respect of normative documents recording and review, which has addressed issues in abuse and excessive use of "red-headed documents".

The legislative affairs body of the State Council also established a collaborative mechanism with the Legislative Affairs Bureau of the CPC's General Office, the Legislative Affairs Commission and the Legislative Affairs Bureau of the CPC Central Military Commission to ensure the conformity of Party and military rules with laws and regulations and achieve coordinated law-based governance of the state, the Party and the armed forces.

2.2 Its Role in Law-Based Government

From 1949 to 1978, the State Council's active engagement in administrative regulations was to meet the needs of regulating the economy and society, and the concept of "law-based administration" had not yet been fully formed. After the reform and opening-up, the Party and the State put greater emphasis on guaranteeing and promoting reform and development through rule of law. As China's democratic legal system's development gains momentum, people's awareness of law and democracy, and aspirations and demands for law-based administration have also steadily increased. The change of situation has made the State Council to strengthen the establishment of legal system, stick to law-based administration and establish law-based government to harness the officials and powers under the rule of law.[27] The concept of "law-based administration" was first proposed in the Government Work Report of State Council in 1993. The 2004 Outline made all-round arrangements

[27] CAO Kangtai, *To Promote Law-based Administration in All Respects and Establish a Law-based Government: Several Reflections on Learning Deng Xiaoping Thought on Democracy and Law*, in Committee for the Forum of Deng Xiaoping's Life and Thoughts ed., Commemoration of the 100th Birthday of Deng Xiaoping: Collection of Papers in the Forum of Deng Xiaoping's Life and Thoughts (Vol. 2), Central Party Literature Press, 2005, p. 859.

on promoting law-based administration, called for "improving the quality of institutional establishment",[28] and imposed stricter requirements. The 2010 Opinions laid out the elaborate requirements on this matter in a more systemic way.

After the Eighteenth CPC National Congress, the Party's Central Committee has taken quick strides to promote rule of law, drawn special attention to the law-based government, and stated plainly that the governance of the country, the exercise of power and the work of administration must always be done according to the law and a law-based country, government and society should be integrated. Among their relation, a law-based government is the main task for promoting rule of law in all respects, which will cause exemplary effect to the construction of a law-based country and society. Again, new requirements were laid out in the Fourth Plenary Session of the Eighteenth CPC Central Committee. According to these requirements, it was stated "to thoroughly advance the administration of government on the basis of the law and accelerate our efforts to build a rule of law government" and listed in detailed the areas subject to more efforts, including the law-based performance of governance functions, sound decision-making mechanism, institutional reform of administrative law enforcement, strict, regulated and impartial enforcement of law, constraint and supervision of administrative power, and transparency of administrative affairs. One main task in the 2015 Outline was to "improve the institutional system of law-based administration" to improve the quality of administrative legislation, make a compete, scientific, standardized and effective system of law-based administration and cause the institutions of government's administration more mature and target-oriented. It also laid out the specific measures for improving the system, for example, to ameliorate the institution and mechanism for government legislation, to strengthen legislation in key areas, to increase public participation in legislation, to enhance the supervision and management of normative documents, and to set up a long-term mechanism for re-examining administrative regulations, rules and normative documents. These tasks and measures have given directions for future efforts and laid out new tasks for the State Council to advance administrative legislation as the times change.

Since the founding of the PRC, especially since the initiation of reform and opening-up, the State Council has made sustained efforts to adapt to the continuous progress of socialist rule of law and to strengthen and improve the work on administrative legislation. It not only provides guidelines to practice law-based administration among the governments at all levels, but also gradually corrects the concepts and practices that do not follow the development of socialist rule of law.

[28] The 2004 Outline specified the measures for improving quality of institutional development: to propose law bills and draft local regulations, formulate administrative regulations, rules and normative documents; to make reasonable and scientific legislative schedules based on the maturity of circumstances and focus of legislation in a coordinated manner; to transform the working methods for government legislation and increase public participation; to actively engage in the explorations for establishing a cost-efficiency analysis of government legislation, especially economic legislation; to establish a practice of regularly revising and abolishing administrative regulations and rules and re-examining rules and normative documents.

This process represents not only self-improvement and self-development for administrative legislation,[29]but also the transformation from a power-based, management-oriented, obedient and relatively closed regulatory government to a responsibility-based, service-oriented, standardized and transparent government characterized by rule of law. Its role in promoting law-based government can be made plain in the transformations: from governance based on red-headed documents, directives and administrative orders to a more mature model of governance characterized by law and institutions; from heavily relying on approval and punishment to one that aims to reasonably formulate standards, improve information disclosure and imposed administrative punishment according to law; from making captain's calls to making scientific, democratic and law-based decisions; from governing people and managing affairs to exercising the power and regulating the officials according to law; from using administrative means to resolve risks to adjusting interest relationships of market entities by respecting the market economy and market means within the framework of rule of law.

In conclusion, the State Council's expanded role in administrative legislation for a more complete system of law-based administration is essential to the construction of a law-based government and an unfailing guarantee for the regulated operations of government under the rule of law.

3 Administrative Legislation and Modernized State Governance System and Capacity

The Party and the State have made steady progress in their conceptions and methods of governance since the founding of the PRC, providing theoretical guidance and directions for the State Council's work on administrative legislation. It is a great responsibility for the State Council to translate the governance principles into legal norms and ensure the effective implementation of laws and regulations in building a law-based government.

[29] It changed from a focus on economic legislation to balanced and integrated legislation of all areas, from the focus on power and management rather than responsibility and protection to the emphasis on correctly handling the relation among power, right and responsibility in order to reasonably define the rights and obligations of citizens, legal persons and other organizations, and to impose both power and responsibility on administrative departments; from limited transparency to full transparency; from performance of primary functions in making regulations and law bills to full scale legislation including formulating, revising, abolish, interpreting and re-examining legal norms; from a low completion rate, long period, and arbitrary violation of upper level laws of supporting legislation to a prompt provision of supporting regulations.

3.1 To Keep Pace with the Times: A Fundamental Reason for Achievements of State Council

China has walked along an arduous path in which the rule by man was finally replaced by rule of law. Liang Qichao put forward the concept of "rule by law" as early as in 1904.[30] However, the sounds of guns and canons prevailed the call for rule by law, and in a period of wars, the rule by law was an illusion. Since the founding of PRC, the Party has led Chinese people to make arduous explorations, though in some time there were failures in building rule of law. As a whole, as the true faithful representative of the people's interests, it has gradually recognized that law-based governance was a much-deserved pursuit during its long-lasting governance of China. Later, it set out it as the fundamental principle of governance, continued to strengthen the work on legislation, made ready a complete national system of laws, and contributed to the promotion of rule of law.

In the Fifteenth CPC National Congress held in 1997, it put forward the goal of "governing the country according to the law and making it a socialist country ruled by the law". Seven years later, it was written down in the Constitutional Amendment, which marked beginning of rule of law as a Constitutional pursuit. Since the Eighteenth CPC National Congress, the Party's Central Committee with Xi Jinping as the core highly valued a comprehensive rule of law and made new ideas, thoughts and strategies for promoting it. As pointed out by Xi Jinping, "the comprehensive advancement of the rule of law is a systematic undertaking and a profound and far-reaching revolution in the governance of our country", and "shrewd people of petty mind attend to trivial matters, of medium wisdom attend to the rule of people, while people with vision attend to legislation. The key to the governance of a country and a society is to make, respect and observe rules. Law is the most important rule for governance of a country. To modernize the national governance system and capacity should strictly follow the rule of law, which is the fundamental, comprehensive and long-lasting institutional guarantee for the Party and the state's undertakings." The proposal of "building rule of law in China", the Resolution of the Central Committee of the CPC on Major Issues Concerning the Enhancement of All-round Law-based Governance and the establishment of Commission for Law-based Governance and the measures for it represent the increasingly deepened understanding of the law for Party's governance, socialist construction and the development of human society. The progress made in the Party and state's understandings and methods provide guidance and directions for the State Council to strengthen administrative legislation and promote law-based government, and are the fundamental reason for the achievements made by the State Council in this regard.

---

[30] Liang Qichao said, "in today's world, each country is closely related with another, and the race for survival is increasingly fierce. Without strictly internal regulations of a country, it will not defend other powers. Rule of law is the only way for survival. And legislation is the most urgent undertaking for the survival of China.", see Liang Qichao, *History of the Development of Chinese Jurisprudence*, in FAN Zhongxin ed., *Liang Qichao's Essays on Jurisprudence*, China University of Political Science and Law Press, 1997, p. 71.

3.2 *To Transform Governance Principles into Legal Norms: A Major Responsibility of State Council*

Only the correct governance principles can be designed as useful public policies or transformed into a set of institutions can they be turned into a dynamic and orderly action in practice. The vitality of an institution lies in its manifestation of governance principles and values, and only with such vitality can the institution be accepted and observed by the public.[31] In this case, legislation in the precondition for advancing a comprehensive rule of law. To play the role of legislation in leading and promoting development is the Party's mastery of legislation in governance and is also an explicit requirement for strengthening and improving the work on legislation. Not all the laws are good for governance, and not all the laws can better governance. A comprehensive rule of law requires good laws for better governance. Therefore, it is the great responsibility for the State Council to effectuate administrative legislation. on one hand, it needs to accelerate legislation in implementing new development principles, perfecting people's democracy, guaranteeing and improving people's livelihood, nurturing civilized habits, innovating social governance, making China beautiful, maintaining national security, promoting law-based administration and carrying out self-improvement, cause the provision of a sound institutional environment and a full set of administrative regulations for quality development, and secure and promote quality development through quality legislation. On the other hand, it needs to continue improving the mechanism for scientific, democratic and law-based legislation, integrate administrative legislation with big data and artificial intelligence, innovate the way of public participation in administrative legislation, increase the public participation and transparency and make timely response to people's anticipations in order to adhere to the universal law, realize people's aspiration and collect their wisdom for administrative legislation and effectually make laws and regulations more scientific, target-oriented and effective.[32]

The magnificent history of PRC's administrative legislation in the past 70 years undergoes the same path with China's socialist modernization and construction of rule of law. It also witnesses the staggering start of PRC, the total destruction in the Cultural Revolution, the rapid development during the reform and opening-up,

---

[31] WANG Yongqing, *To Turn Governance Principles into Systems, Institutions and Mechanisms*, Qiushi Journal, Vol. 24, pp. 37–38 (2007).

[32] An effective public participation in the decision-making of administrative legislation is critical to guaranteeing impartial, reasonable, scientific and democratic legislation. It will not only prevent institutional wrongs in decision-making and mistakes in regulating the system, but also improve administration, working efficiency, and government authority. In addition, effective participation will also strengthen administrative supervision to avoid the lack or abuse of administrative power, balance the interest relations, and help promote the respect, observance and protection of law. In a conclusion, it is of great significance to promote democratic legal system, strengthen and innovate social management, make a more harmonious and stable society and guarantee scientific development of China's economy and society. See QING Feng, *Analysis of the Status of Public Participation in Administrative Legislation for Decision-making*, Journal of Shanghai University of Political Science and Law, No. 6, pp. 1–13(2012).

and the tortuous development for a comprehensive rule of law in the new era. It has lived through these difficulties, made remarkable achievements and contributed to the formation and improvement of the Chinese socialist legal system. As pointed out by Deng Xiaoping, "the experience of successes is valuable, and so is the experience of mistakes and defeats."[33] Thus the experience deserves a full summary. When the Chinese socialism enters the new era, the administrative legislation of State Council also stands on the new starting line, and undertakes more important missions and plays bigger role in promoting the comprehensive rule of law, which certainly will bring about more contributions to the modernization of state governance system and capacity.

[33] Deng Xiaoping, *Selected Works of Deng Xiaoping* (Vol. 3), Foreign Languages Press, 1994, p. 232.

Chapter 7
Local Regulations: History, Status and Function

Luo Huanxing and Qu Di

Abstract This chapter traces the evolution of local regulations in China. From 1954 to 1978, only autonomous regions enjoyed limited rule-making power; provinces and cities had none. The 1979 Local Organization Law first granted provincial legislatures authority to enact "local regulations," and the 1982 Constitution affirmed this tier. The 2000 Legislation Law added "larger cities," and the 2015 amendment extended the power to all prefecture-level cities, creating today's 353 local legislative bodies. It details the four phases, analyzes the features, functions and achievements of local regulations, and summarizes the basic experience from the local legislation.

Keywords Local legislation · Local regulations · Four phases · Features and functions · Basic experience · New demands

As a unified, multi-ethnic and unitary socialist country, China adopts a unified and multi-tiered legislative system. While the National People's Congress (NPC) and its Standing Committee exercise the legislative power of the State, legislative power is also distributed across various levels. The State Council formulates administrative regulations, while the local people's congresses and their standing committees, also vested with legislative power, formulate local regulations. As an important part of the socialist legal system with Chinese characteristics local regulations serve as a vital supplement to national legislation. This legislative power can be exercised by the people's congresses and their standing committees at the level of province, national autonomous regions and municipalities directly under the State Council, cities with subordinate districts and autonomous prefectures. Since the local governments exercised their legislative power, they have aligned with their efforts with the priorities of the Party and the State, taken national legislation as the guide, advanced legislation with the times, kept pace with reforms, and developed with practice.

L. Huanxing (✉) · Q. Di
Beijing, China
e-mail: liujixuan@lawpress.com.cn

Q. Di
e-mail: liujixuan@lawpress.com.cn

C. Shen et al. (eds.), *A History of Legislation in the Past 70 Years in China*,
https://doi.org/10.1007/978-981-95-3799-0_7

These efforts have contributed to the formation, development and improvement of the Chinese socialist legal system as scheduled. As of August 2019, more than 12,000 local regulations were in force, covering various aspects such as economy, politics, culture, society, and ecological environment, which reflects the requirements of the Five-sphere Integrated Plan and Four-pronged Comprehensive Strategy. The local legislation has played an important role in helping form and improve the socialist legal system, building China into a law-based country under the rule of law, and promoting the modernization of the national governance system and capacity.

1 History

To grant legislative power to the local legislatures represents a significant development of China's legislative system and a pivotal step toward strengthening local power.

In the early days of the PRC, the local still retained substantial power, especially inlcuding the legislative power comparable to that of the central government, because the new country had not established a unified and centralized system of state power. According to the Common Program, the NPC shall be the supreme organ of state power, and the Central People's Government shall be the supreme organ for exercising state power when the NPC is not in session. Pending the convocation of the National People's Congress elected by universal franchise, the Plenary Session of the Chinese People's Political Consultative Conference shall exercise the functions and powers of the NPC, enact the Organic Law of the Central People's Government of the People's Republic of China, elect the Central People's Government Council of the People's Republic of China and vest it with the authority to exercise state power. According to the Organic Law of the Central People's Government, the Central People's Government Council had the power to enact and interpret the laws of the state, promulgate decrees and supervise their execution. Based on them, there was also local legislative power. At that time, above the provincial level there were greater administrative areas, i.e. the Northeast, North, East, Central South, Southwest and Northwest China Greater Administrative Regions.

According to the provisions of the General Rules on the Organization of the People's Government Councils of the Greater Administrative Regions adopted on December 16, 1949, each council had the power to enact provisional decrees and regulations on their own administrative affairs, and then report to the State Council for approval or recording. Similar general rules on the organization of the provincial, city and county people's governments also authorized them to make provisional decrees, regulations or separate regulations and then report to the upper level people's government for approval or recording. However, this early exercise of local legislative power was short-lived and, by modern conception of the rule of law, were not technically the formal exercise of legislative power. Then in 1952 the Central People's Government Council issued a decision to change the greater administrative regions into administrative councils as the representatives of the Central Government assigned to lead and supervise the people's governments within their own administrative area. The greater administrative region ceased to be the highest local authority. Two years later, to consolidate national unification, strengthen central government's administration of the local governments, exercise unified and centralized leadership, and fight against decentralization, the Central People's Government put an end to the greater administrative region and appointed these leaders to the central departments.

This shift in central-local relations was also mirrored in the exercise of legislative power. The 1954 Constitution instituted a more centralized legislative system, designating the NPC as the only legislative authority of the state. It empowered it to amend the Constitution, enact laws, supervise the enforcement of the Constitution and other functions and powers, while authorizing its Standing Committee to interpret laws, promulgate decrees and others. The State Council was restricted to formulating administrative measures, issue decisions and orders and verify their execution. The local legislation was significantly curtailed; the local people's congresses could only adopt and issue decisions and local people's council could only issue decisions and orders within the limits of authority prescribed by law. But it also laid down the foundation for self-government legislative power Departments of self-government of all autonomous regions, prefectures and counties were authorized to draw up statutes governing the exercise of autonomy or separate regulations suited to the political, economic and cultural characteristics of the nationality or nationalities in a given area, and report them to the NPC Standing Committee for approval.

Though it helped to maintain the unified exercise of central legislative power, it also brought about some problems and demotivated the local authority. In order to embark on a correct socialist path that suited to China's conditions, Mao Zedong summarized the experience from the Soviet's highly centralized management model, and made his own thinking on how to better simulate the central and local initiative. In *On Ten Major Relationships*, he pointed out that "our attention should now be focused on how to enlarge the powers of the local authorities to some extent, give them greater independence and let them do more, all on the premise that the unified leadership of the central authorities is to be strengthened. This will be advantageous to our task of building a powerful socialist country. Our territory is so vast, our population is so large and the conditions are so complex that it is far better to have the initiative come from both the central and the local authorities than from one source alone", and "according to our Constitution, the legislative powers are all vested in the central authorities. But, provided that the policies of the central authorities are not violated, the local authorities may work out rules, regulations and measures in the light of their specific conditions and the needs of their work, and this is in no way prohibited by the Constitution. We want both unity and particularity. To build a powerful socialist country it is imperative to have a strong and unified central leadership and unified planning and discipline throughout the country; disruption of this indispensable unity is impermissible. At the same time, it is essential to bring the initiative of the local authorities into full play and let each locality enjoy the particularity suited to its local conditions", so "the central authorities should take care to give scope to the initiative of the provinces and municipalities, and the latter in their turn should do the same for the prefectures, counties, districts and townships; in neither case should the lower levels be put in a strait-jacket."[1] However, these problems were not solved due to the left-line mistakes in the Party and other reasons until the start of reform and opening-up.

The local legislative power emerged from the socialist modernization and the requirements laid out by the mission of establishing democratic legal system and the legislation for deepening reform and opening-up. When the Cultural Revolution came to an end, the Third Plenary Session of the Eleventh CPC Central Committee was opportunely convened to summarized the experience and lessons, restore justice and order, turn the focus to socialist modernization, and make the decision of reform and opening-up. In the closed meeting of the Central Work Conference held in December 1978, Ye Jianying stressed that socialist legal system was not yet established. The case of Lin Biao and the Gang of Four had taught us a grave lesson that a state could not stand without laws and systems, and they should be stable and continual…it should possess tremendous authority, and could only be revised through legal procedures rather than the wishes of certain leader. In this meeting, Deng made his famous speech, Emancipate the Mind, Seek Truth from Facts and Unite as One in Looking to the Future. He said that "to ensure people's democracy, we must strengthen our legal system. Democracy has to be institutionalized and written into law, so as to make sure that institutions and laws do not change whenever the leadership changes, or whenever the leaders change their views or shift the focus of their attention", "so we must concentrate on enacting criminal and civil codes, procedural laws and other necessary laws…", "all this will ensure that there are laws to go by, that they are observed and strictly enforced, and that violators are brought to book." The Party leaders also reflect on how to solve the problems of centralized power by reforming the legislative institution, i.e. considering a legislative institution that could give play to the initiative of the central and local authorities. Deng even made detailed instructions on local legislation: "some laws and statutes can be tried out in particular localities and later enacted nationally after the experience has been evaluated and improvements have been made." His directive actually put into practice the visions of Mao Zedong.

The 1979 Local Organization Law prescribed that the standing committees be established in the local people's congresses at or above the county level, and the people's congresses of the provinces, autonomous regions and municipalities directly under the State Council and their standing committees may enact and issue local regulations which do not contravene the Constitution, laws, policies, decrees and orders, and report to the NPC Standing Committee and State Council for the record. To answer the question why the legislative power was granted to the provincial people's congresses, Peng Zhen gave an elaborate reply. He said, as a country with vast land and many ethnic groups, the political, economic and cultural development was uneven in China, even for a province or an autonomous region. Therefore, if everything was left for the central authority to decide and impose one set of rigid standards for the whole nation, it would be hard to adapt to the changes and differences, and there surely came with omissions and arbitrariness. It had been

[1] Mao Zedong, *Selected Works of Mao Zedong (Vol. 5)*, Foreign Languages Press, 1977, pp. 292–294.

proven futile by the practice…so the specific issues could not be decided by the central authority. It would be better to resolve these local issues by referring to the general principles made by the central authority and relying on the actual circumstance of their own. The Decision on Several Provisions on Amending the Constitution issued in the Second Session of the Fifth National People's Congress provided constitutional basis for formulating the Local Organization Law and other relevant laws, which marked a great change of China's law on local legislative power.

In December 1982, the amended Constitution was adopted, which incorporated the provisions on the power of making local regulations by the people's congresses and their standing committees of the provinces and municipalities directly under the State Council and on the power of formulating self-government regulations and separate regulations by the people's congresses of the autonomous regions. For the first time, a comprehensive set of provisions were made for granting local legislative power, which fully mobilized the local enthusiasm and initiative and promoted the work of people's congress at the new historical starting line of reform and opening-up. As pointed by Peng Zhen in his Report on the Draft Constitution, these provisions were purported to strengthen the local power to enable them to engage in local undertakings based on their own conditions under the unified central leadership.

Considering the importance of large cities' political, economic and cultural development and the necessity for them to make local regulations for promoting these developments, the Local Organization Law was also revised in this conference. The revised law empowered the cities where the people's governments of provinces and national autonomous areas reside and the large cities approved by the State Council to draft local regulations, submit them to their provincial standing committees for deliberation and issuance, and then report them to NPC Standing Committee and the State Council for the record. The reason for this provision was that the Constitution did not grant legislative power to the cities other than municipalities directly under the State Council. These cities could only have the power to prepare the drafts and then propose the provincial standing committees for final adoption.

As the institutional reform and practice evolved, the Local Organization Law was revised again in the Eighteenth Session of the Sixth National People's Congress, which prescribed that the people's congresses of the cities where the people's governments of provinces and national autonomous areas reside and the large cities approved by the State Council and their standing committees may formulate local regulations, which did not contravene the Constitution, laws, administrative regulations and local regulations of the province or national autonomous regions, report them to the standing committees of the people's congresses of the provinces and national autonomous areas, which then report to the NPC Standing Committee and the State Council for the record. Within just 7 years, i.e. from 1979 to 1986, a layout of local legislation emerged, vesting the people's congresses of the province and large cities with legislative power. From 1980s to early 1990s, the State Council approved 19 large cities in four times considering their locations, population and economic development: Tangshan, Datong, Baotou, Dalian, Anshan, Fushun, Jilin, Qiqihar, Qingdao, Wuxi, Huainan, Luoyang and Chongqing (later upgraded to municipality directly under the State Council) in 1984, Ningbo in 1988, Zibo, Handan and Benxi in 1992, Suzhou and Xuzhou in 1993. Though the applications never stopped, the State Council did not approve any one of them as large cities.

The NPC made decisions to set up Hainan Province and Chongqing Municipality in 1988 and 1997 respectively, and they were also granted with corresponding legislative power. Further, the NPC also authorized the people's congresses and their standing committees of Hainan Province, Shenzhen, Xiamen, Shantou and Zhuhai to make regulations according to the conditions of these special economic zones and actual needs. The 2000 Law on Legislation stipulated greater legislative power for the cities housing the special economic zones. By that time, the local legislative bodies increased to 31 for the provinces, national autonomous regions and municipalities directly under the State Council and 49 for the large cities.

Another major progress in the development of China's local legislation was made in 2015 Law on Legislation, which granted such power to the people's congresses of cities divided by district and their standing committees. Since the Eighteenth CPC National Congress, the Party's Central Committee with Xi Jinping as the core has provided in-depth thinking on China's legislative system in order to suit the new demands for modernizing state governance system and capacity, meet the new expectations of the people for better life after China's social contradiction was changed and better bring the initiative of both the central and local authorities into full play. Great changes have taken place in local economic and social development since the reform and opening-up, and many cities divided by district are large in scale. According to the new criteria for cities issued by the State Council, there are 87 megacities that are with subordinate districts (with an urban permanent population of more than five million and less than ten million), accounting for 30% of the total, and some urban areas have a permanent population of over ten million (super-cities), such as Linyi in Shandong and Nanyang in Henan; there are 82 type I large cities that are with subordinate districts (with a population of more than three million and less than five million in urban areas), accounting for 29%. The population of these cities is larger than that of some countries in the world, and some are even equivalent to the population of a medium-sized European country. Type I large cities and megacities add up to nearly 60% of total Chinese populations.

As China's economy, society and urbanization are in rapid development, and people's material and cultural living standards are improved, their expectations for a better life continue to increase, but the issues in social governance, including these in land, population, health, education, old-aged care, social security and housing, especially the ones in environment protection, urban construction and management, taxi and ride-hailing services, are increasingly complex and involved with a lot of interest adjustments. The desire of people to express their interest demands through legal means, and they have made more requirements for participating in the management and governance of the state, social, economic and cultural undertakings. Such desire and requirements need to be met through legislation. However, the national laws and regulations cannot extend their reach to every aspect of social life, which requires local legislation to refine and implement national laws and regulations on certain issues. And in order to effectively deal with some problems that are difficult to be solved by provincial legislation, it is necessary to give the cities with subordinate districts with more local legislative powers according to the requirements of building China into a law-based country. Therefore, considering the development of China's economy and society and a law-based China, the local authorities have more actual needs for legislation, and the voice calling for equal legislative power to be given to all districted cities in the administrative division gets louder. Some NPC deputies have repeatedly put forward bills and suggestions to increase the number of larger cities with local legislative power, and some cities with subordinate districts have also continued to apply to the State Council for approval to be larger cities with local power to make laws and regulations.

In order to adapt to the new situation, new tasks and new requirements of promoting the modernization of the state governance system and capacity, and to give better play to the initiative of both the central and local authorities, in the Third Plenary Session of the Eighteenth CPC Central Committee, it was proposed to gradually increase the number of large cities with local legislative power. In its Fourth Plenary Session, it was proposed to improve the legislative system, clarify the limit and scope of local legislative power, and grant it to cities with subordinate districts according to law. The equal granting of local legislative power to cities with subordinate districts was a strategic decision made by the Party's Central Committee to strengthen and improve state governance.

To better implement the major decisions and arrangements made by the Party's Central Committee, the Law on Legislation was revised in the Third Session of the 12th National People's Congress, vesting all the cities with subordinate districts with local legislative power. It made clear that the people's congresses of cities with subordinate districts and their standing committees may make regulations on the urban and rural development and administration, environmental protection, and historic and cultural protection, so long as the local provisions do not contravene the Constitution, laws, administrative regulations, or the local provisions and regulations of that province or autonomous region. It also granted local legislative power to 30 autonomous prefectures and 4 cities with no subordinate districts, namely Jiayuguan, Dongguan, Zhongshan and Sansha. In the First Session of the 13th National People's Congress convened in 2018, the Constitutional Amendment added a provision on the legislative power of cities with subordinate districts, providing a constitutional basis for the legislation of cities with subordinate districts. So far, the number of local legislative bodies in China has increased to 353, including 31 provinces, autonomous regions, and municipalities directly under the State Council, 288 cities with subordinate districts, 30 autonomous prefectures, and 4 cities with no subordinate districts.

2 Development of Local Legislation

The development of the exercise of legislative power by local people's congresses and their standing committees can be categorized into the following four periods.

2.1 Early Explorations (1979–1992)

From the establishment of the Standing Committee of the People's Congress of the Tibet Autonomous Region in August 1979, to June 1980, the people's congresses of 29 provinces, autonomous regions, and municipalities directly under the State Council in China established their own standing committees, and began to exercise local legislative power (Hainan was not yet established as a province, and Chongqing not as a municipality directly under the State Council). On November 29, 1979, the Second Session of the Standing Committee of the Fifth People's Congress of the Xinjiang Uygur Autonomous Region adopted three decisions and resolutions, including the Circular on Strengthening the Work on the Public Security of Border Areas, the first of its kind in China since 1978. As of June 1981, 29 provincial (autonomous regions and municipalities directly under the State Council) standing committees of people's congresses had formulated local regulations, primarily focusing on the implementation rules for community people's congress elections and extension of the time limit for handling criminal cases.

At the Twelfth CPC National Congress held in September 1982, to establish socialism with Chinese characteristics was laid out as a major thesis, and that Chinese people would be comparatively well-off both materially and culturally was the strategic goal for next-phase development. This conference also made elaborations on the nature, direction and mission of reform and opening-up. The decision on reforming economic institutions was adopted at the Third Plenary Session of the Twelfth CPC Central Committee convened in October 1984, which stressed a comprehensive economic institution reform with a focus on urban areas. The local legislation could be carried out according to their own conditions but strictly following the reform decisions and arrangements made by the Party's Central Committee. It mainly focused on three aspects: first, to formulate local regulations to enforce the laws. For example, some local legislative bodies adopted measures for the Land Administration Law, Urban Planning Law, Environment Protection Law, Law on the Protection of Wildlife Animals, Forest Law, Fisheries Law, Law on the Organization of the Urban Residents' Committees, Law on the Organization of the Villagers' Committees, Law on Assemblies, Processions and Demonstrations, Law on the Protection of the Rights and Interests of Returned Overseas Chinese and the like. Second, to carry out innovative legislation and adopt regulations for pilot programs. For example, some local legislature, based on their own actual conditions, carried out legislation on special economic zones, encouragement of foreign investment, commodity quality supervision, agricultural technology promotion, crop seed administration, agricultural machinery accident handling, traditional Chinese medicine management, alcohol management, protection of the rights and interests of the elderly, and prohibition of gambling. For example, the Standing Committee of the Guangdong Provincial People's Congress formulated provisional regulations on land administration for the Shenzhen Special Economic Zone in 1981 according to the provisions of authorized legislation. These regulations, for the first time, made provisions on the separation of land ownership from land use rights and established the system of land use and transfer, a catalyst for the reform of the national land property rights system and a practical basis for the revision of the Land Administration Law. Third, to formulate regulations to strengthen local people's congress. For example, some formulated the rules of procedure for local people's congresses and their standing committees, and some have also formulated rules for the legislative and supervisory work of the people's congresses. For example, on March 5, 1980, Shanghai Municipal People's Congress adopted the Provisional Rules for the Election of Shanghai District and County People's Congress, creating a precedent for local legislation in Shanghai. On October 6, 1980, the Detailed Rules for the Implementation of Direct Elections at the County Level in Gansu Province which was reviewed and approved by the Fourth Session of the Standing Committee of the Fifth National People's Congress of Gansu Province, marked the first step in the local legislation.

2.2 *Striving for A Market Economic System (1992–2002)*

Following the speeches delivered by Deng Xiaoping during his southern tour, the Fourteenth CPC National Congress established the goal of building socialist market economic institution. It outlined the main tasks of speeding up reform and opening-up and promoting overall economic and social development put forward, and it also emphasized the work on legislation, particularly focusing on the enactment of laws and regulations for improving and securing reform and opening-up, strengthening macro-economic administration and regulating micro-economic activities. In the Third Plenary Session of the Fourteenth CPC Central Committee, a lot of higher requirements were laid down, including the focus on the construction of legal system to ensure its integration with reform and opening-up and the expertise in applying the means of law to manage the economy. In the First Session of the Eighth National People's Congress, it was proposed to speed up legislation, especially economic legislation as the most important legislative area to promote reform and opening-up and help establishing the socialist market economic institution. Based on these requirements, in the Fifteenth CPC National Congress, it was made further clear to "advocate rule of law and establish China into a socialist rule of law country", and "the work on legislation should be strengthened and a Chinese socialist legal system would be established till 2010."

The local legislation had resolutely followed and implemented the decisions and arrangements of the Party's Central Committee. They have taken the laws enacted by the NPC Standing Committee as a benchmark, placed the economic legislation at the center of their legislative work, and carried out legislative in a remarkably rapid pace. The most prominent period was between 1993 to 1997, when the average annual legislation in some provinces and cities was about 20, of which economic legislation accounted for a large share, and some even reached more than 50%. For example, the local legislature in Shanghai in the 1990s focused on economic legislation for developing market economy. Only in the term of the Tenth Shanghai Municipal People's

Congress and its Standing Committee between 1993 and 1998, 59 local regulations were promulgated, accounting for nearly half of the total local regulations since the Shanghai Municipal People's Congress and its Standing Committee began to exercise legislative power in 1980. Even more remarkable was the formulation of 31 regulations on economic affairs, accounting for 52%. In these 5 years, the local legislation, together with national legislation, mainly focused on the goal of building a socialist market economic legal system as required by the NPC Standing Committee, thus economic legislation was in its prime. The economic legislation was carried out mainly on the following aspects: First, to promote the economic institution reform. It had formulated the regulations on economic and technological development zones, bonded areas, science and technology parks, approval and liquidation of foreign-invested enterprises, labor relations in Sino-foreign joint ventures, and introduction and absorption of technologies for promoting the development of private and individual economic sectors. Second, to maintain market order. The regulations on price administration, anti-unfair competition, product quality supervision and administration, and supervision of standard contract terms were formulated. Third, to regulate the construction and real estate market. It formulated regulations on urban road and bridge management, construction project quality administration, engineering materials management, project cost, tendering and bidding, registration, development, operation, transfer, evaluation, leasing and pre-sale of real estate property rights, property management and others. Fourth, to promote rural and agricultural development. Regulations on basic farmland protection, water and soil conservation laws and regulations were formulated. Fifth, to protect the rights and interests of workers. Regulations on the employment of migrant workers, enterprise collective contracts, protection of labor rights and interests, labor inspection, and work-related injury insurance were formulated. Sixth, to protect intellectual property rights. Regulations such as patent protection and technical secret protection were formulated. In addition, all local legislative bodies also strengthened legislation in the fields of democratic politics, urban and rural management, and cultural progress, involving the matters on letters and visits, religious affairs management, fire protection, city appearance and health, funeral and interment, consumer rights protection, and libraries.

2.3 Coordinated Promotion of Legislation in All Areas (2003–2012)

The goal of making China a moderately prosperous country in all respects was advocated in the Sixteenth CPC National Congress, and "to make the socialist democracy sounder and socialist legal system more complete and the rule of law as fundamental principle is implemented in all respects" was an important goal for advancing moderately prosperous country. It reiterated the importance of "strengthening the work on legislation, improving legislation quality and forming the socialist legal system with Chinese characteristics by 2010". The Scientific Outlook on Development was proposed in the Third Plenary Session of the Sixteenth CPC Central Committee, which called for improving socialist market institution according to the requirements of coordinated efforts for urban and rural areas, regions, economy and society, man and nature, and domestic development and opening-up. In its Seventeenth Congress, the Party put forward the full-scale practice of the Scientific Outlook on Development as a strategic mission, proposed to "comprehensively implement the rule of law as the fundamental principles, accelerate the construction of socialist law-based country" and "to adhere to legislation in a scientific and democratic manner and improve socialist legal system with Chinese characteristics".

In this period, while focusing on economic legislation, the local legislature implemented the Scientific Outlook on Development, paid attention to promoting legislation on social affairs, cultural progress, ecological environment protection and other areas, made the legislative schedule more specific to coordinate law-making efforts in various areas, and ensured a more robust institutional design for legislation to improve the working mechanisms and institutions of legislation. The local legislation was carried out mainly in the following five aspects: first, to continue economic legislation. They revised and improved the regulations on budget management, transfer payments, financial risk control, labor inspection and the like, and formulated regulations on electronic transactions, promotion of small and medium-sized enterprises, promotion of independent innovation, labor force administration and labor contracts. Second, to safeguard socialist democracy. They improved the system of people's congresses and the community self-governance system, formulated or amended the rules of procedure of the people's congresses, the provisions of the standing committee's bills and methods for hearing special work reports, the regulations on the handling of representatives' suggestions, the detailed rules for the implementation of the law on deputies, the detailed rules for the implementation of the Electoral Law, and the measures for legislative hearings and other regulations. Third, to keep eye on social legislation with focus. The local legislative bodies formulated regulations on road traffic safety, public health emergency response, social insurance fund supervision, work injury insurance, wage payment, employment assistance, taxi management, protection of the rights and interests of the elderly, protection of the rights and interests of the disabled, volunteering services, fireworks management, house engineering and decoration management. Fourth, to strengthen cultural legislation. Regulations on public culture promotion, intangible cultural heritage protection, historical and cultural city protection, and national fitness were formulated. Fifth, to focus on legislation in the field of ecological environment protection. They formulated regulations on forest protection, water pollution prevention, noise pollution prevention, and energy conservation to address the conflict between economic development and environmental resource protection through the framework of legal institutions.

In 2009, in order to ensure the internal harmony and unity of the socialist legal system with Chinese characteristics to be established as scheduled, referring to the arrangements of the NPC Standing Committee, all local legislative bodies carried out a comprehensive review of local regulations to address the inconsistency within the legal system, especially of the ones formulated in the early stage that were obviously not in line with the requirements of the socialist market economy, the laws and administrative regulations, and other local regulations. The cleanup played an important role in the formation of the legal system as scheduled.

Through the joint unremitting efforts of all parties, by the end of 2010, the socialist legal system with Chinese characteristics was formed as scheduled. The legal system is commanded by the Constitution, with laws related to the Constitution, civil and commercial law and other legal departments as the pillars divided by laws, administrative regulations and local regulations. It ensures that there are laws to abide by in the development of economy, politics, culture, society and ecology. It is an important milestone in the history of China's socialist democratic legal system construction, which is also of great practical significance and far-reaching historical significance. As an important part of the Chinese socialist legal system, local regulations play an important role in implementing, making supplements to and carrying out exploratory efforts for the construction of socialist rule of law, and provide the legal guarantee for local economic and social development.

2.4 *Leading and Promoting Comprehensive Reform (After 2013)*

Since the Eighteenth CPC National Congress, the Party's Central Committee with Xi Jinping as the core has put extraordinary attention on rule of law and legislation. As pointed out by its report, "the rule of law is the basic way for running the country", "we should make laws in a scientific way, enforce them strictly, administer justice impartially, and ensure that everyone abides by the law", and "we should improve the socialist system of laws with Chinese characteristics, strengthen legislation in key areas". According to the Third Plenary Session of the Eighteenth CPC Central Committee, the overall goal of deepening the reform comprehensively is to improve and develop socialism with Chinese characteristics, and to promote the modernization of the state governance system and capacity. In the fourth plenary session, the Party issued the Resolution of the Central Committee of the CPC on Major Issues Concerning the Enhancement of All-round Law-based Governance, which laid out the guidelines, overall goal and basic principles and made a full range of arrangements on scientific legislation, strict law enforcement, impartial justice, law observance and team building for rule of law, and the promotion and improvement of the Party's leadership in fully advancing rule of law. Its overall goal is to establish a socialist rule of law system with Chinese characteristics and build China into a law-based country. At the same time, it proposed to improve the socialist legal system with Chinese characteristics with the Constitution as the core, and called for improving the enforcement and supervision system of the Constitution and the legislative system, promoting legislation in a scientific, democratic and law-based manner, strengthening legislation in key areas, and ensuring legislation and reform decision be interconnected and the legislation adapt to the needs of reform and social economic development. As required by the Nineteenth CPC National Congress, the Party should be dedicated to carrying out lawmaking in a well-conceived and democratic way and in accordance with law, so that good laws are made to promote development and ensure good governance. It also proposed a two 15-year plan on advancing comprehensive rule of law: from 2020–2035, the rule of law for the country, the government, and society is basically in place; and from 2035 to the middle of the twenty-first century, modernization of China's system and capacity for governance is achieved.

Thc local legislature's adherence to the Party' Central Committee's decisions and arrangements can be illustrated from the following five aspects:

The first is to lead and promote the local reform and development. By focusing on the overall situation of the state and local development, the local legislatures carry out their work to implement the initiatives for the Pilot Free Trade Zone, the Guangdong-Hong Kong-Macao Greater Bay Area, the Yangtze River Economic Belt, the integration of Beijing-Tianjin-Hebei, and the Yangtze River Delta, so as to give full play to the role of legislation in leading and promoting reform, which finally put into practice the Central Committee's decisions and arrangements and promote local economic and social development.

Second is to carry out legislation on ecological environment protection. They have revised the implementing regulations on environmental protection, air pollution prevention, water resources management, drinking water protection and the like. Some also made regulations on one specific matter to protect the ecological resources including mountains, rivers and lakes. For example, in July 2018, the NPC Standing Committee convened a meeting outside its plan to hear and review the inspection report on the law enforcement of the Law on the Prevention of Air Pollution, and adopted the Resolution on Comprehensively Strengthening Ecological Environment Protection and Promoting the Fight of Pollution Prevention and Control. According to statistics in the law enforcement inspection, 20 provinces (autonomous regions and municipalities directly under the State Council) have formulated relevant regulations on air pollution prevention. The Legislative Affairs Committee issued the Opinions on Strengthening and Accelerating Local Legislation on the Prevention and Control of Air Pollution and Ecological Environmental Protection, which clearly required that the relevant provinces, autonomous regions, and municipalities directly under the State Council should complete the formulation or revision of the local regulations on air pollution prevention by the end of 2018 if they had not.

The third is to make local regulations on people's livelihood. The local regulations on the protection of the disabled, protection of the rights and interests of the elderly, elderly care institutions, pre-hospital medical emergency services, smoking control, population and family planning and others were formulated to respond to the concerns of the people in a timely manner, and to protect the rights and interests of citizens. For example, at the National Health and Health Conference held in August 2016, Xi Jinping and other party and state leaders delivered important speeches, emphasizing that promoting the reform and development of health and health undertakings and building a healthy China were major strategies related to the overall China's modernization drive. To put it into practice, Beijing formulated the

Regulations on National Fitness in Beijing in a timely manner, which highlighted the protection of citizens' health rights and interests and their fitness needs and other civil rights, attached importance to the active role of fitness social organizations and fitness teams, and actively promoted the idea of social co-construction and sharing by the whole people.

The fourth is to focus on legislation in urban and rural construction and administration. They have formulated regulations on social credit, promotion of civilized behaviors, service and management of floating population, food safety, underground space planning, safe operation of rail transit, taxi management, garbage classification, park management, and dog raising management to improve the level of refined urban and rural development and administration.

The last is to make legislation guarantee democratic politics. The detailed rules on public pledge of allegiance to the Constitution to promote the enforcement of the Constitution in their own regions, the local regulations on legislation were revised to make more standardized and institutionalized, and the regulations on village committee elections were also changed to ensure the exercise of the people's democratic rights.

The 2015 Law on Legislation granted all the cities with subordinate districts with legislative power. However, they are large in number and their regional differences also contribute to their different capacity. To make the exercise of their legislative power safe and stable, the people's congresses of the province and autonomous regions and their standing committees are authorized to decide on the steps and time for allowing the cities with subordinate districts and autonomous prefectures to start their work on legislation. After reviewing their population, area, social and economic development, demands for legislation and legislative capability, these upper level people's congresses and standing committees should properly complete such authorization and guide them properly use it in an orderly manner. The reason why the legislative power of the cities with subordinate districts is limited to areas of "urban and rural development and administration, environmental protection, and historic and cultural protection" is that such local legislative power should meet the local needs but also avoid redundant legislation in order to maintain the unity of legal system. However, the scope of these areas varies. For example, the urban and rural development and management includes urban and rural planning, infrastructure construction, municipal administration and the like; the environmental protection, according to the provisions of the Environment Protection Law, includes the air, water, ocean, land, minerals, forests, grasslands, wetlands, wildlife creatures, natural relics, cultural relics, nature reserves, scenic spots, cities and villages and others. As of December 2018, 272 of the 273 cities with subordinate districts (including autonomous prefectures) have been authorized by their upper level people's congress of provinces (including autonomous regions) to begin exercising legislative power. Among them, 249 cities with subordinate districts (including autonomous prefectures) have formulated local laws and regulations, and 848 local regulations have been approved by the standing committees of the provincial (including autonomous region) people's congresses. Among them, 217 regulations are on legislation and 631 on urban and rural development and management, environment protection, historical and cultural protection and other matters. With respect to the proportion of regulations made by these cities, to take Guangdong Province as an example, from late March 2015 to March 2019, the Standing Committee of the Guangdong Provincial People's Congress approved a total of 83 regulations proposed by the cities with subordinate districts: 54 substantive regulations and 17 procedural regulations (the formulation of regulations on making local regulations), 12 revision decisions were made. Among the 54 substantive regulations, 27 were for environmental protection (including 12 for water protection), 19 for urban and rural development and management, and 8 for historical and cultural protection.

3 Characteristics, Role and Effects of Local Legislation

China has a large population, a long history, and a vast territory with uneven development and significant regional differences: it has a population of nearly 1.4 billion, 56 ethnic groups, 14 inland neighbors and 6 maritime bordering countries. The area and population of some provinces are equivalent to those of a medium-sized country. To this end, China has established a legislative system adapted to its national conditions, granting different legislative powers to the provincial people's congresses and their standing committees and those of the cities with subordinate districts.

According to the provisions of the Law on Legislation, local regulations can make provisions on the following matters: (1) Matters for which specific provisions are necessary, based on the actual circumstances of the administrative region, for the implementation of laws or administrative regulations.; (2) Matters for which it is necessary for local practice to formulate local provisions. Except for those matters exclusively subject to national legislation, the local legislature may formulate local provisions, as needed by specific local conditions and work needs. Generally, there are three aspects to be considered in formulating local regulations. First, to enact the regulations for implementing a certain law or administrative regulation based on local realities to ensure the compliance with and enforcement of the Constitution, laws and administrative regulations so that the national systems and provisions are more in line with local realities and more targeted, operable and enforceable. Second, the local regulations enacted within the scope of local authority are often called regulations, procedures and measures which cover a wide range of subjects and reflect distinct local features. Third, within the scope of statutory authority, to enact local regulations as pilot programs to regulate the matters that national law or administrative regulations have not yet covered, including the local regulations of five special economic zones. According to the Law on Legislation, local legislation is essentially supplementary and subordinate, purported to maintain the unity of national legal system. As provided, the people's congresses of the provinces, autonomous regions, and municipalities directly under the State Council and their standing committees may, according to their own circumstances and actual needs, adopt local regulations, which must not contravene the Constitution, the law, administrative rules and regulations, and the people's congresses of the cities with subordinate districts and autonomous prefectures and their standing committees may also adopt local regulations on the urban and rural development and administration, environment protection, and historical and cultural protection, so long as the local provisions do not contravene the Constitution, laws, administrative regulations, or the local provisions and regulations of that province or autonomous region.

The conditions and realities of China and its legislative system and division of legislative power have made local legislation prominent in four aspects: first, it has large space for local legislation. China does not practice a federal system, but the guidelines of the Party's Central Committee and the provisions of laws are always subject to specific performance based on local conditions and realities. Therefore, local regulations should be made accessible to every community for addressing every specific rule of law problems. Second, local legislation is flexible. The local regulations are specific rules for either implementing the upper level legislation, making connections with other laws or regulations, creating new norms, giving answers for certain specified issues, or making exploratory efforts. Third, it is target-oriented. Local legislation is often carried out for resolving specific issues, which is not easy for national legislation. Fourth, it is comprehensive. The formulation of local regulations is based on a comprehensive consideration of the guidelines of the Party's Central Committee, laws, and state policies to make them more adaptable for local needs.

Over the past 40 years, under the firm leadership of the Party's Central Committee and the local party committees, and guided by the principles of conformity, locality and practicability, the local legislature has promulgated a lot of effective and efficient regulations to promote reform, development and innovation, to ensure the enforcement of the Constitution, laws and administrative regulations in their own administrative areas, and to help promote reform and boost local economic and social development. Furthermore, local legislation has also contributed to national legislation helping to foster a complete set of legislative institutions and mechanisms and train a professional workforce. The achievements in this period can be elaborated in the following five aspects.

3.1 Enforcement Legislation for Effective Implementation

With a focus on the undertakings of the Party and the State, and with a view to local conditions, the local legislature has taken a proactive role in promoting local legislation to make the provisions of laws and administrative regulations more refined, operable and practical for addressing local issues and effectively enforce the Constitution, laws and administrative regulations, which is called "enforcement legislation". According to statistics, some legislative bodies have made great efforts to supplement and refine the upper-level legislation on economy, politics, culture, society and ecological environment protection, which takes up more than half of the total local regulations. For example, the Standing Committee of Tianjin Municipal People's Congress revised the Measures for Implementing the Law on Maternal and Infant

Health Care, which prescribed the infant health care should be available to all children under the age of 6, and made detailed provisions on such care, which helped lighten the burden of a lot of families. In Shanxi Province, when the Measures for Implementing the Law on Water and Soil Conservation, that whoever develops should be accountable for protection and restoration and whoever causes soil erosion should be accountable for afforestation and compensations was designated as its guiding principle, and any violation of the Law would be put into personal credit records and announced to the public. The Standing Committee of Liaoning Provincial People's Congress, promulgated the Measures for Implementing the Land Contract Law to address in particular the issues of excessive reserved flexible land and the provision of land for new farmers. The Regulations of Heilongjiang Province on the Protection of Rights and Interests of the Elderly prescribed that there were accumulative 20 days of care leave for the supporter, an only child of the family and 10 days for non-only child supporter if the elder was in hospital. Henan made the Measures for Implementing the Compulsory Education Law, which aimed to protect the legitimate rights and interests of the people in difficulty or in disadvantage.

3.2 Innovative Legislation for Leading Local Reform and Economic Development

Adhering to local features is the vitality for and a quality standard for local legislation. The creative legislation, through which the local legislature may make pioneering regulations to deal with the problems beyond the reach of national legislation based on their needs for social and economic development, can play the role of legislation in promoting reform and boosting local economic and social development and provide guarantee for law-based governance, so these regulations are often applied with a narrower scope and keen to resolving the locality-dependent issues. For example, the formulation of the Regulations on National Fitness, Regulations on Promoting Volunteering Service and Regulations on the Construction and Administration of Accessible Facilities were intended to safeguard the 2008 Olympics held in Beijing. The Regulations of Hebei Province on the Protection of Rights and Interests of Migrant Workers addressed issue in getting paid among the migrant workers by creating the mechanisms such as emergency working funds, surveillance of payment, guaranty deposits for construction companies and enterprise credit system for construction companies. The Regulations on Traditional Mongolian Medicine, Regulations on the Spoken and Written Mongolian Language, and Regulations on the Administration of Prairie were promulgated by the Inner Mongolia to protect the rights and interest of people in the self-government regions and of minority ethnic groups and to consolidate national unity and social economic development in this regions. The Regulations of Jilin Province on the Protection of Black Soil classified it into intensive protection and restoration and defined the focus of protection, which manifested the principle of strictest protection. To promote coordinated regional development, the Regulations of Anhui Province on Promoting the Development of Industrial Transfer Demonstration Zone for Wanjiang Urban Belt. The Regulations of Jiangxi Province on the Prevention and Treatment of Medical Disputes were intended to guide the parties to medical disputes to resort to legitimate procedures for dispute resolution. The Regulations of Guangdong Province on the Promotion of Independent Innovation established various mechanisms to encourage research and creation, promote technology transfer and industrialization, and strengthen the talent pooling and services. The Regulations of Guangxi Zhuang Autonomous Region on the Protection of Stalactite Resources given it is abundant with karst landforms. The Regulations of Guizhou Province on Poverty Alleviation laid down the pattern of overall participation with the greatest efforts to eliminate all the poor. Yunnan Province has been dedicated to protecting the water resources, especially the nine plateau lakes. The regulations on the protection of Dianchi and Erhai were promulgated very early. After more efforts for enhanced protection of these lakes were made, now every prominent plateau lake was under protection of their own regulations in Yunnan. To show its confidence in Tibetan culture, the Regulations on the Protection of Cultural Relics, Regulations on the Administration of the Cultural Market and Regulations on the Protection and Administration of the Potala Palace were successively promulgated, which have help spread Chinese traditional culture and continue to continue improving their affinity with the great country, Chinese nation, Chinese culture, the Party and socialism with Chinese characteristics. With a view to its fragile ecology, drought and few rainfall and the desertification problem, the local legislation in Ningxia has focused on ecological environment protection, and made 49 regulations and decisions on it, 30 of all the local regulations and normative documents. Regulations of Xinjiang Uygur Autonomous Region on De-radicalization provides a legal guarantee for social stability.

3.3 Pilot Legislative Programs for Accumulating Experience

The local people's congresses and their standing committees, as the experiment fields for national legislation, have been actively engaged in implementing legislative programs for pilot programs to accumulate experience. For example, the Regulations on China (Shanghai) Pilot Free-Trade Zone helped to lay down the institutional framework of free trade zone development, explore the experience of innovation that can be repeated and promoted and ensure the law-based operation of these pilot programs. As the earliest pilot province of community correction in China, Jiangsu took the initiative to promulgate the Regulations on the Work of Community Corrections, which provides reference and experience for national legislation in this area. Zhejiang Province is the first one that drew up the local regulations on river chiefs to ensure that over 60 thousand river chiefs in Zhejiang have detailed legal provisions to abide by. As the experiment land for Taiwan related legislation, Fujian Province has made great efforts for new integrated development between

China's mainland and Taiwan region by issuing the Several Provisions of Admitting Taiwan Students, Regulations on the Agricultural Cooperation between Fujian and Taiwan, and Regulations on Promoting the Vocation Education Cooperation between Fujian and Taiwan. To ensure the connection among different dispute resolution methods and procedures and deliver on institutional mechanisms, the Standing Committee of Shandong Provincial People's Congress promulgated the Regulations on the Promotion of Diversified Dispute Resolution, which made provisions on coordinating mediation, arbitration, administrative decision and review, providing flexible, convenient and cost-efficient dispute resolution methods. The Regulations of Hubei Province on the Prevention and Control of Soil Contamination were conducive for national legislation. The Regulations of Hunan Province on Donations Soliciting made detailed provisions on the nature, administration and use of donated properties to improve its transparency and address the issues such as failed donation promises. The Regulations on the Administration of Commercial Registration in the China (Hainan) Pilot Free Trade Zone helped to achieve the one-stop commercial registration system throughout the province, streamline the simplified de-registration procedures, explore the credit restoration, reduce matters for publicity, and allow registration of foreign or other region's enterprise, which is of great significance for accelerating the development of a law-based international and convenient business environment, and a fair, open and efficient integrated market. The Regulations of Chongqing Municipality on the Promotion of Family Education help to lead and promote family education, good family traditions and establish happy and harmonious families. The Regulations of Sichuan Province on the Government Service has consolidated the achievements in administrative approval reform, and provides guarantee for transforming government functions and establishing an institutionalized and regulated government service system. The Regulations on Public Credit Information by the Standing Committee of the Shaanxi Provincial People's Congress are intended for building trustworthy society. The Regulations on the Recycle and Reuse of Waster Agricultural Film were formulated to address the land contamination and the recycle and reuse of agricultural film, which had long been the focus of plastic pollution in the rural areas, which was the first of its kind across the country. The Regulations of Qinghai Province on Sanjiangyuan National Park was the achievement of pilot legislation with respect to national park; the Regulations are essential for promoting law-based park construction and systemic building of ecological environment and laid the foundation for future laws and administrative regulations on national parks.

3.4 A Complete Set of Legislative Institutions and Mechanisms

The local legislatures have been committed to exploring and refining the legislative institutions and mechanisms through years of legislative practices. First, to make local regulations on legislation and establish a uniform deliberation practice. Great attention has been paid to improving the legislative system through the establishment of various institutions and mechanisms to regulate their legislative activities. Almost all the legislatures have revised their local regulations on legislation and set out the standards for making annual legislative plans and schedules, the draft, deliberation, adoption and issuance of regulation bills and their interpretations and recording. A uniform deliberation system was generally made available to them, under which the legislative affairs committees are responsible for the uniform deliberation while the special committees for giving deliberative opinions. It strengthens the integrated efforts and initiatives of all the parties, improve their deliberation capacity, effect and quality. Second, to formulate normative documents to improve the legislative standards. The mechanisms for the Party to exercise leadership over legislation has be established and improved, such as the issuance of opinions to implement the Party's guidance for legislation and the reporting of major legislative programs to the Party groups. The leading role of the people's congress and its standing committee in local legislation is also emphasized with great efforts, such as the practice of coordinating the legislation among the people's congress, government and relevant departments and of the people's congress deputies' participation in legislative decision-making. For example, in Guangxi the people's congress has taken the lead in drafting 17 pieces of comprehensive, all-round and foundational regulations, accounting for 30% of all the regulations under deliberation by this congress. The mechanism for carrying out scientific legislation was established, under which the argumentation on legislative programs, assessment before legislation, assessment after legislation, appointment of advisors to legislation and expert opinions are practiced for better scientific legislation. In addition, a democratic legislation mechanism for local legislature was also set up: the public opinions solicitation for regulation bills, hearings and community liaison offices for legislation established as usual practices to gather people's wisdom and wills for local legislation.

3.5 *Training of Talents*

Legislation requires a good grasp of politics and policies and sound capacity in professional expertise and practice, which should be supported by a high-quality legislation professional team. The establishment of legislative working agencies was particularly emphasized, for example, the provincial people's congress set up the law committee and their standing committees the legislative affairs committees, and the uniform deliberation agencies and legislation working agencies were generally established among the local legislatures. This is also the same with the cities with legislative power. With regard to resource pooling, there are 20–30 people working at the provincial legislative affairs committees and 5–10 for city committees. A good team of legislative professional is essential for the standing committees to better exercise legislative power and to improve legislation quality. The local legislatures also enhance the training of legislative professionals through effective measures, such as bring in new talents and sending out for training, to ensure that the teams are more standardized and professional with high political standing, sound capacity, good behaviors, pragmatic attitudes, and efficient working styles. For example, in Guangdong, the Several Opinions on Strengthening the Building of Legislative Work Team, specified the detailed requirements on the team of legislative professionals and made it a legal provision that about 10 people are required for city legislative affairs committees, except for adding more to Guangzhou and Shenzhen. The qualifications for the members of standing committee and special committees were laid down with detailed rules, based on which the members with legal experience can be added, the knowledge structure and age are imposed more requirements, and the deliberation should be carried out high quality.

4 Experience: A Summary

The history of local legislation over the past four decades has made the following characteristics even more prominent with a view to the basic requirements and the experience.

First, to persist in the Party's leadership to ensure the correct political orientation. As the governing party of China, CPC is the core leadership in developing Chinese socialism. To unswervingly uphold the Party's leadership is the primary political principle and the fundamental guarantee for the work on legislation. The local legislatures strengthen the consciousness of the need to maintain political integrity, think in big-picture terms, follow the leadership core, and keep in alignment with the central Party leadership; they stay confident in the path, theory, system, and culture of socialism with Chinese characteristics, and uphold the unity between the Party's leadership, the running of the country by the people, and law-based governance; they stay unmoved on the correction direction of the socialist legal system with Chinese characteristics, resolutely implement the Party's Central Committee's decisions and arrangements, follow the Party's principles, guidelines and policies, and make legislation promote local development of economy, politics, culture, society, and ecological civilization. Since the Eighteenth CPC National Congress, the local people's congresses have made in-depth study and implementation of Xi Jinping Thought on Socialism with Chinese Characteristics for a New Era, especially the new ideas, concepts and strategies on comprehensive rule of law and the important elaborations on legislation made by him. The system of reporting major matters to the corresponding Party group has been well established. As required by this system, any social or economic legislation involving major institutional or policy adjustment and the political legislation are subject to the decision of the Party committee, the legislative plan and schedules should be reported to the Party committee for approval, and the major issues arising from law making or revisions should be reported to the Party committee. It has guaranteed that legislation promote local economic and social development.

Second, to focus on the central work, serve the general development plan, and take the lead in reform and social economic development. The work of people's congress is an important part of the Party and the State's undertakings. Thus, to better the work on local legislation should focus on the central work of the Party, ready themselves for being connected or integrated with the implementation of major development strategy or major decision of the Party and state and put in the first place the implementation of the Party's principles, guidelines, policies and reform decisions in the legislation. The local legislatures should align with local general development plan and use legislation to address social concerns or social and economic development difficulties. The local people's congress should pay attention to the institutional design, uphold the interconnection between legislative decision-making and reform decision, plan the work on legislation by closely centering on the major decisions and arrangements of the Party's Central Committee and local party committees, actively engage in making regulations to provide institutional support for reform decision, and make great efforts to ensure that each reform decision-making is made according to law and legislation should proactively adapt to the needs of reform and social economic development.

Third, to adopt a people-centered approach to ensure that local legislation serves the people. It is the essential requirement of legislation to uphold the people-centered approach and also an important surety for keeping the vitality of legislation. The local people's congresses have never ceased to adopt the people-centered approach in legislation, tried to coordinate the relationship between public power and private rights, and properly handled the relationships among the interests of the state, collective and individual as well as the interest demands of various social groups. The local legislation has been dedicated to addressing the most pressing, most immediate issues that concern the people the most, safeguarding social fairness justice, and making efforts to ensure that every legislation conforms with the Constitutional principles, reflects people's will and wins people's welcome.

Fourth, to make local features prominent in local legislation based on local realities. On the premise of maintaining the unity of socialist legal system, the local legislation strictly follows the principles for legislative power, procedures and higher-level laws or regulations. Meanwhile, it should start from the real needs of local development and social stability, properly balance universality and particularity, make full use of local legislative power and reflect local characteristics. The local legislative bodies insist on tailoring legislation to local conditions and needs, accentuating the local characteristics, adopting pragmatic attitudes towards legislation. By making local regulations more target-oriented and practicable, while not contradictory with other legislations, they ensure that local legislations are well-founded and effective, striving to address the prominent issues of social and economic development through legislation and giving play to the role of local legislation in the socialist legal system with Chinese characteristics.

Fifth, to carry out legislation in a scientific, democratic and law-based manner to improve its quality. As pointed out by Xi Jinping, the more emphasis is placed on the rule of law, the more legislative quality must be improved. To achieve good laws for good governance, quality is the key. The local legislation has made efforts to promote scientific, democratic and law-based legislation within their own legislative power, to explore the inherent nature of legislation, improve and refine legislation mechanisms, respect people's position as masters, expand the channels for people's orderly participation in legislation and improve local legislation quality to provide guarantee for good laws and good governance.

Sixth, to play the leading role of people's congress and its standing committee in local legislation. Law-making is a comprehensive undertaking, which requires coordination and cooperation among all the parties in all the procedures. To effectively promote the law-making process, it is necessary to assert the leading role of people's congress and its standing committee under the Party's leadership. The local people's congresses have better exercised the legislative power granted by the Constitution and law, striving for their leading role in making legislative programs, drafting and deliberation. This has helped establish a new pattern in the new era for local legislation under which the Party committees practice leadership, the people's congresses take the lead, and the government offers support and other parties are actively engaged. With concerted efforts, clear division of responsibility and cohesion, the work of local legislation has been pursued within the new pattern.

Last, to maintain the unity of national legal system. The local people's congresses have taken the Constitution and law as the basis for their legislative initiatives, developed an accurate grasp of local legislative power, ensured it against abuse of authority and contravention of upper level legislation by following the legal procedures, and resolved the general issues in local social and economic development. It also has firmly positioned itself in the socialist legal system with Chinese characteristics, and taken the effective enforcement of the Constitution and law as its primary mission. In addition, it also put emphasis on strengthening supervision of legislation: it established and improved the institution of normative documents review and recording to ensure every normative document under strict recording and deliberation and every mistaken be corrected if found to maintain the unity of national legal system.

Reviewing the past seven decades, especially the past 40 years since the reform and opening-up, history has proven that granting of local legislative power is the outcome of constructing China's democratic rule of law, as well as the guarantee for promoting such democratic process. The allocation of local legislative power also reveals the fact that the Party has been developing its understanding of how to govern the country according to law and of what methods should resort to; it has provided institutional safeguard for modernizing state governance system and capacity, and demonstrated its adherence and dedication to playing the role of local initiative and enthusiasm.

In the Nineteenth National Congress, the Party made the important judgment that Chinese socialism crossed the threshold into a new era. This is a new historic juncture in China's development. New features and new situations have confronted the work on legislation with new and high requirements. What China now faces is the contradiction between unbalanced and inadequate development and the people's ever-growing needs for a better life. And China's economy has been transitioning from a phase of rapid growth to one of high-quality development. Standing on a higher starting line, when planning and promoting deepened reform in all respects and expansion of opening-up, the Nineteenth CPC National Congress made a lot of important reform measures and laid down many major reform missions. To deepen the comprehensive law-based governance has brought about many new challenges. As pointed by Xi Jinping in the Second Session of the Party's Central Commission for Comprehensive Law-based Governance, development should be high-quality, while legislation should also be high-quality. Therefore, the quality and efficiency of the work on legislation must undergo continuous improvement. The local legislature should also adapt to the new requirements for the new era, adhere to the guidance of Xi Jinping Thought on Socialism with Chinese Characteristics for a New Era, keep a close eye to people's new aspirations for better life, strengthen the awareness of responsibility, dedicate itself to reform and innovation and strive hard to provide quality and efficient provision of institutions to meet people's increasing demands for democracy, rule of law, fairness, justice, security and environment. They should also lead, promote and safeguard steady progress of reform in the new era according to law to make contributions to a sound Chinese socialist legal system with the Constitution as the core and the modernization of state governance system and capacity.

Chapter 8
Legislation for Implementing "One Country Two Systems"

Hu Jian

Abstract This chapter reviews how the "one country two systems" principle has been translated into law since the 1980s. The 1982 Constitution empowered the NPC to create Special Administrative Regions (SARs). It details the five NPC Standing Committee interpretations of the Hong Kong Basic Law, on right of abode, political reform, chief-executive tenure, state immunity and oath-taking, showing how "NPC interpretation" resolves crises while safeguarding sovereign unity. It also tracks the selective application of 13 national legislations in Hong Kong SAR and 12 in Macao SAR via Annex III, emergency powers, and *ad-hoc* NPC decisions. It concludes that this legislative innovation offers a constitutional template for eventual Taiwan reunification.

Keywords One country two systems · Basic law · NPC interpretation · Hong Kong SAR · Macao SAR · Taiwan reunification

When the People's Republic of China was founded on October 1, 1949, Hong Kong, Macao and Taiwan were still separated from the motherland. The first generation of Party's central leadership with Mao Zedong as the core formulated the proposal and plan to peacefully address the questions, especially the Taiwan question, and put them into practice for national reunification. Based on the consideration of long-term fundamental interests and the overall socialist construction, the Party's Central Committee adopted a different approach to Hong Kong and Macao, focusing on long-term exploitation of their status, which successfully ended the western capitalist blockade led by the United States. However, the vicissitudes of international and domestic situations, especially the Cultural Revolution, brought the national reunification to a halt and suspended the work on Hong Kong and Macao.

When the focus of the Party and the State shifted to economic development and socialist modernization in 1978, the national reunification was once again placed on the agenda. In early 1980s, Deng Xiaoping proposed the scientific concept of One

H. Jian (✉)
Beijing, China
e-mail: liujixuan@lawpress.com.cn

C. Shen et al. (eds.), *A History of Legislation in the Past 70 Years in China*,
https://doi.org/10.1007/978-981-95-3799-0_8

Country Two Systems with great wisdom and creativity to address the Hong Kong question. According to Deng Xiaoping and other leaders, the One Country Two Systems means that within the People's Republic of China, the mainland maintaind the socialist system, while the existing capitalist system long practiced in Hong Kong, Macao and Taiwan remain unchanged. This pioneering concept by the CPC and Chinese people represents an innovative model of national governance, reflecting a pragmatic attitude and superior political wisdom.

According to Article 31 of the 1982 Constitution, "the state may establish special administrative regions when necessary. The systems to be instituted in the SARs shall be prescribed by law enacted by the National People's Congress in the light of the specific conditions". This provision transformed the vision of One Country Two Systems into a national system in the Constitution, providing constitutional basis for achieving peaceful national reunification and implementing social systems and policies different from those of the mainland. On April 4, 1990, the Basic Law of Hong Kong Special Administrative Region (Hong Kong SAR) and the decision to establish the Hong Kong SAR were adopted in the Third Session of the Seventh National People's Congress. On March 31, 1993, the Basic Law of the Macao Special Administrative Region (Macao SAR) and the decision to establish the Macao SAR were adopted in the First Session of the Eighth National People's Congress. Two basic laws were enacted based on the Constitution and also made provisions on the systems and policies in SARs; they were institutionalized and legalized One Country Two Systems, which provides legal guarantee for latter's implementation. Deng Xiaoping ever highly commended the Basic Law of Hong Kong SAR as "a law that is of historic and international significance", and "a creative masterpiece".[1] On June 1, 1997, China resumed the exercise of its sovereignty over Hong Kong. The Hong Kong SAR was established, and its Basic Law came into force. On December 20, 1999, China resumed the exercise of its sovereignty over Macao. The Macao SAR was established, and its Basic Law also came into force. The Constitution and Basic Law together has instituted the constitutional basis for the special administrative regions. Since then, Hong Kong and Macao entered the era of One Country Two Systems, under which the people of Hong Kong administer Hong Kong, and the people of Macao administer Macao, both with a high degree of autonomy. This is not only a historic achievement in implementing the policy of One Country Two Systems, but also a great achievement in China's work on legislation since the founding of the People's Republic of China 70 years ago, especially since the reform and opening-up more than 40 years ago. It could be also a Chinese proposal to the countries that have not yet achieved reunification.

The establishment of SARs transformed the constitutional basis of Hong Kong and Macao into the dual authority of the Constitution and Basic Law. Directly under the Central People's Government, they were both incorporated into China's state governance system again. The Central People's Government began its governance over Hong Kong and Macao according to the Constitution and Basic Laws, and also established the corresponding systems and institutions. Since the Constitution is the

[1] DENG Xiaoping, *Selected Works of Deng Xiaoping (Vol. 3)*, Foreign Languages Press, 1994, p. 340.

fundamental law and represent the common will of all Chinese people, it is also the origin of the Basic Laws, which are also the legal basis and practical foundation for implementing the One Country Two Systems. According to Article 18 of the Basic Law of Hong Kong or Macao, two types of laws are enforced in the SARs according to their legislative bodies: one is the laws enacted by the legislature of the regions including previous laws retained by the Basic Law; the other is the national laws applied to the regions enacted by the National People's Congress and its Standing Committee, which includes the following: (1) the Constitution; (2) Basic Law and the interpretations made by the NPC Standing Committee; (3) National laws listed in Annex III to the Basic Law and (4) other laws, regulations, decisions and resolutions made for the regions by the Central People's Government. When reviewing the legislative achievements in the past 70 years, the legislation of Hong Kong and Macao is also inseparable. The following is a summary of such achievements, especially the formulation and enforcement of national laws for the regions, for they are the major ones for maintaining long-term peace and stability in Hong Kong and Macao.

1 The Constitution and Its Enforcement in the SARs

As laid down by the Resolution of the Central Committee of the CPC on Certain Major Issues Concerning Comprehensively Advancing the Law-Based Governance of China, it should ensure "the Constitution has the highest legal position and the highest legal effect, comprehensively and accurately implement the guidelines of 'one country, two systems', 'Hong Kong people administering Hong Kong', and 'Macao people administering Macao', and the policies of high levels of autonomy, conduct affairs strictly according to the Constitution and the Basic Laws, perfect systems and mechanisms connected to the implementation of the Basic Laws, exercise central powers according to the law, guarantee a high level of autonomy according to the law, support the Special Administrative Regions' Chief Executives and governments in governing according to the law, guarantee the development of economic and trade relationships between the mainland, Hong Kong and Macao, and of exchange and cooperation in all areas, prevent and oppose interference by foreign powers in Hong Kong and Macao affairs, guarantee that Hong Kong and Macao remain flourishing and stable in the long run". These remarks reiterate the importance of the Constitution and the Central People's Government in governing the SARs.

As the fundamental law of a state, the Constitution has the highest legal position and the highest legal effect across the whole country, including Hong Kong and Macao, so it should be enforced in these regions. As inseparable parts of China, the SARs should respect the role and effect of the Constitution as well as perform the duties in maintaining national sovereignty, reunification and territorial integrity.

However, opinions varied a lot as to whether the Constitution should be enforced in the SARs. Some thought that only a part of the Constitution could be applied to the SAR, because it practiced the systems different from other regions of China according to the principle of One Country Two Systems. Others argued that only Article 31, the only provision that governed the system of the SAR, could be applied. A third view held that the Constitution should be enforced as a whole. However, the third opinion was expressed as a principle. Though it sounded more comprehensive than the other two, it may be interpreted as a principle overall application but some provisions not applicable.

The problem of the Constitution's enforcement in the SARs was originated from two conceptions: one was that the SARs did not practice socialism or the system of people's congresses and other fundamental systems as prescribed by the Constitution; the other was that the Basic Law was the constitution of the SAR, so the Constitution was no longer needed. Whatever the three opinions and two conceptions were, they were misleading.

First, the special administrative region does not practice socialism by virtue of the grant of the Constitution. In the 1980s, the One Country Two Systems was put forward as a policy to peacefully resolve problem of national reunification, then as a basic principle to address the question of Hong Kong and Macao. When the Constitution was promulgated in 1982, it was stipulated in Article 31. Meanwhile, the enactment of the Hong Kong or Macao Basic Law was based on or granted by the 1982 Constitution.

Second, though the basic laws are constitution-related laws, they are not constitutions themselves. The basic law is a set of specific systems as prescribed by the Constitution, but cannot replace the role of the Constitution as the fundamental law. With a view to the specific affairs, the Constitution governs the state affairs in general, while the basic law governs a portion of the affairs of certain region. It is the Constitution that legetimizes the fact that the SAR does not implement socialism, and without the Constitution, the basic law and the systems will have no legitimate basis. Therefore, the Constitution's enforcement does not contravene the social systems of special administrative region, but provides strong legal guarantee for its own systems. Moreover, the socialism the Constitution provides is generally practiced across the country, not to any one region or agency.

Though the Constitution is enforced in the SAR as a whole, it is also subject to specific conditions. According to the governance and judicial practice of Hong Kong and Macao, its enforcement is also universal. For example, when the SAR governments reported their work to the Central People's Government or proposed bills, the basic laws as well as the Constitution and other related laws should be basis for them. The judgments delivered by the Hong Kong and Macao courts also cited the Constitution, not limited to its Article 31.

In conclusion, the Constitution is universally applied in the SARs, not limited to one provision or several provisions, but all of its provision. It should be noted that this universal application does not mean to interfere the high degree of autonomy of the SARs. If the Constitution and the Basic Law is applied with due respect to such autonomy, the Central People's Government will also show respect to the SAR's autonomy. Only on such common ground can a consensus be achieved to ensure long-term stability of the One Country Two Systems.

2 The Basic Laws as National Laws and Their Implementation

According to Article 18 of the basic laws of Hong Kong and Macao, the laws in force in the regions shall be "this Law", as it made provisions on the politics, economy and cultural systems, rights and duties of the citizens, and the relationship between the central authorities and the regions. "This Law" is the foundation of the SAR's administration, legislation and the judiciary, and the constitutional law that the central authorities and the SARs should observe. The basic laws replaced their original constitutional laws as soon as China resumed exercise of sovereignty of Hong Kong and Macao. The most prominent feature of basic laws lies in its integration to resolve contradictions, such as the integration of the rigidity of principles with flexibility and the integration of sovereignty, reunification and territorial integrity with the high-degree autonomy and prosperity and stability of the SARs. As national laws, they not only secure the implementation of State's basic principles and policies, but also manifest the One Country Two Systems.

The "interpretation of laws by the NPC" is an important institution prescribed by the Constitution, as the NPC Standing Committee is the body that makes law and interprets the Constitution and law and the basic laws of Hong Kong and Macao. The One Country Two Systems is China's basic policy to resolve the question of Hong Kong and Macao, so the interpretation of laws by the NPC is also essential for fully implementing it as well as the basic laws, for the basic laws are also subject to NPC Standing Committee's interpretation for better enforcement and improvement. According to Article 158 of Hong Kong Basic Law and Article 143 of Macao Basic Law, the power of interpretation of this Law resides in the NPC Standing Committee, and as it implies, the NPC Standing Committee may proactively or as requested interpret all the provisions of the basic laws. In addition, the Basic Laws also make clear that the NPC Standing Committee may authorize the courts of the SARs to interpret on their own the provisions of basic laws which are within the limits of the autonomy of the regions when the courts adjudicate cases. These courts may also interpret other provisions of the basic laws in adjudicating cases. However, if the courts need to interpret the provisions of the basic laws concerning affairs which are the responsibility of the Central People's Government, or concerning the relationship between the Central Authorities and the regions, and if such interpretation will affect the judgments on the cases, these courts should seek an interpretation of the relevant provisions from the NPC Standing Committee through the courts of final appeal before making their final judgments which are not appealable. When the NPC Standing Committee makes an interpretation, the courts should follow it when applying those provisions. It should be noted that the NPC Standing Committee's power to make interpretation does not contradict the independence judicial power of Hong Kong and Macao. According to the basic laws, the power of final adjudication and the power to interpret the basic laws can be exercised in parallel. For example, in its judgments, the Court of Final Appeal of Hong Kong explicitly pointed out the power of NPC Standing Committee to interpret the laws was a constitutional one which had undisputable binding force on the courts of Hong Kong, and the courts should adjudicate the cases according to this principle.

There are five cases of Hong Kong Basic interpretations by the NPC Standing Committee,[2] which made respectively in 1999, 2004, 2005, 2011 and 2016 on the right of abode of Chinese nationals born outside of Hong Kong whose parents are Hong Kong permanent residents, the provisions on the procedures for selecting the Chief Executive and the method for forming the Legislative Council, the term of office of the Chief Executive, the application of the doctrine of state immunity and the pledge of allegiance in the Constitutional provisions when assuming public offices. Every interpretation was made to respond to the major issues that confronted Hong Kong, which were directly concerned with the implementation of One Country Two Systems and the prosperity and stability of Hong Kong. The making of interpretations also reflected that the Party's Central Committee and Central People's Government governed Hong Kong in a law-based approach.

2.1 First Interpretation: Right of Abode

The issue of the right of abode of Chinese nationals born in the mainland whose parents are permanent Hong Kong residents had sparked universal social concern in Hong Kong. On January 29, 1999, the Court of Final Appeal made the final

[2] The interpretation of laws by the NPC includes five interpretations of Hong Kong Basic Law. However, the NPC Standing Committee also issued an interpretation of Macao Basic Law after it was returned to motherland. The Interpretation by the National People's Congress Standing Committee Regarding Article 7 of Annex 1 and Article 3 of Annex 2 of the Basic Law of the Macao Special Administrative Region of the People's Republic of China, issued on December 31, 2011, clarified the legal procedures of selecting Macao's chief executive and forming legislative assembly. According to this Interpretation, the provision in the two annexes, that is, "if the need arises to amend" the method for selecting the chief executive and forming the Legislative Assembly in and after 2009, amendments may or may not be amended. The provisions of the two annexes that amendments must be made with the endorsement of a two-thirds majority of all members of the Legislative Assembly and the consent of the chief executive and are to be reported to the NPC Standing Committee for approval or recording means that the method for selecting the chief executive and forming the Legislative Assembly must go through legal procedures. The amendments take effect only if they go through the above procedures, including the final ones for being approved or recorded by the NPC Standing Committee. The Chief Executive of the Macao Special Administrative Region is to submit a report to the NPC Standing Committee as to whether amendments are needed, which is to be decided by the NPC Standing Committee in accordance with the provisions of Article 47 and Article 68 of the Basic Law of the Macao Special Administrative Region and according to the actual circumstances in the Macao Special Administrative Region. Bills for amendments to the methods for selecting the chief executive and forming the Legislative Assembly are to be presented by the government of the Macao Special Administrative Region to the Legislative Assembly. If no amendments are made to the provisions in the two annexes regarding the selection of the chief executive and the forming of the Legislative Assembly, the provision in Annex 1 about the method of selection of the chief executive will continue to apply to the method of selecting the chief executive and the provision in Annex 2 about the method of forming the Legislative Assembly will continue to apply to the method of forming the Legislation Assembly.

judgment, which decided that the children of Hong Kong residents, including the children of either the father or mother before or after he or she became a Hong Kong resident whether the child/children were born in or out of wedlock. It also declared that the "people from other parts of China" entering into Hong Kong in subparagraph 4 of Article 22 of the Hong Kong Basic Law, did not apply to the mentioned children. The judgment changed Hong Kong's exit and entrance system, which sparked wide discussions and social concern. According to the statistics of Hong Kong SAR Government, it may cause serious social problems because there would be over 1.67 million people of mainland residents with the rights of abode in Hong Kong according to the rules set out by the judgment, accounting for nearly 1/4 of its total population. This huge number of potential legitimate residents would cause great pressure on Hong Kong, whose land and social resources could not the needs of education, housing, healthcare, social welfare and others, an immediate challenge to Hong Kong's stability and prosperity.

Therefore, the dispute arose as to whether the judgment conformed with the Basic Law. On May 19, 1999, the Hong Kong Legislative Council adopted a resolution to support the government to request the interpretation of the NPC Standing Committee. One day later, Tung Chee-hwa, the Chief Executive, submitted a report to the State Council. In the report, he thought that the judgment was different from the government's understanding of its Basic Law. After reviewing it, the State Council made a bill to the NPC Standing Committee. On June 26, the NPC Standing Committee promulgated the Interpretation Regarding Paragraph 4 in Article 22 and Category (3) of Paragraph 2 in Article 24 of the Basic Law,[3] which prescribed that people from China mainland, including the children of permanent residents of the Hong Kong SAR born in the mainland with Chinese nationality, should apply for approval from the relevant government department in the place of their resident and enter the Hong Kong SAR with the valid certificates issued by relevant authorities, and it's illegal if without going through the due approval procedures according to laws or regulations. This interpretation made by the NPC Standing Committee eliminated the difference in understanding of Basic Law, harnessed the social disputes, effectively prevented the unsanctioned entry of people from the mainland into Hong Kong, and guaranteed the prosperity, stability and orderly development of Hong Kong.

Moreover, the judgment's opinions expressed that the courts of Hong Kong SAR could review and declare the legislation of NPC and its Standing Committee null, which apparently contravened the provisions of the Basic Law, a serious challenge to the Constitutional position of NPC and its Standing Committee and the One Country Two Systems. On February 8, Xiao Weiyun and other three experts from the mainland who joined the drafting of Hong Kong Basic Law stressed three points: first, the NPC is highest organ of state power, their legislation and decision cannot be challenged or denied by any organization; second, the Hong Kong SAR is a local region directly

[3] The Interpretation by the Standing Committee of the National People's Congress Regarding Paragraph 4 in Article 22 and Category (3) of Paragraph 2 in Article 24 of the Basic Law of the Hong Kong Special Administrative Region of the People's Republic of China, see https://www.basiclaw.gov.hk/en/basiclaw/index.html

under the Central People's Government, and its position has determined that its Court of Final Appeal did not have the authority to review and declare the legislation of NPC and its Standing Committee null. Such act is a denial of China's sovereignty. Third, the jurisdiction of the Court of Final Appeal was limited, so it could not dispute the legislation of the highest organ of state power. In late February, the Court of Final Appeal clarified its judgment, which stated that the NPC Standing Committee's power to interpret the Basic Law and any exercise of power of the NPC and its Standing Committee's power according to the Basic Law and the procedures as prescribed could not be disputed. This judgment was of great significance for it signified the actual implementation of the interpretation of law by the NPC, which was formally incorporated as an important part of Hong Kong's rule of law and a success of the One Country Two Systems guaranteed by the Constitution and Basic Law.

2.2 Second Interpretation: Clarifying the Development Process of Hong Kong's Political System

Before Hong Kong's return to China, the western media sang badly about Hong Kong, believing that the day Hong Kong returned to China was the time when Hong Kong declined. However, after the return of Hong Kong, it not only maintained stability, but also achieved outstanding achievements in various aspects. Moreover, the Central People's Government also attached great importance to the development of a democratic system suitable for Hong Kong's reality in accordance with the Basic Law. Since 2003, discussions on Hong Kong's political system had focused on Annexes 1 and 2[4] of the Basic Law, because they did not clearly stipulate the method of selecting the Chief Executive and the Legislative Council after 2007. Therefore, some people in Hong Kong took advantage of it to advocated the universal suffrage for the election of the third Chief Executive in 2007 and the election of the fourth Legislative Council in 2008, and rejected the Central People's leading role in the development of Hong Kong's political system.

However, the development of Hong Kong's future political system was essential for the implementation of the One Country Two Systems policy and the Basic Law, for the relationship between the central government and the Hong Kong and for the interests of all sectors and the long-term prosperity and stability of Hong Kong. On April 6, 2004, the NPC Standing Committee made an interpretation of Article 7 of Annex I and Article 3 of Annex II of the Basic Law, which clarified the procedures for initiating election reform: in the first step, as to whether the revisions were to be made, the Chief Executive should submit a report to the NPC Standing Committee,

[4] Annex 1: Method for the Selection of the Chief Executive of the Hong Kong Special Administrative Region, Annex 2: Method for the Formation of the Legislative Council of the Hong Kong Special Administrative Region and Its Voting Procedures, see https://www.basiclaw.gov.hk/en/basiclaw/index.html

which would make a decision according to Articles 45 and 68 of the Basic Law in the light of the actual situation and in a gradual and orderly manner; in the second step, the methods for selecting the Chief Executive and the Legislative Council should be proposed by the Hong Kong SAR Government to the Legislative Council; in the third step, the methods for selecting the Chief Executive and the Legislative Council were subject to the approved of 2/3 members of the Legislative Council by a majority voting; in fourth step, if the methods for selecting the Chief Executive and the Legislative Council were revised, the consent of the Chief Executive must be obtained; in the fifth step, after methods were revised, the revision could take effect only after approval or filing by the NPC Standing Committee. This interpretation reiterated that the political system of Hong Kong was prescribed in the Basic Law enacted by the National People's Congress, and Hong Kong had no authority to decide or change its political system on its own. At the same time, it adhered to the principle of developing Hong Kong's political system in a gradual manner, provided clear legal guidance, and also showed the determination and sincerity of the Central People's Government to promote the progressive development of democracy in Hong Kong. It is a landmark in the history of Hong Kong's political system.

2.3 *Third Interpretation: Remainder of the Term of Hong Kong's Chief Executive*

On March 12, 2005, Tung resigned due to health problems. According to relevant provisions of the Basic Law and the Chief Executive Election Ordinance of Hong Kong SAR, a new Chief Executive must be elected on July 10. However, whether the term of the new chief executive should be a new five-year term or the remaining term of the original chief executive (2 years), two different opinions emerged in Hong Kong society. The Government believed that the term of office of the new Chief Executive should be the remainder of the term of the original Chief Executive. Accordingly, the Government needed to amend the Election Ordinance to stipulate the term of office of the new Chief Executive when the office of the Chief Executive became vacant during the term of the original Chief Executive. However, this opinion received strong objection from some Legislative Council members and residents. Some members even openly called for a judicial review of the bill to amend the Chief Executive Election Ordinance. If a judicial review occurred, due to its lengthy period, the new Chief Executive would not be elected, which would have a negative impact on Hong Kong's stability and development. Therefore, Donald Tsang, Acting Chief Executive, made a report to request the NPC Standing Committee give an interpretation of Paragraph 2 of Article 53 of the Basic Law.

The State Council, after research, deemed that the problems faced by the Hong Kong SAR Government concerned the correct implementation of the provision of the Basic Law and the selection of a new Chief Executive, and also important for the appointment of the Chief Executive by the Central People's Government. Therefore, it submitted the bill of Proposal on Requesting Interpretation of Paragraph 2 of Article 53 of the Basic Law of the Hong Kong SAR of the People's Republic of China to the NPC Standing Committee. On April 27, 2005, the Standing Committee issued the interpretation, which prescribed that in the event that the office of Chief Executive became vacant before the expiration of the 5 years prescribed, the term of office of the new Chief Executive shall be the remainder of the term of office of the previous Chief Executive, which successfully prevented a constitutional crisis.

2.4 Fourth Interpretation: Scope of Authority in Foreign Affairs of Hong Kong SAR

On May 2008, an US registered company brought a litigation before the Court of First Instance of the High Court in Hong Kong, which request implementation of two international arbitration awards. The Democratic Republic of Congo ("DRC"), China Railway Group (Hong Kong) Limited and its three affiliated companies were defendants. The defendants argued that the DRC had state immunity, so the courts of Hong Kong had no jurisdiction over DRC; meanwhile, DRC had exchanged ideas with PRC through diplomatic channels. Considering the case concerned national sovereignty and the diplomatic power of the Central People's Government, the Ministry of Foreign Affairs issued three letters to the Secretary for Constitutional and Mainland Affairs of Hong Kong SAR through its Commissioner in Hong Kong. In these letters, the Ministry stated the stance of Central People's Government, pointed out the China had been practicing the principle of state immunity among all the regions of China, including Hong Kong SAR; if it practiced the principle different from the stance of Central People's Government, it would cause damage to China's sovereignty. These letters were delivered to the courts as evidence by the Secretary for Justice of Hong Kong, who joined the adjudication in consideration of a major legal issue in the enforcement of Basic Law. After the adjudications in the Court of First Instance and the Court of Appeal, this case was then delivered to the Court of Final Appeal.

On June 8, 2011, the Court of Final Appeal made a provisional judgment, and referred the matter to the NPC Standing Committee according to Subparagraph 3 of Article 158 of Basic Law since the judgment was directly concerned with the interpretation of the provisions of Basic Law on the administrative affairs of Central People's Government and the relationship between the Central Authorities and the Hong Kong SAR. On August 26, the NPC Standing Committee issued the Interpretation[5] which clarified the power of the Central People's Government in administering the foreign affairs related with Hong Kong. According to this interpretation, the Hong

[5] The Interpretation by the Standing Committee of the National People's Congress Regarding the First Paragraph of Article 13 and Article 19 of the Basic Law of the Hong Kong Special Administrative Region of the People's Republic of China, see https://www.basiclaw.gov.hk/en/basiclaw/index.html

Kong SAR Government shall apply or adopt the rules or policies on state immunity that the Central People's Government had determined, but not apply or adopt any adapted rules or policies or any rules or policies in contravention of those above. Accordingly, the Court of Final Appeal ruled in favor of DRC.

The fourth interpretation of law by NPC emphasized that the rules on state immunity belonged to foreign affairs, courts of Hong Kong had no jurisdiction to adjudicate the cases in which foreign states were the defendants or foreign state properties were involved. It was also the first time for the Court of Final Appeal to proactively seek an interpretation, which was very significant for the exchanges between the Court and the NPC Standing Committee.

2.5 *Fifth Interpretation: Constitutional Meaning of Pledging Allegiance when Assuming Public Offices*

During the Legislative Council election in 2016, some Hong Kong independence supporters also signed up for the election, six of who were not validly nominated as decided by the Chief Electoral Officer according to law. In the inaugural session of the Sixth Legislative Council held on October 12, 2016, a small number of the members-elect intentionally violated the procedures of oath taking, blatantly advocated Hong Kong independence, insulted the country and Chinese nation. Yau Wai-ching even displayed a banner that read "Hong Kong is not China", announced allegiance to "Hong Kong nation", and pronounced "People's Republic of China" as "people's re-fucking of Shina", an extremely vulgar and insulting expression. Leung Chung-hang also wrapped in a flag and pronounced "Shina" as China. In fact, all the members-elect signed a legal declaration which swear to uphold the Basic Law and swear allegiance to the Hong Kong SAR of the People's Republic of China. The Electoral Chamber had issued a confirmation letter before the inaugural session, so that all members-elect could understand the allegiance pledged to the Basic Law included Articles 1, 12 and Paragraph 4 of Article 159. Yau and Leung's oaths were declared invalid, and their derogation and insult against the Chinese nation immediately sparked the protest of Hong Kong society and overseas Chinese. In the day when the farce was on, many Hong Kong media made reports titled as "Anyone who insults fellow countryman is not qualified as a Legislative Council member" and "All Hong Kong citizens angrily denounce the ugliest day in Legislative Council". On the Internet, many Chinese at home and abroad expressed their indignation at the incident.

Article 104 of the Basic Law provides that t the Chief Executive, principal officials, members of the Executive Council and of the Legislative Council, judges of the courts at all levels and other members of the judiciary in the Hong Kong SAR must, in accordance with law, swear to uphold the Basic Law of the Hong Kong SAR of the People's Republic of China and swear allegiance to the Hong Kong SAR of the People's Republic of China. According to Section 21 of the Oaths and Declarations Ordinance, any person who declines or neglects to take an oath duly requested which he is required to take should vacate his office or should be disqualified from entering on his office. The Rules of Procedure of the Legislative Council of Hong Kong also disallow the members who have not taken an oath in accordance with the Oaths and Declarations Ordinance to attend or vote at a meeting of in the Legislative Council. On October 18, 2016, Leung Kwan-yuen, President of the Hong Kong Legislative Council, ruled that the oaths of five elected members who had not taken the oath according to law were invalid, but at the same time allowed them to re-swear in the next day. However, the Hong Kong SAR Government and most citizens were very dissatisfied with this ruling. The Chief Executive and Secretary for Justice urgently applied to the Hong Kong High Court for judicial review and an injunction that evening, requesting that the President of the Legislative Council overturn the approval of Yau and Leung to re-take oath. The High Court heard the case that night and ruled not to issue a temporary injunction, but accepted the judicial review application and decided to pronounce the sentence on November 3. The Hong Kong society, even among the Legislative Council and between the Legislative Council and the Hong Kong SAR government, had diverged opinions on the validity of the declaration and rescheduled oath, which seriously affects the normal operation of the Legislative Council and the political stability of Hong Kong.

Under this emergency, on November 7, 2016, the 24th Session of the Twelfth NPC Standing Committee unanimously adopted the Interpretation of Article 104 of the Basic Law, which clarified the meaning of this article based on its original meaning. The Interpretation gave answers to five matters: first, "to uphold the Basic Law of the Hong Kong SAR of the People's Republic of China" and to bear "allegiance to the Hong Kong SAR of the People's Republic of China" are not only the legal content which must be included in the oath prescribed by the Article, but also the legal requirements and preconditions for standing for election in respect of or taking up the public office specified in the article. Second, the Interpretation made detailed provisions on the form and content of oath taking, which should be accurate, sincere and solemn. Third, it specified that an oath taker should be disqualified forthwith from assuming the public office if he or she declines to take the oath according to law. Fourth, if the person administering the oath determines the oath taking as invalid, no arrangement should be made to retake the oath. Last, the taking of oath is legally binding, and an oath taker who makes a false oath or engages in conduct in breach of the oath after taking the oath should bear legal responsibility. On November 15, the High Court made the ruling to invalidate the qualifications of Yau and Leung as Legislative Council members. In the opinions of the judge, their behaviors had objectively and clearly shown that they did not intend to take the oath in the Legislative Council whether in form or in content according to Article 104 of Basic Law and the Oath and Declarations Ordinance. Therefore, they were both disqualified as Legislative Council members according to Article 21 of Oath and Declarations Ordinance. Yau and Leung then appealed to the Court of Appeal to make a judicial review application. On November 30, the Court of Appeal dismissed their appeal. On December 2, the Department of Justice, on behalf of the Chief Executive, filed a judicial review with the High Court on the oaths of four Legislative Council members, requesting the court to rule their oaths invalid and order the corresponding seats to be vacant. On July 14, 2017, the High Court ruled that the oaths of four members of the Legislative Council, Lau Siu-lai, Law Kwun-Chung Yiu Chung-yim, and Leung Kwok-hung, had no legal effect, and their memberships were cancelled.

This Interpretation was very necessary and timely. It not only clarified the bottom-line principles for the Legislative Council's oath-taking incident, but also resolutely prevented "Hong Kong independence" activists from entering the Legislative Council. It also provided a solid legal basis for opposing and punishing "Hong Kong independence" activities in the future, and maintained authority of the Constitution and the Basic Law of the Hong Kong SAR and the rule of law in Hong Kong.

Reviewing the five interpretations of the NPC Standing Committee, whether it was the NPC's initiative to interpret the law, or the State Council or the Hong Kong Court of Final Appeal requested the NPC to interpret the law, there were real needs for such interpretations and major disputes over the understanding of the provisions of the Basic Law, which could not be solved on Hong Kong's own. Only by the interpretation of the law by the NPC Standing Committee can end the disputes and maintain Hong Kong's prosperity and stability. Interpretation of NPC is an important way of exercising national sovereignty and an important part of the rule of law in Hong Kong after its return, which has played a significant role in ensuring the full and accurate implementation of the One Country Two Systems guideline and the Basic Law, and maintaining Hong Kong's prosperity and stability.

3 Enforcement of Annex III to Basic Laws

According to Article 18 of the basic laws of the Hong Kong and Macao, all national laws listed in Annex III to the Basic Law be applied locally by way of promulgation or legislation by the SAR. That is to say, there are two ways for Hong Kong and Macao to implement the national laws listed in Annex III: one is to directly promulgate and implement them; the other is to adopt local legislation to implement them if the local systems and agencies are required to cooperate when national laws cannot be directly applied. The basic laws allow the SARs to promulgate the national laws or carry out legislation to implement such national laws, which also embody the One Country Two Systems.

3.1 Enforcement of National Laws in Hong Kong SAR

When the Basic Law of the Hong Kong SAR was adopted in 1990, the NPC decided to list 6 national laws in Annex III to the Basic Law. After Hong Kong's return, the NPC Standing Committee added or removed the national laws in Annex III in 1997, 1998, 2005 and 2017. As of the end of August 2019, a total of 13 national laws were in force in Hong Kong.

1. When the Hong Kong Basic Law was adopted in 1990, the NPC decided that 6 national laws shall be applied locally with effect from 1 July 1997 by way of promulgation or legislation by the Hong Kong SAR

   (a) Resolution on the Capital, Calendar, National Anthem and National Flag of the People's Republic of China;
   (b) Resolution on the National Day of the People's Republic of China;
   (c) Order on the National Emblem of the People's Republic of China Proclaimed by the Central People's Government (Attached: Design of the national emblem, notes of explanation and instructions for use);
   (d) Declaration of the Government of the People's Republic of China on the Territorial Sea;
   (e) Nationality Law of the People's Republic of China;
   (f) Regulations of the People's Republic of China Concerning Diplomatic Privileges and Immunities.

2. When Hong Kong returned on July 1, 1997, the NPC Standing Committee decided to add 5 national laws and delete 1 national law to Annex III

   The five national laws added are: National Flag Law, Regulations of the People's Republic of China Concerning Consular Privileges and Immunities, National Emblem Law, Law of the People's Republic of China on the Territorial Sea and the Contiguous Zone, and Law of the People's Republic of China on Garrisoning the Hong Kong SAR.

   The national law deleted is Order on the National Emblem of the People's Republic of China Proclaimed by the Central People's Government (Attached: Design of the national emblem, notes of explanation and instructions for use).
3. On November 4, 1998, the NPC Standing Committee decided to add the national law on the Exclusive Economic Zone and the Continental Shelf of the People's Republic of China to Annex III to the Basic Law.
4. On October 27, 2005, the NPC Standing Committee decided to add a national law to the list of the national laws in Annex III to the Basic Law, i.e., the Law of the People's Republic of China on Judicial Immunity from Compulsory Measures Concerning the Property of Foreign Central Banks.
5. On November 4, 2017, the NPC Standing Committee decided to add the Law of the People's Republic of China on the National Anthem to Annex III of the Basic Law.

The addition of the Law on National Anthem deserves more attention.

After the promulgation of the Law on National Anthem, Hong Kong society generally agreed that this Law is one as stipulated in Paragraph 3 of Article 18 of the Basic Law, which was subject to be in force in Hong Kong SAR. On July 24, 2017, the Hong Kong Basic Law Committee of the NPC Standing Committee held a meeting to make in-depth discussions on the draft Law on National Anthem and its enforcement in Hong Kong and Macao. On September 9, the Standing Committee consulted the Hong Kong Basic Law Committee on adding the Law in Annex III to the Basic Law of the Hong Kong SAR. On September 23, the Hong Kong Basic Law

Committee held another meeting for serious discussions. Members of the Hong Kong Basic Law Committee unanimously agreed to made the addition, and submitted the following opinions to the Standing Committee in accordance with the law:

First, the national flag, national emblem and national anthem are symbols and signs of the state as stipulated in the Constitution, and are important embodiments of the spirits of the state and Chinese nation. It is the duty of every citizen to maintain the dignity of the national flag, national emblem and national anthem. The National Flag Law and National Emblem Law have been added in Annex III to the Basic Law of the Hong Kong SAR. Therefore, addition of the Law National Anthem to Annex III for enforcement in Hong Kong is consistent with the provisions of the Basic Law and in line with other similar laws additions after the return of Hong Kong.

Second, considering the occurrences of disrespect for the national anthem in Hong Kong in recent years, the enforcement of this Law is of more urgency and importance. After the NPC Standing Committee decided to list it in Annex III to the Basic Law, it recommended that the Hong Kong SAR should promptly proceed with local legislation to adapt to the actual situation of Hong Kong according to its provisions, so as to ensure its full enforcement in the Hong Kong SAR.

Third, the Resolution on the Capital, Calendar, National Anthem and National Flag of the People's Republic of China listed in Annex III is still a valid national law. After the NPC Standing Committee decided to list the Law on National Anthem in Annex III, it shall remain in it. The inclusion of the Law and its enforcement in the Hong Kong SAR will effectively prevent and deal with occurrence of disrespect for the national anthem and challenges of the principle of One Country Two Systems and other social values. It is also conducive to the correct use and reverence for the national anthem, and protection of national dignity, and to enhancing conception of state and patriotic awareness of Hong Kong residents.

It should be noted that the enforcement of the 13 national laws listed in Annex III is uneven in Hong Kong. The national laws that have been promulgated and in force include the Resolution on the Capital, Calendar, National Anthem and National Flag, Resolution on the National Day, Declaration of the Government of the People's Republic of China on the Territorial Sea, Nationality Law, Regulations Concerning Diplomatic Privileges and Immunities, Regulations Concerning Consular Privileges and Immunities, Law on the Territorial Sea and the Contiguous Zone, Law on Garrisoning the Hong Kong SAR, and Law on the Exclusive Economic Zone and the Continental Shelf. The National Flag and National Emblem Ordinance was promulgated to enforce two national laws in this regard, and the National Anthem Ordinance was under law-making procedures,[6] but the Law on Judicial Immunity from Compulsory Measures Concerning the Property of Foreign Central Banks has not been promulgated or came into legislation procedures in Hong Kong.

[6] The National Anthem Ordinance came into force on June 12, 2020.

3.2 Enforcement of National Law in Macao SAR

When the Basic Law of Macao SAR was adopted in 1993, the NPC decided to list 8 national laws in Annex III of the Basic Law of Macao SAR for enforcement. Two more national laws were listed as decided by the NPC upon the return of Macao in 1999, and another two listed in 2005 and 2017 respectively. As of the end of August 2019, a total of 12 national laws are in force in Macao.

1. When the Basic Law was adopted in 1993, the NPC decided that 8 national laws should be applied locally with effect from 20 December 1999 by way of promulgation or legislation by the Macao SAR:
   (a) Resolution on the Capital, Calendar, National Anthem and National Flag of the People's Republic of China;
   (b) Resolution on the National Day of the People's Republic of China;
   (c) Nationality Law of the People's Republic of China;
   (d) Regulations of the People's Republic of China Concerning Diplomatic Privileges and Immunities;
   (e) Regulations of the People's Republic of China Concerning Consular Privileges and Immunities;
   (f) Law on the National Flag of the People's Republic of China;
   (g) Law on the National Emblem of the People's Republic of China;
   (h) Law of the People's Republic of China on the Territorial Sea and the Contiguous Zone.
2. When Macao was returned on December 20, 1999, the NPC Standing Committee decided to add 2 national laws for enforcement in Macao: Law on the Exclusive Economic Zone and the Continental Shelf and Law on Garrisoning Macao SAR.
3. On October 27, 2005, the NPC Standing Committee decided to add to Annex III the Law on Judicial Immunity from Compulsory Measures Concerning the Property of Foreign Central Banks.
4. On November 4, 2017, the NPC Standing Committee decided to add the Law on National Anthem to Annex III.

3.3 Enforcement of National Laws in SARs under Unusual Circumstances

The basic laws of Hong Kong and Macao prescribed that the NPC Standing Committee should decide to declare a state of war or, by reason of turmoil within the SARs which endangers national unity or security and is beyond the control of the SARs' governments decide that the SARs are in a state of emergency, and the Central People's Government may issue an order applying the relevant national laws in the SARs.

4 Laws, Regulations, Decisions and Resolutions on SARs

In addition to the Constitution, the Basic Law of Hong Kong or Macao SAR, and the national laws listed in Annex III of each region's Basic Law, the NPC and its Standing Committee have also enacted laws, made decisions and adopted resolutions within the scope of their authority under the Constitution and the Basic Law.

4.1 Measures for Election of Hong Kong and Macao Deputies to NPC

According to Article 21 of the Basic Law of Hong Kong or Macao, the Chinese citizens who are residents of Hong Kong or Macao SAR shall be entitled to participate in the management of state affairs according to law. The system of people's congresses is China's fundamental political system, and the NPC is the highest organ of state power. Therefore, the primary way of participating in managing state affairs for residents of SARs is to join in the activities of the NPC. However, due to the political systems different from China mainland, they do not have people's congress and its standing committee, neither do they adopt the Electoral Law. Furthermore, the election of NPC deputies is not a matter subject to SAR's autonomy or the local legislation on legislative council membership. In a word, the election of the SAR's deputies to NPC can only be a matter subject to the Central Authorities' jurisdiction, which should be governed by a separate law.

In this case, on March 14, 1997, the Fifth Session of the Eighth National People's Congress adopted the Measures for Election of Deputies of the Hong Kong SAR to the Ninth National People's Congress. On October 27, 1998, the NPC Standing Committee of the National People's Congress made a decision on the by-election of Hong Kong SAR deputies who had become vacant to the Ninth National People's Congress; then on January 30, 1999, it made a decision on the Measures for Resignation of Deputies of the Hong Kong SAR to the Ninth National People's Congress. On March 15, in the Second Session of the Ninth National People's Congress the Measures for Election of Macao SAR Deputies to the Ninth National People's Congress were adopted. The two electoral measures were separately enacted by the NPC for the SARs, and are special statutes on the election of deputies to the National People's Congress. From then on, on the last session of each NPC's term these measures would be promulgated after incorporating necessary adjustments or amendments to the previous ones as listed in the follows:

1. On March 12, 2002, the Fifth Session of the Tenth National People's Congress adopted the Measures for Election of Hong Kong SAR Deputies and Measures for Election of Macao SAR Deputies to Tenth National People's Congress;
2. On March 16, 2007, the Fifth Session of the Tenth National People's Congress adopted the Measures for Election of Hong Kong SAR Deputies and the Measures for Election of Macao SAR Deputies to the Eleventh National People's Congress;

3. On March 15, 2017, the Fifth Session of the Twelfth National People's Congress adopted the Measures for Lection of Hong Kong SAR Deputies and Measures for Election of Macao SAR Deputies to the Thirteenth National People's Congress.

4.2 Decisions on the Development of Political System in Hong Kong SAR

An important part of the Basic Law is to promote democracy in Hong Kong in an institutionalized and legalized way. For example, the Chief Executive and principal officials of the Hong Kong SAR Government must be Chinese citizens who are permanent residents of Hong Kong, and the Central Government will not send officials to take posts in the Hong Kong SAR Government. The change from "rule by the UK" to "rule by the people of Hong Kong" is a tremendous progress in Hong Kong's democracy, a vivid manifestation of Hong Kong compatriots taking charge of their own affairs, and a milestone in the development of democracy in Hong Kong. It also prescribes that the Chief Executive and all members of the Legislative Council should be elected by universal suffrage in the light of the actual situation in Hong Kong under the principle of gradual and orderly progress. So the political system as provided for in the Basic Law is a democratic and scientific one. More importantly, it also clearly sets out the principles and steps for the development of Hong Kong's political system and its progress towards democracy, and specifies the direction of development for the eventual realization of comprehensive democracy in Hong Kong. Compared to its previous constitutional laws, the Letters Patent and Royal Instructions, the principles, spirit and content of the Basic Law are very democratic. It is an undeniable fact that it was only after 1997, in accordance with the provisions of the Basic Law, that Hong Kong compatriots began to be masters of their own region and exercise their democratic rights, and that the true democracy of Hong Kong's political system began only after its return and its re-integration into the state governance system of China.

Since 1997, Hong Kong residents have gained unprecedented democratic rights. According to the Basic Law, Hong Kong residents have participated in the election of the Chief Executive in statutory means for the first time in its history. The election results of the Chief Executive are highly consistent with the findings of various prior public opinion polls, indicating that the Chief Executive has a broad public opinion support. Regarding the election of the 60 members of the Legislative Council, the number of directly elected members of the first Legislative Council by geographical constituencies in 1998 was 20, the number was increased to 24 in 2000, and to 30 in 2004, accounting for half of the number of members.

The Hong Kong SAR is a local administrative region directly under the Central People's Government, whose high degree of autonomy derives from the authorization of the Central Authorities. The political structure of the Hong Kong is prescribed by the Basic Law which is also enacted by the National People's Congress. Since China is a unitary country, the local administrations do not have the right to decide or change their political structure on their own. Therefore, the development of Hong Kong's political structure involves the relationship between the Central Authorities and the SAR, which should be carried out within the framework of the Basic Law. The revisions of the measures for Chief Executive election and for forming the Legislative Council is a major issue to the development of the political structure, but the decision on whether and how to revise them rests with the Central Authorities. This is an extremely important principle established by the Constitution and the Basic Law, and is also the proper meaning of the One country, Two Systems principle. Although there are controversies in Hong Kong society about the path of political system development, the Central People's Government's determination to promote democracy in Hong Kong remains unchanged and will not be intimidated into a stop.

On April 6, 2004, in order to further promote the development of democratic politics in Hong Kong, the NPC Standing Committee issued the Interpretation Regarding Article 7 of Annex I and Article 3 of Annex II to the Basic Law of the Hong Kong SAR, which specified the procedures for initiating the development of the political structure. Accordingly, on April 15, Tung Chee-hwa submitted to the NPC Standing Committee a report on whether there was a need to revise the methods for Chief Executive election in 2007 and for forming the Legislative Council in 2008. On April 26, the NPC Standing Committee adopted a decision approving the Hong Kong SAR to revise these measures. According to this decision, Hong Kong SAR Government put forward a more democratic political reform package to the Legislative Council on December 21, 2005 after 18 months of extensive consultation. Although this package was not passed by a 2/3 majority of all Legislative Council members, the Central Authorities and Hong Kong SAR Government indicated that they would further promote the development of democracy in Hong Kong in accordance with the Basic Law.

On December 12, 2007, Donald Tsang, Chief Executive of Hong Kong SAR, submitted to the NPC Standing Committee a consultation report on constitutional development of the Hong Kong SAR and on whether there was a need to amend the methods for selecting the Chief Executive and for forming the Legislative Council in 2012. The Decision of the Standing Committee of the National People's Congress on Issues Relating to the Methods for Selecting the Chief Executive and for Forming the Legislative Council of the Hong Kong SAR in the Year 2012 and on Issues Relating to Universal Suffrage was adopted on 29 December 2007, making it clear that appropriate amendments may be made to the specific methods for selecting the fourth Chief Executive and for forming the fifth Legislative Council of the Hong Kong SAR in 2012. On June 24 and 25, 2010, the Legislative Council passed the motions on the amendments to the methods for selecting the Chief Executive and for forming the Legislative Council in 2012 by a majority of more than two-thirds of all the members, thereby approving the 2012 political reform package of Hong Kong. Based on the proposals, the NPC Standing Committee amended the methods for selecting the Chief Executive and for forming the Legislative Council in 2012 respectively. As to selecting Chief Executive, the Election Committee in 2012 shall be increased from 800 to 1200 members, consisting of 300 people from each of the industrial, commercial and financial sectors, the professions, labor, social services, religious and other sectors with members from the representatives of members of the District Councils, representatives of the Heung Yee Kuk, Hong Kong deputies to the National People's Congress, and representatives of Hong Kong members of the National Committee of the CPPCC. Candidates for the office of Chief Executive may be nominated jointly by not less than 150 members of the Election Committee. With regard to forming the Legislative Council, the number of Legislative Council seats in 2012 shall be increased from 60 to 70, with 35 seats for functional constituencies and constituencies through direct elections respectively. The approval of this reform package was a "big step" in the process of democratic development in Hong Kong.

From December 4, 2013 to May 3, 2014, the Hong Kong SAR Government conducted an extensive and in-depth public consultation on the methods for selecting the Chief Executive in 2017 and for forming the Legislative Council in 2016. During the consultation, the Hong Kong society expressed the hope that the Chief Executive would be elected by universal suffrage in 2017, and they reached a consensus on such important principles as the methods for selecting the Chief Executive by universal suffrage must comply with the Basic Law and the relevant decisions of the NPC Standing Committee, and the Chief Executive must be a patriot of Hong Kong. The Hong Kong community also put forward various views and suggestions on the methods for selecting the Chief Executive by universal suffrage in 2017 and for forming the Legislative Council in 2016. Based on these views and proposals, Leung Chun-ying, the Chief Executive, submitted a report to the NPC Standing Committee on the issues relating to the selection of the Chief Executive by universal suffrage and on the method for forming the Legislative Council in the Year 2016. On August 31, the NPC Standing Committee made the decision regarding the report, which specified the core elements and institutional framework for Chief Executive selection by universal suffrage and determined that the methods for forming the Legislative Council would be unchanged. Based on the explicit wording of the decision, the selection of the Chief Executive may be implemented by the method of universal suffrage from 2017, and when the selection of the Chief Executive is implemented by the method of universal suffrage, a broadly representative nominating committee should be formed, which should nominate two to three candidates for the office of Chief Executive and each of them must have the endorsement of more than half of all the members of the nominating committee. This is not only a major legal decision, but also a major political decision, reflecting the Central Government's firm position on the implementation of universal suffrage for selecting Chief Executive. As a crucial step in the development of Hong Kong's political system, it is also of great significance for better forging social consensus in Hong Kong, achieving the goal of universal suffrage. Through extensive and in-depth public consultation, the Hong Kong SAR Government introduced the bill on universal suffrage for the Chief

Executive to the Legislative Council on April 22, 2015. But it was not passed because it failed to obtain the 2/3 majority support of all members as required by the Basic Law due to the joint veto by opposition members in the Legislative Council.

4.3 New Authorizations for Hong Kong

In 1996, before Hong Kong's return, the NPC Standing Committee authorized the Hong Kong SAR Government to designate the Immigration Department as the authority to receive nationality applications in the Hong Kong SAR and to handle all nationality applications in accordance with the Nationality Law and its interpretations. Ten years later, it again authorized Hong Kong to exercise jurisdiction over the Hong Kong side of the Shenzhen Bay Port in accordance with the laws of the Special Administrative Region, and in 2017, it made another decision to approve the co-location of boundary control facilities, which deserves particular attention.

The Guangzhou-Shenzhen-Hong Kong Express Rail Link (XRL) is a major cooperation project for large-scale infrastructure construction between the mainland and the Hong Kong SAR. In order to achieve interconnection between Hong Kong and national high-speed rail network, and to ensure that the transport, economic and social benefits of the XRL's Hong Kong section are maximized, the relevant departments of the Central People's Government, Guangdong Provincial People's Government and Hong Kong SAR Government have repeatedly studied and made reference to the previous model of setting up a mainland control point area and a Hong Kong control point area at Shenzhen Bay in Guangdong Province and implementing the co-location arrangement. They agreed that the West Kowloon Station was the best solution to the establishment of a control point and the co-location of immigration and customs facilities. According to their scheme, a control point area at the West Kowloon Station would be set up, divided into a Hong Kong port area and a mainland port area, according to whose own laws, the immigration border control, customs supervision, inspection and quarantine and other immigration control would be carried out for the travelers taking the high-speed rail travel between the mainland and the Hong Kong SAR and their belongings and luggage. Considering that this scheme concerned the division of jurisdiction between the mainland and the Hong Kong SAR and the application of the law, it was necessary to clarify the corresponding legal basis and specific implementation methods in accordance with the Basic Law. The relevant departments of the Central Authorities and the Hong Kong SAR Government, after an in-depth study, agreed to take a "three-step" process: the first step, the mainland the Hong Kong SAR signed the Cooperation Arrangement between the Mainland and the Hong Kong Special Administrative Region on the Establishment of the Port at the West Kowloon Station of the Guangzhou-Shenzhen-Hong Kong Express Rail Link for Implementing Co-location Arrangement ("Cooperation Arrangement"); in second step, the State Council submitted the Cooperation Arrangement to the NPC Standing Committee for approval; in third step, the two sides implemented it through their respective legal procedures.

On July 25, 2017, the Hong Kong SAR Government announced the framework arrangement for the co-location of immigration and customs facilities at the West Kowloon Station, and on November 15, the Legislative Council R passed a motion to support its implementation. Authorized by the State Council, on November 18, 2017, Ma Xingrui, Governor of Guangdong Province, signed the Cooperation Arrangement on behalf of the Mainland and Carrie Lam, Chief Executive, completing the first step.

On December 27, the NPC Standing Committee made the decision to approve the Cooperation Arrangement. The Cooperation Arrangement is closely related to the understanding and application of the Basic Law, which covers the following three aspects: first, the source of the authority of Hong Kong SAR to sign the Cooperation Arrangement with the mainland; second, the relationship with the implementation of national laws in Hong Kong SAR; and third, the relationship with the relevant authorizing provisions of the NPC Standing Committee.

According to the Cooperation Arrangement approved by the Standing Committee, all relevant parties have completed the legal procedures and the co-location of border control facilities have also been successfully implemented. Its implementation is conducive to the interconnection of Hong Kong SAR with the national high-speed rail network and the maximization of the transport, economic and social benefits of XRL, the promotion of people-to-people exchanges and economic and trade activities between Hong Kong and the mainland, the deepening of mutually beneficial cooperation, and the better integration of Hong Kong into overall development of the state. It is of great significance for maintaining the long-term prosperity and stability of Hong Kong SAR.

4.4 New Authorizations for Macao

In 1998, the NPC Standing Committee authorized the Macao SAR Government to designate its relevant institutions to handle all nationality applications in accordance with the provisions of the Nationality Law and its interpretations. Unlike Hong Kong, the specificity of the issue of Macao's nationality is manifested by the existence of a population of Portuguese descent with both Chinese and Portuguese origins. They hoped that a flexible and pragmatic solution to their nationality issue could be adopted. Based on this historical background and reality, in April 1994, during the visit of Portuguese Prime Minister Cavaco Silva to China, Premier Li Peng stated the stance that the Chinese government has no intention to force residents of Portuguese descent born in Macau to become Chinese citizens, and allows them to freely choose their nationality according to the principle of voluntariness. In order to ensure free choice of nationality, the NPC Standing Committee made the interpretation which prescribed "any resident in the Macao Special Administrative Region who is of both a Chinese and a Portuguese descent may, out of his or her own wish, choose either the nationality of the People's Republic of China or of the Republic of Portugal. Once he or she decides on one nationality, he or she shall give up the other. The above-mentioned resident in the Macao Special Administrative Region shall, before he or she chooses his or her nationality, enjoy the rights prescribed in the Basic Law of the Macao Special Administrative Region, with the exception of the rights that are restricted by nationality." This provision adopted a flexible, pragmatic and lenient treatment for the nationality of residents of Portuguese descent, which helped maintained social stability and smooth transition and return of Macao.

In 2009, the NPC Standing Committee authorized Macao SAR to exercise jurisdiction over the new campus of the University of Macau, located on Hengqin Island. The University of Macau is currently the largest comprehensive public university in Macao and representative among Macao's higher education institutions, with nearly 6600 students enrolled at that time. With a crowded campus area of only 54,000 square meters, its development was severely constrained. In view of its small size and lack of suitable land for university expansion, the Macao SAR Government made a request to the Central People's Government on April 24, 2009 to provide the University with a new campus site of approximately 1 square kilometer in Hengqin Island, Zhuhai City of Guangdong Province, located across the river from Macao and connected to Macao by a dedicated access road. At the same time, it proposed in the request that in order to make the University relocate to Hengqin Island, the State Council ask the NPC Standing Committee to authorize Macao to exercise jurisdiction over the new campus on Hengqin Island as it did for Hong Kong SAR over the Shenzhen Bay Port Public Transport Interchange. In order to support the development of education and training of talents in Macao and to promote better and faster Macao's development, the State Council agreed. The relocation of the University of Macau to Hengqin Island required the exercise of jurisdiction according to the laws of Macao. In this regard, according to the bill proposed by the State Council, the NPC Standing Committee of the National People's Congress made the decision which prescribed that "the Macao SAR is authorized to exercise jurisdiction over the new campus of the University of Macau on Hengqin Island in accordance with the laws of the Macao Special Administrative Region from the date of its opening of the new campus…". It also stipulated that "the new campus of the University of Macau on Hengqin Island shall be managed separately from other areas of Hengqin Island", the area of the new campus on Hengqin Island shall be stipulated by the State Council and the manner of acquiring the land use right and the period of use should be determined by the State Council in accordance with the provisions of relevant laws. After the authorization decision and the approval of the State Council to the People's Government of Guangdong Province and Macao SAR Government, the Macao SAR Government and the People's Government of Zhuhai City signed a state-owned land lease contract to acquire the land use right. Regarding the location and area of the new campus, after consultation between Zhuhai and Macao, the State Council decided that the site be located in an area of 1.0926 Km^2 on the south of the Hengqin Port, between the East Island Road and the Cross Gate Waterway, with a special access road to Macao. Considering Article 5 of the Basic Law of the Macao Special Administrative Region, which provides that the previous capitalist system and way of life shall remain unchanged for 50 years, and with reference to the provisions of the laws and regulations on land management regarding the maximum period of 50 years for the granting of educational land, the State Council decided that the land use period of the new campus of the University of Macau on Hengqin Island shall be from the date of opening of the campus to December 19, 2049. After both parties negotiate and report to the State Council for approval in accordance with the prescribed procedures, the land use right may be terminated earlier or renewed at the end of the lease period.

Deng Xiaoping's One Country Two Systems, put forward creatively in the 1980s, was initially aimed at solving the Taiwan question. But now, it has been successfully practiced in the Hong Kong Special Administrative Region and the Macao Special Administrative Region, which will also provide useful experience for its implementation in Taiwan. After a retrospect of the legislative practice in implementing the One Country Two Systems policy, it is generally felt that the Constitution and the SAR's Basic Law are a solid legal guarantee of the One Country Two Systems policy and of great significance for long-term prosperity and stability of Hong Kong and Macao. This process has also accumulated important experience for solving the Taiwan question and achieving the complete reunification of the motherland.

In March 1994, the NPC Standing Committee adopted the Law on the Protection of Investments by Taiwan Compatriots; in the Third Session of the Tenth National People's Congress held in March 2005, the Anti-Secession Law was adopted with an overwhelming majority. The Taiwan Provincial deputies have participated actively in the management of state affairs in accordance with the law for a long time. In the Fourth Plenary Session of the Eighteenth CPC Central Committee convened in October 2014, the CPC proposed to "apply the rule of law to consolidate and deepen the peaceful development of cross-strait relations, improve the laws and regulations relating to Taiwan, regulate and safeguard the development of cross-strait relations and promote cross-strait exchanges and cooperation in accordance with the law. We should use legal means to defend the One-China principle, oppose Taiwan independence, enhance the common understanding of upholding the One-China framework, and advance the peaceful reunification of the motherland". On January 2, 2019, in his important speech made at the Meeting Marking the 40th Anniversary of the Issuance of the Message to Compatriots in Taiwan, Xi Jinping put forward a major decision to promote the peaceful development of cross-strait relations, advanced the peaceful reunification of the motherland in the new era, stated explicitly the proposal of exploring Two Systems solution to Taiwan, gave a creative suggestion on initiating consultations and negotiation and laid out the guidelines for making institutional arrangements on peaceful development of cross-straits relations. His speech, in an open, confident and pragmatic attitude, paves a new journey for peaceful reunification in the new era, which certainly has a profound impact on the future of cross-straits relations. It is universally believed that, under strong Party's leadership, the great practice of One Country Two Systems will continue, and Taiwan-related legislation will continue to be improved, which will lay a solid foundation for the rule of law to resolve the Taiwan question and achieve complete reunification of the motherland.

Chapter 9
Human Rights Protection Legislation: History and Achievements

Hou Xiaoguang and Wang Yuanyuan

Abstract This chapter traces the legislative development of human rights protection in China over the past 70 years. The Constitution enshrines the principle that "the State respects and protects human rights," and the NPC and its Standing Committee have built a comprehensive legal framework to secure civil, political, economic, social, and cultural rights. Since the 18th CPC National Congress, the leadership with the core of Xi Jinping has advanced a people-centered development philosophy, promoting the rule of law to protect citizens' rights and strengthen institutional safeguards. In the new era, human rights legislation has become more complete, transforming "rights on paper" into "rights in action." It highlights the unity of CPC leadership, people as the masters of the country, and the rule of law as the foundation of this progress, rooted in China's national conditions and socialist practice. It concludes that the Chinese path to human rights development provides a durable institutional guarantee for continued progress.

Keywords Human rights · NPC · Rule of law · People-centered · Socialist legal system · Enforcement of human rights protection in constitution

As clearly stated in the Constitution, "the state shall respect and protect human rights". Accordingly, to promote legal institutions and mechanisms and advance the respect to and protection of human rights is not only the stance and proposals that the Party have made during long-term explorations but also the mission and goal of NPC and its Standing Committee.[1] Human rights protection in China has

[1] SHEN Chunyao, *To Strengthen the Legal System for Human Rights Protection to Advance Overall Development of China's Undertaking on Human Rights*, in The Department of International Organizations and Conferences of Ministry of Foreign Affairs, PRC ed., Achievements of Human Rights in China (2012–2017), World Affairs Press, 2018, p. 15.

H. Xiaoguang (✉) · W. Yuanyuan
Beijing, China
e-mail: liujixuan@lawpress.com.cn

W. Yuanyuan
e-mail: liujixuan@lawpress.com.cn

C. Shen et al. (eds.), *A History of Legislation in the Past 70 Years in China*,
https://doi.org/10.1007/978-981-95-3799-0_9

witnessed tremendous achievements and remarkable progress over the past 70 years since the founding of the PRC. As the Chinese socialist legal system has gradually matured, a socialist rule of law system is also well under way, which ensures that the Constitution and the laws confirm and protect citizens' rights to survival and development, personal rights, property rights, fundamental political rights and freedoms and rights of labor, education, social security and equality. The protection and development of human rights through the enforcement of the laws have transformed the "rights on paper" into "rights in action".

Since the Eighteenth CPC National Congress, the Central Committee with Xi Jinping as the core has unswervingly adhered to and developed socialism with Chinese characteristics, emphasizing that the people's aspiration for a better life is the goal of the Party's undertakings and adopting a people-centered approach to development. By making unwavering dedication to the comprehensive rule of law, the Party has remained firm in promoting rule of law that is by the people, for the people, and to the benefit and protection of the people by strengthening human rights protection and ensuring citizens' rights protection strictly according to law. As Chinese socialism enters a new era, the conceptions of China's human rights protection will be elevated and more manifest, its legal institutions and mechanism will be more complete, and the path for advancing human rights protection will be pursued with even firmer conviction.

Over the past seven decades, the legislation on human rights protection has adhered to the integration of Party's leadership, the people's position as masters of the country and the rule of law. This reflects the high degree of consistency between the Party's proposals and people's will, as well as the Party's aspiration and mission for establishing and improving the system of people's congresses. The legislation on human rights protection is also rooted in China's actual conditions, seeks truth from facts, and draws its strength from the practice of socialist revolution, development and reform. It demonstrates the socialist superiority for China's rapid social and economic development and increasingly strong national strength. By adopting a people-centered approach, China has written a magnificent chapter in the history of human rights development and protection, and makes full use of institutional advantage for protecting people's rights and benefiting people with more rights and interests. The reason why China's human rights protection has achieved these extraordinary achievements is that we have unswervingly followed the path of human rights development with Chinese characteristics, one that is firmly taking the country's conditions as the basis, people as the center, rule of law as the criteria, and openness as the driving force.[2] In a word, the legislation on human rights protection has provided solid legal and institutional foundation for advancing along this path.

---

[2] WANG Yi, *To Continue the Path of Human Rights Development with Chinese Characteristics*, in The Department of International Organizations and Conferences of Ministry of Foreign Affairs ed., Achievements of Human Rights in China (2012–2017), World Affairs Press, 2018, pp. 3–4.

1 1949: The Start of Human Rights Protection Legislation in the PRC

The founding of the PRC in 1949 declared that the Chinese people had stood up and became the masters of the country. It also provided the conditions and guarantee for carrying out law-making on human rights protection. Moreover, the Common Program laid out the provisions on the rights of people and prescribed various institutions and mechanisms for the people to exercise state power. Since then, China's human rights undertaking has started a new journey.

During the Chinese revolution, the Party took the Marxism-Leninism conceptions on human rights and law as the guidance, adhered to the combination of the Marxist basic principles with the realities of Chinese revolution, which helped to form and develop the Party's own conceptions on human rights. During the New Democratic Revolution, the Party represented by Mao Zedong made explorations on how to establish people's democracy, achieve people's position as the masters of the country and develop and protect people's rights on theory and practice, which generated innovative achievements. After 1949, as China transitioned to socialism, the Party's conceptions on human rights gained new developments and contributed to a series of distinctive theoretical views on it, including the citizens of a socialist country enjoy a broader measure of personal freedom than the people of a capitalist country.[3] The people under socialism enjoy extensive rights, not only the civil rights and political rights, but also the economic, social and cultural rights;[4] the emphasis on the harmony between rights and duties;[5] and the state's guarantee for human rights.[6] In this period,

[3] In his Report on the Draft Constitution of the People's Republic of China in 1954, Liu Shaoqi stated that, "many articles in the Draft Constitution provide for citizens' freedoms and rights...Our state being in a position to concern itself with the freedoms and rights of very citizen is, of course, determined by our state and social systems. The people of no capitalist country enjoy, or can enjoy, as broad a measure of personal freedom as do our people". See LIU Shaoqi, *Selected Works of Liu Shaoqi (Vol. 2)*, Foreign Languages Press, 1991, p. 153. Mao Zedong, in his *On the Correct Handling of Contradictions Among the People*, pointed out that "our Constitution also provides that the organs of state must practice democratic centralism, that they must rely on the masses and that their personnel must serve the people. Our socialist democracy is the broadest kind of democracy, such as is not to be found in any bourgeois state." See Mao Zedong, *Selected Works of Mao Zedong (Vol. 5)*, Foreign Languages Press, 1977, p. 387.

[4] In his speech made on the Eighth CPC National Congress held in September 1956, Dong Biwu said that "the people's democracy is China is the most democratic type of socialism in the world. Under this regime, people have the freedoms of speech, publication, assembly, association, demonstration and others, particularly the freedoms to oppose imperialism, the systems of exploitation and oppression, and wars of aggression for maintaining world peace, to remove the obstacles in the way of social progress, and to improve people's material and cultural life as production develops. Such extremely broad freedoms are absolutely not enjoyed by the people under imperialism". DONG Biwu, *Collection of Dong Biwu's Writings on Politics and Law*, Law Press, 1986, pp. 478–479.

[5] As Liu Shaoqi pointed out, "in our country the people's rights and duties are in complete harmony. No one has duties without enjoying rights, and no one enjoys rights without duties." See LIU Shaoqi, *Selected Works of Liu Shaoqi (Vol. 2)*, Foreign Languages Press, 1991, p. 153.

[6] In Lius Shaoqi's Political Report made for the Eighth CPC National Congress, he said, "Everyone in the country, in order to maintain a normal life and foster production, must be convinced that

the Party's conceptions of human rights directly guided the establishment of national legal system and its practice, which helped to achieve greatly in this regard.

These achievements can be illustrated as follows:

First, the Common Program and the 1954 Constitution provided the fundamental legal basis for protecting human rights. Constitution is the general basis of state laws, regulations and systems, and the fundamental legal guarantee for ensuring people's position as masters of the country and their basic rights. As correctly pointed by Lenin, "what is a constitution? A sheet of paper with the people's rights recorded on it".[7] The Common Program adopted in the First Plenum of CPPCC convened in September 1949 prescribed that Chinese people shall have freedom of thought, speech, publication, assembly, association, correspondence, person, domicile, change of domicile, religious belief and the freedom of holding procession and demonstrations, and women shall enjoy equal rights with men in political, economic, cultural, educational and social life. The 1954 Constitution adopted in the First Session of the First National People's Congress provided for the principle of democracy and socialism, made provisions on China's state system and government system, formally established the system of people's congresses to ensure the power of the state belong to the people; it also set out separate chapters on citizens' fundamental rights, including the right to vote and the right to stand for election, the freedom of speech, press, assembly, association, procession and demonstration, religious belief, person, correspondence, domicile and change of domicile, work, rest and leisure, education and material assistance, and women shall enjoy equal rights with men. Under the guidance of the Common Program and the 1954 Constitution, China gradually transitioned from the new democratic revolution to socialism, completed the socialist transformation of privately owned production materials, eliminated the system of man exploiting man, established the socialist system and walked on the socialist path.

Second, to make laws on state agencies to ensure that the people's position as masters of the country be practiced with a guarantee. The 1953 Electoral Law for the National People's Congress and Local People's Congresses of all Levels guaranteed the exercise of the right to elect and to stand for election in all respects, which marked a new phase of China's people's democratic development. Under this Electoral Law, the elections based on universal suffrage were carried out throughout China to elect deputies for the forthcoming first session of the first National People's Congress. The NPC then promulgated the Organic Law of the National People's Congress, Organic Law of the State Council, Organic Law of the Local People's Congresses and Local People's Councils, Organic Law of the People's Courts, and Organic Law of the People's Procuratorates and the like on state organizations and agencies, and the Organic Regulation on Urban Community Committees, the Organic

as long as he does not violate the law, his civil rights are guaranteed and shall not be encroached upon by any organization or individual. If his civil rights are unlawfully encroached upon, the state will intervene." LIU Shaoqi, *Selected Works of Liu Shaoqi (Vol. 2)*, Foreign Languages Press, 1991, p. 241.

[7] *Between Two Battles*, in Collected Works of V.I. Lenin (Vol. 9), Progress Publishers, 1972, p. 461.

Regulation on Urban Sub-districts for giving legal basis as masters of country and providing organizational guarantee in protecting people's rights and interests.

Third, to enact laws on economic affairs, marriage and family to protect citizens' property rights and rights on marriage and family. The Agrarian Reform Law was promulgated to abolish the land ownership system of feudal exploitation by the landlord class and establish the system of peasant land ownership. Enabled by this law, the 30 million peasants without no land or less land were distributed with 47 million hectares of land and other production materials for free, and the completion of agrarian reform also made an end of peasants' dependence on landlord and made them equal and independent, which helped form a new democratic free social relationship with equal freedoms that was conducive to the modernization drive of China.[8] The Regulation on the Administration of Trademarks was also enacted to protect people's right to trademarks, urge companies to ensure and improve product quality and protect consumers' interests. The Marriage Law adopted in May 1950 completely dismantled the feudal marriage system based on arbitrary and compulsory arrangements and the superiority of man over women, and ignores the children's interests. It established the new democratic marriage system based on free choice, monogamy, equal rights for both genders, and the protection of the lawful interests of women and children. This helped foster new marriage and family relations characterized by mutual respect and love, mutual support and assistance, unity and harmony.

Fourth, to make laws on social affairs to protect citizens' lawful rights and interests. The Trade Union Law adopted in 1950 explicitly defined the legal status of trade unions in the new China, playing an important role in consolidating the state power for people's democratic dictatorship and protecting the workers' lawful rights and interests. The Regulation on Administrative Penalties for Public Security, Regulation on Border Health Quarantine and Regulation on the Supervision Over Fire Protection were promulgated to improve social management and provide legal basis for protecting relevant citizens' lawful rights and interests.

Fifth, to enact laws for administration of justice to strengthen the people's democratic dictatorship and safeguard people's interests. The Statute on Punishment for Counter-Revolutionary Activity adopted in 1951 made provisions on punishing the bandits, secret agents, bullies, core members of reactionary groups, and other anti-revolutionaries that needed to be dealt with according to law, which completely defeated the rampant attacks of the reactionaries, eliminated the security risks against the new people's regime, ensured social stability and people's peaceful life, and ensured the smooth progress of all the undertakings. To give a summary of the experience from the Three Anti Campaigns, the Statute on the Penalties for Corruption were promulgated in 1952. By adhering to the guideline of combining punishment with education and repression with leniency, it made explicit provisions on the crimes and punishments on corruption, and the boundary between punishment and leniency,

---

[8] ZHENG Yougui, *Land Reform is A Great Historical Change: Celebration of the 50th Anniversary of China's Land Reform Law*, Contemporary China History Studies, No. 5, pp. 6–16 (2000).

which served as the legal basis for punishing corruption and protecting people's interests from encroachment according to law. In addition, the Regulation on Arrest and Detention specified the litigation procedures to guarantee people's exercise of rights to bring an action to a certain extent.

However, the Party's Left-line mistake led the whole nation into various political movements from 1957 to the end of the Cultural Revolution, which totally paralyzed the state apparatus. According to the statistics of law-making in the 18 years between 1959 and 1977, there were basically no any legislative activities.[9] The 1975 Constitution adopted at the First Session of the Fourth National People's Congress, which comprehensively amended the 1954 Constitution, prescribed in Article 13 that "speaking out freely, airing views fully, holding great debates and writing big-character posters are new forms of carrying on socialist revolution created by the masses of the people. The state shall ensure to the masses the right to use these forms to create a political situation in which there are both centralism and democracy, both discipline and freedom, both unity of will and personal ease of mind and liveliness, and so help consolidate the leadership of the CPC over the state and consolidate the dictatorship of the proletariat". Soon after the Cultural Revolution went to an end, the Constitution was amended in the First Session of the Fifth National People's Congress held in February 1978. However, the Left-line mistakes remained, the 1978 Constitution still contained the erroneous contents and provisions that did not conform with realities and took class struggle as the basic line of the state. Therefore, the Cultural Revolution was affirmed in the 1978 Constitution, and to speak out freely, air view fully, hold great debates and write big-character posters was stipulated as people's fundamental rights. In order to fully develop socialist democracy, improve the socialist legal system, maintain a political situation of stability and unity, and guarantee the steady progress of socialist modernization, a special meeting of the Third Session of the Fifth National People's Congress was held in 1980 to amend Article 45 of 1978 Constitution, which removed the provision same as in Article 13 of 1975 Constitution. As commented by Deng Xiaoping, "because what they are doing is, precisely, 'speaking out freely, airing their views fully, putting up big-character posters' and producing illegal publications – all of which only creates unrest and brings back the practices of the "cultural revolution". We must keep this evil trend in check. In 1980 the National People's Congress adopted a special resolution to delete from Article 45 of the Constitution the provision that citizens "have the right to speak out freely, air their views fully, hold great debates and write big-character posters"—a provision that had been added during the "cultural revolution". People who worship Western "democracy" are always insisting on those rights. But having gone through the ordeals of the 10-year "cultural revolution", China cannot restore them".[10] When making a summary of the Cultural Revolution in the Sixth Plenary

[9] The NPC Standing Committee only adopted the Regulation on the Administration of Trademarks, Regulation on Military Services of Officers (Revised) in 1963 and Regulation on the Administration of the Entry, Exit, Transition, Residence and Travel of Foreigners in 1964.

[10] DENG Xiaoping, *Selected Works of Deng Xiaoping (Vol. 3)*, Foreign Languages Press, 1994, pp. 129–130.

Session of the Eleventh CPC Central Committee, it was noted that the reason why the mistake of the Cultural Revolution was committed was that "we do not institutionalize and legalize the intra-Party democracy and democracy of state's political and social life, or even if laws were enacted, they did not have the authority that they should have".

2 1978: A New Period for Human Rights Legislation

At the Third Plenary Session of the Eleventh CPC Central Committee held in 1978, after making a profound review of the lessons from the Cultural Revolution, the Party made a historical decision to turn the focus of the Party and state to economic development and carry out reform and opening-up. It also took the socialist democratic legal system as an abiding guideline, emphasized that the socialist democracy should be institutionalized and legalized. The conference initiated a new phase for developing socialist democratic legal system. The CPC members represented by the old generation of proletarian revolutionaries, such as Deng Xiaoping and Peng Zhen, kept deepening their understandings of people's rights protection for implementing this guideline, and created a new situation for carrying on the undertaking of human rights protection in China.

Since the 1990s, the Party has proposed the "human rights" and "rule of law". In 1991, the State Council Information Office issued the Human Rights in China, a white paper. This was the first time that Chinese government adopted the concept of "human rights", outlined the Chinese history of revolution, development and reform and opening-up through the lens of human rights, and articulated the conditions and basic stance for China's human rights.[11] The report of the Fifteenth CPC National Congress proposed "the rule of law and to build China into a socialist rule of law country", and "as a ruling party, the Communist Party leads and supports the people in exercising the power of running the state, holding democratic elections, making policy decisions in a democratic manner, instituting democratic management and supervision, ensuring that the people enjoy extensive rights and freedom endowed by law, and respecting and guaranteeing human rights". This was also the first time that a Party's report established rule of law as the basic line, and made it explicit to "respect and guarantee human rights", thereby achieving an integration of human rights and rule of law. The report of the Sixteenth CPC National Congress reiterated that "it is essential to improve the systems of democracy, develop diverse forms of democracy, expand citizens' participation in political affairs in an orderly way, and ensure that the people go in for democratic elections and decision-making, exercise democratic management and supervision according to law and enjoy extensive rights and freedoms, and that human rights are respected and guaranteed". In the Suggestions of the CPC Central Committee on Revising Parts of the Constitution approved

[11] CHEN Youwu and LI Buyun, *A Historical Development of Rule of Law and Human Rights*, Modern Law Science, No. 2, pp. 3–9 (2015).

in the Third Plenary Session of the Sixteenth CPC Central Committee held in 2003, the Party suggested the NPC to add a provision of "respecting and guaranteeing human rights". In the amendment to the Constitution adopted in the Second Session of the Tenth National People's Congress held in the following year, it incorporated this provision, a milestone for China's history of human rights development. Three years later, it was written into the Party Constitution, which in its General Program laid down the Party's mission and guidelines in this regard.

The achievements of legislation on human rights protection from 1978 to 2012 can be summarized as follows:

(I) To enact and improve the Constitution to strengthen human rights protection

In addition to the state system, government system, fundamental tasks, path for development, objectives, guidelines and principles, the 1982 Constitution, adopted at the Fifth Session of the Fifth National People's Congress held in December 1982, also highly valued the citizens' fundamental rights and duties. Following the structure of the 1954 Constitution, it places this chapter dedicated to fundamental rights and interests between the General Principles and State Structure as the second chapter to highlight the constitutional principle of protecting people's rights and freedoms. It makes various provisions on people's fundamental rights, including the right to be equal before the law, to vote and stand for election, the freedom of speech, press, assembly, association, procession, demonstration, religious belief, personal dignity and the like. Chapter 1 also prescribes that the state protects citizens' private property and the right to inherit according to law and the rights and interests of the individual and private and other non-public sectors of economy, which in effect confirms the protection of citizens' private property.

The past 30 years' history has demonstrated that the 1982 Constitution conforms with China's conditions and realities, and meets the requirements of development. It fully reflects people's common will, protects people's democratic rights, safeguards people's fundamental interests, promotes national development and progress, guarantees people to live a happy life, and ensures the great rejuvenation of the Chinese nation.

During this period, under the Party's leadership, the NPC made a total of 31 articles of amendments to several provisions or some parts of the 1982 Constitution in 1988, 1993, 1999 and 2004 to ensure the Constitution evolves alongside China's reform and opening-up and socialist modernization. These amendments also enrich the provisions for human rights protection from the aspects of fundamental economic system, adjustment of income distribution system, protection of citizens' private property and social security system. In the Second Session of the Tenth National People's Congress convened in March 2004, the adopted amendment incorporated the article of "respecting and protecting human rights" in the Constitution, making it a basic principle in the state's fundamental law. It not only signified a new level of China's socialist democratic and rule of law development, but also pushed forward China's undertaking on human rights.

(II) To strengthen and improve legislation on human rights protection to construct a fairly complete system of human rights laws.

The Constitution is basically enforced by establishing a sound system of laws, regulations, institutions and mechanisms in China, for the various rights in politics, economy, culture and society as prescribed in the Constitution are guaranteed and realized by the enactment and enforcement of specific laws. As of 2010, 30 years into the reform and opening-up, the Chinese socialist legal system has already been set ready with continuous developments after concerted efforts from all relevant parties. In this system, the Constitution is the core, and the Constitution-related law, civil and commercial law, administrative law, economic law, social law, criminal law, and litigation and non-ligation law are the seven pillars, which can also be divided into law, administrative regulations and local regulations from the perspective of law's hierarchy. A large number of legal norms on citizens' fundamental rights and human rights protection are made available in it, which helps to construct a relatively complete system of human rights laws.

1. The system of laws to protect and improve citizens' right to subsistence and development have been gradually established and improved

   The right to subsistence and development is the basis for the citizens to enjoy other rights. China attaches great importance to strengthening the legislation on the environment and security to create a favorable institutional atmosphere in protecting people's right to subsistence and development, and increase people's sense of fulfillment, happiness and security.

   (a) To consolidate and maintain national security through legislation to guarantee the people's right to subsistence and development. The National Security Law, Military Service Law, National Defense Law, Law on the Protection of Military Facilities, State Secrets Protection Law, and the Anti-Secession Law were enacted to maintain national unification and stability and provide security for the people to live and work in peace and happiness.
   (b) To establish and improve the legal system of environmental protection to ensure that the people enjoy a livable environment. The Environment Protection Law, Law on the Protection of Marine Environment Protection, Law on the Prevention and Control of Water Pollution, Law on the Prevention and Control of Air Pollution, Law on the Prevention and Control of Environmental Noise Pollution, Radioactive Pollution Prevention and Control Law, Law on Environmental Impact Assessment, Law on the Prevention and Control of Sand, Island Protection Law and Circular Economy Promotion Law were enacted to promote green development and protect and safeguard citizens' environmental rights.
   (c) To vigorously protect and improve people's livelihood, and strengthen the institutional build-up of public health, social security and other aspects.

The development of Food Safety Law, Agricultural Products Quality and Safety Law, the Prevention and Control of Infectious Diseases Law, Drug Administration Law, Maternal and Child Health Law, Road Traffic Safety Law, Fire Prevention Law, Safe Production Law, and Occupational Disease Prevention Law were formulated to protect the people's right to life and health within a strict system of laws.

2. The legal norms for civil and political rights continue to be improved

   (a) To give full play to the role of the people's congress as the fundamental political system to effectively strengthen the fundamental institutional guarantee of the people's position as masters of the country. The Organization Law of the National People's Congress, Local Organization Law, Organization Law of the State Council, Law on the Organization of People's Courts, Law on the Organization of People's Procuratorates and other laws have been enacted to help establish and improve the system of organization, powers and authority of state agencies. Regional Ethnic Autonomy Law was to implement the system of regional ethnic autonomy, fully respect and guarantee the rights of ethnic minorities in managing their own internal affairs, and safeguard the legitimate rights and interests of ethnic minorities in accordance with the law. The enactments of the Law on the Organization of the Residents' Committees and Law on the Organization of the Villagers' Committees have established the community self-governance system in urban and rural area to ensure people's participation in the community governance.
   (b) To continue improving the system of protecting citizens' political rights. The Law on the Deputies to the National People's Congress and Local People's Congresses at All Levels, Law On Legislation, Budget Law, and the Law on the Supervision of Standing Committees of the People's Congresses at All Levels were formulated to promote and guarantee the exercise of citizens' rights to vote, to stand for election and to be informed, to participate, to express and to supervise in accordance with the law.
   (c) Efforts are made to strengthen judicial protection of human rights and properly resolve people's disputes. The Criminal Law, Criminal Procedure Law, Civil Procedure Law and Administrative Litigation Law and interpretations related to Criminal Law were made to meet the requirements of deepening the judicial system reform and ensuring the fair administration of justice, so as to strengthen judicial protection of human rights. The Arbitration Law, People's Mediation Law, Law on the Mediation and Arbitration of Rural Land Contract Disputes, Law on Labor Dispute Mediation and Arbitration and the like were enacted to give people with diversified dispute resolution choices.
   (d) To regulate the behavior of administrative departments to protect the lawful rights and interests of citizens. The Law on Administrative Reconsideration,

Administrative Penalty Law, Administrative Licensing Law and Administrative Coercion Law are to ensure that administrative departments exercise their powers in accordance with the law and to strengthen the protection of the legitimate rights and interests of citizens. The State Compensation Law was also enacted to help form a state compensation system for effectively protecting the rights of citizens and organizations to obtain state compensation in accordance with the law.

3. The legal institutions and mechanisms on securing people's economic, social and cultural rights are promoted. China adheres to a people-oriented legislative philosophy, striving to improve the protection of citizens' economic, social and cultural rights through legislation for people's better welfare and a fair social atmosphere.

    (a) The General Principles of Civil Law, Contract Law, Property Law, Tort Law, Marriage Law, Inheritance Law, Adoption Law and Law on the Protection of Consumer Rights and Interests were formulated to protect the personal rights and property rights of citizens.
    (b) Constantly refinement of the intellectual property protection system with Patent Law, Trademark Law, Copyright Law as the pillars and the enactments of the Company Law, Partnership Law, Securities Law, Law on the Promotion of Small and Medium-Sized Enterprises, Anti-Unfair Competition Law, Anti-Monopoly Law and other commercial laws were to maintain the socialist market economic order, protect the legitimate rights and interests of market entities, and constantly stimulate the enthusiasm for innovation.
    (c) The Labor Law, Labor Contract Law, Employment Promotion Laws, Trade Union Law and other laws were enacted to protect the rights of citizens in labor and employment and the Social Insurance Law, Public Welfare Donation Law, Red Cross Society Law and the like to continuously improve the social security and social assistance system and protect citizens' right to assistance.
    (d) The Education Law, Compulsory Education Law, Higher Education Law, Law on the Promotion of Privately-run Schools, Teachers Law and others were formulated to protect citizens' right to education.
    (e) The Law on the Protection of Cultural Relics, Intangible Cultural Heritage Law, and Sports Law were to protect citizens' rights to cultural well-being and interests.

4. A sound legal system for protecting the rights of the ethnic minorities and specific groups such as women, minors, the elderly, and the disabled

    (a) The rights of ethnic minorities are protected according to law. China has established a series of institutions and mechanisms to prohibit ethnic discrimination and guarantee the rights of ethnic minorities with the Constitution as the leading one and the Regional Ethnic Autonomy Law, Electoral Law, Labor Law, Employment Promotion Law, Standard Spoken and

Written Chinese Language, Education Law, Criminal Law and other related laws as the primary ones.

(b) The Law on the Protection of Women's Rights and Interests, Law on The Protection of Minors, Law on the Prevention of Juvenile Delinquency, and the Law on the Protection of the Rights and Interests of the Elderly were enacted to protect the legitimate rights and interests of specific groups such as women, minors, and the elderly in accordance with the law, and to constantly enhance institutional protection for these groups by strengthening criminal legislation.

(c) The enactment of the Law on the Protection of the Disabled clarifies that persons with disabilities enjoy equal rights with other citizens in political, economic, cultural, social and family life.

(III) To fulfill international human rights treaties and proactively create rules on international human rights protection

China has ratified or acceded to 26 international human rights conventions,[12] including the International Covenant on Economic, Social and Cultural Rights and International Convention on the Elimination of All Forms of Racial Discrimination. China attaches importance to the important role of international human rights instruments in the promotion and protection of human rights, and proactively fulfills its treaty obligations, such as the connection of domestic legislation and policy formulation with treaty provisions, preparing and timely submitting compliance reports to relevant treaty bodies in accordance with treaty provisions, conducting constructive dialogues with treaty bodies, fully considering the recommendations and opinions put forward by treaty bodies, and adopting and implementing reasonable and feasible recommendations in light of China's national conditions. China has actively participated in the shaping international human rights rules, such as contributing to the development of the Charter of the United Nations, Universal Declaration of Human Rights and a series of international human rights documents inlcuding Vienna Declaration and Program of Action, Declaration on the Right to Development, Convention on the Rights of the Child, Convention on the Rights of Persons with Disabilities, the Declaration on the Right to Peace, and Convention on the Elimination of All Forms of Discrimination against Women. China has made important contributions to the development of the international human rights legal framework.[13]

[12] State Council Information Office, *Development and Progress of China's Undertaking on Human Rights in the Past Forty Years since the Reform and Opening-up*, www.xinhuanet.com/politics/2018-12/12/c_1123841017.htm, last accessed on August 28, 2019.

[13] State Council Information Office, *New Progress in Legal Protection of Human Rights in China*, http://politics.people.com.cn/n1/2017/1215/c1001-29709774.html, last accessed on August 28, 2019.

3 A New Phase of Human Rights Protection Legislation

Since the Eighteenth CPC National Congress, the Party's Central Committee with Xi Jinping as the core has highly valued the comprehensive rule of law, which was brought to a new height as it was incorporated in the Four-pronged Comprehensive Strategy, made a series of major decisions and initiatives, called for adherence to the position of the people as masters of the country, and ensured requirements of representing the people's interests, reflecting their wishes, protecting their rights, and furthering their wellbeing be integrated into the whole process of comprehensive rule of law. In the Nineteenth CPC National Congress, the Party has made an important judgment that the principal contradiction facing Chinese society has evolved, which reflects China's realities of social development and constitutes the important basis for studying the situations, making human rights policies and arranging legislative programs. As directed by its report, "building on continued efforts to sustain development, we must devote great energy to addressing development's imbalances and inadequacies, and push hard to improve the quality and effect of development. With this, we will be better placed to meet the ever-growing economic, political, cultural, social, and ecological needs of our people, and to promote well-rounded human development and all-round social progress". In the new era, the legislation on human rights protection should tally with these requirements, pay close attention to the key links subject to imbalanced or inadequate development, and make greater efforts to enhance legislation for better democratic development, rule of law, fairness, justice, security and environment to achieve shared and well-rounded development of man.

3.1 Xi Jinping's Important Remarks on Human Rights Protection by Law

In the Eighteenth CPC National Congress, to fully "respect and protect human rights" was laid out as an important goal of completing the building of a moderately prosperous society in all respects, which confirmed the strategic importance of human rights undertaking in China. The Constitution of the CPC revised in this congress reiterated the importance of respecting and protecting human rights. Two years later, the Resolution of the Central Committee of the CPC on Major Issues Concerning the Enhancement of All-round Law-based Governance adopted in the Fourth Session of the Eighteenth CPC Central Committee, emphasized "strengthening judicial protection of human rights" and "improving the awareness of respecting and protecting human rights throughout the whole of society" within the framework of modernization of state governance system and capacity as an important strategic undertaking for improving the judicial protection of human rights. When the Xi Jinping Thought on Socialism with Chinese Characteristics was designated as the guiding principles of the Party in the Nineteenth CPC National Congress in 2017, it championed to "strengthen legal protection for human rights to ensure that the people enjoy extensive rights and freedoms as prescribed by law". The Xi Jinping Thought puts forward new and higher requirements for the development of China's human rights in the new era and provides fundamental guidelines for following the road of human rights development with Chinese characteristics and comprehensively promoting China's undertaking of human rights.[14]

Xi's thought on the development of human rights undertaking should be understood from the following six aspects:

1. To adhere to the people-centered approach to integrate and guide the human rights undertakings and legal protection of human rights. Xi has made several profound explanations in various events on the basic line and development principles for implementing the people-centered approach, which are taken as the fundamental guidelines for legislation on human rights protection. For example, he said, "following a people-centered development philosophy, the CPC and the Chinese government have all along placed people's interests above all else, and worked hard to meet people's desire for a better life and improve respect for and protection of the fundamental rights of the Chinese people".[15]
2. To emphasize the basic stances and principles in respecting and protecting human rights. For example, he pointed that "the CPC and the Chinese government always respect and protect human rights",[16] and "the basic system and basic tasks of the state, the core leadership and theoretical guidance of the state…the socialist legal system, the principle of democratic centralism, and the principle of respecting and safeguarding human rights are that we must uphold, implement and develop".[17]
3. To follow the path for human rights development that conforms with China's conditions. For example, he also remarked in his speech that "for a long time, China, by connecting the universality principle of human rights with China's reality, constantly advances social and economic development, improves people's welfare, promotes social fairness and justice, strengthens legal guarantee of human rights and strives for a comprehensive and coordinated development of economic, social and cultural rights as well as civil and political rights. This has significantly elevated the guarantee level of people's existence and development rights and paved a development path for human rights suitable to China's national

[14] State Council Information Office, *Development and Progress of China's Undertaking on Human Rights in the Past Forty Years since the Reform and Opening-up*, www.xinhuanet.com/politics/2018-12/12/c_1123841017.htm, last accessed on August 28, 2019.

[15] Congratulatory Message from President Xi Jinping to the "South-South Human Rights Forum", *People's Daily*, December 8, 2017, p. 1. The English text can be found at http://p.china.org.cn/2017-12/07/content_50091431.htm

[16] Congratulatory Message from President Xi Jinping to Beijing Forum on Human Rights 2015, *People's Daily*, September 17, 2015, p. 1.

[17] Xi Jinping, *Speech at the Meeting of the People from All Walks of Life in Beijing to Commemorate the 30th Anniversary of the Promulgation and Implementation of the Current Constitution (December 4, 2012)*, in The Governance of China, Foreign Languages Press, 2018, p. 153.

conditions",[18] and "for years, China has put the people first during its development, increasing their benefits, ensuring the people are their own masters and supporting development in an all-round way. These are both the starting points and the goals of development. China has effectively safeguarded the people's right to development and carved out a human rights development path with Chinese characteristics".[19]

4. To emphasize the people's rights to subsistence and development as the primary human rights. He said, "China insists on a combination of the principle of human rights' universality and the nation's actual conditions, and insists that the rights to subsistence and development are primary basic human rights",[20] "China integrates the universality principle of human rights with contemporary realities, follows a human rights development path suitable for China's conditions, adopts a people-centered approach to understanding human rights, takes the rights to subsistence and development as the primary basic human rights, strives for a comprehensive and coordinated development of economic, political, social, cultural and environmental rights, spares efforts to maintain social fairness and justice and promotes all-around development of man".[21]
5. To lay emphasis on the legal and judicial protection of human rights. As Xi said, "We must ensure that all citizens enjoy extensive rights in accordance with the law, that their right of the person and property and basic political rights are inviolable, and that their economic, cultural and social rights are exercised. We must safeguard the fundamental interests of the overwhelming majority of the people, and fulfill their aspirations for and pursuit of a better life. We should address public demands impartially and in accordance with the law, enable the people to feel that justice is served in every case before the courts, and eradicate elements that hurt their sentiments or damage their interests".[22] In addition, he proposed to "promote the impartial administration of justice, further judicial reform, expedite the establishment of an impartial, efficient, and authoritative judicial system, improve judicial systems for the protection of human rights,

[18] *Congratulatory Message from President Xi Jinping to Beijing Forum on Human Rights 2015*, People's Daily, September 17, 2015, p. 1.

[19] *Congratulatory Letter from Xi Jinping to the International Symposium on the 30th Anniversary of the Adoption of the United Nations' "Declaration on the Right to Development"*, People's Daily, December 5, 2016, p. 1. The English text can be found at http://english.cctv.com/2016/12/04/ARTIkHZsTbjTJTvokLQQSPne161204.shtml

[20] General Office of NPC Standing Committee and Party Literature Research Center of CPC Central Committee (eds.), *Selected Important Documents on the System of People's Congresses (Vol. 1)*, Central Party Literature Press and China Democratic and Legal System Publishing House, 2015, pp. 216–217, 342.

[21] *Xi Jinping's Letter to Commemorate the 70th Anniversary of the Universal Declaration of Human Rights emphasizes adherence to the path of human rights development in line with national conditions and promoting the all-round development of human beings*, People's Daily, December 11, 2018, p. 1

[22] Xi Jinping, *Speech at the Meeting of the People from All Walks of Life in Beijing to Commemorate the 30th Anniversary of the Promulgation and Implementation of the Current Constitution (December 4, 2012)*, in *The Governance of China*, Foreign Languages Press, 2018, p. 156.

strictly punish judicial corruption, and ensure that people feel they are being treated fairly and justly in each judicial case".[23]

6. To stress the joint efforts in building a global community of shared future for better human rights development. Xi articulated a wish that "the Chinese people would like to work in concert with people in other developing countries and beyond to advance development through cooperation, promote human rights through development, and build a community with a shared future for human beings".[24]

3.2 Constitutional Amendments: Fundamental Legal Guarantee for Strengthening Human Rights Protection

The Xi Jinping Thought was designated as the leading one in the Party in the Nineteenth CPC National Congress and set forth new goals, which is of great significance for guiding and leading the undertakings of the Party and state. In the First Session of the Thirteenth National People's Congress held in 2018, the Constitution amendment was adopted, which laid down the guiding position of the Scientific Outlook on Development and Xi Jinping Thought in national political and social life. The Amendment also adjusted the integrated plan for building Chinese socialism and the second centenary goal with new contents, improved the measures for comprehensive rule of law and enforcement of the Constitution, made new requirements for insisting on and advancing the Party's leadership in all respects, added new provisions for promoting socialist core values, revised the provision on the term of state's president, and specified provisions on the supervision commissions. These revisions have better manifested people's will, made explicit the advantages of Chinese socialism, and conformed with the great socialist practice for the new era. They are also of great and far-reaching significance for promoting the modernization of state governance system and capacity and for advancing and strengthening rule of law and the undertakings in human rights protection.

[23] Xi Jinping, *Speech at the Ceremony Marking the 60th Anniversary of the National People's Congress*, in General Office of NPC Standing Committee and Party Literature Research Center of CPC Central Committee eds., Selected Important Documents on the System of People's Congresses (Vol. 4), Central Party Literature Press and China Democratic and Legal System Publishing House, 2015, p. 1768. The English text can be found at http://en.qstheory.cn/2020-03/20/c_489248.htm

[24] *Congratulatory Message from President Xi Jinping to the "South-South Human Rights Forum,"* People's Daily, December 8, 2017, p. 1.

3.3 Further Development of the Legal Institutions and Mechanisms for Human Rights Protection

The NPC and its Standing Committee have implemented Xi Jinping's new concepts, new thinking and new strategies of comprehensively advancing rule of law and his important remarks on of human rights development, put into practice the constitutional principle of respecting and protecting human rights, strengthened and improved legislation on human rights protection, and constantly improved the people's sense of fulfillment, happiness and security. As of the end of August 2019, there were 274 laws in force, which helped to enforce the constitutional provisions on the basic rights of citizens, achieve connection with the international human rights protection conventions, and developed the connotation, scope and level of human rights protection.

1. To construct a national security legal system to protect the people's right to subsistence and development. National security is an important prerequisite and foundation for the human rights protection. Since the Eighteenth CPC National Congress, National Security Law, Anti-Espionage Law, Anti-Terrorism Law, Law on the Administration of Activities of Overseas Non-Governmental Organizations within the Territory of China, Cyber Security Law, National Intelligence Law and National Defense Transportation Law were enacted one after another to effectively protect national security.
2. To effectively protect citizens' civil and political rights. The enactment of Supervision Law and the revisions of Local Organization Law, Electoral Law, Representation Law and Civil Service Law improved the system of state agencies and their operations, enhanced the capacity of state institutions and their staff to serve the people, close the ties between people's congress deputies and the people, expand citizens' orderly political participation, smooth the channels for expressing and public opinions, and guaranteed citizens' better exercise of the right to vote, to stand for election and to supervision. The Law on Legislation was also revised to strengthen the system of filing and review on regulations, rules and normative documents, clarified the system of proactive review, feedback to review applicants and disclosure to society, and revoke and correct unconstitutional and illegal regulations, rules and normative documents in accordance with the law for better and effective enforcement of the Constitution and law. The enactment of People's Assessors Law and the revisions of the Organization Law of the People's Courts, Organization Law of the People's Procuratorates, Judges Law and Prosecutors Law ensured the people's right to be informed, participate and supervise the judiciary, consolidate the achievements in and deepen the judicial institutions reform, put into practice the judicial accountability system, promote the construction of a fair, efficient and authoritative socialist judicial system with Chinese characteristics for better protecting human rights with judicial practice.
3. To improve the legislation on socialist market economy to continue the protection of citizens' civil and economic rights. The General Principles of Civil Law,

which was intended for protecting people's rights, clarified equality, voluntariness, fairness and honesty as its basic principles, highlighted the autonomy of will and protection of rights and interests, and reflected the pursuit of comprehensive protection of individuals, safeguarding human values and providing conditions for human development as its pursuit. It laid out the provisions for strengthening the protection of property rights, as it did that "the property rights of civil entities are equally protected by law", which extended the equal protection of property rights to equal protection of all property rights. It also increased protection of civil rights of specific entities, the minors in particular, and made protection of the elderly subject to a guardianship system. What's more, the General Principles of Civil Law also built a complete civil rights system, which incorporated the provisions on protection of the right to privacy, personal information, data and virtual property. On its basis, the codification of civil law also gained momentum to ensure the readiness of a civil code that would meet the socialist development by 2020 and conform with China's national conditions and reality with scientific rules, rigorous structure, reasonable norms, and consistent contents for it would undoubtedly enhance the protection of people's legitimate rights and interests in all respects and better maintain their vital interests. The Rural Land Contract Law was revised to set down in law the results of the major reform of the "separation of ownership, contracting and management rights"; and the new law regulates and guarantees the orderly transfer of land management rights, financing security and shareholding and others., and specifies that the state maintaining the long-term stability of rural land contractual relationships in accordance with the law, and further makes farmers enjoy full and guaranteed rights to land.

The making of Tourism Law, Asset Appraisal Law, E-Commerce Law and Foreign Investment Law, and the revisions of the Anti-Unfair Competition Law, Trademark Law, Standardization Law, Advertising Law and the Law on the Protection of Consumer Rights helped to regulate and protect the sound development of market economy, maintain market order and fair competition, and protect the legitimate rights and interests of consumers and investors. In order to implement the principle of statutory taxation, the Environmental Protection Tax Law, Tobacco Tax Law, Ship Tonnage Tax Law, Law on Farmland Occupation Tax, Law on Vehicle Purchase Tax, and Resource Tax Law for better protecting the legitimate rights of taxpayers. The Individual Income Tax Law was revised to promote the transformation from a classified tax system to a combination of comprehensive and classified tax system to ensure that the public enjoys the benefits of tax reduction.

4. To strengthen legislation on people's livelihood to protect the citizens' personal property and promote their well-being. The Mental Health Law, Traditional Chinese Medicine Law and Law on the Administration of Vaccines enacted and Law on the Administration of Drugs and Red Cross Law amended were intended to strengthen the protection of citizens' right to life and health with an effective management system and strict legal responsibilities. The Population and Family Planning Law was revised to implement the universal two-child policy. The Education Law, Higher Education Law, and Law on the Promotion

of Privately-run Schools were revised to promote education fairness, balanced development, and better exercise of citizens' right to education. The revised Employment Promotion Law, Labor Contract Law, Safe Production Law, and Occupational Disease Prevention Law helped to protect the legitimate rights and interests of workers. The Special Equipment Safety Law, Network Safety Law, Nuclear Safety Law, Regulation on Fire and Rescue Ranks formulated and the revised Food Safety Law were conducive to improving the public safety system in accordance with the law, curbing and preventing various social security accidents and risks, and protecting people's personal rights and property rights. The Charity Law was formulated to guarantee the development of charity causes, protect the legitimate rights and interests of participants in charity activities, and promote the sharing of the fruits of development by all.

5. To promote advanced socialist culture and the prosperity of socialist culture, and constantly meet the growing cultural needs of the people. The enactment of the Law on the Guarantee of Public Cultural Services, Film Industry Promotion Law, Public Libraries Law, Law on the Protection of Heroes and Martyrs and the revision of the Law on the Protection of Cultural Relics, strengthened the legal institutions for culture, made available more public services, promoted the equal distribution of standardized basic public cultural services, and protected people's rights to culture and enjoy cultural benefits.
6. To improve the legal norms on ecological environment protection to guard lucid waters, lush mountains and beautiful homes for people. The Law on the Prevention and Control of Soil Pollution enacted and the Environment Protection Law, Law on the Prevention and Control of Air Pollution, Law on Marine Environmental Protection, Law on the Prevention and Control of Water Pollution and Wildlife Animal Protection Law revised helped to strengthen environmental supervision and accountability, improve the public interest litigation system for environmental protection, strive to build the strictest legal system for ecological protection, protect the relevant environmental rights of citizens, and strengthen the institutional development of a beautiful China.
7. To continue to deepen and strive to strengthen judicial protection of human rights. The Decision of the NPC Standing Committee on Repealing Legislation on Reeducation through Labor was finally made. The Ninth Amendment to the Criminal Law abolished death punishment on nine crimes, and the rest death punishment kept in the law, apart from the crimes on corruption and bribery, are directly concerned with national security, public security, people's life and safety and occupational crimes of people in military service. The amendment also improved the provisions on the execution of death punishment for criminals with suspended death sentence, which leveled up the standards on the application of death punishment by changing its provision from "if it is verified that he has committed any intentional crime" to "if he has committed any intentional crime with execrable circumstances". The revised Civil Procedure Law clearly allowed the procuratorates to bring civil public interest litigations. The revised Administrative Litigation Law also improved the institutions on administrative trial, expanded the scope of administrative litigation, relaxed the restrictions on

the eligibility of plaintiffs and third parties, increased the supervision of administrative trial and enforcement of court judgments, and protected the legitimate rights and interests of administrative litigants. The provisions on civil public interest ligation by the procuratorates can better maintain the citizens' rights and public interests. The revised Criminal Procedure Law improved the mechanism for connecting criminal procedures with supervision, introduced the default judgment, leniency on pleading guilty and accepting punishment and speedy adjudication in criminal trials. The Law on International Criminal Judicial Assistance was enacted to improve China's judicial assistance system, which is conducive to deepening international judicial cooperation, combating transnational crimes and safeguarding citizens' legitimate rights and interests.

8. To constantly improve the legal institutions and mechanisms on the protection of women, minors, the elderly and persons with disabilities. The Anti-domestic Violence Law provided for measures and mechanisms on the prevention and treatment of domestic violence, introduced caution letters by the public security departments, personal safety protective orders and mandatory reporting and specified the legal responsibilities of people who commit domestic violence and procedures for punishing them to effectively protect the legitimate rights and interests of victims of domestic violence, especially the minors, the elderly, persons with disabilities, pregnant or breastfeeding women. The revised Criminal Law increased criminal penalties for the buyers of women and children who are abducted and sold, and include all acts of buying women and children who have been abducted and sold in the scope of criminal liability and made clear-cut provisions on those who abuse minors, the elderly, the sick, or the disabled who are under their guardianship or care will be held criminally liable if the circumstances are serious. The Law on the Protection of the Rights and Interests of the Elderly was revised to actively respond to the aging population, lay down the basic framework of the social pension service system, and strive for its establishment and improvement.

3.4 Strengthening of Constitution's Enforcement and Supervision of Its Enforcement for Effective Implementation of Human Rights Protection Laws

The life of the Constitution is in its implementation, and so is its authority. The political, economic, cultural and social rights of citizens as prescribed in the Constitution are strongly guaranteed and fully realized through the enactment and enforcement of relevant laws. China has, for a long time, upheld, implemented and continued to develop state's fundamental and basic political systems to guarantee people's position as masters of the country, carried out the constitutional principle of respecting and protecting human rights, ensured and improved people's livelihood through development, made use of development to strengthen areas of weakness, promoted social fairness and justice, made the gains of reform and development benefit all our people in a fair way, and realized people's aspirations for a better lie. Over the past 70 years since the founding of PRC, especially over the past 40 years since the reform and opening-up, China has attached increasing importance to the enforcement of the Constitution and law and spared greater efforts to ensure their effective enforcement with new institutions and mechanisms such as recording and review of normative documents and law enforcement inspections. Since the Eighteenth CPC National Congress, under the leadership of the Central Committee with Xi Jinping as the core, the Party has taken a series of effective measures to spread the spirits, safeguard the authority, promote the enforcement, and strengthen the supervision of the Constitution, which also generates a lot of significant achievements and progress, thereby carrying out the principles, initiatives and norms on human rights protection in the Constitution and laws.

1. To promote human rights protection by putting into practice the institutions and mechanisms in the Constitution

On one hand, to practice the pledge of allegiance to the Constitution to consolidate the ideals of and urge the state employees to fulfill the mission laid down in the Constitution and better serve the people. On July 2015, the NPC Standing Committee made the decision to practice the oath of allegiance, which was revised in February 2018. The state employees should make a public oath of allegiance to the Constitution when assuming office according to law as stated in the Amendment to the Constitution. In making the oath, they should pledge to be loyal to the PRC Constitution, to safeguard the authority of the Constitution, to perform obligations imposed by law, to be loyal to the country and to the people, to be fully committed in performing their official duties, to have integrity and always work in the interest of the public, to accept the supervision of the people, and to work hard for the great cause of building a strong, democratic, culturally advanced, harmonious, and beautiful socialist country. A solemn oath-taking ceremony will push forward the state employees to improve their awareness of the Constitution, observe its principles, spirits and missions, inspire and educate them to be loyal to, abide by, and safeguard the Constitution for better its enforcement, protection of citizens' fundamental rights, development of human rights undertaking and service to the people.

On the other hand, to practice special pardons for the purpose of fully advancing rule of law and humanitarian spirit. Pardon is to exempt or reduce the penalties for specific criminals by the state according to law, and also an internationally accepted humanitarian practice. According to the Constitution, the NPC Standing Committee may decide on the granting of special pardons and the President may issue the order of special pardons. In 2015, the NPC Standing Committee adopted a decision on granting of special pardons for some criminals who have participated in the War of Resistance against Japanese Aggression, Liberation War and other two kinds of eligible criminals. In 2019, the NPC Standing Committee adopted a decision on granting of special pardons to some criminals of 9 categories, including those who have participated in the Anti-Japanese War, Liberation War, and have fought in the battles to defend the sovereignty, security and territorial integrity of the People's Republic of China. The granting of special pardons helps to demonstrate the Party's image in continuing Chinese traditions of prudent and lenient punishment for education, and the confidence in governance and system; to promote the comprehensive rule of law and form a good atmosphere for Constitution-based administration and governance for deepening the building of China into a law-based country; to implement the criminal polices underlined by a combination of punishment and leniency, draws upon the inspirations from special pardons to eliminate the negative effect for social harmony and stability; to display China's judicial protection of human rights and consolidate China's image of being open, democratic, law-based and civilized.

2. To promote the constitutional review to provide constitutional guarantee for human rights

As pointed out in the report of the Nineteenth CPC National Congress, "we will strengthen oversight to ensure compliance with the Constitution, advance constitutionality review, and safeguard the authority of the Constitution". One of the Constitution's basic principles is to regulate the exercise of power and protect human rights. Human rights is one of the core values advanced by the Constitution. Therefore, if the Constitution enjoys due authority, human rights may have guarantee. The constitutional review is a major institutional reform for protecting human rights.[25] The Law Committee was changed to Constitution and Law Committee based on the 2018 Constitutional Amendment. In the decision on the duties of the Committee, the Constitution and Law Committee would be borne with the responsibilities to promote the work on enforcement and interpretations of the Constitution and constitutional review, strengthen the supervision of the Constitution's enforcement, and cooperate in publicity of the Constitution in addition to continuing the work on unified deliberation of law bills and others matters. The constitutional review ensures that the decisions and resolutions of the NPC and its Standing Committee conform with the provisions and spirits of the Constitution. According to the arrangements of constitutional review, all the regulations, rules, important policies and initiatives should be subject to the constitutional review by the NPC Standing Committee to keep consistent with the provisions and spirits of the Constitution if they concern the understanding of certain Constitution's provisions. For example, if the institutional designs, norms, policies or measures that concern citizens' basic rights are to be made, they should be compatible with the Constitution's principles and provisions on the protection of citizens basic rights and human rights.

3. To establish a sound mechanism for recording and review of normative documents to provide a strong legal guarantee for human rights

All the laws, administrative regulations and local regulations should not contravene the Constitution as prescribed in the Constitution. For this purpose, the NPC

[25] HAN Dayuan, *To Strengthen Human Rights Protection by Law and Promote the Development of the Human Rights Undertaking*, Human Rights, No. 6, pp. 13–16 (2017).

Standing Committee has made ready a connecting and collaborative mechanism for carrying out the recording and review of regulations, rules and normative documents, prepared a set of working procedures, set up a national information platform, listen and deliberate on the working reports on bills review, enhance the constraints on review, and supervise the correction of matters that are contrary to laws or inappropriate. As of December 2018, all the regulations, rules, judicial interpretations and normative documents were incorporated within the sphere of the recording and review mechanism to ensure that every piece of document is under filing, review and correction if any mistakes are found for the purpose of better enforcing the provisions of the Constitution and law on protecting citizens' basic rights and human rights. For any problems found during the filling and review that contravene the Constitution and law or infringe citizens' basic rights, the Legislative Affairs Committee of the NPC Standing Committee will communicate with and send written suggestions or in other means to the enacting bodies after studying the review results. Moreover, the Committee will also enhance its supervision over correction and spare efforts to resolve the issues from review to maintain the unification of China's legal system.

To take the filing and review of the judicial interpretations of the Supreme People's Court and the Supreme People's Procuratorates as an example, the citizens' proposal for review gave impetus for the SPC to revise Article 24 of the Interpretation (II) on Marriage Law. In January 2018, the SPC issued the Interpretation on Issues concerning the Application of Law in the Trial of Cases Involving Marital Debt Disputes, detailing the criteria for determining the marital common property and the burden of proof. This Interpretation resolved the problems raised in the review. In another example, some citizens suggested to review Article 32 of the Rules on Supervision of Civil Proceedings by People's Procuratorates (for Trial Implementation).[26] After exchange of ideas, the SPP ceased to enforce this provision.[27]

To take the example of filing and review of local regulations, some citizens suggested the standing committees of the local people's congresses to revise the wording of "people having more than one child should be dismissed" in their local Regulation on population and family planning. Revisions were then made based on the review results. To take another example, the bicycle of a Hangzhou citizen was detained by the transportation police on account of the Regulations of Hangzhou Municipality on the Administration of Road and Traffic Safety, but he believed that the administrative coercive measure set forth by the Regulations violated the provisions of law. So he proposed a review to the NPC Standing Committee. Upon study, the Legislative Affairs Committee determined that the detention of non-motorized vehicles and forced transport to home of origin as prescribed in the Regulations were

[26] Article 32: Where a party may legally appeal but fails to appeal a civil judgment or ruling rendered by a people's court of first instance, and files a request for supervision with a people's procuratorate in accordance with paragraph 1 (1) or (2) of Article 209 of the Civil Procedure Law of the People's Republic of China, the people's procuratorate shall not accept the application.

[27] In SPP's notice, a request filed by a party for supervision over an effective civil judgment or ruling rendered by a people's court of first instance shall be accepted in accordance with law provided that the request complies with Article 209 of the Civil Procedure Law of the People's Republic of China, no matter whether the party has filed an appeal.

inconsistent with the provisions of the Administrative Coercion Law, and asked the enacting body to revise them. In June 2017, the Standing Committee of Hangzhou Municipal People's Congress made the revisions accordingly.

As Chinese socialism has entered a new era, the work on legislation should also undertake new initiatives. Based on the strategic plan of the Nineteenth CPC National Congress, the NPC Standing Committee has planned its legislative work in the next 5 years, dedicated itself to the coordinated implementation of Five-sphere Integrated Plan and Four-pronged Comprehensive Strategy, made full-range efforts to meet the requirement of "strengthening legal protection for human rights to ensure that the people enjoy extensive rights and freedoms as prescribed by law", and continued to enhance human rights protection through legislation to provide solid legal guarantee for better promoting the development and progress of China's undertaking in human rights.

Chapter 10
International Law and Domestic Legislation in the Past Seventy Years

Mao Yu

Abstract This chapter examines how China respects international law through constitutional endorsement, treaty-making mechanisms, and alignment of national laws with global norms. During economic reforms, compliance with WTO rules catalyzed the largest legal overhaul in PRC history. Beyond trade, Chinese legislators increasingly reference multilateral treaties and soft-law instruments to craft precise, transparent, and human-centered legislation in fields ranging from aviation to climate change. It identifies three emerging trends: converging legal values, synchronized domestic-international legislative agendas, and China's growing capacity to export legal concepts. It concludes by recommending refining statutory precision, expanding foreign-related legislation, improving inter-agency coordination, and cultivating transnational legal expertise, eventually contributing to building a "community with a shared future for mankind".

Keywords International law · Domestic legislation · WTO · Treaty implementation · Community with a shared future for mankind

The People's Republic of China ("PRC") has been an important member of the international community. It has pursued an independent and peaceful foreign policy, respected and implemented international law, observed the well-recognized international and basic rules of international relations, taken full consideration of relevant international treaties and practices, and actively performed its international obligations. Especially after China launched reform and opening-up, its process of globalization was also accelerated, and international law has played an increasingly important role in China's rule of law construction. Though China does not incorporate international law into its domestic legal system, it attaches importance to performing its obligations under international law, which can be demonstrated by China's legislation history in the past 70 years.

M. Yu (✉)
Beijing, China
e-mail: liujixuan@lawpress.com.cn

C. Shen et al. (eds.), *A History of Legislation in the Past 70 Years in China*,
https://doi.org/10.1007/978-981-95-3799-0_10

1 Persistent Stance of China in Respecting and Following the International Law

It has been China's firm stance to respect and follow the international law since its founding. And China has never abandoned this position, as evidenced by its legislation and performance of international obligations in the past seven decades.

A state's stance toward the basic principles of international law reflects its attitude toward international law.[1] China has been dedicated to equality, mutual benefit and mutual respect for territorial and sovereign integrity and other basic international law principles, which collectively characterize China's attitude to international law.

Such respect for international law is first reflected in the state's fundamental law. The Common Program prescribed that "the principle of the foreign policy of the People's Republic of China is protection of the independence, freedom, integrity of territory and sovereignty of the country, upholding of lasting international peace and friendly co-operation between the peoples of all countries, and opposition to the imperialist policy of aggression and war". As laid down in the 1982 Constitution, "China adheres to an independent foreign policy as well as to the five principles of mutual respect for sovereignty and territorial integrity, mutual non-aggression, non-interference in each other's internal affairs, equality and mutual benefit, and peaceful coexistence in developing diplomatic relations and economic and cultural exchanges with other countries". The 1993 and 2018 amendments to the Constitution included "adhering to reform and opening-up" and "promoting the building of a community with shared future" in their preambles, which not only demonstrate China's determination in promoting opening-up and integration with the international community, but also were solemn commitments to the world by way of its fundamental law.

The respect can also be found in the speeches and writings of China's leaders. In the proclamation of Mao Zedong made to foreign countries on October 1, 1949, he announced that "this government is the sole legal government representing all the people of the People's Republic of China. This government is willing to establish diplomatic relations with any foreign government that is willing to observe the principles of equality, mutual benefit, and mutual respect for territorial integrity and sovereignty".[2] When drafting the report for the Third Plenary Session of the Eleventh CPC Central Committee, Deng Xiaoping directed that necessary laws should be formulated, and attention should also be paid to the research on international law, for the more international exchanges, the more likely difficulties and setbacks would rise if it lacked a grasp of international law.[3] Jiang Zemin thought that attention should be paid to the study of international law to improve capabilities in applying international

[1] Li Shishi, *China's Legislation, Treaties and International Law*, in China Society of International Law ed., China International Law Yearbook (1993), China Translation and Publishing Corporation, 1994, p. 263.

[2] Li Zhaojie and Rao Geping, *One China Principle and International Law*, People's Daily, June 5, 2000, p. 5.

[3] Yu Guangyuan, *To Draft the Speeches for Deng Xiaoping*, http://cpc.people.com.cn/n1/2018/0126/c69113-29789388.html, last accessed on May 1, 2019.

law... the skills should be adept for protecting national interests and dignity and for upholding international justice.[4] Hu Jintao also made it clear that "China abides by the purposes and principles of the Charter of the United Nations and observes international law and universally recognized norms governing international relations. We promote democracy, harmony, cooperation and common progress in international relations...We work for a more just and equitable international order".[5] In his keynote speech on promoting international law-based governance and building a community of shared future at the UN Office at Geneva, Xi Jinping said, "as modern history shows, to establish a fair and equitable international order is the goal mankind has always striven for...The relevance of law lies in its enforcement. It is thus incumbent on all countries to uphold the authority of the international rule of law, exercise their rights in accordance with law and fulfill their obligations in good faith. The relevance of law also lies in fairness and justice. All countries and international judicial institutions should ensure equal and uniform application of international law and reject double standards and the practice of applying international law in a selective way, thus ensuring genuine equality and justice in the world".[6]

China has also attached great importance to treaty ratification by establishing and improving the procedures and mechanisms for it, another aspect of its respect and observance of international law. Treaty is an international instrument that legally binds a state, and to observe treaties is a recognized principle of international law. In China's view, ratification of treaty is a stately act because the power to conclude treaties is sovereign and its proper excise needs laws on ratification procedures.[7] The Organic Law of the Central People's Government stipulated that the Central People's Council should excise the power of "ratifying, abrogating or revising treaties and agreements concluded by the People's Republic of China with foreign countries".[8] The NPC Standing Committee was authorized to decide on the ratification or abrogation of treaties by the 1954 Constitution,[9] and the Decision on the Procedures for Ratifying the Treaties Concluded with Foreign Countries adopted in 1954 laid out

---

[4] LUO Guanxing, ZHANG Sutang and WU Hengquan, *Central Committee held a lecture in international law and Jiang Zemin made a speech*, *People's Daily*, December 10, 1996, p. 1.

[5] Hu Jintao, *Continuing Reform and Opening-up and Advancing Win-Win Cooperation*, http://politics.people.com.cn/GB/1024/7112603.html, last accessed on June 19, 2019. The English text can be found at http://www.china.org.cn/business/boaoforum/2008-04/14/content_14949772.htm

[6] XI Jinping, *Work Together to Build a Community of Shared Future for Mankind: Speech at the United Nations Office at Geneva*, http://www.xinhua net.com//politics/2017-01/19/c_1120340081.htm, last accessed on April 25, 2019. Its English text can be found at http://www.xinhuanet.com/english/2017-01/19/c_135994707.htm?isappinstalled=0

[7] QIAN Qichen, *Explanations on the Draft Law of the People's Republic of China On the Procedure of the Conclusion of Treaties*, http://www.npc.gov.cn/wxzl/gongbao/2000-12/27/content_5002493.htm, last accessed on April 26, 2019.

[8] First Session of the First National People's Congress, Constitution of the People's Republic of China, http://www.npc.gov.cn/wxzl/wxzl/2000-12/26/content_4264.htm, last accessed on April 27, 2019.

[9] First Plenary Session of the Chinese People's Political Consultative Conference, *The Organic Law of the Central People's Government of the People's Republic of China*, http://www.npc.gov.cn/wxzl/wxzl/2000-12/10/content_4237.htm, last accessed on April 25, 2019.

the procedures that were to be connected with the provisions of the Constitution.[10] These laws and decisions had played an important role in the work on treaties and treaty laws, especially on re-examining or revising the old treaties in the early years of PRC. To meet the new circumstances and needs after the reform and opening-up was started, the Law On the Procedure of the Conclusion of Treaties, which made detailed provisions on the procedures on treaty ratification, was adopted in 1990. It conformed with the principles and certain provisions of the Constitution, connected itself with existing laws, demonstrated China's treaty ratification practice and suited the international law and practices, laying solid foundation for expanding China's international cooperation.

Active participation in international legislative activities through concluding or acceding to bilateral or multilateral international treaties constitutes the third manifestation of China's respect for international law. As of April 2019, China had concluded a total of 27,000 bilateral and multilateral international treaties, 7230 of them were made available in the Treaty Database of the Ministry of Foreign Affairs.[11] According to the Law On the Procedure of the Conclusion of Treaties, the treaties and important agreements shall be subject to the decision of the NPC Standing Committee for ratification or abrogation.[12] An analysis of these treaties and agreements is of significance for understanding China's participation in treaty-making in the past 70 years. Based on the statistics published in the NPC Standing Committee's gazettes, as of December 2018, a total of 420 international treaties had been ratified by the NPC or its Standing Committee ratified or acceded to upon their decision,[13] including 1 ratified by the NPC,[14] 263 bilateral and 157 multilateral treaties. The timeline of ratifications and accessions to these international treaties is illustrated in Fig. 10.1.

Based on the database classification, a new classification-based analysis may be made as shown in Fig. 10.2. If analyzed from the perspective of treaty types, it can be found that the bilateral treaties were increasingly concerned with political, military, judicial assistance, anti-terrorism, and criminal affairs after 1990 because the types of bilateral international treaties that had gone through the NPC Standing Committee's procedures were strictly defined in the Law On the Procedure of the Conclusion of Treaties; however, as China has broadened its participation

---

[10] First Session of the First National People's Congress, Constitution of the People's Republic of China, *Decision of the Standing Committee of the National People's Congress on the Procedures for Ratifying the Treaties Concluded with Foreign Countries*, http://www.npc.gov.cn/wxzl/wxzl/2000-12/16/content_4271.htm, last accessed on April 28, 2019.

[11] Data retrieved from the Treaty Database, http://treaty.mfa.gov.cn/Treaty/web/index.jsp, last accessed on May 7, 2019.

[12] Standing Committee of the National People's Congress, *Law of the People's Republic of China On the Procedure of the Conclusion of Treaties*, http://www.npc.gov.cn/wxzl/gongbao/2000-12/16/content_5004545.htm, last accessed on June 1, 2019.

[13] The data was based on the NPC Standing Committee's gazettes. One decision may ratify two or more treaties, for example, the Decision on Ratifying Protocols 2 and 3 of the South Pacific Nuclear Free Zone Treaty (Treaty of Rarotonga). So the data may differ with other research findings.

[14] Joint Declaration of the Government of the United Kingdom of Great Britain and Northern Ireland and the Government of the People's Republic of China on the Question of Hong Kong ratified by the decision made in the Third Session of the Sixth National People's Congress in 1985.

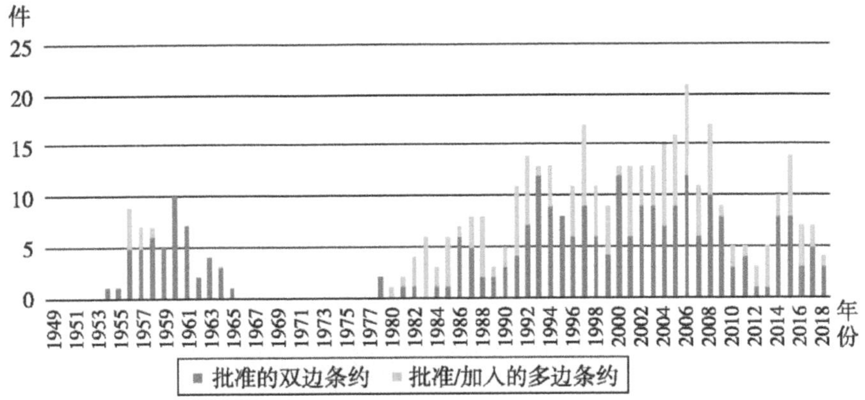

Ratified Bilateral Treaties
Ratified or acceded to Multilateral Treaties

Fig. 10.1 Treaties ratified and acceded to by China's NPC and its standing committee

in international cooperation, the types of multilateral treaties have become more diversified.

In conclusion, the number and scope of international treaties in which China has participated have been on increase since the founding of the PRC. China has never changed its stance and attitude to international law.

2 Particular Influence of International Law on Domestic Legislation

The relationship between international law and domestic law is an important topic of international law study. From the perspective of theoretical development, it can be mainly classified into two theories: the one that believes that domestic law and international law can be incorporated into one legal system and that there should be distinction of effect is monism, while the other that believes they are in different legal systems is dualism,[15] both which have their own merits. However, to absolutely separate international law from domestic law or to generally demand priority of international law or domestic law does not conform with the realities of international community as globalization deepens. As stated by Zhou Gengsheng, a renowned Chinese jurist, "international law and domestic law should not have superiority over each other, nor be in opposition to each other in terms of their substance".[16] The

[15] ZENG Lingliang ed., *International Public Law*, Higher Education Press, 2016, pp. 77–81.

[16] ZHOU Gengsheng, *International Law (Vol. 1)*, Commercial Press, 1976, pp. 19–20.

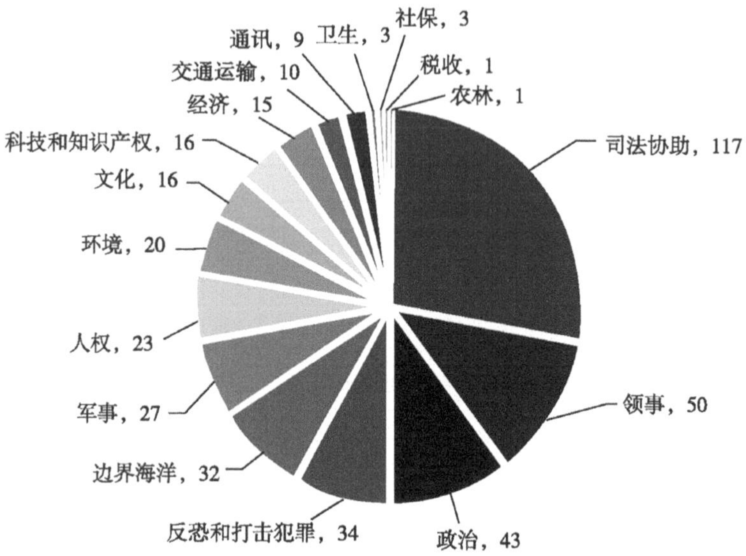

Fig. 10.2 Types of international treaties ratified or acceded to by China's NPC and its standing committee. 科技与知识产权: Technology and intellectual property, 文化: Culture, 环境: Environment, 人权: Human rights, 军事: Military affairs, 边界海洋: Border and marine affairs, 反恐和打击犯罪: Combating terrorism and crimes, 政治: Politics, 领事: Consular affairs, 司法协助: Judicial assistance, 农林: Agriculture and forestry, 税收: Taxation, 社保: Social security, 卫生: Health, 通讯: Communications, 交通运输: Transport, 经济: Economy

key to their relationship is how should the state perform international law obligations, especially how to reflect the principles and spirits of international law through national legislation and apply the specific rules of international law. In the eyes of domestic legislation, China has adhered to a strong and firm stance in international law.[17]

2.1 International Treaties and Practices: Direct Mention or Application in China's Laws

According to statistics, among the 272 laws in force as of April 2019, 61 laws contain the provisions related with international law and its application, accounting for over 1/5. All the seven departments of law, i.e. Constitution and related law, civil and

[17] Li Shishi, *China's Legislation, Treaties and International Law*, in China Society of International Law ed., China International Law Yearbook (1993), China Translation and Publishing Corporation, 1994, p. 263.

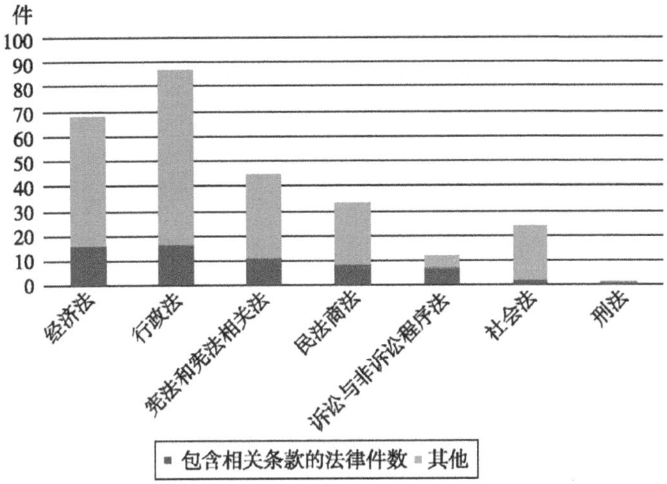

Fig. 10.3 Number of laws that contain provisions related with international law or its application *Note* 经济法: Economic Law行政法: Administrative Law宪法和宪法相关法: Constitution and related Law民法商法: Civil and Commercial Law诉讼与非诉讼程序法: Litigation and Non-Litigation Procedure Law 社会法: Social Law 刑法: Criminal Law.

commercial law, administrative law, economic law, social law, criminal law and litigation and non-litigation law, have these provisions as shown in Fig. 10.3.[18] Most of the provisions in the Constitution and related law are about the competence and procedures of state agencies involved in treaty ratification, and those in litigation and non-litigation law are about the procedural provisions on litigation or other methods of dealing with foreign-related cases. The provisions in other five law departments concern the application and effect of international treaties, which often use the expressions completely or partially consistent or similar with Article 142 of the General Principles of Civil Law.[19]

It has shown different features in different stages of legislation: in the early years of the PRC, some legislations already incorporated the provisions on international

[18] The statistics are based on the texts of National Laws and Regulations Database, which contain the expressions of "(international) treaty", "convention", "agreement", "protocol", or "practice" (the determination of "agreement", "protocol", or "practice" may include their use based on deduction). Classification of laws, decisions on legal issues and departmental laws were made from Legislative Affairs Committee of the NPC Standing Committee, *Laws of the People's Republic of China*, People's Publishing House, 2018.

[19] National People's Congress, General Principles of Civil Law, http://www.npc.gov.cn/wxzl/wxzl/2000-12/06/content_4470.htm, last accessed on May 22, 2019. Article 142: If any international treaty concluded or acceded to by the People's Republic of China contains provisions differing from those in the civil laws of the People's Republic of China, the provisions of the international treaty shall apply, unless the provisions are ones on which the People's Republic of China has announced reservations. International practice may be applied on matters for which neither the law of the People's Republic of China nor any international treaty concluded or acceded to by the People's Republic of China has any provisions.

Table 10.1 Legislation related with international law and its application

Period	Number of legislation
1949–1959	3
1960–1969	0
1970–1979	0
1980–1989	19
1990–1999	29
2000–2009	21
2010–2019	11

law and its application; during 1960s and 1970s, there were no such legislation because the "NPC as the state's top legislature…could not make laws according to the procedures stipulated in the Constitution",[20] which was in line with the "suddenly subdued even abandoned legislative activities" in China.[21] After the reform and opening-up was started, the decision was made to "put the work on legislation as the important agenda of the National People's Congress and its Standing Committee" in the Third Plenary Session of the Eleventh CPC Central Committee,[22] which sped up the efforts on legislation. Furthermore, as the economic institution reform and opening-up gained momentum, "the state legislature should accelerate economic legislation" as proposed in the Third Plenary Session of the Twelfth CPC Central Committee, and the decision made in this conference also proposed to make full use of "two resources" and "two markets", "learn the skills in planning domestic development and developing foreign economic relations",[23] more and more provisions on international law and its application were written down in the domestic laws as shown in Table 10.1.[24]

It deserves special attention that the data retrieved cannot provide a full picture of China's incorporation of provisions on international law and its application in domestic legislation and its performance of international law obligations because the statistical method used in this article only takes the related wording from legal texts as valid data. Some laws and decisions on legal issues, though do not have these

[20] XIN Chunying, *China's Legal System and Its Reform*, Law Press, 1999, p. 16.

[21] ZHOU Wangsheng, *Fifty Years' Legislation in China - A Review of 1949–1999 (Part 1)*, Law and Social Development, Vol. 5, pp. 1–23 (2000).

[22] WAN Qigang, *The Initiation and Development of Rule of Law*, http://www.npc.gov.cn/npc/xinwen/rdlt/fzjs/2014-11/14/content_1886222.htm, last accessed on May 30, 2019.

[23] The Third Plenary Session of the Twelfth CPC Central Committee, *Decision of the Central Committee of the CPC on Economic Institution Reform*, in Party Literature Research Center ed., Selection of Important Documents Since the Twelfth CPC National Congress (Vol. 2), People's Publishing House, 1986, p. 575.

[24] The statistics include the legislation of the CPPCC and Central People's Government Council before the establishment of Standing Committee of the First National People's Congress. The legislation here includes the formulation, revision and alterations of the decisions on law and legal issues as of April 2019.

expressions, are also closely related with its performance of international treaty obligations, respect and observance of international practice. For example, the Law on Exploration for and Development of Resources in the Deep Seabed Area adopted in 2019 does not directly contain international law-related expressions, but many institutions and mechanisms prescribed in this law are derived from the United Conventions on the Law of the Sea. In his explanations on the draft to the Standing Committee, Lu Hao, director of the NPC Environment and Resources Protection Committee, pointed out that the Convention was ratified by the decision issued in the 19th meeting of the Eighth NPC Standing Committee in May 15, 1996. China has been party to the Convention and sponsor of deep seabed area activities since then, and it was necessary to complete the domestic legislation to honor its commitments. According to the relevant provisions on the Contention, to regulate the activities of the contractors in these areas sponsored by China through domestic legislation not only performs its international obligations but also achieves consistency between the performance and reduction of compensation as a state party.[25]

2.2 *WTO Rules: Promotion of Legal Institution Reform for Socialist Market Economy*

To practice socialist market economy is a great revolution in China. It not only continues to liberate people's minds, but also helps to innovate and improve the institutions and mechanisms.[26] As some researchers believed, the establishment of the legal institutions and mechanisms of the socialist market economy has been central to the structural integration of contemporary China's legal system,[27] while in this process the domestic legislation has been engaged in unprecedented "interaction" with international law,[28] the most prominent and influential is the economic legislation around China's accession to WTO.

In 1986, China formally submitted the request too resume its status as a contracting party to the GATT and started negotiations, and in 1995 requested accession to the WTO and carried out negotiations accordingly. As to the demands for "open market" and "accepting WTO rules" for developing countries,[29] Li Peng pointed

[25] Lu Hao, *Explanations on the Draft Law on Exploration for and Development of Resources in the Deep Seabed Area*, http://www.npc.gov.cn/wxzl/gongbao/2016-06/03/content_1993578.htm, last accessed on June 7, 2019.

[26] Xin Chunying, *The Work on Legislation of the National People's Congress and Its Standing Committee since the Reform and Opening-up*, http://theory.people.com.cn/n1/2019/0218/c40531-30759985.html, last accessed on June 7, 2019.

[27] Pang Zheng, *On the Structural Integration and Innovation of Contemporary China's Legal System*, Law and Modernization, No. 9, p. 115 (2004).

[28] Liao Shiping, *Domestic Law Reform Through International Law: Observations on the Alternative to China's Legal System in the Past Forty Years*, China Law Review, No. 5, pp. 145–153 (2018).

[29] Xin Chunying, *To Warn Against the Legal Hegemony during Economic Globalization*, China Economic and Trade Herald Journal, No. 19, p. 30 (2000).

out that "the accession to WTO has made new demands for our work on legislation. We should carry out the necessary initiatives to clean up and revise the existing laws and regulations, take the opportunity to formulate new ones according to the operations of socialist market economy and WTO rules to better meet the WTO requirements…China is still a developing country, so it should enact laws and regulations based on the provisions of WTO rules that suit the conditions of developing countries to ensure the balance of rights and duties, maintain national economic security, and improve competence and opening-up. The WTO rules cover a wide range of areas, and we are not familiar with or do not understand many of them, so it is very meaningful for us to strengthen our learning of these areas".[30] China's legislature had made a systemic study of the WTO's legal system and, since 1999, carried out a comprehensive organizing of relevant laws, administrative regulations, departmental rules and normative documents with reference to its legal system and China's commitment. It had won the commendation of WTO for China "has been working to change its institutional and legal structure in accord with its role as a leading Member of the multilateral trading system".[31]

During the negotiations, the Chinese delegation declared that the revision and abolition of laws would be basically completed before China became a WTO member.[32] According to statistics, as of the end of June 2002, a total of over 190 thousand local regulations, local government rules and other policy measures were revised or abolished based on the results of the initiative carried out in 31 provinces, autonomous regions and municipalities directly under the State Council and 49 large cities.[33] By 2010, China has re-examined over 3000 pieces of laws, regulations and rules and made complete transformation of its trade institutions and policies,[34] the biggest move in PRC's legislative history.

China also carried out collective revision of important laws to make sure China's economic legislation in line with WTO rules. To take national legislation of NPC and its Standing Committee as an example, China made full-range revision of Law on Chinese-Foreign Equity Joint Ventures, Law on Chinese-Foreign Contractual Joint Ventures, Foreign-funded Enterprises Law, Foreign Trade Law and intellectual property-related laws, revised the Customs Law and Law on Import and Export

[30] Li Peng, *Speech at the Seventeenth Law Lecture of the Ninth NPC Standing Committee*, in NPC Training Center ed., Law Lectures of the Ninth NPC Standing Committee, China Democratic and Legal System Publishing House, 2003, p. 386.

[31] WTO Secretariat ed., *Trade Policy Review Report by the Secretariat on People's Republic of China*, translated by Liu Jingdong et al., China Financial and Economic Publishing House, 2006, p. 46. The original English text can be found at https://www.wto.org/english/tratop_e/tpr_e/tp262_e.htm

[32] Li Shishi, *The Revision and Abolition of Laws Basically Completed Before Accession to WTO*, http://news.southcn.com/ztbd/wto/news/200111100397.htm, last accessed on June 7, 2019.

[33] Yang Guohua, *Conceptions of the WTO*, Xiamen University Press, 2012, pp. 234–251.

[34] Ministry of Commerce, *China and WTO: Review and Prospect*, http://www.mofcom.gov.cn/aarticle/ae/ai/201007/20100707037241.html, last accessed on June 7, 2019.

Commodity Inspection and specified provisions in laws on customs, intellectual property rights protection, rules of origin, and export and import commodity inspection to ensure interconnection with relevant legal institutions of WTO rules.

China declared in 2010 that it had honored all the commitments made upon accession to WTO. It has established an economic and trade institution consistent with the WTO rules and evolved into the most open market in the world.[35] Accession to WTO has undoubtedly been the biggest driving force for China to establish a systematic legal system for market economy. As commented by some scholars, "the influence of the WTO on China's rule of law construction is unmatched by any other international organizations".[36]

2.3 *International Treaties and Practices as Important Reference for China's Legislation*

The quality of legislation is the center of the work on legislation. To improve quality, the work on legislation should reflect the objective laws of social development, stand for the policy proposals of the Party and the common will of the people, conform with the realities of China and be operable. To make law in a scientific manner is an important means for legislative quality.[37] Article 6 of the Law on Legislation enacted in 2000 was usually cited as the basis for China's pursuit of scientific legislation.[38] As the superstructure, law must meet the demands of social life, otherwise it would become paper texts.[39] To realize scientific legislation, the work on legislation should adhere to the conditions and realities of the state to make law keep to economic and social development and reasonably regulate social relations.[40] As globalization deepens and reform and opening-up continues, China has been deeply integrated with the world, and international law has also become a part of realities that cannot be ignored when considering China's circumstances. Therefore, it is an important manifestation of China's adherence to realities in the work on legislation to take into full consideration of the relevant principles and provisions of international law and

---

[35] *Ibid.*

[36] Liu Jingdong, *On the Influence of Accession to WTO on China's Rule of Law Construction in the Past Decade*, Journal of International Economic Law, No. 3, pp. 132–158 (2011).

[37] Li Fei, *Seven Aspects for Scientific and Democratic Legislation of the NPC and Its Standing Committee*, https://news.qq.com/a/20110310/002158.htm, last accessed on May 26, 2019.

[38] Lawmaking shall be based on actual circumstances, and shall, in a scientific and reasonable manner, prescribe the rights and obligations of citizens, legal persons and other organizations, and the powers and duties of state organs.

[39] Zhang Chunsheng, *Explanations and Interpretations of the Law on Legislation of the People's Republic of China*, Law Press, 2000, pp. 12–13.

[40] Office of State Law of the Legislative Affairs Committee of the National People's Congress ed., *Explanations and Interpretations on the Law on Legislation of the People's Republic of China*, Law Press, 2015, p. 40.

ensure the consistency between domestic legislation and international law in terms of the spirits and substance of law.

The NPC and its Standing Committee have tried ensure that the treaties to which China has acceded or will accede are properly connected with domestic legislation for better fulfillment of treaty obligations.[41] This is particularly evident in areas where the treaty system is much mature. During NPC and its Standing Committee's work in legislation, international treaties that China have ratified or acceded to are often taken as an important part of the legislative background, and great importance is attached to translating and applying the provisions of international treaties when drafting or deliberating the laws for the purpose of ensuring the integration of faithful enforcement of treaty obligations with scientific legislation. The examples of such kind are great in number. For example, many provisions of the Copyright Law are made by reference to Berne Convention for the Protection of Literary and Artistic Works and Universal Copyright Convention.[42] As pointed out by its enacting body, the copyright enjoyed by foreigners in the works made outside the territory of China under the agreement concluded between China and the country to which they belong or the international treaty to which both countries are parties, should be protected by Chinese law. This provision is not only China's respect for international treaties, but also the realization of mutual benefit, which is one of basic international law principles.[43] In another example, the Seed Law makes separate rules on the sovereign protection of germplasm resources, not only for protecting the safety of China's germplasm resources but also adhering to the international consensus reached in the revision of International Undertaking on Plant Genetic Resources by the Food and Agriculture Organization of the United Nations.[44] In the third example, in his Explanations on the Draft Law of the People's Republic of China on the Territorial Sea and the Contiguous Zone, Yan Hongmo, the Director of State Oceanic Administration, stated the basis of determining breadth of China's territorial sea was the provision of United Nations Convention on the Law of the Sea, which prescribed in Article 3 that "every state has the right to establish the breadth of its territorial sea to a limit not exceeding 12 nautical miles, measured from baselines". Considering China's natural conditions, economic interests and national security, as early as in 1958, the Chinese government declared that "breadth of China's territorial sea is 12 nautical miles" in 1958 to safeguard China's sovereignty and fundamental interests, and maintained

---

[41] SONG Jianli, Several Problems in Applying International Treaties in China, *People's Judicature*, Vol. 5, pp. 51–55 (2015).

[42] LI Shishi, *China's Legislation, Treaties and International Law*, in China Society of International Law ed., China International Law Yearbook (1993), China Translation and Publishing Corporation, 1994, p. 264.

[43] GAO Dezhan, *Explanations on the Draft Seed Law of the People's Republic of China*, http://www.npc.gov.cn/wxzl/gongbao/rlyw/2000-12/17/content_5008912.htm, last accessed on May 28, 2019.

[44] SONG Muwen, *Explanations on the Draft Copyright Law of the People's Republic of China*, http://www.npc.gov.cn/wxzl/gongbao/1989-12/20/content_1479229.htm, last accessed on May 28, 2019.

consistency with the international practice. Therefore, the draft law followed suit to continue China's established position and remain consistent with the Convention.[45]

China has become increasingly engaged in international exchange and has strengthened its work on legal issues concerning foreign affairs and international law developments. When a law bill involves areas covered by international treaties, the legislature will study and draw on experience from the treaties that China have not yet ratified or acceded to but may potentially ratify or accede to, provided that they conform to the principles of the proposed law. In this process, preparations are also made to respond to any potential legal risks. The Civil Aviation Law was a prominent example of this kind. As stressed in the Explanations on the Draft Civil Aviation Law of the People's Republic of China, "this draft adheres to China's conditions, and tries to connect China's legal institutions of civil aviation with international practice after a thorough analysis of the provisions of the convention on international aviation". The draft made a classification of over 20 international treaties on aviation: first, those that China had ratified or acceded to; second, those that China did not ratify or accede but their provisions were not contrary to China's policies; third, those that China did not ratify or accede to, and some of their provisions were contrary to China's realities or policies, though parts of their framework for institutions or others were correct, reasonable and representative of the future development trends; and forth, those that China could not put them into its agenda. China spared great efforts to ensure consistency with the first category, draw on experience from second whose provisions were reasonable and shared the legislative purpose to better deal with the relationship between domestic legislation and international treaties.[46] Another example is the Law On the Procedure of the Conclusion of Treaties. During its enactment, it was clearly asked to take the "conformity international law and international practice" as a principle and stated, with reference to two international conventions,[47] that "the two conventions manifest the rules and practice in international law. Though China does not accede to them, some provisions of them are consistent with our laws and practices. Given this fact, the draft incorporates these provisions to ensure consistency, which may lay the foundation for China ratifying and acceding to the conventions."[48]

The reference to international practice during legislation often occurs in foreign-related civil, commercial and economic legislation, which will consider not only

---

[45] YAN Hongmo, *Explanations on the Draft Law of the People's Republic of China on the Territorial Sea and the Contiguous Zone*, http://www.npc.gov.cn/wxzl/gongbao/2000-12/14/content_5002675.htm, last accessed on May 28, 2019.

[46] CHEN Guangyi, *Explanations on the Draft Civil Aviation Law of the People's Republic of China*, http://www.npc.gov.cn/wxzl/gongbao/1995-06/23/content_1481317.htm, last accessed on May 29, 2019.

[47] Vienna Convention on the Law of Treaties in 1969 and Vienna Convention on the Law of Treaties between States and International Organizations or between International Organizations Signatories in 1986.

[48] QIAN Qichen, *Explanations on the Draft Law of the People's Republic of China On the Procedure of the Conclusion of Treaties*, http://www.npc.gov.cn/wxzl/gongbao/2000-12/27/content_5002493.htm, last accessed on May 29, 2019.

the supranational nature of foreign-related civil, commercial and economic interactions and specific norms on foreign relations, but also the reasonableness of legal provisions under specific context of the times. Before China implemented reform and opening-up, some basic rules of international economic interactions, especially the commercial ones, had already taken shape and been laid down in written texts, and some codified international practices had been widely accepted by the international community. After the reform and opening-up was started, as a latecomer, "it is impossible for us to open up and exchange with the international community without considering international experience and practices",[49] so it became a natural choice for China to "learn, familiarize itself with and implement the rules" of international community in opening-up and integrating itself into the world economic system.[50] A typical example is the enactment of the Contract Law. It referred to both the United Nations Convention on Contracts for the International Sale of Goods (CISG) and Principles of International Commercial Contracts (PICC) after making an in-depth study of international practices. PICC is not an international convention but a set of model texts. It was thus made by considering the different practices of civil law and common law systems and embodies compromised rules on a mutually acceptable basis.[51] Another example is the Maritime Law. It is of great international significance, and highly relevant to import and export. The international commercial practice arises spontaneously from the frequent international commercial activities and are important guarantee for the stability and predictability of these activities. China began to study and organize the drafting of maritime law since the founding of PRC, then interrupted by various political movements and the Cultural Revolution, established in 1982 a drafting committee again, and finally adopted the Maritime Law in 1992, which lasted 4 years. In these years, the drafting had always focused on the study and experience of the related international treaties and international commercial practices, and "start from the national conditions, take the existing international conventions as basis, absorb the private rules reflecting international practices, draw on the widely influential standard contracts, and give consideration of the trend of international maritime legislation's development".[52] The same orientation is also reflected in the provisions of Chinese civil and commercial legislation that concerned the Maritime Law. According to research, the provisions on the contract of carriage in the 1986 General Principles of Civil Law, 1991 Civil Procedure Law, 1992 Maritime Law, and 1999 Special Maritime Procedure Law and Contract Law

---

[49] GU Angran, *Notes on Legislation: Introduction to the Enactment of Some Law in China (1982–2004)*, Law Press, 2006, p. 215.

[50] ZHAO Longyue, *Problems in China's Participation in Making International Rules and the Responses*, Frontiers, No. 16, p. 2 (2012).

[51] GU Angran, *Notes on Legislation: Introduction to the Enactment of Some Law in China (1982–2004)*, Law Press, 2006, p. 294.

[52] YANG Jingyu, *Explanations on the Draft Maritime Law of the People's Republic of China*, http://www.npc.gov.cn/wxzl/gongbao/1992-06/23/content_1479244.htm

and the provisions on ships in the 2007 Property Law, either directly applied or generally recognized the international maritime practices.[53]

Another research believes that various international soft laws[54], including the decisions of international organizations and international standards[55], have also served as important references to domestic legislation as globalization gains momentum and China has participated more and more international organizations.

3 New Developments of the Relationship Between Domestic Legislation and International Law

For any country in the international community, its actions are based on a certain self-positioning, which is also dependent on its understanding of its own strengths, values and pursuits. In the past 70 years, especially since China resumed its legitimate seat in the United Nations in 1971, China has changed from the "victim", "sojourner" to "participant" in the international law system, and its international status also increased. After the end of Cold War, China became an active promoter, a constructor and even a leader of international system, and promoted the international law as a law on coexistence and cooperation.[56] As pointed out in the report of the Nineteenth CPC National Congress, "with decades of hard work, socialism with Chinese characteristics has crossed the threshold into a new era. This is a new historic juncture in China's development...This new era will be an era...that sees China moving closer to the center of stage and making greater contributions to mankind". In this new historical juncture, the relationship between domestic legislation and international law has presented the following three features.

First, the growing resonance domestic governance rules and international rules. Against the backdrop of globalization, China has been committed to the domestic and international imperatives, which has contributed to the values convergence of domestic legislation with international rules.

Rule of law. Over the past 70 years since the founding of PRC, especially over the past 40 years since the reform and opening-up, China has experienced a transition from legal system to rule of law, and its practice of law also transformed from the recognition of making laws to abide to by to comprehensively advancing rule of law, which makes China identify that rule of law is not only essential for achieving quality development, but also important guarantee for the realization great rejuvenation of

[53] CHEN Yaqin, *On the Status of International Maritime Practice in Domestic Law: A Perspective from China's Legislation and Judicial Practices*, Fudan University Dissertation, 2008, pp. 76–110.

[54] HE Zhipeng, *Deglobalization and the Trend of International Soft Law*, Journal of Wuhan University (Philosophy and Social Sciences Edition), N. 4, pp. 54–69 (2017).

[55] ZHU Jingwen, *Socialist Legal System with Chinese Characteristics: Structure, Features and Trend*, Social Sciences in China, No. 3, pp. 87–103 (2011).

[56] HE Zhipeng, CUI Yue and JUAN Xin, *From Confusion to Awakening: China and International Law in the Light of Changing International Relations*, Journal of International Relations and International Law, No. 1, pp. 237–271 (2011).

the Chinese nation. To practice rule of law and implement law-based governance has become a universal acknowledgement in China. Based on the socialist legal system with Chinese characteristics, China will continue to improve it, establish sound legislative institutions, better legislation quality, and ensure state governance according to law. More importantly, with the increasingly frequent exchanges among countries, it has become an imperative for the countries to resolve issues through negotiations, and a consensus of most countries to establish international mechanisms, abide by international rules, and uphold international justice; in a word, international law become more and more important with respect to its status and its role as an important tool and stage for global governance. The rule of law in all respects as advocated by China and the international rule of law share the values, which takes law as the criteria for determining right or wrong and eliminating conflicts and disputes. It should be reminded that the law here includes not only national legislation but also the international legal institutions and mechanisms that reflect the shared interests, values and actions of the mankind.[57]

Humanism. China's legislation and international law share the values on protecting and respecting people's rights. As to domestic legislation, China has put human rights protection throughout the work on legislation since the reform and opening-up. After entering the twenty-first century, to improve people's livelihood and improve social legislation has increasingly become the focus of NPC and its Standing Committee. To take people first and conduct legislation for the people has become one of the most distinctive features of the people's congress legislation in the new era.[58] As to human rights protection in China, the State Council Information Office has issued the National Human Rights Action Plan of China for several consecutive years, which focused on planning the work on human rights protection amelioration through national legislation and the promotion of the development of human rights undertaking. According to the National Human Rights Action Plan of China (2016–2020), based on the constitutional principle and China respects and protects human rights and the spirit of the Universal Declaration of Human Rights and other related international human rights conventions, China would take law-based implementation of human rights protection as the basic principle and conduct regular review and assessment on the human rights protection in all legislative areas.[59] China has established a rather complete normative system for human rights protection to ensure the legal norms on protecting citizens and their political rights under continuous improvements, and deliver on more sound norms on protecting citizens' economic, social and cultural rights.[60] Domestic legislation not only pays attention

---

[57] Liu Zhiyun, *International Law and China's Peaceful Rise in the Perspective of National Interests*, Law Press, 2015, p. 37.

[58] Wang Ping, *To Emphasize People's Livelihood: New Foundation of China's Legislation*, National People's Congress of China, Vol. 17, pp. 28–29 (2014).

[59] State Council Information Office, *National Human Rights Action Plan of China (2016–2020)*, http://www.scio.gov.cn/wz/Document/1492804/1492804_1.htm, last accessed on June 12, 2019.

[60] State Council Information Office, *Progress in Human Rights over the 40 Years of Reform and Opening-up in China*, http://www.scio.gov.cn/zfbps/32832/Document/1643346/1643346.htm, last accessed on June 12, 2019.

to protecting all the people's rights to subsistence and development as a whole, but also insists on proper balance and coordination of overall interests, public interests and individual interests. As the key to improving people's livelihood, it also focuses on legislation on people's welfare such as the laws made for protecting personal life, property rights and legitimate rights and interest of all social groups, regulating labor relations, promoting employment, improving social security system, regulating and promoting the undertakings in people's livelihood including education and medical care, which are also increasingly attuned to the values observed by international law. In modern international law, it is influenced by the humanism, which pays more attention to establishing personal rights and duties and the overall interests of the mankind. What's more, it has become increasingly dedicated to establishing and safeguarding the "individual-based" and "human-based" order based on the establishment and improvement of the peaceful order and development among nations, which helps to contribute to international humanitarian law, human rights law, international criminal law, and international environmental law and other branches of international law. The international law has extended its reach to all aspects of human activities apart from its original functions of the state.[61]

Transparency. One of the defining features in a modern law-based society is the use of publicly accessible laws as the code of conduct and value orientation of all social entities and the emphasis on the transparent legislative process to ensure that the norms of law are scientific and reasonable. This is consistent with the principle of transparency in international law. The principle of transparency has been widely incorporated into international agendas since twentieth century. Now, it is particularly relevant to the international institutions on cross-border investment and trade, human rights and environment, "an important support for the legitimacy of the institutions' procedures."[62] It has promoted the institutions on performance of international obligations, effectively improved the participation of international organizations and other non-state actors in making and implementing international laws. Meanwhile, China has been dedicated to "open-door" legislation, which is also a manifestation of transparency as required by international law. The fifth article of China's Law on Legislation makes it clear to "persist in legislative transparency, and ensure that people are able to participate in the legislation process through various channels". It should also be noted WTO imposed a high bar of requirements on transparency, any judicial judgment or administrative decision "if universally applied, should be issued in the native language, and disclosed if it is not subject to issuance".[63] The rather prevailing conclusion that the WTO's principle of transparency is key to the legislative transparency in China's process of acceding to WTO is not one-sided.

---

[61] ZENG Lingliang, *Trends towards Humanization in Contemporary International Law*, Social Sciences in China, No. 1, pp. 89–103 (2007).

[62] David B. Hunter, *The Emerging Norm of Transparency in International Environmental Governance*, in Padideh Ala'i, Robert G. Vaughn eds., *Research Handbook on Transparency*, Edward Elgar Publishing, 2014, pp. 343–344.

[63] CAO Jianming, *A Comparative Study on the WTO Legal Institutions and Relevant China's Laws, Regulations and Policy Measures*, Study on China Administration for Industry and Commerce, No. 9, pp. 4–7 (2000).

The transparency of China's legislation is determined by the character of people's democracy under the Party's leadership. As early as in 1954 when the draft Constitution was disclosed, China has pursued transparency. After being a WTO member, China accelerated its transparent legislation. in 2008, the Chairman Meeting of the NPC Standing Committee decided to general disclose the law bills for public opinions deliberated by the NPC Standing Committee.[64] Disclosure has evolved into a legislative conception, which gradually converges in the principle of transparency in the development of domestic legislation and international law.

Second, the increasing concurrence of domestic and international legislation. In today's world, new opportunities and challenges continue to emerge, the number of public concerns requiring globally joint efforts is increasing, and global governance has become a consensus among the countries. As China moves closer to the center of the world and plays an increasingly important role in global governance, the concurrence of China's legislative programs with international legislative concerns has become prominent, especially in the emerging law departments including economic law, trade law, oceanic law and environment law. From the perspective of China's legislation, in the legislative plan of the Thirteenth NPC Standing Committee, the legislative programs of these emerging legislative departments take up a large share of the first, second and third categories for legislation.[65] In terms of international law, negotiations in the issues of international private law have picked up speed, multilateral international ocean governance has become an important area of international cooperation, rules in climate and environment have been constantly improved.[66] The emergence of these law departments and new rules can be attributed to the dedication to promoting social productive forces, deepening international exchanges and promoting changes for human development. China's development has been deeply integrated into the world, and in following the road of development, China's demand for institutional supply in these areas is similar with other countries. And such emergence can also be determined by China's domestic legislation and the development of international law in different periods of time. As Chinese socialism enters a new era, a new historic juncture for China's development, the work on domestic legislation follows suit by engaging more in these initiatives: to establish the rule of law system with Chinese characteristics, improve the Chinese socialist legal system with the Constitution as the core, continue to improve legislative quality and efficiency, put more energy on the revision of laws and the formulate and revision of their corresponding regulations and hasten the enactment of new laws that meet the new trends and areas for social and economic development. For international law, the traditional law of war and peace has basically been established, and it gradually

---

[64] LI Shishi, *The Work of NPC Standing Committee on Legislation*, http://www.npc.gov.cn/npc/xinwen/2013-06/25/content_1798343.htm, last accessed on June 12, 2019.

[65] Legislative Plan of the Standing Committee of the Thirteenth National People's Congress, http://www.npc.gov.cn/npc/xinwen/2018-09/10/content_2061041.htm, last accessed on June 11, 2019.

[66] JIA Guide, *Current Trends of International Law and China's Foreign Affairs and Work on Treaty and Law*, http://aoc.ouc.edu.cn/_t719/cb/0e/c9824a248590/page.psp, last accessed on June 11, 2019.

developing into a collection of international rules encompassing more law departments. As the demands of international regulation in outer space, deep sea, polar regions, networks and other emerging areas rises, the requirement of concurrence of domestic legislation with international legislative issues will be further highlighted during the formulation of rules in these areas.

Last, the relationship between domestic legislation and international law changes from one-side influence to rigorous interaction, especially China's legislation has exerted increasing influence on international law. In the early days of reform and opening-up, after the NPC Standing Committee re-examined the laws promulgated before 1978, it found that among 134 pieces of laws and decisions on legal issues, 111, or 81%, had lapsed. The primary basis of constructing China's legal system at that time was the remaining 23 decisions,[67] and there was a substantial gap in the rules of state governance, creating a urgent need to strengthen legislation. In only a dozen years, by the early 1990s, China had enacted more than 200 laws and decisions on legal issues, and over 700 pieces of administrative regulations.[68] In such a rapid legislative process, domestic legislation referred to a large number of principles and rules of international law, and the interaction was dominated by the one-sided influence of international and foreign laws, while the influence or "export" of domestic law was relatively limited. A typical example is the Five Principles of Peaceful Coexistence, which was incorporated into the Preamble of the Constitution and became the cornerstone of China's foreign policy. These principles were gradually accepted as the basic norms governing international relations as well as basic principles of international law through the concerted efforts in practicing them among China and other Asian and African countries.[69]

From the basic theories of international law, the relationship between international law and domestic law influencing each other promotes both the development of domestic law and international law. The channels and modes through which domestic law influences international law are in constant development. Historically, some concepts and institutions arising from domestic legislation would gradually evolve into concepts and institutions of international law, the most conspicuous ones being the law of treaties and the law of state responsibility.[70] This pattern of evolution is developed after a long journey of establishing identity recognition and *opinio juris* through the enduring interactions among states. However, to accelerate the evolution and strengthen the influence of domestic law on international law, the U.S. has gradually developed the "long-arm jurisdiction" since 1945. The long-arm jurisdiction has expanded jurisdiction across federal states to jurisdiction across national borders,

---

[67] XIN Chunying, *China's Legal System and Its Reform*, Law Press, 1999, p. 19.

[68] LI Shishi, *China's Legislation, Treaties and International Law*, in China Society of International Law ed., *China International Law Yearbook (1993)*, China Translation and Publishing Corporation, 1994, p. 266.

[69] XI Jinping, *Carry Forward the Five Principles of Peaceful Coexistence to Build a Better World Through Win-Win Cooperation*, http://www.xinhuanet.com//politics/2014-06/28/c_1111364206.htm, last accessed on June 15, 2019. Its English text can be found at http://www.china.org.cn/world/2014-07/07/content_32876905.htm

[70] WANG Tieya, *Introduction to International Law*, Peking University Press, 1998, p. 194.

which crosses the boundaries of the legislative, judicial and administrative branches and extend its reach in civil and commercial law to the criminal law. It supplements the traditional system of extraterritorial jurisdiction, allowing a country's domestic laws to exert extraterritorial effects across national borders in a "short and quick" manner, which plays a role similar to that of international law in some legal fields. However, it can be easily abused and become a tool for "protectionism", and the implementation of its rules requires a high degree of national institutional innovation, legislative operability and extraterritorial enforcement capacity.

However, China adopts an alternative approach, i.e. enacting and enforcing domestic laws and actively participating in international legislation, especially the treaty-making, to promote law-based development of international relations and improve the interaction between domestic legislation and international law. Relying on this approach, China makes full use of multilateral international organizations, such as the United Nations, to make China heard and put forward its solutions and proposals. China has also taken the initiative to assume the responsibilities as a major country, and position the common needs of other countries. A typical example in this regard is China's coordinated response to climate change by considering both the domestic and international circumstances and rules. As pointed out by Xi Jinping, "to actively respond to climate change is what others tell us to do, but our own initiative, for it is the inherent requirement for China's sustainable development, and the responsibility we have to bear to protect humanity and earth as a major developing country".[71] Therefore, China has resolutely put into practice the provisions of the Law on the Promotion of Circular Economy, Law on the Conservation of Energy and the revised Environment Protection Law, established specialized agencies to coordinate and supervise the practice of United Nations Framework Convention on Climate Change and its two protocols. In the international community, China has proposed its solutions to major disagreements on climate change and proactively assumed the emission-reduction responsibilities, which not only helps to address the current international issues but also sets out its plan for the future. China has won the support and commendation of the international community.[72] Another typical example is China's efforts in steadfastly combating domestic and international corruption and actively advancing institutionalized and law-based initiatives against corruption. With unprecedented vigor and determination, China has stepped up the governance of the Party and supervision over Party members, fought corruption with iron fists, amended the Constitution, enacted the Law on Supervision and made a large number of Party regulations and rules to harness the power within the cage of institutions.[73] For the international community, China has strenuously advocated international cooperation in combating corruption, actively participated in the

[71] State Council Information Council, *Annual Report of 2018 on Responding to Climate Change: China's Policies and Actions*, http://www.gov.cn/xinwen/2018-11/26/content_5343360.htm, last accessed on June 15, 2019.

[72] *To Meet the Challenges Together and Join Hands to Promote Development*, People's Daily (Overseas Edition), December 7, 2015, p. 4.

[73] Yan Yu, *China's Achievements in Combating Corruption awe the World*, Collected Papers on Party Building, No. 7, p. 2 (2017).

making of rules for international anti-corruption cooperation under the multi-lateral frameworks including the United Nations, taken a vigorous and prudent attitude towards the review of the implementation of the United Nations Convention against Corruption and joined the task force in asset recovery and corruption prevention, which have been highly praised among the countries.[74] China has also quickened the interaction of domestic legislation and international rules in emerging areas that do not have rules in China or in the globe. For example, the principle of cyber sovereignty advocated in China's Cyber Security Law corresponds with its National Cyber Security Strategy. After the joint efforts by China, Russia and other countries, the concept of cyber sovereignty has been widely accepted in the international community, and incorporated in the relevant reports of the United Nations Group of Governmental Experts.

The development of the relationship between China's domestic legislation and international governance can, in general, be characterized by three trends: conceptual resonance, concurrence of concerns and increasing international influence of China's domestic legislation. The international law has recently been confronted with the most serious challenges, particularly in the post-Cold War era, because some countries take advantage of their power to abuse international rules and disrupt international order by abrogating international treaties and withdrawing from international cooperation. Nonetheless, the making and observance of rules still prevail, and the value of international law in stabilizing international relations and its role in constructing international order are even more highlighted. China steadfastly supports the international order with the United Nations as the core and international law as the basis, proposes the concepts including a community of shared future for mankind, and faithfully honors its international commitments through domestic legislation, fulfills its international obligations and gives support to multilateralism and multilateral trading system. Such efforts are consistent with the development of international order. In return, in this process China insists on following the trend, and its influence will be further expanded.

4 Reflections on the New Trends of the Relationship Between Domestic Legislation and International Law in the New Era

The new historic juncture at which Chinese socialism enters a new era has put forward new demands for state governance. Since the Eighteenth National Congress, the Central Committee with Xi Jinping as the core has assessed the situation to coordinate

[74] JIANG Jie, *To Show China's Determination in Combating Corruption to the World*, People's Daily, December 10, 2018, p. 5. JIA Guide, *Current Trends of International Law and China's Foreign Affairs and Work on Treaty and Law*, http://aoc.ouc.edu.cn/_t719/cb/0e/c9824a248590/page.psp, last accessed on June 11, 2019.

the development of domestic and international rule of law, which make their development in an unprecedented level.[75] By reviewing the past 70 years' development of their relationship, it can be found that China's rule of law is not borrowed elsewhere, but emerges out of China's own needs as the result of reflections on both the positive and negative experiences that China has accumulated in the construction of democratic legal system. As China gets closer to the center of the stage and its domestic legislation vibes with international law, it is of urgent need for China to consider the domestic legislation and international law in a coordinated way, make it clear the goal of achieving socialist modernization and great rejuvenation, and resolutely become a constructor of word peace, and contributor to global development and protector of international order. To "adhere to rule of law in all respects" and "promote a community of shared future for mankind" are the basic lines of Chinese socialism in the new era, which should be implemented in all aspects. To integrate the comprehensive rule of law with a community of shared future and better follow the new trends of their relationship, China's participation in making international rules should start from its own interests, refer to domestic law to deliver its solutions, insist on consultation, concert of action and sharing, become more adept at making its aspirations known in a way that is more in line with the interests of mankind, and efficiently advance law-based international relations.

These new trends also put forward ever higher requirements for China's domestic legislation. The domestic legislation should uphold "innovation on inheriting traditions and learning from others" and continue its integration of Chinese characteristics with foreign experience. Specifically, China should continue its efforts in strengthening and improving domestic legislation and promote its connection with international law from the following three aspects.

First, to pay more attention to improving the accuracy of law. Understanding is the precondition for international exchanges and cooperation. Deeper mutual understanding will cement and broaden the foundation of international exchanges and cooperation, the more solid the foundation for communication and cooperation will be.[76] Law collectively manifests a state's governance capacity and system, and it is the window for international exchanges. However, to timely adapt Chinese law to changing world, its legislation tends to apply some vague provisions and retain a moderate degree of flexibility of some legal institutions and mechanisms, which to a certain extent helps to form a three-dimensional structure of legal norms,[77] i.e. the components of a legal norm can be found in laws, administrative regulations, local regulations, departmental rules, local governmental rules, various normative

[75] Zhang Wenxian, *Forty Years' Rule of Law in China: History, Features and Experience*, http://sub.cssn.cn/fx/201810/t20181016_4705087_14.shtml, last accessed on June 11, 2019.

[76] XI Jinping, *Speech at the Körber Foundation*, People's Daily, March 30, 2014, p. 2. Its English text can be found at https://www.fmprc.gov.cn/mfa_eng/gjhdq_665435/3265_665445/3296_664550/3298_664554/201404/t20140421_575629.html

[77] XIE Yong, *On the Updates of Theoretical Basis for Local Legislation from the Perspective of the Three-Dimensional Structure of Legal Norms*, China's National People's Congress, No. 20, pp. 31–32 (2017).

documents in all levels and even judicial interpretations, which increases the difficulty for international exchanges of law. Therefore, the future work on legislation should aim at precise and accurate law-making, strive to be specific and clear-cut and effectively improve the relevance, efficacy and practicability of legal norms. To make better language of law, it should further strengthen the research, preparation and implementation of technical standards for legislation to ensure the accuracy and coherence of legislative terms, strive for consistent expressions of the same legal norm at different levels of legislation, try as much as possible to make the expression of legal norm conform with the international legal rules to make it understood and accepted by the international community, so as to provide strong support for China to carry out international exchanges in rule of law and elaborate on the model of China's governance.

Second, to speed up the improvement of the system of foreign-related laws. Since the founding of the PRC, China has established a system of foreign-related laws that suits China's conditions by starting from its national circumstances and fully learning the experience of international law and foreign laws.[78] Of particular importance is the Foreign Investment Law adopted by the Second Session of the Thirteenth National People's Congress in March 2019. The Foreign Investment Law, as China's basic law for foreign investment, integrates Chinese characteristics with international rules. It will expand China's opening-up, promote the development of its legal institutions in foreign investment in line with the changing times, and advance high-quality development of the socialist market economy.[79] Now there is still room for China to improve its foreign-related legislation in land border administration, ocean, and export, their legislative programs are already set out in the plan of the Thirteenth NPC Standing Committee, which will start deliberations in proper time. As the international cooperation for Belt and Road initiative, advocated by China, gains momentum and more and more companies and citizens go abroad, the foreign-related legal relations become increasingly complex, which puts forward higher requirements for domestic legislation to protect the interests of the state, companies and citizens. To further deepen opening and ensure the connection and spillover effect of domestic laws with international law, China should focus on studying the extraterritorial effect of China's foreign-related legislation, especially the relevant provisions from the laws on foreign investment, cyber security, anti-monopoly, trademark and others, revise and refine such provisions for enhanced protection and provide stronger legal basis to protect China's overseas interests.

Considering the particularities in implementing foreign-related legal institutions and mechanisms, it is advised to establish a collaborative platform across departments through legislation, clarify the powers and functions of the departments concerned, improve the cooperation mechanism for information sharing and devote more efforts

---

[78] LI Weihong, JING Yi, YANG Xun and WANG Di, *China's Important Contribution to the Innovation and Development of International Law*, People's Daily, April 17, 2019, p. 17.

[79] WANG Chen, *Explanations on the Draft Foreign Investment Law of the People's Republic of China*, http://www.npc.gov.cn/npc/xinwen/2019-03/15/content_2083626.htm, last accessed on June 21, 2019.

to law enforcement. The publicity and education of law for the companies and citizens should include the training of Chinese and other related countries' laws and of the international law basics and the awareness of compliance. These should also be an important part of the future work on foreign-related legislation.

Third, to improve cross-departmental coordination and communication to strive for consistency of domestic laws with China's international claims. It should be noted that the foreign-related legislation and other legislative programs, as the direct manifestrations of China's governance model, have attracted the attention of the international society as China's comprehensive national strength and international influence have improved. Given current situation, international law and national domestic legislation are simultaneously extending their reach into new areas where international rules have not yet been fully finalized. China's proposals may influence the development of international rules making, and in turn, the international rules will present significant influence on China's domestic legislation. Therefore, China should seize the opportunity, be committed to peace, development, cooperation and win-win, insist on the independent foreign policy of peace, follow the mission of maintaining world peace and promoting shared development, and promote the integration of domestic law with international law. In a short term, the international soft law, represented by resolutions of international organizations, deserves attention. International organizations provide platforms for frequent interactions among countries, and international soft law has an increasingly conspicuous role in guiding and promoting the relevant provisions of international customs and international treaties, which is the best linkage for China to improve the efficiency and quality of interaction between domestic legislation and international law. In new areas such as network governance, social credit, artificial intelligence and biosecurity, domestic legislation should continue to start from China's national conditions and reality, fully investigate and precisely position China's national interests and development needs, and provide basic reference and support for voicing China's position in international occasions. To this end, the legislature should in their daily work strengthen communication with the departments engaged in international exchanges and make judgments upon the analysis of the issues related to the international governance rules. In the long run, to make better use of international law to promote the community of shared future requires China to clarify the status of international law, particularly international treaties, in the socialist legal system with Chinese characteristics. Before making such a clarification, it is necessary for China to comprehensively map out its foreign treaty-making and commitments after thorough research, systematically sort out the performance of international treaties, and then make detailed and refined provisions of laws on the treaty-making powers, functions and procedures of the relevant state departments through legislation or revision of law.

Fourth, to pay more attention to the cultivating the institutional innovation capacity that draws strength from China while serving the international community. The world's social and economic development are now more and more relying on the innovation in theory, institutions, technology and culture, and the international competitive edge is increasingly determined by the ability to innovate. In time of positive changes in international balance of power, despite the obvious rise of emerging markets and developing countries, the Western countries still take dominant positions in the global governance system, which is guaranteed by their strong capacity for institutional innovation. If China is still dedicated to the community of shared future, it must become more adept at transforming its economic strength into influence in shaping international institutions, and make use of institutional innovation to consolidate its achievements in reform and opening-up and social economic development and build itself into a global law-based, convenient, integrated and efficient market. To this end, it should give full play to the leading role of people's congress in domestic legislation, curb departmental interests and local protectionism in legislation, gear legal provisions to be better integrated with the overall national development strategies, and provide efficient and effective legal basis in protecting the status and interests of China in economy, technology and international trade. In this case, consideration should be given to further optimizing the NPC Standing Committee's structure by increasing the number of full-time committee members, especially those who have legal backgrounds or experience in legal practice and by increasing the training of the members of NPC and its Standing Committee in respect of legal knowledge, international law basics, and technical standards for legislation. In addition, the training of talents who have an international vision and are well-versed in international rules and dealing with international legal affairs should be vigorously enhanced. The universities and scientific research institutions should be encouraged to strengthen research and training of professionals in international law and comparative law, and take measures, such as regularly sending outstanding young talents to relevant international organizations for short-term work, to make them learn about how institutional innovation and change in the international community occur and to accumulate experience in and build up strength for putting forward Chinese solutions and making Chinese voice heard in different international arenas.

5 Conclusion

Over the past 70 years since the founding of the PRC, especially over the past 40 years since the reform and opening-up was initiated, China has consistently respected and observed international law, and absorbed the benefits of international rule of law, which have promoted the opening-up and Chinese rule of law. Standing at a new historical starting point in the new era, China should be more confident in its system and adhere to the goal of improving and developing Chinese socialist system, modernizing the national governance system and governance capacity, and practicing the Five Principles of Peaceful Coexistence and the principle of "consultation, concerted action and sharing" in the work on legislation and the legislation on foreign-related matters in particular, so as to truly connect the domestic rule of law with international rule of law through positive and complementary interactions. Through such confidence, adherence and connection, China will contribute its wisdom and solutions to the construction of a community of shared future and the creation of a better future for mankind.

Chapter 11
Enactment, Revision, Repeal and Interpretation: Practice and Development

Luo Xiaoman and Zhao Zhenhong

Abstract This chapter explores the evolution of legislative practice in the PRC, specifically examining the comprehensive framework of "Enacting, Revising, Repealing and Interpreting" laws. It systematically analyzes the shifts in legislative methods and concepts from the founding of PRC to the present day, and highlights how, after the reform and opening-up, China's legislative practice underwent a profound transformation, moving towards a more flexible and diversified approach to meet the demands of rapid economic and social development. Particularly since the 18th Party Congress, this framework has become more frequent and normalized. It demonstrates this through statistical data, showing a marked increase in the number and proportion of legal amendments. It concludes that this shift toward a dynamic and integrated legislative framework is crucial for institutionalizing major reforms and providing a strong legal foundation for the modernization of state governance.

Keywords Enacting, revising, repealing and interpreting · Legislative framework · 18th CPC National Congress · Socialist legal system with Chinese characteristics · Reform and opening-up · Economic and social development

As laid down by Xi Jinping, "the competent manage tasks, the bright govern people, and the wise make laws. The key to governing a country and society well lies in establishing, prioritizing, and adhering to rules. Law is the greatest and most important form of rules in a country's governance. To modernize China's system and capacity for governance, we must maintain our commitment to law-based governance to provide a fundamental, comprehensive, and long-term institutional guarantee for advancing the cause of the Party and country".[1] These remarks are the conclusion

[1] The Party Literature Research Office ed., *The Law-Based Governance of China*, Central Compilation and Translation Press, 2017, p. 14.

L. Xiaoman (✉) · Z. Zhenhong
Beijing, China
e-mail: liujixuan@lawpress.com.cn

C. Shen et al. (eds.), *A History of Legislation in the Past 70 Years in China*,
https://doi.org/10.1007/978-981-95-3799-0_11

drawn by the Party from the history of social revolutions, development and reform and are also the major decision guiding the endeavors of the Party.

The founding of the PRC created a new historical opportunity for China's social development and progress, and laid the foundation for China's modernization of state governance. Over the past 70 years since its founding, especially over the past 40 years since the reform and opening-up was launched, practice has shown that only socialism can save China, and only socialism with Chinese characteristics can lead China to development. Since 1949, the Party has led the Chinese people to carry out arduous tasks in establishing, consolidating, improving and developing socialism, setting up the state powers to achieve the people's position as masters of the country, and making China a great modern socialist power. Through these tasks, the Party has led the people to carve out a path of socialist rule of law development with Chinese characteristics, strive for the socialist legal system with Chinese characteristics and a socialist rule of law country, and finally achieve the modernized state governance system and capacity. In these years, China's legislative system has been established and developed through continuous refinement, and its legislative bodies, procedures and practices have also undergone great changes. In this process, the sources of law and the methods of legislation have become diversified. In the early years of the PRC, the Central People's Government Council was empowered to make and interpret national laws and promulgate decrees; subsequently, the National People's Congress was established with the authority to amend the Constitution and enact law, and its Standing Committee had the power to interpret laws and promulgate decrees. Later, both of the NPC and its Standing Committee were authorized to enact laws. The number of lower-level legislative bodies also increased, as the State Council could make administrative regulations and the people's congresses and their standing committees of the province, autonomous regions, municipalities directly under the State Council, the cities with subordinate districts, autonomous prefectures and four cities with no subordinate districts were authorized to make local regulations. The methods applied in legislation have also diversified and integrated, evolving from the enactment of laws and decrees to a combined use of enactment and revision of laws, and further to the integrated use of enactment, revision, repeal and interpretation after the reform and opening-up so as to better adapt to the social economic development. Of particular significance is the more flexible and frequent use of enactment, revision, repeal, interpretation, grant, decision, compilation and re-examination after the Eighteenth National Congress. The gradually diversified legislative methods and increasingly standardized legislative activities have improved the efficiency of legislation, better manifested the common will of the Party and the people, and enhanced state governance system and capacity for its better modernization drive.

1 Legislative Methods from 1949 to Pre-Reform and Opening-up Period

In this period, the legislation was focused on establishing, consolidating and improving socialism and ensuring national governance under people's democracy. It was a history of starting from scratch, arduous explorations and interruption. The priority after the founding of the PRC was to heal the wounds, restore national economy, suppress anti-revolutionaries, consolidate state power and completely destroy the old social systems and order to build the new ones. Therefore, the legislation was prioritized on making and implementing new legal institutions to guarantee the new-born people's democratic state and their position as masters of the country, ensure the success of the major tasks of the state, create conditions for national stability and development and a better environment for the starting and development of various social undertakings, and lay the foundation for the establishment of the future legal system. Therefore, the legislation in this period was specifically tasked to destroy old laws and make new laws with some revision and repeal, and to make arrangements for the implementation of the legal interpretation institutions. The legislative bodies also shifted from the CPPCC and the Central People's Government Council which were empowered to make and interpret national laws and promulgate decrees, to the National People's Congress established as the only highest legislative organ stipulated in the 1954 Constitution to amend the Constitution and enact laws. Its Standing Committee's power of interpreting law and promulgating decrees was expanded by granting it with the power to make separate regulations and revise laws based on the authorization of the NPC. In conclusion, this period represents the Party's continuous efforts to explore and improve both the practice and theory on state governance. A two-phase illustration would help to understand the process and legislative institutions.

1.1 Central People's Government Council (from 1949 to 1954)

All the legislative activities were carried out based on the Common Program for it stipulated the government system, state system and legislative institutions and mechanisms.

Based on the provisions of the Common Program and the Organic Law of the Central People's Government, the state power of the People's Republic of China belongs to the people, the people's congresses and the people's governments of all levels are the organs for the exercise of state power by the people, and the people's governments shall be the organs for exercising state power at their respective levels when the people's congresses of their respective levels are not in session. The Government of the People's Republic of China is a government of the people's congress system based on the principle of democratic centralism. The Central People's Government had the power to enact and interpret the laws of the state, promulgate decrees and supervise their execution; annul or revise any decisions and orders of the Government Administrative Council (State Council), which did not conform to the laws and decrees of the state. The Government Administrative Council, as the organ for executing the administrative policies of the Central People's Government Council, had the power to issue decisions and orders and verify their executive.

The primary task in this period was to destroy the old and establish the new.

On one hand, to destroy the old legal system. The proclamation of eight conditions on peace talks with KMT, punishment of war criminals and abrogation of KMT's constitution and legal system made by the Party on January 1949 and the Instructions concerning Abolishing the Six Codes of the KMT and Determining Judicial Principles for the Liberated Areas made in the following month directed the establishment of people's democratic legal system. Article 17 of Common Program also stipulated that all laws, decrees and judicial systems of the KMT reactionary government which oppress the people be abolished, and laws and decrees protecting the people's be enacted and the people's judicial system be established. According to this provision, the Central People's Government carried out initiatives to destroy the old legal system and establish the new revolutionary system of law.

On the other hand, to establish a new legal system. According to Article 13 of Common Program, the Chinese People's Political Consultative Conference is the organizational form of the people's democratic united front...Pending the convocation of the National People's Congress...exercise the functions and powers of the National People's Congress. Based on this authorization provision, the Organic Law of the Chinese People's Political Consultative Conference and the Organic Law of the Central People's Government were adopted at the First Plenary Session of the Chinese People's Political Consultative Conference. In the early years of PRC, the Party established the central state authorities and local people's governments based on the organization laws. A nation-wide legislation was also initiated: the formulation of the general principles for the organization of local people's governments and judicial authorities, the enactment of the Trade Union Law, Marriage Law, Agrarian Land Reform Law, Provisional Regulation on the People's Courts, Regulation on Punishing Counter-revolutionaries, Regulation on Punishing Corruption, Electoral Law and Ethnic Regional Autonomy Law and other laws and decrees. All these legislative activities had helped to safeguard the revolution, protect people's interests, consolidate national unity, and the destruction of all the old systems had played an important role in the success of various social democratic and revolutionary movements and the restoration and development of national economy.

The laws and decrees made by the CPPCC and the Central People's Government Council were about people's democracy and political issues. For example, the Program on the Implementation of Ethnic Regional Autonomy adopted in 1952 was the first of its kind to regulate the new system and ethnic policies and relations, helping to develop the economy in ethnic groups areas, deal with ethnic relations, promote and protect ethnic unity, and realize the rights of ethnic groups to govern the country as the masters. The 1953 Electoral Law also provided institutional guarantee for the convocation of the First National People's Congress. Of all these laws, the organization laws were primary ones, such as the General Principles of the Organization of Government Administrative Council and Its Departments, General Principles of the Organization of Provincial People's Congresses, Trade Union Law, General Principles of the Organization of People's Tribunals, Provisional Regulation on the Organization of Supreme People's Procuratorate, Provisional Regulation on the Organization of People's Courts, General Principles of the Organization of the Ethnic Affairs Committees of People's Governments at All Levels, and the Provisional Regulation on the Organization of Militia.

Some other laws and decrees were about social reforms and made during the massive people's movements. For example, the Agrarian Land Reform Law adopted in June 1950 for the purpose of carrying out agricultural land reforms in an orderly manner, was made for the land reform. Once the reform completed, it would no longer be applied. The Regulation on Punishing Counter-Revolutionaries, passed in February 1951 during the oppressing anti-revolutionaries movement were still on, was the first important criminal legislation. The Regulation on Punishing Corruption was adopted when the Three-anti and Five-anti Campaigns were carried out. Some laws and decrees were formulated out of the need for government's efforts in administration, public security, judicial practice, administrative supervision, economy, science and culture and education, such as the Provisional Regulation on the Agricultural Tax in Newly-liberated Areas, Provisional Regulation on the Appointment and Remover of State Employees, and the Marriage Law. The Marriage Law was one of the earliest basic laws in addition to the Common Program and Organic Law of the CPPCC and the first civil legislation, which initiated a great transformation of China's marriage and family system.

From 1949 to 1954, the CPPCC and the Central People's Government, acting jointly as the statutory national legislature, adopted over 30 laws. However, apart from the Common Program, Organic Law of the Central People's Government and Organic Law of CPPCC and the resolution on the capital, calendar, national anthem, and national flag, the CPPCC did not exercise its legislative power again. The legislative procedures in these years had not yet been standardized. Some law bills, after being passing by the Government Administration Council, were issued by the Central People's Government Council,while others were just approved by the President of the Central People's Government without the passing of the Council. For example, the General Principles on the Organization of People's Tribunals, Provisions Regulation on the Protection of State Secrets, General Principles on the Organization of Ethnic Affairs Committee of the People's Governments at All Levels (for Trial Implementation) and the Provisional Regulation on the Organization of Militia were approved by the President. As the highest executive organ, the Government Administration Council did not have legislative power uner law, but it made over 300 pieces of normative documents of a legal nature and established many important institutions and mechanisms.[2] The Military and Administrative Commissions of the

[2] Data from the *Collection of Decrees of the Central People's Government from its 1949 to 1954 editions*, edited by the Legal Affairs Committee of the Central People's Government.

Great Administrative Areas (later renamed administrative commissions) also made many provisional decrees and regulations on local administrative affairs based on the provisions of the General Principles on the Organization of Greater Administrative People's Government Council, the Common Program and other state laws and decrees, and the guidelines of the Central People's Government and the resolutions and orders of the Government Administrative Council. Though they were unevenly distributed, they played an important role of stimulating the various local undertakings. In 1953, China started its first five-year plan for national economic development. The system of greater administrative areas was abolished, and the legislation became more centralized. The people's governments at or above the county level made a lot of provisional decrees, regulations and separate regulations based on the General Principles on the Organization of the Provincial, Municipal and County People's Governments issued in January 1950 by the Government Administrative Council. Though they were not real local legislations as in the contemporary sense, they paved the way for the subsequent development of local legislation.[3]

1.2 National People's Congress and its Standing Committee: From 1954 to Pre-Reform and Opening-up Period

The Constitution adopted in the First Session of the First National People's Congress in September 20, 1954 explicitly established China's legislative system.

Based on the 1954 Constitution, the National People's Congress was the only organ exercising national legislative power, with authority to amend the Constitution and enact laws. Its Standing Committee was empowered to interpret laws and promulgate decrees. The NPC, as the only one with state legislative power granted part of its functions and powers to the Standing Committee. The 1975 and 1978 Constitutions also made similar provisions, demonstrating that the Party's cautious approach to the exercise of legislative power and its view of such power as sacred. In this period, the exercise of legislative power was highly centralized: it was exercised exclusively by the NPC, while its Standing Committee could make lower-level decrees. Decrees refer to the normative and legal documents issued by state departments within the scope of their duties; they are different from laws. However, their legal effect was undeniable. As explained by Dong Biwu, "when the National People's Congress is not in session, its Stand Committee has the power to promulgate decrees that have legal effect". If they are found to contravene the Constitution and other principles, they can be revoked only by the National People's Congress.[4] In a word, the decrees

[3] Office of State Law of the Legislative Affairs Committee of the National People's Congress ed., *Interpretations on the Law on Legislation of the People's Republic of China*, Law Press, 2015, p. 222. From September 1949 to August 1954, there were over 500 laws, decrees and normative documents of legal nature, see LAN Quanpu ed., *Introduction to the Changes of Regulations in China Over the Past 30 Years*, Qunzhong Press, 1980, p. 10.

[4] DONG Biwu, *On the Work of the Party on Promoting People's Political and Legal Awareness (May 18, 1954)*, in Selected Works of Dong Biwu, People's Publishing House, 1985, p. 346.

made by the Standing Committee were not laws, but they had legal force. However, due to its vagueness and the difficulty in determining its legal force, it was deleted from the 1982 Constitution. Although the NPC was the only legislative authority according to the 1954 Constitution, however, it could not be convened frequently due to the large number of its deputies. The NPC alone could not shoulder the heavy legislative burden. In July 1955, it was in the Second Session of the First National People's Congress that decided to authorize "the Standing Committee to enact certain laws in a timely manner according to the spirit of the Constitution and actual needs, i.e. separate regulations". Four years later, in the First Session of the Second National People's Congress the Standing Committee was again authorized to revise and make new provisions of law that were no longer applicable according to the development of the circumstances and the needs of work during the intersessional period of the NPC. However, China's development of democracy and rule of law were gradually put to an end due to Anti-Rightist Campaign and the Cultural Revolution, the authorization made in 1959 was actually put on the shelf. Nonetheless, the two authorizations to the Standing Committee with some national legislative powers had already changed the legislature's structure in which the NPC was the only national legislative authority as laid out in the 1954 Constitution. For local legislation in this period, the general local power in promulgating decrees and regulations was canceled, while only the ethnic autonomous regions had the power to formulate self-governance regulations and separate regulations.

Generally, the legislation in this period was focused on making new laws and decisions on legal issues. But a small number of law revisions and abrogation were also made in this period. For example, the Constitution was amended in 1975 and 1978. However, only two resolutions, one bill and one piece of regulations were made to amend provisions, i.e. the Resolution on Disestablishing Rehe Province and Xikang Province and Revising Item 1 of Subparagraph 2, Article 25 of the Law on the Organization of the Local People's Congresses and Local People's Government Councils at All Levels and the Resolution on Disestablishing the Ministry of Fuel Industry and Establishing the Ministry of Coal Industry, Ministry of Electrical Power Industry, Ministry of Petroleum Industry, and Ministry of Agricultural Products Procurement and Revising Subparagraph 1 of Article 2 of the Law on the Organization of the State Council in 1955, the Bill to Revising Items 4 and 5 of Subparagraph 2, Article 25 of the Law on the Organization of the Local People's Congresses and Local People's Government Councils at All Levels in 1956 and the Regulation of the Chinese People's Liberation Army on the Military Services of Officers adopted in 1963 after revision.

Some laws and regulations were repealed either in express terms or became no longer applicable or ceasing to be enforced. Some of them were to adopt new ones by making a provision on repealing the old in express terms. For example, Article 32 of Regulation on Agricultural Tax adopted in 1958 prescribed that "these Regulations shall come into force as of the date of promulgation. The Provisional Regulation on Agricultural Tax and relevant provisions shall be repealed simultaneously". The Provisional Regulation on Agricultural Tax in the Newly-liberated Areas adopted in September 1950 by the Central People's Government Council was repealed. Others were not repealed expressly, but became no longer applicable or ceased to be enforced due to the change of circumstances, including the Organic Law of the Chinese People's Consultative Conference, Organic Law of the Central People's Government, General Principles for the Organization of Municipal People's Congresses, General Principles for the Organization of County People's Congresses, General Principles for the Organization of the Government Administration Council and Its Departments, Agrarian Land Reform Law and General Principles for the Organization of People's Courts. Others were terminated in general terms by making decisions on legal issues. For example, the resolution adopted in the First Session of the First National People's Congress in September 26, 1954 prescribed that the existing laws and decrees enacted or approved by the Central People's Government remained effective unless they contravened the Constitution. But it did not specify which laws or decrees were contrary to the Constitution making it arguably the first document for re-examining laws since the founding of the PRC.

Institutional arrangements were also made in this period. The Organic Law on the Organization of Central People's Government clarified that its Council had the authority to enact and interpret law. In the 1954, 1978 and 1982 Constitutions, the Standing Committees designated as the body responsible for interpreting law. A resolution adopted in June 1955 during the First NPC Standing Committee laid out the provisions on the bodies of interpreting law and the scope subject to interpretation. However, legal interpretation was not initiated until the reform and opening-up period.

The important laws enacted in this period concerned democratic development and political affairs, for example, the various organization laws adopted in the First Session of the First National People's Congress when the Constitution was passed, helping to establish the fundamental state systems, basic principles of political life in all respects, fundamental rights and duties of the people as affirmed by the Constitution and relevant laws. Some other laws and regulations were then formulated successively based on the Constitution and the line, guidelines and policies of the Party, including ones on government administration, for example, the Regulation on the Appointment and Removal of State Employees by People's Committees at or above the County Level, Resolution on Approving Regulation on Fire Supervision, Regulation on Frontier Health and Quarantine, Regulation on Household Registration, Regulation on Administration of Trademarks and Regulation on Administrative Penalties for Public Security. Some resolutions were also passed to address labor issues, for example, the Standing Committee passed the resolution on the Provisional Regulation of the State Council on Wages and Benefits of Ordinary Workers and Handymen in Enterprises, Institutions and State Departments and the Provisional Regulations of the State Council on the Retirement of Workers and Employees. In addition, some economic regulations and rules were adopted, for example, the Regulation on the Public Debts for Local Economic Construction, Measures of the State Council on Giving Preferential Treatment to Overseas Chinese Nationals Investing in State-Owned Companies Invested by Overseas Chinese Nationals, Decision on

Appropriately Raising the Proportion of Advanced Agricultural Production Cooperative Provident Funds and Supplementary Provisions of the State Council on the Approving Agricultural Production Cooperative Share Funds and others.

1.3 Achievements and Problems

During this period, the Party was generally keen on people's democratic development and legislation by putting some efforts on establishing China's legal system. Despite the Cultural Revolution,remarkable achievements were still made, including the promulgation of the Constitution along with many important laws, decrees and various regulations. As of the breakout of Cultural Revolution, the CPPCC, Central People's Government Council, NPC and its Standing Committee issued 134 pieces of laws and decisions on legal issues,[5] and drafted important laws on criminal law, criminal procedure law, civil law and civil procedure law, and the State Council made over 1,500 pieces of administrative measures, resolutions and orders (equivalent of administrative regulations), laying solid foundation for further promoting the construction of socialist legal system. However, the Left-line mistakes had became dominant in the guiding principles of the Party and state, interrupting the implementation of the Party's correct proposals, line and policies. When the Cultural Revolution drove theses mistakes to the extreme, the socialist legislation was seriously damaged, and the Constitution and laws were just pieces of paper.

However, some urgently needed basic laws, such as criminal law, civil law, procedure laws and labor law, were not enacted yet, and at the same time, some laws were not timely revised, abolished or re-enacted due to the changes of political and economic circumstances. To make matter worse, the provisional measures formulated by the ministries and committees that often played an important role in practice were revised too often and too much. For example, the Procedures on Implementing the Provisional Measures for Administering the Trade of Exchanged Goods were formulated on March 6, 1951 by the Ministry of Trade, but were revised on September 11, and revised for another two times by issuing two notices on the following day. On October 12, they were revised for the fourth time.[6] Too frequent revision not only reflected the unserious attitude, but also the lack of experience and immaturity in state governance.

From the early days of PRC's founding to the pre-reform and opening-up period, despite the enactment of some laws, China made no plans for the entire departments of law and system of laws and the legislation in a whole fell short of the actual needs. During these years, the conception of rule of law was not yet established, so the policies and resolutions made by the Party and government were the primary

[5] XIN Chunying, *History of Chinese Law and Its Origins in Culture*, in Chinese Legal System and Its Reform, Law Press, 1999, p. 19.

[6] DONG Biwu, *On the Work of the Party on Promoting People's Political and Legal Awareness (May 18, 1954)*, in Selected Works of Dong Biwu, People's Publishing House, 1985, p. 349.

means to mediate the social relations, which made them act as laws in practice for a long time and changed as the attention and thinking of the Party and state's leaders and the social situation were changed. For example, in the early days of PRC, to consolidate the new people's democratic state, the Party and state's leaders tended to issue instructions in both the names of the Party and state to deal with various issues and mediate social relations, which were indeed effective. However, as the legal system was under gradual progress, more attention began to be paid to the distinction between the Party and state powers and functions, especially after the 1954 Constitution was promulgated. The documents issued by the Party were more concerned with Party affairs, while the state's policy documents were mostly concerned with government affairs. However, starting from the Anti-Rightist, the number of Party documents and instructions related to the governance and general administration of the country increased. After the Great Leap Forward in 1958, the Party's instructions not only covered the political aspects of the state and society in general, but also penetrated into the fields of agriculture, industry, culture, education, science and health. Although some corrections were made in 1962, during the Four Clean-ups campaign, as "taking class struggle as the key link" became the dominant thinking of the Party's main leaders, the role of state was reduced in governance. From 1964 to 1965, there was a dramatic decrease in the number of national legislation, and the instructions and directives of the Party leaders became more frequently and extensively applied to all aspects of social life as the significant means of state governance.[7]

The confusion of legislative methods and the twists and turns in the path for rule of law reflected the Party and state's lack of proper understanding of the law inherent to socialist construction and state governance, which finally made the imperfect system of law an unavoidable reality in this period. Many reasons could be attributed to it, but the most important one was the historical and cultural soil that impeded the development of legal system and the frail idea of law among the people jointly caused by the feudal aristocracy that had nagged China for 1000 years. As Deng Xiaoping pointed out, "from old China we inherited a strong tradition of feudal autocracy and a weak tradition of democratic legality". The task of legal development confronted the new-born China was insurmountably huge, and it could not be possible as it was imagined that the whole system of laws could be set ready all at once.

2 Evolution of Legislative Methods

Xi Jinping ever said, "History is our greatest teacher. Experience and past lessons have made us keenly aware that the rule of law is indispensable as a means of governance. If the rule of law prevails, the country benefits; if it fails, the country

[7] ZHANG Peitian ed., A *Comprehensive Guide to the Legal History Research of the People's Republic of China*, China University of Political Science and Law Press, 2003, p. 3.

suffers".[8] Since 1978, the Party has reflected on the impact of Left-line mistakes on legal development after 1949, especially the profound lessons from the Cultural Revolution, and decided to take rule of law as the basic principle to lead the Chinese people to govern the country, the law-based administration as the basic method for the party's governance, and put the law as the central theme for considering its undertakings for the country. Under the Party's leadership, the work on promoting rule of law has made tremendous achievements.

Legislation is the foundation for promoting rule of law. Since 1978, while adhering to the Party's leadership and to the development strategies laid out by the Party and the government set in different periods, the NPC and its Standing Committee have proposed the goals in line with the implementation of these strategies, made integrated use of enactment, revision, repeal and interpretation of law and accelerated legislation for establishing and improving the socialist legal system with Chinese characteristics. Particularly since the Eighteenth CPC National Congress, all kinds of legislative methods have been more extensively, frequently applied according to law, and the number of laws enacted, revised and interpreted and the decisions made on legal issued has increased significantly (See Fig. 11.1). With the flexible of various legislative methods, the law can better support the social and economic development more opportunely, reflect the will of the Party and the people, give strong impetus for improving the socialist legal system, and move forward the modernization of state governance system and capacity. From 1979 to the end of August 2019, the NPC and its Standing Committee had adopted 1 Constitution, 5 constitutional amendments, enacted 297 pieces of laws and revised 344 pieces of laws, abolished 4 pieces of laws and decisions on legal issues,[9] issued 25 pieces of legal interpretations and formulated 258 pieces of decisions on legal issues and major issues.

According to statistics, the Twelfth NPC and its Standing Committee enacted 25 pieces of laws (8.74% of all the laws enacted since the fifth NPC, same as follows), revised 127 pieces (44.1%), issued 9 interpretations (36%), adopted 21 pieces of decisions on authorization and reform (63.64%) and other 30 pieces of decisions on legal issues and other major issues (11.85%). Between March 2018 and August 2019, the first year of the Thirteenth NPC and its Standing Committee, 12 pieces of laws and 1 constitutional amendment were adopted, and there were also 60 pieces of law revisions, 5 pieces of decisions on authorization and reform and 9 pieces of decisions on legal issues and other major issues. As China's legal system continues to improve, revision, interpretation and decision on legal issues and other major issues have been more extensively and prominently alongside the enactment of new laws.

[8] The Party Literature Research Office ed., *The Law-Based Governance of China*, Central Compilation and Translation Press, 2017, p. 10.

[9] Including 2 pieces of laws and 2 pieces of decisions.

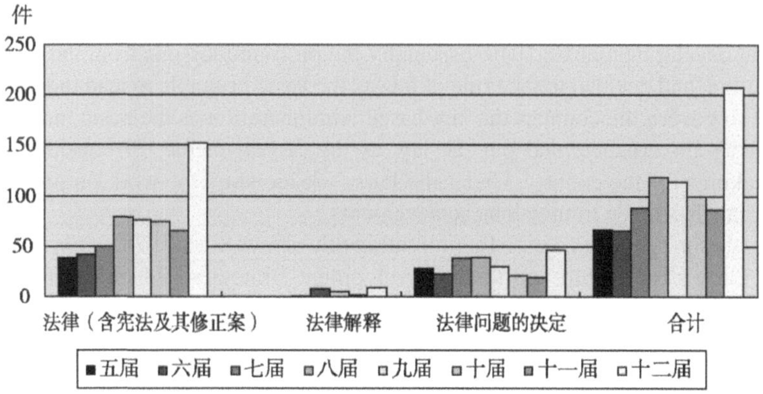

法律（含宪法及其修正案）：Laws (including the Constitution and its Amendments)

法律解释：Interpretation

法律问题的决定：Decisions on Legal Issues

合计：Total

Fig. 11.1 Changes of legislative methods

2.1 To Continue Law-Making for Social and Economic Development

In the Third Plenary Session of the Eleventh Central Committee, the Party reflected on the lessons from Cultural Revolution, and decided to turn the focus of the Party and the State's work to economic development and reform and opening-up. Strengthening the establishment of a socialist democratic legal system was designated as an unswerving principle which emphasized the development of legal system and made the socialist democracy institutionalized by law, so that these institutions and laws would not be changed as the leaders' opinions or attention changed. The Party's successive national congresses also laid out the requirements on developing democracy and legal system, the most prominent of which was the goal of "establishing socialist legal system with Chinese characteristics by 2010" put forward in the fifteenth national congress. The 1982 Constitution set out the state's goal of development and its historical mission, gave the direction for the Chinese people and provided the constitutional basis. In addition to its, the NPC and its Standing Committee also enacted a lot of basic laws that were urgent from social life, which effectively maintained the social stability and ensured the orderly development of society and economy.

According to Fig. 11.2, a lot of new laws were enacted after the reform and opening-up, and the number in each session continued to increase, reaching its peak at the Eighth NPC. After the Ninth NPC, more attention was paid to revising the existing laws to adapt to China's economic transformation. In a session of the Tenth NPC Standing Committee, it was proposed to give priority on legislation quality

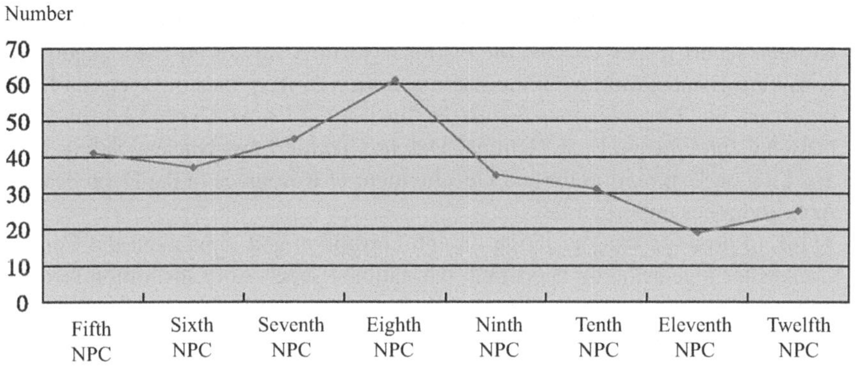

Fig. 11.2 Number of law enactment

while still staying the course of establishing the Chinese socialist legal system with Chinese characteristics. Therefore, the new law-making saw a decrease after the Eighth NPC. With the parallel development of enactment and revision, the socialist legal system was established in 2010 as scheduled, which provided law to abide by in national economic, political, cultural, social and ecological development. Law reflects social practice, and legal institutions and mechanism will change as the social practice changes, and so does the socialist legal system. As of the end of August 2019, there were 274 pieces of laws in force: 45 including the Constitution and related laws, 34 pieces of civil and commercial laws, 88 pieces of administrative laws, 71 pieces of economic laws, 24 pieces of social laws, 11 pieces of laws on litigation and non-litigation procedures, and the criminal law and its 10 amendments.

Since the Eighteenth CPC National Congress, the Central Committee with Xi Jinping as the core has steadfastly deepened reform in all respects and introduced various reform measures to make breakthroughs in key links. The Twelfth and Thirteenth NPCs and their standing committees have resolutely implemented the Central Committee's decisions and arrangements, adhered to connecting the legislative decision with reform decision, actively adapted legislation to the needs of reform and social economic development, promptly transformed the reform decisions of the Central Committee into laws through statutory procedures, and provided legal support for the implementation of major reform measures. The legislation in this period was large in number, important, quick and effective. To respond to the new demands for social and economic development, the NPC and its Standing Committee has strengthened the legislation in key areas to continue the advancement of socialist legal system. The laws enacted for this purpose can be summarized based on the following classification:

First, to improve the legal institutions and mechanisms for the enforcement of the Constitution, the NPC and its Standing Committee enacted the Law on National Medals and Titles of Honor, National Anthem Law, and Law on the Protection of Heroes and Martyrs.

Second, to accelerate the construction of legal institutions and mechanisms on national security, they enacted the National Security Law, Anti-Espionage Law, Anti-Terrorism Law, Law on the Administration of Activities of Overseas Non-Governmental Organizations within the Territory of China, Cyber Security Law, National Intelligence Law, National Defense Traffic Law, Nuclear Safety Law and Law on Exploration for and Development of Resources in the Deep Seabed Area and other important laws.

Third, to promote the legislation on anti-corruption and implement the Central Committee's decision on deepening the national supervisory institution reform, they enacted the Supervision Law.

Fourth, they also enacted the General Provisions of Civil Law to advance the compilation of civil code.

Fifth, to strengthen the legislation on socialist market economy, they enacted the Foreign Investment Law, E-Commerce Law, Tourism Law, Asset Appraisal Law, and Waterway Law.

Sixth, they enacted the Environment Protection Tax Law, Tobacco Tax Law, Vessel Tonnage Tax Law, Law on Farmland Occupation Tax, Law on Vehicle Purchase Tax and Resource Tax Law to implement the principle of statutory taxation.

Seventh, they enacted the Law on the Guarantee of Public Cultural Services, Public Libraries Law and Film Industry Promotion Law to change the stagnation of cultural legislation in China.

Eighth, to give stronger legal guarantee for people's well-being, they enacted the Charity Law, Drug Administration Law, Traditional Chinese Medicine Law, Anti-domestic Violence Law, and Special Equipment Safety Law.

Lastly, they enacted the Law on Prevention and Control of Soil Pollution to ensure the success in the fight for healthy land, and to establish a three-dimensional integrated defense system along with the air and water pollution prevention and control.

As reform continues to deepen, the NPC and its Standing Committee should, in the future, pursue new law-making by centering on the general requirements of the Party and the state to adapt to the new tasks and missions of the new era. It can be concluded from Fig. 11.3 that the newly enacted laws are mainly about the economy and socialist democratic development. In addition to improving the legislation in the economic and political areas, the NPC and its Standing Committee should pay more attention to the following three areas: the first is to accentuate the importance of social legislation to give better guarantee for people's well-being by hastening the law-making in securing citizens' rights, developing social undertakings, perfecting social security, regulating social organizations, strengthening social management, securing people's basic livelihood, and protecting the legitimate rights and interests of special social groups. With such enhanced efforts, it would help to establish a social security system comprising labor employment, social security, social assistance, social welfare, education and health, and public security, and to reasonably adjust the income distribution system. The second is to promote legislation in culture, science and technology. The NPC and its Standing Committee should hasten to establish the legal institutions and mechanisms for promoting the prosperity of cultural industry to meet the increasing demands of the people and spread the core socialist values. They should also make greater efforts to improve the legal institutions and mechanisms to encourage independent innovation and sci-tech progress to strengthen national innovation competence. The third is to attach great importance to legislation in ecological civilization. The top legislature should move faster to create the legal institutions and mechanisms on green economy and climate change to help build a resource-conservation and environment-friendly society, achieve harmony between people and nature, and strive to resolve the contradiction between economic development and the protection of the environment and resources.

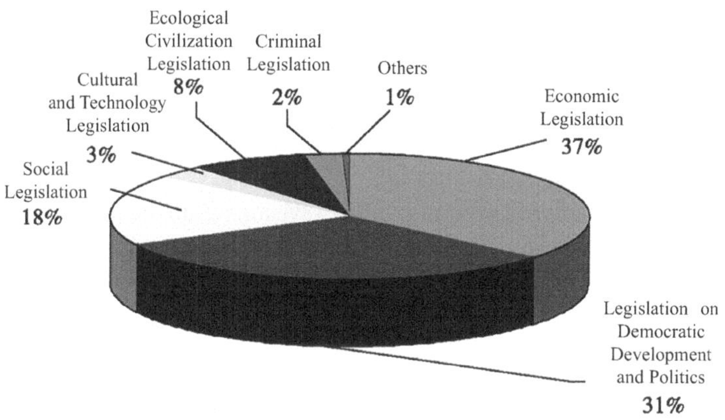

Fig. 11.3 Proportion of area-based new laws since the reform and opening-up (as of August 2019). *Notes* 1. Economic legislation adjusts the social and economic relations arising from the state's performance of its powers and functions in macro-control, market supervision, opening-up and industrial revitalization, including the legal institutions and mechanisms on civil and commercial affairs, finance and taxation. 2. Legislation on democratic development and politics is about the procedures on better election, community-level self-governance, state organizations, and regulation of administrative behaviors to adapt to judicial system reform, improve the exercise of power of state organizations and prevent and punish corruption and other purposes. 3. Social legislation centers around the guarantee and improvement of people's well-being in labor employment, labor protection, social insurance, social assistance, social welfare, income distribution, education, health, housing and social organizations by promoting the social undertakings, improving social security system and innovating social management. 4. Legislation on culture and science and technology is to create legal institutions and mechanisms to improve and support non-profit cultural undertakings, develop cultural industry, encourage innovation in culture and science and technology for promoting cultural system reform and sci-tech progress. 5. Legislation on ecological civilization is to create legal institutions and mechanisms on energy and resource conservation and protection of ecological environment to build a resource conservation and environment-friendly society.

2.2 *To Change the Conception of Legislation and Take Revision as an Important Method*

As the legal institutions and mechanisms continue to improve, the primary laws for all aspects of social life are in place. However, the circumstances change as society and the economy evolve, raising new demands on the existing laws, which are to be revised in a timely manner, so that the law can better adapt to the extensive and profound changes and regulate the social life.

From the statistics over the years since the reform and opening-up, it can be seen that revision has been an important legislative method. In 2000, the number of law revision exceeded those of enactment (See Fig. 11.4). The work on revising the existing laws has been gradually highlighted.

The proportion of the number of laws revised has been on continuous rise (See Fig. 11.5). It can be predicted that the future work on law revision will be heavier. From now on, the NPC and its Standing Committee should spare more efforts to revise and repeal the laws that are not in conformity with the reform in a timely manner. To make law better adapt to the reform in the new era and socialist modernization has been an important legislative pursuit.

As both the number and proportion of law revisions continue to rise, the methods for revision also have also become diversified: complete revision, partial revision and integrated revision. A law can be revised completely or partially based on the importance and scope of such revision.

The first complete revision was applied in the Procedures of the People's Liberation Army on the Election of Deputies to the National People's Congress and Local People's Congresses at or above County Level issued on October 29, 1996. As of the end of August 2019, the NPC and its Standing Committee had applied this method to 55 pieces of laws.

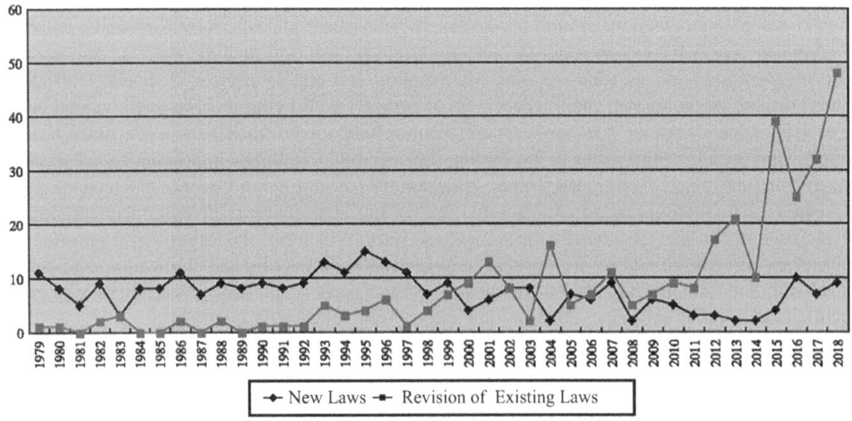

Fig. 11.4 Revision of law

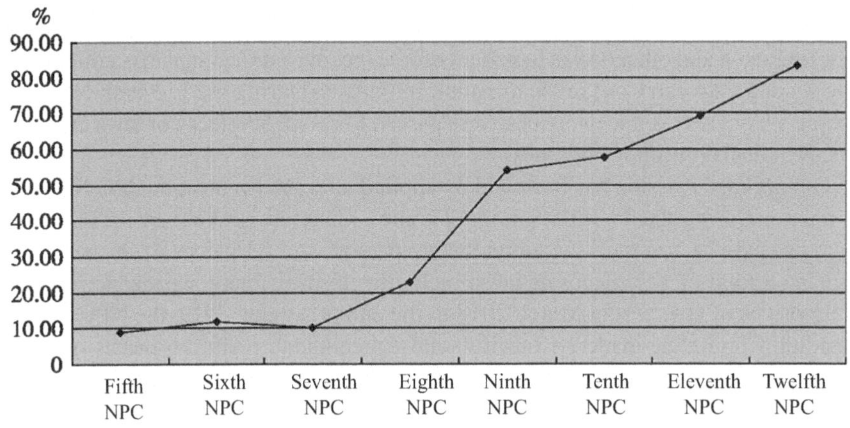

Fig. 11.5 Proportion of law revision

Partial revision is often made by either amendments or decisions on revision. Amendment is only used for the Constitution and the Criminal Law. There have been five Constitutional amendments after 1988 and 10 Criminal Law amendments after 1999. A resolution may also be adopted to revise a law in the early years of reform and opening-up. For example, in the Second Session of the Fifth National People's Congress held in July 1, 1979, the Resolution on Amending Several Provisions of the Constitution of the People's Republic of China was made for the first time by the NPC and its Standing Committee to revise a law. The partial revision was first applied in the Decision of the NPC Standing Committee on Revising the Law on the Organization of the People's Procuratorates adopted in September 2, 1983. As of the end of August 1983, 154 decisions of this kind were issued.

Integrated revision, also known as "package revision", refers to the revision of some law provisions that have a common concern or the same reasons for revision through submitting bills together. Article 43 of the Law on Legislation revised in March 2015 confirmed the status of package revision. However, it was not widely applied before the Twelfth National People's Congress. It was applied once to revise nine pieces of laws during the Tenth National People's Congress, and three times for 68 pieces of laws and decisions on legal issues. During this period, it was often used for two purposes: first was to coordinate the old laws with the new ones. For example, in 2004 the Tenth NPC Standing Committee issued the decision to revise the Highway Law and other eight laws to guarantee the enforcement of Administrative Licensing Law and provide basis for the State Council and local governments to re-examine or revise certain provisions on administrative licensing in relevant administrative and local regulations. This was the first time that the State Council submitted one bill of several draft law revisions to the NPC Standing Committee for deliberation, which later made separate decisions on revisions. When the Eleventh National People's Congress was in session, the NPC and its Standing Committee passed the decisions on revising the Law on Coal Industry and the Law on Construction to ensure they were connected with the Social Insurance Law, and also made the decision on revising the Law on Prison and other 6 laws to better enforce the revised Criminal Procedure Law. The second is to carry out re-examination initiatives. During the Eleventh National People's Congress, some decisions were passed to revise 55 pieces of laws and four pieces of decisions on legal issues.

The package revision has been widely applied after the Eighteenth CPC National Congress. During the Twelfth National People's Congress, there were 12 pieces of laws revised, 2 Criminal Law amendments passed, and 33 pieces of decisions on revising a total of 113 pieces of laws, including 15 decisions for package revision of 95 pieces of laws. From March 2018 to the end of August 2019, the NPC and its Standing Committee made 1 Constitutional Amendment, revised 6 pieces of laws, and made 13 pieces of decisions on revising 60 pieces of laws, including 8 decisions for package revision of 49 pieces of laws.

In conclusion, law revision has become an important part of the NPC and its Standing Committee's work on legislation to meet the needs of promoting reform for the new era and timely legalize and institutionalize the Party's reform decisions to guide, promote and guarantee the progress of reform through legislation. Among the three methods, integrated revision is widely and routinely applied due to its better efficiency and save of legislative resources. However, the integrated revision should also be improved by formulating the implementation standards and methods of voting. Meanwhile, when it is applied, a coordinated plan should be made to avoid frequent revisions of one law in several revision packages, and to exclude the revision of law by taking improper advantage of a revision package.

2.3 To Adopt Various Legislative Methods to Ensure Reform Decisions Law-Based

In addition to law making and revision, methods such as repeal, interpretion, granting, decision, re-examination and law compilation also play significant roles in legislation. To meet the needs of rapid economic and social development, these methods will continue to be applied and even become normalized in legislation.

1. To timely abolish the laws not suitable for new circumstances to eliminate the institutional obstacles to social and economic development.

The repeal of laws is usually driven by the actual needs of economic and social development. Laws that are manifestly out of date and no longer necessary should be abolished in a timely manner after a careful research, thereby eliminating institutional obstacles to economic and social development. From 1978 to the end of August 2019, the NPC and its Standing Committee often repealed laws through the following methods:

First, incorporating specific provisions on repeal in new laws. According to statistics, 41 of 274 laws in force (excluding the laws specially for repealing other laws) are inserted with the provision on repeal. (1) To repeal specific predecessor laws. For example, the Supplementary Provisions of the 1980 Marriage Law prescribed that "the Marriage Law of the People's Republic of China promulgated on May 1, 1950 shall be repealed when this Law comes into force". The 2006 Enterprise Bankruptcy Law also made a similar provision in its Supplementary Provisions that "this Law shall come into force as of June 1, 2007, and the Enterprise Bankruptcy Law of the People's Republic of China (for Trial Implementation) should be repealed simultaneously". The 2014 Anti-Espionage Law also prescribed in the Supplementary Provisions that "this Law shall come into force on the date of promulgation. The National Security Law of the People's Republic of China adopted at the Thirteenth Meeting of the Seventh NPC Standing Committee on February 22, 1993 shall be repealed simultaneously". The 2018 Supervision Law stipulated the same that "this Law shall come into force on the date of promulgation. The Administrative Supervision Law of the People's Republic of China shall be repealed simultaneously". (2) To repeal relevant laws and regulations at the same time. For example, the 2007 Corporate Income Tax Law prescribed that the 1991 Income Tax Law of the People's Republic of China for Enterprises with Foreign Investment and Foreign Enterprises and the 1993 Provisional Regulations of the State Council on Corporate Income Tax shall be repealed simultaneously. (3) To repeal specific administrative regulations. The separate tax laws, including the Law on Vehicle Purchase Tax, Law on Farmland Occupation Tax, Law on Tobacco Leaf Tax and Resource Tax Law, made provisions to repeal the relevant regulations of the State Council.

Second, to enact standalone laws or make decisions to repeal other laws. It has not been widely used in legislation, with only two laws and two decisions of this kind. The two laws include the Decision on Repealing the Regulation on Agricultural Tax in 2005 and the Decision on Repealing Certain Laws in 2009. The two decisions include the Decision of the NPC Standing Committee on Approving the Legal Affairs Committee's Report on the Re-examination of and Opinions on the Laws Promulgated Before the End of 1978 and the Decision on Repealing Certain Legal Provisions on Re-education Through Labor made in 2013 by referring to the spirits of the Third Plenary Session of the Eighteenth CPC Central Committee. The two decisions were typically made as part of the re-examination initiatives.

However, some laws after complete revision or enacted do not expressly state whether the predecessor laws should be repealed. In case the laws cease to be valid, future legislation should explicitly state the repeal the outdated ones, either though explicit language or special legislation.

2. To use legal interpretations to clarify the law provisions for correct and effective implementation of laws

Interpretation of law is crucial for legislation. Its main function is to expound and elaborate on the meanings of the legal provisions, so as to clarify the boundaries of the enforcement of law and ensure the correct understanding and application. In China, the system of legal interpretation evolves from practice and is grounded in law. Despite the institutions on legal interpretation before 1978, the NPC Standing Committee adopted a resolution to strengthen the work on legal interpretation in June 1981 to eliminate the impact of Cultural Revolution on legislation, consolidate the political unity and peace and restore the authority of socialist law. The resolution re-established the system of legal interpretation. On 15 May 1996, the Explanations of Some Questions by the Standing Committee of the National People's Congress Concerning the Implementation of the Nationality Law in the Hong Kong Special Administrative Region was adopted at the Nineteenth Session of the Standing Committee of the Eighth NPC, which was the first legal interpretation made after the reform and opening-up. Section 4 of Chapter 2 of the Law on Legislation makes provisions on legal interpretation. In 2004, in the Chairman's Meeting of the Tenth NPC Standing Committee, a set of working procedures of the NPC Standing Committee on legal interpretation was adopted.

The NPC and its Standing Committee have been actively engaged in interpretating law to ensure the correct enforcement of law. Based on statistics, between 1979 and the end of August 2019, the Standing Committee issued 25 interpretations. Among them there are 2 on the Nationality Law, 5 on the Hong Kong SAR Basic Law, 13 on Criminal Law, 1 on Macao SAR Basic Law, 3 on Criminal Procedure Law, and 1 on General Principles of Civil Law and Marriage Law. Based on the timeline, there are 1 in the Eighth NPC, 8 in the Ninth, 5 in the Tenth, 2 in the Eleventh, and 9 in the Twelfth. The application of interpretation is also closely related with the changing circumstances of society and economy. Since the Eighteenth CPC National Congress, the NPC Standing Committee has steadfastly adhered to a combined use of enactment, revision, repeal and interpretation in legislation, and made efforts to coordinate the connection between old and new and among different laws. From then on, the Standing Committee has paid much more attention to interpretation of law, and adopted 7 interpretations on the Criminal Law and Criminal Procedure Law, 1 on the question of citizens' right in name in the General Principles of Civil Law and Marriage Law and 1 on Article 104 of Hong Kong SAR Basic Law to resolutely deter and fight against so-called Hong Kong independence activities and safeguard the dignity of the Constitution and Basic Law. These interpretations were made by the NPC Standing Committee upon the requests or suggestions of relevant parties to address the practical questions during the enforcement of law. They have helped to resolve the pressing issues and brought in good results. Practice has demonstrated that the application of interpretation is essential for continuously improving Chinese socialist legal system, ensuring the correct and effective implementation of laws and regulations, advancing rule of law in all respects and accelerating the construction of a socialist law-based country.

3. To make authorizations for carrying out pilot programs to support and promote reform

As directed by Xi Jinping, "we must align and coordinate decisions on legislation with those on reform, to ensure legislation meets the needs of reform and plays a positive role in leading, promoting, standardizing, and safeguarding it, while also ensuring that reforms have a legal basis and advance in step with the rule of law such that their effectiveness is increased. Decisions that prove effective and reform measures that are successful should be promptly made into law. For important legislative issues over which there are major disputes between departments, we need to move quickly to facilitate and coordinate resolutions; such issues cannot be left to drag on endlessly. In the case of reforms for which conditions are not yet ripe and trials are still needed, authorization must be granted in accordance with legal procedures before proceeding. While it is not permitted to overstep the line of the law; it is also forbidden to hold up reform simply because there is no legal basis on which to implement it."[10] China is currently in a stage of major historical change and social transformation, and new problems and circumstances will emerge endlessly as the society and the economy develop. The drive for innovation cannot be subdued due to a lack of basis in existing laws and regulations or denied by virtue of no precedent. Rather, the legislature should start from the pursuit of the long-term interests of the nation and people's fundamental interests, weigh the overall work of the Party and the state, take proactive initiative to conduct research and propose the solutions on the problems. If the reform and innovation requires revision of law, the legislature should timely make the revision according to statutory procedures. Where the reform and innovation are still under way, the legislature should draw on the lessons and experience, and grant authorizations to allow for pilot programs, if legislation to promote the proposed reform and innovation is not permissible to ensure reform is carried out according to law under steady progress.

The first authorization was the Resolution of the NPC Standing Committee on Authorizing Guangdong Province and Fujian Province to Formulate Separate Economic Regulations for the Special Economic Zones Which Belong to Them in November 1981. The Standing Committee then made similar resolutions to authorize the people's congresses and their standing committees and the people's governments of Shantou and Zhuhai to formulate regulations and rules for the special economic zones that belong to them. The number of such authorizations was small, because the matters concerned were usually subject to the regulation of normative documents issued by the State Council and local legislatures or the people's governments. They were also very general in terms of the scope and contents, and lacked explicit provisions on the authorization period and the follow-ups when they expired.

When the Law on Legislation was enacted in 2000, the legal basis for authorization with respect to its purpose and scope was laid down, as it prescribed that authorization decisions shall specify the purpose and scope. Then in 2006, the Decision on Authorizing Hong Kong SAR to Exercise Jurisdiction over the Hong Kong Port Area at the Shenzhen bay Port was adopted in the Tenth NPC Standing Committee, which, for the first time, made provisions on authorization's period. Six years later, the NPC Standing Committee made the Decision on Authorizing the State Council to Temporarily Adjust Certain Administrative Approval Items Prescribed in Laws in Guangdong Province, which for the first time specified the follow-ups.

Since the Eighteenth CPC National Congress, to cater to the needs of socialist reform and development for the new era, the NPC Standing Committee made 25 pieces of decisions on authorization and reform Among them, 21 were made in the Twelfth NPC on issues such as the pilot free trade zone, administrative approval,

---

[10] The Party Literature Research Office ed., *The Law-Based Governance of China*, Central Compilation and Translation Press, 2017, pp. 60–61.

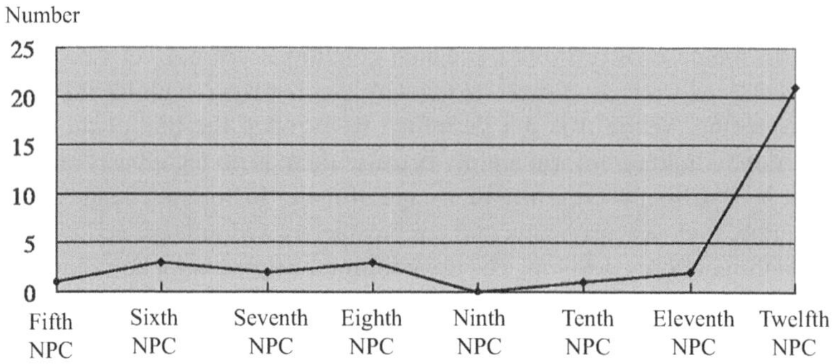

Fig. 11.6 Number of decisions on authorization and reform

rural collective land, judicial system, stock issuance registration, national defense and military affairs, all of which were of great importance to reform. Between March 2018 and August 2019, three decisions on authorization were made in response to the market authorization holder system, rural collective land and local government debt. Compared with the past, these authorizations were not only larger in number (see Fig. 11.6), but also gradually institutionalized, standardized and normalized the application of authorization by improving its working mechanisms and methods. Making authorization decisions in accordance with the law represents the innovative exploration of promoting reform in a law-based way. This not only ensures that legislation precedes reform and law-based major reforms, but also accumulates practical experience for further revising and improving the legal system. They also benefit the legislation in leading and promoting reform, and play an important role in promoting modernization of state governance system and capacity.

First, to standardize the components of an authorization decision. If the reform measures are not in conformity with existing laws, but the conditions for law revision are not yet ripe, pilot programs should be carried to implement the measures, which asks for a decision on authorization or reform. Such a decision should specific the components of the authorization. The 2015 revised Law on Legislation made further provisions on the authorization decision by requiring that it should specify the purpose, subject, scope and period and the principles that the authorized should adhere to. It also prescribed that any authorization decision shall be valid for 5 years, except as otherwise provided by the authorization decision. The authorized shall, 6 months before the expiry of the authorization, report to the authorizing on the implementation of the authorization and submit an opinion on whether or not it is necessary to draft law; if it is necessary to continue the authorization, an opinion may be submitted to that effect, and the NPC and its Standing Committee will make a decision. The authorized shall strictly follow the authorization decision in exercising the authorized powers, and shall not transfer such powers to others. It also prescribed that the NPC and its Standing Committee may, as needed for reform and development, decide to adjust or temporarily suspend the application of some statutory provisions in specific authorization matters in areas such as administrative management for a certain period of time in some areas.

Second, to urge and promote the smooth operation of relevant pilot reforms. To ensure the efficacy of reform authorization and explore the replicable experiences, some authorization decisions explicitly state that the authorized should make a summary of the experience before the pilot reform expires and submit a report to the NPC Standing Committee on the implementation of the authorization. The NPC Standing Committee will deliberate on the reports submitted by the State Council, Supreme People's Court and Supreme People's Procuratorate on the implementation of reform measures and pilot reforms to strengthen its supervision for better future implementation and efficacy.

Third, to explore the mechanisms for the follow-up response when the authorization expires, which can be illustrative from the following three ways. The first is to make a decision to extend the authorization or incorporate into a new pilot initiative if the reform measure should continue. For example, in November 2015, the Decision on Authorizing the State Council to Carry out Pilot Market Authorization Holder Programs for in Certain Areas and on Other Relevant Issues was made in the Twelfth NPC. In October, 2018, 3 years before this decision expired, the decision to extend the authorization was made in the Thirteenth NPC. In February 2015, the Standing Committee issued the Decision on Authorizing the State Council to Temporarily Adjust the Implementation of the Provisions of Relevant Laws in the Administrative Regions of 33 Counties (Cities and Districts) under the Pilot Program Including Daxing District of Beijing Municipality. It was extended in November 2017, and then extended again in December 2018. However, some authorizations were not extended but incorporated into a new decision for authorization. For example, the 2016 Decision on Authorizing the Supreme People's Court and the Supreme People's Procuratorate to Carry Out the Pilot Program of the System for Imposing Lenient Punishments on Those Confessing to Their Crimes and Accepting Punishments in Criminal Cases in Certain Areas incorporated the decision to authorize the Supreme People's Court and the Supreme People's Procuratorate to Carry Out the Pilot Program of Fast-Track Sentencing Procedure for Criminal Cases in Certain Areas made in 2014. The new authorization made improvements on the old one, and continued the old pilot program according to its new rules. The second is to revise relevant laws to promote replicas of the pilot reform measures when the authorization expires if they prove effective. For example, in August 2013, the NPC Standing Committee made a decision on authorizing the State Council to temporarily adjust administrative approval items prescribed in the Foreign-funded Enterprises Law, Law on Chinese-Foreign Equity Joint Ventures and Law on Chinese-Foreign Contractual Joint Ventures. In December 2014, the NPC Standing Committee made another decision on authorizing the State Council to temporarily adjust the same for the pilot free trade zones in Guangdong Province, Tianjin Municipality, Fujian Province and the extensions of Shanghai Pilot Free Trade Zone. To summarize the success of these pilot measures, a decision was made in the Twenty Second Meeting of the Twelfth NPC Standing Committee to revise four laws including the Foreign-funded Enterprises Law, upgrading the reform measures in the pilot free trade zones into laws and making an end to the two decisions. The decision made in the Twelfth NPC Standing Committee to revise the Administrative Litigation Law and Civil Procedure Law was to spread the good practice of public interest litigation through legislation when the Decision on Authorizing the Supreme People's Procuratorate to Carry Out the Pilot Program of Public Interest Litigation in Certain Areas expired. The People's Assessors Law adopted in April 2018 also represented a upgrading of the reform measures proven effective and replicable through practices into law, when both the initial authorization on people's assessor system in 2014 and the second one in 2017 expired. The third is to restore validity of the relevant statutory provisions if the reform measures are proven impracticable. For example, the Decision on Authorizing the State Council to Temporarily Adjust Certain Administrative Approval Items Prescribed in Laws in Guangdong Province involved too many laws, and part of the reform measure was practicable, which were then incorporated into law revisions. However, other parts of the authorization could not change the status quo as demonstrated by practice. When no more bills on law revision were submitted before January 1, 2018, the original statutory provisions were restored.

4. To made decisions on legal issues and other major issues to guarantee the implementation of the Central Committee's major decisions

A decision on legal issues is different from a law. Generally, a law adjusts social relations, directly regulates citizens' rights and ditties on one hand and the functions and powers of state organs on the other hand; laws can create institutional rules that can be repeatedly applied. The decision on legal issues are mainly specific to individual matters, and are no longer once the matter to which it is dedicated is resolved. In a word, the decision cannot be applied to unspecified questions, and other specific issues should be subject to the provisions of law. For example, the Decision on Maintaining the Internet Security made by the NPC Standing Committee was targeted at only one issue, i.e. Internet security. The decision did not create any new institutions or mechanisms, nor did it establish new norms on the rights and duties. If anyone commits an act subject to this decision, that person should be punished by the Criminal Law or Law on Penalties for Administration of Public Security. Such decisions are also made following the procedures that are different from the enactment of law.

Since the Eighteenth CPC National Congress, the Central Committee with Xi Jinping as the core has put more emphasis on the capacity and performance of law-based administration, and has also paid special attention to promoting reform and development through law-based means and thinking. To adapt to new trends and requirements, the Twelfth NPC Standing Committee made timely responses to some important issues based on the Constitution and law, which contributed to 46 decisions on legal issues and other major issues to ensure the implementation of the Central Committee's major decisions, and to promote and safeguard the correct enforcement of the Constitution and law. To be specific, the NPC Standing Committee made a variety of decisions to establish constitutional awareness, demonstrate its authority and promote its enforcement. It also made three decisions on three anniversaries to spread patriotism and core socialist values, and adopted the decision on the election of Hong Kong SAR's Chief Executive by universal franchise to adhere to the One Country Two Systems. Finally, it passed the decision on adjusting the family planning policy to better carry out the two-child policy.

During the first term of the Thirteenth NPC, its Standing Committee had made 14 pieces of decisions, including the Decision on Issues concerning Adjustments to Functions of Administrative Organs Prescribed by Laws as Involved in the Institutional Reform of the State Council to put into force the directives made in the Eighteenth CPC National Congress and the Third Plenary Session of the Nineteenth CPC Central Committee on institutional reform; Decision on Matters concerning the Duties of the Constitution and Law Committee of the National People's Congress to implement the arrangements of the Central Committee and the First Plenary Session of the Thirteenth NPC; Decision on Granting Special Pardons to Some Prisoners on the Occasion of the 70th Anniversary of the Founding of the People's Republic of China according to the arrangements of the Central Committee and the provisions of the Constitution; Decision on Forming the Shanghai Financial Court and Decision on Several Issues concerning Judicial Procedures for Patent and Other Intellectual Property Cases to improve on the deepen the judicial institutional reform; Resolution on Comprehensively Strengthening Ecological Environment Protection and Promoting the Fight of Pollution Prevention and Control to put into practice the Xi Jinping Thought on Ecological Civilization; and Decision on the Exercising of the Marine Right Safeguarding and Law Enforcement Functions and Powers by the China Coast Guard to ensure the coast guard reform under steady progress according to law and smooth transition of powers and responsibilities.

5. To carry out re-examination initiatives in a timely manner to guarantee the internal harmony and unification of the legal system

To ensure that the Chinese socialist legal system is scientific, harmonious and unified, the NPC Standing Committee, the State Council and local people's congresses with legislative power have carried out various comprehensive or specialized initiatives to re-examine the laws and regulations, and have established a self-upgrade mechanism within the system since the reform and opening-up.

In the Twelfth Session of the Fifth NPC Standing Committee held in November 1979, the Resolution on the Question of Validity of the Laws and Decrees Enacted Since the Founding of the People's Republic of China was adopted, which decided that "all the laws and decrees enacted or approved by the Central People's Government since the founding of the People's Republic of China on October 1, 1949 and all laws and decrees enacted or approved by the National People's Congress and its Standing Committees since the enactment of the Constitution of the People's Republic of China by the First Session of the First National People's Congress on September 20, 1954 shall remain in force, except for those that contravene the Constitution and the laws enacted by the Fifth National People's Congress and the decrees enacted or approved by the Standing Committee of the Fifth National People's Congress." This resolution was the first of its kind on re-examination.

In 1987, the NPC Standing Committee carried out a comprehensive re-examination of the laws and decrees enacted or approved between 1949 and the end of 1978. According to the requirement that laws enacted since the founding of PRC should be re-examined, as advanced in the report of the Standing Committee delivered at the Third Session of the Fifth National People's Congress, the Legislative Affairs Committee made a comprehensive re-examination of the laws enacted before the end of 1978, including the decisions on legal issues, and issued a report. The Decision on Approving the Report of the Legislative Affairs Committee on Re-examination and Commenting on the Law Enacted by the End of 1978 was adopted in the Twenty-Third Session of the Sixth NPC Standing Committee. As illustrated in the Report, of the 134 pieces of laws under re-examination, 111 had expired, and 23 were still valid or being studied and revised while they remained valid. The 111 pieces of laws that were invalidated fall into four categories: (1) 11 had been repealed by the provisions of new laws; (2) 41 had been replaced by laws; (3) 29 were no longer applicable or ceased to be effective because of changes in the objects subject to their regulation or the changes of circumstances; and (4) 30 pieces of legally binding decisions or Regulation on specific issues went outdated. With respect to the 111 laws which became invalid, apart from those repealed by the provisions of new laws, the remaining 100 pieces of laws were no longer applicable as declared by the NPC, while the handling of relevant issues in the past based on these laws remained valid. Additionally, 48 pieces of regulations on the organization of people's congress and people's councils in national autonomous areas as approved by the NPC became inapplicable because of changes in the situation as a result of the fact that the new Constitution, Local Organization Law and Regional Ethnic Autonomy Law had been enacted, that the standing committees of the people's congresses in national autonomous areas had been established and that Regulation on self-government in national autonomous areas had either been enacted or were being enacted separately.

Starting from 2008, several initiatives have been carried out to re-examine the laws, administrative regulations and local regulations based on the directive of the NPC Standing Committee. In 2009, the NPC Standing Committee consecutively adopted the Decision on Repealing Some Laws, putting an end to 8 pieces of laws and decisions on legal issues, and the Decision on Revising Some Laws, which made revisions to 141 provisions of 59 pieces of laws in one package. The NPC Standing Committee also repealed 7 and revised 107 administrative regulations, and repealed 455 and revised 1417 pieces of local regulations, which basically addressed the issues of inconsistency, disconnection and incongruity to ensure the legal system scientific, harmonious and unified.

The Thirteenth NPC Standing Committee also pushed forward re-examination initiatives in local legislative bodies and departments regarding normative documents through law enforcement and issuance of decisions. It convened a specialized meeting to deliberate on the inspection report on the implementation of the Law on the Prevention and Control of Air Pollution and made the Resolution on Comprehensively Strengthening Ecological Environment Protection and Promoting the Fight of Pollution Prevention and Control to put into practice the Xi Jinping Thought on Ecological Civilization. It also urged and supervised the formulation and revision of 31 pieces of provincial regulations on air pollution prevention and control and the re-examination of normative documents on ecological protection by revising 514 and repealing 83 pieces of local regulations.

Future efforts should focus more on establishing a sound mechanism for self-upgrade-and-improvement within the legal system by referring to the experience gained in re-examination. A long-term mechanism is essential to normalize the initiative on re-examination. If any inconsistency, disconnection and incongruity is found in the system, the laws or regulations concerned should be timely revised or repealed. When enacting a law, consideration should be given to revising or repealing the laws or provisions of laws that are inconsistent or uncoordinated with it, so as to ensure the synchronized efforts in enactment, revision and repeal. If it cannot be done at the same time, revising or repealing relevant laws or provisions of laws after the law is promulgated is essential for avoiding new inconsistency and incongruity.

6. To compile the laws timely to promote law codification

Law compilation is to integrate and systemize similar laws or laws of one department by way of revision and addition after reviewing them based on statutory powers and procedures by the state legislature. Law compilation is often intended for making a code, so it is also called codification. With systemization of a set of laws, law compilation is conductive to enforcement. In addition, law compilation can change the laws by deleting the outdated or incompatible provisions to reduce redundancy or contradiction, and also make new provisions. As a basic means for codifying and systemizing laws, it can help achieve the unification and integration of national legal system.

China is now working on the codification of civil laws. Civil law is the basic law of the market economy and the foundation for developing market economy in China. The codification of civil laws was proposed as a goal in the Fourth Plenary of the Eighteenth CPC Central Committee. with a high sense of mission and responsibility, the NPC and its Standing Committee have spared no efforts for its codification by proposing a two-step scheme according to the realities first, the promulgation of the General Rules; second, the different parts and final integration of all these parts, which was scheduled to be finished in 2020. In March 2017, the General Rules, which played an overarching role in the code, were adopted in the Fifth Session of the Twelfth National People's Congress. The General Rules adhered to the requirements of comprehensively advancing rule of law, people's position as masters of the country, China's realities, and core socialist values, promoted the fine Chinese traditional culture, summarized the experience of China's civil law practice, and made a full set of basic provisions and general norms for the civil transactions in China by referring to the new demands and trends, which had laid foundation of the codification of civil laws. The new NPC and its Standing Committee had worked to accelerate the codification by preparing a draft Civil Code consisting of six parts with 1034 articles, which were deliberated in August 2018 as a whole. Then deliberations on its parts were separately conducted: on the Contract and Torts parts in December 2018, on Real Rights and Personality Rights in April 2019, Marriage and Family and Inheritance in June and Personality and Torts again in August. With a step-by-step approach, the whole codification was expected to meet the scheduled time of completion in 2020.

The precondition for codification is the availability of a certain number of separate laws of the same kind, on the basis of which deletions and additions are made to form a complete code. Apart from civil laws, China has also enacted the labor, education, environment protection laws, which formed the basis for law codification. In the future, by referring to the systems of relevant laws, the theoretical research and preparatory work, suggestions and working plans can be made for promoting the codification of environment protection laws, education laws and labor laws to make the system of laws more agile in responding to new circumstances and trends and make it more integrated and coordinated for better law enforcement.

Since the Eighteenth CPC National Congress, Chinese socialism has entered a new era. In response to the new demands and trends of development, the legislation in China has also taken proactive steps, which have contributed to a lot of major progress and even breakthroughs. In this process, the legislative methods are also diversified, and the application of enactment, revision, repeal, interpretation, authorization, decision, re-examination and compilation has becomes a new normal. As reform goes further and the economic and social development advances, it can be predicted that these methods will be applied more often than not, as an institutionalized and normalized set of tools. The NPC and its Standing Committee should continue their work on making decisions on authorization and reform and strengthen the efforts in law enactment, revision, repeal and interpretation related with reform to guarantee the rule of law in line with reform. In addition, they should also enhance the integration of legislation by applying these legislative methods for better coordination, consistency and congruity of legal institutions and mechanisms and for a scientific, harmonious and unified legal system.

Appendix: Introduction to the Re-examination of Laws and Regulations in the Past 70 Years

Laws and regulations reflect social practice: their contents are determined by the realities of social and economic development and vice versa. The contents will change as the social and economic development changes. A regular re-examination of laws and regulations to review the gap between their contents and social practice and revise them, is essential for coordinating the relationship among laws and the relationships between law and social change and demands and for promoting healthy, stable, harmonious and orderly development of society.

The social system and economic development have undergone tremendous changes in China in the past 70 years. Accordingly, its legal system also changes. During the socialist modernization, China has never changed its attention to adapting law to the practice of social and economic development, and established an effective working mechanism on re-examination laws and regulations. Especially since the reform and opening-up, this work has been an important measure to maintain the unity of national legal system, help form and improve the socialist legal system and guarantee the scientific, harmonious and unified development of the legal system as the socialist rule of law gains momentum. A summary of the measures for and experience in it in the past 70 years is of great significance for developing socialist rule of law system, building China into a law-based country, and modernizing state governance system and capacity in the new era.

Laws

In the early years of the People's Republic of China, while abolishing outdated laws, the Party issued the successfully experience it had gained during the new-democratic revolution when establishing a legal system for its bases to quickly begin developing and lay the initial foundation for socialist rule of law. In fact, the Party has put emphasis on the construction of legal system in the early days of PRC, and strengthened the efforts in re-examination the outdated laws when enacting laws according to the national economic and social development to maintain the unification and authority of national legal system.

(I) Two Resolutions

1. Resolution on the Continuing Validity of Existing Laws and Decrees

   It was adopted in the First Session of the First NPC held on September 26, 1954 and invalidated on November 24, 1987, which stipulated that the existing laws and decrees enacted or approved by the Central People's Government continued to be effective unless they contravened the Constitution. It was the first of this kind on re-examination laws in China, and an exploration of the Party on law-based governance through law-based means and thinking.
2. Resolution on the Validity of the Laws and Decrees Enacted Since the Founding of PRC

   It was adopted in the Twelfth Session of the Fifth NPC Standing Committee on November 29, 1979. Based on this resolution, all the laws and decrees enacted or approved by the Central People's Governments since the founding of PRC on October 1, 1949 and all laws and decrees enacted or approved by the NPC and its Standing Committee since the enactment of the 1954 Constitution on September 20, 1954 remained in force, except for those that contravened the Constitution and the laws enacted by the Fifth National People's Congress and the decrees enacted or approved by the Standing Committee of the Fifth National People's Congress. It was an important resolution on clarifying the validity of laws and decrees since 1949.

These two resolutions did not specify the names of the laws and decrees, just a general statement for re-examination. Reiterating the validity of old laws and decrees is to protect people's democratic rights, safeguard social order, consolidate the political peace and unity, and ensure the smooth progress in socialist undertakings by resorting to the existing laws. It can also enable the legislature to concentrate on enacting the urgently needed regulations that were not available in the past when the work on legislation was arduous and under capacity. The resolutions are also an important and effective measure to improve the socialist legal system.

(II) Two Specialized Initiatives for Re-examination

1. The NPC Standing Committee's Initiative in 1987 for Re-examining the Laws and Decrees Enacted from the Founding of PRC to the End of 1978

According to the requirement that laws enacted since the founding of PRC should be re-examined, as advanced in the report of the Standing Committee delivered at the Third Session of the Fifth National People's Congress, the Legislative Affairs Committee made a comprehensive re-examination of the 134 pieces of laws (including decisions on legal issues) enacted before the end of 1978 in collaboration with relevant departments and submitted the report to the Twenty-Third Session of the Sixth NPC Standing Committee in November 1987. The NPC Standing Committee approved this report after deliberation. According to the report, from September 1949 up to the end of 1978, in the 134 pieces of laws enacted or approved by the First Session of the CPPCC, the Central People's Government Council, the NPC and its Standing Committee, 111 pieces of laws were invalid, and 23 were still valid or were being studied and revised while they remained valid. Among the 111 invalid, there were 11 repealed by the provisions of new laws, 40 replaced by new laws, 29 no longer applicable or ceasing to be effective because of changes in the objects to be regulated or changes in the situation and 30 legally binding decisions or regulations on specific issues outdated. Additionally, 48 pieces of regulations on the organization of people's congress and people's councils in national autonomous areas as approved by the NPC became inapplicable because of changes in the situation as a result of the fact that the new Constitution, Local Organization Law and Regional Ethnic Autonomy Law had been enacted, that the standing committees of the people's congresses in national autonomous areas had been established and that regulations on self-government in national autonomous areas had either been enacted or were being enacted separately.

This resolution was different from the previous two for it specified the catalogue of laws to be invalidated and repealed, which truly put into practice the institution of re-examination.

2. The NPC Standing Committee's Initiative in 2009 for Re-examination the Laws Enacted before the 1980s

In the second closing meeting of the Eleventh NPC Standing Committee, Wu Bangguo directed that the initiative on re-examination existing laws should be organized to ensure the goal of establishing the Chinese socialist legal system by 2010 was achieved. According to this directive, the laws subject to this initiative had three kinds of problems: first, some provisions of the laws enacted in the 1980s or early

1990s when planned economy still prevailed could not meet the needs of developing socialist market economy; second, some later laws were inconsistent or disconnected with previous laws in some provisions; and third, some laws were not very operable, which could not be guaranteed with effective enforcement.

The Standing Committee decided to carry out re-examination initiatives to address the above three problems to further the efforts in establishing socialist legal system. On July 21, 2008, the General Office of the Standing Committee issued a notice to carry out the re-examination initiative for the laws enacted before the 1990s and not subject to any kind of re-examination, and laid out an implementation scheme on it. According to the arrangements of the Standing Committee, the special committees of NPC, the working agencies of the Standing Committee, Legislative Affairs Office of the State Council, Legislative Affairs Bureau of the Central Military Commission, the Supreme People's Court and the Supreme People's Procuratorate reviewed over 200 laws and made 1972 suggestions based on the division of their responsibility. The Legislative Affairs Committee collected and sorted out these suggestions, and after meetings of deliberation with the Law Committee of NPC, proposed a package of methods including repeal and revision. The report on the package solution was submitted for deliberation in the Ninth and Ten Sessions of the Eleventh NPC Standing Committee in June 27 and August 27 respectively, which then issued the Decision of the NPC Standing Committee on Repealing Some Laws and the Decision of the NPC Standing Committee on Revising Some Laws.

According to this decision, a total of 67 pieces of laws were subject to repeal and revision, 8 and 59 respectively with 141 provisions. The 8 pieces of laws to be repealed included 4 enacted in the early PRC, 1 on specific matters of economic institutional reform, and 3 replaced by new ones given that they were outdated. The provision of General Principles of Civil Law on planned economy and mandatory plans, the provision of Law on Industrial Enterprises Owned by the Whole People on mandatory plans, the provision of the Sports Law on designated examination and approval institutions, the provisions of the Education Law on extra charges of education funds and raising funds for education and the provision of the Flood Control Law on rural compulsory labor and accumulation labor were deleted for obvious inconformity with the social development. To address the inconsistency and disconnection among the provisions of law, 16 laws and regulations were revised to ensure that they keep congruity with the 2004 Constitutional amendment. The provisions of 25 laws that made references to the 1997 Criminal Law were revised. And the provisions of 32 laws that made references to the Regulation on Administrative Penalties for Public Security were revised to ensure consistency with the 2005 Law on Administrative Penalties for Public Security. Revisions were also made to the Military Service Law, Meteorology Law, Regulation on the Police Ranks of the People's Police and Arbitration Law which made reference to the names of laws and ordering of legal provisions. Considering the large number of the laws subject to repeal and revision, the package approached was adopted.

The Standing Committee's initiative in 2009 achieved remarkable phase results, which basically addressed the issue of inconsistency, disconnection and incongruity among laws that did not suit the social and economic development. It was an important measure to ensure the establishment of socialist legal system as scheduled in 2010.

(III) Re-examination Since the Eighteenth CPC National Congress

The regular re-examination by the NPC Standing Committee is conducive to maintaining the socialist legal system scientific, harmonious, and unified. The previous re-examinations also made their contributions. However, one problem of regular re-examination is that before the laws were re-examined, conflicts between legal provisions often bring confusion to law enforcement or administration of justice, and make relevant legal issues in an uncertain state. However, since 2009, when the legal review was carried out intensively, NPC Standing Committee has not carried out any specialized initiative to re-exam the laws, but incorporated it into its daily legislative work. Since the Eighteenth CPC National Congress, the Party has taken rule of law as the means for governance, clearly stated that it is an important foundation for state governance system and capacity, and emphasized that "every major reform must be based on the law." The NPC and its Standing Committee have resolutely implemented the major decisions and arrangements of the Central Committee, adhered to connecting legislative decision-making and reform decision-making, actively adapted legislation to the needs of reform and economic and social development, continuously innovated the legislative working mechanisms, and established a new mechanism on law re-examination and revision. In this mechanism, while formulating a new law, the provisions of other laws that are not in harmony with them and do not meet the needs of reform should be considered at the same time, and then revised through a package approach to coordinate the revision of these provisions and to avoid conflicts. The integrated revision of the law has achieved good results, which are better illustrated as follows:

1. In April, 2011, revisions were made to certain provisions of Coal Industry Law, Construction Law and Road Traffic Safety Law to ensure their consistency with the Social Insurance Law and the Eighth Amendment to the Criminal Law.
2. In October 2012, the provisions of the Law on Prison and other six laws were revised to address their inconsistency with the revised Criminal Procedure Law.
3. On December 2012, certain provisions of the Agricultural Law were revised to ensure consistency with the revised Law on Promotion of Agricultural Technology.
4. To put into practice the decision of State Council on department reform and transformation of government functions, promote the administrative approval system reform according to law, stimulate market and social creativity and vitality, give full play the intimacy of local governments with the people, and advance and ensure the interim-and post-supervision from prior approval, from 2013 to the end of 2018, the provisions on the matters subject to administrative approval, commercial registration, pricing and professional qualifications of 114 laws including the Law on the Protection of Cultural Relics, Marine Environment Protection Law, Insurance Law, Ports Law, Electric Power Law, Compulsory Education Law, Foreign Trade Law, Accounting Law, Bidding Law, Metrology

Law, Law on Frontier Health and Quarantine, Forest Law, Wild Animal Protection Law, Product Quality Law, and Labor Law. These revisions helped to improve the administrative approval procedures and efficiency and make the government administration more scientific and law-based.

5. To revise the laws based on the implementation of relevant authorization decisions. First, based on the decisions on authorizing the State Council to temporarily adjust administrative approval items in the pilot free trade zones of Guangdong Province, Tianjin Municipality, Fujian Province, Shanghai Municipality and the extensions in Shanghai, the NPC Standing Committee, referring to their implementation, decided to revise the Foreign-funded Enterprises Law, Law on Chinese-Foreign Equity Joint Ventures, Law on Chinese-Foreign Contractual Joint Ventures and Law on the Protection of Investments by Taiwan Compatriots. Second, based on the decision on authorizing the Supreme People's Procuratorate to carry out the pilot public interest litigation in certain areas, in June 2017, the Civil Procedure Law and the Administrative Litigation Law were revised accordingly. Third, the Bidding Law and Metrology Law were revised in December 2017 by referring to the implementation of the NPC Standing Committee's decisions on authorizing the State Council to temporarily adjust administrative approval items as prescribed in some laws and the decision on its expiry.
6. To improve the admission to legal professionals, better regulate the national legal profession qualification examination, promote the professional expertise of legal practitioners, some provisions on the legal qualification of 8 laws including the Law on Judges were revised with additions in September 2017.

Administrative Regulations

Administrative regulations are an important part of the socialist legal system with Chinese characteristics, which have played an important role in national economic and social development. Their legal force is second only national laws. To timely re-exam the administrative regulations are of great significance to promote economic and social development and maintain the unity of national legal system. Over the past 70 years, the State Council has carried out 6 comprehensive initiatives and 15 specialized initiatives, which can be briefly introduced as follows:

Comprehensive Re-examination Initiatives

The comprehensive initiatives were intended to re-exam all the administrative regulations by the State Council according to the trend of economic and social development and the needs for practice.

1. In 1956, as directed by Zhou Enlai and the resolution of the State Council's executive meeting on sorting out regulations, the Legislative Affairs Bureau of the State Council, with the help of other departments, carried out the initiative

to sort out over 250 regulations as formulated and approved by the Government Administration Council. and 144 of them were finally repealed and 64 were revised.

2. Between 1983 and 1987, the Legislative Affairs Bureau worked along with other departments of the State Council to re-exam the 3298 administrative regulations and other normative documents promulgated or approved by the State Council (Government Administration Council) from October 1949 to the end of 1984. The report made based on the results stated that the many regulations could not meet the national economic and social development and inconsistency among them which impacted their enforcement and the regulated state of being excessiveness and confusing. After the re-examination, 661 regulations continued to be valid, and some of the remaining 2637 regulations were changed to ordinary documents, repealed or continued to be valid after major revisions.
3. In May 1994, to suit for reform and opening-up and the new trends in constructing the system of socialist market economy, the State Council issued the Decision on Repealing Certain Administrative Regulations Promulgated before the End of 1993, which, after an initiative to re-exam the 684 administrative regulations, repealed 21, replaced 13 with new laws or regulations, and declared 8 invalid due to the change of circumstances, expiry or outdated provisions on the issues they were formulated to address.
4. To adapt to reform and opening-up, the construction of a sound system for socialist market economy and the new trends in China's accession to the WTO, the State Council made an initiative to re-exam the 756 pieces of administrative regulations promulgated before the end of 2000. In October 2001, the State Council issued the Decision on Repealing Certain Administrative Regulations Promulgated before the End of 2000, which repealed 71 of them due to their inconsistency with the new laws, revised laws, the principles and polices of the Party and state, or the changes in such principles and policies, or their being replaced by new laws or regulations, and declared 80 invalid due to their expiry or non-existence of the matters they were originally subject to.
5. On February 25, 2007, the General Office of the State Council issued the Notice on Re-examination Administrative Regulations and Rules, which focused on the 655 pieces of administrative regulations promulgated before the end of 2006. In January 2008, the State Council issued the Decision on Repealing Some Administrative Regulations, which abolished 49 that were already replaced by the new laws or administrative regulations and declared 43 invalid due to their expiry or the non-existence of the matters they were originally subject to. As the largest initiative since the founding of PRC, it was a major step taken by the State Council to better adapt to the accelerated construction of the law-based government and law-based administration in all respects.
6. From early 2010, the Legislative Affairs Office re-examined 691 pieces of administrative regulations that were in force by the end of 2009 according to the joint arrangements of the NPC Standing Committee and the State Council, the fourth one since 1983 initiated by the State Council based on the new situation and demands for social and economic development and deepened reform. In

January 2011, the State Council issued the Decision on Repealing and Revising Some Administrative Regulations, which repealed 7 pieces of administrative regulations, revised 172 articles of 107 pieces of administrative regulations, and changed provisions on expropriation or requisition that were no longer applicable to the socialist market economy and the new situation in social and economic development. All the outdated provisions on "speculation and profiteering" and expressions such as planned economy and mandatory plans were also deleted from the administrative regulations.

Special Re-examination Initiatives

The State Council also carried out specialized initiatives to re-exam area-specific regulations based on the needs of its work.

1. In July 1986, the State Council issued the Notice on Repealing Some Regulations on Finance and Trade, which re-examined administrative regulations and other normative documents on financial, monetary, trade, auditing, pricing and government administration affairs promulgated or approved by the State Council (Government Administration Council) between 1949 and 1984. According to the results, 104 pieces should be repealed, 23 were repealed explicitly, and 359 were automatically invalid due to their expiry or non-existence of the matters they were originally subject to.
2. In September 1986, the State Council issued the Notice on Repealing Some Regulations on Agriculture and Forest, which re-examined the administrative regulations and other normative documents on agriculture (including animal husbandry and fishery), forestry, water conservancy, electric power and meteorology promulgated or approved by the State Council (Government Administration Council) between 1949 and 1984. According to the results, 24 pieces should be repealed, 3 were explicitly repealed, and 76 were automatically invalid due to their expiry or non-existence of the matters they were originally subject to.
3. In January 1987, the State Council issued the Notice on Repealing Some Regulations on Foreign Affairs, Foreign Trade, Industries, Communication and Urban Construction, Labor and Human Resources, Science, Education, Culture and Health promulgated or approved by the State Council (Government Administration Council) between 1949 and 1984. According to the results, 158 pieces of administrative regulations and normative documents should be repealed, 68 were explicitly repealed and 513 were automatically invalid due to their expiry or non-existence of the matters they were originally subject to.
4. In June 1987, the State Council issued the Notice on Repealing Some Political and Legislative, Military, Office Work and Other Regulations promulgated or approved by the State Council (Government Administration Council) between 1949 and 1984. According to the results, 48 pieces should be repealed, 18 were explicitly repealed and 210 were automatically invalid due to their expiry or non-existence of the matters they were originally subject to.

5. In 1988, to adapt to further opening-up and accelerate the implementation of economic development strategies in the coastal areas for promoting the export-oriented economic in these areas, the State Council organized the relevant departments to re-exam the administrative regulations and normative documents on foreign affairs promulgated or approved by the State Council. According to the results, 29 pieces in total were repealed and 27 declared invalid in two batches.
6. To implement the Administrative Licensing Law, in September 2003, the State Council issued the Notice on Implementing the Administrative Licensing Law of the People's Republic of China, which required the local governments to hasten the cleaning of the existing provisions on administrative licensing, revise or repeal the ones that were not in conformity with the Law, upgrade those subject to the jurisdiction of law or regulations, and made available the results to the public. As of the end of 2005, it re-examined over 25,000 pieces of administrative provisions issued by 31 provinces, autonomous regions, municipalities directly under the State Council and 58 departments of the State Council, 3981 of which were repealed and 2493 revised.
7. To implement the Administrative Compulsion Law, in August 2011, the State Council issued the Notice on Implementing the Administrative Compulsion Law of the People's Republic of China, which required its departments to re-exam the provisions on administrative compulsion of existing administration regulations, and to make suggestions on revision or repeal if they were found to be inconsistent with the Law or inadaptable to the trends of social and economic development. In November 2012, the State Council issued the Decision on Revising and Repealing Some Administrative Regulations, which decided to revise 7 articles of 5 administrative regulations and repeal 5 administrative regulations. Some local governments and their departments also carried out the re-examination, which reported the results of 103 pieces of regulations and rules subject to re-examination.
8. The Plan for Restructuring the State Council and Transforming Functions was adopted in the First Session of the Twelfth NPC, which stressed the importance of deepening administrative approval system reform for better transformation of government functions. To regulate the reform and consolidate the achievements already made in this regard, the Legislative Affairs Office collaborated with relevant departments to re-exam the administrative Regulation on cancelling administrative items and delegating approval authority. In July 2013, the State Council issued the Decision on Repealing and Revising Some Administrative Regulations, which repealed the Measures for the Administration of Coal Production Permits and revised some articles of 25 pieces of administrative regulations. In December, the State Council issued the Decision on Revising Some Administrative Regulations which decided to revise 16 administrative regulations by cancelling 11 and delegating 16 administrative approval items to lower levels. In July 2014, the State Council issued another Decision on Revising Some Administrative Regulations, which revises 21 administrative

regulations and 56 articles by cancelling 23 and delegating 7 administrative approval items to the lower levels.

9. To put into practice the convenient industry and commerce registration as required by the Decision of the CPC Central Committee on Some Major Issues Concerning Comprehensively Deepening the Reform, by referring to the decision of the NPC Standing Committee's decision to revise the Company Law, the State Council carried out initiative to re-exam the administrative regulations concerning the capital contribution subscription, publicity of annual reports and credit constraints. In February 2014, the State Council issued the Decision on Repealing and Revising Some Administrative Regulations, which repealed 2 pieces of administrative regulations and revised some provisions of 8 pieces of administrative regulations.
10. In 2015, to promote the overall reforms for simplified administration, streamlined procedures and optimized services, guarantee the reform law-based and achieve connection of legislation with reform decision, the State Council carried out several initiatives to re-exam the administrative regulations on the cancellation of administrative licensing items and other matters that hindered new industries, business models and development models. First, in February 2016, the State Council issued the Decision on Revising Some Administrative Regulations, which revised certain provisions of 66 pieces of administrative regulations by cancelling and changing 146 the administrative approval items and changing 3 measures on price reform and 2 measures on administrative charges. Second, in March 2017, the State Council issued the Decision on Revising and Repealing Some Administrative Regulations, which revised certain provisions of 36 administrative regulations and repealed 3 of this kind. Third, in October 2017, the State Council issued the Decision on Revising Some Administrative Regulations, which revised 15 pieces of administrative regulations. Fourth, in November 2017, the State Council issued the Decision on Revising Some Administrative Regulations, which revised 2 pieces of administrative regulations. Fifth, in March 2018, the State Council issued the Decision on Revising and Repealing Some Administrative Regulations, which revised certain provisions of 18 pieces of administrative regulations and repealed 5. Sixth, in March 2019, to deepen the reform of Internet + Government Services and One-Stop Portal services, the State Council issued the Decision on Revising Some Administrative Regulations, which revised certain provisions of 6 pieces of administrative regulations that did not conform with the requirements on One-Stop Portal services.

Local Regulations

Local regulations are also an important component of socialist legal system with Chinese characteristics. Over the past 40 years since the reform and opening-up, the local legislature has taken a firm standing on the general picture of the Party and the state undertakings, drawn on the strength from the great practice of Chinese socialist modernization, and been responsive to the change of times, reform and practice. The local regulations have made important contributions on the establishment and improvement of socialist legal system with the Constitution as the core, the modernization of state governance system and capacity, and the construction of China into a socialist law-based country. Based on the realities, several initiatives have also been carried out to re-exam the local legislation to maintain the unity of national legal system.

Re-examination Initiatives as Required by Law and Reform

After the reform and opening-up was initiated, the people's congresses and their standing committees of the province, municipalities directly under the State Council and cities with subordinate districts were successively granted with legislative power, which helped them to formulate a large number of local regulations for guaranteeing the enforcement of laws and administrative regulations in their own administrative areas and promoting the local social and economic development. As the legal system continues to improve, the local legislature also carried out the re-examination initiatives by referring to the changes of national reform and development to effectively maintain the unity of national legal system.

1. In 1996, the local legislature carried out initiatives to re-exam the provisions of local regulations that were not compatible with the Administrative Penalty Law as required by the NPC Standing Committee.
2. In 2000, the local legislature re-examined the provisions of local regulations that contravened China's commitment to WTO based on the national initiative.
3. In 2004, the local legislature re-examined the provisions of local regulations that abused the power in making administrative licensing matters as against the Administrative Licensing Law as required by the NPC Standing Committee.
4. In 2009, the local legislature carried out a comprehensive initiative to address the inconsistency and incongruity of local regulations with the upper level laws and regulations to ensure the socialist legal system established as scheduled based on the decision of the NPC Standing Committee.
5. In 2012, the local legislature carried out initiatives to re-exam the provisions of local regulations that were not consistent with the Administrative Compulsion Law as required by the NPC Standing Committee.
6. From 2016, the local legislature has been engaged in re-examination the local regulations that were outdated based on the requirements of simplified administration, streamlined procedures and optimized services and transformation of government functions to ensure these reforms are law-based.
7. In 2018, the local legislature carried out an initiative to re-exam the local regulations that were inconsistent with or contravened the laws, administrative regulations based on the requirements of ecological civilization and environment protection laid out by the NPC Standing Committee, and revised or repealed

them according to the results, which provided sound legal guarantee for the fight against pollution and control.

Re-examination Initiatives as Required by Supervision and to Address Practical Problems

Apart from the local initiatives, the NPC Standing Committee also implemented the initiatives on some specific matters to maintain the unification of legal system.

1. On August 27, 2006, the Law on the Supervision of Standing Committees of People's Congresses at Various Levels were adopted at the Twenty-Third Session of the Tenth NPC Standing Committee and came into force as of January 1, 2007. In the closing session, Wu Bangguo pointed out the local legislature should study this Law and carry out a comprehensive review of local regulations before it went into force, make detailed provisions on those that conformed with the Law and adjust the provisions that did not conform with its provisions and principles. To be well informed about the review of local people's congress standing committees with legislative power, the Legislative Affairs Committee issued a notice asking for the local reports on review before the Law became effective to 80 local people's congress standing committees on November 17, 2006. As of February 5, 2007, all the local legislative had submitted the reports which clarified the provisions on assessment of working reports, supervision of individual cases and procedures in enquires, investigation on specific matter and dismissal. Among them, 55 local people's congress standing committees believed that 219 pieces of local regulations were inconsistent with the provisions and principles of the Law and needed detailed rules. Of these regulations, 22 were revised or repealed, while 180 were to be revised to repealed, and 17 were not listed in the revision plan as they needed further study. The standing committees of other 25 local people's congresses reported that their local regulations were consistent with the provisions and principles of the Law. On April 13, 2007, the Legislative Affairs Committee issued another notice to ask the local legislature to report on the revision and repeal of the local regulations and working documents in line with the Law. As of June 4, 2007, 77 local people's congress standing committees submitted their reports on the review of local Regulation on assessment of working reports, supervision of individual cases, specialized working reports, law enforcement inspection, review and supervision of budgets and final accounts, and investigation of specific matters. Among them, 56 local people's congress standing committees believed that 208 local regulations were inconsistent with the provisions and principles of the Law and subject to revision or repeal. Among them, 94 were already revised and repealed, and 114 were listed in the legislative plan for revision or repeal. The standing committees of 21 local people's congresses reported no problems.
2. On February 22, 2017, the Legislative Affairs Committee issued a Letter of the Research Opinions on Relevant Local Regulation on the Application of Audit Results as the Basis for Determining the Completion of Government-Invested

Construction Projects to the standing committees of the people's congresses of the provinces, autonomous regions and municipalities directly under the State Council. It asked the local legislative to review their local Regulation on audit and to submit their opinions on the application of audit results for determining the completion of government-invested construction projects and the provisions that allow its application in bidding documents or contracts. Based on the local feedback, these problems existed in the local regulations of 11 provincial administrative areas, i.e. Beijing, Hebei, Shanghai, Jiangsu, Zhejiang, Anhui, Shandong, Hainan, Sichuan, Guizhou and Ningxia, of 8 cities with subordinate districts, i.e. Shijiazhuang, Hohhot, Qingdao, Zhengzhou, Luoyang, Wuhan, Guangzhou and Yinchuan, and of 2 special economic zones, i.e. Shenzhen and Shantou. A year later, the Legislative Affairs Committee issued a letter of handling under supervision to the standing committees concerned. According to their feedback reports, they had completed the revision and repeal of the local regulations.

3. In June 2017, the Office of Regulations Recording and Review of the Legislative Affairs Committee carried out special initiative to review nearly 50 local Regulation on natural reserve when the Central Committee publicized the compromised legislation on Qilian Mountain Natural Reserve. It also issued letters twice, in September 2017 and April 2018 respectively, to the local people's congress standing committees, which asked them to carry out compressive review of the local Regulation on ecology and environment protection and to find and correct the compromised regulations with lower standards and loosened control so as to make local regulations consistent the Central Committee's principles, the Constitution and law. As a result, 35 local regulations were either revised or repealed, and 700 were to be revised or repealed according to the feedback of 31 provincial people's congresses.
4. In July 2018, the Resolution on Comprehensively Strengthening Ecological Environment Protection and Promoting the Fight of Pollution Prevention and Control was adopted, which clearly stated that "laws, regulations, judicial interpretations and normative documents on ecological and environment protection shall be comprehensively reviewed without delay, and those contrary to, disconnected with, or unable to adapt to the law, the spirit of the CPC Central Committee, or the requirements of the era, repealed or revised in a timely manner". To put it into practice, the General Office of the NPC Standing Committee issued notices to all the local people's congresses, laid down the requirements on review. The provincial people's congresses expanded the scope of regulations subject to review, and urged local governments to accelerate the review of local rules and normative documents on ecological and environment protection. According to the feedback of 31 provincial people's congresses, a total of 1029 pieces of local regulations were inconsistent with upper level legislation in some respects; among them, 514 were already revised and 83 repealed, and 432 were to be revised or repealed based on the legislative plan. In addition, based on the inspection reports of the NPC Standing Committee, the local governments also enhanced their efforts in formulating and revising the rules on air pollution prevention and control, and the 31 provincial people's congress standing committees finished most of the

work on formulating and revising the local Regulation on it with 17 formulated and 14 revised.

Reflections on the Long-Term Mechanism on Re-examination

As required in the Nineteenth CPC National Congress, great efforts should be made to carry out lawmaking in a well-conceived and democratic way and in accordance with law, so that good laws are made to promote development and ensure good governance. For scientific legislation, it should first ensure the harmony and integration of legal system, in which the laws are coordinated, complete, orderly, well-connected.

China is a unified and unitary socialist country, and its nature determines the unity of socialist legal system, which is also required by the construction of socialist rule of law system and law-based country. The Party and state highly value the re-examination of laws and regulations, and have made the decisions and arrangements for it several times over the past 70 years according to the changes of circumstances and legislative practice. To make the legal system more developed, scientific and complete after its establishment, the NPC Standing Committee has put more emphasis on the re-examination of laws and regulations. In a forum held in January 2011, Wu Bangguo reiterated the importance of re-examining the laws and regulations. In March 2013, Zhang Dejiang also stressed in a speech that more attention should be paid to the revision of law by timely changing the laws not suitable for social and economic development, transforming the legal principles into legal rules to make the law more responsive and systematic and establishing a long-term mechanism on laws and regulations re-examination. The State Council also issued the Outline for Promoting Law-based Administration in an All-round Way which clearly strived for "establishing and improving the working mechanism on revision and repeal of administrative regulations and rules, and the mechanism on regularly re-examination of the rules and normative documents". In this case, with a reference to the experience in the past 70 years, several suggestions are put forward as follows:

To Sum Up Experience

To re-exam the laws and regulations is a major task for ensuring the conformity of law with practice and law-based reforms. As proposed in the Fourth Plenary Session of the Eighteenth CPC Central Committee, the legislative decision should be interconnected with the reform decision, and any laws and regulations that do not adapt to reform should be timely revised or repealed. Therefore, in the future, more efforts should be made to study and explore a long-term mechanism on laws and regulations re-examination, summarize the regular issues in these initiatives, improve the working procedures, and regulate the initiating mechanism, procedures, organization and methods for re-examination to make it more standardized and institutionalized so as to ensure laws and regulations meet the needs of and provide strong legal guarantee for social and economic development.

To Clarify the Working Methods

1. To combine regular initiatives with responsive initiatives
   First, for certain laws and regulations disconnected from realities fail to adapt to the new ideas, institutions and systems, the procedures should be started timely; second, if the laws and regulations are found to be inconsistent with and inadaptable to social and economic development or disconnected or inoperable after law enforcement inspection and post-legislative review after they have come into force, they should be dealt with in a centralized manner, and be incorporated into legislative plan or schedule for regular re-examination.
2. To Enhance the coordinated efforts in law enactment and revision
   The good practices of enacting and revising law since the Eighteenth CPC National Congress, should be summarized, other related laws should be considered when enacting or revising law, and the provisions that are inconsistent, incongruent or even contradictory with others should be revised in a timely manner.
3. To improve package legislation to promote regular re-examination initiatives
   A striking feature of re-examination in 2009 was to revise 59 laws in a package, which not only follows the legislative procedures but also reduces deliberation costs and increases its efficiency. This initiative has been a major historic turn for re-examination of laws and legislative system reform. Since the Eighteenth CPC National Congress, it has been adopted in legislative practice to address the issues of inconsistency and obsoleteness. In the future, it should be adopted in enacting or revising law when any potential contradiction among laws will occur. The package approach to legislation, which helps to eliminate the inconsistency and incongruity among laws if the re-examination is carried out after each legislation, will increase legislative efficiency and reduce its costs, but also prevent any occurrence of legal contradiction in the early stage of legislation.
4. To specify the requirements on supporting regulations
   It is advised that the supporting regulations should be considered when deciding the legislative programs and drafting laws. In this case, the State Council and relevant parties should be urged to hasten their efforts in formulating the corresponding administrative regulations for simultaneous enforcement of laws and their regulations. If not simultaneously, they should be formulated as soon as possible to ensure the effective implementation of laws. The NPC and its Standing Committee should also supervise and guide relevant parties to carry out the initiatives on re-examination administrative and local regulations.

Legislation is the important political activity of the state, a sacred mission for laying down the rules for the state and the society. As Chinese socialism entered a new era, the development should be high-quality, so is the legislation. High-quality legislation to secure and promote the healthy and sustainable economic development should the goal of the legislature. When carrying out the work on legislation, China's actual conditions and the practical problems should be taken into account. When China's economic and social development gain momentum, and the administrative approval system reform and transformation of government continue to be deepened, the legislation should strive to be connected with reform; the reform should be enhanced during the rule of law construction, and the rule of law should be improved in the process of reform. Based on the experience gains from the past initiatives on re-examination laws and regulations, a working mechanism dedicated to it should be gradually established to achieve the upgrade and self-improvement of legal system and meet the needs of socialist economic, political, cultural, social and ecological progress so as to improve the socialist legal system as being more scientific, harmonious and integrated. And more efforts should be made to provide quality provision of institutions and mechanisms for social and economic development, which are intended to ensure the smooth progress in leading, promoting and guaranteeing reform and opening-up and make greater contributions to the socialist legal system with Chinese characteristics in line with the modernization of state governance system and capacity.

Chapter 12
Theory and Practice of Scientific, Democratic and Law-Based Legislation

Ren Caifeng

Abstract This chapter delves into the core principles of China's unique legislative path: scientific legislation, democratic legislation, and law-based legislation. It systematically traces the theoretical and practical development of these principles from the founding of the PRC to the present day. It highlights the intrinsic relationship between the three, positing that law-based legislation serves as the fundamental prerequisite, democratic legislation as the cornerstone for reflecting public will, and scientific legislation as the essential standard for evaluating legislative quality. It explores the historical evolution of these principles, and details how, particularly since the 18th CPC National Congress, the Chinese government has intensified its focus on these principles to institutionalize major reforms and improve governance. It concludes that the continuous refinement of these principles has been crucial for perfecting the socialist legal system with Chinese characteristics.

Keywords Scientific legislation · Democratic legislation · Law-based legislation · Legislative practice · Chinese legal system · Modernization of state governance

In uniting and leading the Chinese people to engage in the New Democratic Revolution and leading the socialist revolution, development and reform, the Party has strictly adhered to the guidance of the principle of Scientific Marxism and the principle of people's democracy, treading on the path of Chinese socialism. In this period, the Party has also followed a path of Chinese socialist legislation, whose striking feature is carrying out legislation in a scientific, democratic and law-based manner. Over the past 70 years, Chinese legislation has persisted in the integration of the Party's leadership, people's position as masters of the country, and rule of law. by starting from China's conditions and realities, the work on legislation respects the law of social development, and adheres to a combination of scientific, democratic and law-based legislation, which has made outstanding achievements both in its theory and practice. To carry out legislation in a scientific, democratic and law-based

R. Caifeng (✉)
Beijing, China
e-mail: liujixuan@lawpress.com.cn

C. Shen et al. (eds.), *A History of Legislation in the Past 70 Years in China*,
https://doi.org/10.1007/978-981-95-3799-0_12

manner is a good practice evolving through the Party's leadership in establishing, consolidating, developing and improving socialist system and through the gradually deepening understanding of the law for the Party to govern the country and engage socialist construction as well as the law for human development, and also the basic principles of legislation during its practice being gradually regulated and institutionalized. The 2000 Law on Legislation laid out specific rules on law-based, democratic and scientific legislation in Article 4, 5 and 6, which made it the statutory principles of China's legislation.[1]

1 Theoretical Significance and Basic Requirements

They are closely related: being law-based is the prerequisite because there is no legitimacy for any law is enacted not based on legal principles; the legislative power comes from the people, and only through democratic in legislation can the legislative decision-making meet the people's demands and realities, and the legislative quality and efficacy be improved; being scientific is not only a methodological guidance for legislation, but also a value measurement of the legislative quality. They are essential for the legislative practice within the Chinese socialist legal system with the Constitution as the core.

1.1 Elaborations and Requirements of the Party and State Leaders

In the early years of the PRC, the Party began to lead the people to explore the socialist legal system. Though they were not formally proposed at that time, the Party and state leaders, including Mao Zedong, also made important elaborations on them when enacting the Common Program and the Constitution, which became the sources of scientific and democratic legislation.[2]

[1] Article 4: Laws shall be made in accordance with the statutory limits of power and procedures, on the basis of the overall interests of the State and for the purpose of safeguarding the uniformity and dignity of the socialist legal system; Article 5 Laws shall be made in order to embody the will of the people, enhance socialist democracy and guarantee that the people participate in legislative activities through various channels. Article 6: Law shall be made by proceeding from reality and scientifically and rationally prescribing the rights and duties of citizens, legal persons and other organizations, and the powers and responsibilities of State organs.

[2] In the Thirtieth Session of the Central People's Government Council held in June 14, 1954, Mao Zedong rejected the proposal of titling the Constitution as Mao Zedong Constitution and asked to delete the provision that "the President of the People's Republic of China is the state leader" from the Draft Constitution. Some said that it was out of exceptional modesty. He explained that, "this is not the way to put it. It is not out of modesty but because inclusion of these articles would be improper, unjustifiable and unscientific. In a people's democratic state like ours such improper articles ought not to be written into the constitution. We have not omitted, out of modesty, what ought to have been

To reflect on the lessons from the Cultural Revolution, it was clearly stated in the Third Session of the Eleventh CPC Central Committee that the socialist legal system should be strengthened to protect people's democracy. As pointed out by Deng Xiaoping, "the socialist democracy and socialist legal system are closely connected. The democracy without socialist legal system, the Party's leadership, or discipline and order is not a socialist one". To fill the gap in legislation, Deng also proposed that "legal provisions will have to be less than perfect to start with, then be gradually improved upon. Some laws and statutes can be tried out in particular localities and later enacted nationally after the experience has been evaluated and improvements have been made. Individual legal provisions can be revised or supplemented one at a time, as necessary; there is no need to wait for a comprehensive revision of an entire body of law. In short, it is better to have some laws than none, and better to have them sooner than later", and "the legal system will be improved only gradually in the course of practice, and we can't wait for that." Peng Zhen also believed that the law was formulated to legalize the policy, when the circumstances were mature, the law should be enacted accordingly and be concise in wording. In 2001, the working report of the NPC Standing Committee proposed to "practice democratic centralism in legislation to strive for democratic and scientific legislation", and in the 2006 working report, it was directed to "summarize the experience to promote legislation being scientific and democratic and make them institutionalized into the legislative procedures". In the Outline of the Eleventh Five-Year Plan for National Economic and Social Development adopted in that session, it was also advocated to "implement the basic principle of rule of law, promote scientific and democratic legislation and form the Chinese socialist legal system". In the report of the Seventeenth National Congress, the Party called for insisting on scientific and democratic legislation to improve the Chinese socialist legal system.

Since the Eighteenth National Congress, the Central Committee with Xi Jinping as the core has made a lot of important remarks on promoting scientific, democratic and law-based legislation. During this conference, it was proposed to "make laws in a scientific way, enforce them strictly, administer justice impartially, and ensure that everyone abides by the law". In the Resolution of the Central Committee of the CPC on Major Issues Concerning the Enhancement of All-round Law-based Governance, it was proposed to "promote the practice of scientific and democratic legislation". The report of the Nineteenth National Congress advocated the promotion of law-based governance and lawmaking in a well-conceived and democratic way and in accordance with law, so that good laws are made to promote development and ensure good governance. In his speech at the first meeting of the Commission for Law-based Governance under the CPC Central Committee, Xi Jinping pointed out that the good laws were the prerequisite of sound governance, and efforts should

---

included. With science, modesty or immodesty is not the issue. Constitution-making is a matter of science. We must believe in science and nothing else...We must do away with blind faith. We should believe in what is correct and not in what is incorrect, be it ancient or modern. Not only that, we should criticize what is incorrect. This alone is the scientific approach". See Mao Zedong, *Selected Works of Mao Zedong (Vol. 5)*, Foreign Languages Press, 1977, p. 146.

be made to improve the legislative plan, legislation in key areas, and advance scientific, democratic and law-based legislation. In the second meeting, he reiterated that quality development should be pursued, so did the legislation; the legislation in key areas should be promoted, and the scientific, democratic and law-based legislation should also be advanced for better quality and efficiency. He also expounded on the connotations of scientific and democratic legislation: the key to scientific legislation is to respect the objective law of development. To observe and understanding this law in legislation requires the adherence to the law of economy, nature, social development and legislative activities to ensure the laws enacted conform with these laws realities. In addition, the key to democratic legislation is for the people and by the people. These remarks are an important part of the new concepts, new thinking and new strategies of the Xi Jinping Thought on Comprehensive Rule of law, which also raises more demanding requirements on scientific, democratic and law-based legislation.

From the founding of the PRC to the formation of the Chinese socialist legal system, the Party's requirements on legislation as an essential part of rule of law, to be conclusive, is to ensure that there are laws to abide by. In the early twenty-first century, as the rule of law practice and theory developed, to carry out scientific and democratic legislation to improve the Chinese socialist legal system was put forward in the Seventeenth CPC National Congress. Scientific legislation was proposed for the first time. In the following congress, the Party proposed a new sixteen-character principles of rule of law, which put more emphasis on scientific legislation and asked to speed up legislation and improve its quality as the same time.

1.2 Theoretical Development Since 2000 Law on Legislation

1. Scientific, democratic and law-based legislation became a statutory principle for legislation and continues to be improved for the new era

The 1982 Constitution laid out the basic legal rules of legislative power enjoyed by the NPC and its Standing Committee and the State Council, but did not specify their division and institutions and mechanisms. In 1992, the goal of establishing socialist market economy was laid down in the Fourteenth CPC National Congress. In this system, the market should play the decisive role in allocation of resources. However, the local governments had issued numerous red-headed documents to intervene in the market and exclude non-local products, leading to local protectionism and market barriers. Unauthorized legislation often happened when matters subject to local regulations were incorporated into government rules to avoid "trouble", some local regulations changed the provisions of law to increase the types and scope of punishments, and the departmental interests were fervently pursued when some departments only eyed for their own interests and tried every means to expand their powers when drafting laws. The rules made by the governments and departments and the local regulations were often contradictory which disabled local law enforcement.[3] All these problems could be resolved by a law on legislation.

In the Third Session of the Ninth NPC, Gu Angran, the director of the Legislative Affairs Committee, pointed out in his Explanations on the Draft Law on Legislation that "China has made significant achievements and accumulated experience since 1979, but some problems still exist, for example, some regulations and rules exceed statutory power, are are contradictory among themselves or with the laws, and suffer from low quality and departmental interests, which have damaged the unification and dignity of the national legal system and caused difficulty to law enforcement". Some of them occurred due to their inconsistency with law that undermined unification of legal system, failure to observe the law of development and a lack of democracy during legislation. The 2000 Law on Legislation made provisions on law-based, democratic and scientific legislation respectively in Articles 4, 5 and 6 as the basic principles, and at the same time, specified the procedures for making laws, regulations and rules for standardization and institutionalization.

The Law put special emphasis on law-based legislation as exemplified by the preceding placement in its general provisions. After its adoption, the problem of failing to enact laws according to legal principles was resolved to a certain extent.

To further regulate legislative activities and promote scientific, democratic and law-based legislation, the basic principles and other provisions of the Law on Legislation were revised in 2005. First, to "improve legislation quality" was laid out as a basic requirement to strive for the laws enacted or revised can accurately reflect the Party's proposals and people's will, to ensure the firm foundation, operability and effectiveness of law and make law definite, responsive, systematic and enforceable. Second, to "play the role of leading and promoting development" was added to Article 1 to put into practice the requirements specified in the Fourth Session of the Eighteenth CPC Central Committee. This addition stressed the application of law to adjust interest relationships and promote development and reform for better coordination of political decision-making with legislative decision-making. Third, the revision also focused on democratic legislation and guaranteed the people with more channels to participate in legislation. For example, it added "adhere to open legislation" to Article 5, improved the provisions on the mechanisms of legislative argumentation, hearing, publicity of draft laws for public opinions, solicitation of opinions from the lower level people's congress, and introduction of experts in drafting laws, involvement of deputies in law drafting and revision, and the feedback on the acceptance of public opinions in law drafting. Fourth, it added "adapt to the requirements of economic and social development and deepening reform in all respects". As China's reform has entered a critical phase, to deepen the reforms in all respects must be reliant on innovation in institutions and mechanisms and to strengthen the institutional development is also essential for improving the legal

[3] QIAO Xiaoyang, *To Conduct the Research on Law on Legislation: Speech at the Seminar on Drafting the Law on Legislation*, Administrative Law Review, No. 3, p. 5 (1994).

system. Therefore, the work on legislation should be enhanced and improved to give a full play to the role of legislation in leading, promoting and securing reform.[4]

The revised Law granted the cities with subordinate districts with power to formulate local regulations on "urban and rural development and administration, environmental protection, and historical culture protection". As of August 2019, there were 322 cities with subordinate districts and autonomous prefectures with legislative power, with an increase of legislative bodies from 80 to over 300. These changes have presented more difficulties in maintaining unification of legal system, and put forward a new mission and requirements of Constitution-based and law-based legislation.

2. Basic Requirements

(1) Basic Requirements on Scientific Legislation

First, legislation should start from realities and adapt to the needs of economic and social development. As stated in the Book of Lord Shang, the emperors "established laws in accordance with what was opportune and regulated rites according to practical requirements".[5] What the legislation starts from realities refers to the full respect and reflection of the social relationships subject to the adjustment of legislation and making responses to economic and social development.[6] The legislators should carry out survey and study, develop a correct grasp of the economic and social development needs in different phases and regions, decide on the demands for legislation and accurately discern the urgency and importance in legislation to strive for each act of law-making conforming with objective requirements.

Second, to scientifically and reasonably determine the powers and responsibilities of state departments, and the rights and duties of citizens, legal persons and other organizations. A key link in the construction of the rule of law is to achieve the legalization of the exercise of state powers and avoid power scrambles and the evasion of responsibilities among the administrative departments. The consistency between powers and responsibilities should be pursued to avoid the legalization of departmental interests through legislative activities, and to assure the necessary powers for

---

[4] Office of State Law of the Legislative Affairs Committee of the National People's Congress ed., *Interpretations on the Law on Legislation of the People's Republic of China*, Law Press, 2015, pp. 4–8, 24–25, 27.

[5] Jan Julius Lodewijk Duyvendak, *The Book of Lord Shang*, Probsthain, 1928, p. 172.

[6] In different periods, the economic and social development may impose different requirements on legislation. For example, at the beginning of reform and opening-up, in response to the situation of no law to abide law, "something is better than nothing", "fast legislation is better than a slow one", and legal provision "could be rough" were the requirements on legislation. In the Decision of the Central Committee of the CPC on Some Issues concerning the Improvement of the Socialist Market Economy, to "strengthen economic legislation" and "establish a socialist market economy legal system" were the requirements. To improve the legal system for connecting with WTO rules was the requirement when China chose to accede to WTO. When the socialism with Chinese characteristics has entered a new era, to promote the Five-Sphere Integrated Plan and the Four-Pronged Comprehensive Strategy, advance comprehensive reform, fight for pollution prevention and control, promote and guarantee quality economic development, and carry out regional development strategies were the new requirements, and people's aspirations for a better life in democracy, rule of law, fairness, justice, security, environment, culture and tourism also constitute new requirements.

social governance. When prescribing the rights and duties, the provisions on citizens' fundamental rights and duties in the Constitution should be adhered to for educating them with the fact law is the weapon to protect rights and the code of conduct that they must observe. Any formulation of laws, regulations, rules and other normative documents should not limit or deprive people of these rights.

Third, to follow the rules of legislative techniques. Legislation is not only an important political activity, but also technical task with demanding expertise. It has its own law of development. To carry out legislation is a science itself, which requires the legislators to follow the rules. These rules include the structure, language, revision, repeal, interpretation, authorization and compilation. To take the rules on language as an example, the provisions of law should be accurate and rigorous to make the language of law standardized and unified, be concise and simple to avoid repetition in contents and expressions, and be characterized as a legal language to avoid copying the policy documents. If the provisions are vague and ambiguous, otherwise there will be no basis to resort to when applying the laws.

(2) Basic Requirements on Democratic Legislation

First, legislation should reflect the people's will. "The public good ought to be the object of the legislator; general utility ought to be the foundation of his reasoning."[7] The nature of the People's Republic of China is a socialist state under the people's democratic dictatorship as prescribed in the Constitution, so the legislation should serve the people's position as masters of the country and their participation in managing state and social affairs, and truly reflect the common will and interests of the majority of the people.

Second, to adhere to open legislation. Openness is a basic principle of the rule of law. To achieve democratic legislation, all the parties concerned should be fully informed of the legislation, its procedures and process. Open legislation is an important measurement of democracy in legislation. Open legislation is conducive to the people's supervision in the first place. The legislative power comes from the people, is responsible to the people, and supervised by the people. There will be no supervision over legislation if it is not open. Open legislation is also helpful to complement the representative legislation in what it might lack. The representative democracy is characterized by efficiency and strong professional expertise, but it lacks enough representation of public opinion. However, open legislation allows the public to directly participate and exercise legislative power and guarantees the people's right to be informed of the legislative process and development. Finally, since legislation is the initial distribution of interests, it should ensure that all the interest parties have equal opportunities to join the process. If the legislation is not sufficiently disclosed, there will be cheating and rent-seeking of power during the legislation by the parties who have a monopoly on information. As a result, the justice in legislation will be compromised. Therefore, open legislation should be

[7] Jeremy Bentham, *Theory of Legislation*, translated by Li Guifang et al., People's Public Security University of China, 2004, p. 1.

strictly upheld, and all the information from all stages of legislation, including planning, drafting, deliberation, assessment prior to adoption, assessment after adoption, regulation re-examination, and recording and review, should be disclosed as much as possible, except for the matters subject to state secrets and other circumstances.[8]

Third, to expand orderly participation. The people's participation in legislation is an important part of citizens' political participation, and it plays an important role in improving democratic politics, quality of legislation, and enforcement of laws. The law-making process itself is an important activity for political decision-making. Full and orderly legislative participation helps to enhance the public's political recognition of the country. Public participation can also improve the legality and fairness of legislative decision-making. In situations where the decision-making process is not democratic and public participation is not sufficient, the laws enacted may only represent the will of a few people, which impairs justice, or be put on the shelf once they are formulated, failing to solve any practical problems. Open, transparent, well-regulated and orderly participation in legislation process also helps guide and educate the public to reflect on the problems, exercise their rights, and reasonably articulate their demands in a law-based manner, help to boost the public's enthusiasm in observing the law, reduce the costs of law enforcement, and improve the outcomes of law enforcement. As Carl Cohen puts it, "the laws may be bad laws (and I may still oppose them) but the process of making them in which I participated obliges me to recognize their legitimacy and to obey them.... The obligation arises from the fact that in part I constitute that community; its laws are my laws; I helped to forge them".[9]

Orderly participation in legislation requires the legislature to choose a reasonable form of participation according to the needs and purposes of different legislative process. For example, the legislature may disclose draft laws for public opinion and convene expert meetings, hearings, consultation meetings, forums, and seminars, and allow citizens to sit on in meetings, and conduct surveys if major interests are involved It is also necessary to make procedures more detailed, including the

---

[8] Open legislation is an international practice. For example, the laws in the US, France, Japan make detailed rules on it. In the US, the draft laws or explanations on laws should be published by a joint notice, otherwise they will not come into force. The US Constitution prescribes that "each House shall keep a Journal of its Proceedings, and from time to time publish the same, excepting such Parts as may in their Judgment require Secrecy". In France, the 1791 Constitution also made similar provision that "the deliberations of the legislative body shall be public, and the procès-verbaux of its sessions shall be printed". The 1958 Constitution also affirmed it, which provided that "the sittings of the two Houses shall be public. A verbatim report of the debates shall be published in the Journal official". The Japanese Constitution also made it clear that "Each House shall keep a record of proceedings. This record shall be published and given general circulation, excepting such parts of proceedings of secret session as may be deemed to require secrecy", and deliberation in each House shall be public. However, a secret meeting may be held where a majority of two-thirds or more of those members present passes a resolution therefor. In conclusion, the records of deliberation on law and of the hearings are generally public. ZHANG Ping, *A Study on the Open Legislation of the Standing Committee of the National People's Congress*, Minzu University of China, Master Thesis, 2017.

[9] Carl Cohen, *Democracy*, translated by NIE Chongxin and ZHU Xiuxian, Commercial Press, 1988, p. 233. Also See Carl Cohen, *Democracy*, MPublishing, 2013, p. 230.

selection of participants, period of participation, deliberation rules, collection and analysis of opinions, feedback, and organizational guarantee. Each of these procedures involves complex considerations, for example, to select the participants should consider their representation, and their ability to deal with complex information, understand deliberation rules, make reasonable analyses and judgment, and reach rational decisions.

(3) Basic Requirements on Law-Based Legislation

First, to carry out legislation grounded in the Constitution. As the state's fundamental law with the highest legal effect, the Constitution is the general basis for establishing national systems and enacting laws and regulations. Article 3 of the Law on Legislation provides that laws are to be made in compliance with the basic principles laid down in the Constitution. As to the origins of law, the Constitution is the basis for the enactment of all laws, while, with respect to their contents, the enactment, revision, repeal and interpretation of all the laws and regulations should conform with the principles and requirements of the Constitution and shall not contravene them. Second, to carry out legislation according to statutory powers. Legislation is essentially an exercise of public power, which should adhere to the principle of "no action unless mandated by law" and strictly apply the statutory legislative power. In addition, the Constitution and the Law on Legislation make explicit provisions on the division of powers between the central authority and local authorities, and between the legislative authorities and administrative departments in respect of their legislative powers. The 2015 Law on Legislation further provides the legislative matters for different jurisdictions of legislative bodies, imposes more rules to regulate and limit the legislation on authorization, and grants legislative powers to cities with subordinate districts in three matters. The legislative bodies should accurately understand the powers and functions of legislation in different hierarchies, better deal with the relationship among the Constitution, law, administrative regulations, local regulations and rules and the relationship between creative and enforcement legislation, and give full play to the role of legislation in different hierarchies to maintain the unity of national legal system and better exercise the legislation according to law.[10]Third, to carry out legislation according to statutory procedures. Procedure precedes rights. Legislative process serves as a channel for resolving interest conflicts and allocating legislative resources. During the drafting, deliberation and promulgation, legislative process provides support to ensure all the legislative activities are carried out according to law. Process is inherent to the quality of legislation: passion, recklessness and arbitrariness will be dissolved by the process one by one, and only the reason will remain; partiality, greed and evil will be stopped one by one by the process, and only justice will remain.[11]The Law on Legislation, Rules of Procedure of the NPC Standing Committee, and the Law on the Organization of the State Council

[10] AN Dong, *To Uphold the Law-based, Scientific and Democratic Legislation and Improve Our Work on Legislation (Part 1)*, Legal Daily, December 14, 2016, p. 12.

[11] SUN Chao and XU Xianghua, *On Improving China's Legislative Process*, China Legal Science, Vol. 5, pp. 55–64 (2003).

and other laws lay down the rules on formulating law, administrative regulations and local regulations, including the rules on making legislative plan, schedule and programs, drafting, deliberation and voting, which is of great significance to prevent and overcome the arbitrariness in legislation and improve the regulation and institutionalization of legislation. Last, to implement the Party's principles and policies. The Constitution's preamble provides that building socialism with Chinese characteristics must adhere to the Party's leadership. Article 1 as amended in 2018 was added with a provision that "leadership by the CPC is the defining feature of socialism with Chinese characteristics". By performing the legislative functions through the system of people's congresses, the Party's proposals are upgraded into the will of the state via statutory process. This creates a code of conduct to be universally observed by all the people, manifesting the integration of the Party's proposals with the people's fundamental interests, which is the core experience accumulated from China's legislative practices.

2 Practices (1949–1978)

On the eve of the founding of PRC, considering that the conditions for convening the national people's congress and enacting a constitution were not ripe, the Party convened the First Plenary Session of the CPPCC, in which the Common Program was adopted as an interim constitution. The new Constitution was adopted in September 1954. However, between 1957 and 1976, the undertakings of the Party and the State were seriously damaged and the state departments were also disabled due to the mistakes in the Party's guiding principles. Except for the Outline on National Agricultural Development (1956–1967) and 1975 Constitution, the NPC, as the only legislative authority in China, did not enact any law of any kind. Therefore, before the reform and opening-up, the Common Program and 1954 Constitution are representative of scientific and democratic legislation.

2.1 Common Program and 1954 Constitution: Living Examples of Scientific and Democratic Legislation

1. Legislative Process and Features of Common Program

Under the Party's leadership, the Common Program was formulated to promote democracy and oppose dictatorship, and the process of its initiation, main participants, and main contents embodied the spirit of striving for science and democracy, which laid the constitutional foundation for founding PRC and acted as an interim constitution.

First, the process of initiating its formulation. Before the Anti-Japanese War was won by the Chinese, Mao Zedong pointed out in his On Coalition Government written in 1945 that "the urgent need is to unite representatives of all political parties and groups and of people without any party affiliation and establish a provisional democratic coalition government... After that it will be necessary to convene a national assembly on a broad democratic basis and set up a formally constituted democratic government, which will also be a coalition and will have a still wider representation of people from all parties and groups or without any party affiliation". In 1948, the Central Committee made a call to convene a political consultative conference as soon as possible to discuss and convene the people's congress and establish a coalition government, which was received with welcome by the Chinese people, democratic parties, people's organizations, nonpartisan democrats, people of minority ethnic groups, and overseas Chinese. The Party had been firm in promoting democracy and opposing dictatorship in addressing the important question of how to establish a new China. Such integration of democracy into political practice has been a good practice since the founding of the PRC, laying the legal and political foundation for founding the PRC.

Second, the participants and process. The Common Program is the achievement of collective wisdom. On June 15, 1949, the organization committee for the political consultative conference was established, which consisted of 134 members of 23 organizations including CPC, other democratic parties, democrats of all social organizations, ethnic minorities and overseas Chinese. In their meeting, it was decided to establish six groups, of which the third one was responsible for drafting the Common Program. The initial draft was prepared by the CPC, which took "serving the people whole-heartedly" as its mission. From the date the draft was submitted to its adoption at the sixth session of the organization committee' standing committee, it was discussed twice by all the deputies (about five to six hundred) in groups, by the drafting group for three times, and by the standing committee twice apart from the internal discussions held in the democratic parties. All of the deputies put their heads together to discuss every word and carefully select the expressions.[12]

Third, collectively representing the people's will and interests. As stipulated in the Common Program, people are the masters of the new China, "the state power belongs to the people", "laws and decrees protecting the people shall be enacted", people has the right to elect and stand for election and other extensive freedoms and rights, women shall enjoy equal rights with men in political, economic, cultural, educational and social life, the freedom of marriage for men and women should be put into effect, all the state agencies and organizations should be named with the expression of "people", and regional autonomy should be practiced in areas

[12] Some opinions were adopted or partially adopted, others were referenced in later revisions. For example, Luo Longji, deputy of China Democratic League, thought that "it did not mention the personal freedom, please give an explanation" since all kinds of freedoms were incorporated in the constitutional text. His opinion was adopted by adding a provision on personal freedom in Article 5. After it was adopted in the Second Plenary Session of CPPCC's organization committee on September 17, 1949, it was revised again. The whole process of its formulation demonstrated the democratically agreed draft which incorporated the opinions of all the parties and reflected the spirit of science. XU Chongde, *The History of the Constitution of the People's Republic of China (Vol. 1)*, Fujian People's Publishing House, 2005, p. 31.

where national minorities are concentrated. These provisions have demonstrated that Common Program is an outline that reflects people's interests.

Fourth, its provisions in conformity with China's conditions and realities. On the eve of the PRC, to continue the War of Liberation until success, to restore national economy, to finish agrarian land reform and to exterminate the feudalism was the central tasks, which were also incorporated in the Common Program. As prescribed by it, the nature of PRC was a new democratic state, the interests of petty bourgeoisie and national bourgeoisie were protected when making economic policies, for example the policies of considering both public and private interests, of benefiting both labor and capital were also made, rather than eliminating the national bourgeoisie. These provisions reflected China's conditions at that time and the realities.

2. Legislative Process and Features of 1954 Constitution

At the end of 1953, Mao Zedong went to Hangzhou along with the constitutional drafting committee to devise the first constitution of the PRC, which was later adopted in the First Session of the First National People's Congress held in September 1954. The process of enacting it demonstrated the spirit of science and democracy, acting as a living example of scientific and democratic legislation. Mao Zedong even proclaimed that "constitution-making is a matter of science", which could be illustrated as follows:

First, to extensively solicit public opinions as to whether the Constitution was to be made. To convene a National People's Congress and enact a constitution were fundamental to the operations of a nation, which required seeking the common foundation among all the communities by negotiating with all social classes, groups and ranks in equal terms before decisions were made in order. However, the opinions varied as to whether to enact a constitution. In order to listen to the views of all social sectors on the issue of constitution-making, Mao Zedong held a discussion with 18 heads of democratic parties on January 11, 1953 and a day later, Zhou Enlai convened a forum of the CPPCC to listen to the opinions on this issue.[13]

Second, the composition of the constitutional drafting commission was very representative. In January 1953, the constitutional drafting commission was established under the Central People's Government Council, and with Mao Zedong as the chairman incorporated delegates from other democratic parties, non-partisan democrats, people's organizations and others.[14]

---

[13] HAN Dayuan, *The Legislative Process of 1954 Constitution*, Law Press, 2014, p. 76.

[14] The Commission consisted of Mao Zedong (chairman), Zhu De, Song Qingling, Li Jishen, Li Weihan, He Xiangning, Shen Junru, Shen Yanbing, Zhou Enlai, Lin Boqu, Lin Feng, Hu Qiaomu, Wu Lanfu, Ma Yinchu, Ma Xulun, Chen Yun, Chen Shutong, Chen Jiageng, Zhang Lan, Guo Moruo, Xi Zhongxun, Huang Yanpei, Peng Dehuai, Chen Qian, Dong Biwu, Liu Shaoqi, Deng Xiaoping, Deng Zihui, Sai Fuding, Bo Yibo and Rao Sushi. Some of them were top leaders, some were representatives of other democratic parties. For example, Ma Xulun was the member of the Central People's Government Council and a renowned representative of a democratic party. Ma Yinchu was the president of Peking University, a representative from the academia. In terms of the composition, it was a high-standard, widely representative and authoritative organization, reflecting the authority and wide-participation in the constitution making. *Ibid.*, pp. 79–80.

Third, from March 23 to June 11, 1954, the constitutional drafting commission held seven plenary sessions. During these sessions, over 8000 people were organized by the National Committee of CPPCC, the leading authorities from the greater administrative areas, provinces and municipalities as well as from local organizations of other democratic parties and people's organizations and armed forces to discuss it, which contributed over 5900 opinions. Some of them were adopted in revision. In the following initiatives to call for people to join the discussion, over 150 million people were involved to study, spread and discuss the draft constitution. At the same time, the people's congress meetings were held in various provinces, municipalities, counties and some towns and townships. From June 15 to September 10, over 1.18 million pieces of opinions were solicited from the Chinese people across the country. After being sent to Beijing, they were summarized and classified by the office of the constitutional drafting commission and printed into 16 volumes of Collection of Opinions of Chinese People on Draft Constitution.

Fourth, to practice democracy and respect expert opinions and reject the "echo chamber". For example, in reviewing the provision that allowed the NPC Standing Committee to exercise the power of ratifying and abrogating the treaties with foreign states, Mao Zedong commented that "this provision should follow the opinions of Zhou Gengsheng",[15] the legal counsel appointed by the commission, who studied in Japan, France and Britain and was an international law expert. Such adherence to the opinions of experts, which could be found in the whole constitution-making process, reflected the democratic spirit that did not judge them correct or wrong simply from their social status and ranks.

Fifth, to learn from the constitution-making experience in China and abroad. As Liu Shaoqi pointed out in his report, the Constitution "is not only the product of the people's revolutionary movement in China, but also a product of the international socialist movement". The 1936 Constitution of Soviet Union, 1946 Constitution of Vietnam, 1947 Constitution of Bulgaria, 1948 Constitution of North Korea, 1949 Constitution of Hungary, 1952 Constitution of Poland and other socialist constitutions had an important influence on the environment and process of China's constitution-making at that time.[16]When preparing the draft constitution in Hangzhou, Mao Zedong mentioned in his telegram to the leaders of Central Committee including Liu Shaoqi that the 1913 Draft Constitution, 1923 Constitution and 1946 Constitution of China, 1946 Constitution of France and other important constitutional texts should be referred to. Some of them were socialist constitutions, while the others were capitalist. In Mao's opinions, the 1912 Provisional Constitution of the Republic of China was good at that time though it was still incomplete and flawed. He also emphasized the features of 1946 Constitution of France, which represented a relatively progressive and complete one of the bourgeois cabinet systems. In analyzing the modern China's constitutional texts from Nineteen Articles enacted in 1911 by the Qing Government to the 1912 Provisional Constitution of the Republic

[15] Mu Zhaoyong, *Records of the First National People's Congress (1954)*, Guang People's Publishing House, p. 136.

[16] Han Dayuan, *The Legislative Process of 1954 Constitution*, Law Press, 2014, p. 62.

of China, he also found what they had in common was the small number of provisions and concise in language, which inspired him. He then proposed that the constitution text under drafting had better have no more than 100 articles, its language should be concise and its provisions should avoid the potential of multiple interpretations.

As the state leader, Mao Zedong's comments on the text also reflected the science and democracy in constitution-making. For example, "the preamble should have an explanation", "this article seems to be moved into the general provisions", "the 'agrarian land reform' is not a full sentence, 'institutional' should be added", "'the suppression of counter-revolutionary' should be added with 'elements'", and "pro-mulgation' had better be omitted to avoid conflicts with the powers and functions of the president". These comments were made mainly on specific institutional designs and use of language in constitution, which reflected that Mao Zedong and other older generation proletarian revolutionaries paid great attention to the characteristics of the constitution as a legal document and to the scientific nature of the constitutional language so as to make it accurately and carefully worded. In addition, when he had different opinions on the draft, he often adopted "had better" and "inappropriate", but did not use his position as a leader to suppress dissenting opinions. In conclusion, in the process of constitution-making, everyone participated in the discussions with equal status, and did not blindly follow authority but respected the science that governs constitution-making.[17]

Last, the effective enforcement of the Constitution proves it scientific. Practice is the sole criterion for testing truth. The 1954 Constitution was subject to the test of practice to determine whether it was good or not. In the first 3 years of promulgation, it was well enforced since all the relevant parties paid attention to it. As Peng Zhen reflected, "when deciding any major issue, Mao Zedong and Zhou Enlai would ask 'does it conform with the Constitution?'" The leaders of the Central Committee made decisions based on the Constitution. In this period, the people's congresses at all levels performed their powers and functions and played their roles in state life of all respects. The NPC and its Standing Committee enacted over 80 laws and decrees and sped up the drafting of Criminal Law and Civil Law; the draft Criminal Law was at its 22nd edition in 1957, which was submitted to NPC deputies for their opinions. The NPC and its Standing Committee also made a lot of important decisions after discussions.[18]The construction of democratic legal system and the people's congresses were under normal operations in this period, and the national political, economic and social undertakings were carried out in an orderly way, all of which were inseparable from the effective implementation of the Constitution.

The process of enacting the 1954 Constitution stands as one of the best examples of scientific and democratic legislation since 1949. The current 1982 Constitution, which was formulated based on the 1954 Constitution, also reflects a continuity and identification with it.

---

[17] *Ibid.*, pp. 93–96.

[18] LIU Zheng, *Why the 1954 Constitution was Abandoned Three Years After Its Promulgation*, The People's Congress of China, Vol. 14, pp. 42–43 (2002).

2.2 *Practices (After 1978)*

Since the reform and opening-up, the NPC and its Standing Committee have adopted a problem-oriented approach to improving the legislative system, innovating and reflecting on their legislative mechanisms, which has contributed to a lot of good practices and helped to institutionalize the scientific, democratic and law-based legislation. This experience and these good practices are elaborated as follows:

1. To insist on thc Party's leadership in legislation

The Party's leadership in legislation is a basic principle for the socialist rule of law. As pointed out by Peng Zhen, laws are enacted for the purpose of formalizing the Party's and the government's guiding principles and policies. In 1979, Peng Zhen drafted a report which required that the issues and opinions for drafting and revision of laws and regulations should be reported the Central Committee, which established the instruction-seeking and reporting system. In 1991, the Central Committee formulated a document on the Party's leadership in legislation based on past experience, which decided that its leadership was to be mainly excised concerning important guidelines and policies, laid down the rules for the discussion of important laws and procedures, and made it clear that it would support and guarantee the NPC and its Standing Committee in fully exercising their legislative power.

Since the Eighteenth CPC National Congress, the Central Committee has paid even more attention to legislation and continued to improve the institutions and mechanisms for exercising its leadership over legislation. In the Fourth Plenary Session of the Eighteenth CPC Central Committee dedicated to advancing rule of law in all respects, the Party laid out the requirements that "any adjustment of major institution or policy by the legislation should be reported to the CPC Central Committee for discussion and final decision" and others. In a document on strengthening the Party's leadership in legislation issued by the Central Committee in 2016, it further clarified the Party's leadership in legislation: the Central Committee should lead the national legislation and decide on the major issues in it, the party committees to which the local legislature corresponds should take the lead in its legislation based on the Central Committee's line and principles, and it was put forward to establish a distribution of functions for legislation in which the Party takes the leading role, the people's congress takes charge of legislation, the government provide support and other parties join in the legislative process. New arrangements and requirement were made clear on advancing rule of law and the work on legislation in the meetings of the Commission for Law-based Governance under the CPC Central Committee held in 2018 and 2019.[19]

[19] In the history of legislative practices, the Party's leadership in legislation can be summarized as follows: General Secretary Xi Jinping and the Central Committee directly assign legislative tasks; the Party's meeting resolutions, documents and other arrangements for legislation; the Central Committee directly proposes to amend the constitution and enact laws; examınes and approves the legislative plans of the NPC Standing Committee and approve important legislative programs; the Central Committee deliberates on relevant parties' instructions-seeking on important legislative matters; formulates intra-Party normative documents to regulate Party's leadership in legislation;

The NPC and its Standing Committee have been strictly adhering to the decisions and put into practice the requirements proposed by the Central Committee, practiced the instruction-seeking and reporting system and strengthened the legislation in key areas. Under the Party's leadership, the work on legislation has made a lot of progress. For example, in the First Session of the Thirteenth National People's Congress, the glorious task of amending the Constitution was finally completed,[20]the guiding position of Xi Jinping Thought on Socialism with Chinese characteristics for a New Era was established for national political and social life, and the overall leadership of the Party was nourished and strengthened. In addition, when enacting the Supervision Law, E-Commerce Law, Law on Prevention and Control of Soil Pollution, all the parts of Civil Code, and revising the Criminal Procedure Law, Rural Land Contract Law, Civil Servants Law, Law on the Organization of People's Courts and Law on the Organization of People's Procuratorates, the Central Committee's decisions and arrangements were unswervingly put in to practice through the Party Group of the NPC Standing Committee seeking instructions and reporting to it.

2. To improve legislative institutions

The Legislative institutions change as the political institution reform, economic development and social transformation take place. Before the revision of the Local Organization Law in 1979, China practiced a highly centralized institution of legislation, i.e. the legislative power was centralized in the National People's Congress, which was also to meet the political demands of practicing a highly centralized planned economic system. However, it only played the role of the central initiative, not the local initiative. Since the Third Plenary Session of the Eleventh CPC Central Committee, to conform to the transformation of focus and stimulate both the central and local initiatives, the legislative institution had been under gradual improvement through the enactment of the Constitution and Local Organization Law, and a sharing of legislative power between the legislature and administrative authorities and between the central and local authorities under the centralized and unified leadership of the Central Committee, which helped to give impetus to the central and local initiatives, provide the people with more opportunities to participate in

strengthen the organizational leadership and supervision of the implementation of the work on legislation; and strengthen the organizational leadership and team building of the Central Committee in the work on legislation. Research Office of the Legislative Affairs Committee of the NPC Standing Committee ed. *Introduction to the Legislative Achievements in the Past 40 Years*, Law Press, 2019, pp. 18–21.

[20] Since the promulgation of 1954 Constitution, China has established a constitutional practice in which the Central Committee proposes the NPC Standing Committee to amend the Constitution according to changes of realities, and the NPC Standing Committee drafts the amendment and submits to NPC for deliberation. After the promulgation of 1982 Constitution, the Central Committee has proposed for five times to the NPC Standing Committee to amend the Constitution based on the practice and development of reform and opening-up and socialist modernization, which makes necessary amendments, in total 52, to provisions and some parts of 1982 Constitution. They also reflect China's economic and social development and the Constitution's adherence to the change of time for better development.

the management of state and social affairs, and make legislation more scientific and democratic.

First, to grant the legislative power of the state to the NPC and its Standing Committee. the 1982 Constitution specified the provisions on the legislative power of the NPC and its Standing Committee. The 2000 Law on Legislation made provisions on the division of legislative powers, and the 2015 Law on Legislation after revision put into practice of statutory taxation by adding the provision that "the establishment of a tax, determination of tax rates, tax collection administration and other basic taxation rules". Second, to grant to the State Council and gradually regulate its exercise of legislative power. The 1982 Constitution granted the power to make regulations to the State Council for the first time, and the 2015 Law on Legislation established the system of authorization based on specific matters and provided details on the content and time limit of such authorization. Third, to grant and increase the legislative power to the local people's congresses and their standing committees. The 1979 Local Organization Law authorized such local legislative power for the first time, which was later confirmed by the 1982 Constitution. The revised 1986 Local Organization Law provided that the people's congresses and their standing committees of the cities where the provincial capital reside and the large cities approved by the State Council have the power to formulate local regulations and implement them after approval of principal people's congresses. The 2000 Law on Legislation specified that the local regulations could be formulated on two matters and granted the people's congresses and their standing committee of the cities where the special economic zones were located with the power to formulate local regulations. To implement the gist of the third and fourth sessions of the Eighteenth CPC Central Committee, the 2015 Law on Legislation allowed the people's congresses and their standing committees of the cities with subordinate districts to formulate local regulations on urban and rural development and administration, environmental protection, and historic and cultural protection, which should be implemented after the approval of their provincial people's congresses.

In addition, the Constitution and Law on Legislation granted the autonomous regions the power to formulate self-governance regulations and separate regulations, and the latter also specified the provisions on department rules and local government rules.

3. To Improve Working Mechanisms

In recent years, based on continuous summary of experience, the NPC Standing Committee has made remarkable achievements in improving relevant legal institutions and establishing legislative working mechanisms, which significantly improves legislative quality and efficiency.

First, to establish mechanisms for collecting legislative programs and conducting argumentation. The NPC Standing Committee formulated a set of procedures on collecting legislative programs and conducting argumentation, which required extensive collection of public opinions on legislative programs when compiling or adjusting the legislative plans and annual legislative schedules.

Second, to establish and improve the mechanism on soliciting public opinion on draft laws. All the draft laws after first and second deliberation should be published online for public opinions.[21] In the document that asked to solicit the opinions of NPC deputies on draft laws issued in 2015, in addition to publishing on the NPC portal for deputies' opinions, it paid more attention to the opinions of the deputies who are engaged in law practices and ever submitted the similar bills and suggestions. The NPC Standing Committee also established community liaison offices for legislation, held forums, hearings and seminars, distributed questionnaires, conducted field surveys and interviews to collect the suggestions of experts, deputies, administrative officials and CPPCC members, and continued to improve the practice of appointing counsellors to legislation.[22]

Third, to improve the deliberation mechanism. The NPC has established a three-step deliberation and reading mechanism on legislation, and a mechanism of a combination of individual and uniform deliberation to take advantage of the expertise of the special committees and the authoritative unification of the Constitution and Law Committee. The NPC Standing Committee also established the mechanism on postponing and terminating the submission for voting.

Fourth, to improve the procedures on draft laws voting. The 2015 Law on Legislation establish the practice of individual voting on important articles, in which the Chairman may decide, based on the Standing Committee's deliberations, to submit individual articles on which opinions greatly differ before the bill subject to voting is passed to the Standing Committee for deliberation and voting.

Fifth, to establish mechanisms for assessment before and after a draft law is passed. Before the Standing Committee deliberates on and passed the draft laws under new enactment, complete revision or revision of important institutions, the assessment on the feasibility and timing of major institutions in the draft laws and the potential social impact and issues will be conducted. When the law is enforced for a period of time, the assessment will also be carried out to review its enforcement and social effect of the institutions stipulated by referring to a combination of qualitative and

[21] In July 2013, in addition to publishing the first law drafts for public opinions, the NPC Standing Committee, for the first time, published the second Draft Law on Environment Protection for public opinions, which received 2434 suggestions and 48 letters. The two disclosures of draft laws received a total of over 14 thousand opinions of 10, 394 people. The practice of publishing the second draft law has been normalized since then.

[22] In 2005, the Law Committee, the Finance and Economy Committee, and the Legislative Affairs Committee held the legislative hearing for the first time on the standards of deductions from wages and income involved in the revision of the Individual Income Tax Law to listen to the opinions of citizens and relevant parties. There were 20 representatives selected from over 5000 applicants, and other 8 representatives from the enacting body, All-China Federation of Trade Unions and the departments of finance and taxation of 4 provinces (including autonomous regions municipalities directly under the State Council). In addition to presenting their opinions, reasons and arguments, another 18 representatives submitted written opinions. Yang Jingyu, the Director of the Law Committee pointed out when he chaired the hearing that "the deductions are concerned with the reasonable adjustment of income and directly involves the interests of people. In the process of deliberating the Draft Individual Income Tax Law by the NPC Standing Committee, this hearing is held for soliciting public opinions, which is an important step to adhere to the mass line, promote democracy, increase legislative transparency, and advance democratic legislation".

quantitative analyses, which is intended to provide basis for improving the law and the work on legislation and enforcement.

Sixth, to specify the working rules for conducting consultations on major interest adjustments in legislation and introducing third-party assessment on the legislative matters that cause major disagreement. To strictly follow the problem-solving approach, these rules will improve the legislative quality and efficiency, avoiding improper and inaccurate decision-making and delays in legislation.

Seventh, to improve the work on legislative field surveys. The NPC Standing Committee adopts various field survey methods through direct contacts to resolve the legislative matters by strictly following the problem-solving approach.

Eighth, to formulate rules on legislative techniques. By continuing to summarize the experience in legislative practices, the Legislative Affairs Committee centralize the common opinions on the matters that are frequent, universal, urgent and easy for agreement in a set of technical rules, i.e. the Rules on Legislative Techniques (for Trial Implementation) exclusive for its staff, which are important for drafting, deliberating on and revising law. According to the directive of the NPC Standing Committee's leaders to study the legislative techniques, the Committee has analyzed the issues arising out of the formulation and implementation of local legislative techniques, actively revised the rules, and published the proposed rules and explanations for public opinion to achieve better standardization.

Ninth, to supervise the formulation of supporting regulations to strive for synchronous drafting, promulgation and implementation. For example, on August 31, 2018, the Individual Income Tax Law was adopted in the Fifth Session of the Thirteenth NPC Standing Committee. To guarantee its enforcement, the State Council proactively revised the Regulation on Implementing the Individual Income Tax Law, which came into force on January 1, 2019, the same date on which the Law also became effective.

Tenth, to play the leading role of the people's congress and its standing committee. The enactment and revision of important law bills must be deliberated by the people's congress, a practice which has been carried out for five consecutive years. The NPC Standing Committee also makes it a institutional practice to organize the special committees and their working agencies to draft important laws, analyze the suggestions of the deputies, continue to expand the channels for their participation in legislation, and invite relevant some of them to join in the surveys and argumentation.

Last, the NPC Standing continues to establish the mechanism for legislative interpretation and has set up the position of spokesman to actively spread the legislative achievements and respond to social concerns.

4. To persist in combining the rule of law and rule of virtue and incorporate the core socialist values into legislation

As Xi Jinping stated, "law is virtue committed to writing, while virtue is law inscribed in people's hearts. Both law and virtue possess the power to achieve certain standards of social behavior and preserve social order. In the governance of our country and society, we need to emphasize both rule of law and rule of virtue, valuing the normative function of law, while also attaching importance to the edifying effect of virtue, so that law and virtue complement each other and rule of law and rule of virtue promote each other."[23] In the Guiding Opinions on Further Integrating Core Socialist Values into Construction of Rule of Law issued by the Central Committee and the State Council in December 2016, it was directed to analyze in depth the need for the legislation on the development of core socialist values and vigorously advance legislation in relevant fields so as to make the laws and regulations better manifest the value pursuits of the country, society and citizens. In May 2018, the Central Committee issued the Plan on Law Enactment and Revision for Integrating Core Socialist Values into the Construction of Rule of Law, which emphasized the complete and full incorporation of core socialist values into the enactment, revision, repeal and interpretation of law and strived to completely incorporate the values into the Chinese socialist legal system in 5–10 years. To put it into practice, the NPC and its Standing Committee paid more attention to promoting the values in legislation. For example, in the General Provisions of Civil Law, "to promote core socialist values" was added into Article 1, and the articles on encouraging voluntary help in dire need regardless of danger and prohibiting the violation of public order and good practices were also laid down. The core socialist values were written down in the Constitution amendment adopted in the First Session of the Thirteenth NPC. The Law on the Protection of Heroes and Martyrs adopted in April 2018 implemented the gist of Xi Jinping's remarks on respecting, defending, learning from and caring about the heroes and martyrs, and it strengthened the protection and punished acts of distorting, defaming, or insulting the heroes and martyrs, which helped to promote the spirit of heroes and martyrs and the spirit of patriotism in the whole society. Its formulation was highly welcomed by the people, and made more manifestations of core socialist values.

5. To strengthen the work on recording and review of regulations

To carry out the recording and review of normative documents is a Constitutional design that conforms with China's conditions and presents its unique characteristics and an institutional development to ensure the enforcement of the Constitution and law and maintain the unity of national legal system. Since the reform and opening-up, the legislative institutions have continued to improve, legislative activities at all levels have gained momentum, and the number of administrative and local regulations has increased. All of these have accentuated the importance of recording and review of regulations. However, this practice was not formally initiated until the formulation of Law on Legislation in 2000. Then it became an institution as the rules of procedure and other normative documents on recording and reviewing administrative regulations, local regulations, self-governance regulations, separate regulations, and regulations of economic zones as well as the judicial interpretations were successively formulated. In 2004, the Legislative Affairs Committee set up the office of regulations recording and review to be in charge of studying and reviewing

[23] The Central Literature Research Office ed., *The Law-Based Governance of China*, Central Party Literature Press, 2017, pp. 33–34.

the administrative regulations, local regulations and judicial interpretations for better serving the performance of NPC Standing Committee in this regard.

Great importance has also been attached by the Central Committee to specifying the requirements on strengthening the capacity for recording and reviewing the normative documents in its third and fourth sessions. Based on these requirements, the NPC Standing Committee has made more efforts in the following two aspects:

On one hand, to strengthen the supervision. The NPC Standing Committee has proactively reviewed the regulations and judicial interpretations one by one and given its opinions on them, consolidated the efforts on reviewing the suggestions proposed by citizens and organizations for reviewing local regulations and judicial interpretations, and issued correction opinions It also carried out specialized reviews, for example, on the 49 local regulations on natural reserve protection according to the Central Committee's circular on the issues and lessons from the Qilian Mountain. The NPC Standing Committee has also promoted a comprehensive initiative on reviewing the normative documents on ecological and environmental protection.

On the other hand, to spare more efforts to improve the mechanism for and build up the capacity for recording and reviewing. The NPC Standing Committee laid down the working rules on giving feedback to the review suggestions made by the citizens and organizations and issued the Rules and Procedures on the Recording and Review of Regulations and Judicial Interpretations in order to make it more institutionalized and standardized. It consolidated the work on improving the national information platform for recording and review, which was established at the end of 2016 and could be connected with the provincial platforms, established a collaboration mechanism with the General Office of the Central Committee on recording and review for an initial interconnecting framework. The NPC Standing Committee also established the practice of listening to the reports on recording and review, and put it into practice from 2017. A unified set of rules on recording and review has also been under progress, the training, study and exchanges carried out, and its guidance on local people's congress's work on it strengthened.

3 Developments

As Chinese socialism enters a new era, people's expectations for legislation are no longer limited to having laws to abide by, but exntend to good, effective and practical laws. The focus of the work on legislation has been shifted from the pursuit for the number of laws to the aspirations for good laws that foster sound governance. Therefore, the work on legislation in the new era should enhance the implementation of the principle of scientific, democratic and law-based legislation, By referring to the transformation of social contradictions and people's aspirations for a better life, it must adhere to the connection of legislative decision with reform decision, strictly follow the logic of legislative activities, strengthen the constraints on any violation of the law of legislation, and strive for better legislative quality.

3.1 To Adhere to the Guidance of Xi Jinping Thought on Socialism with Chinese Characteristics

The Party's leadership is the most essential feature of Chinese socialism and the fundamental guarantee for advancing the rule of law in all respects and accelerating the construction of socialist rule of law country. In this case, legislation should adhere to the guidance of the Xi Jinping Thought on Socialism with Chinese characteristics, implement the new concepts, new thinking and new strategies, and stick to the Party's leadership, and in particular the Central Committee's centralized and unified leadership in legislation in order to ensure the effective implementation of the Party's major decisions for the legislation.

The rule of law thinking and approaches should be strictly applied to help make the Party's leadership in legislation institutionalized, regulated and procedurally sound. The Party's role in exercising overall leadership and coordinating all the respects should be played to ensure the legislation always follows the correct direction. The relationship between the Party's leadership and the people's congress's leading role should be correctly understood: the institutions on Party's leadership in legislation should be strengthened to ensure that the legislation reflects the requirements on the Party and state's undertakings and people's aspirations, while such leadership should be exercised according to the Constitution and law and by respecting the procedures and logic of legislation.

3.2 To Abide by the Constitution and Maintain the Unity of Socialist Legal System

Since the Eighteenth CPC National Congress, the methods for the governance of the Party and state have been profoundly transformed. Xi Jinping has emphasized several times that advancing the rule of law should take Constitution-based governance as the top priority. Legislation should strictly adhere to the Constitution's principles and spirit for effective Constitution enforcement.

First, to keep the Constitution always in mind. Any deliberation and revision of law bills, research of major issues, and design of major institutions should always stick to the Constitution to make every legislation decision conform with the Constitution's spirits. Second, to put into practice the 2018 Constitution Amendment and carry out the law-making on it. For example, it wrote down the "beautiful" country, which required the NPC Standing Committee to strengthen its legislation on ecology and environment protection. Third, to improve the mechanism on interpretation of the Constitution. The problem of understanding the Constitution's provisions is inevitable, and an authoritative, efficient, standardized and orderly constitutional interpretation mechanism should be established to respond to the needs in this regard. Fourth, to actively and prudently promote the work on constitutional review. As advocated in the report of the Nineteenth CPC National Congress, the efforts should be made to strengthen oversight to ensure compliance with the Constitution, advance constitutionality review, and safeguard the authority of the Constitution. Based on the recording and review, it is necessary to improve the institutional arrangements for the work on constitutional review, establishing its working mechanism, innovate its working methods, resolutely correct any violation of the Constitution and law, and protect the authority and dignity of the Constitution.

3.3 To Improve the Investigation and Research Methods and Seek Truth from Facts to Reflect Social Needs

Scientific legislation requires that the provisions of law conform with realities and reflect and address the social needs arising from these realities. Therefore, the legislation should adopt a problem-solving approach with more research and investigations for more effective provisions directly addressed to specific issues. Some laws are not effective due to a lack of in-depth research and investigation, which results in a failure to accurately reflect and respond to real social needs when making the decision and devising the institutions in legislation.

The knowledge comes from practice. Legislation is nothing but a practice. If no in-depth research and investigation are made, there will be no possibility of grasping the intention of the Central Committee's decisions. In this case, the laws enacted cannot be called "good" no matter how skilled the legislature is and how rigorous the legislative logic is. Compared with the work of the courts and procuratorates, the focus of the people's congress's work is to write texts and hold meetings for convergence of ideas. However, to write a good text requires good investigations and research. Investigation is purported to figure out the particularity of a thing, and research to grasp the generality of the things of the same kind. To draft and deliberate on a good article of law, investigation and research are the prerequisites. The work on investigation and research can be characterized into six words: in-depth, solid, detailed, accurate and effective. To be in-depth refers to joining in the people and the communities, making friends with workers, farmers, intellectuals and others, and addressing issues in the farmlands, factories and other places. To be solid refers to adopting intimate style, simplifying official receptions and finding the true ideas, circumstances and problems by field surveys. To be detailed refers to a full grasp of the overall situation by listening to opinions of all relevant parties and an in-depth analysis. To be accurate is not only to develop a comprehensive, in-depth and meticulous understanding of the actual situation, but also to be good at analyzing contradictions, discovering problems, looking at the essence from the surface, and finding the regularities. To be effective means to provide practical solutions, effective measures and produce the best efficiency.[24] In conclusion, to achieve these requires adherence to the truth, not to the books or the ideas of leaders, facing contradictions

---

[24] Xi Jinping, *Zhejiang, China: A New Vision for Development*, Zhejiang People's Publishing House, 2007, p. 1.

and problems head-on, and ensuring the endurance of the legislative solutions and institutions as will be tested by practice.

Now the principal contradiction facing Chinese society has evolved. What we now face is the contradiction between unbalanced and inadequate development and the people's ever-growing needs for a better life. The demands and expectations for rule of law and legislation differ among regions, urban and rural areas and social classes. The legislator should delve themselves into the practice, communities and people, and tirelessly, truly and accurately grasp these needs and expectations, to devise scientific institutions and make law the true stabilizer for allocating social interests, adjusting social relations and resolving social contradictions.

3.4 To Stick to the Combination of Rule of Law and Rule of Virtue to Strengthen Legislation on Promoting Core Socialist Values

Social ethical issues have also become prominent and people are seeking a solution. Therefore, the legislation should focus more efforts on regulating the acts that go against morality. For example, the core values that reflect social morality, good family practices, personal behaviors, excellent traditional culture, red culture and good culture are to be integrated into the legislation to inherit and spread the excellent traditional culture and help build a positive, healthy and upright online cultural atmosphere. In addition, the legislation should also help to resist the culture nihilism in order to form a good social atmosphere of advocating, defending, learning the Heroes and Martyrs and caring for their families, to prevent school bullying and violence, improve the law-abiding and integrity reward mechanism and joint punishment mechanism on illegal and dishonest acts and refine the social assistance system. In a word, the legislation is dedicated to promoting a good social atmosphere of respecting women, caring for minors and the disabled, esteeming the elderly, revering and giving preferential treatment to the veterans and family members of martyrs.

However, we should avoid mechanical implementation of Central Committee's documents and not neglect the difference between law and virtue. They have different functions: law regulates people's external behaviors and safeguards public order, putting emphasis on equal treatment of rights and duties; morality regulates people's inner world and corrects people's mind for goodness. In light of this, they regulate different social relationships. For example, filial piety, friendship and offering seats in public transportation are more appropriate to be promoted through morality education and public opinion rather than through legal obligations. Not all the social relationships can be regulated through legislation. The legislative power should remain modest in expanding its applicable scope, and choose the appropriate social fields to regulate the social morality issues.

Consult history when observing the reality, for reality does not exist without history. The millennia-old Chinese civilization has developed its own value system.

The excellent Chinese traditional culture has become the gene of the Chinese nation, which subtly influences the Chinese people's way of thinking and behavior. Though time changes, the traditional conceptions on state governance that emphasizes on the combination of morality and law and advocacy of attaching importance to the complementarity, compatibility and consistency of the rule of law and the rule of virtue, and the concept of state governance conveyed still have practical significance across time and space, such as "virtue and rites are the foundation while criminal law is the tool for governance", "he who exercises government by means of his virtue may be compared to the north polar star, which keeps its place and all the stars turn towards it", and "ceremonies to direct men's aims aright; music to give harmony to their voices; laws to unify their conduct; and punishments to guard against their tendencies to evil. The end to which ceremonies, music, punishments, and laws conduct is one; they are the instruments by which the minds of the people are assimilated, and good order in government is made to appear." When the Chinese nation is heading toward a great rejuvenation, the legislators should draw on the traditional Chinese culture to find aspirations for the rule of law, summarize the moral consensus from historical facts and people's practices and transform them into the principles or elements of law through modern conceptions on rule of law to make the law so enacted more acceptable by the people and conducive to spreading core socialist values.

3.5 *To Insist on Deepening Democratic Legislation to Better Play the Principal Role People's Congress Deputies*

When affirming the great progress made in China's democratic legislation, it should be noted that deficiencies in open legislation and public participation still exist. For example, the scope subject to legislative openness is still somewhat arbitrary as it is often determined by the legislature. Some law bills are prepared behind closed doors, and the discussions and argumentations on the institutional design that may cause major legislative disputes are often insufficient, which will increases the difficulty and costs of later corrections of errors. In addition, some legislative hearings are of small practical value because they are held as mere formalities, and more attention is paid to collection of public opinions rather than giving feedback after the hearings.

The practice of democratic legislation should be deepened to improve the quality of democratic legislative process and promote the institutional development of democratic legislation. First, to enhance the legislative openness. The draft law texts and explanations, especially on the interpretations, background, reasons and deliberative process of the key and disputable provisions, should be disclosed to the public if no confidentiality is required to expand the public's rights to be informed and participate in legislation as much as possible. Second, to expand the scope and depth of public participation in legislation. The procedural design of participation process should reflect the majority's opinions but also respect the minority's opinions. For example, if the participants are not representative, procedures are not reasonably laid down, process is more of formalities, feedback mechanism is not perfect or opinion acceptance rates are low, the organization and working mechanism should be innovated, the working procedures should be simplified, and people's congress deputies and community representatives should be invited to hear from the people to improve the effectiveness of democratic legislation.

Moreover, the emerging technologies should be proactively adopted to boost the enthusiasm in public participation in legislation. For example, the disclosure, forums, hearings and seminars on legislation and other democratic legislation measures are to be deeply integrated with the Internet, big-data, AI and other modern technologies to reduce the public participation costs and increase its efficiency. Third, the principal role of deputies should be well played. As directed in the report of the Nineteenth CPC National Congress, "we should give better play to the role of deputies to people's congresses, and enable people's congresses at all levels and their standing committees … to truly represent the people and maintain close ties with them". However, apart from the community liaison offices for legislation and inviting of deputies to observe the meetings, the institutions for the deputies to contact the people during legislation are limited, and the channels for people to submit legislative opinions to the deputies are not always smooth. As Chinese socialism enters a new era, people's demands for democracy, rule of law, impartiality, justice, security and environment are increasing, which requires the legislation to establish more institutional breakthroughs. If these demands are not timely responded to and the channels for orderly and regulated democratic legislation are not established, the laws enacted will not be of high quality, nor will they meet the people's expectations for a better life. In this case, the people's sense of participation and political recognition of the nation will be decreased, which may damage the public image of Party's governance. Therefore, the institutional development should be enhanced, and procedures for deputies to contact the people in legislation should be detailed so as to better play their role in representing the people.[25]

[25] When sticking to deepening democratic legislation and improving its effectiveness, it should also be noted that the development of democracy is preconditioned by necessary economic, social and cultural conditions, but such conditions are progressive and gradually developing in the historical process, which cannot be changed all at once. Therefore, the democratic legislation will also experience a gradual process and change according to the actual conditions to adapt to the local economic, social and cultural progress.

3.6 To Observe the Law of Development in Legislation to Promote Innovation of the Working Mechanisms on Legislation

First, to formulate general rules on legislative techniques. After the Law on Legislation was revised in 2015, the number of legislators increased dramatically, and they should be guided by more specific rules on legislation. To formulate the general rules on legislative techniques will not only provide guidelines for the legislative bodies, but also help the standing committee members to master the necessary knowledge. Second, to advance the civil code compilation. After the formation of the socialist legal system with Chinese characteristics, the laws are enacted to achieve basic provision of law-abiding practices, but the overlaps, disconnections and inconsistencies among the separate regulations also arose. Therefore, these regulations should be consolidated based on their categories, the outdated provisions should be repealed, the contradictory provisions should be revised, and the gap in legislation should be filled to promote the codification of some department laws with scientific organization, coordinated arrangement of provisions and sound integration. The compilation of Civil Code has been under steady progress. The success and experience from codifying civil laws in China will be summarized to help promote in a timely manner the codifications of some separate laws which share common rules and are well-connected normative structures-such as environment laws and labor laws-in order to advance legal establishment in relevant fields with a more scientific organization, a more rigorous structure and more harmony. Third, to enhance the exchanges with other legal systems while giving prominence to Chinese socialist legal system for its own benefit and use. In the era of globalization, law-making should not only be based on the national conditions, but also draw on the good legislative experience from other countries. With an inclusive and global vision, the foreign experience should be selectively learned, digested, and absorbed. To learn from foreign experience, it is necessary to give prominent to Chinese socialist legal system for its own benefits and use, insist on learning and assimilating the essence discriminately, and stick to national conditions to transform foreign institutions and mechanisms to ensure conformity with local resources.[26] All these efforts are made to improve

[26] For example, in the era of big data and AI, all the countries in the world are confronted with the issues in personal information and privacy protection and automated driving. In 2012, Singapore adopted the Personal Data Protection Act, the European Parliament passed the General Data Protection Regulation in April 2016 and started to implement from May 2018, which made it the central law on personal information protection in the EU. In 2017, Germany revised the Road Traffic Act (Straßenverkehrsgesetz), the first time the automated driving was incorporated in traffic laws in the world. At the same year, the US issued the Automated Driving Systems 2.0: A Vision for Safety, showing the US Federal Government's support for automated driving technology. These

legislative quality and hastily promote the Chinese socialist legal system with the Constitution as the core.

Over the past 70 years since the founding of the PRC, under the centralized and unified Party leadership, the NPC and its Standing Committee have worked closely around the general picture of the Party and State undertakings, continuing to promote scientific, democratic and law-based legislation and never stopping the pursuit of truth and correcting mistakes. They have followed a legislative path with Chinese characteristics, which has provided strong legal guarantee for establishing, upholding and developing Chinese socialism. As China enters the new era, the continued theoretical innovation in and development of scientific, democratic and law-based legislation practice will, as the great institutional strength, help to improve the Chinese socialist system, modernize the state governance system and capacity, and realize the Chinese dream of great national rejuvenation.

experience may provide good examples for China's future legislation in these fields. In addition, many provinces and cities in China have established friendship with other provinces and cities of other countries. Such friendship may be fully applied to learn their experience and concepts of law-making to improve local rule of law in governance.

Chapter 13
Reflections on the Basic Experience in China's Legislation

Wang Hongyu

Abstract This chapter summarizes the fundamental experiences of China's legislative work over the 70 years since the founding of the People's Republic of China, particularly since the reform and opening-up period. It asserts that China has successfully forged a unique legislative path rooted in the great practice of socialist construction. It identifies several key principles guiding this work, including upholding the leadership of the Communist Party, adhering to the socialist system with Chinese characteristics, and prioritizing the principal status of the people. It details how legislative decisions are grounded in the practice of reform and opening-up, allowing for a strategic relationship between reform and the rule of law. It also highlights the importance of proceeding from China's national conditions, combining the rule of law with the rule of virtue, and ensuring the unity of the socialist legal system to guarantee stability and national cohesion.

Keywords Legislative experience · CPC leadership · Socialist system · National conditions · Rule of law · Rule of virtue

Over the past 70 years, under the centralized and unified Party's leadership, China's work on legislation has followed a path with Chinese characteristics after accomplishing the arduous tasks, such as abolishing the bogus legal system and traditions established by the KMT and making explorations on socialist legal system with the active use of the legal construction experience in the revolutionary period. Over the past 40 years since the reform and opening-up was initiated, China has been firmly rooted in the great practice of socialist undertakings, worked closely around the general picture of the Party and state undertakings, and promoted the construction of legal system in a well-planned, steady, and step-by-step approach. After the concerted efforts of all parties, the Chinese socialist legal system was established in 2010 as scheduled, which deliver on the laws to abide by for the economic, political, cultural, social and ecological progress. Since the Eighteenth CPC National Congress, under

W. Hongyu (✉)
Beijing, China
e-mail: liujixuan@lawpress.com.cn

C. Shen et al. (eds.), *A History of Legislation in the Past 70 Years in China*,
https://doi.org/10.1007/978-981-95-3799-0_13

the leadership of the Central Committee with Xi Jinping as the core, the work on legislation in China has never failed to conform with the profound changes in domestic and international society, to meet the increasing requirements brought by the change of the social principal contradiction, to consider, plan and promote law-making by the coordinated implementation of the Five-sphere Integrated Plan and the Four-pronged Comprehensive Strategy, and to advance law-making in key areas. These efforts, as a result, have continuously improved the Chinese socialist legal system with the Constitution as the core, making it compatible with China's state governance system and capacity, and the socialist rule of law system in China has also made tremendous achievements. In a word, China has accomplished the legislative tasks that are rarely seen in the world and overcome the difficulties of an unprecedented scale, which makes it necessary to reflect on these hard-won achievements and precious experiences.

1 To Uphold and Improve the Socialist System with Chinese Characteristics

As pointed out by Xi Jinping, "the path of socialist rule of law with Chinese characteristics is a crystallization of the achievements and experience in socialist rule of law construction, and is the only correct one for constructing socialist rule of law country".[1]The question of the road directly concerns the success or failure of comprehensive rule of law and socialist rule of law construction, which is the most salient feature of Xi Jinping's new concepts, new thinking and new strategies on comprehensive rule of law. Looking back on the extraordinary history in the past 70 years, the voice of opposition has never faded concerning what banner to raise and what path to follow. The Constitution and law are the legal manifestation of Chinese socialist system. Under the Central Committee's centralized and unified leadership, the NPC and its Standing Committee adhere to the socialist direction, standing and principles and confirm the Chinese socialist political system and basic economic system by enacting and amending the Constitution and relevant laws on state system and agencies to consolidate and safeguard a peaceful political unity and ensure the country's development follows the right path.

The Constitution is the fundamental law of the state and the general charter for governing the country and the state. The Common Program adopted as the interim constitution confirmed the achievements of new democratic revolution and the direction for developing the new China, and clarified that China practiced the system of

[1] Xi Jinping, *Explanations on the Draft Resolution of the Central Committee of the Communist Party of China on Certain Major Issues Concerning Comprehensively Advancing the Law-Based Governance of China*, in The Party Literature Research Office ed., Selection of Important Documents Since the Eighteenth CPC National Congress (Vol. 2), Central Compilation and Translation Press, p. 147.

people's congresses as the fundamental political system, which laid the legal foundation for finalizing Chinese socialist system. The 1954 Constitution confirmed the Party as the governing party in China, the leading role in state's political and social life, and the legitimate role in the Constitutional order in the form of fundamental law. It also instituted the principles of people's democracy and socialism, and required the persistence of the system of people's congresses. The Third Plenary Session of the CPC Central Committee convened in 1978 ushered China into the era of reform and opening-up. In 1982, the Constitution was adopted after amendment. The reform and opening-up marked China's opening of its door to the world, however, it also brought about complicated discussions at home and abroad on where China's reform and opening-up would head in terms of political development. Western politicians and scholars believed that if socialist China started reform and opening-up by accepting foreign capital and market economy, it would also accept the capitalist system. Under such context, the Party established the guiding principles for amending the Constitution, which unequivocally declared adherence to Four Cardinal Principles, i.e. the socialist path, the people's democratic dictatorship, the Party's leadership, and the Marxism-Leninism and Mao Zedong Thought.

The Four Cardinal Principles are the political foundation for uniting the Chinese people and the fundamental political guarantee for the socialist modernization. The incorporation of the four cardinal principles was to declare that the reform and opening-up will not change China as a socialist country. The practice also proves that its corporation along with a series of systems, principles and rules laid out in the Constitution, has provided the fundamental political condition and institutional foundation for reform and opening-up. In line with the reform and opening-up and socialist modernization, the NPC, under the Central Committee's leadership, has consecutively made several amendments to the Constitution in 1988, 1993, 1998, 2004 and 2018, a total of 52 amended provisions, which have helped the Constitution change over time for better upholding and improving Chinese socialist system. From the 1954 Constitution and the 1982 Constitution to the five constitutional amendments, all major political decisions made at critical junctures by the Chinese people under the Party's leadership are the successes in following the path of Chinese socialist rule of law.

Over the past 70 years, with the Constitution as the core, the NPC and its Standing Committee has strengthened the legislation in key areas and continued to promote the improvement of socialist political system with Chinese characteristics. For example, the NPC and its Standing Committee enacted the laws on the organization, powers and functions and operation rules of state agencies to establish the institutions, division of powers, operation methods, principles of work and rules of procedures to ensure the coordinated and efficient operations of state agencies according to law. The laws on the exercise of powers and functions of administrative departments according to law have also been formulated to promote the law-based government as essential for modern social governance. The NPC and its Standing Committee enacted the Ethnic Regional Autonomy Law in 1984 to maintain and develop the socialist ethnic relationships characterized by unity, mutual help and harmony. The 1987 Law on the Organization of the Villagers' Committees and the 1989 Law on the

Organization of the Urban Residents' Committees helped to establish the community democratic institutions and mechanisms with Chinese characteristics. According to the principle of One Country Two Systems, the NPC and its Standing Committee enacted the Hong Kong SAR Basic Law and Macao SAR Basic Law, commended as the Chinese political wisdom among the international community, which has provided legal guarantee for the safe return of Hong Kong and Macao and their long-term prosperity and stability. Since the Eighteenth CPC National Congress, the NPC and its Standing Committee has enacted the National Security Law, Anti-Espionage Law, Anti-Terrorism Law, Law on the Administration of Activities of Overseas Non-Governmental Organizations within the Territory of China, Cyber Security Law and National Intelligence Law to put into practice the holistic view of national security for safeguarding national security and national core interests and ensuring the socialist direction of national progress.

2 To Adhere to the Party's Leadership in Legislation

As Xi Jinping concluded, "the Party's leadership is the defining feature of socialism with Chinese characteristics, and the fundamental guarantee for socialist rule of law".[2] This important conclusion is a summary of the basic experience in building rule of law in the past 70 years from the founding of the PRC, especially during the past 40 years when the reform and opening-up was initiated. It not only reveals the essence of Chinese socialist rule of law, but also addresses the core and key components of socialist rule of law with Chinese characteristics. In this period, the most crucial and significant experience in the tremendous achievements made in the work on legislation is to adhere to the Party's leadership in the legislation, especially its centralized and unified leadership.

To adhere to the Party's leadership means to resolutely maintain the authority of the Central Committee and its centralized and unified leadership, while putting into practice the Party's core role in exercising overall leadership and coordinating efforts of all in the whole process and all respects of the construction of comprehensive rule of law. Over the past 70 years since the founding of the PRC, especially over the past 40 years since the reform and opening-up, the successive central leaderships have reflected on the historical experiences and lessons, gained an accurate grasp of the characteristics of the time, the Party's mission and circumstances of governance. By standing firm on the national conditions and realities while adapting to demands for the construction of socialist legal system they have made sound decisions to prompte the socialist democracy and legal system. Step by step, they have put forward and practiced the governance concepts centered on carrying out work according to law, the rule of law and the law-based governance of the country. Since the Eighteenth CPC National Congress, the Central Committee has made more efforts to improve the institutions and mechanisms on its leadership in legislation, for example, Xi

[2] *Ibid.*, p. 157.

Jinping chaired the meetings of the Political Bureau's Standing Committee to deliberate on the NPC Standing Committee's legislative plans and changes of the plans, which were then distributed in the form of Central Committee's documents. The Central Committee also listened to the reports of the party group of the NPC Standing Committee on the major legislative issues and matters during the formulation and revision of important laws, studied the major issues arising from the work on legislation, deliberated on the major institutional and policy changes concerning the lawmaking, and coordinated the resolution of major legislative disputes. The practice has proven that only the Party's leadership and unswerving implementation of rule of law can ensure the correct political direction of the construction of socialist rule of law with Chinese characteristics, stick to China's conditions and realities of current development stage, and guarantee the realization of the fundamental interests of the majority of people.

During legislation, the NPC and its Standing Committee has been dedicated to adhering to the Party's leadership, implementing Central Committee's opinions on strengthening that leadership, and giving full play to the advantages of the system of people's congresses. This ensures the authority of the Central Committee in exercising overall leadership and coordinating efforts, while putting into practice its major decisions and arrangements in the work on legislation. The NPC and its Standing Committee has also worked to transform the Party's proposals into the will of the state through statutory procedures and into the behavioral norms for the whole society, so as to guarantee the implementation of Party's line, principles and policies and the steady progress of reform and opening-up and socialist modernization. First, the NPC and its Standing Committee keep a close eye on the Party and state's central tasks to plan the work on legislation, scientifically formulate legislative plan and schedules, and actively promote key legislative programs for ensuring the implementation of the Party and the State's major decisions and arrangements. Second, the NPC and its Standing Committee center their work on the Central Committee's decisions and arrangements, initiating the legislative procedures timely for the legislative suggestions of the Central Committee. This ensures a firm political standing consistent with the Central Committee on matters that concern the general situation, have profound influence or involve major differences. third, to insist on the instruction-seeking and reporting system for major legislative programs and issues. The drafting and revision of important laws and other major issues arising from legislation should be reported to the Central Committee for instructions in a timely manner, and its directives and requirements should be put into practice. This instruction-seeking and reporting practice has been routinely implemented and institutionalized. Practice has proven that the adherence to the Party's leadership is of great help to unswervingly implement the Party's proposals and major decisions into the work on legislation and to keep the Central Committee informed of the NPC and its Standing Committee's work on legislation, thereby translating these major decisions and arrangements into the laws for the whole people to abide by through statutory procedures.

3 To Uphold the Socialist Theoretical System with Chinese Characteristics

Law is the institutionalized and standardized manifestation of the Party's line, principles and policies that have proven correct and mature, requiring lasting persistence. To adhere to the correct guiding principles is the basic premise for strengthening democracy and the legal system. The theoretical system of socialism with Chinese characteristics is a scientific framework that includes the Deng Xiaoping Theory, the Important Thought of Three Represents, the Scientific Outlook on Development and the Xi Jinping Thought on Socialism with Chinese characteristics for a New Era This system represents the latest achievement in adapting Marxism to China's realities, the most valuable political and spiritual wealth of the Party, the common theoretical basis for the unity of all ethnic groups, the guiding ideology for the long term, and the fundamental guidelines for all work.

Since the Third Plenary Session of the Eleventh CPC Central Committee, the second Central Committee leadership with Deng Xiaoping as the core proposed the historical mission of "strengthening socialist democracy and improving the socialist legal system", and laid out the principles for socialist legal system construction, i.e. to ensure that "there are laws to abide by, that laws are observed and strictly enforced, and that any violators of law are prosecuted", which were then established as the Deng Xiaoping Theory on legal system. The second generation of Central Committee's leadership with Jiang Zemin as the core, while advancing the reform and opening-up and the socialist modernization and instituting the Important Thought of Three Represents, continued to promote the theoretical innovation. They estalished the rule of law as the basic line for the Party to lead the Chinese people in governing the country, and set the general objective of establishing the Chinese socialist legal system. The Central Committee with Hu Jintao as the core insisted on the Deng Xiaoping Theory and the Important Thought of Three Represents, put forward the Scientific Outlook on Development and the construction of a socialist harmonious society. This approach integrated the Party's leadership, people's position as masters of the country and rule of law, providing a more solid theoretical and practical basis for implementing rule of law.

Since the Eighteenth CPC National Congress, based on a profound understanding of major theoretical questions on the socialist path of rule of law and the Chinese socialist rule of law system with Chinese characteristics, and of the great practice of building China into a socialist rule of law country, Xi Jinping has elaborated on the comprehensive rule of law This has evolved into the new concepts, new thinking and new strategies of rule of law, defining the fundamental guarantees, sources of strengthen, overall objective, path, general mission and strategies for fully advancing rule of law under new historical conditions. These concepts, thinking and strategies respond to the critical questions: where does the Chinese socialist rule of law go, whom will follow, which path will take, what objective will be achieved, how to achieve the objective and other important major questions. They have innovated the theory of socialist rule of law, and are of great theoretical, historical and true significance for advancing the rule of law in all respects, establishing China into a socialist rule of law country, promoting the modernization of state governance system and capacity, and developing China into a great modern socialist country that is prosperous, strong, democratic, culturally advanced, harmonious, and beautiful.

In the work on legislation, the NPC and its Standing Committee have adhered to the guidance of this theoretical system of socialism with Chinese characteristics, using it to achieve consensus and position the legislative principles to ensure the laws and regulations formulated are conducive to developing the Chinese socialist system, unleashing socialist productive forces, and leveraging the advantageous role of the socialist system.

4 To Stick to People's Principal Position

China is a socialist country under the people's democratic dictatorship, where all the state power belongs to the people This determines that the legislation should stick to people's principal position for realizing their master role in governing the country. Therefore, the legislation should be carried out for the people, by relying on the people, and for the benefit and protection of the people. Specifically, the people's interests, expectations, rights and interest and welfare should be considered throughout the legislative process to ensure that laws enacted and their implementation represent people's will. Moreover, the legislation should also be carried out for the sake of people's fundamental interests, protect their extensive rights, freedoms and performance of duties, safeguard social justice and fairness, and promote common prosperity.

During the work on legislation, the NPC and its Standing Committee have insisted on realizing, safeguarding and developing the fundamental interests of the overwhelming majority of the people. They have adopted the people-centered approach either in the law-making process or the formulation of rules, respected people's principal position and their initiative, drawn inspiration from people's creative practices, and gained momentum from the people's demands for development to better realize people's fundamental interests through law-making, and fulfil people's aspirations for a better life, social fairness and justice.

First, to take people's expectations as the guidance and protect their rights and interests. Over the past 70 years, as China's national strength has siginificantly improved, the people have benefited the most. In this period, law has become the most important means to adjust the social interest structures and relationships of rights. The work on legislation has focused on continuously improving the law-making in socialist market economy to increase social wealth and provide material conditions for people's well-being This includes improving the taxation legislation to consolidate the national financial revenue, balance regional development, safeguard public expenditure and adjust the relationships between economy and income distribution. The NPC and its Standing Committee enacted the Charity Law to encourage donations and charitable undertakings to support poverty alleviation, and the Social

Insurance Law and the Law on the Protection of the Rights and Interests of the Elderly to ensure people's right's to employment, medical care and old-age care.

Second, to base legislation on China's national conditions and realities Legislation must observe and grasp the law of development, reflect the social relations subject to adjustment of law, show the humanistic care for people in legal system design, and realize, safeguard and develop the fundamental interests of the overwhelming majority of the people so as to consolidate the institutional foundations for rule of law. Moreover, it should develop a correct understanding of the people's fundamental interests, common interests in the current stage and different interest relationships among different social groups to better coordinate these interests in legislative process. The relation between power and rights, power and responsibilities should be properly handled; the administrative, supervisory, adjudication and procuratorate departments should be granted with necessary powers, but the exercise of such powers should be regulated, checked and supervised to protect the law rights and interests of the citizens, legal persons and other organizations.

Third, to ensure legislation is carried out for the people and by relying on the people. During legislation, the people's opinions should be heard in various means to coordinate the different interests and, with great efforts, make every legislation responding to people's concerns and expectations. The NPC Standing Committee has accentuated the importance of legislative quality, and spared every effort to improve the legislative mechanisms and methods to better scientific and democratic legislation. The NPC and its Standing Committee also strive to give full play to the role of deputies in legislation, continue to expand the orderly participation in legislation, and listen to the opinions of various parties especially from the communities through the disclosure of law bills, forums, seminars and hearings to collect wisdom and reach consensus making the law enacted fully represent people's common will.

5 To Continue Institutional Innovation of State Governance System and Capacity

Over the past 70 years, especially over the past 40 years, the most salient feature of China's legislation has been its close alignment with the reform and opening-up and the development of Chinese socialism Legislation has played a pivotal role in safeguarding and promoting development by eliminating the institutional systems and mechanisms that hinder reform and opening-up, and establishing the new systems with Chinese characteristics under the Party's leadership. By promoting legislation in a well-planned and step by step manner with a focus, China has gradually established the Chinese socialist legal system with the Constitution as the core that conforms with the modernization of state governance system and capacity. This legal system has established the major fundamental systems concerning the overall situation and long-term stability, consolidated the foundation for national prosperity and long-term security, actively promoted and safeguarded socialist economic, political, cultural, social and ecological progress. It is a modernization path that is totally different from the Western model.

First, to promote the fundamental transformation of China's high-centralized planned economy to socialist market economy to ensure the fast and healthy development of economy according to law. Since the reform and opening-up, China's rule of law construction has persisted in economic development with a special attention to learn from the advanced Western experience in management, leading to the enactment and enforcement of Company Law, Contract Law, Property Law, Enterprise Bankruptcy Law, Price Law, Anti-Monopoly Law and other laws. These laws established and improved the socialist market economic institutions from scratch, granting managerial autonomy to the state-owned enterprises and collectively-owned economic organizations, affirming the legal status of the private sector and individual economy and other non-public economic sectors, estbalishing market-oriented allocation of production factors, improving the protection of citizens' lawful properties, and forming a legal system that comprises market entities, property protection, market competition and macro control that conforms with the socialist market economy. The establishment and continuing improvement of the rule of law has broken the shackles of the planned economic system and unleashed the wisdom and strength of millions of Chinese people in developing socialist market economy, thereby providing gives stronger impetus and guarantee for the great transformation and development of Chinese economy.

Second, to promote the institutionalization and standardization of socialist democracy with well-defined procedures for safeguarding people's democracy, citizens' rights and human rights. Over the past 70 years, the legislation has upheld the integration of the Party's leadership, people's position as masters of the country and rule of law, while safeguarding and developing the socialist system and the democratic political system of Chinese socialism. The NPC and its Standing Committee have enacted and made amendments to the Constitution in setp with the times, and formulated the law on deputies, electoral law, organization law of state agencies, supervision law and oversight law and others. These efforts aim to guarantee the Party's leading role, protect people's democratic rights, and establish robust mechanisms and institutions that ensure the people's master position, the supervision over the Party and the State and the exercise of powers. Under the Party's leadership, the NPC and its Standing Committee have established and improved the rule of law, expanded scope of people's democracy, developed socialist democratic politics, and ensured citizens' rights and human rights. This has formed, consolidated and developed a political situation characterized by vitality, stability and unity.

Third, to promote socialist cultural and social progress to ensure cultural prosperity and social harmony and stability. Over the past 70 years, China has attached great importance to cultivating virtue and good conduct through legislation, promoting social civilization, and safeguarding fairness and justice. To be specific, the NPC and its Standing Committee have enacted the Law on the Protection of Heroes and Martyrs, Film Industry Promotion Law, Law on the Protection of Cultural Relics, and Law on the Guarantee of Public Cultural Services to cultivate and practice the core socialist values while promoting socialist cultural prosperity and development; they have also enacted the laws on education, employment, distribution of income, social security, health care, food safety, social assistance, social organizations and social governance to strengthen the efforts on social development, innovate governance, maintain stability and promote harmony; further, the Cyber Security Law and other relevant laws were also enacted to set up a comprehensive network governance system that fosters a clean cyberspace. The work on legislation has also been committed to establishing sound and diverse dispute resolution mechanisms that incorporates litigation, mediation, arbitration, administrative consideration and administrative adjudication. Through the continuous improvement of the rule of law, China has gradually established a social governance model characterized by the combination of law and morality, the integration of the rule of law and the rule of virtue, and the harmony among law, morality and self-governance. This has helped to build a benign social atmosphere where the whole society follows the moral standards and abides by the law, thereby improving people's sense of gain, happiness and security.

Last, to promote green development and ecological civilization to ensure that people live harmoniously with the nature. China's rule of law development regarding ecological civilization began alongside the reform and opening-up. Facing rapid urbanization and industrialization, the NPC and its Standing Committee have enacted over 30 laws, such as the Environment Protection Law, Marine Environment Protection Law, Law on the Prevention and Control of Water Pollution, Law on the Prevention and Control of Air Pollution and Law on the Prevention and Control of Soil Pollution. They have implemented the strictest posssible systems for source protection, damage compensation and accountability, while improving the mechanism for environmental control and ecological restoration. These efforts address the prominent environmental issues and provide a reliable guarantee for building a beautiful China. Through these, China has strengthened its efforts for ecological civilization development creating a situation in which the environment protection and economic development mutually reinforce each other and people are living harmoniously with the nature.

6 To Insist on Making Legislative Decisions Based on the Practice of Reform and Opening-up and Socialist Modernization

Reform and opening-up is the most distinct banner of the Party in the new era. To deal with the relationship between reform and opening-up and legislation is a major political issue for contemporary China. While the goals of reform and the rule of law are fundamentally aligned, they manifest in different forms: the rule of law establishes rules, while reform breaks outdated rules; the rule of law settle issues for stability, while reform drives changes. The rule of law emphasizes maintaining the authority of existing laws and the stability of the economic and social order, whereas reform focuses on the breaking of shackles of established systems and mechanisms. The NPC and its Standing Committee have worked hard to properly handle this relationship, and to ensure that major reforms are grounded in law and that economic and social development remains vigorous, steady and orderly.

First, to authorize reform through legislation. In the early stage of reform and opening-up, the primary task was to gradually dismantle the constraints of the planned economic system on productive forces and establish a vibrant socialist market economy. When the conditions for formulating and revising laws are not yet mature and reform measures required testing, the NPC Standing Committee followed statutory procedures to authorize the State Council and the special economic zones to conduct legislations, which provided legal basis for pilot programs in specific fields or local areas and offered support and a legal guarantee for the reform and opening-up. Since the Eighteenth CPC National Congress, China's reform has sailing in uncharted waters. The Third Plenary Session of the Eighteenth CPC Central Committee identified 336 reform tasks, and the Fourth Plenary Session identified 190 reform tasks. Most of these reform tasks involved adjustments of the legal system. The Twelfth National People's Congress and its Standing Committee have made efforts to play role in leading and promoting legislation and taken the law-based reform decision as the principle of the work on legislation. The 2015 Law on Legislation introduced a provision that "the National People's Congress and its Standing Committee may, as needed for reform and development, decide to authorize the temporary adjustment or temporary suspension of the local application of certain provisions of a law during a specified period regarding specific matters in the administrative management and other fields". This addition serves as the legal basis for authorizing reform through legislation. During the five-year term of the Twelfth NPC, there are a total of 25 laws, 127 revisions, 46 decisions on legal issues and other major issues, and 9 interpretations of law. The number of decisions on authorization was 16, which were made to the State Council, Supreme People's Court, and Supreme People's Procuratorate for adjusting the enforcement of certain legal provisions to conform with the pilot programs. Building on this momentum, the Party has contemplated the deepening of reform and opening-up, and accordingly, the Standing Committee of the Thirteenth NPC have made decisions to authorize the State Council to extend the pilot program of drug marketing authorization holder system.

Second, to lead reform through legislation. The Party laid out the general arrangements for comprehensively deepening reform and advancing rule of law in its Third and Fourth Sessions of the Eighteenth Central Committee, offering new interpretations of the relationship between legislation and reform. The NPC and its Standing Committee have remained committed to aligining the legislative decision-making with reform decisions. They have pushed forward the adaptation of legislative initiatives to the needs of reform and opening-up and economic and social development, made integrated use of enactment, revision, repeal and interpretation and other means to promote reform under the rule of law and improve the rule of law through reform. For example, to fully implement the spirit of the Central Committee on deepening the reform of the fiscal and taxation system and improving the budget administration system, the NPC and its Standing Committee revised the Budget Law in 2014. And to implement the spirit of the Third and Fourth Plenary Sessions of the Eighteenth CPC Central Committee, they also revised the Law on Legislation to improve the legislative institutions, clarify the legislative authority, and improve the mechanism and procedures for better scientific and democratic legislation. In addition, to implement the Central Committee's decision to deepen the national supervision system reform, they enacted the Supervision Law on the basis of two successive pilot reform decisions, which helped to innovate and improve the national supervision system, and promote the work on anti-corruption by adopting rule-of-law thinking and approach.

Third, to revise laws to remove barriers to reform. Existing laws that do not meet the requirements of reform should be revised or abolished in a timely manner, so that outdated legal provisions will not become "stumbling block" for reform. For example, with the intensified reform of the administrative examination and approval system, the NPC Standing Committee established the "package" revision mechanism for revising laws Under this mechanism, some law provisions sharing common concerns or reasons for revision are consolidated into a signle bill. The Standing Committee of the Twelfth NPC adopted 15 such decisions, resulting in 95 reivsions to laws, mainly involving system reforms in areas such as streamlining administration and delegating powers, industrial and commercial registration, and pricing. These integrated revisions provided strong support for the smooth implementation of the administrative examination and approval system reform, but also facilitated the interconnection and harmony within the legal system.

Fourth, to summarize pilot reform experiences in a timely manner and replicate and promote them through revision of law. For reform measures requiring continued explorations, the NPC Standing Committee may decide to extend the pilot period or incorporate them into new pilot programs for improvement; for reform measures that have proven effective in practice and are ripe for replication and promotion, it will make a timely summary to revise and improve the relevant laws. For example, in 2013 and 2014, the NPC Standing Committee made two decisions to authorize the State Council to temporarily adjust the implementation of administrative approval under the relevant laws in the free trade zones in Shanghai, Guangdong, Tianjin and Fujian. Upon the expiry of the two decisions in September 2016, the NPC Standing Committee revised the Foreign-funded Enterprises Law and other three laws, which upgraded the reform measures adopted in the free trade zones into laws and decided to terminate the validity of these decisions. In March 2019, the second session of the 13th NPC considered and adopted the Foreign Investment Law, which incorporated the experience from pilot programs into law again to further improve the legal institutions and mechanisms on reform and opening-up.

From the perspective of changing the established legal rules and order to meet the needs of reform and opening-up, some scholars have described the over 40-year China's reform and opening-up as the "change of law" (bian fa) that has covered the largest population, lasted the longest period of time with the greatest success in the history. Under the centralized and unified leadership of the Party, the "New Deal" (xin zheng) and the "Change of Law" complement each other. In this great process, reform and opening-up have become the driving force of legal development, while the legal system is the institutionalized guarantee. This "dual engine" effect manifests the distinct advantages of China's political system.

7 To Firmly Stand on China's Conditions and Realities

The path of the rule of law a country takes and the legal system it establishes are determined by its basic conditions. As pointed out by Marx, "society is not founded upon the law; this is a legal fiction. On the contrary, the law must be founded upon society, it must express the common interests and needs of society...which arise from the material mode of production prevailing at the given time".[3] The NPC and its Standing Committee have insisted on China's national conditions and realities, taking the great practice of reform and opening-up and socialist modernization as the legislative basis. They have complied with the new requirements as circumstances change and taken a firm hold of the development and changes to form the socialist legal system to ensure conformity with the rejuvenation of Chinese nation over the past 70 years' success in legislation.

First, to establish the legislative institutions and mechanisms that give full play to both the central and local initiatives. As a unified, unitary and multi-ethnic socialist country with a vast territory and a large population, China faces unevenly distributed and insufficient productive forces. Over the past 70 years since the founding of the PRC, especially over the past 40 years, to eliminate the imbalance and inadequacy, a legislative system that reflects these realities and conditions has been established For example, the NPC and its Standing Committee granted the self-governance power to national autonomous regions, the power to formulate local regulations to the people's congresses and their standing committees of the provinces, regional autonomous regions, municipalities directly under the State Council and the cities with subordinate districts. While ensuring the implementation of the national Constitution, laws and administrative regulations and the smooth flow of central government decrees, they have spared efforts to fully stimulate the initiative and play the important role of local legislation in enforcing the laws, making complementary provisions and carrying out exploratory legislation. All these efforts have promoted the formation and improvement of a socialist legal system with Chinese characteristics that is compatible with the state governance system and governance capacity, and provided an effective institutional guarantee for socialist modernization.

Second, to treat the great practice of reform and opening-up and socialist modernization as the basis for legislation and keep a close eye for the central work of the Party and state to carry out legislation. The NPC and its Standing Committee adhere to the objective law of social development and properly balance legal foresight with feasibility: on the one hand, the NPC and its Standing Committee pay attention to extracting the successful experiences of reform into laws, revising the outdated laws

[3] Karl Marx, *Trial of the Rhenish District Committee of Democrats (1849)*, in Karl Marx and Frederick Engels, Collected Works (Vol. 8), Lawrence & Wishart, 1977, p. 323.

in a timely manner to provide reliable legal guarantee for reform; on the other hand, they also pay attention to leaving room for deepening reform and combining the the stability of enacted laws with the fluidity of ongoing reforms to ensure that legislation and the reform and opening-up remain adaptive to the socialist modernization and that the legal framework meets the actual needs of economic and social development.

Third, to ensure legislation reflects real social needs through in-depth analysis and scientific proposals for well-founded, practical and efficient legislation. For example, in the process of revising the Air Pollution Prevention and Control Law, significant efforts were made to grasp the features of economic development in the "new normal" and properly handle the relationship between environment protection and economic development. Recognizing that an over-emphasis on economic benefits rather than environmental benefits has made air pollution a prominent issue, the legislature focused on addressing this through institutional design. In this case, the NPC and its Standing Committee constructed a reasonable system of air prevention and control, using the strictest legal institutions and mechanisms to solve the deep-seated problems They also incorporated provisions on new technology and new energy, though not yet ripe for use, to ensure that the legislation is both grounded in practice and prospective in vision.

Last, to conduct surveys and investigations to grasp the development logic of legislation. Legislation should conform with national conditions, realities and the objective law of development. To this end, survey and investigation should be carried out. The NPC and its Standing Committee should insist on deepening scientific and democratic legislation, pay special attention to strengthening and improving the legislative survey through innovative methods to obtain the first-hand information to the greatest extent, and strive for accurately grasping the essence of the issue concerned and thoroughly studying the solutions. If the status quo is found to be unreasonable, the legislation should not follow so as to prevent the creation of loose institutions that may cause regulation failure. In addition, the legislation should strictly follow the national conditions and realities to prevent the institutional designs from outpacing the current development stage, making them impossible to implement. Through prospective, practical, scientific and reasonable institutional arrangements, the laws enacted will be well-founded, effective and practical as well.

Over the past 70 years since the founding of PRC, especially over the past 40 years since reform and opening-up, China's legislation, while remaining firmly rooted in national conditions and realities, has also drawn on the beneficial achievements of all human civilizations This includes learning from not only the Western legislation in the fields of economy, civil and commercial affairs, environment and resource protection and social affairs, but also some experiences in democratic politics and administration. It has also assimilated lessons from both the civil law and common law systems, as well as foreign countries, Hong Kong SAR, Macao SAR and Taiwan Region, while simultaneously making the traditions of ancient Chinese legal system serve contemporary needs. When enacting various laws, the provisions of foreign laws and regulations are collected for research and comparison to draw on the useful experience. The legislation should take the initiative to absorb the provisions that reflect the regularity and commonality of market economy and the norms and practices of international law during international exchanges. For example, the General Rules of Civil Law, Property Law and Contract Law are made by referring to the various basic institutions of the common law and civil law systems and the spirit and principles of international private law. The principles of proportionality and reliance protection are incorporated in the administrative legislation. In criminal legislation, the Criminal Law and Criminal Procedure Law draw on the basic principles and spirits of legality and public trial as prescribed in foreign legislation.

8 To Stick to the Integration of Rule of Law with Rule of Virtue

Xi Jinping once pointed out that "law is virtue committed to writing, while virtue is law inscribed in people's hearts. Both law and virtue possess the power to achieve certain standards of social behavior and preserve social order. In the governance of our country and society, we need to emphasize both rule of law and rule of virtue, valuing the normative function of law, while also attaching importance to the edifying effect of virtue, so that law and virtue complement each other and rule of law and rule of virtue promote each other…We need to pay more attention to turning basic ethical conventions into laws, ensuring our laws and regulations are more reflective of moral ideals and human concern, and we need to draw on the peremptory power of law to strengthen morality and protect basic moral standards, so as to improve the overall moral fabric of our society…There is a saying, 'A person who knows no shame knows no limits'. Without the nurturing effect of virtue, rule of law culture would be without its source of sustenance and we would lack the solid social foundations needed for laws to be enforced".[4] His elaborations reveal the inherent relationships between law and morality, and between rule of law and rule of virtue, which is of great significance for stimulating new vitality of the co-governance of law and morality. The rule of law should reflect ethical values and strengthen the role of law in promoting moral standards. In return, the civilizing effect of virtue should be applied to nurture the spirit of rule of law and strengthen the role of morality in supporting the rule of law culture.

The work on legislation should focus on integrating the core socialist values into the construction of legal system to carry forward these values and traditional Chinese virtues, nourish social morality, professional ethics, family virtues, and personal moral standards, and improve overall moral standards of the whole nation to create a good humanistic environment for the rule of law.

On one hand, to adhere to the guidance of the core socialist values by incorporating them in the Constitution, laws, regulations and rules to improve public recognition of these values and the consciousness to practice them. To fully implement the gist of the

[4] The Central Literature Research Office ed., *The Law-based Governance of China,* Central Compilation and Translation Press, 2017, pp. 33–35.

core socialist values in legislation requires steadfastly manifesting the requirements of building a powerful modern socialist country that is prosperous, democratic, civilized, and harmonious. It must embody the requirements for constructing socialist rule of law characterized by freedom, equality, impartiality and law-abiding, and reflect the socialist cultural progress requirements such as patriotism, dedication, integrity and friendship. Incorporating these requirements in legislation guarantees that the Chinese socialist legal system with the Constitution as the core reflects Chinese wisdom and unique civilization. It creates institutions and rules that reflect China's mainstream core values, promote the core socialist values, and strengthen the people's self-confidence in the path, system, theory, culture, and the rule of law of socialism with Chinese characteristics.

On the other hand, to stick to a problem-oriented approach and addressing the prominent issue in behaviors that are unethical or violate moral standards. The work on legislation should play the role of law in promoting social moral standards and help foster good civic acts through the compulsory norms and punishments of law to cope with the prominent issue in the violation of core socialist values. For example, to implement the provision that "the state shall champion core socialist values", the NPC and its standing committee enacted the Law on the Protection of Heroes and Martyrs. This law aims to punish the act of distorting, defame, or insult the heroes and martyrs to protect their dignity and lawful rights and interests, promote the spirit of heroes and martyrs and the spirit of patriotism in the whole society, urge the whole society to respect heroes and martyrs, suppress evil and promote goodness, and foster the positive energy for building socialism. Third, the legislation should also promote the ethics of traditional Chinese culture. For example, when revising the draft General Rules of Civil Code, the NPC and its Standing Committee strengthened the awareness of rules, enhanced ethical restraint, advocated for the spirit of contract and public order and good customs, the essential requirements of excellent traditional Chinese culture. By adapting to the features of the time, it reflects the co-governance of morality and law and keeps pace with the times.

9 To Adhere to the Unity of Socialist Legal System

China is a unified, multi-ethnic and unitary socialist country. The unity of socialist legal system is the foundation for national unification, ethnic unity, social stability, a unified modern market system and a socialist rule of law country. It is also an essential requirement for improving the work on legislation and the socialist legal system with Chinese characteristics with the Constitution as the core. In a country with a vast territory and unbalanced development in economy, culture and society, the legislative demands vary. To strengthen the construction of socialist democracy and rule of law while developing the socialist market economy, it is necessary to not only mobilize both the central and local initiatives, but also maintain the unity of socialist legal system and safeguard the authority of the Constitution and law. In recent years, the NPC and its Standing Committee have closely centered around the general situation of the Party and the State undertakings. They have spared efforts to strengthen the enforcement supervision of the Constitution and law through statutory methods and procedures and advance the implementation of the Central Committee's major decisions and arrangements, ensuring that the Central Committee's decisions and directives are implemented without fail and maintain the authority of socialist legal system. The achievements made from these efforts can be summarized as follows:

First, to provide institutional guarantees for establishing the Constitution's authority and safeguarding its enforcement. The NPC Standing Committee adopted the decision to set up the National Constitution Day and made provisions for educational activities to disseminate the knowledge of the Constitution. It also adopted the decision on practicing the public pledge of allegiance to the Constitution, requiring the state employees elected or appointed by the people's congresses and their standing committees or appointed by the people's governments, supervision commissions, people's courts and people's procuratorates to make such an allegiance pledge when assuming offices. This demonstrates the dignity and authority of the Constitution. To meet the requirement of establishing a sound procedural mechanism for Constitutional interpretation advocated in the Fourth Plenary Session of the Eighteenth CPC Central Committee, the party group of the NPC Standing Committee has studied and formulated the procedural rules to promote its institutional design and guarantee the correct and effective enforcement of the Constitution. To this end, the NPC set up the Constitution and Law Committee based on the provisions of the Constitutional Amendment; its Standing Committee adopted a resolution on the responsibilities of this Committee, expanding its role from the unified deliberation of draft laws to include the enforcement of the Constitution, constitutional interpretations, constitutional review, constitution's supervision and support the dissemination of the Constitution to actively advance the enforcement of Constitution and maintain its authority.

Second, to continuously strengthen and improve the work on legislation to maintain the internal rigor, harmony and unity within the legal system. The NPC and its Standing Committee have adopted such methods as argumentation before legislation, survey and investigation during legislation and review after legislation to ensure the connection and coordination between the laws to be enacted and relevant laws and regulations to ensure that they are effectively implemented. Once an important law is enacted, the relevant laws should be timely revised or abolished to address the inconsistency and incongruity. For the provisions of law requiring further clarification or to address new circumstances, the NPC and its Standing Committee issue legislative interpretations to make the provisions more targeted and and effective implementation.

Third, to actively promote the work on recording and review of normative documents. The recording and review of the normative documents is an important supervisory power granted to the county or above people's congresses and their standing committees. This institutional design,which conforms with China's conditions and has Chinese characteristics, is an important step to guarantee the enforcement of the Constitution and law, and safeguard the unity of national legal system. Based on the requirements of the Central Committee, the NPC Standing Committee has included all the normative documents in the scope of recording and review to ensure every normative document under strict recording and deliberation and every mistaken be corrected if found. It has continued to improve the working mechanism on recording and review, strengthened the proactive review, urged the legislature to revise and correct the regulations and other normative documents that conflict with the Constitution and law. By expanding the public participation, piloting feedback mechanisms for review suggestions and disclosing review suggestions to the public., these efforts have strongly safeguarded the unity of the socialist legal system.

Chapter 14
A Vision for a More Complete System of Law and Modernization of State Governance System and Capacity

Hou Xiaoguang

Abstract This chapter reviews the 70-year history of legislative work in the PRC, emphasizing its foundational role in establishing a comprehensive legal framework for modernization of state governance. It details a journey marked by challenging exploration, from the initial period of imitating the Soviet legal system to a political awakening in the mid-1950s that prompted a shift toward "walking its own path". It asserts that the formation of the socialist legal system with Chinese characteristics in 2010 was a monumental achievement, ensuring that state and social life are broadly governed by law. This chapter concludes that China has successfully charted a unique legislative course, providing a new model for global legal civilization.

Keywords Marxism · CPC leadership · 70 years · Reform and opening-up · 18th CPC National Congress · Socialist legal culture

Law is the beginning of order. The enactment of the Constitution and laws are the beginning of state governance by the Chinese people under the Party's leadership after the People's Republic of China was founded. In September 1949, the Party convened the Chinese People's Political Consultative Conference, which invited other democratic parties, people's organizations, local regions, people's liberation army, ethnic groups, overseas Chinese and other patriots. In this conference, the Common Program and the Organic Law of the Central People's Government were adopted, which laid the foundation for the new China. Since then, China has embarked on a long journey of legislative exploration for China's development and reform. Navigating both the adversity and prosperity, the Party has gradually mastered the basic laws for state governance. It has developed a profound understanding of the irreplaceable role of rule of law in promoting the modernization of state governance system and capacity. By the skillfully applying the rule of law methods to deal with the matters arising from the governance and social life, the Party has ushered the comprehensive rule of law in a new era.

H. Xiaoguang (✉)
Beijing, China
e-mail: liujixuan@lawpress.com.cn

C. Shen et al. (eds.), *A History of Legislation in the Past 70 Years in China*,
https://doi.org/10.1007/978-981-95-3799-0_14

Over the past 70 years, the Party has led the Chinese people to reflect on the successes and failures By moving beyond the copy of other countries and the confusion of left-line thinking, the Party has independently blazed the path of socialist rule of law that suits China's national conditions. Over the Party 70 years, by adhering to the Marxist guidance, the Party has adapted the basic Marxist principles of rule of law to China's development and reform, creating and developing a theoretical system of Chinese socialist rule of law. During the past 70 years, the Chinese socialist legal system with the Constitution as the core has been formed and improved, helping to gradually construct the socialist rule of law system and consolidating and developing Chinese socialist system. During the past 70 years, the excellent traditions in Chinese legal system and the combination of law and virtue and the red heritage nurtured in the revolutionary period have been passed down to the new era, and the socialist rule of law culture was nourished and disseminated, which have won the support of people for the socialist rule of law concepts. As the torchbearer of the rule of law undertaking, the legislation has made remarkable achievements in establishing a complete set of institutions, mechanisms and norms under highly efficient and democratic operations, which has played an important and foundational role in incepting, establishing and developing the path, theory, system and culture of socialism.

The legislation in the past 70 years manifests the practices for advancing rule of law in all respects and constructing a socialist law-based country and is the essential part for the system of people's congresses and the development of socialist democratic politics as well as the socialist system with Chinese characteristics. Under the Party's firm leadership and continuous progress in the system of people's congresses, the legislature has put into practice the integration of Party's leadership, people's master position and rule of law, steadfastly pursued the correct political direction, the changes of times, and solid social foundation, and continued to play the role of legislation in leading, promoting, regulating and safeguarding reform. The work on legislation has exercised an increasingly significant role in promoting the modernization of state governance and capacity. The history of legislation in the past 70 years is also a history of the struggles on the socialist path of rule of law, the development of socialist rule of law theory, the improvement of socialist legal system, and the dissemination of socialist rule of law culture.

1 A Marxist Approach to Practice and Path-Finding of China's Socialist Rule of Law

To stand firm on the Chinese socialist path and to advance the rule of law in all respects is the right choice for China. However, this path is not an easy one marked by successes and achievements, but an arduous one involving repeated self-negations, along which the rule of law has been developed and improved through continuous efforts.[1] The initial explorations of this path started in the revolutionary period, and

[1] Qi Guang, *A History of China's Rule of Law Construction*, World Affairs Press, 2011, p. 4.

it then evolved from a new democratic one to a socialist one. After errors were corrected and national circumstances were restored, it entered a new socialist era. In this period, there were attempts to imitate the Soviet Union or simply copy Western countries, but also a political awakening to adhere to Marxist guidance, seek truth from facts and build the country based on national conditions; and there were also compaigns to fight against the counter-revolutionaries and efforts to consolidate the revolutionary regime and systems and continuous correction of left-line mistakes to re-construct the rule of law. Finally, China embarked on the socialist path of the rule of law.

1.1 Legal System Construction in the Revolutionary Base Areas

In the 1920–30s, the Party adopted the constitutional principles and laws to promote the rule of law in the limited regions of the revolutionary base areas, which accumulated valuable experience in state governance. Between 1931 and 1937, the Chinese Soviet Republic established local governments for all the revolutionary base areas according to the Party's line and policies, and enacted many laws and decrees for them. After completely dismantling the KMT's old legal system, it promulgated over 130 laws and decrees including the soviet organization, criminal regulations, land law, labor law and marriage law, which set out an initial new democratic framework for legal system. The Principles of the Constitution was the first constitutional document formulated by the people under the Party's leadership. It has a unique position in the Party's history of constructing state power and legal system and plays an extremely important role in consolidating and developing the Soviet republic.[2] The enactment, promulgation and implementation of various laws have satisfied the needs of social, economic and cultural life within the republic, which consolidated the Soviet regime and ensured the success of revolutionary wars, germinating the seeds for constructing socialist rule of law. The experience in developing the legal system of the revolutionary base areas, such as the Party's leadership, the people's democracy, the principle of socialism, and the voluntary correction of the left-line mistakes and mistakes in imitating the Soviet Union model, is still valuable for today legislation on the implementation of the Four Cardinal Principles, reform and opening-up and socialist modernization, and should be carried forward.[3] In his *Introducing the Communist*, when summarizing the experience of the Chinese Soviet Republic period, Mao Zedong offered a penetrating opinion that "the Party blazed

[2] ZHOU Meng, *Initial Explorations and Practice of the People's Congress System in the Chinese Soviet Republic*, Qiushi Journal, Vol. 5, 2019.

[3] ZHUO Fan, *History of the Legal System of the Chinese Soviet Republic*, Jiangxi Colleges and Universities Publishing House, 1992, Preface I.

the trail of people's political power and thus learned the art of government...These were momentous advances and achievements."[4]

Facing severe external battles during the revolutionary period, the Party developed a more accurate and profound understanding of the basic conditions of the semi-feudal and semi-colonial China, the status of all classes of Chinese society, and the features and laws of the Chinese revolutions It integrated the Marxism-Leninism with the practices of Chinese revolution, and improved its capacity for governing the Party, the State and the armed forces. During this period, the Party also started to explore and accumulate experience in governing regional power and undertaking all-round development. With respect to rule of law, the Marxism-Leninism theory on law was applied to guide the legislation, thereby establishingan initial legal system adapted to the revolutionary base areas. "If there was no such practices, there would no development and progress in the legal system of the revolutionary base areas, neither would the socialist legal system today."[5]

1.2 Transition from New Democratic Rule of Law to Socialist Path of Rule of Law

With the continuous expansion of the liberated areas, the Party had led the Soviet areas, revolutionary base areas and the liberated areas in establishing the revolutionary legal system during the periods of Agrarian Reform, War of Resistance Against Japanese Aggression and the War of Liberation, a process in which the practice of building the rule of law was first carried out regionally and then expanded nationwide. To secure complete victory, the Central Committee issued the Instructions concerning Abolishing the Six Codes of the KMT and Determining Judicial Principles for the Liberated Areas, and then the CPPCC adopted the Common Program which declared that "all laws, decrees and judicial systems of the KMT reactionary government which oppress the people shall be abolished. Laws and decrees protecting the people shall be enacted and the people's judicial system shall be established" This resolution laid the legal foundation for overthrowing the reactionary regime, ensuring the establishment of a new state and constitutional order, and giving directions for the rule of law development for the new state. As pointed by Dong Biwu, "after the victory of revolution is won, our people's democratic government abashed the old laws, which is good, because the old laws must be abolished completely and destroyed without any traces. To destroy, as I say, is to completely destroy its legal system because it stands for the will of the reactionary rule". The abolition of old legal system represented the practical application of the Marxist principles of state building and law for the proletariat, a milestone in China's

[4] MAO Zedong, *Introducing the Communist*, in *Selected Works of Mao Zedong (Vol. 2)*, Foreign Languages Press, 1965, p. 293.

[5] ZHUO Fan, *History of the Legal System of the Chinese Soviet Republic*, Jiangxi Colleges and Universities Publishing House, 1992, Preface I.

history of the rule of law development. It also marked the decisive break between the new and the old, as the experience in new democratic rule of law construction was expanded across the whole nation, the old KMT's governance system characterized by exploitation came to an end, fundamentally changing people's conceptions of the state and law and creating a favorable environment for pursuing the socialist path of rule of law.

Xi Jinping pointed out that "in the early stage of the People's Republic, while abolishing outdated laws, the Party used the successful experience it had gained during the new-democratic revolution when establishing a legal system for its bases to quickly begin developing and lay the initial foundation for socialist rule of law".[6] Specifically, the laws and decrees concerning marriage, land reform, trade union and punishing counter-revolutionary activities and corruption were successively enacted and issued, while the people's judicial system was also in a step-by-step progress. Dong Biwu believed that the revolutionary legal system was of decisive importance for safeguarding the revolutionary order, consolidating the people's democratic regime, protecting people's legitimate rights and interests, and sheltering national economic development. The revolutionary legal system was also established and improved in the continuous fight against various erroneous ideological trends.[7]

In The Chinese Revolution and Chinese Communist Party, Mao Zedong said, "the Chinese revolutionary movement led by the Communist Party embraces the two stages, i.e., the democratic and the socialist revolutions, which are two essentially different revolutionary processes, and that the second process can be carried through only after the first has been completed. The democratic revolution is the necessary preparation for the socialist revolution, and the socialist revolution is the inevitable sequel to the democratic revolution."[8] The period between 1949 and 1956 was a transitional phase from new democratic revolution to socialist revolution. Therefore, the problem in the undertakings for the rule of law was to ensure a smooth transition from revolutionary legal system to a socialist one and to maintain stable and sustainable development of the legal system in this transition. This was also the basic condition for the successful transition from new democratic revolution to socialist revolution and for setting up the socialist political, economic and cultural systems. But it was the first time that the Chinese communists had encountered this task and the first time in the history of the international communist movement, there was no ready-made answer in the Marxist theory, nor any other prior experience in other socialist countries.[9] After the promulgation of the 1954 Constitution, the resolution adopted in the First Session of the First National People's Congress stipulated that the existing

---

[6] Publicity Department of the CPC Central Committee ed., *A Reader's Book on the Important Speeches of Xi Jinping*, Xuexi Press and People's Publishing House, 2016, p. 86.

[7] DONG Biwu, *Several Issues in the Work on Politics and Law and the Issue in Strengthening Law-abiding Education in the Past Five Years*, Collection of Dong Biwu's Writings on Politics and Law, Law Press, 1986, p. 370.

[8] MAO Zedong, *The Chinese Revolution and Chinese Communist Party*, in Selected Works of Mao Zedong (Vol. 2), Foreign Languages Press, 1965, pp. 330–331.

[9] LI Zhongda, *Mao Zedong's Theory on Law and Its Practice*, Shaanxi People's Education Press, 1989, p. 205.

laws and decrees enacted or approved by the Central People's Government since the founding of PRC continued to be effective unless they contravened the Constitution although it did not specify which laws or decrees were contrary to the Constitution. This resolution transformed the eligible new-democratic laws into the legal institutions and mechanisms suited to the new circumstances for the rule of law development, thereby ensuring an effective connection and transition between two revolutionary legal systems. Under the Party's leadership, the Chinese people applied their own wisdom to explore a distinct path, contributing the practice, experience and model of rule of law to human civilization.

1.3 A Socialist Path for Rule of Law with Distinct Chinese Features

The enactment of the Constitution and laws establishes, consolidates and improves socialism, gives impetus to socialist rule of law construction, and reflects and safeguards the fundamental interests of the majority of the Chinese people. The 1954 Constitution, the first one since the founding of the PRC, made a summary of China's experience over nearly a hundred years as well as the experience accumulated during the first five years, thereby laying down the path and direction for socialism. The promulgation of the Constitution marked China's entry into a new stage of political development. The Common Program and the 1954 Constitution provided strong constitutional basis for founding and consolidating the People's Republic of China. During the transition from the Common Program to the 1954 Constitution, the top-level design of national basic political, economic, cultural and social systems was gradually completed, which safeguarded the gradual transition of China from new democratic revolution to socialist revolution. In his remarks on the draft Constitution, Mao Zedong pointed out that "to codify the principles of people's democracy and socialism in the form of a fundamental law, in the form of the constitution, so that there will be a clear course before the people of the whole country and they will feel sure they have a clear, definite and correct path to follow – this will heighten their enthusiasm."[10] Dong Biwu also pointed that to pursue socialist path was the guideline that was widely received by Chinese people, and China's legal system construction also entered a new stage.[11] By closely following this path, the new republic rapidly enacted and promulgated nearly 1,000 laws, decrees and regulations within only two to three years, and spared no effort to draft other basic laws, including the criminal law, civil law, civil procedure law and criminal procedure law, in a bid for laying

---

[10] MAO Zedong, *On the Draft Constitution of the People's Republic of China (June 14, 1954)*, in Selected Works of Mao Zedong (Vol. 5), Foreign Languages Press, 1965, p. 145.

[11] DONG Biwu, *On Further Strengthening People's Democratic Legal System and Ensuring the Socialist Undertakings*, in Collection of Dong Biwu's Writings on Politics and Law, Law Press, 1986, pp. 479–480.

down the basic framework of socialist legal system.[12] However, to construct a grand edifice of the rule of law, the new republic was confronted with heavy and arduous legislative tasks. As advocated in the Party's Eighth National Congress, one of the urgent tasks facing China then was to begin the systematic codification of a fairly complete set of laws and to put the legal system of the country on a sound footing, and the state should gradually and systematically to make a complete set of laws and ensure that there were laws to abide by and law were observed according to its needs. In this period, under the Party's firm leadership, there was a rapid surge in legislation, which promoted the smooth socialist of agriculture, handicrafts and capitalist industry and commerce and provided reliable legal guarantee for establishing the socialist legal system and consolidating the state power under people's democratic dictatorship.

Since the October Revolution in the early twentieth century, the experience of the Soviet Union had been heavily relied on by China, Eastern Europe and other socialist countries. From the legislation in the revolutionary base areas, the Party learned from and, to some extend, imitated the Soviet legal system, drawing on its legislative experience and legal theory to guide the work on legislation. The Outline of the Constitution, the first attempt by the Party to lead Chinese people to enact a constitution, mainly referred to the Soviet experience, for most of its provisions were similar to those of the 1918 Soviet Russia Constitution, and some its provisions on basic democratic rights of the labor workers and peasants were borrowed from the Declaration of Rights of the Laboring and Exploited People in the 1918 Constitution.[13] This reference and submission to the Soviet experience were determined by the historical conditions, political environment and global situation at that time. As Mao Zedong pointed out in On the People's Democratic Dictatorship, "the salvoes of the October Revolution brought us Marxism-Leninism. The October Revolution helped progressives in China, as throughout the world, to adopt the proletarian world outlook as the instrument for studying a nation's destiny and considering anew their own problems. Follow the path of the Russians – that was their conclusion", "The 40 years' experience of Sun Yat-sen and the twenty-eight years' experience of the Communist Party have taught us to lean to one side, and we are firmly convinced that in order to win victory and consolidate it we must lean to one side. In the light of the experiences accumulated in these 40 years and these twenty-eight years, all Chinese without exception must lean either to the side of imperialism or to the side of socialism".[14] To lean toward Soviet Russia in ideology and state systems meant a comprehensive acceptance of the Soviet model, including its legal system.[15] The Soviet Russia also sent expert advisers to China to support its construction, and

---

[12] CAO Kangtai, *Explorations and Development of Rule of Law Construction in the Past 60 Years*, Qiushi Journal, Vol. 14, pp. 32–35 (2009).

[13] HAN Dayuan, *The Dissemination of Soviet Russian Constitution in China and Its Contemporary Significance*, Chinese Journal of Law, No. 5, pp. 189–208 (2018).

[14] MAO Zedong, *On the People's Democratic Dictatorship*, in Selected Works of Mao Zedong (Vol. 4), Foreign Languages Press, 1961, p. 415.

[15] WANG Zhihua, *Some Reflections on the Soviet Law's Influence on Chinese Law*, Journal of East China University of Political Science and Law, No. 1, pp. 95–100 (2008).

the legal experts provided opinions on China's political and legal development for example, by directly participating in the drafting of the laws and regulations enacted or to be enacted, offering suggestions for the political and legal institutions, and introducing the Soviet experience.

Learning from the Soviet laws and leaning to one side were reflected in the legislative process of some important laws in the early stage of the PRC. The legislation not only drew on the guiding thoughts on law, legislative principles and jurisprudence, but also adopted some provisions. For example, as Liu Shaoqi stated in his report on the draft constitution, "the road we are taking is exactly the road traversed by the Soviet Union. About this we have not the slightest doubt. The Soviet road is the road all humanity will eventually take, in accordance with the laws governing historical development. To by-pass this road is impossible". The 1954 Constitution made reference to the 1936 Soviet Union Constitution, the Stalin's report, 1918 Soviet Russian Constitution and the socialist spirits and principles embodied in the constitution.[16] Another example is the draft Crminal Law, which incorporated the criminal law institutions and mechanisms characteristic of the Soviet Union, such as the emphasis on the nature of class, concept of crime and purpose, the rejection of principle of legality but confirmation of the use of analogy and retroactivity.[17] The draft Civil Code is also the example that not only completely imitated the four-part arrangement of the 1922 Civil Code of the Soviet Union, i.e. the General Provisions, Property Rights, Obligations and Inheritance, but was extensively impacted by the Soviet Union in the legislation of the General Provisions part and academic research, for example the adoption of the same stances with the Soviet Union in the matters subject to civil law, civil entities and civil objects, and some important civil law systems and principles.[18] China's creation of marriage and family law was likewise influenced by the Soviet model and experience, becoming an independent department of law widely accepted by the academia and legislative and judicial practice, and exerting decades of influence in China.[19]

Effectively learning from the socialist legal system construction and legislative experience of the Soviet Union had played a tremendous role in helping China's legislature to master the legislative theories and practices, abandon the outdated legal thinking as soon as possible, and rapidly improve the legislative capacity and standards. It provided some similar experience to draw on, shortened the time of legislative preparation, and avoided many detours. At the same time, the Party was also increasingly aware of the problems that had emerged in the Soviet Union, and its own development of the legal system gradually placed more emphasis on its own characteristics and an independent path for China.

---

[16] HAN Dayuan, *The Dissemination of Soviet Russian Constitution in China and Its Contemporary Significance*, Chinese Journal of Law, No. 5, pp. 189–208 (2018).

[17] LI Xiuqing, *A Study on China's Transplant of Criminal Legislation from the Soviet Union*, Law Review, No. 6, pp. 120–126 (2002).

[18] *Ibid.*

[19] LI Xiuqing, *Development of Marriage Law in China and the Impact of the Soviet Union's Model*, Science of Law, No. 4, pp. 76–89 (2002).

In 1956, Mao Zedong made a speech titled On Ten Major Relationships, which summarized China's experience with a reference to the Soviet Union, which made initial explorations for the socialist path adapted to China's conditions. Several years later, when summarizing the experience after the founding of PRC, he still regarded the speech as the turning point, as he wrote "we copied foreign experience in the eight years after its founding. But from the ten major relationships were put forward in 1956, we began to find the path that suits China".[20] In short, the core of his speech is "to follow its own path".

Since this turning point, the Party has developed a more sober and keen understanding of bot the Soviet experience and model and China's own path of exploration and formation. As emphasized in the More On the Historical Experience of Proletarian Dictatorship,[21] "there are different aspects to Soviet experience in revolution and construction as far as its international significance is concerned. Of the successful experience of the Soviet Union, one part is fundamental and of universal significance at the present stage of human history. This is the most important and fundamental phase of Soviet experience. The other part is not of universal significance. In addition, the Soviet Union also had its. mistakes and failures. No country can ever avoid them entirely, though they may vary in form and degree. And it was even more difficult for the Soviet Union to avoid them, because it was the first socialist country and. had no successful experience of others to go by. Such mistakes and failures, however, provide extremely useful lessons for all communists". In his report on the work of government at the Fourth Session of the First National People's Congress, Zhou Enlai pointed out, "we should not copy the experience of other countries mechanically. Even the experience in success must also be carefully selected and combined with the specific conditions of the country when they are applied. We are carrying out a cause that there has no predecessor. When we have not practiced it, it is not easy to choose the experience of other countries, and it is even more difficult to combine it with the specific conditions of the country. To improve the ability in choosing and learning to use it correctly not only takes some time, but also may have to pay a certain price. If we study well, we can shorten out time and pay a smaller price." According to this major transformation in thinking, China's legislation also under went significant changes, placing paid greater emphasis on China's realities and on integrating the Marxism-Leninism theory on law with China's legislative practice. Dong Biwu advocated the requirements on legislation for the new republic: to establish the people's democratic dictatorship and protect and consolidate the new state apparatus for people's victory, the advanced experience of the Soviet Union must be learned and studied; while in learning from its experience in legislation, administration of justice and legal study, the first thing to do is to more frequently adopt the means that can integrate the practices for current Chinese revolution, pay

---

[20] PANG Xianzhi and JIN Chongji, *Before and After the Ten Major Relationships*, Hundred Year Tide, No. 12, pp. 14–24 (2003).

[21] Editorial Department of the People's Daily, *More On the Historical Experience of Proletarian Dictatorship*, People's Daily, December 29, 1956. It was an article prepared by the editorial department of the People's Daily on the basis of a discussion at an enlarged meeting of the Political Bureau of the CPC Central Committee.

more attention to China's historical conditions and the actual social and political environment in order to transform the experience into what is really needed and adapted to China's conditions.[22] Against this backdrop, the second draft Civil Code differed significantly from the first. It demonstrated the attempt to move beyond the Soviet influence and to create a new civil code system with innovative contents on its own, trying to draw a distinction both from the Soviet civil law model and from the capitalist civil law system.[23]

1.4 Stagnation of Legislation and Setbacks in Socialist Path of Rule of Law

The path to socialist rule of law is not easy. From walking the path of the Soviet Union to walking in its own path, the exploration for the path of rule of law tended to emphasize more on China's conditions. By the late 1950s, the left-line thinking started to take over the Party's guiding principles. Till the middle 1960s, due to the serious mistakes in judging the domestic and international situations, the left-line thinking was further promoted, the decade-long Cultural Revolution eventually broke out. This disrupted the work on legislation, put a stop to the legislature and inflicted serious setbacks to the socialist cause of legislation. According to statistics, after March 1964, the NPC and its Standing Committee did not enact any law or decree in 14 years except for the adoption of the 1975 Constitution.

Due to various complex factors, China was not able to achieve the construction of a legal system through large-scale legislation in the early years of the PRC. It failed to establish an institutional "breakwater" capable of protecting law-based state governance through a complete set of institutions and mechanisms; it failed to effectively incorporate the Party's democratic centralism into the construction of state systems and state agency operations so as to achieve the heterogeneous construction of Party's systems and state systems; and it also failed to seize the opportunity to keep firm in the socialist path for rule of law so as to promote the legal system under people's democracy. The resulting inadequacy of legal system and stagnation of legislative activities caused the lack of laws to abide by in many aspects of state governance and social life. Meanwhile, the feudal ignorance of legal system and the serious impact of the left-line thinking aggravated the disconformity with and disloyalty to law. For example, the Criminal Code, Criminal Procedure Code, Civil Code and Civil Procedure Code, laws most concerned with the protection of people's basic rights and general social relationships, were not promulgated. What's more, in some occasions,

---

[22] *Preface*, in Legislative Affairs Committee of the Central People's Government ed. Н. Г. Судариков and Б. С. Беков, Lectures on Soviet State and Law, 1951.

[23] Li Xiuqing, *A Study on China's Transplant of Soviet Union's Civil Law*, Social Sciences in China, No. 5, pp. 125–141, 206 (2002), and Wang Zhihua, *Some Reflections on the Soviet Law's Influence on Chinese Law*, Journal of East China University of Political Science and Law, No. 1, pp. 95–100 (2008).

the general public and even the staff engaged in case investigation, prosecuting and adjudication lacked uniform and clear-cut standards regarding what was lawful or unlawful, what was a crime, what constituted a crime and how punishment should be imposed.[24] As the 1981 "Resolution on Certain Questions in the History of Our party since the Founding of the People's Republic of China" pointed out, to gradually establish a highly democratic socialist political system is one the fundamental tasks for socialist revolution. The lack of emphasis on this task had contributed to the Cultural Revolution, which is a grave lesson that needs to bear in mind.

Though there were twists and turns along the socialist path of the rule of law, the Party has never ceased its footsteps for exploring socialism along with the Chinese people. As pointed out by Xi Jinping, "the process by which the people build socialism under the leadership of the Party can be divided into two historical phases – one that preceded the launch of reform and opening-up in 1978, and a second that followed on from that event. The two phases – at once related to and distinct from each other – are both pragmatic explorations in building socialism conducted by the people under the leadership of the Party. Chinese socialism was initiated after the launch of reform and opening-up and based on more than 20 years of development since the socialist system was established in the 1950s after the PRC was founded".[25] The explorations and development of the rule of law could be characterized by the distinction of phases and consistency. In the two-phase 70 years, the central theme in exploring and promoting Chinese socialist rule of law development remains unchanged, namely to apply the Marxist basic principles to explore and answer the questions of what is socialist rule of law and how to build a socialist rule of law country based on China's conditions. The consistency of the theme determines that the rule of law development in China has also been consistent, and the answers to these questions are also determined by the socialist path of political development with Chinese characteristics.[26] Therefore, Xi Jinping emphasized that the pre-reform-and-opening-up phase should be correctly appraised, "we should neither negate the pre-reform-and-opening-up phase in comparison with the post-reform-and-opening-up phase, nor the converse", the former phase accumulated experience for the latter one, and the latter one insisted in, reformed and developed the former one, so to the former phase "we should adhere to the principles of seeking truth from facts and distinguishing the trunk from the branches. We should uphold truth, rectify our errors, draw on practical experience, and learn lessons. This is the foundation which facilitates further advance of the cause of the Party and the people."[27] This attitude conforms with the dialectical and historical materialism. It should also be recognized that without the develpment of the people's democracy and the legal system, there would be no socialist country under the rule of law; without the establishment of socialist legal thinking, there would be

[24] GONG Pixiang, *Modernization of Chinese Legal System*, China University of Political Science and Law Press, 2004, p. 2004.

[25] XI Jinping, *The Governance of China*, Foreign Languages Press, 2018, pp. 24–25.

[26] QI Guang, *A History of China's Rule of Law Construction*, World Affairs Press, 2011, preface and p. 46.

[27] XI Jinping, *The Governance of China*, Foreign Languages Press, 2018, p. 25.

no correct choice of the basic strategy for governing the country by law; and without the great achivements in building the socialist legal system, there would be no such historic accomplishments in socialist rule of law development. Likewise, without the difficulties, setbacks and detours experienced during the construction of legal system, there would not have been the firm determination to adhere to the goal of building a socialist rule of law country.[28]

1.5 A New Chapter for Socialist Rule of Law

However difficult it might seem, the challenge will be overcome. The legislation in the past 70 years has progressed in tandem with the Chinese socialist cause and reform, so it can also be divided into two phases. Though the trends and missions are different, the work on legislation in the two phases is very similar. The legislation in the early years of PRC was carried out to destroy the outdated legal traditions and abolish KMT's Six Codes, and the understanding of the socialist rule of law was as new as the understanding of the transition from new democratic rule of law to socialist rule of law. The construction of rule of law thus began from scratch. At the beginning of reform and opening-up, there was a vacuum created by the Cultural Revolution and were no resources to depend on. Therefore, the 1982 Constitution was nothing but a total creation. Nonetheless, the Party and the Chinese people have never slackened the efforts for exploring the socialist path of rule of law. The 1982 Constitution inherited and developed the 1954 Constitution, while the enactment of the basic laws including the Criminal Law and Criminal Procedure Law also referred to the socialist practices and experience before the reform and opening-up. In the winding path, there were lessons and experience. Along with the tortuous path of Chinese socialist cause, the socialist path of rule of law has been pursued as the correct one after continuous calibration and adjustment based on the lessons and experience from successes and failures in socialist construction. In a word, "the historical experience of our Party testifies that our Party too has been tempered through struggles against various wrong lines of policy, thus winning great victories in the revolution and in construction".[29] After the Third Plenary Session of the Eleventh CPC Central Committee, the Central Committee made corrections and rectifications, initiated reform and opening-up, summarized the lessons of socialist construction, and attached more importance to the fundamental role of institutional development in enhancing state and social governance and promoting socialist modernization.

---

[28] Qi Guang, *A History of China's Rule of Law Construction*, World Affairs Press, 2011, Preface and p. 51.

[29] Editorial Department of the People's Daily, *On the Historical Experience of Proletarian Dictatorship*, People's Daily, April 5, 1956. It was an article prepared by the editorial department of the People's Daily on the basis of a discussion at an enlarged meeting of the Political Bureau of the CPC Central Committee.

In the new era of reform and opening-up, under the guidance of the theoretical system of socialism with Chinese characteristics, the socialist rule of law construction has a clearer direction, the Chinese characteristics of legislation has become more distinct, and its effectiveness has become more evident. Since the reform and opening-up, our party has adhered to the line of Marxism, continuously explored and answered major theoretical and practical questions, such as what socialism is and how to build socialism, continuously promoted the adaptation of Marxism to Chinese context, opened up the road of socialism with Chinese characteristics, and formed a theoretical system of socialism with Chinese characteristics. The report of the Seventeenth CPC National Congress put forward for the first time the theoretical system of socialism with Chinese characteristics, including Deng Xiaoping Theory, Three Represents and the Scientific Outlook on Development. Under the guidance of this scientific theoretical system, the goals of the socialist path of rule of law proposed by the Party become clearer, drawing up a grand blueprint for legislation. The Fifteenth CPC National Congress proposed to govern the country according to the law and make it a socialist country ruled by the law; the Sixteenth National Congress proposed that the most fundamental task to develop socialist democracy is to integrate the party's leadership, the people's master position and the rule of law; and the Seventeenth National Congress proposed that the rule of law constitutes the essential requirement of socialist democracy and to comprehensively implement the rule of law as a fundamental principle and speed up the building of a socialist country under the rule of law. As the objectives for rule of law country have been were successively articulated, the requirements for the work on legislation were correspondingly clarified. The Fifteenth Congress set out a general legislative mission of "strengthening the work on legislation, improving its quality, establishing the socialist legal system with Chinese characteristics by 2010"; the Sixteenth Congress reiterated the mission and officially put forward the socialist legal system with Chinese characteristics; and the Seventeenth Congress emphasized the need to persist in scientific and democratic legislation to improve the socialist law system with Chinese characteristics.

The system is far-reaching and fundamental. To strengthen legislation in the era of reform and opening-up is to make the socialist system more mature and definitive. After the Third Plenary Session of the Eleventh CPC Central Committee, the Party has applied a completely new perspective to consider the state governance, given emphasis on the overall, stable and long-term character of system, always put institutional development in a prominent place, combined the reform and opening-up with institutional development and strived for institutionalizing the achievements in reform. Deng Xiaoping thought that "system is decisive", so he emphasized that "the problems in the leadership and organizational systems are more fundamental, widespread and long-lasting, and that they have a greater effect on the overall interests of our country. This is a question that has a close bearing on whether our Party and state will change political color and should therefore command the attention of the entire Party",[30] so he asked to "earnestly establish the socialist democratic system

[30] DENG Xiaoping, *On the Reform of the System of Party and State Leadership (August 18, 1980)*, in Selected Works of Deng Xiaoping (Vol. 2), Foreign Languages Press, 1995, p. 332.

and legal system. Only in this way can these problems be solved". The 1982 Constitution laid out the Four Cardinal Principles as a fundamental institutional undertaking, which consolidated the foundation of the Chinese socialist system, improved the setting of state institutions, provided constitutional basis for One Country, Two Systems, further consolidated the state power in the new stage, and safeguarded the Chinese socialist construction. Deng Xiaoping also pointed out with a vision for the future that "it will probably take another thirty years for us to develop a more mature and well-defined system in every field. The principles and policies to be applied under each system will also be more firmly established".[31]

The formation of the Chinese socialist legal system is a major milestone for the development of socialist rule of law with Chinese characteristics. In 1979, the adoption of seven laws, including the Criminal Law, Criminal Procedure Law, Electoral Law and Local Organization Law, marked the beginning of the work on legislation in the new stage. As the China's social economic development and the reform and opening-up advance further, the Chinese socialist system has also transitioned from the "establishment of the legal system for socialist market economy", "initial formation of Chinese socialist legal system", "basic establishment of Chinese legal system" to "the establishment of Chinese socialist legal system". Through concerted efforts by all parties, the Chinese socialist legal system was established in 2010 as scheduled, ensuring that laws were available to govern all the fields of the state governance and social life. This achievement "is a remarkable and significant achievement" as appraised by Xi Jinping in his Explanations on the Draft Resolution of the Central Committee of the CPC on Certain Major Issues Concerning Comprehensively Advancing the Law-Based Governance of China. The formation of the Chinese socialist legal system is an important milestone in the history of socialist legal system development in China and an important symbol of the gradual maturation of the Chinese socialist system, strongly promoting and guaranteed the smooth progress of reform and opening-up and socialist modernization. As of the end of August 2019, there were 274 pieces of laws, more than 600 pieces of administrative regulations and over 12,000 pieces of local regulations in force. As the Chinese socialist legal system continues to improve, it can basically adapt to the needs of China's reform and socialist cause and provide a sound legal framework to promote the modernization of the state governance system and capacity in the new era.

1.6 A Keener Understanding, a Firmer Standing and a More Specific Direction

Since the Eighteenth National Congress, the Central Committee with Xi Jinping as the core has made great efforts to promote the Five-Sphere Integrated Plan and

[31] DENG Xiaoping, *Excerpts from Talks Given in Wuchang, Shenzhen, Zhuhai and Shanghai (January 18–February 21, 1992)*, in Selected Works of Deng Xiaoping (Vol. 3), Foreign Languages Press, 1994, p. 360.

Four-Pronged Comprehensive Strategy in a coordinated manner, while dedicating itself to promoting deepened reform and opening-up on a broader scale and at a deeper level. The Central Committee attaches great importance to the rule of law, emphasizing the implementation of the basic line of rule of law, and accelerating the construction of a socialist rule of law country. It also places more emphasis on giving full play to the important role of the rule of law in state governance and social administration. Xi Jinping pointed out that "the decision to advance the rule of law reflects the Party's will to enhance its governance capacity. It did so not because of pressure", "therefore, our comprehensive efforts to advance the rule of law must be conducive to strengthening and improving the Party's leadership, bolstering its position as the governing party, and accomplishing its position in governing the country. In absolutely no way does this amount to weakening the leadership of the Party."[32]

As laid out in the Third Plenary Session of the Eighteenth CPC Central Committee, the overall goal of deepening the reform comprehensively is improving and developing socialism with Chinese characteristics, and promoting the modernization of the state governance system and capacity. As further emphasized by Xi Jinping, "we are tasked with an important historic mission, that is to make our socialist system with Chinese characteristics more mature and better established, and provide a set of more complete, more stable and more effective systems for the development of the Party and the nation, the well-being of the people, social harmony and stability, and the enduring prosperity and stability of the country".[33] This shows that the Party attaches great importance to institutional development. The state governance system is essentially the system of state institutions, and the state governance capacity is the ability to enforce this system. The representation in law of the state institutional system is the Chinese socialist rule of law system, which emcompasses both the Party's institutional system and the legal system centered on the constittutions. As Chinese socialism enters a new era, the revision of the Party's Constitution provides new guidelines for improving the Party's institutional system to guarantee the interconnection of it with the state legal system; the promulgation of the 2018 Amendment to the Constitution provides new basis for establishing a complete normative system of laws; and a series of new measures made in the Eighteenth and Nineteenth National Congresses provides new plan for guaranteeing the stability of policy and institutional system. The NPC and its Standing Committee also enact a lot of important law, issued interpretations, adopt decisions on reform measures and authorization, and advance the Chinese socialist legal system with the Constitution as the core to a higher level with better quality, which have made contributions to the development of Chinese socialist rule of law system and the socialist rule of law country.

Over the past 70 years, especially over the past 40 years, the construction of rule of has undergone several transitions: from stagnation to revitalization, from

[32] Xi Jinping, *The Governance of China (Vol. 2)*, Foreign Languages Press, 2017, p. 120.

[33] Xi Jinping, *Improve Governance Capacity Through the Socialist System with Chinese Characteristics (February 17, 2014)*, in *The Governance of China*, Foreign Languages Press, 2018, p. 117.

the disruption in the Cultural Revolution to the restration of legislation in the early reform and opening-up period, from the availability of laws and observance of laws, to the emphasis on strict law enforcement and punishment of violation of law, and further to the integrated approach of scientific legislation, strict law enforcement, impartial administration of justice and law-abiding among the whole nation, from legal system to rule of law, from scientific and democratic governance to scientific, democratic and law-based governance, from rule of law to the integration of rule of law and rule of virtue, and from the formation of Chinese socialist legal system to the development of Chinese socialist rule of law system. In deepening its understanding of the relationship between the Party and the law, the Party has gradually upgraded rule of law as the basic means of state governance and gained a better grasp of rule of law in improving and developing Chinese socialist system and promoting the modernization of state governance system and capacity. Through these efforts and understandings, the Party has drawn the important conclusion that its leadership is consistent with the socialist rule of law, namely the socialist rule of law must adhere to the Party's leadership while the Party's leadership must rely on socialist rule of law. To this end, "in the new circumstances, to perform its duty properly in state governance and national rejuvenation, our Party should exercise strict discipline, and govern the country in accordance with the Constitution", "as it leads the people in formulating and implementing the Constitution and laws, the Party must act within the limits prescribed by the Constitution and laws, and ensure that it exercises leadership in legislation, guarantees law enforcement and takes the lead in observing the law". The Party's governance should also operate within the framework of the law, not the other way around. As Xi Jinping pointed out, "it was the Party that proposed the rule of law in China and then made it a fundamental principle by which the Party leads the people in governing the country. In addition, the Party leads the people in advancing the rule of law in practice". In the comprehensive development of the rule of law, to adhere to the Party's leadership in legislation is completely in line with the nature, status and responsibilities of legislative activities. During the reform and opening-up, the Party's leadership in legislation and the exercise of leadership in state and social affairs through rule of law methods constitute the basic experience which the Party has accumulated from practice, not only guaranteeing the correct political direction of Chinese socialist rule of law construction but also pointing toward an even brighter future for the socialist path of rule of law.

2 Theory of Chinese Socialist Rule of Law

Xi Jinping thought that "every form of rule of law is underpinned by a set of political theories; every rule of law model has to it a certain political logic; and every path of rule of law has within it a political position".[34] Only a scientific theory of the rule of law can lead and ensure the long-term and healthy development of practices. The Resolution put forward the task "to develop the socialist rule of law theory that conforms with China's actual circumstances, embodies Chinese characteristics, and reflects the law of social development" for the first time. In his Explanations on the Resolution, Xi Jinping lists the "application of the Chinese socialist rule of law theory", "Party's leadership" and "adherence to Chinese socialist system" as the three key elements for answering the question of "whether the comprehensive rule of law can be completed", which accentuates the importance of the socialist rule of law theory.

Xi Jinping pointed out that the "theory of Chinese socialist rule of law is a theoretical achievement in developing the rule of law".[35] The theory of Chinese socialist rule of law is an important component of the system of the Chinese socialist theory; it carries forward and develops the Marxist classical theories on state and law and scientifically summarizes the experience in integrating the basic principles of Marxist theory of rule of law and China's construction of rule of law. It is also the innovative achievement of carrying forward the heritage of the Party's rule of law practices and the excellent Chinese traditional legal culture, while absorbing the advanced rule of law around the globe. The adaptation of Marxist theory of the rule of law to China's realities, which is a magnificent process that evolves with the times, has greatly promoted the innovation and development of the Chinese socialist rule of law theory.[36] By centering on the basic question of what kind of socialist rule of law country is desired and how to build it, the theory of Chinese socialist rule of law has provided strong theoretical support for exercising the Party's centralized and unified leadership in building China into a law-based country; for the practices and development of scientific legislation, strict law enforcement, impartial administration of justice, and universal observance of law; and for continuously following the Chinese socialist path of rule of law, promoting the Chinese socialist system and developing Chinese socialist rule of law culture.

---

[34] Xi Jinping, *Speech at a seminar for principal provincial and ministerial level leaders on the guiding principles from the Fourth Plenary' Session of the 18th CPC Central Committee and on comprehensively advancing the law-based governance of China (February 2, 2015)*, in Central Party Literature Office ed., *The Law-Based Governance of China*, Central Party Literature Press, 2017, p. 39.

[35] Xi Jinping, *The Governance of China (Vol. 2)*, Foreign Languages Press, 2017, p. 138.

[36] Mo Jihong and Zhai Guoqiang, *New Development of the Chinese Socialist Rule of Law Theory*, People's Daily, March 5, 2018, p. 7; Li Lin, *To Develop the Socialist Rule of Law Theory in the New Era*, People's Daily, July 25, 2018; Gong Pixiang, *The Road to Chinese Socialist Rule of Law Theory*, Social Science Front, Vol. 6, pp. 198–210 (2015). Editorial of Chaoyang Law Review ed., *Essays in Memory of Professor Sun Guohua*, Zhejiang People's Publishing House, 2018, p. 78.

Legislation is the main channel for conducting the exploration of the socialist rule of law theory. The work on legislation in the past 70 years has provided a strong foundation for developing this theory, and the understandings of the law governing legislative activities, the systematic summary of the legislation experience, and the theory of legislation have also become inseparable from the theory of rule of law. The major achievements in socialist rule of law made during different phases of development guide, in return, the legislative practices toward higher quality, high-level development and higher goals.

2.1 Pioneering Efforts in Forming and Improving Socialist Rule of Law Theory

Legislation is the precondition for building China into a rule of law country. In this regard, the socialist rule of law theory was formed on the basis of the socialist legislative practices, underpinned by practices in law enforcement, administration of justice and law-abiding.

The socialist rule of law theory originated from the theory developed in the new democratic period and germinated during the new democratic revolution. The Chinese Communists represented by Mao Zedong attached great importance to the construction of state power when engaging in the revolutionary struggles in order to accumulate the experience in this regard. After a summary of the experience and comparisons, a complete set of theories on the legal system under people's democracy was gradually formed. In the Chinese Soviet Republic period, to distinct the newly born red regime from the KMT's dictatorship and make the republic a democratic and law-based regime "unparalleled by any state in history", Mao Zedong carried out in-depth investigations and studies, summed up the experience from the people, made the universal and typical practices into institutions and laws, drafted and led the formulation of a series of laws and policies for the republic, and put forward a lot of important thoughts, for example, "the thorough and faithful implementation of the Chinese soviet laws and policies should be transferred to all the people of the Chinese Soviet Republic".[37] Under the guidance of the new democratic theories, the Party continued to accumulate valuable experience in constructing the legal system, for example, the legal system for new democratic revolution should be based on the realities of the revolution, the old laws should be abolished and new ones be enacted, and the legal system should protect people's rights. The concepts and principles on rule of law developed from these practices and theories have become the forerunner of the socialist rule of law theory.

The theory of Chinese socialist rule of law started to take shape when the People's Republic of China was founded, especially after the 1954 Constitution. The older generation of proletariat revolutionaries, such as Mao Zedong, Zhou Enlai, Liu

[37] ZHOU Meng, *Initial Explorations and Practice of the People's Congress System in the Chinese Soviet Republic*, Qiushi Journal, Vol. 5, 2019.

Shaoqi, Dong Biwu and Peng Zhen, in their experience in new democratic and socialist revolutions and explorations for building a legal system, creatively put forward a Marxist theory that socialist rule of law should be adapted to the practices in revolution and development and develop its own Chinese characteristics. They also thought that the practices implemented for building socialist rule of law reflected the socialist inheritance, sublation, development and transcendence of the new democratic one.[38] During this transition, the Party applied Marxist theories and methods, drew on the Soviet Union's experience, and made explorations for socialist rule of law theory based on the practices in legislation, law enforcement and adjudication after 1949. An initial framework for this theory includes the concepts, nature, values of law and socialist law,[39] the relationship between state, state power and law (i.e. relationship between the new and old legal systems),[40] the nature, contents, direction and path of socialist legal system, etc.[41] During this period, the Party continued its

---

[38] ZHANG Wenxian, *On Scientifically Positing the Chinese Socialist Rule of Law Theory, Law Science*, Vol. 11, pp. 3–8 (2015).

[39] Mao Zedong pointed out, "law is the superstructure. Our law is made by the working people. It maintains the revolutionary order, protects people's interests, and safeguards the socialist economic foundation and productive forces". Dong Biwu said, "what is law? In Lenin's words, law is formulated by the state highest authority based on prescribed procedures and reflects the will of the ruling class". Xie Juezai thought, "law is a summary of people's will for their interests, and formulated by the representatives and government that they elect though studies and discussions, so every citizen should observe the law". Peng Zhen pointed out that "our law does not transcend any class, it is marked with characteristics of class; it reflects people's interests but goes against any anti-revolutionaries. Our law represents the long-term interests of the majority of people under the leadership of the working class; to enforce the law is to protect the interests of the majority of people, conform with their interests and protect their legitimate rights and interests". WANG Yuming ed., *Collection of Mao Zedong Thought on Law*, China University of Political Science and Law Press, 1993, pp. 7, 9, 406.

[40] Mao Zedong pointed out that "to abolish all the old laws and decrees that hinder the people's patriotic movements, and promulgate new revolutionary laws and decrees". Dong Biwu thought "to treat the KMT's Six Codes with contempt and critical attitude and all the anti-people laws of the capitalist countries and regions including Europe, US and Japan, and apply the revolutionary spirits to study the legal theories of Marxism-Leninism and Mao Zedong Thought, study the new democratic policies, outlines, laws, orders, regulations and resolutions, in order to collect the experience of the people governing the country and make a new and relatively compete set of laws". Xie Juezai pointed out that "we should destroy the capitalist laws and enact the socialist laws. We have done a lot of work in these years to destroy the capitalist laws, and through judicial reform we have criticized them. The destruction of capitalist laws has laid the foundation for establishing socialist law and theory". *Ibid.*, pp. 14–15.

[41] As directed by Liu Shaoqi, "the proletariat legal system is socialist one under people's democracy. The legal system may not be on dictatorship, there should be legal system among the people". Dong Biwu said, "our legal system under people's democracy is the will of the people under the working class's leadership expressed by the state agencies, and an important tool for China to ensure people's democratic dictatorship". He also pointed out that "I think to do things according to law is the central link for us to further strengthen the legal system under people's democracy", "to do things according to law has two meanings: first, there should be laws to abide by; second, the laws should be observed". Xie Juezai pointed out that "the connection of the universal truth in the Marxist theory of law with the practices of people's administration of justice is the line for us to carry out legislation". *Ibid.*, pp. 42–43, 49.

tradition of summarizing experience and theoretical development. Dong Biwu, the most exemplary of them, made explorations for the theory of new China's rule of law with great courage and wisdom. In May 1959, in his speech at a conference, he pointed out "all the knowledge comes from practice, and theory is the summary of experience. To organize and systemize the experience, there will be a theory; after a theory is ready, it will guide the practice."[42] He led the Chinese Society of Political Science and Law to do a lot of work on how to promote legal system construction and legal studies that conform with China's revolution and development, and made significant achievements in theoretical development.[43] In the Eighth CPC National Congress held in 1956, he pointed out the legal system under people's democracy had vitality and rigor for several reasons: first, it was formed during the struggles to destroy the old legal system, reflected people's will and served the people; second, it was gradually developed out of the urgent need of China's development; third, it mobilized people's initiative and promoted the social productive forces; forth, it sought the truths from the people's struggles and implemented the mass line; fifth, it absorbed all the good experience from China's history and other countries that could benefit the people, especially the Soviet experience.[44] It was the first systematic summary of the Party's experience in establishing a legal system for new China, reflecting the Chinese Communists' initiative in developing rule of law theories. It was also then gradually incorporated into the Chinese socialist rule of law theory as the early theoretical achievements through its integration with the Mao Zedong Thought. However, these hard-won theoretical innovations were ignored due to the expansion of class struggles and Cultural Revolution, inflicting serious setbacks to the development of socialist rule of law theory.

Since the reform and opening-up, the large-scale legislation has greatly promoted the development of socialist rule of law theory, and the theoretical explorations becomes more vibrant and the theoretical research more in-depth. After the Cultural Revolution, the Party summarized the lessons and realized the urgency of practicing law-based governance. When reflecting on the failure in socialist construction by Deng Xiaoping, Ye Jianying, Peng Zhen and other old generation of proletarian revolutionaries, with a global vision for the future, put forward a series of important elaborations on the socialist legal system, which then became an important part of Deng Xiaoping Thought and the origins of the theory of Chinese socialist rule of law. In this period, there were three basic tasks for the work on legislation: first, to revise the Constitution with great haste to provide fundamental legal guarantee for the development of reform and opening-up in the new development stage; second, to

[42] DONG Biwu, *To Sum Up Experience Based on the Facts and Do a Better Job in the Work on Politics and Law*, in Collection of Dong Biwu's Writings on Politics and Law, Law Press, 1986, p. 544.

[43] CHEN Jiping, *To Summarize the Experience in Rule of Law Construction and Comprehensively Advance Rule of Law*, in Collection of Essays on Dong Biwu's Thoughts on Law and the Theory of Chinese Socialist Rule of Law, People's Court Press, 2017, pp. 4–13.

[44] DONG Biwu, *On Further Strengthening People's Democratic Legal System and Ensuring the Socialist Undertakings*, in *Collection of Dong Biwu's Writings on Politics and Law*, Law Press, 1986, pp. 478–481.

fill the vacuum of basic laws left in the first 30 years since PRC's founding, such as the organization law, criminal law, civil and procedure law, in order to restore the social stability through rule of law; third, to enact future-oriented laws that conformed with the new trends of reform and opening-up, including the laws on commodity economy and introducing foreign capital in order the steer the course of China's economic and social development into the track of law. These three tasks were the starting point for China towards modernized state governance system and capacity. With the deepening reform and opening-up and the rapid progress of socialist modernization, the undertakings for socialist rule of law have continued to advance, and the legislation witnessed a rapid growth. Between 1979 and 2013, the top legislature made an average of 18.5 pieces of legislation, including the enactment and revision of law, legal interpretations and decisions on legal issues, which laid solid foundation for socialist rule of law construction. In this period, the concepts and strategy transitioned from "legal system" to "rule of law", the Constitution laid out the objective of socialist law-based country, the Chinese socialist legal system was formed and developed under continuous improvement, the reform decision-making was more closely connected with the legislative decision-making, and the socialist cultural progress played an even more significant role in rule of law construction. These developments and innovations both in theory and practice have effectively promoted the Chinese socialist rule of law theory to a new and high level. The socialist rule of law theory that was reborn in the early reform and opening-up period largely inherited the achievements of the theory of the rule of law in the early years of the founding of the PRC, successively adapted to the new trends, new tasks and new requirements, and gained further development and improvement. The main contents of this theory can be summarized in the following: a thoughtful summary of the experience and lessons from construction of the legal system,[45] persistence in the

[45] Deng Xiaoping pointed out that "the democratic rights of the people were trampled upon when Lin Biao and the Gang of Four were in power. Since the downfall of the Gang of Four, and especially since the Third Plenary Session of the Eleventh Central Committee, we have been endeavoring to promote democracy. But much remains to be done and we should continue our efforts". Ye Jianying also pointed out that "China's socialist legal system has yet come into form since the founding of PRC. Lin Biao and the Gang of Four took advantage of our incomplete legal system, and under the guise of 'strengthening the proletariat dictatorship to enforce a fascist dictatorship and to arrest people as they pleased. This lesson has made us realize that a must has laws and systems'". Peng Zhen said, "in reviewing the history since the founding of PRC, we can make a conclusion: to develop socialist democracy and improve the socialist legal system reflects the essential for the development of PRC, and complies with the interests of the Chinese people of all ethnic groups. When we follow this law, the country will be united and peaceful, able to withstand all kinds of risks, and ensure the smooth socialist modernization; when we violate the law, we will have to suffer. This is not determined by any will of the people, but the historical inevitability. Therefore, we must not and should never neglect and waver on it". WANG Yuming ed., *Collection of Mao Zedong Thought on Law*, China University of Political Science and Law Press, 1993, pp. 42–43, 49.

Party's leadership in the socialist legal system,[46] the Party must act within the scope of the Constitution and law,[47] the empiricism of "crossing the river by touching the

[46] As Deng Xiaoping pointed out, "we must firmly maintain the Four Cardinal Principles—namely, keeping to the socialist road, upholding the people's democratic dictatorship (that is, the dictatorship of the proletariat), upholding leadership by the Communist Party and upholding Marxism-Leninism and Mao Zedong Thought. No one should be allowed to undermine these principles, and they should be codified in an appropriate form". Peng Zhen pointed out in his report that "the Preamble of the Draft Constitution upholds the Four Cardinal Principles, i.e. upholding the socialism, the people's democratic dictatorship, the Party's leadership and the Marxism-Leninism and Mao Zedong Thought. It is the summary of the experience of modern China's history, the truth tested by practice and reflects the law of China's historical development", he then emphasized that "the Party's leadership is consistent with doing things according to law. If we emphasize the socialist democracy and improve socialist legal system, do we still need the Party's leadership? Yes, and we should strengthen and improve the Party's leadership. The political and legal departments should adhere to and be subject to the Party's leadership, and any major issue should be reported to the Party committee for instructions. In our country, the Party leads the people to enact the Constitution and law and to abide by and enforce the Constitution and law, and the Party should act within the scope of the Constitution and law. If the socialist legal system is not led by the Party, no one would do better". *Ibid.*, pp. 42–43, 49.

[47] As Deng Xiaoping pointed out, "Stalin gravely damaged socialist legality, doing things which Comrade Mao Zedong once said would have been impossible in Western countries like Britain, France and the United States. Yet although Comrade Mao was aware of this, he did not in practice solve the problems in our system of leadership. Together with other factors, this led to the decade of catastrophe known as the "Cultural Revolution". There is a most profound lesson to be learned from this. I do not mean that the individuals concerned should not bear their share of responsibility, but rather that the problems in the leadership and organizational systems are more fundamental, widespread and long-lasting, and that they have a greater effect on the overall interests of our country. This is a question that has a close bearing on whether our Party and state will change political color and should therefore command the attention of the entire Party". Peng Zhen also said, "the Party's leadership and doing things according to law are integrated and consistent. The Party leads the people to enact the Constitution and law and to abide by and enforce them. The Party's Constitution also clearly provides that the Party's organizations and members should act within the scope of the Constitution and law, which is written down after ten years of painful domestic unrest. So the party members and cadres should become models of knowing, understanding and abiding by the law. As long as we formulate correct policies, establish and improve the legal system, we can make them into laws, so that everyone must abide by them. In this way, it will not be easy for the careerists and conspirators to usurp the leadership of the Party and the state". *Ibid.*, pp. 63–64.

stones",[48] the relationship between the socialist legal system and cultural progress,[49] etc. The legislators represented by Peng Zhen attached great importance to theoretical research on the rule of law, began paying attention to systematic, empirical and comparative research with a world view on the regularity of rule of construction, which helped him make a lot of theoretical achievements. He dedicated himself to this undertaking, often summarizing the experience and regularity during legislation and setting a good example. He said, "the experience demonstrates that to enact any law on new and major issue or reform must have the people's initiative to carry out pilot programs, i.e. a stage of the social practice testing. Based on testing and comparative research on typical cases and experience, a law can be enacted. It is a general practice or a law, if we say, in the legislation. We should proactively master and apply it."[50] He also asked to NPC Standing Committee's employees "to study the theory and get familiar with the realities and laws; only correct legal theory and familiarity with the realities can the sound provisions of law be formulated. Legislation should adopt a theory, not just about provisions; and the familiarity with realities is also necessary, otherwise the legislation will not be good only with a theory. In a word, we should develop a systematic Marxist-Leninist theory of law and keep familiar with China's realities."[51] In the early stage of reform and opening-up, to integrate the basic Marxist-Leninist Principles and China's realities, explore the laws based on China's rule of law practice and test these laws in practice was the path for developing Chinese socialist rule of law theory.

Since the Eighteenth Congress, the Central Committee with Xi Jinping as the core has attached great importance to comprehensive rule of law, and has upgraded it into

---

[48] As Deng Xiaoping said, "there is a lot of legislative work to do, and we don't have enough trained people. Therefore, legal provisions will have to be less than perfect to start with, then be gradually improved upon. Some laws and statutes can be tried out in particular localities and later enacted nationally after the experience has been evaluated and improvements have been made. Individual legal provisions can be revised or supplemented one at a time, as necessary; there is no need to wait for a comprehensive revision of an entire body of law. In short, it is better to have some laws than none, and better to have them sooner than later. Moreover, we should intensify our study of international law". Peng Zhen expressed a similar point, "now the opening-up and economic system reform is under steady progress, what is urgently needed is not law, but some provisional provisions or regulations to ensure our work can be carried out in an orderly manner. In the current stage, many new issues await exploration. A law can be enacted only the practice has proved it. Therefore, the NPC Standing Committee put forward a proposal that the State Council is authorized to formulate provisional provisions or regulations in the pilot or trial stage. This proposal was approved by the Standing Committee of the Political Bureau of the Central Committee". He then emphasized that "a law can only be enacted if the practice has proved its practicability with typical cases developed in a scientifically manner other than out of objective manipulation. If so, the laws can be enacted one by one or part by part; if the circumstances are not ripe, we can formulate outlines and drafts, and continue to test them in practices, summarize experience and solicit opinions and make them into laws if permitted". *Ibid*., pp. 63–64.

[49] More elaborations will be made in Part IV of this chapter.

[50] PENG Zhen, *On the Legislative Work (January 23, 1985)*, in *Selected Writings of Peng Zhen (1941–1990)*, People's Publishing House, 1991, p. 507.

[51] PENG Zhen, *The NPC Should Work for Legislation (October 29, 1954)*, in Selected Writings of Peng Zhen (1941–1990), People's Publishing House, 1991, p. 262.

the Four-Pronged Comprehensive Strategy. Resolution of the Central Committee of the CPC on Major Issues Concerning the Enhancement of All-round Law-based Governance was the first ever Central Committee's document on socialist rule of law construction, which gave the Chinese people with confidence and determination in engaging in building China into a law-based country. The Central Committee highly values the work on legislation, adheres to governance according to the Constitution and law, places legislation in the first place and continues to strengthen its leadership in the work on legislation, which helps to make important progress and prominent achievements in legislation. In over 6 years, the NPC and its Standing Committee amended the Constitution for the first time, enacted the Supervision Law, National Security Law, Anti-Terrorism Law, and Law on Prevention and Control of Soil Pollution, revised the organization laws on people's courts and people's procuratoartes, and Civil Servants Law, and made a lot of decisions on authorization for reform and major issues, helping to improve and develop the Chinese socialist legal system. As the premise of rule of law, legislation kept close with the features and demands as Chinese socialism entered a new era, provided constitutional guarantee for advancing a full-scale moderately prosperous country, deepened reform in all respects and strictly disciplining the Party; together with the practice in strict law enforcement, impartial administration of justice, and law-abiding by the whole people, it has helped to form and establish a socialist rule of law theory with Chinese characteristics underpinned by the features of the new era.

2.2 Theoretical Summary of Legislative Experience as an Important Part of Socialist Rule of Law Theory

When leading the Chinese revolution, development and reform, the Party has never stopped exploring the path for socialist rule of law, making summaries of legislative experience and finding the law that governs legislative activities, thereby establishing and improving the legislative theory with Chinese characteristics. These theories have their own features in different phases of development. In the new democratic revolution period, some primary thoughts and principles were developed from the legislative activities during the Chinese Soviet Republic, Shaan-Gan-Ning Border Region, various Anti-Japanese bases and liberated areas, which included the insistence on the foundation and decisive role of Constitution in establishing and consolidating state power; adherence to resolving the issues on meeting peasants' demand for land through legal means; practice of new marriage institution, liberation of women, and protection of worker's rights and interests; persistence in severely suppressing counter-revolutionaries and traitors with severe criminal punishments and protecting people.[52] After the People's Republic of China was founded, the Party extended its

[52] ZHANG Jinfan, *The History of Chinese Legal System*, Commercial Press, 2010, pp. 495–507. LAN Quanpu, *An Overview of Law in the Past 70 Years*, Law Press, 1997, pp. 1–161. ZHUO Fan, *History of the Legal System of the Chinese Soviet Republic*, Jiangxi Colleges and Universities Publishing

local experience to the whole country, abolished the KMT's pseudo legal traditions, and realized the transformation from new democratic legislation to the socialist rule of law with respect to legislative practice and theory, which marked a new start for China's construction of rule of law. Some important points of legislative thoughts and theories can be summarized as follows: the theory of making and enforcing socialist constitution,[53] persistence in "starting from the practice and summarizing the experience" and other basic principles for legislation,[54] the protection of people's

House, 1992. HAN Yanlong ed., *A General History of the Legal System of the People's Republic of China (Vol. 1)*, Central Party School Press, 1998, pp. 5–20.

[53] In this respect, Mao Zedong pointed out that "it sums up the experience of the past, especially that in our revolution and construction over the last five years. It sums up our experience in the people's revolution led by the proletariat against imperialism, feudalism and bureaucrat-capitalism as well as our experience in social reform, economic construction, cultural construction and government work over the last few years. Besides, it sums up the experience in constitution-making since the last years of the Qing Dynasty, that is, from the Nineteen Constitutional Articles in the final days of the Qing Dynasty to the Provisional Constitution of the Republic of China in 1912, the various constitutions and draft constitutions under the governments of the Northern warlords, the Provisional Constitution of the Republic of China in the Period Under Political Tutelage of the reactionary Chiang Kai-shek regime and right up to Chiang Kai-shek's bogus constitution…Our constitution is of a socialist type. It is based mainly on our own experience but has drawn upon what is good in the constitutions of the Soviet Union and the People's Democracies". He then stated that "our Draft Constitution combines principle with flexibility. There are two basic principles, the principle of democracy and the principle of socialism. Our democracy is not bourgeois democracy but people's democracy, that is, a people's democratic dictatorship led by the proletariat and based on the worker-peasant alliance. The principle of people's democracy runs through the whole constitution", and "Constitution-making is a matter of science. We must believe in science and nothing else, that is to say, we must not have blind faith in anything". Liu Shaoqi also pointed out that "the draft Constitution is an epitome of historical experience. In drawing up the Constitution, we have worked on a basis of facts. But what are these facts? That we Chinese people have won complete victory in our long-drawn-out revolutionary struggles against imperialism, feudalism and bureaucrat-capitalism; that our people's democratic state, led by the working class and based on an alliance of workers and peasants, has been solidly established; that the socialist sector in China's economy has now assumed a position of vigorous leadership; and that our country has embarked on a systematic socialist transformation and is in gradual transition towards a socialist society. From these facts it naturally follows that our Constitution must be a people's democratic constitution. It is a socialist constitution, not a bourgeois one. The Draft Constitution we have submitted is the epitome of the historical experience of more than a hundred years of heroic struggles waged by the Chinese people; it also epitomizes historical experience on the question of constitutions and the constitutional movement in modem China", he then further clarified that "Since 1953 China has been in a period of planned economic development with socialism as its goal. It is, therefore, essential for us now to take another step forward on the basis of the Common Program, to adopt a constitution like the one now submitted to you, in order to set down in legal form the fundamental task of our country in the transition period". WANG Yuming ed., *Collection of Mao Zedong Thought on Law*, China University of Political Science and Law Press, 1993, pp. 97–98, 100.

[54] As Zhou Enlai stated, "In the early years of PRC, especially in the transitional period, the political and economic situation changes rapidly, and it is difficult to formulate fundamental and long-term applicable laws in all aspects. For example, civil law and criminal law are difficult to formulate before the socialist transformation of the private ownership of the means of production has been basically completed and the socialist ownership system has not been fully established. In this case, it is necessary and appropriate for the state to issue provisional regulations, decisions, instructions and others as working norms to be followed by all. Only based on these effective regulations,

rights, and some other thoughts on criminal, civil and litigation affairs, for example, a criminal law policy by combining the punishment and leniency, equality of men and women, freedom of marriage, liberation of women and other legal policy on family and marriage, all the citizens equal in the application of law, and the litigation principle that the facts are the basis and the law is the criterion. Although the Cultural Revolution disrupted the exploration for legal theory, it continued the socialist rule of law in the reform and opening-up period, and took the opportunity of amending the Constitution and large-scale legislation to nourish and develop itself. From the legislative practices of reform and opening-up and socialist modernization, the following ideas and theoretical points can be summarized: to establish a legal system compatible with the socialist market economy, the state respects and protects human rights, to lay down and strengthen the principle of legality, to pay attention to the application of litigation procedures to protect the litigant's rights and interests, to regulate the administrative power of the government, to emphasize the independent and law-based exercise of powers and functions of the judiciary and the procuratorates, to strengthen the protection of minors, the elderly, women, the disabled and other special groups, to promote scientific and democratic legislation, and to safeguard the unity of the socialist legal system, etc. Since the Eighteenth Congress, under the correct leadership of the Central Committee, major progress and remarkable achievements have been made in legislation, from which lots of useful experience is accumulated and the scientific method for observing the laws of legislation is mastered.

All these reflections, understandings and theoretical explorations in legislation are major theoretical innovation made by the Party by adapting the Marxist basic theory on law to Chinese context, answers to the major questions arising from legislative practices after 1949 and nourished and developed the socialist rule of law theory. In this process, the Party has developed and persisted in the following basic principles that have run though the legislative activities:

First, to unswervingly persist in, strengthen and improve the Party's leadership in the work on legislation. An important principle of Marxist theory on state power is that the proletariat should control the legislative power and enact laws to ensure that the proletarian principles and missions can be achieved under the Party's leadership. Some classic Marxists have made their points clear. Engels said, "An active socialist party is impossible without such demands, like any political party. The demands

decisions and instructions, can we sum up the experience and enact long-term applicable laws. Even the laws of capitalist countries were incomplete in their early stages, and were gradually enacted over a long period of time. At present, the socialist transformation of private ownership of the means of production has been basically completed, socialist ownership established, and the state has accumulated some experience in the practice of various undertakings. It gives us the possibility to enacted various socialist laws based on the experience and review of the past regulations, for example, we have preliminary draft of criminal law, and the civil law and regulation on administrative penalties for public security are now drafted by relevant departments", Dong Biwu pointed out that "the laws of our country are not thought out in advance, written down and then enforced, rather they are practiced, and then enacted based on the summary of experience". Xie Juezai also pointed out that "Our laws must proceed from realities, i.e. from the specific conditions and practice experience to find out the regularity". *Ibid.*, pp. 70 and 73–74, 100.

that derive from the common interests of a class can only be put into effect by this class taking over political power and securing universal validity for its demands by making them law. Every class in struggle must therefore set forth its demands in the form of legal demands in a program".[55] In Lenin's opinion, "After it has seized power, the working class maintains it, preserves it and consolidates it as every other class does, namely, by a change of property relations and by a new constitution."[56] To adhere to the socialist path with Chinese characteristics requires the Party's leadership. Xi Jinping also directed that Party leadership is the soul of socialist rule of law with Chinese characteristics and the greatest difference between our rule of law and that of Western capitalist countries. Without Party leadership, there would be no progress in building a socialist rule of law system with Chinese characteristics or in developing China into a socialist rule of law country.[57] The Party's leadership in the work on legislation is an important political principle that the work should adhere to, the summary of Party's success in this regard since the Chinese Soviet Republic period, and the basic experience in uninterrupted progress and development over the past 70 years especially over the past 40 years. As it leads the people in formulating and implementing the Constitution and laws, the Party must act within the limits prescribed by the Constitution and laws, and ensure that it exercises leadership in legislation, supports administration of justice, guarantees law enforcement and takes the lead in observing the law. Though the Central Committee has attached importance to legislation, it has not institutionalized it until after the reform and opening-up was initiated. In 1991, the Central Committee issued the opinions on strengthening the Party's leadership in national legislation, and based on its experience accumulated, revised these opinions in 2016 to provide guidelines on the Party's leadership in the work on legislation. Specifically, all the legislative bodies should steadfastly and proactively adhere to the Party's leadership, earnestly implement the Central Committee's opinions on enhancing its leadership in it, focus on the legislative objectives and tasks laid out by the Central Committee, adopt a well-conceived approach to making legislative plans, unwaveringly report to and seek instructions from the Central Committee or their corresponding party committees on major legislative programs and major issues in legislation, and timely put into practice the Party's lines, principles and policies, so as to turn the Party's proposals into the will of the state through statutory procedures and the code of conduct and guidelines for activities across the nation.

Second, to persist in the people-centered approach, proceed from China's realities and steadfastly adhere to the rule of law path that conforms with China's conditions.

---

[55] Frederick Engels, *Lawyer's Socialism*, in Marx et al., Complete Works of Marx and Engels (Vol. 21), People's Publishing House, 1965, pp. 567–568.

[56] V. I. Lenin, *Ninth All-Russia Congress of Soviets*, in Collected Works of V. I. Lenin (2nd Edition) (Vol. 31), Progress Publishers, 1965, pp. 141–181.

[57] Xi Jinping, *Speech at a seminar for principal provincial and ministerial level leaders on the guiding principles from the Fourth Plenary Session of the 18th CPC Central Committee and on comprehensively advancing the law-based governance of China(February 2, 2015)*, in Party Literature Research Office ed., *The Law-Based Governance of China*, Central Compilation and Translation Press, 2017, p. 40.

"People" is a key Marxist term, the classic Marxist writers have made profound expositions on the historical status and role of the people. As Marx said, only "the law is the conscious expression of the popular will, and therefore originates with it and is created by it".[58] Xi Jinping also pointed out in his speech at the first meeting of the Central Commission for Law-based Governance that rule of law should be for the people and rely on them, and it must benefit and protect them. Social equity and justice, the goal of rule of law, should be upheld, and it should make sure that the people can see that equity and justice are served in every law, every law enforcement action, and every judicial case. It should represent the people's interests, and improve their wellbeing, and ensure that people, under the Party's leadership, are able to administer state affairs, and manage economic, cultural and social affairs through various channels and in various ways as provided by law. The report of the Nineteenth Congress stated that the people are the creators of history; they are the fundamental force that determines the future of the Party and state. It is the essential requirement of socialist rule of law, the starting point and mission of the work on legislation to adhere to the people-centered approach, fully reflect people's wishes, protect their rights and interests, and keep up with people's ever-growing expectations for a better life. The people's centered approach is also the fundamental momentum and origin of force for the great achievements made by the Party in exercising leadership in legislation. The people-centered approach to legislation means that it starts from the practical issues that people concern most and affect them most and from the realities of their current social, material, cultural life. China's legislation has fully reflected this approach and people's will. The legislation on politics of socialist democracy safeguards people's master position, ensures that all the power belongs to the people; the legislation on socialist market economy promoted and guarantees the rapid development of productive forces and economy, which meets people's demands for materials; the legislation on social wellbeing provides social security and benefits across the life of people; the legislation on culture promotes cultural progress and meets people's spiritual nourishments; the legislation on environment and resource protection keeps a beautiful world and enables an livable environment; and the legislation on national security provides a sound legal environment for realizing the long-term stability of the country and enabling people a peaceful and safe living environment.

The people-centered approach adopted in legislation is determined by the nature of the state. China is a socialist state under the people's democratic dictatorship led by the working class and based on the alliance of workers and peasants, the most important reality and the most important national condition on which the legislation is based. As Mao Zedong pointed out, "a clear understanding of the nature of Chinese society, that is, of Chinese conditions, is therefore the key to a clear understanding of all the problems of the revolution".[59] In Deng Xiaoping's view, "The universal truth of Marxism-Leninism must be integrated with the concrete practice

---

[58] Marx, *The Divorce Bill*, in Marx et al., *Complete Works of Marx and Engels*, People's Publishing House, 1957, p. 184.

[59] MAO Zedong, *The Chinese Revolution and The Chinese Communist Party (December 1939)*, in Selected Works of Mao Zedong (Vol. 2), Foreign Languages Press, 1965, p. 315.

of a country-a formulation which is itself a universal truth. It embraces two aspects-universal truth and the integration of that truth with a country's concrete conditions. We have consistently held that neither aspect can be ignored".[60] That legislation should stand on the basic conditions of social and economic development in various phases refers that it should adapt to people's wishes and demands in different phases. It should stand still nor surpass the current, because we have successes and failures in this respect. From the Agrarian Revolution, the Anti-Japanese War to the War of Liberation, the Party never stopped adjusting its laws and policies according to the characteristics of the different stages of the Chinese revolution, which made great successes; after 1949, the Party expanded the application of this experience in the liberated areas when speeding up the legislation, and put equal emphasis on drawing on the Soviet Union's experience and on China's specific conditions, which helped the Party to accumulate useful experience. However, there was also a grave lesson in the "Cultural Revolution" when the legal system was severely damaged. All these have given the Party valuable experience to find and walk on the socialist path of rule of law with Chinese characteristics. Since the reform and opening-up, the Party has further stressed on its own path and devoted itself to solving various issues on the road of advancing modernization of state governance system and capacity, a remarkable achievement unseen in the world. Under no circumstances should China imitate the models and practices of other countries or adopt the Western models of "constitutionalism", "separation of powers", or "judicial independence".

Third, to insist on the leading role of the Constitution and promote the enforcement of the Constitution with a complete set of laws to maintain the unity of socialist legal system. As a state's fundamental law with the highest legal authority and effect, the Constitution is the foundation for establishing national systems and enacting laws and regulations. It has played an extremely important role in China's governance system. The Constitution establishes and consolidates the state power under the Party's leadership, sets out and develops socialist system, protects and safeguards people's rights, and provides a fundamental legal guarantee for building a modern socialist country that is prosperous, strong, democratic, culturally advanced, harmonious and beautiful, and realizing the great rejuvenation of the Chinese nation. That the construction of a socialist rule of law country keeps pace with the times means in the first place that the Constitution keeps to the times. The Constitution of China constantly adapts to new situations, absorbs new experiences, confirms new achievements, and continues to develop as the Party and the State's undertakings develop. The 1982 Constitution has been amended for five times, and each amendment proactively confirmed the success and upgraded the major innovations in theory, practice and institutions made by the Party and people into constitutional provisions to better play the role of the Constitution in regulating, leading, promoting and safeguarding reform and development. The stability of the Constitution is the ballast for reform and opening-up, while its keeping up with the times can boost the reform and opening. The current Constitution is a good one, which brings institutional dividend that promotes

---

60 DENG Xiaoping, *Integrate Marxism-Leninism with the Concrete Conditions of China (November 17, 1956)*, in Selected Works of Deng Xiaoping (Vol. 1), Foreign Languages Press, 1995, p. 257.

smooth reform and opening-up and the realization of two centenary goals. It is an important channel and method to advance the comprehensive implementation of the Constitution to ready a full set of laws. Since the Constitution lays downs the state system, government system, and basic political and economic systems, and provides general provisions on citizens' basic rights and duties, the state agencies and symbols of the nation, all these systems and general provisions need to be specific through laws. The Constitution is the core around which the socialist legal system is formed and develops. Only with a socialist legal system with the Constitution as the core can the systems and principles set out in the Constitution be realized in full swing and can the reform and opening as the basic national policy be observed effectively. To maintain the unity of national legal system is necessary for fully advancing rule of law, and is also a success for establishing the socialist rule of law. In a long period after the founding of the PRC, the legislative power was centralized with only the National People's Congress. From the reform and opening-up to the revision of the Law on Legislation in 2015, China's legislative system has more legislative bodies and a multi-level pattern. The NPC and its Standing Committee have made great efforts to improve the legislative institutions and mechanisms, lay out a clear-cut division of legislative powers, standardized the legislative procedures and strengthen the work on recording and review of normative documents to maintain the harmony and unity of legal system in a well-conceived manner. What's more, they have also been dedicated to the unity of socialist legal system, preventing fragmented decision-making and local protectionism and other problems, and providing a legal guarantee for maintaining Central Committee's authority, encouraging healthy competition, preventing regional barriers and establishing an integrated market during the course of reform and opening-up.

Fourth, to properly handle the relationship between the rule of law and reform. As Xi Jinping stated, "Reform and the rule of law are like the two wings of a bird or the two wheels of a cart", a scientific conclusion made after numerous twists and turns in the Party's leadership in the practice and theoretical explorations of reform and rule of law. The reform and opening-up in the past 40 years have answered the questions of how to catch up with the changes of times and social progress, how to realize connection of reform decision-making with legislative decision-marking, how to integrate deepening of reform, in-depth development with legislation, and how to integrate scientific, democratic and law-based decision-making through legislation. in the early reform and opening-up period, though with the lack of practical experience and ideological constraints, the Central Committee made proper decisions with great resolute, and the NPC and its Standing Committee opportunely put the legislation into the agenda and enacted a series of laws. The Sino-Foreign Equity Joint Venture Enterprise Law enacted in 1975 was an outstanding example of connecting legislative decision-making with reform decision-making, which provided legal guarantee for China to open to the outside world, introduce foreign capital, speed up socialist modernization, a substantive step to promote reform and opening-up. Even in today, the legislation has dedicated to summarizing experience and consolidating reform achievements to promote the continuous growth and spiraling upward of reform and opening-up. Deng Xiaoping ever emphasized that democracy and our legal system should be promoted for they are like a person's two hands. Xi Jinping often pointed out that any major reform should be made according to law, the reform decision-making and the decision for legislation be better connected, a problem-oriented approach be adopted to make the law specific, responsive, systematic and practicable, and the role of legislation in leading and promoting reform and development be better played. The methods and channels for dealing with the relationship between legislation and reform have been under explorations. Apart from the traditional legislative methods of enactment, revision, repeal and interpretation, other means such as decision on authorization and reform and package legislation have also been adopted to flexibly and effectively adapt legislation to reform underpinned by adequate leeway.

2.3 Major Theoretical Achievements for Socialist Legislation Undertakings in Various Phases

The Chinese socialist rule of law theory keeps up the times proactively and makes innovation, and the major theoretical achievements have been made one by one along the socialist path of rule of law. Over the past 70 years especially over the past 40 years, the socialist rule of law theory has transformed from the availability of laws and observance of law, the availability of laws to abide by, observance of law, strict law enforcement, and punishments on violators of laws, to scientific legislation, strict law enforcement, impartial administration of justice and universal observance of law. During this period, it also changes from legal system under people's democracy to socialist rule of law, from rule of law to the combination of rule of law and rule of virtue, and from Chinese socialist legal system to Chinese socialist rule of law system. During the formation and development of this theory, the central leaderships with their representatives including Deng Xiaoping, Jiang Zemin, Hu Jintao and Xi Jinping have played irreplaceable role in leading and promoting the socialist rule of law construction and practicing the rule of law. Considering the strategic position of reforming and opening-up, establishing a socialist market economy, developing socialist democratic politics, building a moderately prosperous society in an all-round way, and realizing long-term stability, they raised questions, reflected on the lessons, and summarized experience based on China's national conditions and the practice of socialist rule of law construction. With rich experience in hands, they have helped to form the socialist rule of law theory and promoted its continuous innovation and development. The original concepts and theoretical points expounded by them have constituted the basic structure of the theory of Chinese socialist rule of law.[61] These achievements in each phase have been faithfully recorded and manifested in the documents of the Party's national congresses, central committees and their guiding principles, thus providing theoretical guidance for the work on legislation to uphold,

[61] ZHANG Wenxian, *On Scientifically Positing the Chinese Socialist Rule of Law Theory*, *Law Science*, Vol. 11, 2015, pp. 3–8.

ensuring the correct political orientation in legislation, and effectively utilizing the legal system for modernizing state governance system and capacity.

After 1949, the Party had made some achievements in its explorations for socialist rule of law theory, but did not institutionalize them, failing to avoid the impact of legal nihilism and the severe damage caused by the Cultural Revolution. Their reach and influence were limited. However, the conception of the rule of law never faded away, and the Party never gave up its original aspirations for building a law-based country, planting the seeds for forming and developing this theory. After the Third Plenary Session of the Eleventh CPC National Congress, the second generation of central leadership with Deng Xiaoping as the core reflected on the serious consequences and grave lessons of China's neglect of democratic politics construction, and put forward many important insights, such as "to develop socialist democracy and improve socialist legal system", "to strengthen development and reform as well as the legal system at the same time with equal strength", and "there must be laws for people to follow, these laws must be observed, their enforcement must be strict and law breakers must be dealt with".[62] From 1990s to early twenty-first century, the third generation of central leadership with Jiang Zemin as the core proposed the "integration of Party's leadership, people's master position and rule of law", that "rule of law is the fundamental principle by which the Party leads the people in governing the country" and "combining rule of law with rule of virtue" and other great theoretical insights.[63] From early twenty-first century to the pre-18th congress,

[62] In "Emancipate the Mind, Seek Truth from Facts and Unite as One in Looking to the Future", Deng Xiaoping stated that "to ensure people's democracy, we must strengthen our legal system. Democracy has to be institutionalized and written into law, so as to make sure that institutions and laws do not change whenever the leadership changes, or whenever the leaders change their views or shift the focus of their attention". See DENG Xiaoping, *Selected Works of Deng Xiaoping (Vol. 2)*, Foreign Languages Press, 1995, p. 156. The Communique of the Third Plenary Session of the Eleventh CPC Central Committee, "to safeguard people's democracy, it is imperative to strengthen the socialist legal system so that democracy is systematized and written into law in such a way as to ensure the stability, continuity and full authority of this democratic system and these laws; there must be laws for people to follow, these laws must be observed, their enforcement must be strict and law breakers must be dealt with". The report of the CPC Twelfth Congress, "Create a New Situation in All Fields of Socialist Modernization", stated that "we must closely link the building of socialist democracy with that of the socialist legal system so that socialist democracy is institutionalized and codified into laws". In the report of the Thirteenth National Congress, "Advance along the Road of Socialism with Chinese Characteristics", it put forward that "socialist democracy is inseparable from a socialist legal system. We must attend to legislation and to economic development and reform at the same time. During the whole process of reform we must go on building our legal system…we should see to it that legislation guarantees good order in economic development and reform and consolidates achievements scored in reform. We should try to define, in terms of laws or rules, what should be encouraged and what should be rejected". Education Office of Central Party School ed., *Selection of Important Documents of the Party and State Since the Third Plenary Session of the Eleventh CPC Central Committee (December 1978 to October 2014)*, Central Party School Press, 2015, pp. 5, 16, 115, 172.

[63] According to the report of the Fourteenth Congress, "Accelerating the Reform, the Opening to the Outside World and the Drive for Modernization, so as to Achieve Greater Successes in Building Socialism with Chinese Characteristics", "while making economic development our central task,

the central committee with Hu Jintao as the General Secretary continued to emphasize the "integration of Party's leadership, people's master position and rule of law", and based on goal of "full-scale implementation of rule of law, speeding construction of socialist rule of law country", put forward "scientific, democratic and law-based governance", "scientific legislation, strict law enforcement, impartial administration of justice and universal observance of law" and "promoting the spirits of socialist rule of law and consolidating the socialist rule of law conceptions" and others alike.[64]

---

we should also improve our socialist democracy, legal system, culture and ethics, so as to ensure all-round social progress", "all due attention should be given to the legal system. To establish a socialist market economy, we urgently need to strengthen legislation. In particular, we need to draw up laws and regulations that will ensure smooth progress of the reform and the opening-up, and provide for better management of the overall economy and standardize the economic behavior of enterprises and individuals". In the "Decision of the CPC Central Committee on Some Issues Concerning the Establishment of a Socialist Market Economic Structure" adopted at the Third Session of the Fourteenth CPC Central Committee held in 1993, it proposed that to establish and improve the socialist market economy should be under the regulation and guarantee of a complete legal system; more attention should be paid to the construction of legal system to ensure its integration with reform and opening-up. The goal of legal system construction was to initially establish a legal system that was adapted to the socialist market economy by the end of the twentieth century; the unity of socialist legal system should be promoted. The reform decision should be closely connected with the legislative decision-making. The legislation should reflect the spirits of reform, and the laws should be applied to lead, promote and guarantee the reform. In "Hold High the Great Banner of Deng Xiaoping Theory for an All-round Advancement of the Cause of Building Socialism With Chinese Characteristics' Into the 21st Century", reported at the Fifteenth National Congress, it was stated to "improve the socialist legal system, governing the country according to law and making it a socialist country ruled by law…Ruling the country by law is the basic strategy employed by the Party in leading the people in running the country…form a socialist legal system with Chinese characteristics by the year 2010." In "Build a Well-off Society in an All-round Way and Create a New Situation in Building Socialism with Chinese Characteristics", report of the Sixteenth CPC National Congress, it was stated that "the key to developing socialist democracy is to combine the need to uphold the Party's leadership and to ensure that the people are the masters of the country with the need to rule the country by law…strengthen legislation and improve its quality and will have formulated a socialist system of laws with Chinese characteristics by the year 2010…Ruling the country by law and ruling the country by virtue complement each other". Education Office of Central Party School ed., *Selection of Important Documents of the Party and State Since the Third Plenary Session of the Eleventh CPC Central Committee (December 1978 to October 2014)*, Central Party School Press, 2015, pp. 200, 207, 231, 257, 264, 265, 331, 332, 334.

64 The Decision of the Central Committee of the CPC about Strengthening the Party's Governance Capability adopted in the Fourth Session of the Sixteenth Central Committee held in 2004 stated that the Party "must adhere to the rule of law, ensure that it exercises leadership in legislation, guarantees law enforcement and takes the lead in observing the law, continue to subject the national economy, politics, culture, and social life to law, adhere to the integration of Party's leadership, people's master position, and rule of law, and implement the fundamental principle of rule law to improve the governance capabilities. The Decision on Major Issues in Building a Harmonious Socialist Society adopted in the Sixth Plenary Session of the Sixteenth Central Committee proposed to implement the fundamental principle of rule of law, construction socialist rule of law country, consolidate the conception of socialist rule of law, strengthen the awareness of law among the society, subject the national economy, politics, culture and social life to law, gradually form a social security system and promote social fairness and justice. The Party should also adhere to scientific, democratic and law-based governance, improve the legal system and consolidate the legal basis for social harmony; safeguard the unity and dignity of socialist legal system and establish its authority;

Since the Eighteenth National Congress, the Central Committee with Xi Jinping as the core, with a thorough understanding of the Chinese socialist path of rule of law and system and other major theoretical issues, has made a lot of important decisions, put forward new concepts, new thinking and new strategies for comprehensive rule of law, attached importance of the Party's leadership to it, persisted in the people's master position, and adhered to the socialist path of rule of law. They have also been dedicated to the construction of Chinese socialist rule of law system, promoting law-based governance, exercise of state power and administration of government, adopting a holistic approach to building a country, a government and a society where the rule of law prevails, practicing the Constitution-based governance and administration, and advancing law-making that is well-conceived, that the law is enforced strictly, that justice is administered impartially, and that the law is observed by all. They have also properly handled the dialectical relationship about comprehensive rule of law, built a team of legal task force with moral integrity and professional competence, focused on a small number of key officials, and clarified the guiding principles, path, working plan and key tasks for advancing rule of law in all respects. These concepts, thinking and strategies have contributed to clearer expositions on the comprehensive rule of law and on building a socialist state under the rule of law, achieving a significant development of the Chinese socialist rule of law theory.

Under the guidance of these theories, the legislature has worked hard to speed up legislation while focusing on improving its quality to quickly establish a complete legal system. A lot of achievements have thus been made. The Local Organization Law, Criminal Law, Criminal Procedure Law, Sino-Foreign Equity Joint Venture Enterprise Law and other three laws were adopted in the Second Session of the Fifth National People's Congress held in 1979. Through concerted efforts, the goal of forming the Chinese socialist legal system by 2010 was achieved as declared in the Fifteenth National Congress. In the Fourth Session of the Eleventh National People's

---

and adhere to combining rule of law with rule of virtue". In "Hold High the Great Banner of Socialism with Chinese Characteristics and Strive for New Victories in Building a Moderately Prosperous Society in All Respects", report of the Seventh National Congress, with a socialist law system with Chinese characteristics basically in place and effective implementation of the rule of law as a fundamental principle, it was laid out to "comprehensively implement the rule of law as a fundamental principle and speed up the building of a socialist country under the rule of law...persist in scientific and democratic legislation to improve the socialist law system with Chinese characteristics". In his speech at a meeting commemorating the 90th anniversary of the founding of CPC, Hu Jintao said, "we will fully implement law-based governance as a fundamental policy, raise public awareness of the rule of law under socialism throughout society, improve law making, ensure strict law enforcement, impartial administration of justice, and observance of law by everyone...insist on the combination of rule of law and rule of virtue". In the Firmly March On the Path of Socialism with Chinese Characteristics and Strive to Complete the Building of A Moderately Prosperous Society in All Respects, Report of the Eighteenth National Congress, it stated to "promote law-based governance of the country in an all-around way... the rule of law is the basic way for running the country...give greater scope to the important role the rule of law plays in the country's governance and in social management...strengthen legislation in key areas...foster socialist spirit of the rule of law and adopt the socialist concept of law-based governance...enhance system building to promote ecological progress". *Ibid.*, pp. 360, 364, 428, 429, 435, 456, 539, 589, 593.

Congress convened in March 2011, Wu Bangguo declared when making his work report, "the departments of law that regulated all social relations were complete, the basic and major laws for each department were enacted, the regulations that corresponded with laws were also relatively complete, making a generally harmonious and unified system within itself. a socialist system of laws with Chinese characteristics has been formed which is based on the situation and realities in China; complies with the requirements for reform, opening-up and socialist modernization; represents the will of the Party and the people; is rooted in the Constitution; has several types of laws including laws related to the Constitution, civil laws and commercial laws, as its backbone; and has different levels of legal force, reflected in laws, administrative regulations, and local statutes. There are laws to cover every area of economic, political, cultural, social and ecological development in the country". "It is a remarkable and significant achievement", Xi Jinping said in the Explanations on the Resolution. The establishment of the socialist legal system with Chinese characteristics was an important milestone in China's history of socialist legal system construction and a significant symbol of the mature Chinese socialism; it was of great practical significance and far-reaching historical significance. Since the Eighteenth Party's National Congress, the Central Committee with Xi Jinping at the core has united and led the people of all ethnic groups in the country, and with firm determination, full confidence and sincere actions, continued to strive to promote the Chinese socialist legal system, and advanced the modernization of the state governance system and capacity, which has ushered China in a new era of socialist rule of law. In the country where there are laws to abide by, the Party has focused closely on the Five-Sphere Integrated Plan and Four-Pronged Comprehensive Strategy, spared unremitting efforts to strengthen and improve the work on legislation, taken solid steps to promote legislation in key areas, and made breakthroughs in legislation of national security, state agencies, ecology and environment, social and wellbeing affairs and in the compilation of civil code. The constitution-centered Chinese socialist legal system that adapts to the modernization of state governance system and capacity continues to improve, the efforts to improve socialist rule of law system are still on the way, and a socialist rule of law country is taking shape.

3 Chinese Socialist Legal System and Rule of Law System for Chinese Socialist System

The general goal of comprehensive deepening reform is to improve and develop the socialist system with Chinese characteristics and promote the modernization of state governance system and capacity, as it was proposed in the Third Plenary Session of the Eighteenth CPC Central Committee. In the next session, the general goal of comprehensively promoting rule of law is to establish the Chinese socialist rule of law system and build China into a socialist rule of law country. The decisions of the two session have formed a companion piece. Reform and the rule of law are like two wings of a bird and two wheels of a car, and jointly promote the development of the cause of socialist modernization. Building a Chinese socialist rule of law system will improve and develop the Chinese socialist system, while building a socialist rule of law country will promote the modernization of the state governance system and governance capacity.

What is socialist system with Chinese characteristics? The report of the Eighteenth CPC National Congress gave an answer, "the socialist system with Chinese characteristics includes the following: the fundamental political system – the system of people's congresses; the basic political systems – the system of multiparty cooperation and political consultation under the leadership of the CPC, the system of regional ethnic autonomy, and the system of community-level self-governance; the socialist system of laws with Chinese characteristics; the basic economic system in which public ownership is the mainstay and economic entities of diverse ownership develop together; and the specific economic, political, cultural, and social institutions based on these systems". The foreground of constructing the Chinese socialist rule of law system is to form a complete set of laws and norms, the Chinese socialist legal system with the Constitution as the core in particular, which is not only an important part of Chinese socialist system but also an inseparable carrier for the Chinese socialist system to play its role in all respects. Over the past 70 years, the legislature has been actively engaged in the work on legislation, dedicated to the formation and improvement of Chinese socialist legal system, and dedicated itself to providing a legal guarantee for the founding of the PRC, the transition from new democratic revolution to socialist revolution and developing the socialism with Chinese characteristics. From 1978 to the end of August 2019, the NPC and its Standing Committee have adopted the Constitution and its five amendments, formulated or amended 643 laws, 25 interpretations and 258 decisions concerning some legal and other major issues. The number of laws in force reached 274. In addition, the State Council has formulated over 600 administrative regulations, the people's congresses and their standing committees that have legislative power had adopted over 12,000 regulations on local affairs. With such abundance in legislation, the Chinese socialist legal system continues to improve, which also makes the Chinese socialism more mature and better-defined.

3.1 Jurisprudential Foundation for New China

In February 1949, seven months before the new republic, the Central Committee issued the Instructions concerning Abolishing the Six Codes of the KMT and Determining Judicial Principles for the Liberated Areas, which declared that "all KMT's laws can only be tools to maintain the reactionary rule of landlords, compradors and bureaucratic capital, and weapons to suppress and constrain the broad popular masses", and claimed that "under the people's democratic dictatorship, led by the proletariat and with the alliance between workers and peasants at the core, the Six Codes of the KMT should be abolished. People's judicial work can no longer be based on the Six Codes, but should be based on new laws of the people", a statement that make all the laws, decrees, political system, political structure, and power under the KMT's reactionary rule were null and void, and completely denied by the people.[65] On March 31, Dong Biwu, then President of the North-China People's Government, issued the Order on Abolishing the KMT's Six Code and All the Reactionary Law, which required that the court judgments should not refer to any of such provisions.[66] To dismantle the KMT's legal system was both an important political and legal decision, which served as the guidelines for legislation before and after the PRC's founding and provided jurisprudential basis for overthrowing the KMT's reactionary rule, founding the People's Republic of China and the path of socialism.

Mao Zedong confidently claimed that "we are not only good at destroying the old world, we are also good at building the new".[67] When destroying the old world, the Party had prepared to "legislate" a new one. According to the Instructions, "until new people's laws have been systematically promulgated, it should be based on the policies of the Communist Party, as well as all programs, laws, regulations and resolutions published by People's Governments and the People's Liberation Army". With respect to the application of law in the preceding provision, it also called for studying and grasping the view of the state and view of law in Marxism and Mao Zedong Thought and the New Democracy's policies, programs, laws, decrees, regulations and resolutions, and finding and studying people's own experience in governance to make new and complete laws. The achievements of constructing a legal system made in the revolutionary base areas and liberated areas led by the Party had become the main sources of law on the eve of PRC's founding, and the essence of revolutionary practices of law were carried forward and developed in the new stage.

To take the land law system as an example. As Mao Zedong pointed out, "the peasant problem becomes the basic problem of the Chinese revolution and the strength of the peasants is the main strength of the Chinese revolution".[68] Land is what people concern most and also concerns the most people. The Party has always attached importance to land revolution and dedicated itself to resolving it through legislation. From the Jinggangshan Period, the Party enacted the Land Law of Jinggangshan (1928), and then the Land Law of Xingguo (1929), Land Law of the Chinese Soviet Republic (1931), Draft Regulation Shaan-Gan-Ning Border Region on Land Tenancy (1942), Principles of Shaan-Gan-Ning Border Region on Handling

[65] *On Abolishing Bogus Legal System (February 24, 1949)*, People's Daily, February 16, 1949, in *Selected Documents on Constitution (Vol. 2)*, Constitution Teaching Office of Law Department of Peking University ed., Peking University Press, 1982, pp. 240–242.

[66] DONG Biwu, *Collection of Dong Biwu's Writings on Politics and Law*, Law Press, 1986, pp. 45–47.

[67] MAO Zedong, *Report to the Second Plenary Session of the Seventh Central Committee of the CPC (March 5, 1949)*, in Selected Works of Mao Zedong (Vol. 4), Foreign Languages Press, 1961, p. 374.

[68] MAO Zedong, *On New Democracy (January 1940)*, in Selected Works of Mao Zedong (Vol. 2), Foreign Languages Press, 1965, p. 367.

Land Pawn Disputes and Outstanding Debt Disputes (1943), and Regulations of Jin-Cha-Ji Border Area on the Interests of Rent and Tenancy Debts.[69] In the War of Liberation period, the Central Committee issued the Directive on the Land Question (generally known as the May Fourth Directive for it was issued on May 4, 1946), which decided to change the policy of reducing rent and interest to one of confiscating the land of the landlords and distributing it among the peasants. On October 1947, the Central Committee promulgated the Outline Land Law of China, which put the land reform in the liberated areas into a law-based footing, making the legal basis for carrying out land reform.[70]

3.2 Constitution and Law Making Along a Winding Path Between October 1949 and Pre-reform

The Common Program, Organic Law of the Chinese People's Political Consultative Conference, and Organic Law of the Central People's Government, which were adopted in the First Plenary Session of the CPPPCC in September 1949, were the direct constitutional and legal basis for the founding of PRC and the Central People's Government. After the founding of the Central People's Government Council, it enacted a lot of laws: for important national political system and state agencies, it enacted the Program on the Implementation of Ethnic Regional Autonomy, the General Principles of the Organization of Government Administrative Council and Its Departments, general principles of the organization of provincial, municipal and county people's congresses, and laws on the organization of people's courts and procuratorates, and laid down the national symbols including capital, anthem and flag; for important areas of social life, it enacted the Marriage Law, Agrarian Land Reform Law and Trade Union law; in respect of criminal legislation, it formulated the Regulation on Punishing Counter-revolutionaries and Regulation on Punishing Corruption. However, legislation in economic affairs were small in number, and the primary ones in this regard were Provisional Regulation on the Agricultural Tax in Newly-liberated Areas and annual Regulation on the Public Debts for National Economic Construction. Though the number of the legislation in this period was small, it had helped to consolidate the state power and socialist systems, and promoted the reform in marriage, reform and land ownership, which contributed to releasing the social productive forces and stimulating people's enthusiasm for engaging in the construction of socialism. To realize the transformation of new democratic laws to socialist laws, the First Session of the First National People's Congress adopted the Resolution on the Validity of the Laws and Decrees Enacted Since the Founding of PRC, which addressed the question of validity of those laws and decrees through a constitutionality confirmation.

---

[69] HAN Yanlong ed., *A General History of the Legal System of the People's Republic of China (Vol. 1)*, Central Party School Press, 1998, p. 9.

[70] ZHANG Jinfan, *The History of Chinese Legal System*, Commercial Press, 2010, p. 505.

The socialist development was turned into a new chapter when the Constitution was adopted in the First Session of the First National People's Congress, for it provided a fundamental legal guarantee for the founding of the PRC and the establishment and development of socialist system. From its promulgation to 1958, the NPC and its Standing Committee had dedicated themselves to building a socialist legal system with 13.2 pieces of legislation in a year.[71] Based on the actual needs at that time, the legislation focused on strengthening the organization and development of state power, and promoting socialist transformation and supporting economic development.[72] A summary of these legislative achievements can be informed by taking a glance of following aspects:

First, to enact the laws on state agencies in a timely manner to basically realize the institutionalization of organizing the state power. These laws were mainly on the organization of National People's Congress, State Council, state council. People's courts, local people's congresses and local people's committees and people's procuratorates, and the regulations on police stations, urban community committees and urban sub-districts. Some decisions on the powers, functions and procedures of people's congresses at all levels were also made to address the conflicts of practices with certain legal principles.[73]

Second, to make law in some urgently needed areas of the state and social life. To regulate economic development, the NPC adopted Model Articles of Association for Agricultural Producers' Cooperatives, Model Articles of Association for Advanced Agricultural Producers' Cooperatives, Regulation of 1957 on the Public Debts for National Economic Construction, Regulation on the Public Debts for Local Economic Construction, Regulation on the Cultural Recreation Tax and Regulation

---

[71] General Office of the Standing Committee of the National People's Congress ed., *Chronology of the National People's Congress and Its Standing Committee (1954–2014)*, China Democratic and Legal Publishing House, 2014, Appendix I.

[72] SUN Guohua ed., *Study on the Socialist Legal System with Chinese Characteristics: Concepts, Theory and Structure*, China Democratic and Legal Publishing House, 2009, p. 33.

[73] For example, Decision on the Filling of Vacancies of Governors of Provinces, Chairmen of Autonomous Regions, Mayors, Prefects and Heads of Counties, Districts, Townships and Towns and Presidents of Local People's Courts in Periods When the Local People's Congresses Are Not in Session, Decision Regarding Whether the Membership of the Local People's Committees Shall Be Restricted to Deputies to the People's Congresses at the Corresponding Levels, Decision Regarding Whether the Presidents of the Local People's Courts and of the Local People's Procuratorates May Concurrently Be Members of the People's Committees at Various Levels, Decision on Meeting Foreign Envoys by the Chairman of the Standing Committee of the National People's Congress while the Chairman and Vice-Chairman of the People's Republic of China are on Vacation or Visits, Decision on the Procedure for Selecting Presidents of Provincial People's Procuratorates in Periods When the People's Congresses of Provinces Are Not in Session, Decision on the Term of Office of Each People's Congress and Each People's Committee of an Autonomous Prefecture, Decision on the Numbers of Deputies to the People's Congresses of Counties, Cities, Municipal Districts, Townships, Nationality Townships and Towns and on Other Matters, Decision on Specifying That the People's Congresses of Provinces and of Municipalities Directly Under the Central Government May Meet Once a Year, Resolution on the Interpretation of the Law, and Resolution of the Second Session of the First National People's Congress on Authorizing Its Standing Committee to Formulate Separate Regulations.

on Agricultural Tax, approved the Regulation on the Consolidated Industrial and Commercial Tax (Draft), Regulation on the Requisition of Land by the State for Construction and Regulation on the Administration of Trademarks. For better social management, the NPC made the Regulation on Household Registration, Regulation on Fire Supervision, Regulation on Frontier Health and Quarantine and the Decision on Handling the Illegal Books and Magazines. To reinforce national defense, the Military Service Law, Regulation of the Chinese People's Liberation Army on the Military Services of Officers and Regulation on Granting Honorary Titles and Medals to Meritorious Persons of the Chinese People's Liberation Army during the Chinese People's Revolutionary War. Moreover, some decisions on the management and guarantee for cadres and employees were also adopted.[74]

Third, to actively pursue the drafting of basic criminal, civil and litigation laws and formulate separate regulations to strive for institutional provision for the state and social life. Mao Zedong attached significant importance to the drafting of criminal and civil laws, as he ever directed, "not only do we need a Criminal Law, we also need a Civil Law; now there is absolutely no law at all. We not do without law, and we must have the Criminal Law and Civil Law. Not only should we enact laws, but also compile cases".[75] Under the Party's leadership, more haste was made to draft the Criminal Law, Civil Law, Criminal Procedure Law and Civil Procedure Law.[76] However, the legislation in these laws were not completed even before the reform and opening-up period, failing to meet the urgent needs for state governance and filling key institutional loopholes.[77] The Regulation on Arrest and Detention, Regulation on

[74] For example, Provisional Regulation of the State Council on Punishing and Rewarding the State Employees, P Provisional Regulations of the State Council on the Retirement of Workers and Employees, Provisional Regulation of the State Council on Wages and Benefits of Ordinary Workers and Handymen in Enterprises, Institutions and State Departments, Provisional Regulation of the State Council on the Period of Training and Financial Subsidies for Apprentices in State-Run, Joint State-Private and Individually-Operated Enterprises and Institutions, Provisional Regulation of the State Council on the Periods of Home Leave for Workers and Staff and Their Salaries During Such Periods and Provisional Regulation of the State Council on the Handling of the Resignation of Workers and Employees.

[75] ZHAO Cangbi, *Speech at the Forum on Legal System Construction*, People's Daily, October 29, 1978, p. 2.

[76] Before the constitution was enacted in 1954, two drafts of the Criminal Law had been prepared. By 1957, 22 drafts had been revised and sent to deputies to the National People's Congress for comments. By the 1960s, the draft Criminal Law was revised for the 33rd time. The draft Civil Law was mostly completed and started to solicit opinions from relevant departments. In 1962, according to the instructions of Mao Zedong, a civil law research group was re-established to resume the drafting of the civil law. In July 1964, a proposed draft of the civil law was made ready. The Criminal Procedure Law was also started and the first draft was completed in June 1957.

[77] Zhao said that the enactment of a Criminal Code was to realize Chairman Mao's last wish, as he said, "our draft Criminal Law was sent to some local governments and departments for comments after it was revised in 1963, and has not yet been deliberated and approved by the national legislature. Even so, some judicial departments have cited the provisions of the draft Criminal Law as a reference for sentencing. All these show that there is an urgent need for a criminal code in judicial practice, so that our sentencing can be accurate and law enforcement can be law-based". See ZHAO Cangbi, *Speech at the Forum on Legal System Construction*, People's Daily, October 29, 1978, p. 2.

People's Police and Regulation on Administrative Penalties for Public Security were formulated, the Decision of the State Council on Re-education through Labor was approved, and some decisions on certain litigation procedures were also adopted,[78] which provided basis for law enforcement and administration of justice.

By the autumn of 1959, the conception that "policy is law" had emerged. From the end of 1959, legislation had been basically suspended.[79] Accoding to some statistics, from 1959 to 1966, only one to two pieces of legislation were adopted every year; however, from 1966 to 1977, the NPC and its Standing Committee did not engage in any legislative activities except for the 1975 Constitution and the decision on granting special pardons.[80] In the 30 years before the reform and opening-up, China did not realize the establishment of a legal system, and the legislation only contributed to establishing the socialist system and consolidating state power, but failed to promote the improvement and development of socialist system with the power of institutions. Therefore, the incomplete and immature legal system could not withstand the erosion of left-line mistakes and legal nihilism. What's worse, the legal system was totally put on shelf, and lost its function in regulating, guiding and guaranteeing social life. The socialist rule of law construction was severely damaged.

3.3 Filling Gaps and Economic Development for Preparing Legal System for Socialist Market Economy from 1978 to Early Twenty-First Century

"Law is what people wish for". The whole Party and all the Chinese people have reached a consensus on how to understand the relationship between reform and opening-up and building legal system after the Cultural Revolution. That the socialist legal system should be strengthened is the consensus. To correspond with the methods

[78] For example, Decision on Cases That Are Not Heard Publicly, Decision Regarding Whether Persons Deprived of Political Rights Can Serve as Defenders during the Deprivation, Decision on Public Surveillance Over All Counter-Revolutionaries that Are Subject to People's Court Judgments, Decision on Leniently Handling and Settling the Remnant Counter-Revolutionaries in Urban Areas, Resolution on Cases Involving the Death Penalty That Are Subject to the Supreme People's Court Judgments or Approvals, Written Reply to the Supreme People's Court on the Implementation of the Resolution on Cases Involving the Death Penalty That Are Subject to the Supreme People's Court Judgments or Approvals.

[79] SUN Guohua ed., *Study on the Socialist Legal System with Chinese Characteristics: Concepts, Theory and Structure*, China Democratic and Legal Publishing House, 2009, p. 35.

[80] The Second NPC and its Standing Committee (April 1959 to December 1964) passed nine pieces of laws, legal interpretations and decisions on related legal issues; the Third NPC and its Standing Committee (December 1964 to December 1974) passed three pieces of laws, legal interpretations and decisions on related legal issues; the Fourth NPC and its Standing Committee (January 1975 to February 1978) passed only one piece of laws, legal interpretations and decisions on legal issues. General Office of the Standing Committee of the National People's Congress ed., *Chronology of the National People's Congress and Its Standing Committee (1954–2014)*, China Democratic and Legal Publishing House, 2014, p. 87, 125, 151, Appendix I.

of state governance, the Party made a significant change from the obsolete conception that policy was law, to an integration of policy and law, and then to a stress on the foundational role of law and practice of rule of law. To adapt to the needs of rule of law and give more impetus to legislation, the legislative system was the first to embrace the reform as soon as the reform and opening-up was started; this reform changed the situation where only the NPC could make laws, its Standing Committee had only the power to enact decrees while the local people's congresses had not legislative power. The 1979 Local Organization Law granted the provincial people's congresses and their standing committees with proper legislative powers. To advance the reform further, the 1982 Constitution confirmed that the NPC and its Standing Committee were authorized to exercise the national legislative power and the State Council had the power to make administrative regulations. To support the work on legislation, the Sixth Session of the Fifth NPC convened in February 1979 voted to establish the Legislative Affairs Committee to assist the Standing Committee strengthening the work on building legal system. The Committee consisted of 80 members with Peng Zhen serving as the director. Since then, the socialist cause of legislation has been on the fast track and undertaken three important mission of the times: first, to amend the Constitution, inherited the courage and initiative of following its own path in the 1950s, and created the socialist path with Chinese characteristics; second, to fill the vacuum of law created in the 30 years to lay general foundation for consolidating state power and maintain social stability; third, to forge ahead with greater innovation and aspirations, improve and develop the Chinese socialist system and realize the goal of building a prosperous, strong, democratic and culturally advanced country.

First, to stay true to the original aspirations, carry forward traditions and adopt the Constitution. The 1982 Constitution carried forward and improved the basic principles of the 1954 Constitution, reflected on the experience of socialist development in China in all respects, manifested the line, principles and policies as established in the Third Plenary Session of the Eleventh CPC Central Committee, and met the demands of reform and opening-up and socialist modernization. It is a sound constitution in line with China's conditions. Over the past 40 years, it has been amended for five times. These amendments have guaranteed the smooth progress of socialist modernization that generated remarkable achievements, and continued to burden the responsibility of realizing the two centenary goals. As Peng Zhen pointed out, "the Constitution mainly proceeds from the current realities, but it needs to look for the future. "[81] The steady implementation of the Constitution and its advancement with the times have ensured the steady development of the socialist cause under the Party's leadership, the progress towards a more mature and complete and the bright future of Chinese socialist path of rule of law.

Second, to enact basic laws in criminal and civil affairs and state agencies, and restore the pillars of socialist legal system. In the 30 years before the reform and opening-up, in terms of key areas, China only made several basic laws in state agencies, and most of the legislation was black in the criminal, civil and litigation affairs.

[81] ZENG Jianhui and XU Minhe, *For the Greatest Interests of the Biggest Majority of Chinese People: Peng Zhen on the Draft Constitution of People's Republic of China*, Outlook, No. 5, pp. 5–7 (1982).

After the reform and opening-up was launched, especially after the promulgation of the 1982 Constitution, the state agency laws were also adjusted. The NPC and its Standing Committee, referring to the spirits and principles of the Constitution, had successively enacted the Law on the Organization of National People's Congress, Rule of Procedures of the National People's Congress, Law on Deputies to the National People's Congress and the Local People's Congresses, Law on Legislation, Law on the Organization of State Council, Regional Ethnic Autonomy Law, Law on the Organization of the Villagers' Committees (for Trial Implementation), Law on the Organization of the Urban Residents' Committees, Basic Law of Hong Kong SAR, Basic Law of Macao SAR, National Flag Law and National Emblem Law, revised the Local Organization Law, Electoral Law, Organization Law of the People's Courts, and Organization Law of the People's Procuratorates. The systems prescribed in the Constitution, including the people's congress system as China's fundamental political system, the regional autonomy and community-level self-governance and other basic political systems along with the special administrative area and national symbols were established and operated on their own laws. In civil legislation, "civil law involves a wide range of areas, and is very complicated, the reform of economic institutions has just started, we lack the experience, the conditions for enacting a complete civil code are not yet mature, so we have to formulate separate laws for those urgently needed and mature parts".[82] The NPC and its Standing Committee enacted the General Principles of Civil Law, Economic Contract Law, Law on Economic Contracts Involving Foreign Interest, Technology Contract Law, Contract Law, Law on the Protection of Consumer Rights and Interests, Patent Law, Trademark Law, Copyright Law, Marriage Law, Inheritance Law, Maritime Law and Enterprise Bankruptcy Law (for Trial Implementation), which provided legal support and code of conduct for socialist civil activities and served as the institutional foundation for establishing the socialist market economy in the 1990s. For criminal legislation, though the Criminal Law was promulgated in 1979, the social structure had undergone complete transformation which was brought by reform and opening-up and socialist modernization, so the crimes also changed. To address such incompatibility and respond to the criminal policy of the Central Committee laid down in 1981 on more quickly and severely punishing the crimes, the NPC Standing Committee adopted the decision on severely punishing economic crimes. As of 1997 Amendment to the Criminal Law, the NPC had promulgated 24 pieces of separate criminal provisions successively.[83] In terms of litigation procedures, three major procedural laws, i.e. the Criminal Procedure Law, Civil Procedure Law, and Administrative Procedure Law, were formulated to regulate litigation activities with sound procedures, protect human rights and realize procedural justice.

---

[82] WANG Hanbin, *Explanations on the Draft General Principles of Civil Law of the People's Republic of China*, April 2, 1986, delivered at the Fourth Session of the Sixth National People's Congress.

[83] SUN Guohua ed., *Study on the Socialist Legal System with Chinese Characteristics: Concepts, Theory and Structure*, China Democratic and Legal Publishing House, 2009, p. 242.

Third, to implement the conception that market economy must be a rule-of-law economy, and strive for establishing the legal system for socialist market economy. After the launch of reform and opening-up, to attract foreign investment and expand international economic cooperation and technological exchanges, the NPC and its Standing Committee enacted the Law on Chinese-Foreign Equity Joint Ventures, Foreign-funded Enterprises Law and Law on Chinese-Foreign Contractual Joint Ventures (collectively known as 3 foreign capital laws), which opened Chinese door to the market and global economy. The dedication to civil legislation not only heightened the socialist commodity economy, but also helped build favorable legal conditions for establishing and improving the socialist market economic system. To better resolve the contradiction between rapid economic institution change and stagnation of legislation, the NPC and its Standing Committee issued two decisions to the State Council, i.e. the Decision on Authorizing the State Council to Reform the System of Industrial and Commercial Taxes and Issue Relevant Draft Tax Regulations for Trial Implementation and the Decision on Authorizing the State Council to Formulate Interim Provisions or Regulations Concerning the Reform of the Economic Structure and the Opening-up. In 1992, the Central Committee made it clear to establish the socialist market economic system. And the 1993 Constitutional Amendment prescribed that the state practices socialist market economy and stressed the importance of economic legislation. Accordingly, the NPC and its Standing Committee focused on deepening reform, expanding reform and establishing socialist market economic system and accelerated the pace of legislation, especially putting the economic legislation in the prominent position, in order to promote the establishment of the legal system for socialist market economy.[84] At that time, the NPC Standing Committee put forward the legislative objectives and tasks for forming a legal system framework for socialist market economy: first, to enact the laws on regulating market entities, including the Company Law, Partnership Enterprise Law, Town/Township Enterprise Law and Law on Individual Proprietorship Enterprises and revised the 3 foreign capital laws when it was opportune; second, to enact the laws on adjusting market entities relationships and safeguarding fair competition, including Anti-Unfair Competition Law, Securities Law, Negotiable Instruments Law, Arbitration Law, Auction Law, Bidding Law, Insurance Law, and Trust Law; third, to enact the laws on improving macro control and promote coordinated economic development, including the Budge Law, Commercial Banking Law, Foreign Trade Law, Law on Tax Collection and Administration, Law on the Protection of Investments by Taiwan Compatriots and Law on the Promotion of Small and Medium-Sized Enterprises, and issued the Decision on Applying the Provisional Regulations Concerning Taxations Including Value-Added Tax, Consumption Tax and Business Tax Applicable to Enterprise with Foreign Investment and Foreign Enterprises; fourth, to establish and improve the laws for social security, including

[84] General Office of the Standing Committee of the National People's Congress ed., *Chronology of the Establishment of the Socialist Legal System with Chinese Characteristics (1978–2010)*, China Democratic and Legal Publishing House, 2011, pp. 102–107.

the Labor Law, Trade Union Law, Safe Production Law and Occupational Disease Prevention Law.

Moreover, the NPC and its Standing Committee also focused on legislation for environment protection institutions, including Marine Environment Protection Law, Law on the Prevention and Control of Water Pollution, Law on the Prevention and Control of Air Pollution, Environment Protection, Law on the Prevention of Control of Solid Waste, Law on the Prevention and Control of Environmental Noise Pollution and Law on Environmental Impact Assessment.

3.4 Social Legislation and Legal System Readiness for a Harmonious Society and Balanced Legislative Development

Since the reform and opening-up, China's work on legislation has been in line with the overall process of its reform and opening-up and socialist modernization, while advancing in an all-round way, it has always adhered to and served economic development. In a process of strengthening the economic legislation, the legal system for socialist market economy has been basically established and developed under continuous improvement. However, it should be noted that there were obvious imbalances in the social and economic legislation, which presents a considerable gap with the requirements of thoroughly implementing the Scientific Outlook on Development and building China into a socialist harmonious society, an issue that could not be ignored in the construction of the legal system.[85] The Decision on Major Issues in Building a Harmonious Socialist Society adopted by the Central Committee in 2006 proposed to improve the laws and regulations on protecting citizens' rights, promoting social undertakings, improving social security, regulating social organizations and enhancing social management. Since 2007, the NPC Standing Committee had emphasized for several times that the social legislation keen to improving social wellbeing should be enhanced by referring to the Party's requirements, dedicated itself to addressing the most pressing and relevant problems that are of the utmost concern to the people, strived for applying legal institutions and mechanisms to ensure that all the people enjoy the rights to education, employment, medical and old-age care and housing to promote social fairness and justice. The social legislation is a shortcoming of the socialist legal system. So resolving some problems brought about by the development of the market economy through legislation can help to promote social fairness and justice while keep its efficiency and reflect the socialist people-centered principle.

To this end, the Legislative Plan of the Eleventh NPC Standing Committee made arrangements for strengthening social legislation, and proposed programs to be

[85] SHEN Chunyao, *On Several Issues on Strengthening Legislation in the Social Field*, Ninth Lecture of the Eleventh NPC Standing Committee.

formulated in the next 5 years, mainly including: first, to improve the laws and regulations on social security, and gradually establish a social security system covering urban and rural residents that connects social insurance, social assistance, social welfare and charities causes, such as the social insurance law, social assistance law and charity law; second, to enact laws and regulations for social undertakings, such as enacting the law on the promotion of basic medical and health care, mental health law, traditional Chinese medicine law, and revising the Drug Administration Law, Vocational Education Law, Intangible Cultural Heritage Protection Law, and Public Libraries Law; third, to enact laws and regulations to protect people's basic life, such as the formulation of the food safety law and the housing security law; fourth, to improve the laws and regulations for the protection of the legitimate rights and interests of special groups, such as revising the Law on the Protection of the Rights and Interests of the Elderly; fifth, the laws and regulations on regulating social organizations and social management, such as the formulation of the people's mediation law.

In this period, the NPC Standing Committee had enacted or revised the Law on the Protection of the Disabled, Law on Earthquake Prevention and Disaster Reduction, Law on the Mediation and Arbitration of Rural Land Contract Disputes, Tort Law, State Compensation Law, People's Mediation Law, Social Insurance Law, and Military Insurance Law. Laws in the social field, such as the Insurance Law and the Intangible Cultural Heritage Law and other laws that were directly related to the people's interests. These laws had greatly strengthened the social legislation. "Because the promotion of legislation in the social field often directly involves the adjustment of interest relations, coupled with some other reasons, legislation in the social field often encounters great difficulties in forming social consensus, and the interests of vested interests and those who strive for interests are coordinated. It brings new challenges to the legislative work".[86] Therefore, other programs in the plan were not accomplished as scheduled, and some legislation were not completed until after the Eighteenth National Congress, such as the Charity Law and the Traditional Chinese Medicine Law; some have been submitted for deliberation only recently, such as Law on the Promotion of Basic Medical and Health Care; some had not yet fully met the legislative conditions and were difficult to amend, so the State Council formulated regulations to pilot explorations, such as the Social Assistance Law and the Housing Security Law. Although the progress of strengthening legislation in the social field did not achieve the expected results at that time, these achievements and efforts made greatly promoted the balanced development of the socialist legal system, and promoted fairness and justice as an important core of the socialist rule of law and socialist system. It has laid the foundation for the improvement and development of the legal system in the social field after the Eighteenth National Congress.

[86] SHEN Chunyao, *On Several Issues on Strengthening Legislation in the Social Field*, Ninth Lecture of the Eleventh NPC Standing Committee.

3.5 Five-Sphere Integrated Plan and Chinese Socialist Legal System for a More Mature and Well-Defined Socialist System

Since the Eighteenth National Congress, the NPC and its Standing Committee have conscientiously studied and implemented Xi Jinping Thought on Socialism with Chinese characteristics for a New Era by firmly adhering to the integration of the Party's leadership, the people's master position and the rule of law, and resolutely implemented the major decisions and arrangements of the Central Committee. By closely centering on the coordinated promotion of the Five-Sphere Integrated Plan and the Four-Pronged Comprehensive Strategy, the NPC and its Standing Committee have steadfastly improved the Chinese socialist legal system with the Constitution as the core, made greater strides and progress in legislation and adopted a large number of important laws quickly which caused positive social effect, which has opened a new chapter of the work on legislation in the new era. Since the Congress (as of the end of August 2019), the NPC and its Standing Committee have passed 1 amendment to the Constitution, enacted 37 pieces of new laws, and passed 70 pieces of decisions on revisions, amendments and changes, involving 191 pieces of revisions, 9 pieces of legal interpretations, and 62 pieces of decisions on legal issues and major issues. The Chinese socialist legal system with the Constitution as the core has gained comprehensive improvement and development, and the socialist system has become more mature and complete.

First, to strengthen legislation in key areas and improve all the respects of Chinese socialist legal system. For political construction, the NPC and its Standing Committee continue to improve the institutionalization of socialist democratic politics. The 2018 Constitution Amendment has helped realize the state's guiding principles keep with the times; it improved the state system and institutions, consolidated its foundation in socialist development for a new era. The Supervision Law was enacted, which established the supervision institution and advanced the development and improvement of state agencies; the Law on Legislation, Local Organization Law, Electoral Law, Law on the Deputies and Civil Servants Law were revised to improve the people's congress system, legislative system and judicial system. To implement relevant provisions of the Constitution, the Law on National Medals and National Honorary Titles and the National Anthem Law were formulated to promote the enforcement of the systems laid out in the Constitution. The People's Assessors Law and Law on International Criminal Judicial Assistance were promulgated to advance the judicial system reform and improve judicial institutions and mechanisms. The Law on the Organization of People's Courts, Law on the Organization of People's Procuratorates, Judges Law and Procurators Law. The NPC and its Standing Committee has enacted the National Security Law, Anti-Espionage Law, Anti-Terrorism Law, Law on the Administration of Activities of Overseas Non-Governmental Organizations within the Territory of China, Cyber Security Law and National Intelligence Law to put into practice the holistic view of national security and institute a system of law for national security for safeguarding national security and national core and major interests.

In terms of economic development, legislation in the field of socialist market economy has been continuously strengthened. A number of important laws have been formulated and revised to improve macro control and market supervision and promoting industrial revitalization. For enhancing macro control, the Budget Law, Law on Securities Investment Fund and Commercial Banking Law were revised; in regulating market behaviors, strengthening market supervision, and maintaining market order, the Tourism Law, Asset Appraisal Law, E-Commerce Law and Foreign Investment Law were enacted, and the Anti-Unfair Competition Law, Trademark Law, Standardization Law, Advertising Law, Surveying and Mapping Law, Specialized Farmers' Cooperatives Law and Company Law were revised; in terms of promoting scientific and technological innovation and industrial revitalization, the Law on Transformation of Scientific and Technological Achievements, Seed Law and Law on the Promotion of Small and Medium-Sized Enterprises were revised and the Waterway Law was formulated. To regulate civil activities, the General Provisions of Civil Law was enacted while the Rural Land Contract Law was revised. Important steps were taken in implementing the principle of statutory taxation, the Environmental Protection Tax Law, Tobacco Leaf Tax Law, Ship Tonnage Tax Law, Farmland Occupation Tax Law, Vehicle Purchase Tax Law and Resource Tax Law were enacted and the Corporate Income Tax Law and the Individual Income Tax Law were revised, which was accorded with the timetable and roadmap approved by the Central Committee.

In terms of social construction, the NPC and its Standing Committee have sped up the protection and improvement of people's livelihood with good laws, and promoted the innovation of the social governance system. The Standing Committee adheres to a problem-oriented approach and strengthens the legislative work by focusing on issues of general concern to the people. In promoting the development of social undertakings, the Charity Law and Traditional Chinese Medicine Law were enacted, while Population and Family Planning Law, Red Cross Law, Education Law, Higher Education Law and Law on the Promotion of Privately-run Schools were revised. The Law on the Protection of Consumer Rights and Interests, Labor Contract Law, Social Insurance Law, Law on the Protection of the Rights and Interests of the Elderly were revised, and the Anti-Domestic Violence Law was enacted. To innovate social management and maintain the safety of people's life and properties, the Food Safety Law, Drug Administration Law and Safe Production Law were revised, while the Special Equipment Safety Law, Cyber Security Law, Nuclear Safety Law and Regulation on Fire and Rescue Ranks were formulated. The NPC and its Standing Committee also adopted the Ninth and Tenth Amendments to the Criminal Law. They also revised the Administrative Procedure Law and Criminal Procedure Law to protect citizens' rights in litigation procedures.

The pace of legislation to promote cultural progress has been accelerated. To promote advanced socialist culture and the prosperity of socialist culture, boost cultural creativity of the Chinese nation, consolidate cultural confidence, promote the absorption of core socialist values in legislation, and actively advance the work on cultural legislation, the NPC and its Standing Committee has enacted the Law on the Guarantee of Public Cultural Services, Law on the Protection of Heroes and

Martyrs, Public Libraries Law and Film Industry Promotion Law and revised the Cultural Relic Protection Law.

For advancing ecological civilization, upgrading the legislative conceptions and institutional design and improving the institutional development for "Beautiful China", the NPC and its Standing Committee have formulated the Environmental Protection Tax Law, Law on the Prevention and Control of Soil Pollution, and Law on Exploration for and Development of Resources in the Deep Seabed Area, and revised the Environment Protection Law, Law on the Prevention and Control of Air Pollution, Marine Environment Protection Law, Law on the Prevention and Control of Water Pollution, and Wildlife Animal Protection Law in a bid to build the most stringent legal system for ecology and environment protection.

Second, to improve the quality of the Chinese socialist legal system in all respects, make the institutional design more adapted to the requirements of the times and present new features of the times. As Chinese socialism entered a new era, the legislature has undertaken a new mission, embarked on a new journey and exemplified a new character of the times. The Xi Jinping Thought on Socialism with Chinese characteristics for a New Era is the new character of the Chinese socialist legal system, which consolidates the confidence in the Chinese socialist system.

To compile a civil code that truly belongs to Chinese people has been the long-cherished wish of generations of the Chinese people since 1949. And the Party along with the legislature launched several initiatives in 1954, 1962, 1979 and 2001 respectively. "The ups and downs in the drafting of China's civil law do not mean that Chinese society does not need civil law. On the contrary, it means that there is a fundamental reason that underlies such need. Only the reason exists, and only China finds it, Chinese civil law will be inevitable regardless of anyone's will".[87] Due to the lack of enough social practice, theoretical research and legislative techniques, the first two attempts did not make any practical results. However, by adopting a one by one approach, in the latter two attempts, the working methods were changed, and the General Principles, Inheritance Law, Guaranty Law, Contract Law, Property Law, Tort Law, and Law on the Laws Applicable to Foreign-related Civil Relations and other separate laws alike were formulated, which gradually established a rather complete normative system for civil legislation. Since the Eighteenth National Congress, the Central Committee with Xi Jinping as the core has attached great importance to the compilation of civil code, and designated it a major legislative task in the Fourth Session of the Eighteenth CPC Central Committee. The General Principles of Civil Law was enacted, and the parts of Civil Code are now under deliberation and revision according to the prescribed timetable and roadmap for it. "A Civil Code that conforms with the development of Chinese socialism, China's conditions and realities, and possesses a scientific system, a rigorous structure, reasonable standards and consistency" is around the corner. It is believed that the forthcoming Civil Code marked a successful culmination of civil legislation, a milestone for China's rule of

[87] YANG Zhenshan, *A Basic Law with Historical Significance: To Commemorate the Tenth Anniversary of General Principles of Civil Law*, China Legal Science, No. 1, pp. 3–11 (1997).

law construction in the new era, a major achievement in the work on legislation, and a new stage of improving and developing Chinese socialist legal system.

To implement the gist of the Forth Plenary Session, the NPC and its Standing Committee revised the Law on Legislation to better the legislative system and clarify the powers, functions and scope of local legislative power. This revision also gave the cities with subordinate districts the legislative power, which was later confirmed in the 2018 Constitutional Amendment. As of March 2019, there were 322 cities with subordinate districts and autonomous prefectures with legislative power, including 288 cities with subordinate districts, 30 autonomous prefectures and 4 cities with no subordinate districts. This is a major development of China's legislative system over the past 70 years, especially over the past 40 years, and of tremendous significance for improving local governance capacity, encouraging the cities with subordinate districts to engage in rule of law practice and promote local economic and social development according to law. It will also help to release the great potential of local legislation in the new era, and in concerted efforts, contribute to the Chinese socialist rule of law system and build China into a socialist rule of law country.

"Clear waters and green mountains as good as mountains of gold and silver", and "the best institutional arrangements and the strictest rule of law to protect the environment" and other important remarks made by Xi Jinping are the guiding principles that should be observed in the environment protection legislation in the new era. To implement Xi Jinping thought on ecological civilization, the NPC Standing Committee made up for shortcomings: to enact the Law on the Prevention and Control of Soil Pollution to resolve the long-ignored issue of soil pollution with the strictest legal institutions; to revise most of the current environment protection laws, reshape the protection system, pay attention to the overall integration of various links and procedures in environment protection and strive for setting up a strictest system of environment protection laws; to adopt the Resolution of the Standing Committee of the National People's Congress on Comprehensively Tightening Ecological and Environmental Protection and Lawfully Promoting Triumph in the Uphill Battle for Prevention and Control of Pollution, which demonstrated the determination and resolve of people's congresses and their standing committees to perform the responsibilities prescribed in the Constitution and law, to resolve the pollution issue with laws as the weapon, and protect the ecological environment under the rule law. As emphasized by Li Zhanshu, to protect ecological environment must rely on rule of law and observe the law, making the legal system bare its teeth to environment protection.[88]

Third, to adopt more flexible and diversified methods to improve and develop Chinese socialist legal system and constantly enhance the adaptability of the static legal system to dynamic economic and social development. When Chinese socialism entered a new era, China's development is also steered in a new historical juncture; the main social contradiction will change, the missions for reform and opening-up will be tougher, harder and more fastidious, and given the increasingly complicated

[88] Li Zhanshu, *To Administer Water Pollution and Protect Water Environment according to Law, and Paint a New Future for Beautiful China in the New Era*, People's Daily, June 7, 2019, p. 1.

world situation, the work on legislation will be heavier and more demanding and pose greater responsibilities. The responsiveness and adaptability of socialist legal system will withstand new challenges. Under the Party's firm leadership and scientific decision-making, the NPC and its Standing Committee have relied on the traditional methods of enacting, revising, repealing and interpreting laws and explored more flexible methods of legislation to better lead, promote, regulate and guarantee reform and development. First, to more frequently apply the package legislation to centrally handle the cancellation of and delegation of power in the administrative approval. Second, to make decisions on authorization and reform. The decisions will permit pilot programs in certain administrative areas and scope for resolving certain matter according to the authorization even if the corresponding law is not revised as the matter requires; and then the experience on certain pilot programs will be summarized, the replicable and mature of the reform measures for it can be upgraded to law, making it a nation-wide institution and mechanism. The decision on authorization and reform is more flexible and effective. For example, upon the NPC Standing Committee's authorization, the China (Shanghai) Pilot Free Trade Zone innovated the foreign investment system, and practiced the system of pre-entry national treatment plus a negative list management for foreign investment. Its success had laid the foundation for revising the three laws on foreign capital and enacting the Foreign Investment Law. third, to coordinate and promote the local guarantee for strengthening regional integrated development. To promote the Yangtze River Economic Belt, the integration of Beijing-Tianjin-Hebei and other regional development strategies is a new challenge in the new era. As a response, the legislature has constantly explored and adopted new legislative methods, provided more specific and earmarked institutional designs, making legislation timely reflect the practice and adapt to the socialist modernization in the new era.

In addition, China attaches great importance to the establishment of an efficient rule of law implementation system. The NPC Standing Committee adopts various methods such as law enforcement inspections and constitutional review to promote the effective implementation of the Constitution and laws. It also makes sure that each normative document is recorded, each recorded one is reviewed and each reviewed one is subject to corrections if any mistakes are found, so as to resolutely safeguard the unity of the socialist legal system. It values a strong rule of law guarantee system, continuously strengthens the awareness of the rule of law among the Chinese people, promotes China as a rule-of-law society, and creates a sound implementation system for the rule of law. Moreover, it has also spared efforts to build a high-level rule of law task force to support the all-round development of the rule of law.

4 A Summary

"A given culture is the ideological reflection of the politics and economics of a given society."[89] Xi Jinping also stressed, "socialist culture with Chinese characteristics is derived from China's fine traditional culture, which was born of the Chinese civilization and nurtured over more than 5,000 years; it has grown out of the revolutionary and advanced socialist culture that developed over the course of the Chinese people's revolution, construction, and reform under the Party's leadership; and it is rooted in the great practice of socialism with Chinese characteristics."[90] Over the past 70 years, especially over the past 40 years, the Chinese socialist culture has developed along the progress of the socialist system and socialist market economy, and the Chinese socialist rule of law culture has also developed by drawing from the great practice of socialist rule of law. By advocating "to promote the spirit of socialist rule of law and construct the socialist rule of law culture" in the Fourth Plenary Session of the Eighteenth Central Committee, the Party, for the first time, decided to incorporate the development of the "socialist rule of law culture", representing its keen grasp of the importance, urgency and regularity of establishing the rule of law culture.

What is rule of law culture? What does it mean? The answers made by the academia can be classified as following three opinions: (1) the rule of law culture embodies the rule of law concepts (spirits) and institutions (systems)[91]; (2) the rule of law culture embodies the rule of law spirits, systems and practice[92] (or material, institutions

[89] Mao Zedong, *On New Democracy (January 1940)*, in Selected Works of Mao Zedong (Vol. 2), Foreign Languages Press, 1965, p. 369.

[90] Publicity Department of the CPC Central Committee ed., *Thirty Lectures on Xi Jinping Thought on Socialism with Chinese Characteristics for a New Era*, Study Press, 2018, p. 195.

[91] For example, Jiang Chuanguang thought the culture of rule of law is a cultural form and social way of life formed in the process of establishing a society under the rule of law, the core of which is the establishment of the concept of rule of law and rule of law thinking, as well as the establishment and operations of its corresponding systems and organizations. In the study of the rule of law theory, all the connotations of the rule of law revealed, the description and summary of the social representation and principles of rule of law and the practices for constructing the operation mechanisms for rule of law. For example, the pursuit of the values, concepts and spirits, institution design, operations and realization of rule of law, all belong to the content of the rule of law culture. Jiang Chuanguang, To Make the Chinese Socialist Rule of Law Culture Prosper with More Efforts, *Study Times*, June 12, 2017, p. 3. In Liu Zuoxiang's opinion, the rule of law culture consists of a surface structure and a deep structure, the former including legal norms, legal system, and their organizations and facilities, etc., while the latter including psychology and awareness of law and a system of legal thought. The rule of law culture is the ideology of law and the social system and organizational institutions that adapt to it. Liu Zuoxiang, *Several Theoretical Issues on Rule of Law Culture*, Legal Forum, Vol. 1, pp. 5–10 (2012).

[92] Li Lin deemed that the socialist rule of law culture in its broad sense refers to the cultural advancement and rule of law progress in its values, spirits, awareness, thinking and theories that are essential for socialist advanced culture, the legal system, norms and measures that can characterize the socialist democratic politics and the behaviors such as doing things according to law and abiding by law. See Li Lin, *Several Issues on the Concept of Socialist Rule of Law Culture*, Journal of Beijing Union University (Humanities and Social Sciences), No. 2, pp. 5–12, 19 (2012). Liu Bin pointed out that rule of law culture refers to the awareness, principles, spirits, legal acts and pursuit of values in

and spirits)[93]; (3) the rule of law culture embodies spirits, institutions, practices and materials[94] (or institutions, spirits, practices and environment).[95] These answers make a consensus on rule of law culture, in which the socialist systems established by law-making, the conceptions, spirits, behaviors and habits nurtured by these systems are the important parts of socialist rule of law culture. As Dong Biwu pointed out, "when there was human civilization in history, legal system was a basic component of it though not the only one. To simply put it, a state that has no legal system cannot be established".[96] Systems possess an overarching position and plays an inseparable role in the socialist rule of law culture, as they control other cultural elements, embody the spirits and values, shape people's behaviors and guide people to develop a common way of life and habits through effective implementation.[97]

Legislation is the most elementary, effective and direct source for building systems in the socialist legal culture. It not only creates the socialist system, promotes the development of socialist culture for systems, nurtures the socialist rule of law spirits by giving full play to the role of legal system in leading, promoting, regulating and securing development, but also guides people to develop the habit of observing and applying the law in daily life. In a word, legislation has provided a strong institutional support for socialist rule of law culture. The socialist rule of law culture is a national, scientific, and people-oriented one. Its national character is prominently manifested in the Chinese socialist system developed in the rule of law construction in the past

---

people's heart and behaviors, the cultural connotations embodied in a country's legal system, legal institutions and facilities, and the behavior involving rule of law in their daily life and work. See LIU Bin, *Theoretical Proposal for Contemporary Rule of Law Culture*, Journal of China University of Political Science and Law, No. 1, pp. 15–19 (2007). In Zhang Xiaolian's opinion, rule of law culture is a set of ideas, values and behavioral system, including the rule of law spirit and beliefs rooted in people's hearts, the rule of law values and authority engraved in the legal system, and the habits and codes of conduct reflected in daily life. ZHANG Xiaolian, *To Vigorously Build the Socialist Rule of Law Culture*, Qiushi Journal, Vol. 9, 2015.

[93] He Qinhua believed that the socialist rule of law culture is the aggregate of material achievements (courts, procuratorates and prison), system (socialist legal system) and spirits (concepts and awareness of socialist law) that have been made under the Party's leadership after the arduous explorations and innovation during the process of the great practice of building socialist country since 1949. See CHANG Feng, *To Start A New Journey of Constructing a Socialist Rule of Law Culture: An Interview with Prof. He Qinhua*, People's Procuratorial Semimonthly, No. 21, pp. 49–52 (2017).

[94] In Xu Xianming's opinion, the rule of law culture includes four elements: spirit, system, behavior, and material bearing. The core is institutional culture. The core of building a socialist rule of law culture is to institute a socialist effective legal system. XU Xianming, *The Core of Socialist Rule of Law Culture is the Culture of Institutions*, Legal Daily, December 18, 2013, p. 9.

[95] Zhang Zhonghou believed that socialist rule of law culture is a grand conceptual system, which, in brief, can be understood as an aggregate of a scientific and complete legal system, fairness and justice, law-abiding and law application and the environment in which the law and the authority of the rule of law are respected. ZHANG Zhonghou, *Cultivation of Legal Belief: The Core of Constructing Socialist Rule of Law Culture*, People's Court Daily, May 23, 2012, p. 5.

[96] DONG Biwu, *Speech at the Meeting of the Chief Procurator of the Military Procuratorate and the President of the Military Court (March 8, 1957)*, in Collection of Dong Biwu's Writings on Politics and Law, Law Press, 1986, p. 45.

[97] XU Xianming, *The Core of Socialist Rule of Law Culture is the Culture of Institutions*, Legal Daily, December 18, 2013, p. 9.

70 years; its scientific character is reflected in its integration of rule of law and rule of virtue; the people-oriented socialist rule of law culture means that a people-centered approach is adopted in legislation, legislation is for the people, all the people should observe the law, the building of a rule of law society should be promoted and the law should be the people's shared belief and code of conduct.

4.1 Chinese Socialist Civilization of Systems as a Significant Representation of Socialist Rule of Law's National Form

Mao Zedong, when commenting on a national, scientific and people's oriented culture, said, "similarly, in applying Marxism to China, Chinese communists must fully and properly integrate the universal truth of Marxism with the concrete practice of the Chinese revolution, or in other words, the universal truth of Marxism must be combined with specific national characteristics and acquire a definite national form if it is to be useful, and in no circumstances can it be applied subjectively as a mere formula. Marxists who make a fetish of formulas are simply playing the fool with Marxism and the Chinese revolution, and there is no room for them in the ranks of the Chinese revolution. Chinese culture should have its own form, its own national form."[98] After arduous explorations and practices, the socialist path with Chinese characteristics has been forged, a complete set of efficient socialist systems through the enactment of the Constitution and law is established, making it possible to cultivate and disseminate the socialist rule of law culture. In contemporary China, the national character primarily means endowing institutions with more distinctly Chinese characteristics and styles.

How can this be achieved? It may be understood from the following three dimensions.

First, it is necessary to carry forward and promote the red heritage developed during the revolution, development and reform led by the Party, and translate such heritage into institutional arrangements so as to ensure that the Party's leadership is upheld throughout the development of socialist rule of law culture and guarantee the socialist direction of its development. Over the past 98 years since the founding of the CPC, the Party has been dedicated to the rule of law, and the red heritage generated by its pursuit has consolidated the socialist Constitution and maintained strong continuity within socialist legal system, demonstrating remarkable despite severe challenges; the socialist cause under the Party's leadership continues to flourish. This is the lifeblood of the socialist culture. To take democratic centralism as an example. According to the Party's Constitution, the Party is an integral body organized under its own program and Constitution and on the basis of democratic centralism. Democratic centralism has been the Party's fundamental organizational and leadership principle and has played a foundational role, because "it correctly regulates the intra-Party's

[98] Mao Zedong, *On New Democracy (January 1940)*, in Selected Works of Mao Zedong (Vol. 2), Foreign Languages Press, 1965, p. 381.

political life, serves as the basic guidelines for dealing with the intra-Party relations, reflects and represents the interests and wishes of the Party members and the Chinese people, is a scientific, reasonable and efficient system which ensures that the Party's line, principles and policies are correctly formulated and enforced".[99] As a sound system deeply rooted in the Party's organizational and leadership institutions, the democratic centralism was further transformed into the state organizational principle after 1949, and has been implemented through the establishment and operations of state agencies through the provisions of the Constitution and other laws. In this way, the Party has successfully incorporated the democratic deliberation and collective decision-making into the state institutional building and operations, achieving the homogeneous construction of both the Party and state systems, so that they are mutually complementary, cooperative and coordinated. This not only demonstrates the great advantages of socialist system, but also consolidates and protects socialist systems through legislation, thereby making it a deeply-rooted component of the rule of law culture. Today, a mere mention of the democratic centralism evokes the institutional spirit of the Party and the State. It represents a form of rule of law culture developed the Party through adapting the Marxist-Leninist state theory to China's context, while also reflecting its distinctive Chinese characteristics and features of the contemporary era.

Second, the civilization of socialist system draws upon and carries forward the cultural traditions and legal traditions of the Chinese nation, ensuring the continuity of Chinese civilization through innovation while demonstrating its profound cultural heritage. The Chinese traditional culture is the spiritual soul of Chinese nation. Over the long course of human civilization, Chinese people has created its distinctive cultural traditions, providing enduring spiritual support for national growth and development. And these traditional concepts have also embodied profound insights and aspirations regarding the understanding and transformation of the world and the governance of the state.[100] They have also provided guidance on how to establish and develop socialism and construct socialist rule of law. The ethical norms inherent to it, for example, the Chinese sense of responsibility, patriotism, prevailing social aspirations and sense of honor and disgrace, are essential for integrating rule of law and rule of virtue and for incorporating core socialist values into the rule of law construction, and constitute the spiritual core that supports China's legal system. The Chinese legal system is an important component and a distinctive symbol of ancient Chinese civilization. It has never been interrupted, and many of its experience and theories transcend time and space with universal values are still the core of the civilization of the rule of law, for example, "when the law of the land under heaven is good, there will be order in the land under heaven; when the laws of the state are good, there will be order in the state", "in the governance of a country, it is the enforcement, not the enactment, of law that presents the greatest challenge", and

---

[99] Xi Jinping, *To Steadfastly Uphold and Comprehensively Give A Play to the Party's Unique Advantages*, *Qiushi Journal*, Vol. 15, 2012.

[100] Publicity Department of the CPC Central Committee ed., *Thirty Lectures on Xi Jinping Thought on Socialism with Chinese Characteristics for a New Era*, Study Press, 2018, p. 206.

"once enacted, a law must be enforced and anyone who violates it must be held to account".[101] These essential traditions have been deeply embedded in the construction of rule of law and norms of law. In the practice for a new era, they should be further enriched, expanded and improved to promote creative transformation and development thereby highlighting the distinctive contemporary features of Chinese socialism. For traditional Chinese legal culture, it is necessary to undertake scientific transform and sublation them based on contemporary practice, integrating these traditions that are compatible with science, reason, democracy, freedom, fairness, human rights, rule of law, peace, order and efficiency with the theory, system and practice for rule of law, so as to form an organic unity between the national ethos and the spirit of the times embodied in the Chinese socialist rule of law theory.[102]

Third, the civilization of socialist system draws upon and assimilates the experience of advanced foreign rule of law civilizations in a reasonably manner, so as to fill the gaps and enrich Chinese socialist rule of law culture, and integrate its characteristics with a global perspective. As expressly stated by Mao Zedong, "China needs to assimilate a good deal of foreign progressive culture, not enough of which was done in the past. We should assimilate whatever is useful to us today not only from the present-day socialist and new-democratic cultures but also from the earlier cultures of other nations, for example, from the culture of the various capitalist countries in the Age of Enlightenment."[103] Throughout all the phases of revolution, development and reform, the Party has consistently confronted situations in which no ready-made experience or models were available. Therefore, by self-reliance and hardworking, it has integrated the Marxist-Leninist basic principles with China's realities and practice, explored and pioneered its own path, which has become a fundamental principle consistently developed and upheld by the Party. The Party also pays attention to foreign experience. For example, it has taken the Soviet Union as the teacher, and after the reform and opening-up was initiated, it further broadened its vision and learned from developed Western countries, which has been an important external factor contributing to China's rapid development and prosperity. In terms of legal system, it absorbed the fine achievements of the Western rule of law civilizations, including both the civil law and common law systems, and has learnt from their reasonable and effective approaches to state governance system and modernization of governance capacity. By transforming them into China's systems and an important component of China's institutional civilization, China's socialist system and norms of law continue to be improved. For example, the compilation of Civil Code drew on the laws of civil law and common law systems. However, the "wholesale westernization" and "complete transplant" are firmly rejected, as Mao Zedong ever warned that "China has suffered a great deal from the mechanical absorption of foreign

---

[101] Commentary Department of People's Daily ed., *Xi Jinping: Wit and Vision—Selected Quotations and Commentary*, People's Daily Press, 2015, pp. 267–279.

[102] ZHANG Wenxian, *On Scientifically Positing the Chinese Socialist Rule of Law Theory*, Law Science, No. 11, pp. 3–8 (2015).

[103] MAO Zedong, *On New Democracy (January 1940)*, in Selected Works of Mao Zedong (No. 2), Foreign Languages Press, 1965, p. 380.

material". In this regard, it is necessary to place China's needs first and carefully discern between the good and the bad, and adopt foreign experience in a selective and appropriate manner, with the aim of absorbing the fine rule of law achievements of other countries. As Xi Jinping stressed, civilizations have become richer and more colorful with exchanges and mutual learning, in that they can help Chinese socialist rule of law culture develop a broader global vision and engage in more frequent and in-depth interaction with other civilizations, but also allow it to present its Chinese characters and fashion and its proposal to the world.

4.2 Culture of Institutions as a Manifestation of Socialist Rule of Law Culture

A peaceful society is governed by law, while a peaceful mind in people is nourished by virtue. The Chinese socialist path of rule of law is marked by the integration of the rule of law with the rule of virtue, with equal emphasis placed on both.[104] Their integration has shaped the national character of Chinese legal system, inherited the core experience of China's traditional excellence in state governance, and continued to evolve with the times under the guidance of basic Marxist principles. It not only conforms with the requirements of modernizing China's state governance, the realities of Chinese socialist rule of law construction, but also is consistent with Chinese people's understanding and acceptance of the rule of law and reflects their cultural and humanistic traditions in this regard. It demonstrates theoretical soundness, institutional innovation and practical significance of the times.

As soon as the PRC was founded, the Party attached importance to the role of ethics in promoting socialist rule of law and spared efforts to utilize socialist ethics to educate people through institutional arrangements. For example, the Common Program called for eradicating the influence of feudal, comprador and fascist ideologies, and promoting the principle of serving the people in cultural and educational work under the leadership of the people's government. It prescribed the people's duties to abide by the law, observe labor discipline, protect public property and the like, and advocated love for the motherland, the people, labor, science and public property. What's more, the 1954 Constitution adhered to the democratic centralism, and prescribed that the state forbade any person to use his private property to the detriment of the public interest, so as to better handle the relationship between personal interests and public interests. It also made provisions on citizens' duties, including abiding by the Constitution and the law, upholding discipline at work, keeping public order and respecting social ethics. Liu Shaoqi also made the similar point in his explanation on the 1954 Constitution that "ours is a state capable of inspiring the people to take an active part in the public activities of the country and society. It enables the masses to take a collective viewpoint and voluntarily fulfill their obligations to society

[104] Xi Jinping, *The Rule of Law and the Rule of Virtue*, in The Governance of China (Vol. 2), Foreign Languages Press, 2017, p. 134.

and the country in their public activities. This is proof that our system of people's democracy corresponds to the interests of the people."[105] The 1950 Marriage Law implemented the new democratic and socialist ethics by ordering an end to the feudal marriage system which was based on the superiority of man over woman and to other outdated practices, and promoting equal rights for both man and woman and the free choice of partners. This provided an institutional foundation for transforming social customs and uplifting public morality.

After the Third Plenary Session of the Eleventh Central Committee, the Central Committee proposed to strengthen the socialist cultural progress and to put equal emphasis on material advancement and cultural-ethical progress. A striking feature of the 1982 Constitution was its special attention to consolidating the provisions on socialist cultural development. For example, it made specific provisions on each aspect of cultural development, i.e. education, science, health and sports and literature and art, from Articles 19 to 22. The Preamble and Article 24 also laid out the principles on socialist cultural development.[106] For citizens' basic rights and duties, as Peng Zhen reported, the requirements of socialist cultural development were in fact embodied in many of the articles in the draft on the fundamental rights and duties on citizens.[107] The socialist constitutions not only take the substantive parts of socialist cultural development, such as well-developed education and prosperous scientific and cultural prosperity, as regulatory objects, but also make provisions concerning its ideological dimensions, which prominently reflects the essential characteristics of

[105] General Office of NPC Standing Committee and Party Literature Research Center of CPC Central Committee eds., *Selected Important Documents on the System of People's Congresses (Vol. 2)*, Central Party Literature Press and China Democratic and Legal System Publishing House, 2015, p. 218.

[106] WU Daying and SHEN Zongling, *Basic Theories on Chinese Socialist Law*, Law Press, 1987, p. 124.

[107] Peng Zhen made detailed explanations on it, "in our socialist country, ideological education, public opinion, standards of social conduct and the law are interrelated. Our Constitution provides for the rights of citizens and at the same time requires that they raise their consciousness as masters of the country and society and safeguard and exercise their rights in a correct manner. Safeguarding one's own rights and respecting those of others are inseparable. This requires that every citizen should safeguard the interests of the state, society and the collective and respect the freedoms and rights of others while safeguarding his own rights. The duties of citizens stipulated in the Constitution are legally obligatory. But it is more important that, as the country's masters. Citizens should enhance their sense of responsibility to the state, to society and to other citizens and conscientiously perform their duties, including those of safeguarding the socialist system and the unity of the country and of all our nationalities, safeguarding the security, honor and interests of the. Motherland. observing the Constitution, the law. Discipline and public order, and taking care of public property. In order to build socialist spiritual civilization in the whole society, it is important that all citizens raise such consciousness and sense of responsibility, handle their relations with the state and society and with other citizens on the principles of socialism and collectivism, cultivate a recognition of their rights and duties and a sense of organization and discipline consonant with the socialist political system, and acquire awareness as socialist citizens". General Office of NPC Standing Committee and Party Literature Research Center of CPC Central Committee eds., *Selected Important Documents on the System of People's Congresses (Vol. 2)*, Central Party Literature Press and China Democratic and Legal System Publishing House, 2015, p. 566.

the socialist constitutions and accentuate its superiority and advanced nature.[108] The requirements for promoting socialist cultural development are manifested in every aspect of China's legal institutions and implemented throughout the legislation on civil affairs, education, science and culture. They also serve as an important guiding principles for making legislative plan, designing legal institutions and enacting law, thereby delivering positive legal outcomes and effective implementation results.

The Central Committee has advocated that socialist cultural progress is an important attribute of socialism with Chinese characteristics, and to govern the country by combining the rule of law with the rule of virtue since the Sixteenth National Congress. Since the Eighteen National Congress, the Central Committee with Xi Jinping as the core has summarized the experience and lessons learned in building a law-based socialist country, developed a clear understanding of the laws of governance and emphasized the integration of rule of law with the rule of virtue with equal importance on both. This has enabled the two to complement and reinforce each other in promoting the modernization of state governance system and capacity. As Xi Jingping stated, "law is a set of virtues in writing, while virtue is law inscribed in people's hearts; Ethics should also be included in the development of the rule of law… Socialist ethical standards and core values should be embodied throughout the legislation, law enforcement and judicial process so that socialist rule of law is equipped with a sound legal system and a sensible governance system".[109]

The core socialist values are the soul of socialist rule of law construction; therefore, to integrate them into the construction is an essential requirement for adhering to the principle of combining rule of law with rule of virtue and an important channel for strengthening the promotion of core socialist values. To implement the new concepts, new thinking and new strategies of Xi Jinping for it, the General Office of the Central Committee and the General Office of the State Council issued the Guiding Opinions on Further Integrating Core Socialist Values into Construction of the Rule of Law, which provided ideological and policy guidelines for promoting correct value pursuits to the society through laws and public policies and integrating the core values with socialist rule of law construction. In May 2018, the Central Committee issued the Plan on Law Enactment and Revision for Integrating Core Socialist Values into the Construction of Rule of Law, which proposed the comprehensive incorporation of the core values into the enactment, revision, repeal and interpretation so as to ensure more explicit, definitive and stronger orientation for legislation. It also proposed to completely incorporate the values into the Chinese socialist legal system through 5–10 years' efforts. The NPC and its Standing Committee have attached great importance to translating such requirements into the spirits, fundamental principles and guidelines of law and actively promoted the incorporation of core values into laws and regulations, so that each law can better reflect the ethical standards and humanistic

[108] CHEN Yunsheng, *Constitution and Cultural Progress*, in ZHANG Youyu et.al ed., Collected Essays on Constitution, Qunzhong Press, 1982, p. 138.

[109] XI Jinping, *The Rule of Law and the Rule of Virtue*, in The Governance of China (Vol. 2), Foreign Languages Press, 2017, p. 134.

care as much as possible. In this way, the Chinese socialist legal system is saturated with the core values and its role of promoting the practice of socialist ethics will be strengthened. For example, General Provisions of Civil Law enthusiastically embraces the core socialist values, promotes the fine traditional Chinese virtues, strengthens people's awareness of rules, enhances the regulation of ethics, spreads the spirit of contract and advances public order and good customs. Another example is the Law on the Protection of Heroes and Martyrs which was enacted based on the principles and spirit of the constitution to strengthen the protection of heroes and martyrs, to inherit and promote their spirits and patriotism, to safeguard the public interests, and to cultivate and practice the core socialist values. Similarly, the National Anthem Law was formulated to safeguard the dignity of the national anthem, regulate the playing, singing, broadcasting of the national anthem, enhance citizens' sense of national identity and promote patriotism.

4.3 People-Centered Approach to Legislation for a People's Socialist Rule of Law Culture

Standing on the people's side represents the fundamental political stance of the Party, and it is what distinguishes a Marxist political party from other political parties. The Party stands together with the people in times of both prosperity and adversity, maintaining its close bond with them no matter what fate may bring. This is a fundamental guarantee that enables the Party to overcome all difficulties and dangers. As the saying goes, "he who wins over the people wins the country; he who loses the people loses the country."[110] In his speech Serve the People, Mao Zedong said, "these battalions of ours are wholly dedicated to the liberation of the people and work entirely in the people's interests."[111] According to the Party's Constitution, serving the people wholeheartedly is the basic principle of our Party. The report of the Nineteenth National Congress, the Party incorporated "committing to a people-centered approach" as one of fourteen fundamental principles in the Xi Jinping Thought on Socialism with Chinese characteristics. To put people first is central to the socialist rule of law construction: it calls for the adherence to the people-centered approach to constructing socialist rule of law culture, steadfastly standing for the people, and fully promoting the socialist democracy. To this end, it is necessary to strengthen the publicity and education on rule of law, encourage all the people to understand and abide by the law and accelerate the construction of a law-based country in which all the people are admiring, proactively observing and defending the law.

[110] Xi Jinping, *Speech at a Ceremony Marking the Centenary of the Communist Party of China (July 1, 2016)*, in Selected Documents of Important Speeches of Xi Jinping on CPC's Original Aspirations and Mission, Party Building Readings Press and Central Party Literature Press, 2019, p. 235.

[111] Mao Zedong, *Serve the People (September 8, 1940)*, in Selected Works of Mao Zedong (Vol. 3), Foreign Languages Press, 1965, p. 227.

First, to constantly strengthen people's belief and support for rule of law through good laws and sound governance to establish the authority of the Constitution, law and socialist rule of law. The authority of law comes from people's sincere support and belief. What kind of the law do the people believes in? What kind of the law do they support? These are two fundamental questions that must be answered in building socialist rule of law. Over the years, the Party has exercised the power for the people and led the legislation for the people, taking the people's support, approval, satisfaction, and consent as the fundamental criteria for evaluating legislative quality and the success and failure of the work on legislation, and striving to improve people's sense of gain, happiness and security through the institutional guarantees. The reason why the socialist legal system can be constantly improved is that the legislation has taken a strong hold of Party's basic line, which is also the lifeline of the state and a guarantee for the people's happiness, unwaveringly adhered to the mass line, and resolutely committed to the increasing people's demand and aspiration for a better life. If the good laws enacted by the people under the Party's leadership win the sincere support of all the Chinese people, the authority of the Constitution and law will be established, and the socialist rule of law will take roots among the people. Standing on the timeframe of the new era, the report of the Nineteenth National Congress made a historical judgment that China's principal social contradiction was transformed, and stressed that the needs to be met for the people to live better lives have been increasingly broad. Not only have their material and cultural needs grown; their demands for democracy, rule of law, fairness and justice, security, and a better environment are increasing. Therefore, the work on legislation is also confronted with the new trends and new requirements brought by the new era. To respond to these changes and requirements, the scientific and democratic legislation should be promoted with greater strength, the people-centered approach should be adopted, the principle of justice, fairness and openness should be observed throughout the process of legislation. The laws enacted should be scientific, targeted and effective, so that each piece of legislation accords with the Constitutional principles, reflects people's will and wins their support. In this way, the function of law in inspiring and educating the people will be better applied, and people's sincere support and belief in the Constitution and law will be guaranteed, internalizing the norms of law into people's code of conduct to better maintain the authority of the Constitution and law.

Second, to strengthen publicity and education on rule of law, improve people's awareness of rule of law and promote the spirits of socialist rule of law so as to provide a sound social environment for building China into a law-based country. The awareness and spirits of the rule of law are internal foundations for people to act according to law and observe it. To improve them is inseparable from enhancing the publicity and education on socialist rule of law. It has been the Party's traditions in publicity and education. The publicity and education on rule of law has also received continuous emphasis and efforts. After the PRC's founding, to address the problems in the transition of legal system, the Party and the State adopted various measures to disseminate the legal policies to the people for study, so that the legal knowledge and conceptions of the people experiencing social transformation could be changed. After the reform and opening-up was launched, to deal with the lingering effects of the Cultural Revolution, Deng Xiaoping took people's understanding of the rule of law as the basis for strengthening legal system, and put forward that "education about the law should begin at an early age".[112] Peng Zhen also emphasized the need to carry out education on socialist legal system, eliminate the harmful influences that could undermine the socialist legal system and social order, and resist the erosion of foreign bourgeois ideology.[113] In 1985, the NPC Standing Committee issued the Resolution on Acquainting Citizens with Basic Knowledge of Law, which started the initiative of popularizing law in China. There have been 7 five-year plans on it up to now. Since the Eighteenth National Congress, for implementing Xi Jinping's requirements on comprehensive rule of law, advancing rule of law in all respects, promoting people's consciousness of upholding, studying, observing and applying the law, and promoting the modernization of state governance system and capacity, the NPC Standing Committee issued a resolution on the seventh five-year plan on popularizing the law in 2016 to strengthen the rule of law conception in the whole society, improve the legal thinking and capacity in doing things according to law, and establish a social environment that upholds the rule of law. After 30 years' development, the task has been upgraded from dissemination of basic legal knowledge to improvement of rule of law conception, legal thinking and capacity. The upgrade is a great achievement in constructing socialist rule of law in China and reflects people's embrace of socialist rule of law culture, which provides a good social environment for building China into a law-based country.

Third, to promote universal compliance with law among the people with greater efforts, consolidate the social foundation for rule of law, and promote the coordinated development of law-based country, government and society. To observe the Constitution and law is the basic duty of citizens and the foundation of building a rule of law country. According to the Constitution, the people of all ethnic groups, all state agencies and armed forces, all political parties and social organizations, and all enterprises and public institutions in China must treat the Constitution as the fundamental standard of conduct. And they have a duty to uphold the dignity of the Constitution and ensure its compliance. As Mao Zedong ever stressed that law must be observed, no one should destroy the revolutionary legal system, and all the people were required to observe it. Considering the historical conditions and people's psychology in the early years of PRC, Dong Biwu made an incisive discussion on "why it is important to nurture people's consciousness of observing law?".[114] Xie

---

[112] DENG Xiaoping, *Help the People Understand the Importance of the Rule of Law (June 28, 1986)*, in Selected Works of Deng Xiaoping (Vol. 3), Foreign Languages Press, 1994, p. 166.

[113] PENG Zhen, *Speech at the Forum on Public Security of Five Cities*, in Selected Writings of Peng Zhen, People's Publishing House, 1991, p. 415.

[114] He pointed out that the people before the liberation had extreme hatred and distrust of all reactionary laws, which was understandable in the old society. Since the people had seized the state power, a revolutionary order should be established, and a legal order that was based on their own revolutionary ideals should be maintained. However, it was not easy to make it… in the past, people hated and distrusted the reactionary laws, but it would not be good if such hatred and distrust continued after the revolution succeeded. In other words, the country under people's democratic dictatorship should make every effort to change them from disbelief and disloyalty. Though it was

Juezai also pointed out that fostering people's awareness of law compliance was a major task in the future.[115] Since the reform and opening-up, people have been under continuous education initiatives to observe the Constitution and the law, establishing the conception of law and learning how to apply it.

Since the Eighteenth National Congress, the Central Committee has attached great importance to the fundamental role of universal law compliance law in building a rule of law country, and incorporated into the 16-character principles and the four elements of rule of law. Such universal compliance requires all the citizens, social organizations and state agencies to treat the Constitution and law as their code of conduct, and exercise their rights or powers and perform their duties according to the Constitution and the law. People are the principal actors in implementing the law, the fundamental driving force of advancing rule of law in all respects. Their knowledge of, faith in and compliance with law is the foundation for implementing the fundamental principle of the rule of law. If the development of a rule of law society is neglected and people do not observe the law, the construction of rule of law country and government will lose people's support, like a river without source or a tree without roots.[116]

Over the past 70 years, China's socialist rule of law construction has endured difficulties, trials and hardships, and has steadfastly forged a socialist path of rule of law. Over the past 70 years, the socialist rule of law theory has adapted to changes of the times and finally achieved its formation; over the past 70 years, the Chinese socialist legal system has been established and constantly developed, ensuring the increasing maturity and completeness of the socialist system. Over the past 70 years, the spirit and conceptions of rule of law have been continuously innovated, and the socialist rule of law culture has nurtured people's minds. As Xi Jinping said, "as everything moves forward, we must remember the path we have trodden". The NPC and its Standing Committee has carried forward the legacy of the revolutionary predecessors on rule of law, drawn on the essences of their thoughts, and remained true to the original aspiration and the founding mission. Under the Party's firm and strong leadership, the NPC and its Standing Committee have remained dedicated to following the socialist path of rule of law, intensified efforts to build China into a law-based country at a faster speed, promoted the modernization of state governance system and capacity, and provided powerful driving force, strong support and comprehensive guarantees for the great rejuvenation of Chinese nation.

---

a rather difficult task, we must accomplish it. We had done a lot in this regard, but not enough. We need to solve it with a long period of time. DONG Biwu, *On the Work of the Party on Promoting People's Political and Legal Awareness (May 18, 1954)*, in Selected Works of Dong Biwu, People's Publishing House, 1985, pp. 330–331.

[115] XIE Juezai, *Speech at the Judicial Training School (January 1949)*, in Collected Works of Xie Juezai, People's Publishing House, 1989, p. 650.

[116] *Questions and Answers for the Study of the Resolution Made in the Fourth Plenary Session of the Eighteenth CPC Central Committee*, Party Building Readings Press and Study Press, 2014, pp. 113–114.

Epilogue

Over the past 70 years since the founding of the People's Republic of China, the legislation has undergone an arduous but glorious path and made tremendous achievements that have attracted worldwide attention. The socialist legal system with Chinese characteristics with the Constitution as the core has been steadily established, which has promoted the improvement of Chinese socialist system and state governance system and capacity. The glorious path and achievements have provided state system and legal guarantee for the Party to lead the Chinese people to create the miracle of economic development and political stability that is rarely seen in the world and to achieve the tremendous transformation from standing up and becoming prosperous to growing strong.

In his southern tour in 1992, Deng Xiaoping pointed out that "it will take a very long historical period to consolidate and develop the socialist system, and it will require persistent struggle by many generations, a dozen or even several dozens. We can never rest on our oars", and "it will probably take another thirty years for us to develop a more mature and well-defined system in every field". Soon after the closing of the Eighteenth CPC National Congress in 2012, at the first group study session of the Political Bureau of the 18th CPC Central Committee Xi Jinping made a speech, "To Study, Disseminate and Implement the Guiding Principles of The 18th National Congress with Emphasis On Adhering to and Developing Socialism with Chinese characteristics" and reiterated Deng Xiaoping's ideas. He emphasized that "it is imperative to give top priority to the building of systems while giving full play to the superiority of the socialist political system in China. We must improve current systems and promote institutional innovation with theoretical innovation based on practice. We must proceed from reality, formulate new systems in a timely fashion, and put in place a well-developed, systematically and rationally regulated, and effective framework of systems to ensure that all systems and institutions are working properly and functioning well, and thereby provide a more effective institutional guarantee for new victories".

Since the Eighteenth CPC National Congress, the Central Committee with Xi Jinping as the core has attached great importance to institutional development,

C. Shen et al. (eds.), *A History of Legislation in the Past 70 Years in China*,
https://doi.org/10.1007/978-981-95-3799-0

focused on the coordinated implementation of Five-sphere Integrated Plan and Four-pronged Comprehensive Strategy, insisted on improving and developing Chinese socialist system and the modernization of state governance system and capacity, and drawn strength from China's realities, Chinese culture and Chinese people to engage in the great innovation and practice, and made new strides in the progress of the socialist legal system with Chinese characteristics. As advocated in the Eighteenth Congress, "we should make laws in a scientific way, enforce them strictly, administer justice impartially, and ensure that everyone abides by the law", and "we should improve the socialist system of laws with Chinese characteristics, strengthen legislation in key areas". As put forward in the Third Plenary Session of the Eighteenth CPC Central Committee, "the overall goal of deepening the reform comprehensively is to improve and develop socialism with Chinese characteristics, and to promote the modernization of the national governance system and capacity". And in the following plenary session, "the general goal of advancing rule of law in all respects is to form a socialist rule of law system with Chinese characteristics and build China into a socialist rule of law country." There is a rigorous internal logic between the two sessions, on a sequence of time the general strategy is successively laid out, which makes the comprehensive deepening of reform and opening-up and rule of law jointly promote the construction of China into a moderately prosperous country in all respects. To resolutely implement the decisions and arrangements of the Central Committee, the Twelfth NPC Standing Committee has strengthened the legislation in key areas, basically made the national security law system ready, made major progress in the compilation of Civil Code, continued efforts in social and people's wellbeing legislation, advanced the public cultural service legislation, and set a gradually complete system for ecological civilization, taken advantage of various legislative methods and completed the legislative tasks urgently needed by reform. All these efforts have made the systems of state more complete, mature and definitive, the socialist legal system more well-conceived, and delivered on new historical progress in state systems and governance, which will provide strong legal guarantee for political stability, economic development, cultural prosperity, national unity, social peace and national reunification.

The world is now going through major changes unseen in a century, and the great rejuvenation of Chinese nation has come to a critical juncture. A major judgment was made in the Nineteenth CPC National Congress that "with decades of hard work, socialism with Chinese characteristics has crossed the threshold into a new era. This is a new historic juncture in China's development." To this end, new initiatives should be undertaken and more great successes should be achieved. To keep abreast of the trend of the times and the change of China's social contradiction, and to continuously meet the people's expectations for a better life, in the Nineteenth Congress, the Party has laid out the strategic arrangements and formulated a development blueprint for China's future, stated the two centenary goals and put forward new and higher requirements for rule of law, emphasizing the need to carry out lawmaking in a well-conceived and democratic way and in accordance with law so that good laws are made to promote development and ensure good governance. It also set forth the two fifteen-year goals based on the achievement of moderately prosperous society, i.e.

from 2020 to 2035, the law-based country, government, and society are basically in place and the modernization of China's system and capacity for governance is basically achieved; in the second stage from 2035 to the middle of the twenty-first century, to build China into a great modern socialist country in all respects and achieve the modernization of state governance system and capacity.

The term of the Thirteenth NPC Standing Committee is a decisive period for accomplishing a moderately prosperous country in all respects and the period during which the two centenary goals converge. Many major reform measures and arrangements advocated by the Central Committee need to be implemented through legislation to make a good start and lay a more solid legal foundation. To fully put into practice the Central Committee's strategic arrangements, and give priority to the goal of accomplishing a moderately prosperous country, the NPC Standing Committee has insisted on reform and innovation, formulated the five-year legislative plan to better organize the current legislative work, and specified the legislative goals and tasks based on the development of China's social contradiction and the demands for quality economic development. Upon the completion of the plan, there will be more solid foundation for promoting continuous improvement of Chinese socialist legal system, adherence and improvement of Chinese socialist systems, and modernization of state governance system and capacity.

In 1956, Mao Zedong said that "China ...ought to make a greater contribution to humanity". It is believed among the Chinese people that the great rejuvenation of Chinese nation by the middle of the twenty-first century is sure to be realized. At that time, China will be a great modern socialist country that is prosperous, strong, democratic, culturally advanced, harmonious, and beautiful; new heights will be reached in every dimension of material, political, cultural and ethical, social, and ecological advancement, the modernization of China's system and capacity for governance will be realized, and China will become a state with global significance in terms of composite national strength and international influence. China as a socialist rule of law country will offer Chinese wisdom and Chinese approaches to global governance and human civilization, and Chinese nation will become a proud and active member of the community of nations with advanced democracy, rule of law and civilization.

The manufacturer's authorised representative in the EU is Springer Nature Customer Service Centre GmbH, Europaplatz 3, 69115 Heidelberg, Germany. If you have any concerns regarding our products, please contact ProductSafety@springernature.com

Printed and bound by CPI Group (UK) Ltd, Croydon, CR0 4YY
07/10/2026
02229352-0009